We Are America

We Are America

SECOND EDITION

ANNA JOY

Sacramento City College

Harcourt Brace College Publishers

Fort Worth Philadelphia San Diego New York Orlando Austin San Antonio
Toronto Montreal London Sydney Tokyo

Vice President, Publisher	Ted Buchholz
Senior Acquisitions Editor	Carol Wada
Editorial Assistant	Tammi Price
Senior Project Editor	Charles J. Dierker
Production Manager	Cynthia Young
Art Director	Burl Sloan

ISBN: 0-15-501480-3

Library of Congress Catalog Card Number: 93-81364

Cover illustration by Dennis Farris

Address for Editorial Correspondence: Harcourt Brace College Publishers, 301 Commerce Street, Suite 3700, Fort Worth, TX 76102.

Address for Orders: Harcourt Brace & Company, 6277 Sea Harbor Drive, Orlando, FL 32887-6777. 1-800-782-4479, or 1-800-433-0001 (in Florida).

Preface

Thehe purpose of *We Are America,* Second Edition, is to introduce beginning writers to the writing process, to basic reading skills, and to the essential
elements of effective writing—unity, coherence, completeness, and sentence
skills. Unlike other textbooks written for developmental writers, this book
includes a thematic reader composed of selections that reflect culturally and
ethnically diverse points of view. Readings, discussion questions, and lists of
topics for writing are designed to increase students' sensitivity to experiences
and cultural perspectives different from their own and to encourage students
to see themselves, their ideas, and their cultural or ethnic group as an important part of the larger (and increasingly more complex) American experience.

ORGANIZATION

The selection and organization of material in this book reflect the goals outlined above. Part One is an introduction to the writing process and a guide to
active reading. Journal and freewriting exercises in Chapter 1 give students the
writing practice they need to gain confidence in their writing. Models of marginal notes and sample summaries in Chapter 2 illustrate active reading techniques, which students practice in a series of exercises. Chapters 3 and 5 introduce the writing process and explain how the steps in the writing process can
be used to compose a paragraph and an essay. Writing samples in these two
chapters present writing as a method of inquiry and discovery that is both
dynamic and recursive. Once students observe the thinking that goes into each
stage of the process, they complete a series of exercises that help them turn
their own ideas into paragraphs and essays. Chapters 4 and 6 introduce the
principles behind well-written paragraphs and essays and ask students to
revise for unity, development, and coherence.

Part Two is a cross-cultural reader and guide to writing designed to help
students master several writing strategies. Most of the chapters in this part
include an overview of the material presented in the chapter, a discussion of
one writing strategy (such as narrating, describing, explaining, evaluating, or

persuading), a model essay written by a professional or student writer, and additional suggestions for applying the writing process to papers that employ the strategy featured in the chapter.* "For Further Reading," the last section of the chapters in Part Two, provides additional readings and examples of student writing consistent with the chapter's theme. Chapter sections on the writing process make the all-important but sometimes-neglected connection between polished writing and students' own writing. Discussions of model essays support the premise that students will become better writers if they can identify the key features, and rhetorical and organizational patterns in the writing of others.

Part Three is aimed at improving students' sentence skills. Workbook exercises provide a review of basic grammar to help students find and correct errors in their own writing. In addition, sentence-combining exercises target sentence fluency and correctness in student writing.

Taken together, the three parts of this textbook provide students with a complete writing program the elements of which form a coherent whole. In Chapter 2, for example, instructions for active reading and for writing summaries give students information they need to critically read selections in Part Two. Instructions on the writing process in Chapters 3 and 5 prepare students to write paragraphs or essays in response to topics that follow readings. Exercises in Parts One and Three help students revise their own writing for coherence and development as well as for sentence correctness.

FEATURES

Clear explanations followed by practice exercises characterize the material introduced in Part One. Basic writing and active reading techniques introduced in this section prepare students for more demanding tasks in Part Two.

The range of reading abilities and interests addressed in Part Two, the cross-cultural reader, gives instructors a great deal of flexibility in putting together courses to fit their students' needs. Chapters are arranged thematically and by the level of complexity of the writing strategy they introduce. In addition, the readings progress from first-person narration to more challenging modes of expository writing, making the textbook appropriate for several class levels of developmental writing. The *Instructor's Manual* offers several sample syllabi that may prove useful in designing courses.

"For Practice" exercises in Part One and the freewriting exercises, "Questions for Discussion" and "Topics for Writing" that follow the reading selections in Parts One and Two, help students connect what they have read to their own writing. These exercises also give students the frequent critical thinking and writing practice that is so crucial for beginning writers.

---

* Chapter 16, "Getting an Education," provides a slight variation on the usual chapter format.

Like the professional selections in this textbook, the examples of student writing reflect a broad spectrum of personal and cultural issues and address many of the concerns of novice writers. In Part One, student samples are used to illustrate journal writing (Chapter 1), techniques for active reading (Chapter 2), and the process of composing paragraphs and essays (Chapters 3 and 5). In Part Two, student writing may illustrate particular writing strategies or reinforce a chapter's theme. Many of the exercises in Part Three are taken directly from students' writing.

Vocabulary lists and occasional explanations of word usage follow a few of the readings in Part One and all of the readings in Part Two. These vocabulary sections give students practice in using the techniques introduced in Chapter 2 to improve their word-recognition skills.

Four appendixes following Part Three provide students with questionnaires for generating and evaluating ideas.

NEW IN THIS EDITION

This second edition retains the vision of *We Are America* as a text that provides the elements of an effective writing course—an introduction to rhetoric, a reader, and a handbook of sentence skills. In addition, new reading selections continue to reflect culturally and ethnically diverse perspectives. While the vision of the text has not changed, thanks to instructors' suggestions, several features of the text are augmented or improved.

Chapters in Part Two—the reader—are rearranged to reflect a new progression of writing strategies and increasingly complex reading selections. Chapter 15 features a discussion of problem solving, a writing strategy new to this edition.

Some changes were made with an eye for better coherence. For example, the explanation of writing oral histories now follows the discussion of interviewing techniques. An explanation of deductive and inductive reasoning completes the chapter on drawing inferences, Chapter 16.

Of the forty-one reading selections, nine are new. Two student samples are also new in this revision. These selections add to the number of analytical pieces in the text. The new pieces also introduce students to several controversial issues and ask them to identify the author's purpose in writing the piece, to discuss the author's approach to the subject, and to decide whether the arguments are convincing or not. In Chapter 16, for example, Henry Louis Gates, Jr. and Donald Kagan debate the importance of cultural diversity in college curriculum. Freewriting exercises and discussion questions encourage students to evaluate each side of this debate and to explore the impact of such curriculum changes on their own education.

Chapter 3 has been rewritten with a new student sample to demonstrate the process for writing a paragraph. A new student essay in Chapter 15 illustrates explaining causes and effects and also provides a third sample of an essay using research material to support ideas.

Several exercises in Chapters 4 and 6 and in the chapters in Part Three have been expanded; some exercises are new.

Finally, an index of key terms, authors' names, and titles of reading selections makes the text easier to use. A fourth appendix provides a conveniently located list of conjunctions used to connect phrases and clauses.

ACKNOWLEDGMENTS

This textbook is the product of thirteen years of work with sensitive, conscientious students in my basic writing classes. Many of them contributed their ideas and writings to this textbook. Supportive editors at Harcourt Brace have provided invaluable suggestions and, at times, much-needed emotional support. In particular, I would like to thank Carol Wada, acquisitions editor; Tammi Price, editorial assistant; Charlie Dierker, project editor; Cindy Young, production manager; and Burl Sloan, art director. I would also like to thank the following reviewers, who took the time to offer helpful comments on the text: Ann Rohovec, Dona Ana Community College; Anitra Dark, Ohlone College; Sheryl Holt, University of Minnesota; and Dean Pettinger, College of Southern Idaho. To friends and relatives who have endured my often obsessive preoccupation with the tasks of writing and revising this textbook goes my heartfelt appreciation. Finally, special thanks go to my husband, Chuck, who recommends this book to everyone he meets.

Anna Joy

Contents

Preface   *v*

PART ONE
An Overview of the Writing Process

1 FIRST STEPS 3
Taking Stock 3
Gathering Your Thoughts....................................... 5
   Freewriting 5
   Keeping a Journal.. 6
   Looking Ahead 11

2 WRITING ABOUT READING......................... 12
Active Reading 12
   Techniques for Active Reading 13
   Why Use the Active Reading Method? 13
      Student Writing "The Tonto Syndrome," Leah Eskin 14
Writing Summaries 17
   Reading and Summarizing 18
      "Get Found, Kid!" Robert Fulghum 19
Responding to the Reading 23
   Building Your Vocabulary 25
   Questions for Discussion 27
Topics for Writing... 27
   Looking Ahead 28

3 THE WRITING PROCESS: WRITING A PARAGRAPH 29

What is the Writing Process? 29

What is a Paragraph? 30

Steps to Writing 30

Step One: Developing a Topic 30

Step Two: Thinking about Your Audience 34

Step Three: Preliminary Writing 38

Step Four: Organizing Ideas 41

Step Five: Writing a Fast Draft 50

Step Six: Editing and Proofreading 50

Step Seven: Sharing Your Writing 52

Step Eight: Making Final Revisions 54

Topics for Writing 55

4 REFINING PARAGRAPHS 56

Basic Paragraph Structure 56

Revising Paragraphs 63

Writing Unified Paragraphs 64

Writing Well-Developed Paragraphs 65

Writing Coherent Paragraphs 69

Transitional Words and Phrases 70

Looking Ahead 73

5 THE WRITING PROCESS: WRITING AN ESSAY 74

What Is an Essay? 74

Questions for Discussion 78

Steps to Writing an Essay 78

Step One: Developing a Topic 79

Step Two: Thinking about Your Audience 80

Step Three: Preliminary Writing 80

Step Four: Organizing Ideas 83

Step Five: Writing a Fast Draft 85

Step Six: Editing and Proofreading 86

Step Seven: Sharing Your Writing 89

Step Eight: Making Final Revisions 92

Topics for Writing 94
    Looking Ahead 95

6 REFINING ESSAYS **96**
Basic Essay Structure 96
Revising Essays 96
    Writing an Introductions 96
    Writing a Thesis 101
    Writing a Title. 106
    Developing Body Paragraphs. 108
    Writing a Conclusion 113
    Looking Ahead 115

PART TWO

A Cross-Cultural Reader

7 FAMILY AND THE SENSE OF SELF 119
Narrating 121
    Characteristics of Narrating. 121
Describing and Explaining 124
    Characteristics of Describing and Explaining 125
      "Mother," Russell Baker 126
Responding to the Reading. 130
    Freewriting 130
    Building Your Vocabulary 130
    Questions for Discussion 131
Topics for Writing 132
The Writing Process: Narrating 133
    Additional Considerations for Developing a Topic. 133
    Additional Considerations for Thinking about Your Audience . . . 134
    Additional Considerations for Preliminary Writing 134
    Additional Considerations for Organizing Ideas 135
    Additional Considerations for Writing a Fast Draft 135
    Additional Considerations for Sharing Your
    Writing and Making Final Revisions. 135
      Student Writing "One Mistake," Betty Tilman 136
    Questions for Discussion 137

For Further Reading 138
    "Girl," Jamaica Kincaid 138
Responding to the Reading 139
    Freewriting 139
    Building Your Vocabulary 139
    Questions for Discussion 140
Topics for Writing 140
    "Fathers Playing Catch with Sons," Donald Hall 141
Responding to the Reading 143
    Freewriting 143
    Building Your Vocabulary 143
    Questions for Discussion 144
Topics for Writing 144

8 A SENSE OF PLACE 147
Describing 148
    Characteristics of Describing 148
    "Rules of the Game," Amy Tan 151
Responding to the Reading 153
    Freewriting 153
    Building Your Vocabulary 153
    Questions for Discussion 154
Topics for Writing 154
The Writing Process: Describing 155
    Additional Considerations for Developing a Topic 155
    Additional Considerations for Thinking about Your Audience . . . 156
    Additional Considerations for Preliminary Writing 156
    Additional Considerations for Organizing Ideas 158
    Additional Considerations for Making Final Revisions 158
    Student Writing "My First Experience with
    Television," Wayne Onuki 158
    Questions for Discussion 159
    Student Writing "I Miss You, Mr. Fish," Arina Hung 159
    Questions for Discussion 159
For Further Reading 160
    "Self and World," Annie Dillard 160
Responding to the Reading 162
    Freewriting 162

Building Your Vocabulary 163
Questions for Discussion 164
Topics for Writing 164
   "The First Morning," Edward Abbey 165
Responding to the Reading 169
Freewriting 169
Building Your Vocabulary 170
Questions for Discussion 171
Topics for Writing 171
   Student Writing "An Awful Wilderness Adventure,"
   Pamela Vickers 172
Questions for Discussion 173

9 THE RICHNESS OF TRADITION 175
Process Analysis 176
Characteristics of Process Analysis 176
Possible Reliance on Other Writing Strategies 178
   "The Art of Lion Dancing," Donald Inn 179
Questions for Discussion 180
Topics for Writing 180
The Writing Process: Process Analysis 180
Additional Considerations for Developing a Topic 181
Additional Considerations for Thinking about Your Audience . . . 181
Additional Considerations for Preliminary Writing 181
Additional Considerations for Organizing Ideas 182
Additional Considerations for Writing a Fast Draft 182
Additional Considerations for Sharing and Revising 183
For Further Reading 183
   "Kwanzaa: Holiday of 'Principles to Live By,'" Eugene Morris 183
Responding to the Reading 185
Freewriting 185
Building Your Vocabulary 185
Questions for Discussion 185
Topics for Writing 186
   "Japanese Tea Ceremony," Vance Horne 186
Responding to the Reading 189
Freewriting 189
Building Your Vocabulary 189
Questions for Discussion 189

Topics for Writing 190
 Student Writing "Memories of Thanksgiving Day," Norma Davis . . . 190
 Questions for Discussion 192
 Student Writing "The Making of a *Quinceañera*,"
 Miguel A. Rodriguez 192
 Questions for Discussion 194
 Student Writing "Football on Monday Nights," Patricia Caldera 194
 Questions for Discussion 195
Interviewing 195
 Questions for Discussion 199
The Writing Process: Writing an Oral History 199
 Additional Considerations for Developing a Topic. 199
 Additional Considerations for Preliminary Writing 200
 Additional Considerations for Organizing Ideas 201
 Additional Considerations for Writing a Fast Draft 201
 Additional Considerations for Sharing
 Your Writing and for Making Final Revisions 202
  Student Writing "To Be Thankful," Sam Masuno 203
 Questions for Discussion 205
Topics for Writing 205

10 SELF AND OTHERS 207
Classifying 208
 Characteristics of Classifying. 208
  "What Ever Happened to Friendship?" Art Jahnke 211
Responding to the Reading 217
 Freewriting 217
 Building Your Vocabulary 217
 Questions for Discussion 218
Topics for Writing 218
The Writing Process: Classifying 219
 Additional Considerations for Developing a Topic. 219
 Additional Considerations for Thinking about Your Audience . . . 220
 Additional Considerations for Preliminary Writing 220
 Additional Considerations for Organizing Ideas 221
 Additional Considerations for Sharing Your
 Writing and Making Final Revisions. 221
For Further Reading 222
  "Personal Politics: A Lesson in Straight Talk," Lindsy Van Gelder . . 222

Responding to the Reading 223
   Freewriting 223
   Building Your Vocabulary 224
   Questions for Discussion 224
Topics for Writing 224
   "Just Walk On By: A Black Man Ponders His
   Power to Alter Public Space," Brent Staples 225
Responding to the Reading 228
   Freewriting 228
   Building Your Vocabulary 228
   Questions for Discussion 229
Topics for Writing 229
   Student Writing "The Good Samaritans," Stella Hallsted 230
   Questions for Discussion 231

11 MEN AND WOMEN 233
Comparing and Contrasting 234
   Characteristics of Comparing and Contrasting 235
   "Why Can't He Hear What I'm Saying?" Deborah Tannen 239
Responding to the Reading 244
   Freewriting 244
   Building Your Vocabulary 244
   Questions for Discussion 245
Topics for Writing 245
The Writing Process: Comparing and Contrasting 246
   Additional Considerations for Developing a Topic 246
   Additional Considerations for Preliminary Writing 246
   Additional Considerations for Thinking about Your Audience . . . 246
   Additional Considerations for Organizing Ideas 247
   Additional Considerations for Sharing Your
   Writing and Making Final Revisions 249
For Further Reading 249
   "George and Ophelia," Gloria Naylor 249
Responding to the Reading 256
   Freewriting 256
   Building Your Vocabulary 257
   Questions for Discussion 257
Topics for Writing 257
   "A Thinly Disguised Message," Deborah Marquardt 258

Responding to the Reading 260
  Freewriting 260
  Building Your Vocabulary 260
  Questions for Discussion 260
Topics for Writing 260
  "Iron John," Robert Bly 262
Responding to the Reading 272
  Freewriting 272
  Building Your Vocabulary 272
  Questions for Discussion 272
Topics for Writing 273
  Student Writing "Relationships," Dan Krum 274
  Questions for Discussion 275

12 IMMIGRANTS 277
Explaining Causes and Effects 278
  Characteristics of Causal Analysis 278
    "The Immigrants: How They're Helping to Revitalize the
    U.S. Economy," Michael J. Mandel and Christopher Farrell 282
Responding to the Reading 288
  Freewriting 288
  Building Your Vocabulary 288
  Questions for Discussion 289
Topics for Writing 290
The Writing Process: Causal Analysis 290
  Additional Considerations for Developing a Topic 290
  Additional Considerations for Thinking about Your Audience . . . 290
  Additional Considerations for Preliminary Writing 291
  Additional Considerations for Organizing Ideas 291
  Additional Considerations for Writing a Fast Draft 292
  Additional Considerations for Sharing Your
  Writing and Making Final Revisions 292
For Further Reading 293
  "Memoirs of a Chinese Mother," Amy Tan 293
Responding to the Reading 298
  Freewriting 298
  Building Your Vocabulary 298
  Questions for Discussion 299

Topics for Writing 299
  "Walking in Lucky Shoes," Bette Bao Lord 300
Responding to the Reading 302
  Freewriting 302
  Building Your Vocabulary 302
  Questions for Discussion 303
Topics for Writing 303
  Student Writing "Coming to America," Gabriel Ramirez 304
  Questions for Discussion 305

13 BETWEEN TWO CULTURES 307
Defining 308
  Characteristics of Defining 308
    "Border Culture," Marjorie Miller and Ricardo Chavira 312
Responding to the Reading 316
  Freewriting 316
  Building Your Vocabulary 317
  Questions for Discussion 317
Topics for Writing 317
The Writing Process: Defining 318
  Additional Considerations for Developing a Topic 318
  Additional Considerations for Preliminary Writing 318
  Additional Considerations for Organizing Ideas 318
  Additional Considerations for Sharing Your
  Writing and Making Final Revisions 319
For Further Reading 319
  "Complexion," Richard Rodriguez 319
Responding to the Reading 326
  Freewriting 326
  Building Your Vocabulary 326
  Questions for Discussion 326
Topics for Writing 326
  "The Black and White Truth about Basketball," Jeff Greenfield 328
Responding to the Reading 332
  Freewriting 332
  Building Your Vocabulary 332
  Questions for Discussion 333

Topics for Writing 333
  Student Writing "Can You Really Go Back Home?" Norma Davis . . . 334
  Questions for Discussion 335

14 EVALUATING EXPERIENCE 337
  Evaluating 338
    Characteristics of Evaluating 338
      "Hypocrisy," Jamie Myers 341
    Questions for Discussion 343
  The Writing Process: Evaluating 343
    Additional Considerations for Developing a Topic 343
    Additional Considerations for Preliminary Writing 343
    Additional Considerations for Organizing Ideas 344
    Additional Considerations for Sharing Your
    Writing and Making Final Revisions 345
  For Further Reading 345
    "The First Cure," Black Elk 345
  Responding to the Reading 350
    Freewriting 350
    Building Your Vocabulary 351
    Questions for Discussion 351
  Topics for Writing 351
    "The Shock of Alienation," Oscar Handlin 352
  Responding to the Reading 360
    Freewriting 360
    Building Your Vocabulary 361
    Questions for Discussion 362
  Topics for Writing 362
    "I'm Black, You're White, Who's Innocent?" Shelby Steele 362
  Responding to the Reading 374
    Freewriting 374
    Building Your Vocabulary 374
    Questions for Discussion 375
  Topics for Writing 377
    Student Writing "Love and War: An Evaluation of
    Dr. Zhivago," Sheryl Little 378
    Questions for Discussion 379

15 THE WORK PLACE 381

Problem Solving 382
   Characteristics of Problem Solving 383
      "The Workforce and the Future of Business," Evon Emerson 388

Responding to the Reading 393
   Freewriting 393
   Building Your Vocabulary 393
   Questions for Discussion 394

Topics for Writing 394

The Writing Process: Problem Solving 395
   Additional Considerations for Developing a Topic 395
   Additional Considerations for Thinking about Your Audience . . . 396
   Additional Considerations for Preliminary Writing 396
   Additional Considerations for Organizing Ideas 397
   Additional Considerations for Sharing Your
   Writing and Making Final Revisions 398

For Further Reading 399
   "The Organizer," Studs Terkel 399

Responding to the Reading 403
   Freewriting 403
   Building Your Vocabulary 403
   Questions for Discussion 403

Topics for Writing 404
   "Jobs," Tran Thi Nga 404

Responding to the Reading 406
   Freewriting 406
   Questions for Discussion 406

Topic for Writing 406
   "The Perfect Job," David Owen 406

Responding to the Reading 408
   Freewriting 408
   Building Your Vocabulary 408
   Questions for Discussion 408

Topics for Writing 409
   Student Writing "Emergency Room," Ernesto Morales 409
   Questions for Discussion 411
   Student Writing "Women in Law Enforcement," Gloria Moulder . . . 412
   Questions for Discussion 415

16 GETTING AN EDUCATION.......................... 417

Drawing Inferences 418
   Sample T-Graph 419
   Drawing Inferences from Details in Your Reading 420
      "The Struggle to Be an All-American Girl," Elizabeth Wong....... 422

Responding to the Reading............................. 424
   Freewriting 424
   Building Your Vocabulary 424
   Questions for Discussion 424

Topics for Writing...................................... 425

Inductive Reasoning..................................... 425

Deductive Reasoning 427
   "If We Stand, They Will Deliver," David Pierpont Gardner........ 428

Responding to the Reading............................. 431
   Freewriting 431
   Building Your Vocabulary 432
   Questions for Discussion 433

Topics for Writing...................................... 433
   "Theme for English B," Langston Hughes.................. 434

Responding to the Reading............................. 435
   Freewriting 435
   Questions for Discussion 436

Topics for Writing...................................... 436
   "Whose Culture Is It, Anyway?" Henry Louis Gates, Jr. 436

Responding to the Reading............................. 438
   Freewriting 438
   Building Your Vocabulary 438
   Questions for Discussion 439

Topics for Writing...................................... 439
   "Western Values Are Central," Donald Kagan 439

Responding to the Reading............................. 441
   Freewriting 441
   Building Your Vocabulary 441
   Questions for Discussion 441

Topics for Writing 442
   Student Writing "The Truth about High School," Thomas Carbone.. 442
   Questions for Discussion 443

17 EXAMINING STEREOTYPES 445

Taking a Stand 446
Characteristics of Essays That Take a Stand 446
"Speaking of Stereotypes," Bruce Ogilvie 449

Responding to the Reading 451
Freewriting 451
Building Your Vocabulary 451
Questions for Discussion 451

Topics for Writing 452

The Writing Process: Taking a Stand 452
Additional Considerations for Developing a Topic 452
Additional Considerations for Thinking about Your Audience . . . 453
Additional Considerations for Preliminary Writing 453
Additional Considerations for Organizing Ideas 454
Additional Considerations for Sharing Your
Writing and Making Final Revisions 454

For Further Reading 455
"Song for the Old Ones," Maya Angelou 455

Responding to the Reading 456
Freewriting 456
Building Your Vocabulary 456
Questions for Discussion 456

Topics for Writing 457
"The Arabs' Image," Mustafa Nabil 457

Responding to the Reading 459
Freewriting 459
Building Your Vocabulary 459
Questions for Discussion 459

Topics for Writing 461
"C'mon, They Don't All Drive Fast Cars!" Roy Blount, Jr. 461

Responding to the Reading 464
Freewriting 464
Building Your Vocabulary 464
Questions for Discussion 465

Topics for Writing 465
Student Writing "And 'How!'" Rebecca Valencia 465
Questions for Discussion 466
Student Writing "Love in Black and White," Gary Gilbert 467
Questions for Discussion 471

18 AGAINST INJUSTICE 473

Persuading 474
  Characteristics of Persuading 474
    "Letter from the Birmingham Jail," Martin Luther King, Jr. 480
Responding to the Reading 490
  Freewriting 490
  Building Your Vocabulary 490
  Questions for Discussion 491
Topics for Writing 491
The Writing Process: Persuading 492
  Additional Considerations for Organizing Ideas 492
  Additional Considerations for Sharing Your
  Writing and Making Final Revisions 493
For Further Reading 493
  "Homelessness in America," Charles E. King 493
Responding to the Reading 496
  Freewriting 496
  Building Your Vocabulary 496
  Questions for Discussion 497
Topics for Writing 497
  "My Anger and Sadness over Pesticides," Cesar Chavez 497
Responding to the Reading 502
  Freewriting 502
  Building Your Vocabulary 502
  Questions for Discussion 502
Topics for Writing 503
  Student Writing "Fathers Should Pay," Linda Lozano 503
  Questions for Discussion 506

PART THREE
Revising Sentences: A Writing Skills Workbook

19 RECOGNIZING VERBS 509

The Present Tense 509
  Verb Forms in the Present Tense 511
The Past Tense 513
  Verb Forms in the Past Tense 513

The Future Tense. 516
  Verb Forms in the Future Tense 516
Writing Exercise 517

20 WORKING WITH VERBS AND SUBJECTS. 518
Identifying Verbs and Subjects 518
  Questions to Help You Find Verb and Subject. 519
  Multiple Subjects 520
  Multiple Verbs 522
  Linking Verbs 523
  Auxiliary or Helping Verbs. 524
  Verbs and Subjects in Commands. 527
  Verbs and Subjects in Questions 528
  Differentiating Verbs and Subjects from
  Introductory Words and Phrases. 529
Writing Exercises 530

21 REVISING FOR VERB-SUBJECT AND
NOUN-PRONOUN AGREEMENT 531
Making Verbs and Subjects Agree. 531
  Using Third-Person Singular Verbs. 531
  Prepositional Phrases. 536
  Indefinite Pronouns 539
  Subjects Joined by *or* or *nor* 542
Making Nouns and Pronouns Agree 543
Writing Exercise 545

22 COORDINATING CONJUNCTIONS AND
OTHER CONNECTING WORDS 546
Connecting Independent Clauses 546
  Coordinating Conjunctions 546
  Transitional Words (Conjunctive Adverbs). 550
Writing Exercise 553

23 SUBORDINATING CONJUNCTIONS
AND RELATIVE PRONOUNS 554
Connecting Dependent and Independent Clauses 554

Patterns of Subordination 555
Relative Pronouns. 561
Writing Exercise 568

24 CORRECTING FRAGMENTS AND RUN-ON SENTENCES 569
Correcting Fragments with Words Omitted 570
Correcting Infinitive and -ing Fragments. 571
Infinitive Fragments. 571
-ing Fragments 572
Correcting Subordination Fragments 574
Correcting Run-on Sentences. 576
Writing Exercise 579

25 MAKING LOGICAL CONNECTIONS 580
Phrases in a Series 580
Prepositional Phrases. 580
Verb Phrases 582
Correcting Illogically Joined Sentences 583
Connecting Other Verb Phrases Correctly 585
Connecting Dangling Modifiers. 587
Writing Exercise 590

26 CONSISTENCY OF PERSON AND TENSE 591
Consistency of Person 591
Consistency of Tense 594
Writing Exercise 596

27 MECHANICS: A FEW BASIC RULES FOR WRITERS 597
Punctuation. 597
Commas 597
Semicolons 599
Colons 600
Apostrophes 600
Spelling. 601

Basic Spelling Rules 601
Commonly Confused Words 602
Capitalization 604

APPENDIX A 606

APPENDIX B 606

APPENDIX C 606

APPENDIX D 607

COPYRIGHTS AND ACKNOWLEDGMENTS 608

INDEX 610

PART ONE

An Overview of the Writing Process

First Steps

Writing probably plays some part in your life already, whether you write a memo to fellow workers, take a phone message for a roommate or family member, jot down items for a grocery list, or write to a relative who is having a birthday. As a student, of course, you can expect your instructors to give you writing assignments that require a great deal of planning and critical thinking.

Part One of this book prepares you for the formal writing assignments required in your college courses. The explanations and exercises in each chapter are designed to help you improve your reading and writing skills. After working through both Parts One and Two, the reading and writing sections of this book, you should find yourself a more efficient, careful, and confident writer.

In this chapter you examine your feelings about writing, and see how doing freewriting exercises and keeping a journal can make writing a little easier.

TAKING STOCK

The following survey helps you "take stock" of the kinds of writing you do and explore some of your ideas about writing.

1. What writing have you done for personal reasons during the past few weeks?

_____

_____

_____

2. What kinds of writing do you like to do? _____

_____

_____

_____

3. Write about a time you felt good about something you wrote. Briefly describe what you wrote and why you were proud of it. _____

_____

_____

_____

_____

_____

4. What do you find most difficult about writing for class assignments?

_____

_____

_____

5. If you were giving advice to a friend, what would you say are the most important things to remember when writing a paper for a class?_____

_____

_____

_____

_____

_____

There are lots of good suggestions to make about writing, and your collective answers to and discussion of question 5 (above) will give you a class list of ideas for successful writing. Here are two suggestions from professional writers that you may find useful when beginning a writing task.

1. *"Meaning is not what you start out with but what you end up with. . . . Think of writing then not as a way to transmit a message but as a way to grow and cook a message."—Peter Elbow*

Don't think you must know exactly what you want to say *before* you begin writing. As Peter Elbow points out, it takes time to "grow and cook" your ideas. Writer's block, the feeling that you have nothing to say, often comes from having the mistaken idea that something is wrong with you if you can't dash off perfect paragraphs, or if ideas don't flow effortlessly from your pen or computer the first time you sit down to work. The truth is, writing takes work, and it is work for *everybody* who writes.

> 2. *"There are days when the result is so bad that no fewer than five revisions are required. In contrast, when I'm greatly inspired, only four revisions are needed."—John Kenneth Galbraith*

Instead of worrying when the words don't come easily or you aren't happy with what you have written, accept the fact that you won't be satisfied with your earliest efforts. Expect to do quite a bit of preliminary writing, drafting, and revising before you write something that you genuinely like.

GATHERING YOUR THOUGHTS

If you are like many writers, getting started is your most difficult task. Freewriting and keeping a journal are two methods you can use to start writing and keep writing.

Freewriting

What Is Freewriting?

Freewriting means writing continuously about whatever comes to mind without worrying about how it sounds or stopping to check wording and spelling. Initially, you might feel like saying, "I have nothing to write," but because your mind is constantly processing sounds, smells, sights, memories, and ideas, you can always record what is going on inside your head. Chapters 3 and 5 show how these thoughts provide the raw material for paragraphs and essays.

How Does It Work?

When freewriting, write *anything* to keep yourself going. If, for example, you are thinking, "I hate to write, and I hate this stupid assignment," write *that*. If you get stuck and can't think of anything to write, try writing about how hard it is to get started. Regardless of where you begin, you will soon find yourself following your own thoughts and having plenty to say. It doesn't really matter *what* you write as long as you keep writing.

Sample of Freewriting

Tamara Baumann wrote this freewriting exercise on a day when she thought she didn't have anything to write.

I hate having to write what's on my mind without thinking about it. My mind grabs onto a total blank, and I can't find a thing. I don't like writing much because it takes me too long to find something to write about. If I'm listening to music, then I can write about something. The music relaxes me, and I can find all kinds of things to write about. My ceramics teacher said the right side of the brain starts to work when music is playing. Maybe that is true. I don't know. Someday I'll try an experiment on it. I have a lot of things on my mind, but when I have to write something, I go blank. Maybe if I didn't think so much and wrote more, this wouldn't happen.

Although she thought she didn't have anything to say, Tamara wrote about 130 words. In the process, she made an important discovery about her writing: It might be easier to write if she didn't worry so much about it—at least not when she is getting started.

FOR PRACTICE

Exercise 1a.   Now you try it. Take out a piece of paper, or get ready to type if your class uses computers. Record the date, note the time, and begin writing. Write steadily for ten minutes. Keep your pen moving across the page (or your fingers moving on the keyboard), and record your thoughts as they come to you. Whatever you do, don't stop to look back; don't correct anything. Just let the words roll out of you as they will.

Keeping a Journal

Reserve a section of your loose-leaf notebook, or buy a separate binder, and begin keeping a **journal.** Writing regularly in this journal is an excellent way to explore ideas, record observations, and experiment with language. The word *journal* comes from the French word meaning "daily," and you may occasionally feel like writing every day. Most of us should write as often as we exercise—about three times a week. Like regular running or swimming, frequent writing can become a familiar, even comfortable, exercise.

Sample Journal Entries

Journal entries are as diverse as the people who write them. The following samples illustrate a few ways to use your journal for comments and sketches. For a list of other possible topics, see "Ideas for Journal Entries" at the end of this chapter.

RECORDING INCIDENTS AND MAKING OBSERVATIONS

2/13

What happens in a child's world? About four months ago, I was standing in the kitchen cooking dinner. All of a sudden my youngest son came running in the door. His shirt was torn, he had red marks on his face and neck. I immediately ran after him to try to find out what had happened. He told me six boys had started hitting him. They chased him home, took his coat from him. I ran immediately to the school, which is only a block away, and explained to the principal what had happened. The next day we were all in the office. I asked them why this happened and got the old standard answer, "I don't know." When I looked at the boys, I couldn't help but wonder what kind of home life they had. They were so young yet so hard. That's one of the many reasons I decided to become a counselor. I feel if we can help children in some way, no matter how small, maybe, just maybe, we can keep a few out of prison or off drugs. Maybe I can help them to love themselves as human beings.

—Norma Davis

RESPONDING TO A MOVIE, CONCERT, OR OTHER ACTIVITY

4/3

I'm at home, thinking about the movie Fatal Attraction. Why? Why did Michael Douglas fall for Glenn Close? He had it all—marriage, a beautiful little girl, money, a wonderful life. Why? Michael Douglas' wife was far more beautiful than Glenn Close—so it can't be that his wife was letting herself go or anything because he was still attracted to her. Was it just convenience or maybe just another "roll in the hay"? Now I'll tell you what I think—Glenn Close (MiMi) knew what she wanted the first time they met. She was a sick woman, as they disclosed later in the movie. Michael Douglas was, by all means, attracted to her (she wasn't ugly). But remember, his wife was out of town, and before you knew it he was having dinner with this semi-attractive woman, and he was probably feeling pretty good after a couple of drinks. Too bad for him because she ends up nearly killing him and his wife later in the movie. And all it was for, especially to him, was a "fatal attraction."

—Doug Gonzales

REFLECTING ON YOUR WRITING

10/5

Today I don't feel very good. I still have a cold, but it seems as though my cold is getting worse. I don't even want to go to school, but I hate missing school because you get behind when you miss. I don't know what to write about today. I haven't been writing in my journal three times a week, but this week I am determined to do so. You know sometimes just picking up my journal and writing makes me feel better—especially when I'm lonely. Writing in my journal is like talking to someone. It kind of helps me to say things that I would not usually say. I think I'm starting to like this journal writing exercise. I'm beginning to see writing as a way of expressing myself, not just in journals, but in the assignments I have done on subjects that interest me, like drug babies.

—Renita Phillips

RESPONDING TO SOMETHING YOU HAVE READ

9/13

After reading Gail Godwin's "The Watcher at the Gate," I began to understand why it seems so difficult for me to commit my ideas to paper, why I find it hard to develop the ideas I get, and why I waste so much paper.

I too have a "watcher." A very egocentric one, at that. He always has to have it his way. He's a perfectionist and has the ability to influence things and people around me, creating every possible distraction. If I try to write outside, for instance, he calls for a car whose muffler has a hole in it. If I'm inside the house, he'll let in a fly to pester me until I give up. Of course, I have some control over his actions. When I put myself in a public place, I invite distractions. When I stay up late and listen to my old punk tapes, however, I can drive him off (as well as most of my family) and get some work done. In the end, writing is a tug-of-war.

—Christian Cinder

—Richard Hansard

Make a Commitment to Writing

Here are a few additional techniques that experienced writers have used to help them write. Practice them a few times and see if they make writing a little easier for you.

1. Write at the same time every day or every other day. When you do, you are keeping a promise to yourself to write regularly.
2. Make your writing sessions brief so that you don't feel overwhelmed by the task. Start by writing for five minutes and work up to ten or fifteen. On some days you will not want to stop, so you may occasionally write for twenty minutes.

3. Write in the same place several days in a row to associate the habit of writing with a particular spot. Start anywhere—your bedroom, the cafeteria, or the library at school.
4. Sneak up on yourself. Get up a few minutes early, and before you have a chance to think, "Oh no, I'm trying to write something," pick up a pencil or pen and begin writing in your journal or on a notepad that you keep beside your bed. Another good time to write is just before going to bed. You might also try jotting down journal entries while waiting for class to begin.

FOR PRACTICE

Exercise 1b.   Journal entries are often reflections on topics like those listed below. Choose one of these topics and take about ten minutes to write a one-page entry in your journal. Share your writing with classmates.

- An event in your life
- Observations you have made
- A recent controversy at school, work, or in the news
- Something you have heard about, seen, or experienced
- Issues about your own writing

Ideas for Journal Entries

1. Describe your surroundings. Where are you right now? What does the place look like, smell like, and feel like? Who usually goes there? Why?
2. Write about how your classes are going.
3. Describe a few of the people you have met this semester.
4. Write a letter to a friend explaining what has been on your mind lately.
5. Discuss your plans for the near future.
6. If you are working, describe the kind of work you do. What do you like or dislike about your job? If you know of a conflict or problem, describe it and explain what you would do to resolve it.
7. Describe what it is like to get up in the morning.
8. Pick a family member or friend you haven't seen for a while but have some feelings for, and write that person a letter.
9. Discuss what your friends have been doing lately.
10. Describe activities or sports that you enjoy.
11. List any special skills that you have. Describe a few in detail.
12. Write about an interesting article you have read or a good movie you have seen.
13. Write about a time when you couldn't stop laughing.
14. Describe something you did that got you into trouble.

Looking Ahead

In college you are often asked to write about something you have read. The next chapter suggests several techniques for understanding, remembering, and responding to what you read. Part Two, the reading section in this book, gives you additional practice in writing about reading and generating papers based on what you have read.

2

Writing about Reading

Most writing assignments in college require that you read about a subject before you write. For example, your sociology instructor might have you read several articles that describe the facts and myths about AIDS and write an analysis of your findings. You also might see a question on a biology exam that asks you to write about characteristics of the seed-producing plants covered in your textbook. Your English teacher might ask you to find articles on a subject of interest to you, summarize a problem that you identify, and offer solutions. To help you prepare for such assignments, this chapter gives you practice summarizing main ideas, thinking about these points, and developing a letter or paragraph in response to your reading.

ACTIVE READING

To be successful in college, you must participate in the learning process. That means taking notes in class, asking questions, and making appointments with instructors to go over ideas that you don't understand. Learning to *read actively* is equally important for college success.

You may have had the experience of reading a textbook or newspaper article and suddenly realizing that your eyes have been scanning the words, but you have not really "read" anything on the page. This is a good example of "passive reading"—you read words but don't think about what they mean. **Active reading,** on the other hand, involves thinking on paper—making notes in the margins of your books, jotting down journal entries as you read, drawing pictures, and making diagrams of what you think the writer is saying—in short, doing anything that helps you visualize what you are reading and keeps you alert to the author's ideas.

Techniques for Active Reading

1. Preview for Main Ideas

The first time you read an assignment, skim the material to locate the writer's main points. Read the title, the introduction (the first paragraph or two), any headings the writer uses, the topic sentences (usually the first sentence or two of each paragraph), and the conclusion. If the passage is a long one, section off groups of paragraphs that focus on the same point, and note in the margin what each section is about.

FOR PRACTICE

Exercise 2a.   Preview one of your textbooks for this term by scanning the table of contents, which is essentially a list of the topic ideas covered in the book. Without looking back at what you have read, write a paragraph explaining what you think the text will be about.

2. Reread Carefully

After reading for the main ideas, reread the material, this time looking for evidence that supports the main points. As you read a second time, keep yourself *active*—highlight or underline key words, consult a dictionary if you aren't sure about the meaning of a word, use the margins to summarize main ideas or note them in your journal, and mark the places where you have questions or disagree with the writer.

3. Respond to What You Read

When ideas in reading assignments stir memories, cause emotional responses, or raise questions in your mind, note these reactions in the margin as well. You might save the left-hand margin for your responses and put notes about main points in the margin on the right. If, on the other hand, you wish to reserve one margin for all of your notes, try using different colored ink to separate the two kinds of notations—blue for main ideas and black for your reactions—or put your reactions in parentheses.

Why Use the Active Reading Method?

1. Previewing, or "viewing in advance," gives you an overview of the material and prepares you to do a more careful reading later.
2. Your comprehension and reading speed should increase with this second reading because you have some familiarity with the subject.

3. Active reading also prepares you to take objective tests, to generate ideas for writing assignments, and to write summaries.

Sample of Active Reading

Here is a sample of one student's active reading notes on "The Tonto Syndrome." He first previewed the article and then reread it more carefully, underlining key ideas and making notes in the margin. His personal responses appear in parentheses.

The Tonto Syndrome
Leah Eskin

Stereotypes of Native Americans

The Lone Ranger, that "daring and resourceful masked rider of the plains," streaks across the screen, trumpets blaring, credits rolling, riding "a fiery horse with the speed of light, a cloud of dust, and a hearty 'Hi-Yo Silver!' " But <u>Tonto</u>, his "faithful Indian companion," <u>is nowhere to be seen.</u> Several minutes into "Six Gun Sanctuary," a typical episode of the popular 1950s TV series, Tonto finally shows up. He spots a wounded man. "Him shot in back, Kimosabee," Tonto states gravely. Then he looks up at his masked friend and asks, "What we do?"

Opening scene — Tonto absent

Tonto's not having a bad day; he's merely acting the part of the <u>typical TV Indian</u>. "The stereotype of Indians is that we're silent, ignorant, and we all talk the same language, which is 'ug,' " says Collins Oakgrove, a professor of American Indian Studies at the University of Minnesota. "It's what I call the (Tonto Syndrome) Tonto follows the white man around and speaks with grunts. In reality, we communicate with our own language, eloquently, and most of us are bilingual. I see the stereotype every day, and it bothers me."

Speaks broken English (He really sounds dumb — guess that's the point.)

Definition of Tonto Syndrome

From settlers' stories of the (1600s) to slick advertisements of the (1980s) Native Americans have suffered from the Tonto Syndrome. They have been typecast as solemn, stupid savages, as drunk, harmless has-beens, or as peace-loving, pipe-smoking friends of the Earth. But rarely have American Indians been cast in the role they most desire—as themselves.

History of stereotyping

Cowboys and Indians

Most non-Indians form their <u>first impressions of Native Americans on the playground</u>. "When little kids play cowboys and Indians," says Robert Thomas of the University of Arizona, "the Indians are always the bad guys. The cowboys win, the Indians get defeated. Children learn that Indians are bad."

Such games, and the stories that inspire them, seek to <u>reenact the conflict between Native Americans and the first white settlers,</u> who arrived in this country in the early 1600s. The problem, say most scholars, is that they draw on a <u>one-sided view of history.</u> "From contact with the first European settlers, the people writing the books were the Europeans," says Duane Hale of the American Indian Institute at the University of Oklahoma. "There were very few Indian writers giving an Indian account of the story. Down through the pages of history, Indians became people without names and faces, people who are very stoic, and have no feelings."

This game forms our ideas about Native Americans

(In my family, my little brother had to be the Indian—not a good thing to be.)

Whites wrote biased history.

(This sure changes my view of cowboys and Indians.)

Buffalo Bill's Wild West

The myth of the American Indian was further <u>refined by frontiersman William Frederick Cody,</u> better known as Buffalo Bill. In 1883, Cody formed Buffalo Bill's Wild West, a traveling show. The act included a <u>mock battle with Indians,</u> played, for the most part, by members of the Lakota Sioux tribe. Because Buffalo Bill's Wild West was as close as most Americans got to "real" Indians, Sioux traditions became, in the public mind, synonymous with all Indian customs.

By the time "Injuns" made it to the Western <u>movies of the 1950s,</u> directors generalized many Sioux traditions—such as hunting and feather headdresses—to all Indians. In fact, the hundreds of Native American tribes each have their own customs. The Hopi, for example, lived in villages, cultivated corn, and crafted elegant pottery.

"The old movies rely on a <u>homogenized Indian,</u>" says Karen Biestman of the University of California. "He is usually male, wears buckskin,

Cody contributed to stereotypes

Indians look alike in Westerns

beads, feathers, has a pinto pony, and is savage, uncaring, and brutal. But it's a <u>shallow image</u>. We don't see families, caring, a sense of community, spirituality, or day-to-day life."

What's missing from "shallow image"

And much of what we do see is simply made up. "We <u>rarely see women,</u>" says Biestman. "If we do, it's the princess, the daughter of a chief. But there's no such thing as royalty in Indian culture. These images are largely perpetrated by non-Indians. They are simply <u>inventions</u>."

Those inventions live on in the form of <u>cigar-store Indians</u>, and roadside attractions such as giant Indian statues, made-for-tourist <u>totem poles</u>, and "<u>ceremonial" dance pageants</u>. The Tomahawk Indian Store in Lupton, Arizona, for instance, looks like an enormous yellow brick teepee, but actually serves as an Indian craft giftshop and restaurant.

Chief Wahoo

Debate over Wahoo

Today, the <u>controversy has largely shifted to sports teams</u> calling themselves "Indians." The Cleveland Indians, for example, changed its name from the Cleveland Spiders more than 70 years ago to honor Louis Sockolexis, a Maine Indian who was the first Native American to play pro baseball. But many Native Americans view the name, and the team's logo, an "Indian" known as Chief Wahoo, as offensive.

Image is offensive

The team recently agreed to pay $30,000 to the Cleveland American Indian Center, but it continues to use the logo. "The claim was that the baseball club's use of the logo was demeaning and degrading to the American Indian," says Terry Gilbert, an attorney who brought suit against the team. "It depicts American Indians in a very goofy way."

lawsuit (But I don't even think of an Indian when I see Wahoo. It's just in fun. He's right, though, other ethnic groups wouldn't like to see these mascots.)

"Do you ever hear of the San Diego Negroes or the Miami Mexicans or the Minneapolis Polish people?" says Oakgrove. "Making a mascot of American Indian imagery is subhuman."

Some Native Americans, on the other hand, call it an acknowledgment of Indian contributions to American history. And the teams defend their mascots with pride. "It was never meant to be a racist symbol," says Christine Linnenbach, 18, a non-Indian student at Lowell High School in San

Image is positive

Francisco. Lowell's symbol, the Indian, was recently banned. "It's always been used with pride. It has hurt the morale of many students to have it taken away."

Whether a badge of honor or a humiliating stereotype, most American Indians agree that such two-dimensional images won't be corrected until Indians themselves play a leading role behind the camera, on screen, and in board rooms. But until then, some Native Americans are taking the long view. "If Indians ever have a team," says Thomas, "we'll just call ourselves the Americans."

Native Americans need larger role in film industry

FOR PRACTICE

Exercise 2b.   Apply the techniques for active reading to one chapter of a textbook you are using this term. First skim it for main ideas; then reread more carefully, making notes as you go.

WRITING SUMMARIES

You can apply your active reading skills to writing **summaries.** Summaries are paragraphs or outlines that paraphrase (state in your own words) the main ideas in something you have read. You may occasionally wish to quote a word or phrase if it helps you clarify the writer's point. In general, you will remember the ideas you have restated in your own words.

Summaries may consist of a short paragraph or a more detailed paper, depending on your purpose for writing. Because they record *main points,* summaries usually omit minor details that support the writer's ideas. You should also omit personal observations or reactions to what you have read.

Summaries are extremely useful in preparing for essay examinations and other writing assignments. For example, if you write summaries for chapters in your textbook on cultural anthropology, you will find it much easier to study for a midterm or final exam. Instead of rereading all the chapters, you can review the main points, additional comments of your own, and any notes you have from lectures.

After previewing and rereading "The Tonto Syndrome," and making marginal notes, one student wrote the following one-paragraph summary of Eskin's main ideas.

Summary of "The Tonto Syndrome"

In the article "The Tonto Syndrome," Leah Eskin shows how Native Americans have been stereotyped from their first contact with whites to present-day television programs, movies, and sports. Native Americans have always been "typecast" as losers and drunks who can't speak good English. Thanks to Buffalo Bill's Wild West shows, we think of all Native Americans as being alike in dress and behavior, and associate them with the cigar-store Indian, the totem pole, and the teepee. Some people argue that Chief Wahoo, symbol of the Cleveland Indians, portrays Native Americans "in a very goofy way." But such stereotypes probably won't change until Native Americans play a bigger role behind the scenes in the film industry.

Another student's more detailed summary of the Eskin article mentions additional topic ideas and key supporting details.

Summary of "The Tonto Syndrome"

In "The Tonto Syndrome," Leah Eskin shows how Native Americans have been stereotyped from their first contact with whites to present-day depictions in television programs, movies, and sports.

Tonto, television's stereotype of the Native American, is a typical case. He is the white man's sidekick who speaks broken English. Tonto and his kind have been with us since whites began writing their lopsided history of the western migration. As children, we reenact battles between whites and Indians that are much like those staged by Buffalo Bill Cody for his Wild West shows. Cody's idea of Native Americans appeared in the movies of the 1950s in which all Indians look alike, dress alike, and act alike—without regard to the differences between Indian populations. Consequently, the cigar-store Indian, the totem pole, tomahawk, and teepee symbolize all Indian cultures.

For some, the stereotypical Indian is alive today in images like Chief Wahoo, mascot of the Cleveland Indians. Outraged Native Americans received a $30,000 settlement for the insult, but the team has not changed its emblem. Perhaps real changes won't come until Native Americans have more control over the film industry.

Reading and Summarizing

Your first reading assignment is a short piece by Robert Fulghum entitled, "Get Found, Kid!" Practice reading actively by first previewing the article, reading more carefully for details, and taking notes in the margins or in your journal.

Get Found, Kid!
Robert Fulghum

In the early dry dark of an October's Saturday evening, the neighborhood children are playing hide-and-seek. How long since I played hide-and-seek? Thirty years; maybe more. I remember how. I could become part of the game in a moment, if invited. Adults don't play hide-and-seek. Not for fun, anyway. Too bad.

Did you have a kid in your neighborhood who always hid so good, nobody could find him? We did. After a while we would give up on him and go off, leaving him to rot wherever he was. Sooner or later he would show up, all mad because we didn't keep looking for him. And we would get mad back because he wasn't playing the game the way it was supposed to be played. There's *hiding* and there's *finding*, we'd say. And he'd say it was hide-and-seek, not hide-and-give-UP, and we'd all yell about who made the rules and who cared about who, anyway, and how we wouldn't play with him anymore if he didn't get it straight and who needed him anyhow, and things like that. Hide-and-seek-and-yell. No matter what, though, the next time he would hide too good again. He's probably still hidden somewhere, for all I know.

As I write this, the neighborhood game goes on, and there is a kid under a pile of leaves in the yard just under my window. He has been there a long time now, and everybody else is found and they are about to give up on him over at the base. I considered going out to the base and telling them where he is hiding. And I thought about setting the leaves on fire to drive him out. Finally, I just yelled, "GET FOUND, KID!" out the window. And scared him so bad he probably wet his pants and started crying and ran home to tell his mother. It's real hard to know how to be helpful sometimes.

A man I know found out last year he had terminal cancer. He was a doctor. And knew about dying, and he didn't want to make his family and friends suffer through that with him. So he kept his secret. And died. Everybody said how brave he was to bear his suffering in silence and not tell everybody, and so on and so forth. But privately his family and friends said how angry they were that he didn't need them, didn't trust their strength. And it hurt that he didn't say good-bye.

He hid too well. Getting found would have kept him in the game. Hide-and-seek, grown-up style. Wanting to hide. Needing to be sought. Confused about being found. "I don't want anyone to know." "What will people think?" "I don't want to bother anyone."

Better than hide-and-seek, I like the game called Sardines. In Sardines the person who is It goes and hides, and everybody goes looking for him. When you find him, you get in with him and hide there with him. Pretty soon everybody is hiding together, all stacked in a small space like puppies in a pile. And pretty soon somebody giggles and somebody laughs and everybody gets found.

Medieval theologians even described God in hide-and-seek terms, calling him *Deus Absconditus*. But me, I think old God is a Sardine player. And will be found the same way everybody gets found in Sardines—by the sound of laughter of those heaped together at the end.

"Olly-olly-oxen-free." The kids out in the street are hollering the cry that says "Come on in, wherever you are. It's a new game." And so say I. To all those who have hid too good. *Get found, kid!* Olly-olly-oxen-free.

You may have noticed that Fulghum doesn't always write complete sentences—"Thirty years; maybe more" and "Too bad" are examples. He also uses "good" in place of the correct adverb "well" ("He hid too good"). Also, "It's real hard" is "it's really hard" in standard English. These nonstandard expressions mimic one variety of spoken English.

FOR PRACTICE

Exercise 2c.   What is the effect of Fulghum's use of nonstandard English in place of more formal expressions?

In the exercises that follow you will apply your active reading skills to find the main ideas in Fulghum's paragraphs. Here is the first paragraph with the main idea stated for you:

> In the early dry dark of an October's Saturday evening, the neighborhood children are playing hide-and-seek. How long since I played hide-and-seek? Thirty years; maybe more. I remember how. I could become part of the game in a moment, if invited. Adults don't play hide-and-seek. Not for fun, anyway. Too bad.

Main Idea: Fulghum says it's "too bad" that adults don't play hide-and-seek.

FOR PRACTICE

Exercise 2d.   Write the main idea for the remaining paragraphs.

> Did you have a kid in your neighborhood who always hid so good, nobody could find him? We did. After a while we would give up on him and go off, leaving him to rot wherever he was. Sooner or later he would show up, all mad because we didn't keep looking for him. And we would get mad back because he wasn't playing the game the way it was supposed to be played. There's *hiding* and there's *finding*, we'd say. And he'd

say it was hide-and-seek, not hide-and-give-UP, and we'd all yell about who made the rules and who cared about who, anyway, and how we wouldn't play with him anymore if he didn't get it straight and who needed him anyhow, and things like that. Hide-and-seek-and-yell. No matter what, though, the next time he would hide too good again. He's probably still hidden somewhere, for all I know.

Main Idea: _____

_____

_____

As I write this, the neighborhood game goes on, and there is a kid under a pile of leaves in the yard just under my window. He has been there a long time now, and everybody else is found and they are about to give up on him over at the base. I considered going out to the base and telling them where he is hiding. And I thought about setting the leaves on fire to drive him out. Finally, I just yelled, "GET FOUND, KID!" out the window. And scared him so bad he probably wet his pants and started crying and ran home to tell his mother. It's real hard to know how to be helpful sometimes.

The main idea in paragraph three is not as obvious as it was in the first two.

What do you think this paragraph is about?_____

_____

_____

A man I know found out last year he had terminal cancer. He was a doctor. And knew about dying, and he didn't want to make his family and friends suffer through that with him. So he kept his secret. And died. Everybody said how brave he was to bear his suffering in silence and not tell everybody, and so on and so forth. But privately his family and friends said how angry they were that he didn't need them, didn't trust their strength. And it hurt that he didn't say good-bye.

Main Idea: _____

_____

_____

He hid too well. Getting found would have kept him in the game. Hide-and-seek, grown-up style. Wanting to hide. Needing to be sought. Confused about being found. "I don't want anyone to know." "What will people think?" "I don't want to bother anyone."

Main Idea: _____

_____

_____

Better than hide-and-seek, I like the game called Sardines. In Sardines the person who is It goes and hides, and everybody goes looking for him. When you find him, you get in with him and hide there with him. Pretty soon everybody is hiding together, all stacked in a small space like puppies in a pile. And pretty soon somebody giggles and somebody laughs and everybody gets found.

Main Idea: _____

_____

_____

Medieval theologians even described God in hide-and-seek terms, calling him *Deus Absconditus*. But me, I think old God is a Sardine player. And will be found the same way everybody gets found in Sardines—by the sound of laughter of those heaped together at the end.

Main Idea: _____

_____

_____

"Olly-olly-oxen-free." The kids out in the street are hollering the cry that says "Come on in, wherever you are. It's a new game." And so say I. To all those who have hid too good. *Get found, kid!* Olly-olly-oxen-free.

Main Idea: _____

_____

_____

Exercise 2e.   Write a summary of Fulghum's article. First write a sentence or two in which you state the main point or thesis *in your own words.* Then, again using your own words, summarize the other general points or topic sentences Fulghum uses to support that thesis.

_____

_____

_____

_____

_____

_____

_____

_____

_____

_____

_____

_____

_____

_____

_____

_____

_____

_____

_____

_____

Exercise 2f.   Select an article from one of the chapters in Part Two of this book. Use the techniques for active reading; then write a summary.

RESPONDING TO THE READING

Summarizing ideas is an important part of understanding what you have read. But active reading also means *responding* in some way to what the writer has said. You can, for example, record the initial satisfaction, surprise, anger, or sadness you felt as you were reading; you may note your disagreement with something you read; the reading may remind you of experiences you have had that are either similar to or different from the writer's; or you can jot down questions for class discussion. Your responses may take the form of notes in the margin or journal entries. In either case, as you write your responses, try imagining that you are talking directly to the writer; this tactic will help you become more involved with the reading.

Exercise 2g.   Write a journal entry in which you respond in some way to Robert Fulghum's "Get Found, Kid!" You can record feelings, experiences, or questions you have in response to particular passages. Share your entries with classmates. Here are a few sample responses.

1. The part about holding things in really touched me because I am one to hold things in. My mom tells me all the time about holding back my feelings. She says that I could get sick if I don't talk about things that bother me. I'm always even-tempered, at least I seem that way, and only people who really know me can tell when I'm upset or sad about something. My mom tells me my dad was the same way, and it's in the genes. I think she's the only person I can really talk to about anything, but sometimes I choose to hold back, even with her. But you know what, she always knows when something's wrong.

2. I think the doctor who hid his cancer from his family was wrong. I can't believe he let himself die alone like that. If I had a friend who was dying of cancer, I would tell him to tell his family at once because he will need their support. Families need to stay together at such times because they give each other strength. Everybody needs somebody. My dad's mom is dying of can- cer, and she talks openly about it. By talking about her cancer, she gets over the pain of dying. So to me, talking about it is the best way to handle any- thing, no matter how large or small.

3. Fulghum makes "getting found" sound great. Everyone ends up friendly and together, but in my own life, I haven't found that many people I want to play Sardines with. No matter what Fulghum says, I think there are times when it is best not to share things. Take me, for instance. I hide my past from people because it was so bad. My older sister says I have had a worse life than most people my age. I don't think I can reveal my deepest secrets to anyone except my closest friend who has just moved to Chico. People would misunderstand and judge me because of the life I've led. There just aren't that many people you can trust.

Exercise 2h.   Choose a passage or two from Leah Eskin's "The Tonto Syndrome" that you feel strongly about or that interests you in some way. Then write a letter to Eskin explaining your reaction.

Exercise 2i.   Freewrite about someone, such as a parent, friend, or spouse, with whom you share your most private feelings.

Building Your Vocabulary

Your teacher may ask you to set aside a section of your journal for a vocabulary list. You will need three columns for your list—one for the word you want to find, another for the definition *you* write based on context clues, and a third for the dictionary's definition.

Techniques for Recognizing Words

In your second column, labeled "My Definition," *before* you consult your dictionary, write your own idea of what the word means. To do that, look for clues from the **context**—the other words near the word you want to find and the ideas in the paragraph—to help you figure out the most likely meaning for the word. For example, *Deus Absconditus* is a Latin phrase that you probably would not understand if you read it by itself. But Fulghum gives you several clues about its meaning when he says, "medieval theologians . . . described God in hide-and-seek terms." He adds that these same theologians called God *Deus Absconditus* (see paragraph 7 of Fulghum's article).

What do you think *Deus* means? _____

_____

To figure out the meaning of *Absconditus,* remember that Fulghum told us this phrase was used to describe God "in hide-and-seek terms." What do you think *Absconditus* means? _____

_____

Another good technique for decoding a word is to break it apart and see if it is composed of other words that are more familiar. If, for example, you see the word *triviality,* you can isolate the word *trivia,* which you may recognize from the name of the game Trivial Pursuit. Like *trivia, triviality* also means a piece of unimportant or insignificant information.

The beginnings and endings of words also offer clues to words' meanings. Here are a few common suffixes and prefixes with sample words.

COMMON PREFIXES AND EXAMPLES

Prefix	Meaning	Sample Word
bi-	two	**bi**sect (cut in two)
de-	take away from	**de**grade (cut in rank, diminish)
ex-	out of, from	**ex**claim (to cry out)
mis-	bad, wrong	**mis**behave (behave badly)
post-/pre-	after/before	**post**war (after a war)/**pre**war (before a war)
sub-	beneath	**sub**marine (beneath the ocean)

COMMON SUFFIXES AND EXAMPLES

Suffix	Meaning	Sample Word
-able	worthy of	depend**able** (worthy of trust)
-ant	person	defend**ant** (person defending himself/herself)
-less	without	hope**less** (without hope)
-ness	quality or state	happi**ness** (state of being happy)

Consulting a Dictionary

You should look up all unfamiliar words in a dictionary. When you compare your definition to the dictionary's, don't forget to look at the etymology of the word. The etymology gives the history of the word—its original form, language, and meaning. Under *abscond*, for example, you will find an entry similar to this one from *The American Heritage Dictionary*.

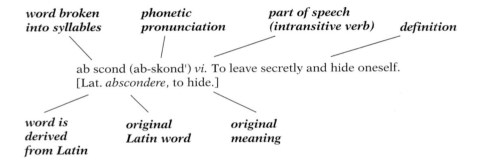

In this case, the etymology of *abscond* helps you translate the Latin phrase "Deus absconditus"—the hidden God.

Below is a student's vocabulary list entry for the word *medieval*. The parenthetical number refers to the paragraph where the word appears in Fulghum's essay.

VOCABULARY LIST

Words to Look Up	My Definition (based on context clues)	Dictionary Definition
medieval (7)	ancient	Of, pertaining to, or typical of the Middle Ages, 700–1500 A.D.

FOR PRACTICE

Exercise 2j.   Record an entry for *theologians* (from Fulghum's paragraph 7) in your vocabulary list.

Questions for Discussion

The following questions, and similar questions in the chapters that follow, are designed to improve your comprehension and ability to draw conclusions and evaluate what you read. Freewriting exercises and marginal notes you make as you read prepare you to think about what the writer is saying and to draw conclusions based on the information in the reading. This kind of critical thinking will give you ideas to explore further in your writing assignments.

1. You may have noticed that you enjoy or reject what you read depending on how the writer "speaks" to you. Authors adopt a particular "tone of voice" or attitude toward their subjects, and, if they are consistent, they maintain a single point of view. Textbooks in your classes, for example, usually have an impersonal voice that is quite different from the way a family member or close friend writes. Use the following questions to identify Fulghum's writing "voice":
   a. Where is Fulghum as he writes?
   b. What scene is he watching?
   c. What memories does he write about?
   d. What is Fulghum's attitude toward "hide-and-seek"? How do you know?
   e. How does Fulghum feel about the game of Sardines? What clues does he give you about why he has this attitude?
2. In the fourth paragraph Fulghum says, "A man I know found out last year he had terminal cancer. . . ." What does this discussion have to do with his description of children playing hide-and-seek?
3. Why does Fulghum think it is important to "get found"?
4. What are some ways people hide from each other?

TOPICS FOR WRITING

Topic 1.   Pick a passage from Fulghum's article and write a letter to the author asking him questions or telling him what you appreciated about his essay.

Topic 2.   Which is the best way for you to express your feelings—in person or in writing? Explain how this communication works with particular people.

Topic 3.   Look over your freewriting notes and see if there is a topic you would like to explore in a paragraph. Freewrite again to gather more details, examples, and information. Then write a draft, and revise it carefully to better communicate your ideas to another reader.

Looking Ahead

Chapters 3 and 5 illustrate how two students used the writing process to compose a paragraph-length assignment (Chapter 3) and an essay (Chapter 5). Exercises in Chapters 4 and 6 help you refine your paragraph and essay structure.

The Writing Process: Writing a Paragraph

T his chapter introduces the writing process, which is a step-by-step approach to writing that takes you from initial ideas to a finished paper. The eight steps in the writing process are used throughout this book, first in this chapter as a guide to writing paragraphs, and then in Chapter 5 as a guide for writing essays. They reappear in most of the chapters in Part Two, where the writing process is applied to specific writing tasks that require narrating, describing, explaining, evaluating, taking a stand, or arguing a point. This chapter shows how one student, Sarah Kaplan, used the writing process to compose a paragraph.

WHAT IS THE WRITING PROCESS?

Most experienced writers look at writing as a *process*—a series of steps they can take to generate, arrange, refine, expand, and revise their ideas. If you look at writing as a series of small steps, it isn't nearly as frightening as it is if you think you must produce a perfect, error-free paper the first time you sit down to write.

As you practice using the techniques for writing described in this chapter, keep in mind the following:

1. You probably won't know exactly what you want to say before you begin writing. In the process of writing, however, you will create new approaches to your subject that you hadn't thought of before you began.

2. You will need to add, cross out, and rearrange ideas as you write and revise your work. Neatness counts only at the end of the writing process.

As you become familiar with the steps in the writing process, you will develop a procedure for writing that works best for you. That may mean completing a step out of order, repeating it at different stages, or choosing one writing technique over another. At this stage it is important for you to learn what your choices are, experiment with steps that are new to you, and, above all, *keep writing.*

WHAT IS A PARAGRAPH?

A **paragraph** is a group of closely related sentences that support one point or main idea. Like the one-paragraph summaries you wrote in Chapter 2, paragraphs may be written to stand alone. This chapter gives you practice writing single paragraphs. Paragraphs are often part of the body of an essay, and they support the larger idea or **thesis**. (Chapter 5 discusses thesis and body paragraphs in greater detail.)

STEPS TO WRITING

Step One: Developing a Topic

In many college classes, you will respond to assignments that instructors have given you. When you get such assignments, take some time to think about what they ask you to do. In particular, underline key words that identify the subject and tell you how to approach it.

Sample Assigned Topics

Key words in the topics listed here are underlined for you and explained in the second column.

Topic	Explanation
Explain why you decided to go to college.	Subject: Your decision to go to college Task: Explain, which means to make clear, by giving reasons why Procedure: Show how people, events, or circumstances influenced your decision to go to college.

Sometimes topics appear as questions. Here is an example:

Topic	Explanation
In what <u>situations</u> could you <u>justify lying</u> to someone?	Subject: <u>Lying</u> Task is implied. Give examples and explain why you chose them Procedure: Explain <u>why lying</u> might be acceptable in certain <u>situations</u>.

FOR PRACTICE

Exercise 3a.   Underline the key words in these topics. Use the lines in the second column to explain your strategy for responding to the topic.

1. Describe someone you know well.

   Subject: _____

   Task: _____

   _____

   Procedure: _____

   _____

2. What are the advantages of living alone?

   Subject: _____

   Task: _____

   _____

   Procedure: _____

   _____

3. Explain to a friend why he or she should vote in the next election.

   Subject: _____

   Task: _____

   _____

   Procedure: _____

   _____

   _____

Choosing Your Own Topic

Sometimes you will be asked to develop your own topic for a paragraph or paper. In this case, you might focus on a subject that has been discussed in class. If the topic is open, you could write about your interests, something that has happened to you, or people you have observed. Another alternative is to find a journal entry that mentions a subject you want to explore. With your writing task in mind, reread your journal entries, and circle words and phrases that suggest a topic. Freewrite in your journal again to gather more information on this topic. (See the list of questions for your journal at the end of Chapter 1.)

Student Sample

The rest of this chapter shows how one student, Sarah Kaplan, used the steps in the writing process to create a topic, generate and arrange ideas, draft a paragraph, and revise it. Accompanying exercises help you become familiar with each of these steps.

Sarah's English teacher asked the class to write a paragraph describing a person who has some significance for them. Sarah wrote this journal entry to get ideas about someone she might describe.

3/3

What shall I write about? I could describe my Dad's friend Raymond. The three of us used to sit in Dad's car on a road near the airport and watch air-planes land. It was a popular place, so we had to go early on a Sunday after-noon to get a spot. Raymond was an interesting man. He knew all about engines. I remember he once spent several hours explaining to my dad and me how a rotary engine works. He was soft-spoken, religious. As a child, I was fascinated with the knowledge he had of jet propulsion.

It wasn't surprising that he didn't get along very well with my Aunt Rumania. She wasn't much like him or other aunts for that matter—she didn't bake cookies, wear flower-print dresses, or pin her hair in a bun the way aunts sometimes do. She was literally a Gypsy—part of her at least. Her grandmother was a Gypsy from Romania, and she was a mixture of other cultures. She traveled a lot, too. She was really beautiful, even in her fifties. She was wearing bright colors whenever I saw her, and she loved silver bracelets and necklaces. Her fingernails were usually painted. Since she died three years ago, I've thought about her a lot. I think she was the most inter-esting member of my family.

Narrowing the Topic

Sarah started with three possible topics for her descriptive paragraph—trips to the airport runway with her father and his friend Raymond, a portrait of Raymond himself, and a description of her aunt, Rumania Tesslav. Although she found all three topics appealing, Sarah was most interested in writing about her aunt. With this topic in mind, she underlined ideas in her journal she thought she could use—She wasn't much like him or other aunts for that matter—she didn't bake cookies, wear flower-print dresses, or pin her hair in a bun the way aunts sometimes do. She was literally a Gypsy. Her grandmother was a Gypsy from Romania. She traveled a lot, too. She was wearing bright colors whenever I saw her, and she loved silver bracelets and necklaces.

Sarah wrote another journal entry, this time focusing on some of the ways Aunt Rumania looked and acted that made her different from other people.

3/4

My aunt, Rumania Tesslav, lived like a Gypsy, traveling all over the country. When I was a little girl, she'd send me postcards from Wenatchee, Washington; Orlando, Florida; and Columbus, Ohio—all in the same year. She changed locations the way most of us change clothes. She never minded what other people thought about how she lived, even members of her family. Her bright clothes—flowing skirts and loud colors—made her look wild. She embarrassed me once when she came to carnival night in junior high school. The kids stared at her red harem pants and orange blouse, her hair tied back with a scarf. I tried to pass her off as a wacky friend of my father. My aunt wasn't affected by their stares or my embarrassment. She said, "Why should you care what they think? They don't know anything about me." I'm not ashamed of her any more.

Sarah's entries suggested several possible ways to organize the description of her aunt. She could, for example, discuss (1) how Rumania compared with other aunts, (2) her aunt's heritage, (3) her flamboyant way of dressing, or (4) her nomadic life.

FOR PRACTICE

Exercise 3b.   What other topics can you think of that are related to Sarah's journal entries on her aunt Rumania?

Exercise 3c.   Spend ten or fifteen minutes freewriting about someone memorable in your life. After you have finished, review what you have written and pick out several topics you could develop in a paragraph.

Exercise 3d.   Reread several journal entries you have written this semester. Pick one that interests you and list possible topics for a descriptive paragraph.

Step Two: Thinking about Your Audience

Often in your life you are aware of an "audience." When you talk to a friend or relative on the telephone, you probably picture the person at the other end of the line. You might imagine that person's surroundings and how his or her facial expressions change in response to what you say. Similarly, when you write, try picturing someone actually reading your work. Imagining your audience in this way helps you think of your writing as a communication between you and your reader, and is one of the most effective tools for narrowing your topic.

STUDENT SAMPLE.   To help her shape her topic to her audience, Sarah Kaplan asked herself two questions:

> *Who is my audience?*

I am writing for students who, like me, may have just started to appreciate their families. I'm writing for myself, too, because I want to write down everything I can remember about the way my Aunt Rumania dressed and acted before I forget those details.

> *Why am I writing for this audience?*

A well-written description of my aunt might give other students ideas about how to describe a family member or another person who has been important to them. I would like to think I could inspire someone else to write about a person who means a lot to them.

I am also writing because some people have misconceptions about what Gypsies are like, and I would like my readers to see that Gypsies are like anybody else—they have families and are warm, loving people.

Sarah's answers to these questions helped her choose her topic: A tribute to Aunt Rumania.

FOR PRACTICE

Exercise 3e.   Who else might be interested in reading about Sarah's topic?

_____

_____

Exercise 3f.   Describe two possible audiences for the topics listed here.

Example: The importance of exercise

    1. Forty-year-olds who are skeptical about starting an exercise program
    2. Students of all ages who have difficulty finding time to exercise

Parking problems on campus

1. _____

2. _____

Choosing the proper roommate

1. _____

2. _____

Benefits of wearing contact lenses

1. _____

2. _____

Overcoming computer fears

1. _____

2. _____

Air pollution

1. _____

2. _____

Writing for Different Audiences

Your audience helps you decide the tone or attitude to take toward your subject, the style of writing to use (slang or more formal English), and the kind of information to include. An assignment for an English class, for example, requires that you use a writing style free of slang and one that helps you to explain your ideas in some depth. If, however, you are writing a letter to a close friend or scribbling a note to a roommate, you are more likely to use an informal, more personal style and to state your message briefly.

FOR PRACTICE

Exercise 3g.   Read the following paragraphs carefully, noting the differences in writing styles and in the kind of information presented. Then identify a possible audience for each paragraph.

1. I have had it with Omar. I really wanted to go to that dance last night. I was wearing the nicest, slinkiest dress I own. I had fixed my hair and put on my makeup and was ready at 9:30, but I waited and waited—9:30, 10:00—no Omar. I called his apartment, his mother's house, and the printing company where he works—still no Omar. I was really mad at that jerk! My friend Lana happened to be home watching a movie with Patrice. They didn't feel like going out, so I changed clothes and went over there. This morning Omar called and said he just couldn't make it. Ha! I flat out told him to forget it and hung up. I got so hot about it I couldn't even talk to that creep. I'm better off without him.

Possible audience: _____

_____

2. Last night I decided to break up with Omar. He usually picks me up half an hour late. Sometimes he has been drinking and I end up driving myself and having a miserable time. But last night he didn't show up at all. He had told me he would come by at 9:30, and we would go dancing, but he never bothered to call when he found out he couldn't make it. It isn't as though I didn't try to find him, either. I called his apartment, his mother's house, and even the printing company where he works to see if he might have been working late. He wasn't at any of those places, and no one knew where he was. Instead of feeling depressed and rejected, I decided to break up with him. I called my friend, Lana, and joined her and her cousin, Patrice, for a VCR party. Lana had rented three films she thought Patrice might like, so we ate popcorn and watched movies on her VCR until 3:00 in the morning. The good time I had with my friend and her cousin convinced me that my decision to break up with Omar was the right one; I can have much more fun without him.

Possible audience: _____

_____

Exercise 3h.   The writer of the next two paragraphs describes what happened at a student council meeting. Suggest a possible audience for each paragraph.

1. I went to my first student council meeting last week and learned that student council meetings can be very explosive. The President made a motion that all candidates for offices in student government should be at least on the sophomore level and be taking 12 units a semester. One of the council members pointed out that she could not vote for the measure because she herself had held the Treasurer's position her second semester of college. Another member said he thought that students themselves would make that decision by either voting or not voting for freshmen. A third member thought that if the President's measure passed, well-qualified candidates who happened to be freshmen would not have the chance to run for office. Once he saw that he had little chance of getting the measure passed, the President got very angry and told the other council members that he expected to get better cooperation from his cabinet. He resented the fact that they had agreed with him when he had talked to them individually, yet refused to support him when he asked for a vote. Eventually, he got up and left the meeting, shouting that they could have his resignation and run the elections any way they wished. After he left, the council voted to accept his resignation.

Possible audience: _____

_____

2. I regret to inform you that Mark Stuart, the former Student Body President, resigned his post last Wednesday afternoon. Mark had a disagreement with several of his cabinet members that he was apparently unable to resolve, and as a result, gave his notice verbally at the end of the last council meeting. As Security Officer for Student Council, I have accepted Mr. Stuart's resignation, effective September 26, 1991.

Sincerely,

Samantha Tarin

Samantha Tarin

Possible audience: _____

_____

Exercise 3i. Pretend you witnessed the accident whose details are listed here. Write descriptions for the audiences described in a, b, and c below.

A red Acura is going south on Birch Street in the middle lane.
Birch is a one-way street.
A motorcycle is in the right-hand lane.
A couple is on the motorcycle, both wearing helmets.
The driver of the Acura is Remy Sims.
The couple are Jennine and Ron Collie.
Sims makes a sharp right-hand turn and cuts across the right lane.
The right side of his car strikes the front wheel of the motorcycle.
The couple is thrown against his car.
Sims stops and asks a neighbor to call an ambulance.
Jennine Collie suffers three broken ribs in the collision.
She also tears a ligament when her left knee hits the pavement.
Ron Collie has skin lacerations on his left arm.
His right leg breaks when the motorcycle falls on it.

a. You are a journalism student who has been asked to describe the accident for the school newspaper. Write your report for students at your college who know both Ron and Jennine Collie. Caution: Change present tense verbs to the past tense.
b. Write a letter to the parents of Jennine Collie explaining what happened. Again, use the past tense when recounting the events.
c. Write a letter of explanation to Remy Sims' wife.

Exercise 3j.   Choose a subject from the list below. Write two responses, each for a different audience.

1. a. Write a letter to your parents describing your best vacation.
   b. Describe the same events in a letter to a close friend.
2. Think of an argument you witnessed that did not involve you directly.
   a. Explain to a friend who was not there what was being argued and your position on the issue.
   b. Explain your view of the argument to one of the people involved.
3. Give reasons why teenagers should not drink and drive.
   a. Write to convince the parents of teenagers why their children and their children's friends should not drink and drive.
   b. Write a plea to teenagers themselves, explaining why they should not drink and drive.

Step Three: Preliminary Writing

Once you have your topic and know something about your audience, use the following techniques to generate the subtopics, details, and examples you need to communicate your ideas to your audience. As you become familiar with these techniques, you may wish to use them in a different order, or you may find that you favor one over the others.

1. Ask Yourself Questions

You have already seen how Sarah Kaplan used a question-and-answer technique to explore ideas about her audience. You will also find this method useful for generating ideas, and if you suffer from writer's block, answering questions will help you keep writing.

"What am I trying to say?" is one of the best questions you can ask. If you ask and answer that question frequently, you are likely to stick to your topic. In addition, expand the journalist's questions—*who, what, where, when, why,* and *how*—into full sentences that relate to your topic. Answers to these questions provide the subtopics and supporting examples for your paragraph. (If you have difficulty coming up with questions on your own, consult "Questions for Expanding Ideas," Appendix B at the back of this book.)

2. Draw an Idea Wheel

Your next response to a topic might be to draw an idea wheel—a cluster of ideas connected to one another like spokes on a wheel. This technique is also called "clustering" or "branching." It is one way to visualize your ideas and make connections between them.

3. Make a List of Ideas

The technique of listing ideas should be familiar to you because of lists you have made of household chores, groceries, or homework assignments. The lists of ideas you make for writing are just as practical as these other lists; you can use them to generate ideas and details about your topic, and to select, group, and arrange those ideas as you move to Step Four—Organizing Ideas.

STUDENT SAMPLE.   Sarah reviewed her topic from Step One as well as her purpose for writing from Step Two:

> Topic: A tribute to Aunt Rumania.
> Purpose: To write a sympathetic description of my aunt and to inspire other students to write about people who have been close to them.

To get a better idea about the information she might include in her paragraph, Sarah asked herself these questions:

What do I want to say about my aunt?

I want to capture her free spirit and somehow convey her importance to me.

How can I describe this freedom?

I can show the way she traveled from place to place, her love of brightly colored clothes, and perhaps her attitude toward people who did not appreciate the way she looked or the way she lived.

How did she dress?

She wore bright colors, reds, oranges, and yellows. Her clothes were flowing and loose-fitting, and she loved to wear scarves.

Why was she important to me?

In spite of her nomadic life, Aunt Rumania was attached to her family. I was her favorite. Although I could not be like her, I appreciate the sense of freedom and individuality she brought to my life.

To help her gather more details about her aunt, and to visualize ideas and the connections between them, Sarah drew this idea wheel:

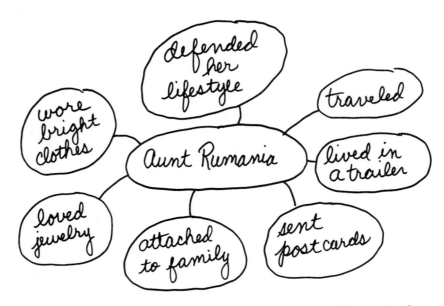

Next, Sarah wrote down all the details about her aunt Rumania she could think of, deleting some details and adding new ones to those already in her journal entries and idea wheel.

bright red blouses

long skirts
   (pinks, yellows, oranges)

harem pants

silk scarves

prints from India

silver jewelry

opals and turquoise

lived in apartments

embarrassed me once
   kids stared at her

ignored what people thought

no pets

attached to people

lived in a travel trailer six years

sent me postcards from many cities

my father (her brother)
   criticized her lifestyle

loved her life

had family loyalty

wanted me to travel with her

true individual

FOR PRACTICE

Exercise 3k.   Choose one of the topics from Exercise 3f (listed below) and apply the preliminary writing techniques: (1) ask yourself questions, (2) draw an idea wheel, and (3) make a list of whatever comes to mind about the topic you selected.

> The importance of exercise
> Parking problems on campus
> Choosing the proper roommate
> Benefits of wearing contact lenses
> Overcoming computer fears
> Air pollution

Step Four: Organizing Ideas

When ideas are clearly organized, another reader can easily follow and make sense of them. To create a good organization for your paper, first gather the information from your responses to questions, idea wheels, and any lists you have made. Then group ideas and details that are similar. With this step, you are identifying two, three, or four points for your topic sentences and selecting details and examples that support them.

The difficult part is that you will not be able to use all the information you have gathered. The ideas that don't quite fit are probably the ones you need to drop. Record these extra ideas in your journal; you might be able to use them in another writing assignment.

A branching diagram can be useful when selecting ideas for papers. If, for example, you discover that you have too many ideas and need to choose among them, this branching technique can help you visualize the ideas you have and determine the relative importance of each.

STUDENT SAMPLE. Sarah Kaplan felt that she had more information than she could use in a paragraph. To help her determine which ideas to keep, she used a branching diagram (see page 42) to group subtopics and details about her aunt. She added a few details and deleted others as she refined her ideas.

Her diagram of branching ideas showed Sarah not only how her aunt dressed and lived but also how closely her aunt's life was tied to family and friends—a subtlety that had not occurred to her before she drew this diagram. To emphasize these two seemingly contradictory sides of her aunt, Sarah chose two main points to discuss in her paragraph—her aunt Rumania's nomadic life and her ties to other people. Sarah hoped to include examples of Rumania's defense of her lifestyle under the discussion of her travels. She also thought she could fit a few descriptions of the way Rumania dressed in the examples of her aunt's retorts to critics.

FOR PRACTICE

Exercise 3l. Choose one of the preliminary writing exercises you completed for Exercise 3k and draw a branching diagram that helps you arrange topics, subtopics, and details you created for the exercise.

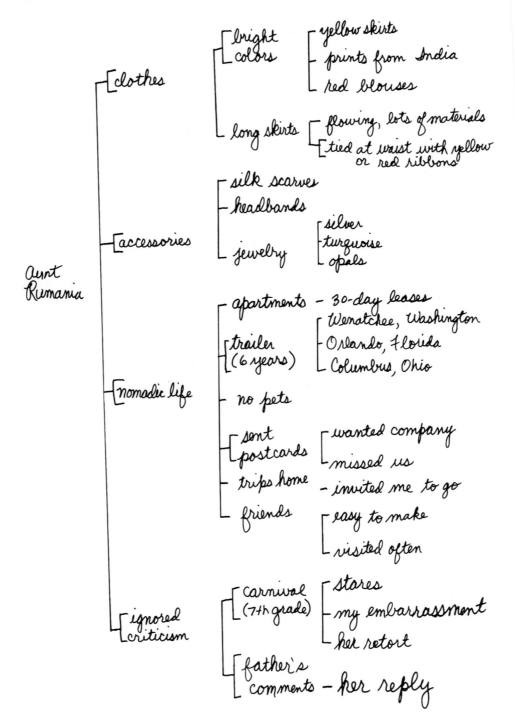

To get a clearer picture of her two main points (her aunt's nomadic life and her ties to other people), Sarah drew another idea wheel with topics and subtopics.

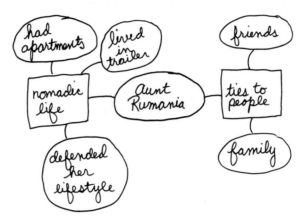

Sarah drew a final idea wheel and added the details associated with each subtopic.

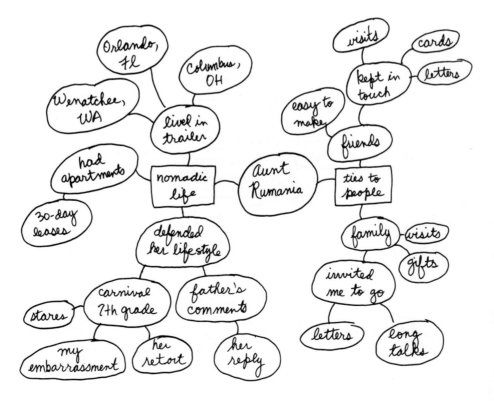

Now Sarah's topic ideas are clear (nomadic life and ties to people) and her subtopics (lived in trailer, had apartments, and defended her lifestyle; and friends and family) connect to her topic idea (the two sides of Aunt Rumania). In addition, specific examples illustrate each subtopic.

FOR PRACTICE

Exercise 3m.   To practice this technique for generating ideas, complete the following idea wheels by filling in details and examples for subtopics. Add spokes as needed. If you need more room, copy the idea wheels on separate sheets of paper.

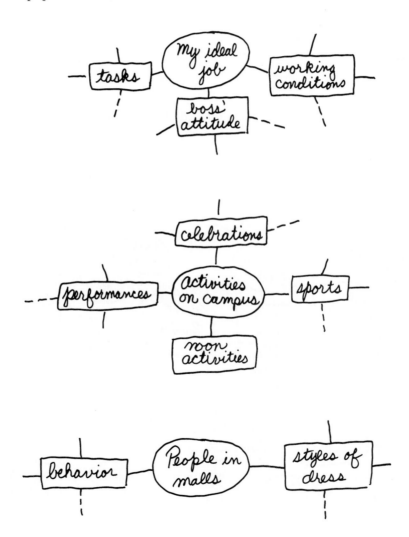

Exercise 3n. Fill in subtopics and details for the following topics.

Patterns of Organization

There are several patterns of organization you may choose when you write. Their use depends on your subject and purpose for writing. If, for example, you are writing about something that happened to you or an event you witnessed, you will probably put those events in **chronological** order—the order in which they occurred.

Example:

Moving On

I remember my childhood in bits and pieces, a blur of different houses and new neighborhoods. In my earliest memory I see the giant gray porch at my grandfather's house in Ohio. I recall lying on the front porch in the summer waiting for the ice-cream truck. Then one day my father received orders for Oklahoma, and we moved for the first time, leaving our relatives behind. I remember one Halloween in Oklahoma when I was in the second grade. The neighbor kids decided to visit the haunted house just down the block from where I lived. We were sure that a doll haunted the house, and when someone yelled that the doll was coming down from the second floor to get us, we all screamed and ran home. In the middle of the third grade, my father left for Vietnam; I didn't see him again for three and a half years. We packed up and left Oklahoma, this time for Sacramento, California. There I made friends with the kids on the block—Harold, Westly, and Bill—and started life all over again. This life lasted until I finished tenth grade and my father came home from Vietnam. My mother and father discovered that they were virtual strangers and decided to separate. I finished the eleventh and twelfth grades in Syracuse, New York; Paul, Gary, and Chris were my best friends. Once we made the news as the four crazies who ran wild on the airport runway late one night. The pattern of my life hasn't changed much over the years. I usually stay a few years in one place, make friends, then move on.

Annotations (right margin):

- *Topic sentence—childhood memories*
- *Earliest memory*
- *Move to Oklahoma*
- *Move to Sacramento, California*
- *Parents' separation and move to Syracuse, New York*
- *Current lifestyle*

If you are writing a description of a room, a painting, or a photograph, you will probably use **spatial** organization to describe details from top to bottom, foreground to background, or left to right.

Example:

In the photograph of my grandmother taken in 1945 sits a woman whom I can barely recognize. — *Topic sentence*

In that forty-five-year-old picture, my grandmother is sitting on the steps of her house in Old Land Park with my mother on her lap. A huge camellia bush hangs gracefully over the porch. — *Background—location, pose*

She is dressed like a little girl, wearing penny loafers, a plaid skirt, and matching blue sweater. — *Clothing*

In the photograph, the wind is blowing her curly, dark brown hair away from her face as she leans over to put her thinner face next to my mother's little fat one. — *Hair*

Grandmother's skin looks slightly tanned next to my mother's rosy cheeks. She smiles radiantly as she looks at the camera, her face quite youthful and free of the deep lines near the corners of her mouth and under her eyes with — *Face*

which I am familiar. In spite of how much she has aged since this picture was taken, the youthful happiness I see in the photograph is there, even now, in her eyes. — *Eyes (central feature)*

If you want to explain causes or effects, or argue a point, you might use **order-of-importance** organization or **emphatic** order, saving your strongest point for the end of the discussion.

Example:

There are several reasons why students drop out of college. A few leave school because they lack — *Topic sentence*

patience. My friend Rita, for example, attended City last semester but ended up dropping her classes and enrolling in a trade school. She felt she — *A few lack patience (least frequent cause)*

was wasting her time getting a general education.
Instead, she decided to get a skill and find a job
quickly rather than take five or six years to
complete a degree. Other students are also parents
and find it hard to play both roles. My friend
Sharmie eventually left school because her   *Difficulties for parents*
daughter, Erin, was always getting colds from
taking buses so early in the morning. Sharmie
found it impossible to care for her sick child,
change her diapers, and feed her while trying to
attend school and study for classes. She hopes to
return to school when Erin is a little older. Most
students quit college for economic reasons. Even in
a community college, students pay at least fifty
dollars in fees every semester, buy several
hundred dollars' worth of books, and either   *Most cannot afford to go*
purchase a bus pass or pay expenses on a car. Two   *(most frequent cause)*
of my best friends had to drop out this semester
because they ran out of money. They couldn't work
enough hours to pay their living expenses, yet
increasing their hours at work meant they had no
time for homework. It isn't easy to stay in college,
but luckily, most of us find a way.

STUDENT SAMPLE.   Let's return to Sarah Kaplan's list of ideas. When
choosing an organizational pattern for her paragraph, Sarah decided to
arrange her ideas according to their importance and discuss Aunt Rumania's
love of travel before discussing her aunt's attachment to people. Sarah
selected this arrangement because she wanted to emphasize the value
Rumania placed on friends and family. Once she had an order for her ideas,
Sarah wrote a rough outline, using the lowest numbers for general ideas, the
higher numbers—3s and 4s—for details.

Outline on Aunt Rumania

1. The two sides of my aunt, Rumania Tesslav
  2. Nomadic life
     3. Lived in a trailer for six years
        4. Had five addresses

        4. Sent postcards from Orlando, Wenatchee, and Columbus
   3. Apartments
        4. 30-day leases
   3. Defended her lifestyle
        4. Seventh-grade carnival
           5. Stares
           5. My embarrassment
           5. Her retort
        4. Dad said to settle down
           5. She said, "I'm happy. Are you?"
2. Ties to people
   3. Friends
        4. Easy for her to make
           5. Friends she met at work
           5. Traveling friends
           5. Neighbors who became friends
        4. Kept in touch
           5. Three address books
           5. Wrote several letters a week
           5. Occasional visits to friends
   3. Family
        4. Visited once a year
           5. Brought gifts for everyone
           5. Did not want to be forgotten
        4. Invited me to travel with her
           5. Long talks during visits
           5. Letters

    When Sarah reviewed her outline, she decided she had too many ideas to develop in a paragraph. To narrow her focus, she concentrated on Rumania's attachment to her family and omitted the discussion of friends.

FOR PRACTICE

Exercise 3o.   Write an outline based on one of the idea wheels you drew for either Exercise 3m or 3n, or the branching diagram you made in Exercise 3l. Note in the margin the pattern of organization you use.

Step Five: Writing a Fast Draft

The purpose of this step is to get your ideas on paper in sentence and paragraph form. With your plan or outline in front of you, begin writing, and write steadily without stopping. Avoid correcting any awkward-sounding sentences or looking up words in the dictionary until you have completed your draft.

STUDENT SAMPLE.   Sarah Kaplan used her revised outline to write a fast draft.

Two Sides of Aunt Rumania

My aunt, Rumania Tesslav, my father's sister, was a Gypsy. She once lived for six years in a trailer. She loved that little travel trailer of hers because it gave her such freedom. She had five addresses during the six years she owned it. My father and I got postcards from places as far apart as Orlando, Florida, and Wenatchee, Washington. Tired of trailer living, she rented apartments with 30-day leases for a while. My father once asked her why she didn't settle down, and she answered, "I'm happy with my life. Are you?" Aunt Rumania once embarrassed me by showing up at carnival night at my junior high wearing red harem pants and a bright orange blouse, her hair tied back with a scarf. When she saw me turn red with embarrassment, she said, "Why do you care what these kids think? They don't know anything about me!" Aunt Rumania always remembered her family. She wrote to us every few weeks and tried to see us once a year, which sometimes meant driving halfway across the country. She brought gifts for my father and me, her other brother and sister, and nieces and nephews to make sure we didn't forget her. I felt important when she asked me to travel with her. The cards she sent told me she was coming to pick me up. When she arrived, she told me about all the things she had seen. Now that she is gone, I regret not following her.

FOR PRACTICE

Exercise 3p.   Write a paragraph based on the outline you completed for Exercise 3o.

Step Six: Editing and Proofreading

This step marks the second time that you will need to stop and think seriously about your audience's needs. Early in our discussion of the writing process (Step Two), you saw how considering her audience's interests helped Sarah Kaplan narrow the topic for her paragraph about her aunt's nomadic life. By the time you reach the sixth step in the writing process, you are ready to concentrate on whether the ideas in your paragraph are arranged and supported in such a way that your readers can understand and appreciate the points you want to make. These considerations about organization and support are **editing** considerations. A thorough editing should involve the following procedures:

1. Write a second outline to see if your ideas follow a distinct chronological or spatial order, or if you have arranged them clearly according to their order of importance.
2. Move sentences, add examples, and delete information when such changes make your ideas clearer to your reader.
3. Rewrite sentences that do not say quite what you mean.

When **proofreading,** you are concentrating on individual words, phrases, and sentences in your writing. Your goal when you proofread is to find and correct errors in sentence structure, grammar, and mechanics—spelling, punctuation, and capitalization. If you have a particular problem with your writing, your instructor may refer you to the discussion and exercises in Part Three that cover this problem. You might also refer to the rules for punctuation, spelling, and capitalization in Chapter 27 of this book as you proofread your essay. In addition, it is useful to keep the following suggestions in mind when you are proofreading:

1. Proofread your paragraph several times, checking for words and phrases you may have omitted in your fast draft.
2. Keep a list of mistakes that recur in your writing, and when you proofread, go through your paragraph looking for each type of error one at a time. If, for example, you frequently drop the past tense (-ed) endings from verbs and tend to write fragments, read your paragraph once to check your verb forms; then read it a second time to find any fragments you may have written. (You might also want to check the explanations in Chapter 24, "Correcting Fragments and Run-on Sentences.")
3. Read your paragraph aloud and, if you can, tape record it. This procedure usually makes writers look more carefully at what they have written.
4. After proofreading your paragraph on your own, share your writing with another student. Like most people, you may not be able to catch all the errors in your own writing; that's why having someone else look at your writing (Step Seven in the writing process) is another good way of finding mistakes.

Here is Sarah's draft after editing and proofreading.

Two Sides of Aunt Rumania

My aunt, Rumania Tesslav, my father's sister, lived a nomadic life. When I was very young, she lived for six years in a trailer. She loved that little travel trailer of hers because it gave her such freedom. She had five addresses during the six years she owned it. My father and I got postcards from places as far apart as Orlando, Florida, and Wenatchee, Washington. The messages were brief—"Bored with Columbus. Miss you both," or "See you in a month." She rented apartments with 30-day leases for a while. She stood up to my father when he criticized her for not settling down. She said, "I'm happy with my life. Are you?" There was another side to my Aunt Rumania that people rarely saw. No matter how much she traveled, she stayed close to her family. She wrote to us every few weeks. She sent gifts for my father and me on birthdays and holidays, and she also mailed packages to her other brother and sister, and her nieces and nephews. She tried to see us once a year, which sometimes meant driving halfway across the country. I guess I was her favorite. She always made me feel that she had come home just to ask me to travel with her. I waited for the cards that would say, "I'm taking Sarah with me next time I come." When she arrived, she talked for hours describing the people and places she had seen. Now that she is gone, I regret not following her.

FOR PRACTICE

Exercise 3q.   Compare Sarah's fast draft with her revised paragraph on Aunt Rumania. What changes did she make? Were these effective changes? If so, what made them effective? Would additional editing and proofreading improve the paragraph? Explain your answer.

Step Seven: Sharing Your Writing

It is extremely important to read your paper to a classmate—or better yet, have a classmate read it aloud to you. When a classmate reads it, he or she is less likely to fill in missing words or reconstruct sentences for you.

Begin by dividing into small groups with three or four students in each. One member of each group (not necessarily the author of the paper being discussed) should act as recorder and write down the group's ideas. You may wish to have a different recorder for each paper. When your paper is read, you will probably want to make additional notes to yourself. Be sure to discuss each paper thoroughly before going on to the next.

When it is your turn, ask your readers what they liked about the paper, and have them write out any questions they think you've left unanswered.

(Consult Appendix C, "Questions for Shared Writing," at the back of this text-book for additional guidelines for sharing your papers.)

STUDENT SAMPLE.   The recorder for Sarah's group wrote the following observations.

What did you like about the paragraph?

We could appreciate Sarah's attachment to her aunt. The details like the places her aunt lived and the quotes were good, too.

Does it have a beginning that helps you focus on the subject?

The first sentence is about her aunt's nomadic life, but she also talks about how much Rumania cared about her family. She may need to write two paragraphs or rewrite the topic sentence to include both points.

Would you like more information about any of the general ideas?

Yes. Something about why she was her aunt's favorite or what her aunt meant to her.

Did you have difficulty following the writer's ideas or reading some of the sentences? Explain.

The paragraph jumps from topic to topic pretty fast. Maybe she should add transitions between some ideas to make it smoother.

Does the paragraph come to a logical end?

The ending seems sudden.

In response to her work in the group, Sarah wrote the following entry in her journal:

My group was really encouraging. I was glad they noticed the details and quotations I included in the paragraph. They made some good suggestions, too. I knew I was rushing toward the end, probably because I still have too many general ideas. I'm going to add details and explanations wherever I can, especially for the last few points about our relationship. I also need to add transitions to make the sentences more connected, take out points I don't want to develop, and focus on those I do. Then I'll rewrite the topic sentence so it covers both ideas presented in the paragraph.

Exercise 3r.   Compare your response to the questions in Exercise 3q with the response Sarah got from students in her peer response group. Did you anticipate any of their responses? Did you make suggestions they overlooked?

Step Eight: Making Final Revisions

Here is Sarah Kaplan's final paragraph.

The Double Life of Aunt Rumania

To people who didn't know her, my aunt, Rumania Tesslav, led a carefree, nomadic life, but I knew how attached she was to her family. During the years I was in elementary school, my aunt traveled all over the country in a tiny travel trailer she hitched to a rented truck. She had five addresses during the six years she owned it. My father and I got postcards from places as far apart as Orlando, Florida, and Wenatchee, Washington. The messages were usually brief—"Bored with Columbus. Miss you both," or "See you in a month." When she arrived for her annual visit, my father usually waited until dinner was over to scold her for refusing to settle down. "Why don't you get a house, have a family like other people?" One day she said, "I'm happy with my life. Are you?" There was another side to Aunt Rumania that people rarely saw. She was very attached to her family and never went more than a month without writing to us or calling. She tried to see us at least once a year, even if it meant traveling halfway across the country. I remember one time she left a job she had as a sous-chef in a hotel and traveled a thousand miles because she wanted to see me on my birthday. That was the summer I turned fifteen. For years she had been asking me to travel with her. I remember reading cards she'd written to my father saying, "I'm taking Sarah with me next time I come." When she arrived that summer, she spent hours describing the people and places she had seen, the diners, restaurants, and hotels where she had worked, and the magnificent mountains, seashores, and lakes where she had lived, as if to lure me away. In the end I did not go with her because, like my father, I am attached to my home and to my friends. Now I can appreciate how hard life must have been for a person like Aunt Rumania, who needed to travel yet loved the closeness of family.

Exercise 3s.   On a separate piece of paper, write a summary of the major changes Sarah made in her last revision. State briefly why you think she made them.

Exercise 3t.   Do you have any suggestions or additional comments about her final paragraph?

TOPICS FOR WRITING

Write a paragraph on one of these topics. Use the steps in the writing process to gather ideas and plan your paragraph.

Topic 1.   Write a detailed portrait of a family member or of someone who means a lot to you.

Topic 2.   Describe people and/or circumstances that cause stress in your life.

Topic 3.   Write a paragraph about an adventure you had.

Topic 4.   Write a paragraph explaining why you decided to enroll in college.

Topic 5.   Write a paragraph on a topic of your choice.

4

Refining Paragraphs

This chapter introduces basic paragraph structure—topic sentences, supporting sentences, and concluding sentences—and gives you practice writing paragraphs that have a clear focus. You will also learn to revise for unity, development, and coherence—crucial elements in well-written paragraphs.

BASIC PARAGRAPH STRUCTURE

The **topic sentence** states the main idea you want to discuss in any paragraph that you write. The rest of the paragraph is about this idea. **Key words** in your topic sentence announce the subject you will discuss and predict how you will discuss it. The topic sentence usually begins the paragraph. In published writing, you may find the main idea in the second or third sentence, or at the end of a paragraph. Occasionally it is not stated at all but merely implied by the discussion. Until you gain confidence in your writing skills, it is best to begin your paragraphs with a topic sentence to make the point of the paragraph clear to both you and your reader.

Supporting sentences of the paragraph provide subtopics, facts, details, examples, and explanations to support the main idea stated in your topic sentence. Think of these supporting sentences as links in a chain; each sentence you write has a logical connection to the one before it and anticipates those that follow it. Most paragraphs must be six to ten sentences long to provide adequate support for the main idea.

The **concluding sentence** (or two) brings the paragraph to a satisfying close.

Sample Paragraph

In the paragraph below, Gary Gilbert promises to discuss how *difficult* it is *to go to school*. The rest of the paragraph discusses how distractions at home and concern about his relationship with his son make it hard for him to attend school. Transitional phrases connect ideas, which are organized by order of importance; Gary's relationship with his son is his last subtopic. In his conclusion, Gary acknowledges his family's patience and looks forward to graduation.

Getting through School

indent about 1/2 inch   *transition*

    It is difficult for me to go to school. For one ⌐ *Topic sentence*
thing, the distractions at home make it hard for me ⌐ *Subtopic*
to concentrate on homework. Just as I'm about to
solve a math problem, my son runs screaming
through the house with my wife in hot pursuit.   *Examples*
transition
Then there are the phone calls from family,
friends, and solicitors that interrupt my thoughts
and make me wonder if I will ever get my work
transition
done. I also worry that my relationship with my   *Subtopic*
son will suffer because I'm not with him as much
transition
as I want to be. I feel especially guilty if I don't get
home in time for dinner, or I have to rush off to
the library on a Sunday afternoon instead of
playing catch with him. I can always tell when he   *Examples*
thinks I have been neglecting him. Sometimes he
refuses to give me a goodnight kiss, or he flips on
the television while I'm trying to hold a family
discussion. It won't be easy on my family but with
the commitment and patience of us all, I'll get   *Concluding sentence*
through school.

—Gary Gilbert

FOR PRACTICE

Exercise 4a.   Read the following paragraphs carefully. Then underline the topic sentences. Keep in mind that the topic sentence is the general idea supported by the rest of the discussion.

1. For transportation around town, I prefer riding my bike to driving my truck. I look forward to the workout I get on the mornings when I ride my 18-speed mountain bike. By the time I have cycled the five miles to school, I can feel the muscles in my legs. On the other hand, it takes very little energy to drive my truck because the machine moves and stops when I apply the slightest pressure to the accelerator or brake. Another thing I enjoy about my bike is the way it hums like a bee as I move freely and gracefully through quiet residential streets. In contrast, when I drive my truck, I feel trapped inside the cab like a crab in its shell. With traffic all around me, I seem to crawl along the crowded thoroughfares. Every time I drive my truck, I am reminded of how much more sense it makes to take my bike across town.

2. When you live alone, yours is the only mess you have to clean up. No roommate lets his dishes pile up in the sink because he is too busy working overtime to wash them. If there are dirty clothes left in the bathroom, they are yours and not someone else's greasy jeans. In addition, you have much more privacy living by yourself. Fewer phone calls come in, and, unless you turn them on yourself, no television programs prevent you from doing your homework. Furthermore, you needn't worry about someone else's friends dropping over unexpectedly while you are taking a bath. There is nothing like settling down in the tub, a good book in hand, without fear of interruptions. Living alone certainly has its advantages.

3. News reporting on the air and in print feeds on sensationalism. The latest multiple-car crash, burn victim, or drive-by murder is sure to make the morning headlines or the evening news. It could be argued that viewers and readers are eager for negative news, and they get what they want. But I think there is more to it than that. We suffocate people with the grim, the horrible, and the pessimistic because we have forgotten that people who are helping and saving others are even more newsworthy than the legion of killers, rapists, and child abusers who march across the news columns and fill the tube. What we need is nothing less than a revolution in the way we define journalism.

4. When I worked for Union Carbide Chemical Plant, I had a foreman who always gave me and my partner all the worst jobs. We lifted heavy boxes, dismantled scaffoldings, and did other heavy labor. The foreman would come around and watch us as if he thought we didn't know what we were doing. He told us that he gave us the menial jobs because we were the best people in his crew. I figure that if we were the best people he had, he should have stopped wasting us on such mindless tasks. The foreman also had the habit of yelling at us for no particular reason. One day when he was screaming about a welding job I had done, I threatened to report him to the general manager. Even though the manager usually took our side, that foreman always managed to find ways to make our lives miserable.

Exercise 4b.   Underline the key words in the following topic sentences.

Example: <u>John McEnroe</u> is famous for his <u>outbursts</u> on the <u>tennis court.</u>

1. Shy people sometimes have difficulty showing emotion in public.
2. My parents were too strict when I was growing up.
3. I look forward to the day when we have a metal detector at Winthrop Stadium.
4. Lassen is my favorite national park.
5. Peer pressure is a major cause of drug and alcohol addiction.

Exercise 4c.   Circle the key words in the topic sentences that you underlined in Exercise 4a.

Narrowing Topics

It is important to write topic sentences that are narrow enough to give your paragraphs a clear direction yet broad enough that you can add supporting ideas and examples. If a topic is too broad, you will not have a clear idea of how to discuss it.

You may need a bit of practice in limiting the topics of your paragraphs. The following topic, for example, is too broad: Relationships can be difficult. First of all, the subject, "relationships," is so broad that the paragraph could be about relationships between family members, intimate partners, or casual friends. A more focused topic sentence would mention the relationship the writer will discuss and what is "difficult" about it.

To narrow this topic, the writer can ask a question: What kind of relationships do I want to discuss—male–female, mother–son, high-school friendships? The answer to this question helps the author replace "relationships" with key words that narrow the subject and give the paragraph more direction. Asking another question, What is difficult about this relationship? gets the writer to focus on the way the paragraph will discuss that relationship.

Possible topic sentences:

The relationship   the difficulty

1. Marriage can be confining.

The relationship   the difficulty

2. Being a parent often means you have very little time for yourself.

To narrow the topic sentence "Music brings back memories," the writer might ask, What music will I discuss, and whose memories do I want to use?
Possible topic sentence:

Songs by the Pointer Sisters remind me of the years I was living a bachelor's life in San Francisco.

Is this topic sentence narrow enough? Why or why not? _____

_____

FOR PRACTICE

Exercise 4d.   Write more focused topic sentences for "Classes can be challenging."

1. _____

2. _____

Exercise 4e.   Below are several topic sentences. Underline the word or words that predict what the writer will say. If the topic sentence is too broad, write a more focused topic sentence below it.

Example: I always look forward to holidays.

Focused alternative: I love Thanksgiving because that's the one time of year when my whole family gets together.

1. People always seem to do the wrong thing. _____

_____

2. Professionals work very hard at what they do. _____

_____

3. The life of a lawyer involves more hard work than glamor. _____

_____

4. I am happy to be in school. _____

_____

5. Alcoholism is a terrible problem. _____

_____

Statements of Fact

Statements of fact do not usually make good topic sentences because they may leave you with nothing else to say about the topic. "My mother is more than six feet tall" is a statement of fact. If it were used as a topic sentence, it would leave the writer little to discuss in the rest of the paragraph. "My mother is an imposing woman" is a better topic sentence because it points to a discussion of the ways mother is imposing. Her height, her strength, and her assertiveness are possible subtopics that explain why she is imposing.

"I registered for school last week" is another statement of fact. A topic sentence on the subject of registering for school needs to mention something about the experience that the writer can discuss in a paragraph.

Possible topic sentence:

Trying to register for classes was a frustrating experience.

Is this a good topic sentence? Why or why not? _____

_____

FOR PRACTICE

Exercise 4f.　　In each of the following sentences, underline the subject and words that narrow it. If the subject is too broad or too narrow, write an alternative.

Example: The divorce rate has been climbing steadily since 1975.

Alternative: Many women who get divorced find that they are much worse off financially.

1. Mt. Everest is more than 29,000 feet high. _____

_____

2. The Beatles' songs remind me of the years when my oldest sister was still dating. _____

_____

3. Cats can have as many as seven kittens. _____

_____

4. Television can harm our minds. _____

_____

5. When I was in high school I had the mistaken idea that college classes would be much too hard for me. _____

_____

Exercise 4g.　　Read the following paragraphs carefully. Then create topic sentences that express the main idea in each.

1. _____

_____

It is often difficult just to get seated. After waiting thirty to forty minutes, a waiter may show you to a table that has not been cleared of dishes and crumbs. Eventually a different waiter brings you a menu that you will have difficulty opening because the pages are stuck together with catsup. Finally, a waitress, chewing gum, asks you rudely if you are ready to order. By this time you should know what to expect. Your hamburger will arrive at the table nearly as cold as it was when it was taken from the refrigerator and slapped on the grill. Your partner's burger may be warmer, but it will be smaller than yours because the heat lamps have dried out the bun. By the time your water and cokes arrive, you are just about finished with your meal. That's the Sky-burger Restaurant—at your service!

2. _____

_____

Whether he was conscious of it or not, he passed his love of working with students on to me. My father, who taught art in high school, would come home every afternoon and tell me about the accomplishments of students in his art classes. Sometimes he brought home samples of their work and displayed them in the den. It didn't take much to get him to tell me how each student was improving: Melissa was developing a stronger brushstroke; Gabriel's recent compositions showed greater depth than did any of his earlier drawings. In addition to my father's love of teaching, his love of art came to me through the splendid paintings I saw in books in his library. His bookshelves were filled with books about mural art in Mexico, Italian Renaissance painting, and traditional African masks.

3.   When my grandmother was a teenager, premarital sex was the farthest thing from her mind. Not only did she blush if anyone asked to hold her hand, she didn't have the slightest idea how babies were conceived. Now, of course, people often talk about having sex before they are married, and many young women have had intercourse before turning twenty. In my grandmother's day, a woman married the man she "loved," and she married him for life. The current statistics on divorce in this country would probably make her think we have given up trying to keep families together.

_____

_____

_____

4. _____

_____

In one supermarket, a display on aisle three said, "Please don't squeeze the Charmin." An elderly woman approached the sign, read it carefully, walked over to squeeze a package, then dropped it in her basket. Behind her, a ten-year-old boy read the sign out loud, picked up a package, and hugged it to his chest. When his mother caught up with him, he tossed the toilet paper into her cart. A little further down the aisle, a twelve-foot sign pictured a mountain of soap; its caption read, "Want to make your hands look younger while you do the dishes?" The words framed the picture of a mother and daughter comparing their equally young-looking hands. Sure enough, only women with their teenaged daughters were selecting bars of soap from this display.

5. Most parents lecture their children about something. _____

_____

They believe that in America education is the key to success. "Without an education," they would say, "you probably will work at McDonald's all your life." When they weren't trying to scare me about the kind of job I'd have to take, they were comparing me to my older brother. "Look at your brother John. He is so smart and does so well in school that he got a scholarship to U.C. Berkeley." My parents convinced me that if I didn't do well in school, I would pay heavily afterwards. "Study and work hard now, and it will pay off later," they assured me. I hope they are right.

Exercise 4h.　　Use your journal to freewrite and ask yourself questions about one of the following topics. Then write a topic sentence whose key words narrow the topic.

> a bad habit
> an athletic event
> dating
> an important change
> an unfair situation
> a family tradition

Exercise 4i.　　Write a paragraph that develops the topic sentence that you wrote for Exercise 4h.

REVISING PARAGRAPHS

In the revision stage of your writing, it is important to check your paragraph for *unity, development,* and *coherence*—three characteristics of a well-written paragraph. The following exercises give you practice checking for these elements.

Writing Unified Paragraphs

Strong paragraphs are *unified.* For the paragraph to be unified, sentences in the body should stick to the idea stated in your topic sentence. In freewriting, you may wander from one idea to another, but this freedom is characteristic of preliminary writing, not revised, polished paragraphs. If you are writing a paragraph and find yourself straying from your topic, take out your journal and freewrite until the irrelevant ideas have played themselves out. Then return to your paragraph and continue developing your support for the main idea. After you have finished writing, check the paragraph to see if all the ideas and examples support the topic sentence.

FOR PRACTICE

Exercise 4j.   To practice revising for unity, read the following paragraphs carefully. Pick out the topic sentence, noting the key words that state the subject and narrow it. If you find any sentences that wander from that topic, cross them out.

1. I was very close to my father when I was a child because he paid so much attention to me. Whenever he went into town, he always brought me something from the store. I once admired a stuffed cocker spaniel that looked just like Rowdy, my brother's dog, and the very next week Dad bought it for me. We had a lot of pets when I was a child and still do to this day. We must have had over a dozen pets including cats, dogs, birds, and hamsters. My father always encouraged me to try new things to see what I could do. He put me on our neighbor's pony when I was three-and-a-half years old and entered me in a horse show at the age of four. I took second place. He was so proud of me that he bought me a horse of my own. I still have lots of pictures of my Dad with his arms around me.

2. Before I went to college, I worked at the Crystal Theater. Frank, a chronic repeater, was a customer I remember well. Every time he asked for popcorn, he repeated it four times in four different ways: "I'd like a popcorn." "Gimme a popcorn, please." "One large popcorn." "I'll take a big box of popcorn." I think he did it just to see if I would get so nervous that I'd forget to ask for his money. I usually brought a magazine to work with me in case things got dull. Thelma the Inquisitor came every time we had a new movie—usually on Thursday nights. She would catch me at the ticket window and hold up the line to ask, "What do you know about this film? What other movies has the director made? Does it have a happy ending? Is it worth seeing?" I never had to worry about answering Thelma's questions because she barked them out, one after another, without pausing for a reply. Rudy was my favorite. He was about twenty years old, used a walking stick, and acted like an old man on a long hike. He usually arrived about half an hour before the movie started, but rather than sit in the theater and wait for the film to start, he paced back and forth in the lobby as though he were waiting for someone. When the credits started to roll, he went in alone. On reflection, I think the people that came to the Crystal were more interesting than anything I saw on the screen.

3. Ten years ago computer nuts rarely strayed from their habitat on New York's Wall Street or on Wilshire Boulevard in Los Angeles. Now they are commonly found in offices and homes across the country. Their sunken eyes and fixed stares make them easy to identify. You will find them sitting at their computers with their heads thrust forward as if they are about to dive into the screen. They own a variety of computers, including Macintosh, IBM personal computers, Commodores, and Hewlett-Packards, to name a few. It is not unusual for computer nuts to work sixteen to twenty hours straight. To keep themselves going, they eat and drink for quick energy, preferring foods and beverages that have sugar or caffeine, like coffee, strong tea, coke, and choco-late candy. The best candy bars for staying awake have "sugar" listed first in the description of ingredients. Sometimes computer nuts are so intent on their work that it is difficult to distinguish them from their machines.

4. My grandfather loves to tell me stories about the old days in Mexico. In most of the stories he is young, likes to gamble, and travels around Mexico looking for work. He tells one story about meeting and falling in love with my grandmother. There wasn't much law and order in their small town, so thieves were often apprehended and sentenced by townspeople. In those days, cou-ples married young and once a girl turned fifteen she was considered old enough to marry in the Catholic Church. On my grandmother's fifteenth birth-day, he simply kidnapped and married her. When he advises me to do the same thing with my girlfriends, I tell him I can't do that at this time and in this country.

Writing Well-Developed Paragraphs

Strong paragraphs *develop* the topic idea. Your topic sentences have strong sup-port when you include enough details, examples, and explanations that the reader can *see* and *understand* the point you want to make about your subject. Most paragraphs have several levels of support—the general idea (topic sen-tence), ideas that narrow the topic sentence (subtopics), and examples that sup-port it. To help you visualize how a paragraph moves from a general idea to sup-porting explanations and examples, the sentences in Gary Gilbert's paragraph on the difficulties of going to school are numbered for you below. The general point in the paragraph, the topic sentence, is number one; subtopics are num-ber two; and details and examples are numbers three and four.

(1) It is difficult for me to go to school.
   (2) For one thing, the distractions at home make it hard for me to concentrate on homework.

(3) Just as I'm about to solve a math problem, my son runs screaming through the house with my wife in hot pursuit.

(3) Then there are the phone calls from family, friends, and solicitors that interrupt my thoughts and make me wonder if I will ever get my work done.

(2) I also worry that my relationship with my son will suffer because I'm not with him as much as I want to be.

(3) I feel especially guilty if I don't get home in time for dinner, or I have to rush off to the library on a Sunday afternoon instead of playing catch with him.

(3) I can always tell when he thinks I have been neglecting him.

(4) Sometimes he refuses to give me a goodnight kiss, or he flips on the television while I'm trying to hold a family discussion.

(2) It won't be easy on my family but with the commitment and patience of us all, I'll get through school.

Try numbering sentences in your own paragraphs to determine whether you have adequate development for your ideas. This process will also tell you when you have sentences that do not belong in the paragraph because they don't clearly support the main idea. Keep in mind that the topic sentence, the sentence you will label number one, is not always the first sentence in the paragraph.

FOR PRACTICE

Exercise 4k.   Use the numbering system discussed above to chart the following three paragraphs from Exercise 4g.

1. The service and the food at the Skyburger Restaurant are the worst I have ever seen. It is often difficult just to get seated. After waiting thirty to forty minutes, a waiter may show you to a table that has not been cleared of dishes and crumbs. Eventually, a different waiter brings you a menu that you will have difficulty opening because the pages are stuck together with catsup. Finally, a waitress, chewing gum, asks you rudely if you are ready to order. By this time you should know what to expect. Your hamburger will arrive at the table nearly as cold as it was when it was taken from the refrigerator and slapped on the grill. Your partner's burger may be warmer, but it will be smaller than yours because the heat lamps have dried out the bun. By the time your water and cokes arrive, you are just about finished with your meal. That's the Skyburger Restaurant—at your service!

2. I decided to become an art teacher because of my father's love of teaching and of art. Whether he was conscious of it or not, he passed his love of working with students on to me. My father, who taught art in high school, would come home every afternoon and tell me about the accomplishments of

students in his art classes. Sometimes he brought home samples of their work and displayed them in the den. It didn't take much to get him to tell me how each student was improving: Melissa was developing a stronger brushstroke; Gabriel's recent compositions showed greater depth than did any of his earlier drawings. In addition to my father's love of teaching, his love of art came to me through the splendid paintings I saw in books in his library. His bookshelves were filled with books about mural art in Mexico, Italian Renaissance painting, and traditional African masks.

3. When my grandmother was a teenager, premarital sex was the farthest thing from her mind. Not only did she blush if anyone asked to hold her hand, she didn't have the slightest idea how babies were conceived. Now, of course, people often talk about having sex before they are married, and many young women have had intercourse before turning twenty. In my grandmother's day, a woman married the man she "loved," and she married him for life. The current statistics on divorce in this country would probably make her think we have given up trying to keep families together. It's amazing how much ideas about love and marriage have changed since grandmother's day.

4. Most parents lecture their children about something. When I was in high school, my parents kept telling me I had to go to college. They believe that in America education is the key to success. "Without an education," they would say, "you probably will work at McDonald's all your life." When they weren't trying to scare me about the kind of job I'd have to take, they were comparing me to my older brother. "Look at your brother John. He is so smart and does so well in school that he got a scholarship to U.C. Berkeley." My parents convinced me that if I didn't do well in school, I would pay heavily afterwards. "Study and work hard now, and it will pay off later," they assured me. I hope they are right.

Supporting details personalize your writing and make it interesting to read. Notice the difference that details make in the following paragraphs.

Changing our habits just a little can go a long way toward helping the environment. One obvious thing we should do is stop littering. We can also fight air pollution by taking public transportation whenever possible. Recycling is another important way to conserve resources. It makes good sense to be more conscious about the environment.

Here is the revised paragraph with supporting examples and explanations. Take a minute to <u>underline</u> the additions.

Changing our habits just a little should go a long way toward helping the environment. One obvious thing we should do is stop littering. Instead of tossing aluminum cans and plastic cups out the car window when we are through with them, we should put them in a sack and take them home. We can also fight air pollution by taking public transportation whenever possible. By learning the schedule of subways and busses, we can leave our cars at home when we go to work or school. With a little bit of planning, we can ride the bus rather than drive to a doctor's appointment. Recycling is another important way to conserve resources. It takes little effort to keep separate containers for aluminum cans, bottles, and newspapers. A trip to the recycling center every other week takes just a few minutes of our time, but saves trees and conserves areas that might otherwise be used as landfills. It makes good sense to be more conscious about the environment.

FOR PRACTICE

Exercise 4l.   After a careful reading of the preceding sample paragraphs, use your own experience, observations, and imagination to fill in details and examples that support the general ideas in these paragraphs.

1. The clothes I wear reflect the different roles I play during the day. In the morning I am the student, casual and comfortable in my going-to-school clothes. In the afternoon I must look professional to please the travel agency I work for. In the evening I might have a PTA meeting, school play, or teacher's conference to attend, so I must look responsible and parental.

2. There are several ways to fight writer's block. First, be sure you have all the tools you need to write. Next, find a place where you will be comfortable. You should also take steps to be sure you will not be distracted.

3. Just because a person is old doesn't mean he or she is debilitated or feebleminded. Many elderly people travel. They do volunteer work in the community. They may even go back to school and take subjects they are interested in but never had time for.

4. It's difficult to make love relationships work. Sometimes partners aren't sure what they want out of the relationship. Even when they are, they may discover that what they want doesn't have much to do with what their partner wants.

5. College classes are difficult for me because I have such trouble taking tests. For one thing, I have a strong physical reaction every time one of my teachers hands out an exam. What's worse, my mind won't cooperate any better than my body. If things don't improve, I'll have to ask my teachers if I can take oral exams instead.

Exercise 4m. Write unified, well-developed paragraphs for two of the following topic sentences. Make sure you include enough details and examples to support your points.

1. Finding time to do homework requires good planning.
2. The best teachers present their subjects clearly and encourage students to ask questions.
3. Characters in _____ , one of my favorite movies, are very believable.
4. There are a few things you should think about when buying a used car.
5. It takes a lot of discipline to become a good college football player.
6. For many people the idea of commitment makes love a four-letter word.

Writing Coherent Paragraphs

Strong paragraphs are *coherent*. In a coherent paragraph, sentences follow one another logically; each sentence looks forward to the next and at the same time is logically linked to the preceding sentence. Writers commonly achieve coherence in paragraphs by using transitional words and phrases. In the following paragraph about chemical weaponry, transitions are underlined to show you how they move the reader from one idea to the next.

My military training taught me contradictory things about chemical weapons. My drill instructors trained me to use chemical weapons. In contrast, the medical courses I took showed me and the other recruits how inhumane these weapons really are. In tactical training, we were told that we had to learn how to conduct chemical warfare because the Russians were training 20 percent harder than we were. Consequently, we learned the parts of the missiles used to carry these deadly weapons and how to clean and care for them. Later we practiced loading and firing the missiles. Proper handling of chemical agents was another part of our training. While I was learning how to use chemical weapons, I was also finding out what they are capable of doing to human beings. The instructors in my medical classes showed me how nerve agents enter the body through the skin and cause such damage that the victims lose all control of their internal organs. As a result, convulsions, urination, defecation, vomiting, and crying precede death. In addition, I learned that some agents prevent the blood from carrying oxygen. One medic said that death would come slowly; like a fish out of water, the victim might flop around for two or three days. Then I learned that the blister agents are the most painful of all. If a droplet gets on your skin, it will swell up to the size of a fat apple. The only good thing about this agent is that if it is inhaled, death is immediate. As my training intensified, it became harder and harder to reconcile the technical and inhumane sides of chemical warfare.

Transitional Words and Phrases

The following chart lists commonly used transitions and their functions. Use them when you complete the exercises that follow, and refer to them when writing your own paragraphs.

Function	Transitional Words and Phrases
To add ideas	above all, also, and, another, besides, in addition, furthermore, for one thing, too
To order ideas in time	after, before, briefly, by this time, currently, during, eventually, finally, first, now, later, meanwhile, next, presently, recently, second, so far, soon, then, third, when, while
To order ideas in space	above, behind, below, beside, next to, in front of, on top of, in the foreground/background, to the right, to the left, under
To introduce examples	especially, for example, for instance, namely, for one thing, in particular, the most, one of the most
To show contrast	although, but, however, in contrast, more than, nevertheless, on the other hand, than, unlike
To show similarity	as, like, likewise, in both cases, in comparison, in the same way, similarly, too
To draw conclusions or show results	as a result, because, because of, consequently, for, for this reason, in fact, therefore, thus, unfortunately

FOR PRACTICE

Exercise 4n.   Circle the transitional words and phrases in the following paragraphs.

1. Competition brings out the best in all of us. If we feel someone is doing better in math or is faster in track than we are, we will probably try to do better. Take me, for example. When I was younger, particularly in high school, I was always competing with my niece. She got A's and B's in English and math while I would get by with a C. Then I noticed that everyone in my family praised her for every little thing she did. Eventually I decided I should do something to get more attention at home. From then on, I tried harder in school and raised my grades. My attitude toward schoolwork improved, too. By the time we graduated from high school, there were only five points difference in our grade-point averages.

2. City College has one of the best college athletic programs in the country. Specifically, the football program here at City ranked fifth in the nation last year and is again in the top twenty this season. These rankings are excellent, especially since over 300 junior colleges participate in the football program. Most of our athletes are strong players who try out but can't quite compete for an athletic scholarship to a university. On the other hand, some players do receive scholarships but can't adjust to university life and flunk out. In both cases, the alternative is to go back home and attend City College.

Exercise 4o. Read the following sentences carefully. Then add a transition that links ideas logically. Try to find transitions on your own before consulting the list.

1. According to Mollie Stevenson Neely, one-third of all cowboys were black _____ you'd never know it from watching TV westerns.
2. Some were slaves who migrated west with their owners. _____ , when they were freed, they stayed on in the area.
3. Many black cowboys lived in Texas. Bill Pickett, _____ , was a famous black Texas cowboy of the late 1800s.
4. Pickett is said to have originated the rodeo technique of "bulldogging"—a method of wrestling a steer to the ground. _____ most cowboys, who simply grab the steer's neck or horns with their hands, Pickett used to bring the beast down by biting its nose with his teeth.
5. Another famous black cowboy was Nat Love. _____ competing in a shooting contest in Deadwood, South Dakota, in 1876, he was given the name "Deadwood Dick."
6. Black women like "Stagecoach Mary" _____ were part of the western cowboy tradition.
7. Mary was very tall and heavy. _____ she was about six feet tall and weighed over 300 pounds.
8. Mary always carried a shotgun; _____ , she looked dangerous.

Exercise 4p. In the numbered exercises below several sentences are given that are part of a paragraph whose topic sentence is listed first. Use transitional phrases to write a coherent paragraph. You may need to change the original wording slightly, but stay as close as you can to the original.

Example:

Success means different things to different people.

> Some people are materialistic.
> Success means having an expensive car, living in a $300,000 house, and earning $100,000 a year.
> They may not consider themselves wealthy enough to be truly "successful."

Other people see healthy, happy children as the measure of their
   success.
They consider themselves successful when their sons and daughters
   do well in sports, become class president, or get a 3.0 on their
   report cards.

Here is one possible combination with the transitional words and phrases
underlined for you.

Success means different things to different people. For instance, some
people are materialistic. Consequently, they think success means having an
expensive car, living in a $300,000 house, and earning $100,000 a year. In
spite of having all that money, they still may not consider themselves
wealthy enough to be truly "successful." In contrast, other people see
healthy, happy children as the measure of their success. For this reason,
they value their children's achievements and consider themselves successful
when their sons and daughters do well in sports, become class president, or
get a 3.0 on their report cards.

1. Mollie Neely and her foreman, Howard "Cowboy" Beauchamo, are spreading the word about the black cowboy.

> They have attracted attention not only in Houston but also across the
>   country.
> Beauchamo teaches horseback riding.
> He lectures on cowboy history.
> He made a 2,500-mile journey on horseback from Houston to Newark,
>   New Jersey, to call attention to the black cowboy's contribution to
>   settling the Old West.
> An article about Neely appeared in *Essence Magazine.*
> She was bombarded with mail from all over the country.
> One writer, noting the picture of Neely on horseback, said she had
>   never seen a black woman riding before.
> Neely and Beauchamo have done a great deal to inform people about
>   black participation in the settlement of the American West.

2. It is important to prepare yourself well before going to a job interview.

> You should think carefully about what you want to wear.
> If the job involves labor or a technical skill, you might come dressed
>   to work.
> You might be asked to demonstrate a welding technique or safety
>   procedure.
> If you are applying for an office job, you'll probably want to wear a suit
>   or a dress that makes you look professional.

Take examples of your work.
Carpenters might bring photographs of kitchens and bathrooms they
have remodeled.
Analysts can bring examples of proposals, handbooks, or regulations
they have written.
It is important to show that you can do the job.

3. When I think of my Salvadorean heritage, oppression comes to mind.

The Spanish conquered Central America.
They subjugated my ancestors.
In the name of Christianity, they destroyed their rich culture.
I am very proud of my ancestry.
My people, the Pipiles, were part of the great Mayan civilization.
The Spanish mixed with the "Indians," as they were incorrectly called.
From that mixture comes the ethnicity of most Salvadoreans.
I always have a question in my mind: What would have happened if our
original culture had been left alone?

Exercise 4q.   Choose a topic from the following list and write your own
paragraph. Use the techniques discussed in Chapter 3 to help you generate
ideas. When you revise, check for unity, development, and coherence.

the benefits of a particular sport
a family problem
dealing with misunderstandings between partners
reasons why you chose a specific career
reasons why you like or dislike the town where you live
something you experienced that you felt was unfair

FOR REVIEW

1. What is a paragraph? _____

_____

2. What is a topic sentence? _____

_____

Looking Ahead

In the next two chapters you practice writing longer papers. Chapter 5 shows how
one student used the writing process to plan, write, and revise an essay. The information and exercises in Chapter 6 prepare you to revise and polish your essays.

5

The Writing Process:
Writing an Essay

This chapter prepares you to write longer papers. The opening discussion compares the structures of paragraphs and essays. The rest of the chapter follows one student's progress as he uses the writing process to compose an essay.

WHAT IS AN ESSAY?

Just as sentences in paragraphs support a main idea with details, the closely related paragraphs in an essay develop *one idea*, which is usually stated in a **thesis.** The thesis is usually found in the essay's **introduction,** generally the first paragraph. The paragraphs that follow the introduction, called **body paragraphs,** develop support for the thesis. The **conclusion** of the essay returns to the thesis idea. The diagram on page 75 illustrates the relationship between a paragraph and an essay.

Compare the student's paragraph about sports fanatics on page 76 to his essay, pages 76–78, on the same subject. Topic sentences, subtopics, and supporting details are labeled for you in the student's paragraph and in the first several paragraphs of his essay.

The Essay

Thesis (main idea of
    the essay) — *Introduction*

The Paragraph

Topic Sentence
    (main idea of para-
    graph)
Supporting ideas or
    "subtopics"
Details, examples,
    and explanations
    that support
    subtopics
Concluding point

Topic Sentence
    (main idea of para-
    graph)
Supporting ideas or
    "subtopics"
Details, examples,
    and explanations
    that support
    subtopics

Topic Sentence
    (main idea of para-
    graph)
Supporting ideas or
    "subtopics"
Details, examples,
    and explanations
    that support
    subtopics — *Body paragraphs*

Topic Sentence
    (main idea of para-
    graph)
Supporting ideas or
    "subtopics"
Details, examples,
    and explanations
    that support
    subtopics

Return to idea stated
    in thesis
Concluding point — *Conclusion*

A Sports Fanatic

Most leisure time in the life of a sports fanatic   — *Topic sentence*
involves some kind of sporting activity. A fanatic
will surround himself with sports paraphernalia   — *Subtopic: sports*
like wall posters, baseball cards, and bumper   *paraphernalia*
stickers. He probably has T-shirts that say "Go   — *Examples*
Raiders" or "Celtics Rule." If he takes time to
watch television or read, he watches a program   — *Subtopic: television, reading*
about sports or reads an article from <u>Sports   — *Examples*
Illustrated</u>. In his more active moments, the
sportsaholic, who is usually a pretty good athlete   — *Subtopic: plays sports*
himself, plays some sort of sport. You may find
him at the local YMCA shooting baskets with his   — *Examples*
friends, or he may have joined a baseball league
through his job. No matter what he does, the sports — *Concluding point*
fanatic finds some way to express his dedication
to sports.

The Life of a Sports Fanatic

Most of us have known a sports fanatic at   — *Introduces subject*
some time in our lives. They are the kids with
collections of baseball caps and team pennants. As   — *Examples of paraphernalia*
adults, they pull the sports section out of the paper — *Example of reading about*
before anyone else can grab it. They are also the   *sports*
husbands whose love of football makes Monday   — *Example of television*
night widows of their wives. If they are tennis   *watching*
buffs, they play several sets every evening and
compete in tournaments on weekends. Sports   — *Example of playing sports*
fanatics usually find ways to fill their lives with
sporting activities.   — *Thesis*
    The dedicated sports fan places sports-related
items around him. He probably has a favorite   — *Topic sentence*
team's bumper sticker on his car or a superstar's
poster on the wall in his room. A friend of mine,   — *Subtopic: paraphernalia*
for example, has a Cowboys bumper sticker on his   *(implied)*
4 x 4 Bronco and a life-sized poster of Michael   — *Examples of paraphernalia*

Jordan in his room. The avid sports fan also wears clothes with the team logo of his favorite football or baseball clubs. Take me for example; I wear my Dodgers baseball cap every day during the season and also enjoy wearing my Laker sweats.

Subtopic: clothes

Examples

Label the last three paragraphs on your own.

A sports fanatic fills his relaxing and lounging-around-time watching a sports program or reading an article about an athlete or a local team he admires. If he reads a book, it is usually a superstar's biography or a couple of pages from a sports magazine. I love to read about sports myself and just finished a biography on Brian Bosworth called The Boz. I also subscribe to Sports Illustrated and have been known to read it cover to cover in one sitting. When watching television, the sports enthusiast watches the baseball game of the week, Monday Night Football, or a Lakers game. Just last month I watched more television than usual because of the World Series.

Not only does a sportsaholic love to watch games and read about sports, but he also loves to play. He never gets tired of one sport because he can play several sports well. Some afternoons you may find him shooting baskets at the local park, playing catch with his friends, or joining a neighborhood pick-up game. My friends and I are the perfect examples of athletic sports fans. We love to take a whole Saturday and devote it to playing many different sports. We often play volleyball at the YMCA in the morning and basketball at the local high school in the afternoon. Then we do a little swimming and try batting cages later in the evening.

Most people have run across a sports fanatic at some time in their lives, but if you are still having trouble recognizing one, here's a final rundown. He is in good physical condition from year-round sports activities and is usually decked out in sweats with "Raiders" across his chest. His sports car will have a Lakers or Jets bumper sticker, and his room will have a poster of James Worthy on the wall. He has subscriptions to both <u>Sports Illustrated</u> and <u>The Sporting News</u>, as well as videos of all the professional golf tours. Last, but not least, the sports fanatic will be the easiest person on your Christmas list to buy for. You just have to get him tickets to see the Reds or Dolphins, a new pair of Champion sweats, or a subscription to <u>Baseball Digest</u>.

Questions for Discussion

1. What are similarities between the paragraph titled "A Sports Fanatic" and the essay titled "The Life of a Sports Fanatic"?
2. What differences did you notice?
3. Why do you think this writer focused on male sports enthusiasts?

Although the topics and supporting information in the papers you write for college classes may be dramatically different, the structure for most body paragraphs and essays is remarkably alike:

Begin with the main idea (topic sentence or thesis),
    followed by subtopics or supporting points,
        followed by specific examples and explanations that support your topic ideas.

By learning this pattern, completing the exercises in this book, and writing paragraphs and essays for practice, you will become a more confident, proficient writer.

STEPS TO WRITING AN ESSAY

The steps in the writing process that work for generating paragraphs also work for writing essays. Review them carefully each time you write. They are printed on the inside cover of this book for easy reference.

The rest of this chapter illustrates how one student, Doug Gonzales, followed the steps from initial idea to finished essay.

Step One: Developing a Topic

For an assignment in his English class, Doug Gonzales was asked to write a paper on stress. He remembered a journal entry he had written on the article, "Get Found, Kid!" (see Chapter 2). He reread the entry and underlined ideas he thought would make good topics.

I really enjoyed reading about all those kids who got found. It makes me wish I had time to get in a big pile and hug everybody! But who has time??? I have <u>no time at all for myself</u>, much less a pile of strangers. I mean, it's 9 P.M. and I've been up since 6 A.M. STRESS!!! I wake up, still tired. <u>At school</u> I get stressed. My <u>girlfriend</u> threatens to break up with me if I don't spend more time with her. My <u>mom</u> gets on my case about yard work. My <u>boss</u> says I have to work harder. I have to find some way to relax, right? <u>We all cope with stress in different ways.</u> I used to <u>smoke</u>. Now I <u>exercise</u> to escape stress. Some people take <u>drugs</u>, others drink <u>beer</u>. Not me, that's just another kind of stress. Gotta go now—I've got math homework and more STRESS!!!

Doug reviewed the ideas he had underlined and saw that he had several possible topics for his paper. He drew up the following list of possible topics.

1. We cope with stress in different ways.
2. I give up a lot to go to school. (This topic came from Doug's journal entry statement that he had no time at all for himself.)
3. The stress in my life comes from school, my girlfriend, my mom, and my boss.
4. I have several ways of coping with stress. (This topic idea came to Doug when he read his entry notes about smoking and exercise.)

His work with the next step, "Thinking about Your Audience," helped him choose a focus for his essay.

FOR PRACTICE

Exercise 5a.   Spend ten minutes writing whatever comes to mind about one of the following topics. When the time is up, reread what you have written and underline possible ideas for essay topics. Then list several topics you could discuss in an essay.

problems in my community
drug use in schools

looking for careers
restaurant food

Step Two: Thinking about Your Audience

Doug answered a few questions to help him picture his reader and select a topic for his essay:

> *What subject do I want to write about?*
>   Coping with stress.
> *Who am I writing for and why did I choose this audience?*
>   My classmates are my audience. They have some of the same stresses
>   I have and should appreciate the subject.
> *What is the main idea I want to communicate to my audience?*
>   I want students to see that there are several ways to cope with stress.

After answering his questions, Doug reread the four topics he had written for Step One and selected the first topic, "We cope with stress in different ways," as the most appropriate for his audience and purpose.

FOR PRACTICE

Exercise 5b.   Use the questions Doug used and those in Appendix A, "Preliminary Questions for Writing," to narrow one of the topics you listed in Exercise 5a.

Step Three: Preliminary Writing

The diagram at the beginning of this chapter shows that paragraphs are composed of general statements (topic sentences) supported by subtopics, which are, in turn, supported by details, examples, and explanations. Preliminary writing techniques (introduced in Chapter 3) are useful tools for generating supporting information for your paragraphs.

When Doug Gonzales reached this point in his writing, he asked himself what information his readers would need to know about ways to cope with stress. To answer that question, he considered the options outlined in Chapter 3:

Ask additional questions
Draw an idea wheel
List ideas

Doug decided to draw an idea wheel first to help him visualize his ideas about coping with stress. His idea wheel shows his topic, subtopic, and some supporting details.

Coping with Stress

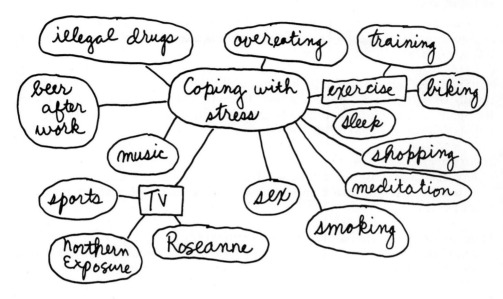

Next, Doug listed his ideas. He saw that he could group some of them according to forms of exercise, and legal and illegal drugs.

Coping with Stress

exercise
   training
   biking
sleep
meditation
using legal drugs
   smoking
   drinking beer
using illegal drugs
   cocaine
overeating
shopping
music
TV
   sitcoms
   sports
sex

Exercise 5c.   Rearrange Doug's list of ideas so that it begins with what you consider the least effective methods for coping with stress and ends with the more important methods.

Doug thought he probably had more ideas than he could write about in detail. To help him decide which ones he could actually support, he read his list again, asking himself additional questions formed from some of the journalists' questions—*who, what, where, when, why,* and *how.*

What *kind of exercise works?*
Exercise is an easy topic; I've got lots to say about the exercise program I use. I do weight lifting and aerobics, and I also bike, play racquetball, and swim.

How *do people use meditation and sleep to relax?*
Marlease does meditation, and maybe I can ask her what it is like. I'm not sure I can say much about this topic, though. I don't think I have much to say about sleep, either.

What *do I have to say about taking drugs, drinking, or smoking?*
I used to smoke, so I can talk about my experiences, and I have some ideas about cocaine use. Maybe I can use my ex-friend Ricky as an example of a person who used drugs to relax. I know people at work who drink to cope with their stress.

Who *do I know that overeats?*
I have a cousin who overeats. That's not a good way to deal with stress, though. I'll have to see whether that fits.

How *does shopping relieve stress?*
I'm not sure I can say much about shopping. My mom shops for relaxation, but I think this idea doesn't seem very interesting to me now.

Who *do I know that listens to music to relax and* **what** *kind of music works for them?*
For music, Mom and Dad listen to Mexican-style music to relax, my little brother listens to rap, and I like salsa.

Who *uses television to cope with stress?* **What** *do they watch?*
Everyone in my family watches television to relax. My parents watch soaps. I watch a variety of programs like *Northern Exposure,* sports, and *Roseanne.*

How *can I work "sex" into my paper?*
Sex might make a good conclusion—it's catchy.

By asking himself questions, Doug was able to identify topic ideas and supporting examples for paragraphs about watching television, exercising, listening to music, and using drugs as ways to relieve stress.

FOR PRACTICE

Exercise 5d. Look again at the topics you created for Exercise 5a. Choose one of your topics and draw an idea wheel, ask yourself questions, or make a list of ideas in preparation for writing an essay. Appendix B, "Questions for Expanding Ideas," gives you additional journalistic questions.

Step Four: Organizing Ideas

The two-step process of grouping ideas by subtopics and arranging them according to a logical pattern works as well for essays as it does for paragraphs. In fact, you will probably spend more time doing preliminary writing when working on an essay simply because it is longer and the task is necessarily more complex.

Doug had already done some organizing by the time he got to Step Four. By drawing his idea wheel, arranging his thoughts in a list, and deciding to omit some ideas while expanding others, he was already making choices about the content of his paper and the order of his ideas.

He was able to organize his ideas even more clearly when he noticed that the ways of relieving stress in his list of ideas were either healthy or unhealthy. He made these the main categories for his essay because he could arrange all the subtopics under these two headings.

In addition, Doug planned his introduction. To get the reader's attention, he thought he might use the brief scenes in his original journal entry on stress to recreate the feeling of stress for his reader.

Creating a Thesis

At this stage in the writing process, it is a good idea to create at least a tentative thesis to help you stay on track as you generate and arrange ideas for the essay. The thesis statement tells your reader what you intend to discuss in the essay. To create your thesis, you may find it useful to ask yourself (as Doug did earlier) what the main idea is that you want to communicate to your audience. When Doug originally thought about his audience and asked himself this question (see Step Two), he answered that he wanted students to see that there are many ways to cope with stress. Then, after completing Step Three and part of Step Four, he knew his thesis would include healthy and unhealthy ways of relieving stress, so he revised his original answer to read: I want to discuss both healthy and unhealthy ways of coping with stress. With this purpose in mind, Doug wrote the following thesis: People have different ways of relieving stress, but some are healthier than others.

Arranging Ideas

Once Doug had a tentative thesis, he rearranged his ideas as either harmful or healthy ways to relieve stress. Using the order-of-importance organizational pattern, he began with the more negative ideas—legal and illegal drugs—and ended with the more positive ways to relieve stress. He wanted to discuss exercise last because he considered it the most positive way to cope with stress, and he felt he had the most to say about it.

Next, Doug created the following outline for his paper. To help him see the levels of his ideas—from the most general to the most specific—he numbered them using an arabic numeral one for the thesis, twos for topic ideas, threes for subtopics, and fours, fives, and sixes for more specific details.

Outline on Relieving Stress

   2. A portrait of my personal stress
       3. Mom's orders
          4. Do the yard work.
       3. Teacher says I'm not passing.
          4. Do more work to pass.
       3. Boss
          4. Work harder at job!
             5. More sales
       3. Girlfriend
          4. Calls me at work
          4. Pay more attention to me!
1. Thesis: People have different ways of relieving stress, but some are healthier than others.
   2. Unhealthy, even harmful ways of dealing with stress
       3. Drugs
          4. Ricky
             5. Drug test at work
       3. Drinking beer
          4. People at work
       3. Smoking
          4. My experience
   2. Healthy ways to relieve stress
       3. Television shows
          4. Mom and Dad
             5. Mexican soaps
          4. I watch my own programs.
             5. Sports

      5. "Northern Exposure"
      5. "Roseanne"
   3. Music
      4. Mom and Dad listen to Mexican music like mariachis.
      4. My little brother listens to rap.
      4. I like salsa.
   3. Exercise
      4. Jogging
      4. My plan for exercise
         5. Basic training workout
            6. Aerobics
            6. Weights
         5. Racquetball
         5. Swimming
         5. Biking
            6. Long-distance
            6. Leisure
 3. Sex as a way to relax

Once he had revised his outline, Doug was ready to write a draft.

FOR PRACTICE

Exercise 5e.   Spend about half an hour grouping your ideas and writing an outline for the information you gathered during your practice with Step Three, Preliminary Writing. You will probably need to write several drafts of the outline. Once you have an outline, number the thesis, topic sentences, subtopics, and details from general (1, 2, and 3) to specific (4, 5, and 6).

Step Five: Writing a Fast Draft

When writing a fast draft, keep your outline by your side, and write ideas quickly, recognizing that you will rework them later. Here is Doug's fast draft:

Stress!!!

    I just got home from work its 9 P.M. and I've been up since 6 A.M. I am stressed out!! I think I have good reasons for feeling this way. This was my day. I wake up, and I'm still tired from the day before. I go to school, and my teacher told me I have to work just a little harder if I want to pass the class (STRESS!!). I went to work and my boss says he has some complaints about me (STRESS!!). Finally, at 9 P.M. I get to go home after a long, stressful day. I walk in the door and the first thing my mom says is that the yard looks terrible. When do I have time to clean the yard? (STRESS!!) This is just an example of my very stressful day. With all these "highs" going on in my life. How do I come back down? What are some ways other people come back down? People have different ways of relieving stress, but some are healthier than others.

Some ways of relieving stress are unhealthy, even harmful. Take drugs, for example. My friend Ricky is a perfect example of someone who used cocaine and eventually lost his job. One day his employer make him take a drug test. Ricky got fired. I also have a stressful job. When 5 P.M. rolls around, most people I work with say "It's beer time." That is just another way people cope with stress they drink beer. I think stress is one of the big reasons people start smoking. I used to smoke. A cigeret always seemed to calm me right down. It will also kill you.

My whole family watches television to relax and forget about work. Mom and Dad watch Mexican soaps. I watch my own programs—sports is my favorite, but I also like "Northern Exposure" and "Roseanne". Music is another way my family has of relaxing. Mom and Dad listen to Mexican music like mariachi bands, my little brother, Ray, likes rap, and I listen to salsa.

The best way to handle stress, I have found, is through exercise. I found a workout system that works for me. I like to play racquetball and do whats called "Basic Training Workout." A complete workout system that deals with everything from aerobics to weight training. I take long bike rides. Especially in the evening. And sometimes I swim at the Y.

I wasn't going to mention sex, but sex is one of the most common ways people relieve stress. Its good exercise, too, you feel good, and its a healthy activity that relieves stress. I guess we all have our own ways of coping.

FOR PRACTICE

Exercise 5f.   Use the outline you wrote for Step Four to write a fast draft of an essay.

Step Six: Editing and Proofreading

This is an important step in the writing process, one that beginning writers should never omit. Editing involves reading your essay as a whole and making substantial changes in the way your ideas are arranged or developed. A thorough editing involves the following procedures:

1. Writing an outline of your essay to see if your ideas follow a distinct chronological or spatial order, or if you have arranged them clearly according to their order of importance.
2. Moving sentences and paragraphs, adding examples, and deleting information when such changes make your ideas clearer.
3. Rewriting sentences that do not say quite what you mean.

When you proofread, you look more closely at individual words, phrases, and sentences. Your goal is to find and correct errors in grammar, sentence structure, spelling, punctuation, and capitalization. Exercises in Part Three of this book give you practice checking for grammar mistakes and errors in sentence structure. Chapter 27 provides a summary of spelling, punctuation, and capitalization rules. You may wish to refer to these rules as you proofread your essays. It is also useful to keep the following suggestions in mind when you are proofreading.

1. Proofread your essay several times, checking for words and phrases you may have omitted in your fast draft.
2. Keep a list of mistakes that recur in your writing, and when you proofread, go through your essay looking for each error one at a time. If you know, for example, that you have difficulty writing parallel sentences and using commas correctly, read your essay once to check the logic of your sentences; then read it a second time to catch errors in comma usage. (Chapter 27 provides a useful list of rules for using commas correctly.)
3. Read your essay aloud and, if you can, tape record it. This procedure usually makes writers look more carefully at what they have written.
4. After proofreading your essay on your own, share your writing with another student. Like most people, you may not be able to catch all the errors in your own writing; that's why sharing writing (Step Seven in the writing process) is another good way of finding mistakes.

Study the following description of Doug Gonzales's considerations as he applied these editing and proofreading techniques to his essay on ways to relieve stress.

When he had finished writing his fast draft, Doug read his paper out loud to make sure he had included all his topics and subtopics, and that each supported his thesis. He noticed that he needed a topic sentence in paragraph three showing the transition from unhealthy to healthy ways of coping with stress. He also decided to put the events in the introduction in chronological order according to when they occur on an average weekday. Overall, he was pleased with the order of ideas in the body paragraphs, but he made a note to add more information because they sounded sketchy and rushed. He wasn't altogether happy with the conclusion, either, but decided to wait and see what his readers would say when he shared his essay with other students.

Doug read his essay again to catch words he might have left out and find mistakes in sentence structure (he knew he had to watch for run-ons and fragments) or punctuation. He also looked up the spelling for "cigarette." Here is his revised draft.

Stress!!!

I just got home from work. It's 9 P.M. and I've been up since 6 A.M. I am stressed out!! I think I have good reasons for feeling this way. This was my day. I woke up and was still tired from the day before. I went to school, and my teacher told me I have to work just a little harder if I want to pass the class (STRESS!!). I got to work, and my boss said he had some complaints about me last week (STRESS!!). Finally, at 9 P.M. I went home after a long, stressful day. I walked in the door, and the first thing my mom said was that the yard looks terrible. "When do you have time to clean the yard?" she asked me (STRESS!!). With all these "highs" going on in my life, how do I come back down? What are some ways other people come back down? People cope with stress in many different ways, but some are healthier than others.

Some ways of relieving stress are unhealthy, even harmful. Drugs, for example, are very harmful. My friend Ricky is a perfect example of someone who used cocaine and eventually lost his job over it. One day his employer made him take a drug test, and Ricky got fired. I also have a stressful job with an insurance agency. I am constantly dealing with angry claimants. When five o'clock rolls around, most people I work with say "It's beer time." That is just another way people cope with stress. They drink beer. I think stress is one of the main reasons why people smoke. I used to smoke. A cigarette always seemed to calm me right down. Of course it could also kill me.

Many people have found healthier ways to escape the stresses we all fight every day. My whole family watches television to relax and forget about work. Mom and Dad, for instance, watch Mexican soaps. I watch my own programs—sports is my favorite, but I also like "Northern Exposure" and "Roseanne." Music is another way my family has of relaxing. Mom and Dad listen to Mexican music like mariachi bands, my little brother, Ray, likes rap, and I listen to salsa.

The best way to handle stress, I have found, is through exercise. I have a workout system that is perfect for me. I play racquetball and do what's called "Basic Training Workout," a complete workout system that deals with everything from aerobics to interval training. I also like to take long bike rides, especially in the evening, and sometimes I swim at the Y.

Sex is one of the most common ways people relieve stress. It's good exercise, too, you feel good, and it's a healthy activity that relieves stress. I guess we all have our own ways of coping with stress.

FOR PRACTICE

Exercise 5g.   Compare Doug's fast draft with his revised essay on stress. What changes did he make? How effective were these changes? Might additional changes strengthen the essay?

Exercise 5h.   Edit the fast draft you wrote for Exercise 5f by checking paragraphs for (1) topic sentences that support your thesis, (2) logical sequence of ideas between sentences and paragraphs, and (3) examples and explanations that support subtopics. Proofread for (1) words omitted, (2) sentence errors, and (3) punctuation and spelling errors.

Step Seven: Sharing Your Writing

At first, the idea of sharing what you have written with other students may make you uncomfortable or may even seem frightening. But once you have done it a few times, you will find that your fellow students can give you support and encouragement as well as good suggestions for clarifying your ideas. Sharing your writing is also beneficial because you can see how other students write. As a result, you may discover ways of organizing and developing ideas that you can use in future papers.

During an in-class workshop, Doug and two of his classmates shared ideas about their work. They used the following questionnaire to comment on each other's essays. (These questions are reproduced in Appendix C.)

Questions for Shared Writing

1. *What did you like about the essay you read?*
    Doug was pleased that both of his readers liked the opening of his essay. One classmate commented: "I get stressed out just reading this." That was exactly the effect Doug wanted. The other student wrote, "I liked seeing some of the ways that I relax. He had a pretty good list. . . . It was good to put the drugs in there, too, because so many people use drugs to escape, and those can be dangerous." The readers also thought the essay was well organized and that the transitions made Doug's paragraphs easy to follow.

2. *Does the opening paragraph get you interested? Explain why or why not.*
   Both students thought the introduction to Doug's essay was one of the strong points because it put them in the mood to read about stress.
3. *Does the introduction include the main point of the paper—its thesis—either stated or implied?*
   Both readers agreed that the thesis was the last sentence in the introduction. One student suggested that Doug write a more specific thesis mentioning the ways of coping with stress that he discusses in the paper. One student thought he asked so many questions near the end of the introduction that she couldn't be sure which one he was going to answer in the paper.
   Doug thought about this criticism and made a late change. He crossed out the questions "How do I come back down?" and "What are some ways other people come back down?" and wrote this tentative thesis: "If you are a student, you probably have some of the same pressures in your life that I have, and like me, you must find ways to cope with stress. Unfortunately, some ways of relieving stress are more harmful than helpful. The trick is to avoid those unhealthy ways (drug use) and find healthy ways (like music and exercise) to relieve stress."
4. *Would you like more information about any of these general ideas? If so, which ones?*
   One reader listed "workout system." She couldn't tell whether the workout system was Doug's own creation or if it was part of the "basic training workout" at a gym. Another reader asked, "How does all this reduce stress?"
   In responding to these comments, Doug explained which exercises he does during different seasons of the year—the basic training workout is just one part of his year-round exercise program.
   In response to the other student's comment, he reread the paper to see which stress-relieving activities he needed to explain more fully.
5. *Were there paragraphs that seemed off the topic and unrelated to the thesis?*
   Students agreed that the paragraphs were about either unhealthy or healthy ways to relieve stress.
6. *Were there places you had difficulty following the ideas or reading the sentences?*
   One student wrote that Doug's essay "jumped around too much—from drugs to drinking to smoking, and then from TV to music." In response, Doug decided to add transitions and additional information, but he wanted to discuss this comment with his teacher first.
7. *Does the paper come to a logical conclusion? What is it?*
   Doug's readers talked about better ways to end the paper. One wrote that "it just seems to stop." Another reader suggested he bring in the two ideas in his thesis.
8. *Would you like to ask the writer anything or do you have any additional point you would like to make?*
   One student said, "I had trouble with the topic in the last paragraph. I agree that sex can be relaxing, but it's not always that 'healthy.' " Doug's

other reader added, "AIDS and other diseases can make sex very unhealthy."

Doug decided that he hadn't really felt comfortable discussing sex in the first place; he felt it was too complex an issue for him to deal with in this essay, so he omitted it.

Teacher's Conference

Doug scheduled an appointment with his teacher to go over some of the comments he received during the student workshop. When he asked about his classmate's feeling that the essay "jumped around too much," his teacher suggested that his readers may have felt he jumped around because he didn't give much detail about the subtopics, particularly in the last few paragraphs. She agreed that adding transitions and explanations would clarify connections between his ideas.

After his meeting with his teacher, Doug changed his essay to explain in greater detail how watching a program on television, listening to music, or exercising relieves tension. Because of the added explanations, he divided his third paragraph and wrote a separate paragraph on television and another on music.

Doug also reorganized the paragraph on drugs in order to begin with legal drugs and end with the most harmful addiction—Ricky's cocaine habit. After writing a reorganized draft of the paragraph, Doug decided to write a separate paragraph on Ricky.

FOR PRACTICE

Exercise 5i.   Take the draft that you edited and proofread, and share it with a few of your classmates. Use the list of questions for responding to essays in Appendix C, "Questions for Shared Writing." When you have completed the questionnaire in Appendix C, answer these additional questions:

1. What is the most important thing you learned about your draft?

_____

_____

2. What changes will you make as a result of other students' comments?

_____

_____

_____

_____

_____

Step Eight: Making Final Revisions

After thinking about the comments from fellow students and his teacher, Doug drafted a new version of his essay. Here is Doug's final, corrected essay.

Coping with Stress

I just got home from work. It's 9 P.M., and I've been up since 6 A.M. I am stressed out!! I think I have good reasons for feeling this way. When I woke up, I was still tired from the day before. I went to school, and my math teacher told me I have to work just a little harder if I want to pass the class (STRESS!!). I arrived at work, and my boss said he had some complaints about me last week (STRESS!!). Finally, at 9 P.M. I went home after a long, stressful day. I walked in the door, and the first thing my mom said was, "The yard looks terrible. When do you have time to clean it?" (STRESS!!). If you are a student, you probably have some of the same pressures in your life, and, like me, you must find ways to cope with stress. The trick is to avoid the more harmful methods of relieving stress, like taking drugs, and to find healthier outlets, like music and exercise, to relieve stress.

Some ways of relieving stress are unhealthy, even harmful. I think stress is one of the main reasons why people smoke. I was a heavy smoker until recently. I work for an insurance agency and spend most of my day dealing with angry claimants. Smoking a cigarette after work used to calm me down after a long, stressful day. Because of the risk of lung cancer and heart disease, I quit smoking a few months ago. Most people I work with drink after work to relieve stress. When five o'clock rolls around, I will hear someone say, "It's beer time." Drinking becomes a problem for everyone on the road if an intoxicated person tries to drive. My co-workers are smart enough to take public transportation or appoint someone as the "designated driver." He or she stays liquor-free and drives everyone else home. But that arrangement doesn't solve the health problems people may develop because they drink.

Illegal drugs can be even more damaging. My friend Ricky is a perfect example of someone who misused drugs, and eventually lost his job because of them. He had a very stressful job and used cocaine to escape. At work he spent eight hours a day loading trucks as fast as he could. By the time he got home, he was dead tired. To feel better, he started using cocaine. At first no one knew, not even his friends. Then he got careless and began using it at work to keep himself going. One day his employer made him take a drug test, and Ricky got fired. He not only lost his job but also changed his life for the worse. Last time I heard he was in jail on a drugs charge.

My family and I have found healthier ways to relieve stress. We often watch television to relax and forget about work. Mom and Dad, for instance, watch Mexican soaps. My mom, especially, gets very involved with the characters' lives and forgets about her own aches and pains. I watch my own programs—sports is my favorite. I love to watch golf games because the players aren't like football players who try to knock each other down. Instead, golf is a slow-moving sport that requires a lot of thinking and concentration. Besides, the setting is always beautiful and makes me feel at ease. I also enjoy watching baseball because even though it is exciting when your team gets a double play or their opponents score a home run, there are still long stretches in between where the manager, pitcher, and catcher are figuring out what to do.

Music is another way my family has of relaxing. Mom, Dad, and my sister listen to Mexican music. Dad likes Carlos Guardel, who sings love songs and ballads that remind him of Mexico. Mom and my sister Ida enjoy listening to mariachi bands, that wonderful music from the Mexican Revolution. My little brother, Ray, likes rap music. I have no idea how he is able to relax while that is on, but he just loves it and seems to be in a world of his own as he listens to his headphones. I am a little older than Ray, and I am happiest listening to salsa, especially the music of Ruben Blades. Music is a great way of taking your mind off your troubles.

The best way to handle stress, I have found, is through exercise. My family joined the YMCA a few years ago, and I have been going regularly since I stopped smoking. In the winter months I swim at the Y, play racquetball on weekends, and do a "Basic Training Workout" during the week. The program at the Y offers a complete workout with everything from aerobics to weight training, and it always ends with a long period of stretching. When summer comes and the weather is right, I also like to take long bike rides, especially in the evening. When I ride on those warm nights, the summer breeze is very soothing, and my body always feels better for the exercise.

With the stress most of us have in our lives, we must find ways to calm down without threatening our health. My family and I find watching television and listening to music effective ways to forget about our problems. Exercise, however, offers the best alternative for me because it makes me feel equal to my tasks at work and school.

Exercise 5j.   List the major changes Doug made in his final essay. State briefly why you think he made these changes.

Exercise 5k.   Write a note to Doug suggesting additional changes he might make to improve his essay.

Exercise 5l.   Use the comments you received from fellow students and your teacher, and any additional insights you have had yourself, to make one or two revisions of your paper.

Exercise 5m.   Exchange your draft and final revision with a fellow student. Identify the changes the student made, and explain the effects of each.

TOPICS FOR WRITING

Topic 1.   Pick a topic from the list below. Use the steps in the writing process to narrow the topic, identify your audience, gather details and information, organize, write, and revise a short paper.

> Write a detailed description of the worst or best restaurant in town.
> Explain how you establish friendships.
> Write an essay about a problem in your life and ways to solve it.
> Discuss the two or three reasons why you became angry with someone recently.

Topic 2.   Write a paper explaining why you are attending college at this time in your life. Be sure to mention the two or three reasons in your thesis. Use the writing process to narrow your topic, do preliminary writing, organize, draft, and revise.

FOR REVIEW

1. What is an essay? _____

_____

_____

2. What are the three kinds of paragraphs in an essay?_____

_____

_____

Looking Ahead

Chapter 6 shows how to refine introductions, thesis statements, body paragraphs, and conclusions—the basic components of an essay. Exercises in that chapter ask you to write focused thesis statements and to use several patterns of development to write introductions and conclusions.

6

Refining Essays

This chapter stresses basic essay structure—introduction, thesis, body paragraphs, and conclusion. In preparation for revising your own essays, you will compose thesis statements, use several patterns of development to support ideas in body paragraphs, and explore strategies for writing introductions and conclusions.

BASIC ESSAY STRUCTURE

The **introduction,** the first paragraph of an essay, introduces your audience to your subject and catches their interest. The **thesis,** usually the last sentence of your introduction, states your approach to your subject. The **body** of the essay consists of paragraphs, sometimes called **body paragraphs,** that contain topic sentences, subtopics, and supporting information that expand, support, and substantiate the thesis statement. The **conclusion** is usually the last paragraph or last few sentences of an essay. Whereas the introduction anticipates the writer's approach to a subject, the conclusion provides a satisfying sense of completion.

REVISING ESSAYS

Writing an Introduction

Students sometimes have difficulty writing papers because they try to write the introduction before they are ready. If you find yourself having this sort of difficulty, write the body paragraphs first; then write the introduction. That way you will know what the essay actually says before writing the opening paragraph.

Remember, too, that the introduction is *not* the place to write a detailed explanation of a point you want to make. Because its purpose is to ease the reader into the essay, the introduction is one of the most general paragraphs in the essay. Support, explanations, details, and examples belong in the body paragraphs.

Effective Patterns for Introductions

No single, "right way" exists to write introductory paragraphs. However, some of the more common patterns appear below. Notice that each ends with the thesis.

1. Begin with a general statement of the subject.

I guess it is always difficult for immigrants to adjust to life in a new culture. That was certainly true for me. When I first came to the United States, I found learning English to be very difficult. I had trouble orienting myself to the physical layout of this city, and I had problems socializing with American students in school and people in general.

2. Begin with a specific scene.

I can still remember the distinct smell of cow manure that filled our van as my boyfriend and I crossed the border into Mexico. That smell stayed with us as we drove through Mexicali. The roads in Mexicali were like mazes and dogs were everywhere. Dented buses that belched smoke passed us on the shoulder; trucks cut us off. At first I was afraid of this chaotic place, but eventually I came to appreciate the warmth, humor, and pride of the people.

3. Begin with a question that you answer in the introduction.

Have you ever envied popular musicians their wealth and fame? If you have, you may not realize how much time, work, and dedication it takes to succeed in this highly competitive business. Members of bands like the local Smokin' Jax must sacrifice much of their personal lives and abandon other potential careers as they struggle to compete for auditions, bookings, and recording contracts.

4. Begin with facts or statistics.

According to the American Cancer Society, smoking is responsible for 83 percent of all cases of lung cancer in the United States. People who smoke two packs of cigarettes a day are 15–25 percent more likely to die of lung cancer than nonsmokers. The American Heart Association has found that smokers die of heart attacks two to four times more often than nonsmokers do. With such overwhelming evidence of the health risks related to smoking, why do thousands of Americans continue to smoke? Some people see smoking as a way to relax. Others smoke socially. Most smokers continue to smoke because they believe their habit is too hard to break.

5. Begin with a quotation.

In the sixties, John Lennon told us, "All you need is love." He made life sound so simple, as though it would be easy to be happy. Now that I have reached forty, have been through a divorce and the death of a child, I know that you need more than love to survive—you also need strength to get through the bad times and determination to grow from your experiences.

6. Begin with a contrast.

Images we see on television and at the movies suggest that the life of a lawyer is filled with exciting cases and jurors who are easily impressed. When television-lawyers aren't driving around in their Porsches, they are impressing the jury with their uncanny insights. But the truth is much different. Lawyers, particularly new ones, are chained to a desk most of the day, writing briefs and motions. When they do appear in court, the opposing lawyer may convince the judge to postpone their trial. If the trial proceeds, it is likely to be quite routine, even boring. Lawyers are frequently "in it for the money," and greed can take the heart out of the work.

FOR PRACTICE

Exercise 6a.   Use these six patterns to create introductions that end with the following thesis statements:

1. People who experiment with drugs think they can control their habit, but eventually the habit controls them.
2. Friendships can be lost because friends grow apart or simply neglect one another.
3. Many high school freshmen think their college classmates will be much smarter than they are and teachers will be indifferent to students' problems with course material.
4. Music puts us in the right mood to study, takes our minds off our troubles, and helps us remember the past.

5. Computers are wonderful tools for writing because there is such a variety of programs for word processing, learning grammar skills, and composing papers.

Exercise 6b. Pick one of the topics that follow the example below. To help you narrow the subject, draw an idea wheel, make a list of ideas, or ask yourself questions. Then try writing a thesis. Once you have your thesis, write two different introductions for it.

Example:

1. One student chose the topic, "teachers."

2. To narrow her subject, this student used the idea wheel, list of ideas, and questions to help her gather information about her topic. Notice that as she listed her ideas about teachers, she thought of questions that helped her narrow her topic.

> I've had good and bad teachers.
> Some teachers encourage students to talk in class.
> Some care about students, but others don't.
> Some will insult you rather than explain things.
> Some teachers talk to themselves and not to students.

Am I being too general? Which teachers have I seen acting in these ways?

> math teachers I had
> Riley and Jackson in high school
> completely different styles
> One liked his job; the other didn't.
> Riley came in late, took out her notes, and read every word even if we weren't listening.
> no questions in her class
> Jackson explained everything, sometimes more than once.

What am I trying to show in this paper?

> The difference between the teaching styles of two high-school math teachers—Ms. Riley and Mr. Jackson

To arrange her ideas more clearly, she drew this idea wheel.

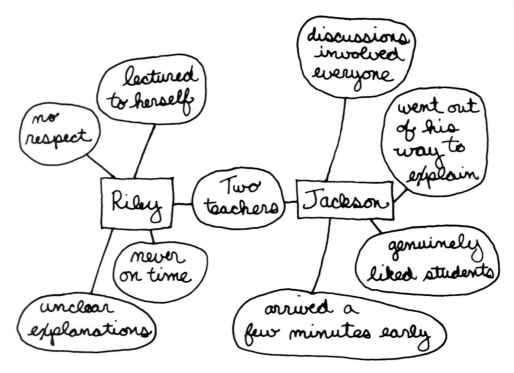

3. Next, the student wrote the following thesis: The difference in teaching styles and attitude toward students made Mr. Jackson the better teacher.

4. The student then wrote two introductions. One began with a general statement of the subject and the second started with a specific scene.

(1) The math teachers I have had over the years have been as different as night and day. Ms. Riley and Mr. Jackson illustrate the extreme differences between the two types of teachers. The difference in teaching styles and attitude toward students made Mr. Jackson the better teacher.

(2) Students in Ms. Riley's Math 1 class stir restlessly in their seats. Splat! Someone throws a spitwad and hits Letitia Briggs in the neck. Ms. Riley keeps writing examples from her notes on the chalkboard. Next door the teacher sits among the students and listens as one of his pupils explains how he solved one of the math problems he did for homework. Several students have their hands raised, waiting to ask questions. I was in both of these classes in high school and saw for myself why the difference in teaching styles and attitude toward students made Mr. Jackson the better teacher.

Now, pick one of the topics below and follow the directions at the beginning of this exercise. Refer to the example again if you need help.

teachers	a movie
commuting to school	student athletes
family problems	the dating game
your writing	parents

Writing a Thesis

The **thesis** is the main idea you will discuss in your essay. You might also look at the thesis as a promise you make to yourself and your readers about the subject you will discuss and the way you will discuss it. Because it determines what will appear in the rest of your paper, the thesis is the most important sentence in the essay.

The thesis is usually the last sentence in the introduction. In that position, it pulls your readers into the essay and tells them what to expect. Experienced writers sometimes put the thesis at the beginning of the introduction or in the conclusion, and if the essay is particularly long, the writer may restate it halfway through the essay. As a beginning writer, you will have an easier time sticking to your subject if you state your thesis at the end of the introduction.

Key words in your thesis, like the key words in your topic sentences, announce the subject you will discuss and predict how you will discuss it.

Thesis Statement

subject
↓

Example: I become a <u>compulsive shopper</u> whenever I get unbearably

causes
↓   ↓

<u>bored</u> or feel <u>pressured</u> to take on more work than I can possibly complete.

In this thesis, the writer promises to discuss why she becomes a "compulsive shopper"—it happens because she gets bored or feels pressured at work. If she fulfills this promise, her topic sentences will focus on one of the two causes. Her body paragraphs will offer supporting examples and explanations to show how each cause triggers her compulsive desire to go shopping.

FOR PRACTICE

Exercise 6c.   Underline the subject and words that narrow it in the following thesis statements.

1. There are a few practical steps women can take to protect themselves from assault.
2. Our newest immigrants contribute more dollars to the economy than they take in public benefits.
3. A large percentage of young black males are dying in America, not from natural causes, but from gang-related violence.
4. Once I became a working mother, I was torn between my desire for independence and the traditional role of woman-as-homemaker that I had known all my life.
5. Members of a band who are struggling to be discovered sacrifice a great deal of time and money.

Narrowing the Thesis

Like topic sentences, thesis statements must be narrow enough that you can support them in body paragraphs. If the thesis is not sufficiently narrow, you will not have a clear guide for the essay, and will be more likely to wander from topic to topic without a sense of logical progression or purpose.

Here is a thesis that is not narrow enough to produce a well-focused paper: *My family is very wasteful.* This sentence has a subject—the writer's family—and includes the general point the writer intends to make about that family—they are "wasteful." This thesis statement lacks a clear direction, however, because the subject is so general that the essay could be about anything vaguely related to being wasteful. The writer's family might, for example, waste water, paper, food, electricity, or time. To help narrow this thesis statement the writer asked several questions:

> Exactly *how* is my family wasteful?
> *What* do they waste?
> *Who* is wasteful in my family?

The answers lead to the following thesis and topic sentences for a well-focused essay.

Revised Thesis:

> My family wastes water, electricity, and paper products.

Topic Sentences:

> My brother and sister waste gallons of water every day.
> My father is no better—he always forgets to turn off the lights and unplug small appliances.
> Every week we throw away several feet of newspapers and computer paper.

FOR PRACTICE

Exercise 6d.   Compare these thesis statements:

    a. My trip to Mexico turned out to be very interesting.
    b. My trip to Mexico turned out to be an interesting adventure that led us to several of the beaches along the western coast, the Aztec ruins in Mexico City, and the badlands of central Mexico.

Which would make the best thesis for an essay?_____

Explain your answer: _____

_____

Exercise 6e.   Narrow each of the following sentences to create a well-focused thesis statement. Use the journalistic questions to help you.

1. Smoking gets on my nerves.

Narrowed: _____

_____

2. I have a terrible job.

Narrowed: _____

_____

3. It is difficult to be an athlete.

Narrowed: _____

_____

4. Divorce can be an awful experience.

Narrowed: _____

_____

5. Addicts are not all alike.

Narrowed: _____

_____

Exercise 6f.   Develop topic sentences for three of the thesis statements you wrote for Exercise 6e. (You may have two, three, or four topic sentences.) If you have difficulty, check to see if your thesis is narrow enough.

Thesis: _____

_____

    Topic sentence: _____

_____

    Topic sentence: _____

_____

    Topic sentence: _____

_____

    Topic sentence: _____

_____

Thesis: _____

_____

    Topic sentence: _____

_____

    Topic sentence: _____

_____

    Topic sentence: _____

_____

    Topic sentence: _____

Thesis: _____

_____

    Topic sentence: _____

_____

    Topic sentence: _____

_____

    Topic sentence: _____

_____

    Topic sentence: _____

_____

      Thesis statements can be too narrow. Like topic sentences, thesis statements must be general enough to give you something to discuss in your essay.

The following sentence states a fact, but is not a good thesis because it leaves you with nothing else to say: *I got divorced last year.* A better thesis statement suggests ideas for several body paragraphs: *I gained independence but lost companionship and financial security when I got divorced last year.* This expanded version suggests one advantage of getting divorced (gaining independence) and two disadvantages (the losses of companionship and financial security).

Here is another thesis statement: People decide to return to college for are several reasons.

What is the subject of this thesis? _____

What will the writer say about this subject? _____

_____

What specific reasons might the writer discuss? _____

_____

_____

FOR PRACTICE

Exercise 6g. The topic sentences for several essays are grouped together in the exercises below. Write a thesis for an essay that develops these ideas.

Example:

Competing in sports helps children set goals.
Children who play sports learn to make decisions.
Team involvement is another important benefit for children who play organized sports.

Possible Thesis: Children who play organized sports learn to set goals, make their own decisions, and cooperate with others.

Possible Thesis: Playing organized sports helps children develop self-confidence and teaches them valuable social skills.

1. The store owners and waitresses in Malberg are hostile to servicemen.
   It is difficult to get on a bus or hail a cab without being either ignored or insulted.
   When servicemen go to nightclubs in Malberg, they must sit in a segregated section in the bar.

Possible Thesis: _____

_____

2. Football players must be in excellent physical shape.
   Members of a football team must also be mentally prepared for
   the games.
   Most important of all, players must learn to work together.

Possible Thesis: _____

_____

3. Friends may begin asking "When are you getting married?" after a
   man and woman have been dating for only a few months.
   Family members often add to the couple's discomfort by assuming
   that because they enjoy spending time together they'll eventually
   marry.

Possible Thesis: _____

_____

4. Tobacco use makes the smoker very unappealing.
   Not only is smoking a socially obnoxious habit, it is considered the
   number one cause of heart and lung disease in the United States.
   Smoking endangers other people's health as well.

Possible Thesis: _____

_____

5. Sioux Falls, South Dakota, has fewer opportunities for entertainment
   than does San Francisco.
   San Francisco also has Sioux Falls beat in terms of job opportunities.
   The crime rate is a major problem in San Francisco, however, and a
   minor consideration in Sioux Falls.
   The costs of housing, food, clothing, and utilities make it much more
   difficult to live in San Francisco than in Sioux Falls.

Possible Thesis: _____

_____

Writing a Title

The title of your essay introduces your subject. Because it is usually the first
thing your readers see, it should be interesting enough that they will want to
keep reading.

A title is usually a phrase (not a complete sentence) containing words that
are closely related to those in the thesis. Here are a few possible titles matched
with their thesis statements:

Title: Making Adjustments
Thesis: When I got married, I had to adjust my social life, household responsibilities, and financial goals.

Title: Trashing America
Thesis: I see garbage everywhere these days—on campus, in parks, and in my
  own neighborhood.

Title: Defensive Moves
Thesis: Using a few practical techniques helps women to protect themselves
  from assault.

FOR PRACTICE

Exercise 6h.   Write a title for each of the following thesis statements.

1. Thesis: Playing organized sports helps children develop self-confidence
  and teaches them valuable social skills.

Title: _____

2. Thesis: Members of a band who are struggling to be discovered sacrifice a
  great deal of time and money.

Title: _____

3. Thesis: A large percentage of young, black males are dying in America, not
  from natural causes, but from gang-related violence.

Title: _____

4. Thesis: Once I became a working mother, I was torn between my desire for
  independence and the traditional role of woman-as-homemaker
  that I had known all my life.

Title: _____

5. Thesis: Our newest immigrants contribute more dollars to the economy
  than they take in public benefits.

Title: _____

Exercise 6i.   Write several alternate titles for the most recent essay you
wrote or an essay that you are currently writing. _____

_____

_____

Which title do you prefer?_____

Why?_____

_____

Developing Body Paragraphs

The supporting information in an essay usually comes from examples, details, and case histories based on the writer's experience and observations. Occasionally writers conduct interviews and do other kinds of research to gather information for an essay.

Strategies for Developing Ideas

Depending on your subject and the information you wish to discuss, you may use one of several strategies for developing your ideas:

1. Narrating.   When you narrate events, you are telling about something that happened. The event may have happened to you or to other people; in either case, you will usually follow a chronological sequence when organizing a narrative essay. Occasionally the entire essay may narrate or tell the story of something that happened. In that case, it is important to use the writing process, especially the questions in Step Two, to determine what central idea or impression you wish your narrative to convey.

2. Describing.   In descriptions, you record the details, sensual impressions, and observations you have made about an object, place, person, or event. Well-written descriptions convey one important idea about the subject or create a dominant impression.

3. Explaining.   When you explain something, you essentially break it apart into smaller ideas to show how it works. Here are some examples of things you might write about using explanation:

> the importance of an event in your life (analysis)
> a complex task you perform at work or the steps involved in forming a
>   friendship (process analysis)
> several learning disabilities (definition)
> factors that made you decide to attend a particular college or choose a
>   specific major (causal analysis)
> how two things, people, places, or events are similar or different (com-
>   pare/contrast)
> a problem and several solutions to that problem (problem/solution)

4. Evaluating.   When you evaluate a subject, you judge it on the basis of criteria you have identified. You might, for example, evaluate the performance of your favorite baseball team based on examples of individual players and overall teamwork. Perhaps you will evaluate a concert you went to, a book you read, or a restaurant you tried. Each of these subjects requires its own criteria for evaluation.

5. Persuading.   In persuasive essays you are trying to use enough evidence and common-sense arguments to convince your audience that your position on a particular issue is valid. The potential subjects for persuasive essays are virtually limitless. Here are two:

> Persuade the non-voting population in your state to vote in the next election.
> Persuade your reader that smoking in public places should be illegal.

The following excerpt from "Stories Make a Family," by Elizabeth Stone, illustrates how writers combine these patterns in their essays.

Many families build self-esteem through stories about money and self-made men. But in my family there wasn't a single story like that. What the	*Contrasts*
Bongiornos substituted was a sense that they came from a long line of people with talent, a talent that was innate, nearly genetic. Their celebration of the artist and their conviction that art was in their blood dated back to an unnamed (and probably apocryphal) court musician who had lived before the beginning of family time. And of course this talent was invoked again in the story in which my great-grandmother, the tale's moral center, fell in love with that poor but talented musical postman.	*Explains family identity*
The motif of art and talent was too important and too powerful a symbol to live in those two stories alone, and so it flourished in many. One of the	*Explains importance*
oldest stories in our family was about my great-grandfather long after his elopement. He could play any instrument he laid eyes on, it was said. And so could his sons who, like my grandmother, inherited his musical genes. In the evenings after dinner, he and his sons would go into the courtyard, each with his instrument, and play music together for several hours. People would come "from miles around" just to listen.	*Narrates*
My grandmother, the youngest of his children, had a lovely singing voice, and this was the subject of one very important family story set during her childhood in Sicily. One day she was at home with her mother, singing as she did some chore around the house. Suddenly, her mother looked out the	*Narrates*

window and saw the parish priest ambling up the road. "Be quiet! Be quiet!" she hissed to my grandmother. "The *padre* will hear you singing, and he will again tell us that we must send you to Rome for singing lessons, and you know we don't have the money for that."

My grandmother never did have voice lessons, but 30 years later she was still singing. By then, she and her six children were living on Vanderbilt Street in a second-floor apartment over a grocery store run by a man named Mr. Peterson. Every Friday morning, my grandmother would get down on her hands and knees and wash the tile floor in the first-floor entry hall. She loved opera, and as she scrubbed the floor, she would sing one aria or another. As the story goes, Mr. Peterson would invariably stop whatever he was doing and hush his customers in order to listen to her without interruption.

I wonder about these stories now. How could a man with a postman's income afford to buy all those instruments? And would a nineteenth-century parish priest in a small Sicilian village really encourage a family to send their preadolescent daughter hundreds of miles away to Rome? And would he do it for as secular an undertaking as singing lessons? And did Mr. Peterson really stop everything to listen?

No one ever noticed the oddities in these stories. In part, it was because they inhabited a strangely protected realm, half real, half fanciful; they were too useful for us to question whether they were true or not. But literal truth was never the point. What all these stories did was give us something strong and important to hold onto for as long as we needed it—a sense of belonging in the world. When I was growing up, my sense of what the future might hold was shaped by the stories I'd heard about our past.

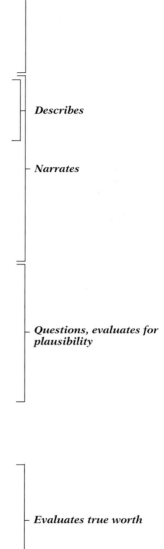

Describes

Narrates

Questions, evaluates for plausibility

Evaluates true worth

Coherence

Just as transitions and references to preceding ideas link sentences within paragraphs, they also provide logical connections between paragraphs.

Here is a summary of techniques for achieving coherence between paragraphs in an essay:

Refer to an idea in the thesis
Use transitional words and expressions (see list on page 70)
Refer to an idea expressed earlier in the paragraph
Refer to an idea in a preceding paragraph

FOR PRACTICE

Exercise 6j.   The thesis and topic sentences from Doug Gonzales's final, corrected essay, "Coping with Stress" (see Chapter 5), are reprinted below. Circle the words that Doug used to make logical connections between his paragraphs.

    . . . If you are a student, you probably have some of the same pressures in your life, and, like me, you must find ways to cope with stress. The trick is to avoid the more harmful methods of relieving stress, like taking drugs, and to find healthier outlets, like music and exercise, to relieve stress.

> Some ways of relieving stress are unhealthy, even harmful.
> Illegal drugs can be even more damaging.
> My family and I have found healthier ways to relieve stress. We often
>   watch television to relax and forget about work.
> Music is another way my family has of relaxing.
> The best way to handle stress, I have found, is through exercise.
> With the stress most of us have in our lives, we must find ways to calm
>   down without threatening our health.

Exercise 6k.   Create topic sentences for paragraphs 2 through 6 in the following essay. Remember that the topic sentence should state the main point discussed in the paragraph as well as connect logically to ideas in the thesis and preceding paragraphs.

Starting the Day

1. I am a creature of habit. There is no better proof of this than the morning ritual I have been following since I left my parents' house many years ago. My multiple alarms, morning bath, carefully-paced cups of coffee, and the final rituals of dressing, putting on makeup, and fixing my hair are as much a part of my morning as breathing.

2. (Topic sentence) _____

_____

_____

The first alarm goes off at six o'clock, though I have no intention of getting up then. Instead, it's a signal for my little dog, Frito, to jump onto the bed and snuggle with me. I relax with Frito until the second alarm sounds at six eighteen; some days I get up, but I know a third alarm will go off at six thirty. The six-thirty alarm has the ring of authority; it is the loudest, and the most obnoxious of the three. I respond immediately by making the bed as I am getting out of it. Where I acquired that habit is a mystery.

3. (Topic sentence) _____

_____

_____

I have a huge, claw-foot tub and every morning I climb in and settle down while it is filling. I built a wooden rack on the side of the tub for my coffee. I relax in water hot enough to turn my skin a rosy pink while I read the morning paper—first the front-page news, then local stories, the travel section, and the comics. I can usually hear my three dogs romping outside the door while I enjoy my coffee, newspaper, and hot bath. Then I take a few minutes to look over my daily calendar. Generally I'm out of the tub before six fifty-five as yet a fourth alarm warns me that it's time to pull the plug.

4. (Topic sentence) _____

_____

_____

On the way back to my bedroom I pour myself a second cup of coffee. I choose a suit or dress from my closet that fits my mood—dark colors for somber, professional meetings, bright prints for times when I wish the sun was shining. I iron-as-I-wear, so next I iron my choice for the day. If I were following the advice of cosmetics companies, I would coordinate the color of my foundation and blush with the clothes I wear. But that sort of nonsense would take too much time, disrupt my schedule, and confuse me. I brush my hair a vigorous sixty strokes and arrange it swept to one side or falling evenly around my face. A rather stubborn hair spray completes my preparations.

5. (Topic sentence) _____

_____

_____

By the time I pull on my shoes, grab my purse, and flick off the bedroom light, the seven twenty-five alarm has gone off. I have just ten minutes to straighten up the bathroom—hang up wet towels, wipe out the tub, and put away my nightclothes while I brush my teeth—before the final seven thirty-five alarm goes off.

6. (Topic sentence) _____

_____

_____

_____

In the old days I would get up late, rush around in a panic, forget my shoes, put on my makeup while driving, or drive recklessly in an attempt to make up ten or fifteen minutes, and arrive late anyway. Now I have time for a leisurely drive to work. The best part is that when I say "Good morning" to fellow workers, I mean it.

Writing a Conclusion

A good conclusion gives the audience the feeling that the writer has brought ideas to a logical end and has said what he or she wanted to say. The best conclusions leave readers with an interesting or thought-provoking idea. Like the introduction, the conclusion is usually a general paragraph; its purpose is to ease the reader out of the essay.

Students sometimes have difficulty deciding what to say in their conclusions. If you find yourself in this situation, try rereading your essay to remind yourself of what you actually wrote. Your general goal is to write a conclusion that is closely related to the ideas you presented in the paper.

As with introductions, writers commonly rely on one of several patterns for writing conclusions. See if you can match the conclusions here with the appropriate introductions on pages 97–98.

1. End with a summary of the main ideas.

I hope to do a lot of traveling in my life, but I will probably be tempted to measure my new destinations by the experiences I had in Mexicali. Whenever I arrive as a stranger in a new country, I will remember the people who welcomed us at hotels as though we were long-lost relatives. If I have trouble making myself understood in another culture, I will remember the kind waitress who made good-humored jokes about my poor Spanish. In countries with much older cultures than that of the United States, I will look for people like the elderly man in the National Museum of Anthropology who wasn't rich enough to travel to other countries, but who took great pride in the art and culture of ancient Mexico.

2. End with a discussion of the outcome or consequences.

As the years went by, I overcame most of my difficulties with English. I learned the areas of the city pretty well by traveling around every day. In addition, I improved my understanding of English by reading books by Mark Twain, Helen Keller, and other writers. The most important step for me was learning to speak English well enough to communicate with American students, teachers, and people off campus.

3. End with a prediction about what will happen.

Musicians give up a great deal for the chance to become well-known performers. But in spite of the tremendous pressures and hard economic times, the results can really be rewarding when the recording contracts start coming in and the band plays to capacity crowds. At first it may not seem possible, but occasionally the self-sacrifices do lead to recognition. As for Smokin' Jax, the crowds are coming earlier and staying later, and agents are more interested than they were a few years ago. In short, their future looks bright.

4. Ask the reader to take action.

No amount of relaxation can make up for the shortness of breath, chest pains, and fatal diseases caused by smoking. And if smoking seems to be an impossible habit to break, smokers should remember what they are doing to their health and their family's peace of mind. The relatives of smokers suffer because they have to watch their husband, wife, child, or parent get sick and die. If smokers can't think of themselves, they should consider the agony they cause their families and stop smoking today.

5. End with a question.

Who could have guessed that life would be so much more complex and painful than John Lennon predicted? I have learned that it takes more than love to survive this life. It takes the strength to go on when you are alone and grieving, or when it seems as though you can't face another day. Learning to survive despite the difficulties makes you a stronger person than you ever imagined you could be.

FOR PRACTICE

Exercise 6l.   Use one of the patterns for writing conclusions to create a concluding paragraph for one of the introductions you wrote in Exercise 6a.

Exercise 6m.   Locate an essay that you have written recently. First, identify the kind of conclusion you have written; then write a different conclusion using another of the patterns suggested above.

Looking Ahead

Part Two, "A Cross-Cultural Reader," provides practice for some of the reading and writing skills covered in Part One. In addition, the chapters in Part Two introduce several strategies for developing your writing—narrating, describing, analyzing, problem solving, evaluating, and arguing. After each discussion you will find an explanation of how the writing process works with each of these strategies.

PART TWO

A Cross-Cultural Reader

7

Family and the Sense of Self

We all come from the past, and children ought to know what it was that went into their making, to know that life is a braided cord of humanity stretching up from time long gone, and that it cannot be defined by the span of a single journey from diaper to shroud.

—Russell Baker

My father and I played catch as I grew up. Like so much else between fathers and sons, playing catch was tender and tense at the same time.

—Donald Hall

The readings in Part Two of this book, "A Cross-Cultural Reader," are arranged in chapters according to theme—"Family and the Sense of Self," "A Sense of Place," "The Richness of Tradition," "Self and Others," "Men and Women," "Immigrants," "Between Two Cultures," "Evaluating Experience," "The Workplace," "Getting an Education," "Examining Stereotypes," and "Against Injustice." The selections in these chapters present a variety of cultural and personal points of view. As a whole, the readings reflect the diversity of American culture.

Most of the chapters in Part Two have two main sections—a discussion of one of the writing strategies introduced in Chapter 6 (narrating, describing, explaining, evaluating, and persuading) and additional thematic essays for further reading. Within the section on writing strategies you will also find (1) characteristics of the writing strategy featured in the chapter, (2) a sample of that strategy written by a professional or student writer, and (3) additional considerations for applying steps in the writing process to the writing strategy introduced in the chapter.

One of the chapters in Part Two does not follow the format outlined above for presenting a writing strategy. Instead, Chapter 16, "Getting an Education," introduces techniques for making careful observations, and discusses patterns of inductive and deductive reasoning.

"For Further Reading," a section common to all chapters in Part Two, includes essays that develop the chapter's theme. Each reading selection is followed by sections that ask you to respond to the reading in several ways. "Freewriting" contains exercises that help you formulate a response to what you have read. The "Questions for Discussion" ask you to think critically about the reading and to discuss your ideas with classmates. "Topics for Writing," which closes each reading selection, may ask you to employ the writing strategy discussed in the chapter or to use strategies introduced in other chapters.

The first three chapters in Part Two focus on several ways that family, neighborhood, landscape, tradition, and heritage form our ideas of who we are. Here in Chapter 7 the authors of the selections you will be reading use memories of people, events, and stories from childhood to show how families connect us to the past. In "Mother," Russell Baker writes an entertaining account of his strong-willed mother at several stages of her life. Jamaica Kincaid's "Girl" records a mother's voice telling her daughter what to do and how to act. In "Fathers Playing Catch with Sons," Donald Hall remembers the "tender and tense" moments when he played baseball with his father, and he speculates about what his father's chances of playing professionally might have been.

The prominent writing strategy in this chapter—narrating—is introduced below. Examples from "Mother," an excerpt from the first chapter of Russell Baker's autobiography, *Growing Up*, illustrate writing techniques typical of narratives.

NARRATING

Human beings are natural storytellers. Think about the conversations that take place in your classroom before the teacher arrives. In a typical classroom scene, one student might tell another what happened after her car broke down on the highway the previous afternoon. Another might reply with an account of an annoying series of events that happened in an auto repair shop a few months earlier. A few seats away one student might be telling another about the agonies he went through before his math test that morning. In a third conversation, a student might be recounting a funny story about his son's first attempt to eat a cheese pizza. Such conversations show you that everyone has stories to tell, and these stories come out naturally.

When we tell our stories to others or write privately for ourselves, we are organizing experiences in coherent patterns that help us understand what people, places, and events really mean to us. At times, we may be explaining what an experience taught us; at other times, we may be presenting ideas we hope can teach others. We also may be attempting to preserve details and feelings that are important to us. When we wish to convey such meanings to an audience, it is helpful to know how other writers have made their stories interesting and meaningful. In the following discussion, passages from Russell Baker's "Mother" are used to illustrate characteristics common to well-written narratives.

Characteristics of Narrating

A Distinct Point of View

Narratives are usually told from a single point of view with an author or character using the first person, "I," to tell what happened. The writer frequently establishes point of view, time, and place in the opening paragraphs of an article or essay. For example, in his autobiographical portrait of his mother (page 126), Russell Baker introduces himself, his subject, and his perspective on that subject in the first paragraph.

> At the age of eighty my mother had her last bad fall, and after   1
> that her mind wandered free through time. Some days she went to
> weddings and funerals that had taken place half a century earlier.
> On others she presided over family dinners cooked on Sunday after-
> noons for children who were now gray with age. Through all this
> she lay in bed but moved across time, traveling among the dead
> decades with a speed and ease beyond the gift of physical science.

Because he is writing an autobiography, Baker uses his own "voice," identifying himself as a grown man who speaks from the bedside of his declining mother. His perspective is important because he can make sense of his mother's mental "travels" in a way that she cannot. As recorder and interpreter, he places each event that she imagines in its proper place in the past, sometimes as much as "half a century earlier" than the moment of his writing.

A Sense of Audience and Purpose

Writers can choose from among several reasons for writing. They may wish *to inform* their audiences of a particular situation, as Doug Gonzales did when he wrote to inform students that there are positive as well as potentially harmful ways to relieve stress. Writers may have other purposes as well. They may, for example, write *to entertain* their readers. In this case they may use humor or an unusual approach to their subject. Another common purpose in writing is *to explain* something that happened, a condition that exists, or the expected result of a situation. Writers may also explain why something happened, what it meant, how something works, or why it is important. In other instances, authors may write *to persuade* their readers to change their minds about an issue, or they may urge them to take action. Authors often write for several of these reasons.

In writing about his mother, Russell Baker includes lively descriptions to entertain us and to illustrate her strong-willed personality. Here is one passage from paragraphs 14 and 15 that suggests these purposes:

> . . . In that time when I had known her best, my mother had 14
> hurled herself at life with chin thrust forward, eyes blazing, and an
> energy that made her seem always on the run.
> She ran after squawking chickens, an axe in her hand, deter- 15
> mined on a beheading that would put dinner in the pot. She ran
> when she made the beds, ran when she set the table. One Thanks-
> giving she burned herself badly when, running up from the cellar
> oven with the ceremonial turkey, she tripped on the stairs and tum-
> bled back down, ending at the bottom in the debris of giblets, hot
> gravy, and battered turkey.

Baker also writes for himself in order to capture his own memories of his mother and to speculate about her memories of times before he was born. In yet another passage from "Mother," he complains about how much of his mother's past he has lost:

> . . . Of my mother's childhood and her people, of their time 39
> and place, I knew very little. A world had lived and died, and though
> it was part of my blood and bone, I knew little more about it than I
> knew of the world of the pharaohs. It was useless now to ask for
> help from my mother. The orbits of her mind rarely touched pre-
> sent interrogators for more than a moment.

If Baker hopes to preserve anything from the past, he must write down what he remembers about his mother and his own childhood before he himself is beyond remembering.

Conflict or Complexity

A well-written narrative usually has some edge, some conflict or uncertainty that may remind us of conflicts in our own lives. In Russell Baker's narrative, his insistence that his mother stop imagining herself as a younger, more vital woman living in a completely different time and place conflicts with her inability to stay in the present "for more than a moment." Controlled by her illness, his mother ignores her son's objections and seems to go wherever she wishes. Baker writes:

> . . . For a time I could not accept the inevitable. As I sat by her 16
> bed, my impulse was to argue her back to reality. On my first visit
> to the hospital in Baltimore, she asked who I was.
>> "Russell," I said.   17
>> "Russell's way out west," she advised me.   18
>> "No, I'm right here."   19
>> "Guess where I came from today?" was her response.   20
>> "Where?"   21
>> "All the way from New Jersey."   22
>> "When?"   23
>> "Tonight."   24
>> "No. You've been in the hospital for three days," I insisted.   25
>> "I suggest the thing to do is calm down a little bit," she replied. 26
> "Go over to the house and shut the door."

Baker's conflict with his mother is resolved when he finally stops trying to bring her back to the present. He realizes that "after the last bad fall, she seemed to have broken chains that imprisoned her in a life she had come to hate and to return to a time inhabited by people who loved her, a time in which she was needed." He concludes that it is best to let her relive the times when she was truly happy.

Chronological Organization

In the word *chronological, chron-* is derived from the Greek word *khronos,* meaning time. Hence, *chronological* refers to the arrangement of events as they occur in time. Many professional writers like Russell Baker change this order by using "flashback," a technique you are probably familiar with from watching movies that interrupt the chronological order to show events that took place before the story started. As you have seen, Baker begins his narration as an adult describing his eighty-year-old mother and, through a series of flashbacks, he remembers her as a young woman who "hurled herself at life."

Use of Transitions to Connect Events

It is important to separate scenes, events, and reflections so that the reader can tell where one ends and another begins. This is especially true of narratives that use flashbacks. Writers use transitional words and phrases to link events in a steady, even stream without gaps or abrupt stops. The opening paragraph of Russell Baker's "Mother" is repeated below with transitions underlined to show how several memories can be linked effectively with the help of transitions.

> At the age of eighty my mother had her last bad fall, and <u>after</u>   1 <u>that</u> her mind wandered free through time. <u>Some days</u> she went to weddings and funerals that had taken place half a century earlier. On others she presided over family dinners cooked on Sunday afternoons for children who were <u>now</u> gray with age. <u>Through all this</u> she lay in bed but moved across time, traveling among the dead decades with a speed and ease beyond the gift of physical science.

The connecting words that are most useful for linking scenes and events in narratives are reprinted here from the list of transitional words and phrases in Chapter 4.

To order ideas in time	after, before, briefly, by this time, currently, during, eventually, finally, first, now, later, meanwhile, next, presently, recently, second, so far, soon, then, third, when, while

DESCRIBING AND EXPLAINING

Writers may include two other writing strategies—describing and explaining—in their narratives in order to clarify what was meaningful about a person or scene. When using description, writers appeal to the senses (sight, hearing, smell, touch, and taste) to create vivid descriptions of people, places, objects, and events. Explaining allows writers to interpret what an experience means to them. As addressed in Chapter 8, describing may be the prominent writing strategy of a piece. Authors also may choose explaining as their principal writing strategy.* In the discussion that follows you can see how strategies of describing and explaining can supplement narratives.

In the descriptive writing in this chapter, the writers use the senses to record vivid memories of their families. In Russell Baker's description of his mother, for example, we not only see her but also hear her voice—strong, uncompromising, and full of self-assurance. (In the passage repeated below, sense impressions are underlined for you.)

---

* Later chapters address various forms of explaining, including process analysis (Chapter 9), classifying (Chapter 10), comparing and contrasting (Chapter 11), explaining causes and effects (Chapter 12), evaluating (Chapter 14), and problem solving (Chapter 15).

She had always been a <u>small</u> woman—short, <u>light-boned, del-</u> 10
<u>icately structured</u>—but now, under the <u>white hospital sheet, she</u>
was becoming <u>tiny</u>. I thought of a <u>doll</u> with <u>huge, fierce eyes</u>. There
had always been a fierceness in her. It showed in that angry, challenging <u>thrust of the chin</u> when she issued an opinion, and a great
one she <u>had always been</u> for issuing opinions.

"<u>I tell people exactly what's on my mind</u>," she had been fond of 11
boasting. "<u>I tell them what I think whether they like it or not</u>." Often
they had not liked it. She could be sarcastic to people in whom she
detected evidence of the ignoramus or the fool.

"It's not always good policy to tell people exactly what's on 12
your mind," I used to caution her.

"<u>If they don't like it, that's too bad</u>," was her customary reply, 13
"<u>because that's the way I am</u>."

And so she was. A formidable woman. 14

In addition to the more obvious visual and auditory details that Baker uses to
describe his mother, he also uses an analogy or comparison: ". . . under the
white hospital sheet, she was becoming tiny. I thought of a doll with huge,
fierce eyes." This comparison between the woman who is wasting away and a
child's doll helps us see the rather startling contrast between her tiny size,
which would make her seem harmless, and her fighting spirit—a spirit
reflected in her eyes.

Characteristics of Describing and Explaining

A Dominant Impression or Idea

Descriptions offer a single, dominant impression of the person, place, object,
or event being described. In addition, writers frequently explain the larger
meaning of impressions they provide. For example, after using many sense
impressions to describe his mother, Russell Baker tells the reader what they
suggest about the sort of person she was. After describing her "huge, fierce
eyes," he tells us, "There had always been a fierceness in her." He adds, "a
great one she had always been for issuing opinions. . . . She could be sarcastic
to people in whom she detected evidence of the ignoramus or the fool." He
concludes this passage by stating this dominant impression: "And so she was.
A formidable woman."

Clarify Connections

Writers also use explanations to show how events in the past are somehow
meaningful to the present. Russell Baker makes this point clear by using his
memories of his mother to explain the connections between his experiences
and those of all children:

Sitting at her bedside, forever out of touch with her, I won- 40
dered about my own children, and their children, and children in
general, and about the disconnections between children and parents that prevent them from knowing each other. . . .

These hopeless end-of-the-line visits with my mother made me 49
wish I had not thrown off my own past so carelessly. We all come
from the past, and children ought to know what it was that went
into their making; to know that life is a braided cord of humanity
stretching up from time long gone, and that it cannot be defined by
the span of a single journey from diaper to shroud.[1]

In drawing this conclusion, Baker speaks not only to his children, but to "children in general" about the importance of knowing that there is more to their
lives than can be understood by the relatively short time allotted us from birth
to death. We are each part of a family history, he implies, and heritage is
important because it tells us who we are and something of the history of
which we are a part. It is interesting to note that Baker's autobiography,
Growing Up, from which these passages are taken, has sold about 22 million
copies and was on *The New York Times'* best-seller list. It appears that he has
reached a very broad audience.

Mother
Russell Baker

Russell Baker, a columnist for The New York Times, *won the Pulitzer Prize for
commentary in 1979. In "Mother," a passage from the first volume of his autobiography,*
Growing Up, *Baker writes an entertaining account of his mother at several stages in her
life. He also contends that her history, like that of all parents, provides an important
connection to the past.*

At the age of eighty my mother had her last bad fall, and after that her 1
mind wandered free through time. Some days she went to weddings and
funerals that had taken place half a century earlier. On others she presided
over family dinners cooked on Sunday afternoons for children who were now
gray with age. Through all this she lay in bed but moved across time, traveling
among the dead decades with a speed and ease beyond the gift of physical
science.

"Where's Russell?" she asked one day when I came to visit at the nursing 2
home.

"I'm Russell," I said.   3

She gazed at this improbably overgrown figure out of an inconceivable 4
future and promptly dismissed it.

---

[1]A sheet used to wrap a body for burial.

"Russell's only this big," she said, holding her hand, palm down, two feet 5
from the floor. That day she was a young country wife with chickens in the
backyard and a view of hazy blue Virginia mountains behind the apple
orchard, and I was a stranger old enough to be her father.

Early one morning she phoned me in New York. "Are you coming to my 6
funeral today?" she asked.

It was an awkward question with which to be awakened. "What are you 7
talking about, for God's sake?" was the best reply I could manage.

"I'm being buried today," she declared briskly, as though announcing an 8
important social event.

"I'll phone you back," I said and hung up, and when I did phone back 9
she was all right, although she wasn't all right, of course, and we all knew she
wasn't.

She had always been a small woman—short, light-boned, delicately struc- 10
tured—but now, under the white hospital sheet, she was becoming tiny. I
thought of a doll with huge, fierce eyes. There had always been a fierceness in
her. It showed in that angry, challenging thrust of the chin when she issued an
opinion, and a great one she had always been for issuing opinions.

"I tell people exactly what's on my mind," she had been fond of boasting. 11
"I tell them what I think, whether they like it or not." Often they had not liked
it. She could be sarcastic to people in whom she detected evidence of the ignoramus or the fool.

"It's not always good policy to tell people exactly what's on your mind," I 12
used to caution her.

"If they don't like it, that's too bad," was her customary reply, "because 13
that's the way I am."

And so she was. A formidable woman. Determined to speak her mind, 14
determined to have her way, determined to bend those who opposed her. In
that time when I had known her best, my mother had hurled herself at life
with chin thrust forward, eyes blazing, and an energy that made her seem
always on the run.

She ran after squawking chickens, an axe in her hand, determined on a 15
beheading that would put dinner in the pot. She ran when she made the beds,
ran when she set the table. One Thanksgiving she burned herself badly when,
running up from the cellar oven with the ceremonial turkey, she tripped on
the stairs and tumbled back down, ending at the bottom in the debris of
giblets, hot gravy, and battered turkey. Life was combat, and victory was not
to the lazy, the timid, the slugabed, the drugstore cowboy, the libertine, the
mushmouth afraid to tell people exactly what was on his mind whether people
liked it or not. She ran.

But now the running was over. For a time I could not accept the 16
inevitable. As I sat by her bed, my impulse was to argue her back to reality. On
my first visit to the hospital in Baltimore, she asked who I was.

"Russell," I said.   17

"Russell's way out west," she advised me.   18

"No, I'm right here."   19

"Guess where I came from today?" was her response.   20

"Where?"   21

"All the way from New Jersey."   22

"When?"   23

"Tonight."   24

"No. You've been in the hospital for three days," I insisted.   25

"I suggest the thing to do is calm down a little bit," she replied. "Go over   26
to the house and shut the door."

Now she was years deep into the past, living in the neighborhood where   27
she had settled forty years earlier, and she had just been talking with Mrs.
Hoffman, a neighbor across the street.

"It's like Mrs. Hoffman said today: The children always wander back to   28
where they come from," she remarked.

"Mrs. Hoffman has been dead for fifteen years."   29

"Russ got married today," she replied.   30

"I got married in 1950," I said, which was the fact.   31

"The house is unlocked," she said. . . .   32

The doctors diagnosed a hopeless senility. Not unusual, they said.   33
"Hardening of the arteries" was the explanation for laymen. I thought it was
more complicated than that. For ten years or more the ferocity with which she
had once attacked life had been turning to a rage against the weakness, the
boredom, and the absence of love that too much age had brought her. Now,
after the last bad fall, she seemed to have broken chains that imprisoned her
in a life she had come to hate and to return to a time inhabited by people who
loved her, a time in which she was needed. Gradually I understood. It was the
first time in years I had seen her happy. . . .

After the last bad fall, she had managed to forget the fatigue and loneliness   34
and, in these free-wheeling excursions back through time, to recapture happiness. I soon stopped trying to wrest her back to what I considered the real
world and tried to travel along with her on those fantastic swoops into the
past. One day when I arrived at her bedside she was radiant.

"Feeling good today," I said.   35

"Why shouldn't I feel good?" she asked. "Papa's going to take me up to   36
Baltimore on the boat today."

At that moment she was a young girl standing on a wharf at Merry Point,   37
Virginia, waiting for the Chesapeake Bay steamer with her father, who had
been dead sixty-one years. William Howard Taft was in the White House,
Europe still drowsed in the dusk of the great century of peace, America was a
young country, and the future stretched before it in beams of crystal sunlight.
"The greatest country on God's green earth," her father might have said, if I had
been able to step into my mother's time machine and join him on the wharf
with the satchels packed for Baltimore.

I could imagine her there quite clearly. She was wearing a blue dress with   38
big puffy sleeves and long black stockings. There was a ribbon in her hair and
a big bow tied on the side of her head. There had been a childhood photograph

in her bedroom which showed all this, although the colors of course had been added years later by a restorer who tinted the picture.

About her father, my grandfather, I could only guess, and indeed, about the girl on the wharf with the bow in her hair, I was merely sentimentalizing. Of my mother's childhood and her people, of their time and place, I knew very little. A world had lived and died, and though it was part of my blood and bone, I knew little more about it than I knew of the world of the pharaohs. It was useless now to ask for help from my mother. The orbits of her mind rarely touched present interrogators for more than a moment.   39

Sitting at her bedside, forever out of touch with her, I wondered about my own children, and their children, and children in general, and about the disconnections between children and parents that prevent them from knowing each other. Children rarely want to know who their parents were before they were parents, and when age finally stirs their curiosity there is no parent left to tell them. If a parent does lift the curtain a bit, it is often only to stun the young with some exemplary tale of how much harder life was in the old days.   40

I had been guilty of this when my children were small in the early 1960s and living the affluent life. It galled me that their childhoods should be, as I thought, so easy when my own had been, as I thought, so hard. I had developed the habit, when they complained about the steak being overcooked or the television being cut off, of lecturing them on the harshness of life in my day.   41

"In my day all we got for dinner was macaroni and cheese, and we were glad to get it."   42

"In my day we didn't have any television."   43

"In my day . . ."   44

"In my day . . ."   45

At dinner one evening a son had offended me with an inadequate report card, and as I leaned back and cleared my throat to lecture, he gazed at me with an expression of unutterable resignation and said, "Tell me how it was in your days, Dad."   46

I was angry with him for that, but angrier with myself for having become one of those ancient bores whose highly selective memories of the past become transparently dishonest even to small children. I tried to break the habit, but must have failed. A few years later my son was referring to me when I was out of earshot as "the old-timer." Between us there was a dispute about time. He looked upon the time that had been my future in a disturbing way. My future was his past, and being young, he was indifferent to the past.   47

As I hovered over my mother's bed listening for muffled signals from her childhood, I realized that this same dispute had existed between her and me. When she was young, with life ahead of her, I had been her future and resented it. Instinctively, I wanted to break free, cease being a creature defined by her time, consign her future to the past, and create my own. Well, I had finally done that, and then with my own children I had seen my exciting future become their boring past.   48

These hopeless end-of-the-line visits with my mother made me wish I had   49
not thrown off my own past so carelessly. We all come from the past, and children ought to know what it was that went into their making, to know that life
is a braided cord of humanity stretching up from time long gone, and that it
cannot be defined by the span of a single journey from diaper to shroud.

RESPONDING TO THE READING

Freewriting

Chapter 1 explains "freewriting" as writing quickly without pausing to correct
mistakes. In freewriting exercises your goal is to write as much as you can in ten
to fifteen minutes. (See page 5 for a more detailed explanation of freewriting.)

Exercise 7a.   Freewrite about the most vivid images, phrases, or ideas that
you remember from Russell Baker's essay.

Exercise 7b.   Write several journal entries about your earliest memories of
your mother, father, or guardian. Then record your memories of that person
from the time when you were a teenager. If you have more recent memories,
write a few additional entries to summarize the more recent period.

Exercise 7c.   Exchange freewriting samples you wrote in Exercise 7b with
classmates or read them aloud in small groups. Write a letter to each of the
other members of your group explaining your response to what he or she
wrote. When you finish, share your reactions.

Building Your Vocabulary

Record unfamiliar words and their definitions in a section of your journal set
aside for your vocabulary list. Make three columns for words and their definitions
as shown below; include your own definitions based on clues from the reading.

VOCABULARY LIST

Words to Look Up	My Definition	Dictionary Definition
presided (1)[*]		
improbably (4)		
inconceivable (4)		
briskly (8)		
ignoramus (11)		
formidable (14)		

[*]Numbers refer to paragraphs in Russell Baker's narrative.

debris (15)
slugabed (15)
libertine (15)
inevitable (16)
impulse (16)
diagnosed (33)
senility (33)
layman (33)

Thinking about Words

Chapter 2 introduces several techniques for recognizing unfamiliar words: read for context clues, break words apart, and learn prefixes and suffixes. You will find these techniques quite helpful as you read the articles in this and other chapters in Part Two.

Looking for context clues works especially well, and you will find that authors often either define a word for you or suggest a word's meaning. For example, Russell Baker tells you that a "mushmouth" is someone who is "afraid to tell people exactly what [is] on his mind."

Many words in English are formed from other words, and breaking them apart will often help you figure out the meaning of the reassembled word. A composite word like "slugabed" carries the idea of *slug* (the slimy wormlike creature found eating our plants) and *abed,* which contains the word *bed.* Put them together and you have a lazy, slow-moving person who stays abed (in bed)—a sort of pre-television "couch potato."

Questions for Discussion

1. The discussion of purpose at the beginning of this chapter points out that writers may write for a variety of reasons; they may wish to entertain, inform, explain, explore causes or effects, interpret, or persuade. Russell Baker writes for several of these reasons. What was his main purpose for writing his narrative? Share your responses with your classmates.
2. How does Baker feel about his mother? How can you tell?
3. Baker draws several portraits of his mother at various stages of her life. Based on his descriptions, what kind of a person do you think she is?
4. Near the end of his story Baker writes, "Gradually I understood." Use your own words to explain what he finally "understood" about his mother's illness.
5. Why does Baker think it is important to remember the past? What are your feelings about this subject with regard to your own family?

TOPICS FOR WRITING

Topic 1.   Using the techniques you practiced in Chapter 2, write a two- or three-sentence summary of Russell Baker's "Mother."

Topic 2.   Write a letter to Russell Baker telling him what you appreciated about his portrait of his mother. Be as specific as you can about what appealed to you.

Topic 3.   Reread your journal entry for Exercise 7b. Using Baker's conversations with his mother as a model, write your own portrait of someone you remember well. Include dialogue involving your mother, father, or guardian to let the reader "hear" this person's voice. Follow the steps in the writing process discussed on the next few pages to gather details, organize, and revise your paper.

Topic 4.   Baker explains that he is writing to help his own children understand their family history because he realizes that, like him, they may not become curious about their own history until he is no longer capable of explaining it. Think of an important event in your life, one that you feel would tell your children the most about who you are or what it was like growing up when you did. Write a letter to real or imaginary children in which you recreate that experience for them. Freewrite to gather information you can use, do some preliminary writing to add subtopics and details, and arrange your narrative chronologically or use flashbacks. Be sure to include descriptions and explanations to convey what the experience meant to you. (For additional help in writing about an event, see pages 156–157.)

Topic 5.   Russell Baker eventually realizes that his mother's lapses of memory allow her to relive moments in the past when she was truly happy. Think of a day in your life when something made you happy. Perhaps it was a day when you did something that made you proud of yourself, or maybe it was a day when you felt really loved and needed. Write about what happened and how you felt on that occasion.

Topic 6.   Write about a time when you had a misunderstanding with a parent or guardian. Decide whose point of view you will use to record your memories of that event. You might, for example, record (1) what you saw as you lived through this misunderstanding, (2) your view of things as you reflect on the experience, or (3) your parent's perspective on what happened.

Topic 7.   Russell Baker says that his son "looked upon the time that had been my future in a disturbing way. My future was his past, and being young, he was indifferent to the past." Write a paper in which you describe your parents' references to the past and your reactions to their stories. Explain why their stories interested or bored you, or show how your attitude toward their memories has changed over the years.

THE WRITING PROCESS: NARRATING

Chapters 3 and 5 apply the steps in the writing process to the tasks of writing a paragraph and an essay. (To review the steps, see the inside cover of this book.) This section and others in Part Two give you additional suggestions for applying the writing process to narration and the other patterns for developing ideas that were introduced in Chapter 6.

Remember that the steps in the writing process are meant to provide a manageable progression from the inception of an idea to the final draft of a paragraph or essay. They need not, however, be followed in order. Instead, you should use them so that they enhance your own methods of writing. If, for example, you work best by writing a "fast draft" shortly after thinking of a topic, your sequence of steps might be One (Developing a Topic), Two (Thinking about Your Audience), Five (Writing a Fast Draft), Four (Organizing Ideas), Three (Preliminary Writing), Six (Editing and Proofreading), Seven (Sharing Your Writing), and Eight (Making Final Revisions). Moreover, your writing strategy will probably change from paper to paper. You may discover, for example, that for one paper you will follow the sequence outlined above, but for the next, you might follow the steps in numerical order from your initial idea to revision.

The discussion on the next few pages gives you additional considerations for applying the writing process to writing narratives about a person you want to remember. These considerations will help you produce well-written narratives with a distinct point of view, a sense of your audience, a well-defined purpose for writing, chronological organization with clear transitions between events, and elements of conflict or complexity—the characteristics of narrating illustrated earlier in this chapter. In Chapter 8 similar considerations are applied to the task of describing places, objects, and events.

Additional Considerations for Developing a Topic

If you have difficulty developing a topic for a paper about someone you wish to remember, try answering a few of the questions below that interest you most.

> What are some of the earliest memories you have of people, family members, or close friends?
> Which of your teachers made an impression on you?
> Who was your first boss, or the boss that made the biggest impression on you?
> What person do you remember when you listen to a particular song?
> Who has had a major influence on your life?

Additional Considerations for Thinking about Your Audience

Before you gather subtopics and details for your narrative, it is a good idea to clarify your topic, purpose, audience, and dominant impression. Put these concerns in the form of questions too:

> Who am I writing about?
> Why am I writing about this topic?
> Who am I writing for?
> What is the main idea or dominant impression I want to convey?

Additional Considerations for Preliminary Writing

When you develop your writing, you may find that some memories are easier to write about than others. Journal writing is valuable for recording memories because the more you rely on your journal, the easier it will be to retrieve specific details and events. You may find it helpful to write several entries about the memory you want to recapture, especially if it seems to be coming back to you a little at a time.

The following questions may prove helpful as you gather details about a person you wish to remember.

> What did this person look like?
> How did he or she dress?
> What distinctive characteristics do you remember?
> How did he or she walk? talk?
> What was his or her general "pace" in life—slow, moderate, fast?
> What did this person enjoy doing? Hate doing?
> What was his or her "role" in life?
> Did he or she work in the home or have an outside job? What was it?
> What conversations do you remember that illustrate something about
>   this person?
> How have other people described him or her?
> Who were this person's other friends? What were they like?
> How close were you to this person? How did the two of you display
>   closeness or separation?
> Did you do things together? If so, what? When? Where?
> What sort of person was he or she? What did this person do or say to
>   illustrate this trait?
> What caused the person to be the way he or she was?
> Did you have a different view of this person at different times?
> Has anything about this person changed?

In addition to asking yourself these questions, you might list ideas or draw an idea wheel to record details and associations as they come to you. Details can also be revived by speaking into a tape recorder, recounting incidents orally to a friend or classmate, or talking to someone who shares the memory. If you like to doodle or draw, you might try sketching this person to illustrate some behavior, conversation, or situation that you remember.

Additional Considerations for Organizing Ideas

Several patterns can help you organize material for your narrative. Put the events, descriptions, or explanations about the person you are discussing in chronological order, at least at first. That will help you determine whether you have all the details you need or if you should omit some that don't seem appropriate.

If you wish to experiment with the order of events, you might try using the flashback technique, as Russell Baker does, to make your ideas more vivid or to add interest to the sequence of events you are narrating. (The student essay that follows this discussion gives you a second example.) Regardless of whether you use straight chronological order or flashbacks, write an outline of the sequence of events you plan to follow.

Additional Considerations for Writing a Fast Draft

Reread your answers to the questions about subject and purpose before you begin writing your fast draft. Use your outline for guidance and include plenty of descriptions, details, and dialogue in this draft.

Additional Considerations for Sharing Your Writing and Making Final Revisions

You may use the general questions in Appendix C at the end of this book for responding to paragraphs or essays. The checklist below is especially useful for writing narratives. Check each question as you complete it.

Checklist

- ❏ Is it clear to the reader *who* I am writing about and *why* I am writing?
- ❏ Have I shown the reader exactly what this person is like?
- ❏ Are there any additional details in the descriptions or examples that would make the memory more vivid?
- ❏ Will adding explanations clarify the meaning of these details?
- ❏ Overall, have I successfully recreated what I remember?
- ❏ Have I proofread this description carefully enough to catch spelling mistakes I may have made and words I may have omitted?
- ❏ Have I checked my sentences for errors like fragments and run-ons?

When you write your revised draft, keep in mind that your goal is to recreate this person for someone who does not know him or her and has no way of imagining this person without your help.

Student Writing

Betty Tilman wrote about the effects that her father's alcoholism had on her family. Here are her answers to some questions about audience and purpose.

> *What is my subject?*
> I want to write about my father's alcoholism.
> *Why am I writing about this person?*
> I want to show how his drinking affected my family.
> *Who am I writing for?*
> I want my father to read this so he will understand what he did. The essay might also have meaning for other alcoholics and children of alcoholics.
> *What is the dominant impression or main idea?*
> I will show how irrational and violent my father became when he drank and how terrifying that behavior was for his children.

When she thought about arranging her ideas, Betty decided to use flashbacks to illustrate how her childhood fears influenced her own decision not to drink.

One Mistake

It is bed time. My children are down for the night. It has been just a few weeks since my husband left home, and I know he is not coming back. I remember a bottle of whiskey he left in the kitchen cupboard. As I reach for it, memories of children the same age as my own flood my thoughts. . . .

It is eight o'clock, and I lie in my bed staring into the darkness. My eyes are adjusting to the dark, and I can make out some of the things in my room: the maple dresser, the nightstand with the white lamp on it, and the chair that sits over in the corner with today's clothes draped over it. I am four years old, and I can't sleep. The arguing in the next room keeps me awake. My father is accusing my mother of having an affair with her boss because he gave her a ride home after she waited two hours for my father to pick her up. She, in turn, accuses him of drinking with his buddies when he should have been picking her up. I am holding the doll that I got for Christmas close to my chest. Lately, my doll has been the only person I can confide in. She knows about the times I have cheated my sister out of candy, put dirty clothes underneath my bed or stuffed them back in the drawer instead of putting them in the laundry hamper. She knows about my fear of cats and the fear I have of waking up one morning and finding my mother dead at the hands of my father.

The arguing in the next room is getting louder and louder. They are still arguing over my mother's ride home. I think it is the guilt of drinking that makes my father falsely accuse my mother of any wrong-doing. Oh, God, I am scared. He is so big, at least six feet two inches tall, and he weighs at least two hundred and five pounds. My mother is a little over four feet eleven inches tall and weighs one hundred fifteen pounds. If he hit her, even slightly, she would be seriously injured. I wish he would go far, far away and leave us alone. He becomes so mean when he has been drinking. He throws dishes, breaks furniture, and abuses my mother. The arguing in the next room is becoming louder and louder, and I am holding my doll tighter and tighter. I close my eyes as if to shut out the scene I'm imagining. I can feel the tears moistening my face and one hundred butterflies flying around in my stomach. I want to scream, "Leave her alone. She has not done anything wrong, except to work hard, take care of us kids, and pay off the debts you have accumulated at liquor stores." But I am too scared to say anything.

There is the sound of a glass breaking. I have to get up and see if my mother is all right, but I am so scared. Will this be like the time my father came home and accused my mother of taking his money? She told him she had paid the rent and bills that were due, and that he had not given her any money the previous month. My brothers, my sister, and I were awakened from our sleep by my mother's scream. My father picked her up and threw her against the wall. The four of us rushed in and stood in front of her so that he would have to hit us before he hurt her again. With hatred and pain in our eyes, we dared him to make one move toward her. He looked down, ashamed of himself, and walked out of the house.

With the memory of my earlier defiance in my mind, I tiptoe over to the door and lean against it; there are no sounds coming from the room. I turn the handle very slowly and peek in; there I see my mother picking up the pieces of what was once a glass filled with dark liquor. My father is slumped over his cold dinner, passed out from the alcohol. My mother looks up at me with tears in her eyes and tells me she is all right and to go back to bed.

Years later, I am standing in the kitchen with the wreck of my own life all around me. My husband's bottle of whiskey is in my hand. With tears in my eyes, I replace the bottle. I will not give my own children memories like the ones I have.

Questions for Discussion

1. What is Tilman's purpose for writing?
2. What details in this narrative help her achieve this purpose? Are there sections of the essay that could be developed in greater detail?

3. Describe the tone or mood of Tilman's essay. Is this tone appropriate for
    her purpose?
4. What other arrangement might she have used to record her memories?
    Which do you think is more effective? Why?
5. Tilman uses the present tense to describe the night her father threw a glass
    against the wall. What is the effect of using the present tense to describe
    this scene?

FOR FURTHER READING

Girl
Jamaica Kincaid

Jamaica Kincaid was born in the West Indies in St. John's, Antigua. She writes for The
New Yorker *magazine and has published several novels and short stories. "Girl" is the
opening chapter of her first novel,* At the Bottom of the River. *Kincaid writes this
narrative in the voice of a girl's mother as she tells her daughter what to do and how to
behave. The daughter's replies appear in italic type. To fully appreciate the effect of the
"voice" in this selection, read "Girl" aloud or ask someone to read it to you.*

Wash the white clothes on Monday and put them on the stone heap; wash
the color clothes on Tuesday and put them on the clothesline to dry; don't walk
barehead in the hot sun; cook pumpkin fritters in very hot sweet oil; soak your
little cloths right after you take them off; when buying cotton to make yourself
a nice blouse, be sure that it doesn't have gum on it, because that way it won't
hold up well after a wash; soak salt fish overnight before you cook it; is it true
that you sing benna[1] in Sunday school?; always eat your food in such a way that
it won't turn someone else's stomach; on Sundays try to walk like a lady and not
like the slut you are so bent on becoming; don't sing benna in Sunday school;
you mustn't speak to wharf-rat boys, not even to give directions; don't eat fruits
on the street—flies will follow you; *but I don't sing benna on Sundays at all and
never in Sunday school;* this is how to sew on a button; this is how to make a but-
tonhole for the button you have just sewed on; this is how to hem a dress when
you see the hem coming down and so to prevent yourself from looking like the
slut I know you are so bent on becoming; this is how you iron your father's khaki
shirt so that it doesn't have a crease; this is how you iron your father's khaki
pants so that they don't have a crease; this is how you grow okra—far from the
house, because okra tree harbors red ants; when you are growing dasheen,
make sure it gets plenty of water or else it makes your throat itch when you are
eating it; this is how you sweep a corner; this is how you sweep a whole house;
this is how you sweep a yard; this is how you smile to someone you don't like too
much; this is how you smile to someone you don't like at all; this is how you

---

[1]Calypso folksong.

smile to someone you like completely; this is how you set a table for tea; this is how you set a table for dinner; this is how you set a table for dinner with an important guest; this is how you set a table for lunch; this is how you set a table for breakfast; this is how to behave in the presence of men who don't know you very well, and this way they won't recognize immediately the slut I have warned you against becoming; be sure to wash every day, even if it is with your own spit; don't squat down to play marbles—you are not a boy, you know; don't pick people's flowers—you might catch something; don't throw stones at blackbirds, because it might not be a blackbird at all; this is how to make a bread pudding; this is how to make doukona; this is how to make pepper pot: this is how to make a good medicine for a cold; this is how to make a good medicine to throw away a child before it even becomes a child; this is how to catch a fish; this is how to throw back a fish you don't like, and that way something bad won't fall on you; this is how to bully a man; this is how a man bullies you; this is how to love a man, and if this doesn't work there are other ways, and if they don't work don't feel too bad about giving up; this is how to spit up in the air if you feel like it, and this is how to move quick so that it doesn't fall on you; this is how to make ends meet; always squeeze bread to make sure it's fresh; *but what if the baker won't let me feel the bread?;* you mean to say that after all you are really going to be the kind of woman who the baker won't let near the bread?

RESPONDING TO THE READING

Freewriting

Exercise 7d.   Without looking back at what you read, freewrite about your impressions of the mother and daughter in "Girl." Write without stopping until you have filled a page or two in your journal.

Exercise 7e.   Record your earliest memories of the "voice" of one of the adults who raised you.

Building Your Vocabulary

VOCABULARY LIST

Words to Look Up	My Definition	Dictionary Definition
fritters		
khaki		
okra		

Thinking about Words

Check in your local library for *Webster's Third New International Dictionary* or an equivalent to look up the words "dasheen" (or *taro*) and "pepper pot."

"Doukona" is a banana pudding. These are colloquial or informal terms used in the West Indies that you won't find in most dictionaries. Why might these terms be appropriate for this particular narrative?

Questions for Discussion

1. Underline key phrases from "Girl" that tell you the kind of person the writer's mother is. Then write a brief evaluation of her. Share your responses.
2. What are some lessons this mother is trying to teach her daughter? How are they typical of or different from the lessons you were taught?
3. The daughter's words (in italics) appear only twice in "Girl." Each time her reply begins with the word "but." Look at the passages where her responses appear and decide how well she defends herself.
4. What would change if this narration were written entirely in the voice of the girl? Which would be more effective? Explain your reasoning.
5. "Girl" is written as one long sentence with semicolons between clauses. What is the effect of writing "Girl" this way?
6. Describe the emotions you felt as you read "Girl" or heard it read aloud. Did you laugh at some point? Why?
7. The girl and her mother are from a culture that is probably different from the one you are used to. What differences do you notice in the language they use, their daily habits, and the things they are worried about? What is similar about the daughter's experience or her mother's experience and your own?
8. What similarities and differences do you notice about the portraits of mothers in "Girl" and in Russell Baker's "Mother"? How might the authors' differing points of view affect the way these mothers are portrayed?

TOPICS FOR WRITING

Topic 1.   Remember a time when you felt your parents were being either overprotective or too hard on you. Freewrite about the incident. Then explain to someone who is not familiar with your family exactly what happened. Try to include your parent's or guardian's voice so the reader can "hear" what he or she said to you.

Topic 2.   Pick someone whose "voice" is familiar to you—a parent, spouse, brother or sister, aunt, teacher, or some other important person in your life. Freewrite in that person's voice, trying to capture his or her personality and relationship to you. Now write a paragraph using this person's voice, as Kincaid does in "Girl."

Topic 3.   Identify a voice that you would like to imitate. (A nagging relative, an insincere person, or a nervous person might make good voices for imitation.) Write a letter to a friend, using the voice you have chosen, to explain something that has happened lately. Exchange letters with your classmates and ask them to respond in any voice they choose. Write a journal entry about how easy or difficult it was to assume a different voice. Explain why in either case.

Topic 4.   Think of a personality you know well enough to imitate—a character in a movie, a singer, a television personality, or someone in your family. Observe that person, paying particular attention to his or her speech. Write a page or two in which you imitate that person's "voice." You might, for example, pretend that you are writing as Madonna or another recording artist and discuss your most recent music; or you might adopt the voice of a sports announcer to explain what happens during a particularly exciting play.

Fathers Playing Catch with Sons
Donald Hall

Donald Hall is a poet, essayist, and author of several textbooks on writing. In the following passage from his book, Fathers Playing Catch with Sons, *he writes about his memories of his father and the guilt he feels for having changed his father's life.*

My father and I played catch as I grew up. Like so much else between fathers and sons, playing catch was tender and tense at the same time. He wanted to play with me. He wanted me to be good. He seemed to *demand* that I be good. I threw the ball into his catcher's mitt. Atta boy. Put her right there. I threw straight. Then I tried to put something on it; it flew twenty feet over his head. Or it banged into the sidewalk in front of him, breaking stitches and ricocheting off a pebble into the gutter of Greenway Street. Or it went wide to his right and lost itself in Mrs. Davis's bushes. Or it went wide to his left and rolled across the street while drivers swerved their cars.   1

I was wild. I was *wild.* I had to be wild for my father. What else could I be? Would you have wanted me to have *control?*   2

But I was, myself, the control on him. He had wanted to teach school, to coach and teach history at Cushing Academy in Ashburnham, Massachusetts, and he had done it for two years before he was married. The salary was minuscule and in the twenties people didn't get married until they had the money to live on. Since he wanted to marry my mother, he made the only decision he could make: he quit Cushing and went into the family business, and he hated business, and he wept when he fired people, and he wept when he was criticized, and his head shook at night, and he coughed from all the cigarettes, and he couldn't sleep, and he almost died when an ulcer hemorrhaged when he was forty-two, and ten years later, at fifty-two, he died of lung cancer.   3

But the scene I remember—at night in the restaurant, after a happy, fool- 4
ish day in the uniform of a Pittsburgh Pirate—happened when he was twenty-
five and I was almost one year old. So I do not "remember" it at all. It simply
rolls itself before my eyes with the intensity of a lost memory suddenly found
again, more intense than the moment itself ever is.

It is 1929, July, a hot Saturday afternoon. At the ballpark near East Rock, 5
in New Haven, Connecticut, just over the Hamden line, my father is playing
semipro baseball. I don't know the names of the teams. My mother has
brought me in a basket, and she sits under a tree, in the shade, and lets me
crawl when I wake up.

My father is very young, very skinny. When he takes off his cap—the uni- 6
form is gray, the bill of the cap blue—his fine hair is parted in the middle. His
face is very smooth. Though he is twenty-five, he could pass for twenty. He
plays shortstop, and he is paid twenty-five dollars a game. I don't know where
the money comes from. Do they pass the hat? They would never raise so much
money. Do they charge admission? They must charge admission, or I am
wrong that it was semipro and that he was paid. Or the whole thing is wrong,
a memory I concocted. But of course the reality of 1929—and my mother and
the basket and the shade and the heat—does not matter, not to the memory of
the living nor to the bones of the dead nor even to the fragmentary images of
broken light from that day which wander light-years away in unrecoverable
space. What matters is the clear and fine knowledge of this day as it happens
now, permanently and repeatedly, on a deep layer of the personal Troy.

There, where this Saturday afternoon of July in 1929 rehearses itself, my 7
slim father performs brilliantly at shortstop. He dives for a low line drive and
catches it backhand, somersaults, and stands up holding the ball. Sprinting
into left field with his back to the plate, he catches a fly ball that almost drops
for a Texas leaguer. He knocks down a ground ball, deep in the hole and nearly
to third base, picks it up, and throws the man out at first with a peg as flat as
the tape a runner breaks. When he comes up to bat, he feels lucky. The opposing pitcher is a side-armer. He always hits side-armers. So he hits two doubles
and a triple, drives in two runs and scores two runs, and his team wins 4 to 3.
After the game a man approaches him, while he stands, sweating and tired,
with my mother and me in the shade of the elm tree at the rising side of the
field. The man is a baseball scout. He offers my father a contract to play baseball with the Baltimore Orioles, at that time a double-A minor league team.
My father is grateful and gratified; he is proud to be offered the job, but he
must refuse. After all, he has just started working at the dairy for his father. It
wouldn't be possible to leave the job that had been such a decision to take. And
besides, he adds, there is the baby.

My father didn't tell me he turned it down because of me. All he told me, 8
or that I think he told me: he was playing semipro at twenty-five dollars a
game; he had a good day in the field, catching a ball over his shoulder running
away from the plate; he had a good day hitting, too, because he could always
hit a side-armer. But he turned down the Baltimore Oriole offer. He couldn't

leave the dairy then, and besides, he knew that he had just been lucky that day. He wasn't really that good.

But maybe he didn't even tell me that. My mother remembers nothing of this. Or rather she remembers that he played on the team for the dairy, against other businesses, and that she took me to the games when I was a baby. But she remembers nothing of semipro, of the afternoon with the side-armer, of the offered contract. Did I make it up? Did my father exaggerate? Men tell stories to their sons, loving and being loved. 9

I don't care. 10

Baseball is fathers and sons. Football is brothers beating each other up in the backyard, violent and superficial. Baseball is the generations, looping backward forever with a million apparitions of sticks and balls, cricket and rounders, and the games the Iroquois played in Connecticut before the English came. Baseball is fathers and sons playing catch, lazy and murderous, wild and controlled, the profound archaic song of birth, growth, age, and death. This diamond encloses what we are. 11

RESPONDING TO THE READING

Freewriting

Exercise 7f.   Without looking back at Hall's essay, write a brief summary of the scenes and ideas you remember.

Exercise 7g.   Freewrite about sacrifices a relative or friend has made for you. What were they? How did you feel at the time? How do you feel now?

Exercise 7h.   Write a few questions you have about Hall's essay to share with the class.

Building Your Vocabulary

VOCABULARY LIST

Words to Look Up	My Definition	Dictionary Definition
minuscule (3)		
hemorrhaged (3)		
intensity (4)		
semipro (5)		
concocted (6)		
fragmentary (6)		
unrecoverable (6)		
rehearses (7)		

Words to Look Up	My Definition	Dictionary Definition
exaggerate (9)		
apparitions (11)		
archaic (11)		

Questions for Discussion

1. What is the dominant impression of Hall's father? Which descriptions support this impression?
2. Briefly describe the relationship between father and son. What are the sources of tension between them?
3. What pressures do you feel from family members? How do they compare with the pressure Hall felt from his father?
4. Hall half remembers, half imagines that his father made several sacrifices for his family. What were they? Why do you think he decided to make them? What would you have done in his place? Explain your choice.
5. Characterize the point of view Hall adopts in this essay. How does it differ from his mother's point of view? How do you explain this difference?
6. What is Hall's purpose in writing this reminiscence of his father? How is it similar to or different from Russell Baker's purpose in writing "Mother"?
7. Part of Donald Hall's intention is to write about how memory works. He part remembers and part creates the past. How well does Hall really remember what happened (paragraphs 4, 5, 6, and 9)? Why isn't it important that he retell exactly what happened (paragraph 6)?
8. Notice the long sentence at the end of paragraph 3 that begins with "Since he wanted to marry my mother" and ends with "he died of lung cancer." Remember that Jamaica Kincaid wrote one long sentence covering several pages to record her mother's constant scolding. Why do you think Donald Hall ends paragraph 3 with such a long sentence?

TOPICS FOR WRITING

Topic 1.   Briefly summarize the sacrifices Donald Hall's father made for his family. Explain what you would have done in his place. Be sure to explain why you would make these decisions.

Topic 2.   Think of a family member or friend who has just done something you consider unwise. Write this person a letter in which you briefly describe what he or she has done that you oppose. Then explain why you disagree with the decision. Finally, suggest what can be done to remedy the situation.

Topic 3.   Do some freewriting about a time when you made an important sacrifice. Use the steps in the writing process and the following questions to write about this sacrifice. What was the sacrifice? Who was it for? Was it worth making at the time? As you look back on it now, do you think you made a good decision? Why or why not?

Topic 4.   Freewrite about something you did that you now consider unforgivably selfish. Discuss what you did, your motives at the time, and your present opinion of the deed.

Topic 5.   Hall tells us that his "memory" of his father's starring game in New Haven is not really a memory at all, but an event that he has pieced together of what his parents have said, and what he, himself, can imagine. Freewrite about some stories you "remember" from your childhood that you can't quite remember living, but your parents or other relatives like to discuss. Then shape your memories and theirs into an account of the past. Check to see that your narration has a dominant idea or impression.

Topic 6.   Write a long letter to Donald Hall in which you do <u>one</u> of the following: (a) summarize Donald Hall's opinions of baseball, and explain the reasons you agree with his assessment, or (b) write a defense of football as more than "brothers beating each other up in the backyard, violent and superficial" (paragraph 11).

8

A Sense of Place

We lived in San Francisco's Chinatown. Like most of the other Chinese children who played in the back alleys of restaurants and curio shops, I didn't think we were poor. My bowl was always full, three five-course meals every day, beginning with a soup full of mysterious things I didn't want to know the names of.

—*Amy Tan*

This is the most beautiful place on earth. There are many such places. Every man, every woman, carries in heart and mind the image of the ideal place, the right place, the one true home, known or unknown, actual or visionary.

—*Edward Abbey*

In this chapter student and professional writers examine the significance of certain places, objects, and events in their lives. "Place" is their principal focus, as they write about places that have shaped their identities and values, or their sense of who they are. In the selection from Amy Tan's novel, *The Joy Luck Club,* the character Waverly Sun describes the importance her neighborhood had for her when she was growing up. Annie Dillard's special place was the bedroom of her family's house in Pittsburgh, where, as a child, she suffered the terrifying nightly visits of a creature that destroyed her sleep. For Edward Abbey, Arches National Monument in Utah is where he feels at home in the universe.

Describing is the prominent writing strategy discussed in this chapter. Passages from "Rules of the Game," the excerpt from Amy Tan's novel, illustrate some of the characteristics of well-written descriptions.

DESCRIBING

Techniques for writing narration—attention to point of view, purpose, and organization—are also useful for writing descriptions of places, objects, and events. Writers who record their observations rely primarily on detailed descriptions and explanations to recreate a particular place, object, or event, and to interpret its significance.

Characteristics of Describing

A Distinct Point of View

Chapter 7 explains that point of view plays an important part in shaping narratives. Russell Baker's point of view as an adult determined which incidents he used to illustrate his mother's slow retreat into the past. Point of view is equally important when describing places, objects, and events. Here, too, writers must clarify their stance and their relationship to their subject. In the case of fiction, writers do not speak in their own voice. Instead, like Amy Tan, they write through the voice of their characters. In the opening paragraphs of "Rules of the Game," for example, Tan's character, Waverly Sun, describes an event from her childhood and introduces herself and her mother.

> I was six when my mother taught me the art of invisible 1
> strength. It was a strategy for winning arguments, respect from oth-
> ers, and eventually, though neither of us knew it at the time, chess
> games.
> "Bite back your tongue," scolded my mother when I cried 2
> loudly, yanking her hand toward the store that sold bags of salted
> plums. At home, she said, "Wise guy, he not go against wind. In

Chinese we say, Come from South, blow with wind—poom!—North will follow. Strongest wind cannot be seen."

The next week I bit back my tongue as we entered the store 3 with the forbidden candies. When my mother finished her shopping, she quietly plucked a small bag of plums from the rack and put it on the counter with the rest of the items.

Tan has her character speak in the first person and writes from the perspective of an adult remembering when she was six years old and her mother taught her "the art of invisible strength." Waverly describes two trips to the store, one before the lesson and one after, in order to help the reader understand her mother's prominence in her life.

Reliance on Details and Sense Impressions

In order to recreate an experience for the reader, a writer might describe sights, sounds, smells, tastes, and tactile sensations. The paragraph that follows illustrates Amy Tan's use of sense impressions to describe the apartment in Chinatown where Waverly lived with her family:

> We lived on Waverly Place, in a warm, clean, two-bedroom flat 5 that sat above a small Chinese bakery specializing in steamed pastries and dim sum. In the early morning, when the alley was still quiet, I could smell fragrant red beans as they were cooked down to a pasty sweetness. By daybreak, our flat was heavy with the odor of fried sesame balls and sweet curried chicken crescents. From my bed, I would listen as my father got ready for work, then locked the door behind him, one-two-three clicks.

Tan has her character describe the "clean, two-bedroom flat" and helps us imagine its location "above a small Chinese bakery." Next, we smell the "fragrant red beans," and she suggests that if we were to taste them, we would notice a "pasty sweetness." She also recalls the "odor of fried sesame balls and sweet curried chicken crescents." The last sense impressions are the sounds of her father getting ready for work and his locking the door behind him—"one-two-three clicks."

A Dominant Impression or Idea

As seen at the beginning of Chapter 7, a writer includes particular details to create a dominant impression or idea. In the preceding passage, the description of Waverly's room in the early morning conveys the impression of a comforting home, rich with sights, sounds, and smells.

Spatial Arrangement

In contrast to narratives, descriptions are arrangements in space rather than time. Here, Waverly Sun describes the alley behind her family's apartment:

> At the end of our two-block alley was a small sandlot play- 6 ground with swings and slides well-shined down the middle with use. The play area was bordered by wood-slat benches where old-country people sat cracking roasted watermelon seeds with their golden teeth and scattering the husks to an impatient gathering of gurgling pigeons. The best playground, however, was the dark alley itself. It was crammed with daily mysteries and adventures. My brothers and I would peer into the medicinal herb shop, watching old Li dole out onto a stiff sheet of white paper the right amount of insect shells, saffron-colored seeds, and pungent leaves for his ailing customers. . . . Next to the pharmacy was a printer who specialized in gold-embossed wedding invitations and festive red banners.
>
> Farther down the street was Ping Yuen Fish Market. The front 7 window displayed a tank crowded with doomed fish and turtles struggling to gain footing on the slimy green-tiled sides. A handwritten sign informed tourists, "Within this store, is all for food, not for pet." Inside, the butchers with their blood-stained white smocks deftly gutted the fish while customers cried out their orders and shouted, "Give me your freshest," to which the butchers always protested, "All are freshest."

This detailed description moves us down the block from the playground to its border of "wood-slat benches" and on "to the dark alley itself." There we follow Waverly and her brothers first to the pharmacy, then to the printer next door, and finally to the fish market where we progress from the window display to the interior, each location rich with sense impressions.

FOR PRACTICE

Underline sense impressions in the description of Waverly's neighborhood. Label the sense to which each impression appeals. What is the overall effect that these details create?

Use of Transitions to Link Details

To organize details in their descriptions, writers use directional cues to move readers from one point to another. The list of transitional words and phrases most useful for writing descriptions is reprinted on the next page from Chapter 4:

Transitions that order ideas in space   above, behind, below, beside, next to, in front of, inside, on top of, in the foreground/background, to the right, to the left, under

Reliance on Explaining

As seen in Chapter 7, writers use explanations to clarify meaning for their readers. Amy Tan frequently interprets a description for her readers by simply telling them what the description means. For example, after Waverly describes the trips with her mother to the grocery store, she explains the importance of her mother's lesson and how well her mother protected her from knowledge of the family's "circumstances":

> My mother imparted her daily truths so she could help my 4
> older brothers and me rise above our circumstances. We lived in
> San Francisco's Chinatown. Like most of the other Chinese chil-
> dren who played in the back alleys of restaurants and curio shops, I
> didn't think we were poor. My bowl was always full, three five-
> course meals every day, beginning with a soup full of mysterious
> things I didn't want to know the names of.

Rules of the Game
Amy Tan

Amy Tan was born in Oakland, California, in 1952, two and one-half years after her parents immigrated from China to the United States. The following passage is taken from her first novel, The Joy Luck Club, *published in 1989.*

I was six when my mother taught me the art of invisible strength. It was a 1
strategy for winning arguments, respect from others, and eventually, though
neither of us knew it at the time, chess games.

"Bite back your tongue," scolded my mother when I cried loudly, yanking 2
her hand toward the store that sold bags of salted plums. At home, she said,
"Wise guy, he not go against wind. In Chinese we say, Come from South, blow
with wind—poom!—North will follow. Strongest wind cannot be seen."

The next week I bit back my tongue as we entered the store with the for- 3
bidden candies. When my mother finished her shopping, she quietly plucked
a small bag of plums from the rack and put it on the counter with the rest of
the items.

My mother imparted her daily truths so she could help my older brothers 4
and me rise above our circumstances. We lived in San Francisco's Chinatown.
Like most of the other Chinese children who played in the back alleys of
restaurants and curio shops, I didn't think we were poor. My bowl was always

full, three five-course meals every day, beginning with a soup full of mysterious things I didn't want to know the names of.

We lived on Waverly Place, in a warm, clean, two-bedroom flat that sat 5 above a small Chinese bakery specializing in steamed pastries and dim sum. In the early morning, when the alley was still quiet, I could smell fragrant red beans as they were cooked down to a pasty sweetness. By daybreak, our flat was heavy with the odor of fried sesame balls and sweet curried chicken crescents. From my bed, I would listen as my father got ready for work, then locked the door behind him, one-two-three clicks.

At the end of our two-block alley was a small sandlot playground with 6 swings and slides well-shined down the middle with use. The play area was bordered by wood-slat benches where old-country people sat cracking roasted watermelon seeds with their golden teeth and scattering the husks to an impatient gathering of gurgling pigeons. The best playground, however, was the dark alley itself. It was crammed with daily mysteries and adventures. My brothers and I would peer into the medicinal herb shop, watching old Li dole out onto a stiff sheet of white paper the right amount of insect shells, saffron-colored seeds, and pungent leaves for his ailing customers. It was said that he once cured a woman dying of an ancestral curse that had eluded the best of American doctors. Next to the pharmacy was a printer who specialized in gold-embossed wedding invitations and festive red banners.

Farther down the street was Ping Yuen Fish Market. The front window dis- 7 played a tank crowded with doomed fish and turtles struggling to gain footing on the slimy green-tiled sides. A hand-written sign informed tourists, "Within this store, is all for food, not for pet." Inside, the butchers with their blood-stained white smocks deftly gutted the fish while customers cried out their orders and shouted, "Give me your freshest," to which the butchers always protested, "All are freshest." On less crowded market days, we would inspect the crates of live frogs and crabs which we were warned not to poke, boxes of dried cuttlefish, and row upon row of iced prawns, squid, and slippery fish. The sanddabs made me shiver each time; their eyes lay on one flattened side and reminded me of my mother's story of a careless girl who ran into a crowded street and was crushed by a cab. "Was smash flat," reported my mother.

At the corner of the alley was Hong Sing's, a four-table café with a 8 recessed stairwell in front that led to a door marked "Tradesmen." My brothers and I believed the bad people emerged from this door at night. Tourists never went to Hong Sing's since the menu was printed only in Chinese. A Caucasian man with a big camera once posed me and my playmates in front of the restaurant. He had us move to the side of the picture window so the photo would capture the roasted duck with its head dangling from a juice-covered rope. After he took the picture, I told him he should go into Hong Sing's and eat dinner. When he smiled and asked me what they served, I shouted, "Guts and duck's feet and octopus gizzards!" Then I ran off with my friends, shrieking with laughter as we scampered across the alley and hid in the entryway grotto of the China Gem Company, my heart pounding with hope that he would chase us.

My mother named me after the street that we lived on: Waverly Place Jong, 9
my official name for important American documents. But my family called me
Meimei, "Little Sister." I was the youngest, the only daughter. Each morning
before school, my mother would twist and yank on my thick black hair until she
had formed two tightly wound pigtails. One day, as she struggled to weave a
hard-toothed comb through my disobedient hair, I had a sly thought.

I asked her, "Ma, what is Chinese torture?" My mother shook her head. A 10
bobby pin was wedged between her lips. She wetted her palm and smoothed
the hair above my ear, then pushed the pin in so that it nicked sharply against
my scalp.

"Who say this word?" she asked without a trace of knowing how wicked I 11
was being. I shrugged my shoulders and said, "Some boy in my class said
Chinese people do Chinese torture."

"Chinese people do many things," she said simply. "Chinese people do 12
business, do medicine, do painting. Not lazy like American people. We do torture. Best torture."

RESPONDING TO THE READING

Freewriting

Exercise 8a.   Record your first impressions of the place where Amy Tan's
character, Waverly, grew up.

Exercise 8b.   Freewrite about the street where you grew up. Don't worry
about the order of details or events; just record as much as you can remember.
How does Waverly's neighborhood compare to one that you remember?

Exercise 8c.   Freewrite about one or two streets that are familiar to you in
the town where you currently live.

Building Your Vocabulary

VOCABULARY LIST

Words to Look Up	My Definition	Dictionary Definition
imparted (4)		
curio (4)		
saffron (6)		
pungent (6)		
deftly (7)		
cuttlefish (7)		
sanddabs (7)		
grotto (8)		

Questions for Discussion

1. Choose a few favorite scenes from "Rules of the Game." What makes these scenes effective? Compare your responses with those of your classmates.

2. Amy Tan's description of her neighborhood is also an introduction to the Chinese community in San Francisco. What do you "see" in her description that you find either inviting or offensive? Explain your choice.

3. Amy Tan obviously considers Waverly's mother an important force in her character's life. What is the dominant impression conveyed by her behavior and speech?

4. In paragraph 2 Waverly's mother advises her daughter: " 'Wise guy, he not go against wind.' " Then she quotes a Chinese proverb: " 'In Chinese we say, Come from South, blow with wind—poom!—North will follow. Strongest wind cannot be seen.' " Examine paragraphs 1 through 4 carefully and decide how this advice applies to Waverly. What is Waverly's mother trying to teach her?

5. Reread the last exchange between Waverly and her mother at the end of paragraph 9, beginning with the sentence, "One day, as she struggled to weave a hard-toothed comb through my disobedient hair, I had a sly thought. . . ." Write a one-sentence summary of what happens next. What does the dialogue imply that is not stated directly?

6. If you have read "Girl" by Jamaica Kincaid or Russell Baker's "Mother," discuss similarities or differences between one of these mothers and Waverly's mother.

TOPICS FOR WRITING

Topic 1.   Reread your freewriting notes for Exercise 8b. Using techniques for preliminary writing—asking questions, making lists, and drawing an idea wheel—add new details to the memories of the street where you grew up. Then take your reader on a walk through your neighborhood. Be sure to use transitions to move the reader from one spot to another. Your descriptions should convey a dominant impression of that street.

Topic 2.   Use your freewriting notes for Exercise 8c and write a few paragraphs that describe the sights, sounds, and smells of a place in the town where you currently live. The questions for remembering places (at the beginning of this chapter) and Amy Tan's vivid descriptions will help you generate details for your paper.

Topic 3.   Write a letter to a friend in which you describe an event that occurred in your neighborhood or community when you were a child. Write the letter quickly to catch as much about the place, people, circumstances, and details as you can remember. Treat this letter as a freewriting exercise, adding details that you may have omitted. Then group similar details and arrange them in the order you would like to follow for a class assignment. Finally, rewrite the letter, recreating the event for your friend. What would you change about this description if you were writing it for your teacher?

Topic 4.   Write about an event that taught you something important about your parents or another adult authority. In writing this paper you might explain the "rules of the game" you learned in this encounter with the adult world.

THE WRITING PROCESS: DESCRIBING

In general, the steps in the writing process are useful for writing any kind of paragraph or essay. The suggestions and questions below offer more specific help in writing descriptions.

Additional Considerations for Developing a Topic

The Topics for Writing that follow each reading selection in this chapter give you ample opportunity to use your memories and observations to write about a place, object, or event. Journal entries and freewriting exercises in this chapter and class discussions may suggest additional topics. The following questions may help you as you explore your topic and shape details and subtopics into a paper.

QUESTIONS FOR REMEMBERING PLACES

> What are some of your earliest memories of a neighborhood and home? Make a list of the places you have lived. Which do you remember most vividly? Why?
> What schools have you attended? Which did you like or dislike most?
> If you have taken trips to the mountains, desert, or seashore, what were your impressions?
> What was your first job like?
> How would you describe your favorite place or the least attractive place you have worked?
> What place was special to you as a child or teenager?
> Is there a place that has special meaning to you as an adult?
> Where do you go to have fun?
> Where did you go to have fun when you were a child?

QUESTIONS FOR REMEMBERING OBJECTS

What have you owned that has meant something to you?

Is there a particular feature in your home, like a fireplace or wall hanging, that interests you?

Is there a special object you remember from the house or apartment where you lived as a child?

Is there something that terrified you when you were little?

Do you own something now that you can't live without? How long have you had it? Why is it important to you?

QUESTIONS FOR REMEMBERING EVENTS

What was it like to do something for the first time, like drive a car, attend your first college class, fly in an airplane, hike, or camp?

Think of a song that has special meaning for you. What events come to mind when you play it?

What embarrassing, rewarding, or maddening things happened on your first job?

Which school year do you remember best? What do you remember about it?

What have you done especially well in your life?

What have you found to be particularly difficult to do?

What is the worst conflict you have ever experienced? Who was involved? What happened? How was it resolved, if at all?

Additional Considerations for Thinking about Your Audience

When you write a description, your goal is to recreate an experience as vividly as you can. Some students find it easier to write specifically if they have an audience in mind that has never seen the place or object they are describing. Then the writer must be the reader's eyes and ears.

The following questions will help you narrow your topic and decide what you want your description to accomplish:

What do I want to describe?

Who is my intended audience?

What point of view will I adopt?

What is the dominant impression I want to create?

Additional Considerations for Preliminary Writing

You may wish to use these additional questions to generate details, examples, ideas, and explanations for your descriptions:

QUESTIONS FOR DESCRIBING PLACES

What did this place look like from the inside or outside?
What distinctive characteristics do you remember about it?
What was your relationship to this place?
What generally happened here?
Were any people involved with the place? How were they involved? What were they like? What conversations do you remember?
How did other people describe this place?
Has this place changed over the years? If so, how?
Have you had different views of this place at different times in your life? Describe these perspectives. How do you explain the differences?

QUESTIONS FOR DESCRIBING OBJECTS

What did this object look like from the inside or outside?
What distinctive characteristics about it do you remember?
How did other people describe it?
Were other people involved with the object? How? What were they like?
Did you have a different view of this object at different times?
What was your relationship to it? Did you observe it, own it, or have it given to you?
Has anything about this object changed over the years? What might have caused these changes?

QUESTIONS FOR DESCRIBING EVENTS

What was important about the event you want to describe?
What have other people said about this event?
What sights, smells, sounds, tastes, or feelings are associated with this event?
How were you involved in what happened?
Were any other people involved? How?
What conversations took place at the time?
Why might things have happened the way they did? What was the result?
Have you had a different view of this event at different times or in different moods?
How close were you to this event? What did it mean to you?

You might arrange your answers to the questions you select by drawing an idea wheel or listing ideas. Again, speaking your memories into a tape recorder, or talking to a friend or classmate might prove fruitful as you recall and shape events. Sketching significant details might also help you recreate your experience.

Additional Considerations for Organizing Ideas

Most descriptions follow a spatial order; left to right, top to bottom, or inside to outside are a few possible arrangements. If you are writing about the place where you grew up, it might be helpful to imagine yourself walking through the neighborhood, much as Waverly Sun remembers walking through her Chinatown neighborhood, and to describe what you are seeing on this walk. If possible, visit the place you want to describe before you write about it. You might actually take a walk there, jotting down what you see, smell, hear, taste, and touch.

Additional Considerations for Making Final Revisions

Once you have written a few drafts of your paper, use the following checklist to make revisions. Check each question as you complete it.

Checklist

☐ Will it be clear to a reader *what* I am describing and my purpose for writing?
☐ Does this description have a dominant impression?
☐ Would additional details, examples, dialogue, or comparisons make this description more vivid?
☐ Should I add explanations to clarify the importance of this scene?
☐ In general, have I recreated this place or experience successfully?

Student Writing

In this paragraph, Wayne Onuki describes a mysterious "thing" that appeared in his life when he was a child.

My First Experience with Television

I remember a long time ago when my little brother and I were playing in the family room. After we stopped playing, my brother came up to me and said he wanted to show me something. Being curious, I asked him what he had and why he was being so cagey. He said nothing and walked over to a big huge block made of wood with a black window for a face. Then he made a noise and across the black window a colorful bar grew lengthwise, and with a bright flash of colorful light, the screen opened like a book. I stared attentively and with awe. It was amazing. It was better than a book. While I was watching it, already a convert, a budding devotee, my brother turned the thing "off." I was upset by his cruelty and told him to make it come back.

Then I heard the patter of little feet as he ran to his room and locked the door. I tried activating the box myself by turning everything I saw, but I could not bring back the magic and began to cry. I had become like a drug user, an addict. I was hooked. I watched television every day from then on.

Questions for Discussion

1. What is Onuki's purpose for writing this description?
2. Imagine that you have read this paragraph for an in-class workshop. What would you say are its strengths? Do you have suggestions for improving it?
3. Do you think television viewing can become "addictive," as Onuki suggests? What examples can you think of to support your answer?

In another student sample, Arina Hung writes about an event that made a strong impression on her when she was growing up in Hong Kong.

I Miss You Mr. Fish

I used to go to a market with my mom every Sunday morning in Hong Kong when I was a little girl. In the market there was a fish shop owner named Mr. Fish. I named him that since I thought he was the President of Fish.

One Sunday morning my mom and I went to the market to buy some food. We went to Mr. Fish's shop as we usually did and bought two fish. While we were at his shop, we met his wife and children for the first time. During our conversation, my mom told Mr. Fish that he was pretty lucky to have such a beautiful wife and such cute children.

On our way home, we had gone not more than fifty feet from his shop when I heard a loud crash. We immediately turned back and saw that a car had smashed into Mr. Fish's shop. Tears started running down my face. The glass in the front window had shattered and the window frame had fallen apart. The fish tanks had been shattered, too, and all the fish were jumping around on the floor, outside, and everywhere. Blood was flowing all over. Every member of Mr. Fish's beautiful family had been injured. I could see blood coming from wounds on Mr. Fish's hands and mouth. Two of the children were crying, and Mr. Fish's wife was unconscious. The shop was just a mess, and I felt very sad.

The careless driver was hurt, too. The windshield of his car was lying in a million tiny pieces on the dashboard, or sprinkled like confetti on the seat.

The whole car was surrounded by fish, some gasping in silence, others already dead. I could tell from the way he was hanging over the steering wheel that the driver, too, was at the point of death.

I heard ambulances coming from far away, and the sound seemed to wake me up. My own cries mixed with the wail of the sirens, and I ran madly into the shop. I told Mr. Fish that everything would be all right, and not to worry as the paramedics put him and his family into the ambulances and drove to a hospital.

That night I couldn't sleep. I lay awake thinking about the fish jumping and dying, and Mr. Fish and his family all bloody and crying. The next morning I learned that everybody was still alive. However, I found out that Mr. Fish had lost his hands in the accident. After that day, we didn't see him in the market selling fish.

Today, after seven years, his strong, clear voice and happy face still appear in my mind. Mr. Fish, I miss you.

Questions for Discussion

1. What was Arina Hung's purpose in writing this essay? What details, examples, and explanations help her achieve this purpose? What else might she have done?
2. What organizational pattern does Hung use? How else might the events in this essay have been arranged? What would Hung gain or lose by using some other arrangement?
3. How well does Hung develop her description? Where might additional details or explanations make this description more interesting?
4. What events in your own life did Hung's essay evoke for you? How are they similar or different from the events she describes?

FOR FURTHER READING

Self and World
Annie Dillard

Annie Dillard has published seven books, including Pilgrim at Tinker Creek *and* Teaching a Stone to Talk. *This excerpt is from* An American Childhood, *her book about growing up in Pittsburgh in the 1950s.*

When I was five, growing up in Pittsburgh in 1950, I would not go to bed   1
willingly because something came into my room. This was a private matter between me and it. If I spoke of it, it would kill me.

Who could breathe as this thing searched for me over the very corners of 2
the room? Who could ever breathe freely again? I lay in the dark.

My sister Amy, two years old, was asleep in the other bed. What did she 3
know? She was innocent of evil. Even at two, she composed herself attractively
for sleep. She folded the top sheet tidily under her prettily outstretched arm;
she laid her perfect head lightly on an unwrinkled pillow, where her thick curls
spread evenly in rays like petals. All night long she slept smoothly in a series of
pleasant and serene, if artificial-looking, positions, a faint smile on her closed
lips, as if she were posing for an ad for sheets. There was no messiness in her,
no roughness for things to cling to, only a charming and charmed innocence
that seemed then to protect her, an innocence I needed but couldn't muster.
Since Amy was asleep, furthermore, and since when I needed someone most I
was afraid to stir enough to wake her, she was useless.

I lay alone and was almost asleep when the damned thing entered the 4
room by flattening itself against the open door and sliding in. It was a trans-
parent, luminous oblong. I could see the door whiten at its touch; I could see
the blue wall turn pale where it raced over it, and see the maple headboard of
Amy's bed glow. It was a swift spirit; it was an awareness. It made noise. It had
two joined parts, a head and a tail, like a Chinese dragon. It found the door,
wall, and headboard; and it swiped them, charging them with its luminous
glance. After its fleet, searching passage, things looked the same, but weren't.

I dared not blink or breathe; I tried to hush my whooping blood. If it found 5
another awareness, it would destroy it.

Every night before it got to me it gave up. It hit my wall's corner and could- 6
n't get past. It shrank completely into itself and vanished like a cobra down a
hole. I heard the rising roar it made when it died or left. I still couldn't breathe.
I knew—it was the worst fact I knew, a very hard fact—that it could return
again alive that same night.

Sometimes it came back, sometimes it didn't. Most often, restless, it came 7
back. The light stripe slipped in the door, ran searching over Amy's wall,
stopped, stretched lunatic at the first corner, raced wailing toward my wall,
and vanished into the second corner with a cry. So I wouldn't go to bed.

It was a passing car whose windshield reflected the corner streetlight out- 8
side. I figured it out one night.

Figuring it out was as memorable as the oblong itself. Figuring it out was 9
a long and forced ascent to the very rim of being, to the membrane of skin that
both separates and connects the inner life and the outer world. I climbed
deliberately from the depths like a diver who releases the monster in his arms
and hauls himself hand over hand up an anchor chain till he meets the ocean's
sparkling membrane and bursts through it; he sights the sunlit, becalmed hull
of his boat, which had bulked so ominously from below.

I recognized the noise it made when it left. That is, the noise it made called 10
to mind, at last, my daytime sensations when a car passed—the sight and
noise together. A car came roaring down hushed Edgerton Avenue in front of
our house, stopped at the corner stop sign, and passed on shrieking as its

engine shifted up the gears. What, precisely, came into the bedroom? A reflection from the car's oblong windshield. Why did it travel in two parts? The window sash split the light and cast a shadow.

Night after night I labored up the same long chain of reasoning, as night after night the thing burst into the room where I lay awake and Amy slept prettily and my loud heart thrashed and I froze.   11

There was a world outside my window and contiguous to it. If I was so all-fired bright, as my parents, who had patently no basis for comparison, seemed to think, why did I have to keep learning this same thing over and over? For I had learned it a summer ago, when men with jackhammers broke up Edgerton Avenue. I had watched them from the yard; the street came up in jagged slabs like floes. When I lay to nap, I listened. One restless afternoon I connected the new noise in my bedroom with the jackhammer men I had been seeing outside. I understood abruptly that these worlds met, the outside and the inside. I traveled the route in my mind: You walked downstairs from here, and outside from downstairs. "Outside," then, was conceivably just beyond my windows. It was the same world I reached by going out the front or the back door. I forced my imagination yet again over this route.   12

The world did not have me in mind; it had no mind. It was a coincidental collection of things and people, of items, and I myself was one such item—a child walking up the sidewalk, whom anyone could see or ignore. The things in the world did not necessarily cause my overwhelming feelings; the feelings were inside me, beneath my skin, behind my ribs, within my skull. They were even, to some extent, under my control.   13

I could be connected to the outer world by reason, if I chose, or I could yield to what amounted to a narrative fiction, to a tale of terror whispered to me by the blood in my ears, a show in light projected on the room's blue walls. As time passed, I learned to amuse myself in bed in the darkened room by entering the fiction deliberately and replacing it by reason deliberately.   14

When the low roar drew nigh and the oblong slid in the door, I threw my own switches for pleasure. It's coming after me; it's a car outside. It's after me. It's a car. It raced over the wall, lighting it blue wherever it ran; it bumped over Amy's maple headboard in a rush, paused, slithered elongate over the corner, shrank, flew my way, and vanished into itself with a wail. It was a car.   15

RESPONDING TO THE READING

Freewriting

Exercise 8d.   As soon as you finish reading "Self and World," freewrite about the passages you found most interesting or those that somehow spoke to your own experience.

Exercise 8e.   Freewrite about a few childhood fantasies you remember or dreams that have pleased or terrified you.

Building Your Vocabulary

VOCABULARY LIST

Words to Look Up	My Definition	Dictionary Definition
serene (3)		
transparent (4)		
luminous (4)		
oblong (4)		
membrane (9)		
ominously (9)		
contiguous (12)		
patently (12)		
floes (12)		
conceivably (12)		
coincidental (4)		
slithered (15)		

Thinking about Words

You have probably had the experience of looking up a word and still not understanding an author's use of it. A writer like Annie Dillard creates new combinations of words. For example, she uses the following phrases to describe the thing that kept coming into her room and her own terror of it:

> my whooping blood (paragraph 5)
> [The thing] stretched lunatic at the first corner (paragraph 7)
> [The ship's hull] had bulked so ominously from below (paragraph 9)

The first phrase, "my whooping blood," imitates the sound of a gasp or cry usually associated with "whooping cranes," "whooping cough," or the stereotypical war whoops of Indians in cowboy movies. Here Dillard uses the word to create an image of her terror as she imagines her very blood gasping and crying out for help.

FOR PRACTICE

Reread the passages in paragraphs 7 and 9 that contain the other two phrases and list any associations that come to your mind. Use these associations to explain what the underlined words above might mean.

Another element that characterizes Dillard's writing style is her use of comparisons or *analogies*. For example, she describes how the "monster" in her room "hit [the] wall's corner and couldn't get past." She traces its movement as "it shrank completely into itself and vanished <u>like a cobra down a hole.</u>" The underlined phrase draws an *analogy* or comparison between the streak of light as it disappeared into the corner, and a cobra vanishing into its hole. Writers frequently use this technique to help their readers picture an experience by describing what it was *like,* so the reader can compare it to something more familiar or more easily imagined.

Annie Dillard uses an extended *analogy* when she compares her ascent from fantasy to reason with a diver's swim from the depths to the surface of the sea (paragraph 9).

FOR PRACTICE

Reread paragraph 9, where the diver analogy appears. In what specific ways are Annie Dillard's discoveries of the differences between the "inner" and "outer" worlds analogous to the diver's ascent from the depths of the ocean?

Questions for Discussion

1. Choose two scenes that you feel are especially vivid in "Self and World," and make a list of the sights and sounds Dillard uses to recreate these scenes.
2. What is Dillard's purpose for writing about this childhood experience?
3. Write the thesis for "Self and World." What, in your view, is Dillard's best support for this thesis?
4. How do you explain the break in the story at paragraph 8? What idea unifies the seven paragraphs that precede it? What do the paragraphs that follow (9 through 15) have in common?
5. Briefly summarize the characteristics of the "inner" and "outer" worlds described in Dillard's narrative. Explain why the discovery of this separation was important for her.
6. What are the differences between the way Dillard and her sister, Amy, perceive the world? Are there similarly startling differences between your own point of view and that of another member of your family?
7. Annie Dillard and Amy Tan write from a child's point of view: Tan uses the voice of six-year-old Waverly Sun, and Dillard writes about what she saw and felt when she was five years old. How do their attitudes toward the events and objects they describe differ? What words and phrases characterize this difference?

TOPICS FOR WRITING

Topic 1.   Write a paragraph or short essay about a time when something you experienced triggered a strong emotion. Use the freewriting you did for

Exercise 8e to get you started. Then follow the steps in the writing process to do your preliminary writing, organizing, drafting, and revising.

Topic 2.   Imagine that there is a room next to your bedroom. One night you discover that you can walk through the wall to enter this room. Imagine what happens there. Describe the room, the people you see, and what goes on in this room.

Topic 3.   Sketch a word-picture of someone you know in a particular position (as Dillard describes her sleeping sister) or doing a particular activity such as playing, eating, studying, listening to music, or dancing. Try drawing a picture of your subject to help you visualize the details of your description. You might also freewrite about your first impressions. Are any analogies appropriate for this description? Organize, draft, and revise your description.

Topic 4.   Write about a time when you first understood something. The true worth of a person, the turmoil in a friend's life, the experience of pain, or a time someone let you down are possible topics. Do some freewriting and preliminary writing about this experience. Use any questions for remembering objects and events (listed earlier in this chapter) that apply to your topic. Arrange your details and explanations in chronological order; rearrange them if you wish to use a flashback. Write, share, and revise your draft.

The First Morning
Edward Abbey

Edward Abbey began writing about nature while he was working as a ranger for the National Park Service. His books include the novel The Monkey Wrench Gang, *and several nonfiction works. The following excerpt is from* Desert Solitaire: A Season in the Wilderness.

This is the most beautiful place on earth.   1

There are many such places. Every man, every woman, carries in heart   2
and mind the image of the ideal place, the right place, the one true home,
known or unknown, actual or visionary. A houseboat in Kashmir, a view down
Atlantic Avenue in Brooklyn, a gray gothic farmhouse two stories high at the
end of a red dog road in the Allegheny Mountains, a cabin on the shore of a
blue lake in spruce and fir country, a greasy alley near the Hoboken water-
front, or even, possibly, for those of a less demanding sensibility, the world to
be seen from a comfortable apartment high in the tender, velvety smog of
Manhattan, Chicago, Paris, Tokyo, Rio or Rome—there's no limit to the
human capacity for the homing sentiment. Theologians, sky pilots, astronauts
have even felt the appeal of home calling to them from up above, in the cold
black outback of interstellar space.

For myself I'll take Moab, Utah. I don't mean the town itself, of course, but 3
the country which surrounds it—the canyonlands. The slickrock desert. The
red dust and the burnt cliffs and the lonely sky—all that which lies beyond the
end of the roads.

The choice became apparent to me this morning when I stepped out of a 4
Park Service housetrailer—my caravan—to watch for the first time in my life
the sun come up over the hoodoo stone of Arches National Monument.

I wasn't able to see much of it last night. After driving all day from 5
Albuquerque—450 miles—I reached Moab after dark in cold, windy, clouded
weather. At park headquarters north of town I met the superintendent and the
chief ranger, the only permanent employees, except for one maintenance
man, in this particular unit of America's national park system. After coffee
they gave me a key to the housetrailer and directions on how to reach it; I am
required to live and work not at headquarters but at this one-man station
some twenty miles back in the interior, on my own. The way I wanted it, naturally, or I'd never have asked for the job.

Leaving the headquarters area and the lights of Moab, I drove twelve 6
miles farther north on the highway until I came to a dirt road on the right,
where a small wooden sign pointed the way: Arches National Monument
Eight Miles. I left the pavement, turned east into the howling wilderness.
Wind roaring out of the northwest, black clouds across the stars—all I could
see were clumps of brush and scattered junipers along the roadside. Then
another modest signboard:

WARNING: QUICKSAND
DO NOT CROSS WASH
WHEN WATER IS RUNNING

The wash looked perfectly dry in my headlights. I drove down, across, up 7
the other side and on into the night. Glimpses of weird humps of pale rock on
either side, like petrified elephants, dinosaurs, stone-age hobgoblins. Now and
then something alive scurried across the road: kangaroo mice, a jackrabbit, an
animal that looked like a cross between a raccoon and a squirrel—the ringtail
cat. Farther on a pair of mule deer started from the brush and bounded
obliquely through the beams of my lights, raising puffs of dust which the
wind, moving faster than my pickup truck, caught and carried ahead of me
out of sight into the dark. The road, narrow and rocky, twisted sharply left and
right, dipped in and out of tight ravines, climbing by degrees toward a summit
which I would see only in the light of the coming day.

Snow was swirling through the air when I crossed the unfenced line and 8
passed the boundary marker of the park. A quarter-mile beyond I found the
ranger station—a wide place in the road, an informational display under a
lean-to shelter, and fifty yards away the little tin government housetrailer
where I would be living for the next six months.

A cold night, a cold wind, the snow falling like confetti. In the lights of the   9
truck I unlocked the housetrailer, got out bedroll and baggage and moved in.
By flashlight I found the bed, unrolled my sleeping bag, pulled off my boots
and crawled in and went to sleep at once. The last I knew was the shaking of
the trailer in the wind and the sound, from inside, of hungry mice scampering
around with the good news that their long lean lonesome winter was over—
their friend and provider had finally arrived.

This morning I awake before sunrise, stick my head out of the sack, peer   10
through a frosty window at a scene dim and vague with flowing mists, dark
fantastic shapes looming beyond. An unlikely landscape.

I get up, moving about in long underwear and socks, stooping carefully   11
under the low ceiling and lower doorways of the housetrailer, a machine for
living built so efficiently and compactly there's hardly room for a man to
breathe. An iron lung it is, with windows and venetian blinds.

The mice are silent, watching me from their hiding places, but the wind is   12
still blowing and outside the ground is covered with snow. Cold as a tomb, a
jail, a cave; I lie down on the dusty floor, on the cold linoleum sprinkled with
mouse turds, and light the pilot on the butane heater. Once this thing gets
going the place warms up fast, in a dense unhealthy way, with a layer of heat
under the ceiling where my head is and nothing but frigid air from the knees
down. But we've got all the indispensable conveniences: gas cookstove, gas
refrigerator, hot water heater, sink with running water (if the pipes aren't
frozen), storage cabinets and shelves, everything within arm's reach of everything else. The gas comes from two steel bottles in a shed outside; the water
comes by gravity flow from a tank buried in a hill close by. Quite luxurious for
the wilds. There's even a shower stall and a flush toilet with a dead rat in the
bowl. Pretty soft. My poor mother raised five children without any of these
luxuries and might be doing without them yet if it hadn't been for Hitler, war
and general prosperity.

Time to get dressed, get out and have a look at the lay of the land, fix a   13
breakfast. I try to pull on my boots but they're stiff as iron from the cold. I
light a burner on the stove and hold the boots upside down above the flame
until they are malleable enough to force my feet into. I put on a coat and step
outside. Into the center of the world, God's navel, Abbey's country, the red
wasteland.

The sun is not yet in sight but signs of the advent are plain to see. Lavender   14
clouds sail like a fleet of ships across the pale green dawn; each cloud, planed
flat on the wind, has a base of fiery gold. Southeast, twenty miles by iine of
sight, stand the peaks of the Sierra La Sal, twelve to thirteen thousand feet
above sea level, all covered with snow and rosy in the morning sunlight. The
air is dry and clear as well as cold; the last fogbanks left over from last night's
storm are scudding away like ghosts, fading into nothing before the wind and
the sunrise.

The view is open and perfect in all directions except to the west where the   15
ground rises and the skyline is only a few hundred yards away. Looking
toward the mountains I can see the dark gorge of the Colorado River five or six

miles away, carved through the sandstone mesa, though nothing of the river itself down inside the gorge. Southward, on the far side of the river, lies the Moab valley between thousand-foot walls of rock, with the town of Moab somewhere on the valley floor, too small to be seen from here. Beyond the Moab valley is more canyon and tableland stretching away to the Blue Mountains fifty miles south. On the north and northwest I see the Roan Cliffs and the Book Cliffs, the two-level face of the Uinta Plateau. Along the foot of those cliffs, maybe thirty miles off, invisible from where I stand, runs U.S. 6–50, a major east-west artery of commerce, traffic and rubbish, and the main line of the Denver–Rio Grande Railroad. To the east, under the spreading sunrise, are more mesas, more canyons, league on league of red cliff and arid tablelands, extending through purple haze over the bulging curve of the planet to the ranges of Colorado—a sea of desert.

Within this vast perimeter, in the middle ground and foreground of the picture, a rather personal demesne, are the 33,000 acres of Arches National Monument of which I am now sole inhabitant, usufructuary, observer and custodian.   16

What are the Arches? From my place in front of the housetrailer I can see several of the hundred or more of them which have been discovered in the park. These are natural arches, holes in the rock, windows in stone, no two alike, as varied in form as in dimension. They range in size from holes just big enough to walk through to openings large enough to contain the dome of the Capitol building in Washington, D.C. Some resemble jug handles or flying buttresses, others natural bridges but with this technical distinction: a natural bridge spans a watercourse—a natural arch does not. The arches were formed through hundreds of thousands of years by the weathering of the huge sandstone walls, or fins, in which they are found. Not the work of a cosmic hand, nor sculptured by sand-bearing winds, as many people prefer to believe, the arches came into being and continue to come into being through the modest wedging action of rainwater, melting snow, frost, and ice, aided by gravity. In color they shade from off-white through buff, pink, brown and red, tones which also change with the time of day and the moods of the light, the weather, the sky.   17

Standing there, gaping at this monstrous and inhuman spectacle of rock and cloud and sky and space, I feel a ridiculous greed and possessiveness come over me. I want to know it all, possess it all, embrace the entire scene intimately, deeply, totally, as a man desires a beautiful woman. An insane wish? Perhaps not—at least there's nothing else, no one human, to dispute possession with me.   18

The snow-covered ground glimmers with a dull blue light, reflecting the sky and the approaching sunrise. Leading away from me the narrow dirt road, an alluring and primitive track into nowhere, meanders down the slope and toward the heart of the labyrinth of naked stone. Near the first group of arches, looming over a bend in the road, is a balanced rock about fifty feet high, mounted on a pedestal of equal height; it looks like a head from Easter Island, a stone god or a petrified ogre.   19

Like a god, like an ogre? The personification of the natural is exactly the   20
tendency I wish to suppress in myself, to eliminate for good. I am here not
only to evade for a while the clamor and filth and confusion of the cultural
apparatus but also to confront, immediately and directly if it's possible, the
bare bones of existence, the elemental and fundamental, the bedrock which
sustains us. I want to be able to look at and into a juniper tree, a piece of
quartz, a vulture, a spider, and see it as it is in itself, devoid of all humanly
ascribed qualities, anti-Kantian,[1] even the categories of scientific description.
To meet God or Medusa face to face, even if it means risking everything
human in myself. I dream of a hard and brutal mysticism in which the naked
self merges with a nonhuman world and yet somehow survives still intact,
individual, separate. Paradox and bedrock.

Well—the sun will be up in a few minutes and I haven't even begun to   21
make coffee. I take more baggage from my pickup, the grub box and cooking
gear, go back in the trailer and start breakfast. Simply breathing, in a place
like this, arouses the appetite. The orange juice is frozen, the milk slushy with
ice. Still chilly enough inside the trailer to turn my breath to vapor. When the
first rays of the sun strike the cliffs I fill a mug with steaming coffee and sit in
the doorway facing the sunrise, hungry for the warmth.

Suddenly it comes, the flaming globe, blazing on the pinnacles and   22
minarets and balanced rocks, on the canyon walls and through the windows
in the sandstone fins. We greet each other, sun and I, across the black void of
ninety-three million miles. The snow glitters between us, acres of diamonds
almost painful to look at. Within an hour all the snow exposed to the sunlight
will be gone and the rock will be damp and steaming. Within minutes, even as
I watch, melting snow begins to drip from the branches of a juniper nearby;
drops of water streak slowly down the side of the trailerhouse.

I am not alone after all. Three ravens are wheeling near the balanced rock,   23
squawking at each other and at the dawn. I'm sure they're as delighted by the
return of the sun as I am and I wish I knew the language. I'd sooner exchange
ideas with the birds on earth than learn to carry on intergalactic communications with some obscure race of humanoids on a satellite planet from the
world of Betelgeuse. First things first. The ravens cry out in husky voices,
blue-black wings flapping against the golden sky. Over my shoulder comes the
sizzle and smell of frying bacon.

That's the way it was this morning.   24

RESPONDING TO THE READING

Freewriting

Exercise 8f.   Freewrite about the passage you found most interesting or
puzzling.

---

[1]Immanuel Kant (1724–1804). Philosopher who said we cannot know things as they are.

Exercise 8g.   What questions do you have about Abbey's experience that you would like to discuss in class?

Exercise 8h.   Freewrite about a time you visited a national park or some other natural setting.

Building Your Vocabulary

VOCABULARY LIST

Words to Look Up	My Definition	Dictionary Definition
sensibility (2)		
theologians (2)		
interstellar (2)		
hoodoo (4)		
petrified (7)		
hobgoblins (7)		
obliquely (7)		
malleable (13)		
advent (14)		
demesne (16)		
usufructuary (16)		
meanders (19)		
pedestal (19)		
Easter Island (19)		
ogre (19)		
personification (20)		
Medusa (20)		
paradox (20)		
pinnacles (22)		
minarets (22)		
intergalactic (23)		
humanoids (23)		

Thinking about Words

Edward Abbey uses analogies to compare the objects in the desert to more fantastical things. One analogy compares the way the natural formations appear at night: "weird humps of pale rock" to "petrified elephants, dinosaurs, stone-age hobgoblins." Notice, too, that Abbey strings together details and descriptive phrases: "petrified elephants, dinosaurs, stone-age hobgoblins." Here is another example: "These are natural arches, holes in the rock, windows in stone, no two alike, as varied in form as in dimension."

FOR PRACTICE

Do you think Abbey's technique of using multiple phrases to describe natural objects is effective or not? Explain your answer.

Questions for Discussion

1. Why do you think Abbey wrote his observations of Arches National Monument? Who is his audience?
2. How is the title, "The First Morning," connected to the rest of the essay? What associations do you have with the idea of "the first morning"? What might these associations add to your understanding of Abbey's essay?
3. Summarize any self-discoveries Abbey makes on his first day in the wilderness. What is he trying to change about himself and why?
4. What is the dominant impression of the desert near Moab, Utah, that Abbey creates? Refer to the passage in Abbey's description that best conveys this impression. Be prepared to explain to the class why you picked this passage.
5. Apart from his being in the desert as an employee of the National Park Service, why did Abbey decide to live near Moab, Utah? What does he hope to do or see? What is he leaving behind? Would you make the same choice? Explain your answer.

TOPICS FOR WRITING

Topic 1.   Abbey writes that "every man, every woman, carries in heart and mind the image of the ideal place, the right place, the one true home, known or unknown, actual or visionary." Write a description of your "ideal place." Do some freewriting to gather details, choose an organization for the details, and write your description. Your "ideal place" need not be in the wilds like Abbey's but can be anywhere you wish it to be.

Topic 2.   List the things about Abbey's desert experience that you find inviting. On a separate sheet of paper, list those you find threatening. Ponder your reactions; then decide whether or not you would take Abbey's job for six months if given the chance. If your answer is yes, explain what you would most enjoy and how you would deal with the things you find threatening. If you would refuse the offer, explain why it is unappealing, and contrast the distasteful elements in Abbey's desert home with characteristics of places you do find inviting.

Topic 3.   Try to schedule a trip to the woods, desert, mountains, or seashore. Record your impressions of what you see by dividing a piece of paper into thirds and writing the details you observe on the left and your impressions or reactions in the middle column. Match as many of your own impressions as you can with Abbey's comments about Arches National Monument. Record these on the right side. As you think about your topic, ask yourself these questions: What attitude do I have toward my subject? Am I respectful, even reverent about the place I'm describing, as Abbey is, or am I more critical? Your answers to these questions will help you decide the approach you will take and the dominant impression you will create. A hike in the mountains, for example, might produce a list with the following comments:

MY HIKE IN THE CASCADES

Details	My Reaction	Abbey's Description
had a soggy tuna fish sandwich for lunch	worst meal of my life	smells sizzling bacon
my egg was raw, not boiled enough		
no place to go to the bathroom, except in the open	I was really embarrassed about using the outdoors as a toilet.	trailer has all the "conveniences"
blue jay kept squawking at my dog, Pete	These birds are obnoxious.	considers the ravens as companions he likes to "exchange ideas with"

This writer is ready to write a contrast between her own impressions of "nature" and Abbey's. Because her attitude is so different from his more respectful tone, her details lend themselves to a humorous paper that explains why Abbey can have his wilderness—she'll take "civilization" any time.

Topic 4.   Use the questions in the writing process section earlier in this chapter to develop your own topic on a place or event you would like to describe.

Student Writing

An Awful Wilderness Adventure

In "The First Morning," Edward Abbey describes the desert near Moab, Utah, as a place where he can get close to God and nature, a place where he can see some breathtaking scenery. Abbey obviously enjoys his wilderness experiences. I, however, have taken one hiking trip in my life, and on that trip I discovered that Abbey's experiences and mine were very different.

For one thing, the meals that Edward Abbey and I had in the wilderness were nothing alike. Abbey used his gas stove to cook hot meals. From his trailer, he enjoyed the comforting smell of frying bacon. In contrast, when I hiked up Mt. Lassen last spring, I had no way to prepare a home-cooked meal. I also had bad luck with the weather, which changed as I was making the climb. I started in 80-degree heat but soon walked into a 60-degree rain-storm. By the time I found shelter under an outcropping of rock and was able to eat my lunch, the tuna fish sandwich I had packed for the climb was so soggy it tasted like a wet sock. To make things worse, the egg I had boiled at a friend's house that morning was practically raw because I had forgotten that it takes a long time to boil water at higher elevations.

At one point in my hike I would have given anything to have Abbey's flush toilet, even though a dead rat was floating in the bowl. The area on the mountain where I was hiking was so exposed that I could not relieve myself without fear of being discovered by other hikers. I finally resorted to going off the trail several hundred feet and sheltering myself with my raincoat.

Edward Abbey had a very different experience of birdlife as well. He felt completely at home with his fellow creature, the raven. At one point he even considered the ravens as companions he would like to "exchange ideas with." I had a few words with a bird myself on my trip but did not find him nearly as sympathetic. When I got back to my car after a long, exhausting climb and descent, I had just settled down with a soda when an obnoxious blue jay swooped down from a tree and pecked my dog Pete on the head. Pete ran off howling to hide under a picnic table, but in his panic, he smashed into some-body's ice chest and knocked it over. I spent the next twenty minutes helping the owners of the ice chest pick up ham sandwiches, cheese, and cans of soda. It was no thanks to the jay that they didn't ask me to buy them dinner.

I have sometimes wondered if I just had a streak of bad luck my first time in the wilds, but I suspect that even if I had had good weather, plenty of dry food, and a good rapport with the birds, I still would not have had the enthusiasm for the wilderness that Abbey had for his desert home.

—Pamela Vickers

Questions for Discussion

1. Describe the tone or attitude that Pamela Vickers has toward the wilder-ness. What words help her establish this tone? Do you find her attitude convincing? Explain why or why not.
2. How effective are the development and organization in Vickers's essay? Would you advise her to revise any portion of the essay?
3. What response do you think Edward Abbey might have had to this stu-dent's complaints about her hiking trip?
4. Are your own feelings about the wilderness closer to those of Pamela Vickers or Edward Abbey?

9

The Richness of Tradition

"We try to send the message during Kwanzaa that it is more important to give of yourselves than to spend money on presents."

—Ikenna Ubaka

The [Japanese tea] ceremony is a way of making a group of people harmonious in a little space. . . . Basically, it is done by feeding them and giving them tea.

—Vance Horne

I n this chapter student and professional writers record their observations about customs that connect them to a larger culture. A few of these traditions, like Thanksgiving, are observed by most people who live in the United States. Other writers describe customs typically observed in Asian, African-American, and Latino communities. Hence, you will read about cultural events like the quinceañera, Kwanzaa, and the Japanese tea ceremony, events that may be quite new to you.

The writing strategies discussed in Chapters 7 and 8—narrating, describing, and explaining—also appear in the readings for this chapter. Two additional techniques for writing are introduced here too: process analysis— a writing strategy for explaining how something works, and interviewing—a technique for gathering information from another source. You use this interviewing technique to gather information about a classmate's traditions and cultural background. At the end of this chapter, you use your interviewing skills to gather information and write an oral history.

PROCESS ANALYSIS

Process analysis is the writing strategy that allows you to break a subject into parts, stages, or categories in order to define or explain something about the parts you have identified. The readings in this chapter use process analysis to explain activities involved in certain traditions. Donald Inn's essay, "The Art of Lion Dancing," provides examples for the discussion of process analysis.

Characteristics of Process Analysis

A Clear Purpose and Point of View

A process analysis may be written from the perspective of an observer, or as a personal experience. Essays in this chapter are written from a variety of points of view. Donald Inn ("The Art of Lion Dancing") and Eugene Morris ("Kwanzaa: Holiday of 'Principles to Live by' ") write objective, third-person explanations of their topics. A third writer, Vance Horne, writes his first-person observations of the Japanese tea ceremony, a custom that is not familiar to him. The purpose behind these essays may be to explain a custom to the audience, and, perhaps, to convince them of the value or importance of that tradition.

With process analysis, as with most writing strategies, the writer's approach to the subject, as well as the purpose for writing, is often stated in the introductory paragraphs. Purpose, audience, point of view, and thesis are evident in Donald Inn's opening paragraph:

For centuries, the Chinese people have practiced the art of lion 1 dancing to celebrate the new year. This custom still goes on even in America to show respect for the gods and to symbolize the chasing away of evil and bad luck. Most Americans have seen the lion costume in magazines and may have watched part of the dance on the news. But very few who are not Chinese know much about the head, the tail and the teaser—the three different roles played in lion dancing.

Donald Inn writes his essay in order to explain to a non-Chinese audience what lion dancing is and what it means. In his thesis statement he promises to examine the three roles in the dance—the head, the tail, and the teaser. His point of view is objective: he uses the third person ("he," "they") to discuss a subject that he knows well.

A Clear Sequence

Like narration, a process analysis is often organized chronologically, that is, according to the order in which things occur during the process. Occasionally, writers explain actions that occur simultaneously, as Donald Inn does when he describes the separate roles in the lion dance. To organize this kind of analysis, writers divide the topic into parts and explain each part in turn. They may organize these divisions according to importance—ending with the most significant, or for emphasis—closing with a category they wish to stress. One of the challenges in writing process analysis is to make smooth transitions between each part of the process.

The topic sentences for Donald Inn's essay illustrate how one writer lets the reader know when he changes his focus from one part of the lion to the next. Phrases that signal a new subject or compare one part of the lion to another are underlined for you. Inn uses order of importance to organize his discussion.

> The lion's head, the most obvious and fearsome part of the beast, is supported on the shoulders of the man inside. (Topic sentence for paragraph 2)

> Operating the tail does not require as many intricate movements as does working with the head. (Topic sentence for paragraph 3)

> The teaser, although not part of the lion-body itself, is an essential player in the lion dance. (Topic sentence for paragraph 4)

Inn uses a spatial order—beginning with the head, the most obvious part of the lion; moving to the tail, the lesser of the two parts; and ending with the teaser, a role that is not part of the lion's body. Because the teaser has the most personality and is the most mobile of the three parts, the essay ends with a discussion of the most interesting character in the lion dance.

Possible Reliance on Other Writing Strategies

To add interest to their process analysis, writers may use narrating, describing, explaining, and other writing strategies in addition to process analysis. In the paragraph on the teaser, for example, Donald Inn relies on several additional strategies to convey the importance of that role. These strategies are identified for you in the margin.

> The teaser, although not part of the lion-body itself, is an essential player in the lion dance. He wears a painted, Mardi Gras-type mask and represents the evil being who torments the lion until it strikes back and chases the evil one away. The teaser carries a little paper lantern, and he makes his appearance ten minutes after the lion completes his bow. He waves the lantern in front of the lion's face, challenging him to give chase. Once the lion charges, the teaser must travel, on a path of his choice, down the streets of Chinatown. The teaser does not have any set rules or footwork. He randomly runs and jumps in front of the lion, zig-zags through the street, and occasionally pauses to playfully tease some of the small children watching from the sidewalk.

4

Describes teaser's appearance
Explains teaser's meaning

Process or sequence of actions

Relates Parts to the Whole

Writers of process analysis are careful not to discuss the parts or categories of a process in isolation; instead, they remind their readers of how each piece contributes to the process as a whole. For example, in the preceding paragraph from "The Art of Lion Dancing," Donald Inn explains the teaser's symbolic importance as an "evil being," whom the lion must chase from the streets of Chinatown. Moreover, the teaser and the lion act together in the dance. The teaser "torments the lion until it strikes back and chases the evil one away." Hence, the teaser's role is an integral part of the action and meaning of the dance.

Freewriting

Exercise 9a.   Before reading Donald Inn's easy on the lion dance, write your own description of this custom. Where did you get your impressions of the dance?

The Art of Lion Dancing
Donald Inn

Donald Inn wrote this essay as a college freshman. He now holds a graduate degree in civil engineering.

For centuries, the Chinese people have practiced the art of lion dancing to 1 celebrate the new year. This custom still goes on even in America to show respect for the gods and to symbolize the chasing away of evil and bad luck. Most Americans have seen the lion costume in magazines and may have watched part of the dance on the news. But very few who are not Chinese know much about the head, the tail and the teaser—the three different roles played in lion dancing.

The lion's head, the most obvious and fearsome part of the beast, is sup- 2 ported on the shoulders of the man inside. His most important task is to learn how to bow. Bowing with the lion's head on your shoulders isn't just a simple matter of bending over. Rather, the bow is part of an elaborate, well-choreographed dance the lion must perform. First, he takes three steps forward with the head raised, lowers and raises the head gracefully, then walks backwards four or five steps, swinging the head from side to side. This movement creates the feeling that the lion is being courteous while keeping a watchful eye for anything evil. Next, he does several leg kicks while simultaneously positioning the lion's head to look up in the direction of the kicking leg. At the same time, the person operating the head must open and close the eyes and mouth and flap the ears. His hands operate the lion's mouth while his own mouth pulls on a string controlling the lion's eyes and ears. After about ten minutes, he is free to do any leg movements he chooses and to raise the head, turn, and shake it. The rest of the dance consists of improvisations created by the person in the head as he maintains the interest of the crowd.

Operating the tail does not require as many intricate movements as does 3 working with the head. Three people work underneath the flowing, velvet tail connected to the back of the head. Their hands grasp the outer edge of the material; they lean forward, bringing their backs parallel to the ground, and point their arms at the ground. They flap their arms in coordination with each other to create a smooth, rippling effect up and down the length of the tail. Their eyes must look forward at all times to anticipate which direction the head will move so they can keep the head and tail looking united. Although their footwork needn't be as exact as the little ballet performed by the dancer inside the lion's head, they have the important job of keeping the tail looking alive, not dragging along behind the head. Also keep in mind that they must continue dancing with their backs bent uncomfortably toward the ground.

The teaser, although not part of the lion-body itself, is an essential player in 4 the lion dance. He wears a painted, Mardi Gras-type mask and represents the evil being who torments the lion until it strikes back and chases the evil one away. The teaser carries a little paper lantern, and he makes his appearance ten minutes after the lion completes his bow. He waves the lantern in front of the lion's face, challenging him to give chase. Once the lion charges, the teaser must travel, on a path of his choice, down the streets of Chinatown. The teaser does not have any set rules or footwork. He randomly runs and jumps in front of the lion, zigzags through the street, and occasionally pauses to playfully tease some of the small children watching from the sidewalk.

Though performing the lion dance might seem to be just for fun, there are   5 rewards that many people are unaware of. While the lion moves through Chinatown, shop owners hang traditional red envelopes with money inside on a stick outside their shops. As the lion passes the shops, someone comes out and waves the money in front of the lion to attract its attention. The beast grabs their money with its mouth, offers a bow of thanks, and moves on. At the end of the day, the lion dancers divide the well-earned money equally among themselves. Lion dancing takes a lot of hard work, but with practice and persistence, the dancers can reap monetary rewards and be proud of their part in this important seasonal dance.

Questions for Discussion

1. What are your impressions of the lion dance now that you have read Donald Inn's essay?
2. Who is Donald Inn's intended audience? What clues in the essay suggest that he is writing for this audience?
3. How effectively does Inn explain the art of lion dancing? Is there anything else you would like to know about the dance?

TOPICS FOR WRITING

Topic 1.   Write a letter in which you use your own words to explain the significance of lion dancing to someone who knows very little about the dance. Your goal in this letter is to communicate how important the lion dance is to people in the Chinese community.

Topic 2.   Think of a ceremony or custom with which you are familiar. Write an explanation of that tradition for someone who knows very little about it. Be sure to do more than summarize what happens; you should break your subject into parts or steps and explain what each is about, why it is important, and if possible, what it means.

THE WRITING PROCESS: PROCESS ANALYSIS

When you give directions to a lost motorist, explain to a fellow student the procedures for writing a paper, or recite a recipe for chocolate mousse, you are analyzing a process. That is, you are breaking down a larger process in order to explain how to get the desired results. Your ability to explain a process will help you write papers for a variety of subjects. You might, for example, describe the process of photosynthesis for a biology class, explain in a political science exam how to pass a bill in the state legislature, or, in a paper for an English class, advise fellow students about the procedures and pitfalls involved in registering for college classes. Many of the writing assignments in this chapter ask you to apply your skills in explaining a process to writing about traditions and rituals that you will observe, read about, or investigate through interviewing.

Additional Considerations for Developing a Topic

An instructor may give you an assignment to write a process analysis that demonstrates your understanding of course material. If you must generate a topic of your own, it is best to pick one with which you are familiar or one in which you have a genuine interest. From the reader's point of view, the most interesting papers explore unfamiliar subjects or introduce a perspective that most people overlook.

If you have difficulty thinking of a topic, the topics for writing that follow the readings in this chapter offer some suggestions. The following questions can also help you identify an interesting topic:

> Have you taken part in a holiday or celebration lately? What happened? How does the ceremony work?
> Do you have any hobbies whose workings might make interesting reading?
> Are any tasks where you work engaging or dangerous?
> What stages do you or people you know seem to go through when they apply for a job, fall in love, or purchase an automobile?

Additional Considerations for Thinking about Your Audience

As with descriptive writing, your task is to recreate the custom or ritual for your reader. Before gathering details for your descriptions of a process, it is important to have a good idea about your purpose, audience, and point of view. The following questions will help you make these decisions:

> What process am I describing?
> What are the major stages, parts, or categories in this process?
> What is my purpose in explaining this process?
> Who is my audience?

Additional Considerations for Preliminary Writing

When drawing an idea wheel or listing ideas, try separating your topic into parts and generating details for each part. Donald Inn, for example, might have drawn the following idea wheel to collect details for his descriptions of

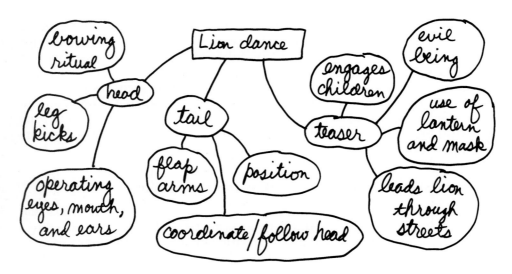

the lion dance. To generate details and explanations about your subtopics, ask
yourself a few of the following questions. Although the word *part* is used in
these questions, you might wish to substitute *stage, step, category,* or *procedure,* depending on your topic.

> What details can I use to describe each part?
> Do any of these parts need defining?
> What is the function of each part?
> What does it contribute to the overall process?
> How do the parts of this process work together?
> Are there problems that should be avoided? What are the consequences
>   of not avoiding them?
> Will a comparison with another topic or activity clarify my point?

Additional Considerations for Organizing Ideas

Make an outline from your list of ideas or idea wheel that represents the order
of ideas you will follow in your paper. Try several different arrangements until
you find one that makes the most sense to you. You may choose to follow the
chronological order of the process or, like Donald Inn, use a spatial arrangement (from lion's head to body to teaser). You might also emphasize the most
important category by discussing it last.

Additional Considerations for Writing a Fast Draft

With your outline beside you, write a fast draft to record as much detail as you
can about the process you are discussing. Revise the essay several times, filling in details that add to your descriptions and explaining the importance of

each part. Be sure to proofread for omissions, sentence structure, spelling, and punctuation.

Additional Considerations for Sharing and Revising

Use the checklist below to revise your paper.

Checklist

❑ Do I have a main point that clarifies my approach to the topic?
❑ What point of view have I used?
❑ Is the point of view consistent throughout the paper? (In other words, if the paper begins with the first person, does it maintain that perspective throughout?)
❑ Are parts of the process distinct from one another?
❑ Do any sections of the paper appear to be out of order?
❑ Are discussions detailed enough or would some benefit from a more detailed description?

FOR FURTHER READING

Kwanzaa: Holiday of "Principles to Live By"
Eugene Morris

Eugene Morris is a writer for The Journal, *a newspaper published in Atlanta, Georgia. For his article on Kwanzaa, Morris interviewed several people who celebrate this African-American harvest festival.*

Alice Lovelace said her five children don't complain each holiday season when 1
they get handmade African toys and books written by African-American authors instead of computerized laser games and combat-fighter planes.

They also understand why their home is decorated with candies, fruit, and 2
place mats instead of a Christmas tree and stockings.

Like millions of other black Americans, the Lovelace family celebrates 3
Kwanzaa (also spelled *Kwanza*), a holiday when African-Americans give thanks for their heritage. Beginning today, Kwanzaa is celebrated the seven days after Christmas.

Derived from an East African Swahili phrase *matunda ya kwanza* or "first 4
fruits," Kwanzaa is neither an African holiday nor a black Christmas. It is an African-American cultural celebration that draws on African harvest festival traditions, like giving thanks for the first crops of the year. It also stresses principles for better living and offers guides to achieve inner peace.

"We started celebrating Kwanzaa as an alternative to the commercializa- 5
tion of Christmas and because Kwanzaa is grounded in moral and cultural
values," said Ms. Lovelace, executive director of an art gallery.

"Kwanzaa teaches principles to live by," she said, "and we thought that 6
was more valuable than celebrating Christmas, which has become so commercial."

Kwanzaa was founded in 1966 by Dr. Maulana Karenga, a black studies 7
professor at California State University campuses in Los Angeles and Long
Beach. Karenga initiated the holiday because he felt blacks needed a holiday
that had historical relevance for blacks and Africans.

Longtime Kwanzaa observers said small celebrations also began about the 8
same time in Atlanta in the homes of some blacks. Other programs and celebrations were held at community centers, black college campuses, and other sites.

Akbar Imhotep, co-chairman of the Atlanta Kwanzaa Committee, said 9
about 900 people attended last year's public displays. He believes some 3,000
to 4,000 Atlantans celebrate on their own.

National Kwanzaa officials said more than 13 million African-Americans 10
celebrate Kwanzaa.

In Atlanta, Kwanzaa '87 celebrations will include displays and demonstra- 11
tions throughout the city. . . .

Kwanzaa was founded under seven principles, referred to as the *Nguzo* 12
Saba. They are unity, self-determination, collective work and responsibility,
cooperative economics, purpose, creativity, and faith.

During Kwanzaa, traditional holiday decorations are replaced by red, 13
black, and green African colors of liberation. Kwanzaa symbols are placed
upon a *mkeka* or place mat, which represents the African foundation of the
holiday. A *kinara* (seven-piece candleholder) and the *mishumaa saba* (seven
candles) are also displayed. One candle is lighted each day.

Other displays include *vibunzi* (corn), which symbolizes children, *mazao* 14
(fruits, nuts, and vegetables), which represent the holiday's origins, African
harvest, the rewards of collective efforts, and the *zawadi* (gifts) primarily given
to the children. However the gifts should be creative, cultural, and educational
and not merely for entertainment.

Each night some families sip a libation (or *tambiko*) from a unity cup (or 15
kikombe) to honor black ancestors. Songs and dances are also performed.

Although Ikenna Ubaka and her daughter celebrate Kwanzaa and 16
Christmas, Ms. Ubaka stresses the religious impact of Christmas and down-
plays its commercialization.

"We try to send the message during Kwanzaa that it is more important to 17
give of yourselves than to spend money on presents," she said. "Kwanzaa deals
with our heritage and our culture."

Dr. Omowale Amuleru-Marshall, a member of the Atlanta Chapter of the 18
Association of Black Psychologists and the faculty of the Morehouse School of
Medicine, said his family celebrates Kwanzaa because of a disillusionment
with Christmas.

"My rejection of Christmas is not a rejection of Christ," he said, "just the   19
way the holiday creates a psychological denial of one's own self and one's own
culture."

RESPONDING TO THE READING

Freewriting

Exercise 9b.   Freewrite about passages that interested you or raised questions for you. Discuss your responses.

Exercise 9c.   Take fifteen minutes or so to freewrite about holidays you celebrate that remind you of Kwanzaa. Are there differences between these holidays?

Building Your Vocabulary

VOCABULARY LIST

Words to Look Up	My Definition	Dictionary Definition
initiated (7)		
self-determination (12)		
libation (15)		

Thinking about Words

Some of the vocabulary in Morris's article on Kwanzaa is probably quite new to you. How does he communicate the definitions of Swahili words to readers who are not likely to be familiar with this language?

Questions for Discussion

1. What facts about Kwanzaa did you learn from reading Morris's article? What explanations about its meaning does Morris record?
2. Write a summary of Morris's article. Imagine that you are writing for someone who has not read this article on Kwanzaa and is not familiar with the tradition and its importance for African Americans.
3. What objections to Christmas are expressed by people Morris interviewed? How do they compare with your own opinion of the holiday?
4. Because Eugene Morris wrote his article on Kwanzaa for a newspaper, most of his paragraphs are only two or three sentences long. These short paragraphs make his article easy to read when the information is printed

in the long columns you see in newspapers. Reread Morris's article and determine which sentences are topic sentences and which are supporting sentences. Indicate in the margins of your textbook where paragraph breaks would be if Morris had used a standard essay format.

TOPICS FOR WRITING

Topic 1.   In his article on Kwanzaa, Eugene Morris explains that the holiday is, in part, a response to the commercialism of Christmas. Write a paper in which you rely on your own memories and observations of Christmas to explain whether you think it is too commercial. Toward the end of the paper offer alternatives to commercialism.

Topic 2.   A harvest festival or spring celebration is usually observed by a whole community, but many customs have significance for individuals as well. Use your own memories and observations to explain what happens at a ceremony that focuses on an individual rite of passage. You might, for example, describe a wedding, funeral, dating ritual, or christening that you have observed. Be careful to do more than just list what happens; also explain the dynamics and meaning behind the rituals, as Donald Inn does for the Lion Dance and Eugene Morris does for Kwanzaa.

Topic 3.   Write a paper explaining key strategies in football or some other sport or activity that you know well. Write your paper for someone who is not as familiar with the sport as you are.

Japanese Tea Ceremony
Vance Horne

In the following article, Vance Horne, a writer for The Olympian, *published in Olympia, Washington, records his observations of one of the most delicate and painstaking of rituals—the Japanese tea ceremony.*

So Choku Naoko, usually known as Mrs. Gower, is kneeling on a Japanese *tatami* mat in her tea room, trying to tell two Westerners about tea.   1

The Westerners are kneeling, too, and their knees are hurting.   2

"If on the one hand people stop striving to achieve more, civilization will stop," she says. "But on the other hand, you have to accept yourself as you are."   3

She pauses long enough for the Westerners to quit thinking about their knees and contemplate this unshakeable paradox. "This is what you have to learn," she says, smiling at the dry humor of it.   4

She is dressed in a beautiful kimono and, except for her eyeglasses, there 5 is nothing about her or her tea room to suggest the modern world. This is what she does for a living, showing people how to leave this world briefly through the Japanese tea ceremony.

In January she performed parts of the ceremony at The Evergreen State 6 College's Tribute to Japan. I had written a few words telling the public that she would do that. Afterwards she invited me to her Burien home to partake of a full ceremony.

I am writing this in the first person because I was one of the two 7 Westerners in the tea room and because I want to confess that the tea ceremony not only impressed me, it baffled me.

The centuries-old ceremony is as tidy as algebra but as full of gestures as 8 an opera. It probably is the most Japanese thing there is. Mrs. Gower, a certified teacher, comes from a tea ceremony school in Japan that has 12,000 students, and she estimates that there are 20 to 30 such schools.

For years I have heard that if you want to understand Japan, you must 9 understand the tea ceremony.

Mrs. Gower's tea room is perhaps 10 feet by 10 feet and a little over 6 feet 10 high. Inside, you see only wood, bamboo, grass mats, rice paper, a sunken pit for a water pot, a small simple chest that holds tea utensils, and a calligraphy scroll.

She built the room inside her son's bedroom when he went to college. 11 After years of living in America with her importer/exporter husband, William, she wanted a room that was totally Japanese.

It is too small for Westerners to gather in comfortably, but that is part of 12 what the ceremony is about, learning to co-exist.

"One-on-one human relationships aren't hard," she says. "But if you have 13 more people, it can become difficult."

The ceremony is a way of making a group of people harmonious in a little 14 space, she explains. Basically, it is done by feeding them and giving them tea.

She enters the tea room on her knees, bowing. Her guests are against one 15 wall, kneeling, and they must know when they, too, must bow. A girls enters, bearing small but beautiful servings of food in black lacquer serving trays.

The guests bow over the food, just as the girl bows. Everyone is in equal- 16 ity, because everyone must know and follow the rituals. Although the girl seems to be a servant, the guests must obey the same rules as she does.

Picking up a food bowl, the guests observe the food as if it were a painting. 17 They turn and inspect the bowls in precise gestures. Eating is a dance, and not a simple one.

"Tea ceremony has certain unavoidable rules," Mrs. Gower says. "We are 18 living in a do-your-own-thing world. This is totally the reverse."

As they finish with a food bowl, the guests take folded paper from their 19 kimonos and wipe the bowl. Then they appreciate its beauty.

The girl pours wine in shallow bowls, and the guests drink, but it's not 20 much wine.

"Tea ceremony was begun by men," Mrs. Gower explains. "About 100   21
years ago we had a big cultural revolution in Japan, and men no longer control everything. Today, 95 to 97 percent of the tea industry is controlled by
females."

"Traditionally, the men drank a lot. Now we don't drink so much; we eat   22
instead." She laughs about this turn of events.

Everything moves slowly in the ceremony, and it takes a long time to get   23
to the tea part of it. The Japanese relish their time in the tea room.

"We are leading a very stressful life," Mrs. Gower says, "and people are try-   24
ing to escape in many ways. As you walk in a Japanese garden, you leave your
stresses behind, and once you enter the tea room you're in a very ideal world."

"In an ideal world we talk only of pleasant subjects, to make people happy.   25
I am actually leading you to a utopian life. I am leading you to the beauty
of life."

But such beauty evades the hand or brain that would enclose it. It is the   26
beauty of *u gen*—the unknown.

But although the beauty is of the unknown, it isn't necessarily unearthly.   27
In trying to explain it Mrs. Gower even speaks of the beauty of an unknown
woman's body beneath her clothes.

When Mrs. Gower finally comes to the tea, she carefully opens the chest   28
and takes implements from it. Before she uses them, she inspects them for
their beauty, turning them this way and that in a ritual of observation.

There is a small ceramic bowl for the tea, a small container holding bright   29
green powdered tea, a simple wood implement that works like a spoon for
measuring the tea, a long-handled wooden dipper for getting water from the
pot and a curious whisk device for stirring the tea.

Her tea room actually is a school room, and she teaches Japanese-   30
Americans the use of these utensils and the rituals of the ceremony as a whole.
There are maybe 18 certified teachers in the Seattle area, she thinks, but she
has one of only two tea rooms.

Actually, she has one American student, a man. The fact that there is but   31
one American makes it clear how Japanese the ceremony is. To learn the ceremony fully usually takes three years.

Using her utensils of ancient design, she makes the tea. It is hard to say in   32
words how careful she is. Perhaps it is what one would imagine heart surgery
to be.

With appropriate bowing on all parts, she serves the tea, and the partici-   33
pants turn the bowls in their hands, admiring them, and at last they drink the
bright green and pleasantly bitter tea, and then they clean their bowls.

Not much has happened in the physical sense. A simple meal that might   34
take 15 minutes has been drawn out to two hours. Although there is much ritual, there is no invoking of gods, no trading of Zen jests.

Mrs. Gower talks of it as a matter of her entertaining guests. "Primarily,   35
entertainment is the love of giving," she says. "Entertainment means nothing
if you just call up the caterer. You must give your time and, if I may say it,
your compassion."

In the end, it is important to see Mrs. Gower as she is. She is not a myste- 36
rious and delicate being, conversing only in Buddhistic subtleties. She is an
outgoing woman full of humor, and she loves to use American slang.

I came away glad to be out of the tea room, because I am not used to such 37
confinement or to such silent ritual or such foreignness. Yet I would like to go
back. I am intrigued.

A plane ticket to Tokyo and two weeks in a hotel might not take me as 38
close to Japan.

In the end, the ceremony reminds me a little of baseball, which is a sport 39
of ritual and of careful geometry, where almost nothing ever happens but it
takes a long time. It too is popular in Japan.

RESPONDING TO THE READING

Freewriting

Exercise 9d.   Freewrite about passages that best explain the Japanese tea
ceremony.

Exercise 9e.   Freewrite about eating habits in your culture that are similar
to or quite different from the tea ceremony.

Building Your Vocabulary

VOCABULARY LIST

Words to Look Up	My Definition	Dictionary Definition
paradox (4)		
partake (6)		
baffled (7)		
calligraphy (10)		
utopian (25)		

Questions for Discussion

1. What is Vance Horne's purpose in writing this article on the Japanese tea
   ceremony?
2. Horne says that the tea ceremony "probably is the most Japanese thing
   there is" (paragraph 8). What can you infer about Japanese culture from
   this ceremony?
3. How has the tea ceremony changed in recent history? How do you explain
   this change?

4. What value might the tea ceremony have for people who " 'are living in a do-your-own-thing world,' " as Mrs. Gower describes it? Discuss an activity in which you participate that demands you behave by the rules of the group.

TOPICS FOR WRITING

Topic 1.   Think of an interesting activity or ceremony you have witnessed. If, for example, you have been somewhere that most people don't know about or have had a unique cultural experience, describe that place or experience in detail. Be sure to explain the meaning or importance of each scene or action you describe.

Topic 2.   Observe a celebration, festival, or ceremony that you have never seen before, and write a description of your experience. To get ideas, you might look in the local newspaper for a Ukranian, Greek, Japanese, or Cajun food festival. Such events often feature folk dancing, which might make for some rich descriptions. Look for tours of ethnic neighborhoods that might be offered in your area, or ask to witness a ceremony in a church, temple, or synagogue that you have never visited.

Topic 3.   One of the values of the Japanese tea ceremony is that it helps the participants relax. Think about ways to relax that are familiar to you. Then, with the help of the writing process, write an essay explaining effective ways to relax. Illustrate each method with detailed examples and explanations.

Topic 4.   If you have further interest in the customs described in this chapter or would like to learn about a different ritual or tradition, ask a librarian to help you find your subject on the INFOTRAC, NEWSBANK, or other computerized information system in your college or local library. If you do not have access to one of these systems, locate the subject in the *Reader's Guide to Periodical Literature.* Use your journal to summarize the information you gather. Then write an explanation of how the ritual or custom you selected is performed and what it means. If you use information from other sources, credit them with a lead-in like "As Jenna Singh says, . . ." or "According to Dr. Edward Lum of the Center for Ethnic Studies, . . ." Consult the readings in this chapter for other examples of lead-ins to source information.

Additional Student Writing

Memories of Thanksgiving Day

When I was eleven, my brother, sister, and I fell in love with the family's main dish. That year mother had brought a turkey home in a cage and we were supposed to fatten it up. Because I was the oldest child, I was responsible for the care and feeding of this ugly bird. But taking care of the turkey turned out to be easier than any of us thought it would be. The hard part came near the end.

I remember so well my sister Molly running from the house with bread crumbs to give the turkey. We had so much fun watching this big bird's neck wiggle every time it gulped down some of the crumbs. It made the funniest sound: "gobble-gobble" but faster than any human could say it. We had a hard time naming this silly creature, but we finally decided on Sam. Every day we would run home from school and play with old Sam, who was starting to look cute, even with that ugly red skin hanging from his chin.

When the big day finally arrived none of us were really ready for it. I guess we were distracted by the preparations; I can still smell the pies and cakes baking the night before. Aunt Helen was at the house early that morning to help mother with the baking and cooking. Around ten Mother yelled from the kitchen, "Norma, go get the cage and put it on the back porch." Dead silence. My brother looked at me; dread filled us both because we knew old Sam's fate. "Is Mom going to kill Sam?" my brother asked. "Not if I can help it. Come on Felton," I shouted. "We've got work to do."

We ran as fast as we could down to the barn. When we opened the cage to set him free, Sam thought it was time to play. He started waddling around looking for food. I remember thinking, "You dummy, you are the food." We had a hard time getting him to run off into the woods. Finally all three of us had to charge him, yelling and screaming like fools.

I will never forget the look on my mother's face when she saw the empty cage. Her mouth was drawn tight across her face. Her eyes were almost shut. She just stood there glaring at us. But Aunt Helen saved the day when she started laughing. While taking some chickens out of the freezer, she reminded mother of the things they used to do as children.

I'm grown now, with children of my own. We all come together on Thanksgiving Day, just as my aunts and uncles did years ago, and share stories about things that happened in years past while the children were growing up. The stories they share with me on Thanksgiving Day are incredible. For example, I cooked a thirty pound turkey one year. It turned out so beautifully, so nice and brown. I put it on the counter while I baked the pies. One of the boys went by and cut a big piece of meat out of the top of it. I was so angry when I discovered it that I could have screamed, and I became even angrier when neither of them would tell me who did it. I was just about to punish both of them when I remembered how I felt when my mother was so angry about our letting Sam go.

When my son turned eighteen, we were talking about past holidays and the things we did. Tim said, "Mom, remember five years ago when someone couldn't wait until dinner and tore a chunk out of the turkey?" I said, "Yes." "Well it was me," he said. This opened the discussion for other confessions. My son David said, "Yeah, Mom, and I'm the one who filled your gas tank with frogs that year, too."

In my family, Thanksgiving Day is a time of remembering, truthtelling, and forgiveness for some of the things we've done over the years. Our custom of telling stories and sharing love and memories has persisted through the generations; it links us with our past and connects us to the future.

—Norma Davis

Questions for Discussion

1. What would you say was the writer's purpose in relating these events?
2. Without looking back at what you read, jot down your general impression of the person writing this recollection. What sort of person is she?
3. What are the most important ideas that Davis communicated to you?
4. What organizational pattern does Davis use? How does she connect the childhood scenes with scenes from her adulthood? Are these connections effective?

The Making of a Quinceañera

A quinceañera is a Mexican-American celebration of a young girl's coming of age, "a sweet 15" party. This celebration mixes the tradition of the Catholic church and local social customs to make one huge birthday party. It includes a morning mass, a reception, a dinner party, and a dance. If a family has a daughter, they begin planning months ahead because a quinceañera takes lots of work and, above all, lots of money.

The actual preparations for a quinceañera should begin at least three to six months before the day arrives. I should know; my family and I have made quinceañeras for each of my two sisters. We started by finding out who would be able to participate in the celebration because it takes lots of family and friends to help make the quinceañera. For example, we needed fourteen damas or female escorts, fourteen chambelanes, male escorts, and eight pairs of godparents, padrinos and madrinas, who accompany the quinceañera herself. One chambelán is the girl's main escort. There are fifteen couples in all, one for each of the girl's fifteen years. The teens in the quinceañera party are usually her awkward, shy friends from school. The taller girls always seem to tower over the short, embarrassed boys.

The godparents are essential to the success of the quinceañera because they pay for just about everything, including the liquor, which is often as much as five kegs of beer and a case of hard liquor. The girl's family must also find godparents to pay for the eight-layer birthday cake, ten cases of champagne, the reception hall, a mariachi band for entertainment during the meal, a live band and D.J. for the dance party, invitations, and finally, the dress, ring, shoes, medallion, crown, and rosario or bible for the young quinceañera.

Once the family finds people who can afford to sponsor the quinceañera, they have to decide on the colors of the dresses that the damas and godmothers will be wearing. Then there are the colors of the tuxedos to choose for the chambelánes and godfathers; each group wears a different color to match the damas and godmothers.

One month before the celebration the damas, chambelanes, godparents and parents of the quinceañera and her escort practice at least twice a week for a month so they will be able to do the traditional waltz at the beginning of the party. The birthday girl dances the first waltz with her father, after which everyone at the reception yells "Happy Birthday," and the dancing opens up for everyone.

About a week before the quinceañera, the parents of the girl must decide on what they are going to serve for dinner and how many people they must feed. The most common dishes served at a quinceañera are carnitas, pork meat, beans, rice, and salad. Each dish usually serves from two to three hundred guests.

On the night before the quinceañera, everyone involved attends church. There the priest shows them the order for entering and exiting the church and also where the godparents, damas, chambelanes, and quinceañera will be sitting during the church ceremony. After practice, everyone goes to the reception hall to practice the waltz for the last time and to help decorate the reception hall.

Finally, on the day of the quinceañera, everyone is happy, nervous, and relieved that the work, time, and money put into this one special day is about to give them something they are proud of. This day will belong to a young, fifteen-year-old <u>quinceañera</u> who will cherish this day, along with her family and friends, who have made this day possible, for the rest of her life.

—Miguel A. Rodriguez

Questions for Discussion

1. Evaluate Miguel Rodriguez's essay in small groups. What are the strengths of this essay? Do you have suggestions for improving the organization or descriptions in "The Making of a *Quinceañera*"?
2. Why might Rodriguez have used Spanish terms in his essay? In general, are his words well-chosen?
3. How is Miguel Rodriguez's description of a *quinceañera* similar to or different from events for teenagers you have attended?
4. Imagine that a relative has expressed interest in putting on a wedding, graduation, baptism, or other family celebration. What advice would you give about how to prepare for the event?

Football on Monday Nights

Since the age of eighteen I have watched "Monday Night Football." I am not alone in participating in this ritual. Across the country and now, thanks to satellite programming, in some European countries, fans turn on their sets and wait for the announcer to introduce the players. But if the game itself hasn't changed much since I was a girl, the fans have. Right in keeping with the woman's movement, football now acknowledges its female viewers, and we have a degree of legitimacy I did not enjoy before.

In the old days football was a man's game. My father came home from work, kicked off his shoes, gathered my brothers around him, and called for beer and peanuts. I was exiled to the kitchen with my mother, doomed to see the game in short glimpses as I trudged in with popcorn and soft drinks for my brothers. My mother hated the game, as she hated scrubbing the floors and doing the laundry. The game, to her, was just another sign of the lack of equality in the household. But it took me years to make the connection, and meanwhile, because I loved my brothers and wanted to be like them, I loved football, too.

Times have changed, and with them, my own patterns of watching football. Now I love the game, not because of my brothers, but because I can express my feelings without worrying what people are thinking as they hear me yelling for my team. Twenty years ago, if a woman yelled over a game, she would have been thought crude, or worse, she would be hounded out of the place. But today it is different. It is a time when friends get together; they bring their own popcorn and drinks, and nobody is sentenced to an evening in the kitchen.

On the occasions when I have gone to a bar to watch a game rather than have friends over, I have noticed that couples and even groups of women are watching the large-screen TV, laughing, drinking, and eating the special dishes served up for the Monday night crowd. Most bars offer free popcorn and nuts—no more kitchen-prep for moms and their daughters. Some bars and restaurants have begun promoting the event in a big way. I have heard of bars that offer specials on drinks for "ladies," have a Tee-shirt giveaway to the first ten customers, and sell earrings in the shape of your favorite team's logo. Thanks to their booming business, these bars welcome women to a sport that once was reserved exclusively for men.

Now a woman living in more liberated times, I no longer feel less important than the men around me as I did when my father and brothers had exclusive use of the living room for Monday night games. I have the same freedom to laugh, drink, and offer my opinion of a team's performance that they did. I don't feel as isolated, either—the drudge in the kitchen who comes out with the snacks but is never invited to stay. I for one appreciate the change.

—Patricia Caldera

Questions for Discussion

1. Which of Patricia Caldera's descriptions is developed most effectively? Should she consider adding details or explanations to any of her descriptions to make them more vivid?
2. Compare what was expected of Patricia Caldera's mother to your own mother's role in the household when you were growing up.
3. Describe a time when you have felt that you did not have the freedom to express yourself.
4. Have you noticed any changes in your lifetime in the way women (or men) are excluded from particular events?

INTERVIEWING

Most of the information you read in your local and campus newspapers is obtained from interviewing. For example, during the crisis in Somalia, local newspapers and television stations interviewed soldiers returning from Mogadishu and the members of their families who had been left behind. For papers you will write in college, interviewing can be an important part of preliminary writing because the authorities, expert witnesses, and other people you wish to survey may provide evidence in support of your points. If, for example, you are writing a paper about whether parents should force their children to take piano lessons, join girl scouts, or attend Chinese or Hebrew school to preserve their heritage, you might ask parents you know, teachers, and classmates to explain their positions on this issue. The resulting survey will give you several people's reasoning about the topic—reasoning that you can use to write an informational paper about the advantages or disadvantages of enrolling children in programs "for their own good."

For some of the topics in this chapter you can interview fellow students, or experts in your community or on campus. If you decide to interview someone outside the classroom, consult the instructions for conducting interviews and writing oral history that appear at the end of this chapter.

FOR PRACTICE

Pair up with a classmate from a different culture and interview each other to find out more about that person and his or her culture. You may wish to use the questions below to get you started.

Where were you born? ZAMBALES,
What is your family's history? 2 TAGALOG
What was your first language? What other languages are spoken in your
    family?
How big is your family? BIG
What is unique about your family?
What sorts of food did you eat at home? FILIPINO
Does your family practice a religion? How great a role does religion
    play in your family? VERY GREAT
What does your family value? (Consider such things as strength, intelligence, honesty, good cooking, money, education, and loyalty.)
What examples can you think of that illustrate these values?
What stories did you read about or hear when you were growing up?
Do you still feel that you are a part of the culture you were born into?
    How do you maintain that culture, or if you don't, what cultural values have you adopted?

Student Writing

When Liz Ann Larson was assigned to interview Randy Lozoya, she began by asking some of the questions for interviewing listed above. She found that some of the questions got better responses than others, so she asked follow-up questions on those. As she was interviewing Randy, she noticed that he talked a lot about the languages that his parents spoke at home. She went back through her notes once she had finished the interview and looked for ideas, examples, and situations that related to language and then grouped what she found in the following rough outline.

Introduction

Randy's parents' background:
    Where they are from
    How they met
    One speaks English; the other, Spanish
    Maybe start with a conversation between them
Spanish dominant language at home
    Why? Father at work
    Children's first language is Spanish
    Problem: Oldest brother understands very little at school
    "Problem" got better for younger children
Randy sees value in knowing more than one language
    Example: translates at the hospital where he works
Randy wants his daughter to be bilingual
    Doesn't want her to be confused in school
        Won't speak Spanish to her until she's started kindergarten
Conclusion
    Randy wants to provide the best possible life for his daughter
        He will stress different things than his family did
        He will emphasize education
        He wants to provide a stable home life and to be a good example for his daughter

When she had completed her outline, Liz Ann developed each of the ideas she listed, adding details and explanations where she needed them.

Randy: The Best of Two Cultures

"Good morning! How's it going?"
¿Comó amaneciste?"
"Huh?"
"¿Has almorzado?"
"What was that?"
"¿Qué?"

So I imagine the first conversation between Ramón and his new co-worker, Rosie, in the warehouse where they worked. Rosie, a beautiful young woman from Aguaprieta, Mexico, spoke no English. Ramón, a Mexican-American born in Sacramento, spoke little Spanish. Yet they were able to teach each other enough English and Spanish to communicate with each other, fall in love, get married, and raise a family.

Randy was the second child to be born into this bilingual family. But just because his father spoke English and his mother spoke Spanish doesn't mean that Randy and his siblings had no language problems. Since Ramón was always at work, Rosie naturally talked to her children in Spanish, which became the dominant language at home. As a result, when Randy's older brother, Ron, started kindergarten, he had a difficult time because he didn't know English. Ron learned English in school and taught some to his younger brother Randy, which made entering school a little easier for him. Their younger sister had the easiest time learning English, for once they started school, both Ron and Randy spoke English to her.

At the time, Randy and his brother thought that speaking only Spanish before starting kindergarten put them at a disadvantage. If their teacher spoke too fast, they could not understand her instructions. It was also embarrassing when they could not respond to what a classmate was saying because he or she was using words that were not familiar to them. Learning to read presented a special challenge because Randy and Ron weren't just learning new words and phrases; they were learning a whole new language as well. However, Randy now sees great value in being bilingual. He is proud to be able to speak both English and Spanish well. He even translates for the doctors at Mercy Hospital, where he works as a medical technician. One night at work, Randy's language skills proved indispensable when he helped out a Spanish-speaking family. The husband had had a heart attack, and Randy was the only one in the hospital who could explain to the woman what was wrong with her husband and what the doctors were going to do to try and save him.

Now that Randy has a daughter of his own, he would like her to take advantage of being bilingual. But he is a little afraid of confusing three-year-old Rene with two languages at this time. He has decided to speak English to her for the present so that she won't have the trouble in school that he and his brother had. After Rene has learned the basics and has started kinder-garten, Randy plans to teach her Spanish.

Randy has learned not only to get along in English but also to thrive. He now understands the value of getting an education, a value that wasn't

emphasized when he was a child. In contrast, Randy wants to stress education for his daughter, he wants to provide a stable, caring home life for her,
and he wants to be a good example for her. As Randy has such clear, worthwhile goals and the drive to attain them, I am sure he will succeed. In fact,
he is already on his way.

Questions for Discussion

1. What is the thesis of this essay? Does it appear anywhere in Liz Ann
    Larson's paper, or is it implied?
2. Reread the opening dialogue of "Randy: The Best of Two Cultures." How
    well did this opening piqué your interest? Is it an effective introduction for
    the rest of the essay?
3. Why was Randy's older brother, Ron, so important to his early education?
    How have family members, friends, or teachers helped you when you were
    having difficulties in school?
4. Based on Randy's experience, what are the advantages and disadvantages
    of growing up in a bilingual household? How do Randy's own difficulties
    and concerns compare with your experience and the experiences of people
    you know?

THE WRITING PROCESS: WRITING ORAL HISTORY

If you completed the preceding writing assignment that asked you to interview
a classmate and write a paper based on the information you gathered, you have
already had some practice writing an oral history. Assignments in this and
other chapters ask you to incorporate information you obtain about other people—friends, family, or people knowledgeable about your topic—into your
writing. The following suggestions are to help you apply the steps in the writing process to the writing of an oral history or to other research projects.

Additional Considerations for Developing a Topic

Sometimes the most difficult part of writing an oral history is choosing a person to interview. Some students can think of a dozen people they would like to
know more about; their problem is how to choose among them. Other students have difficulty thinking of anyone they would like to interview. Most of
the time, a family member or acquaintance who has an interesting personal
history or an unusual lifestyle makes a good subject for an oral history essay.
Individuals' lives are often caught up in the history of a region, a country, or
sometimes several regions or countries, so usually after giving it some
thought, most students are able to find someone whose story is worth telling.

Additional Considerations for Preliminary Writing

Interviewing Techniques

Interviewing can prove a valuable source of information for papers and oral projects in college classes. The instructions that follow will prepare you to interview family members, friends, or acquaintances to gather information for oral histories. Here are some general suggestions that will help you conduct your interviews.

1. Pin down your topic, purpose, and audience before you meet the person you want to interview. (For example, if you want to write about the poor coverage of community college football in the local newspapers, be sure you have identified both a purpose and an audience before you go to interview the college football coach. Knowing that you hope to convince the local newspapers to cover more games will help you choose questions to ask the coach.)

2. Develop questions that relate to your purpose for writing. You will have difficulty getting much information that you can use in a paper unless you have written down what you want to know. (Refer to the preceding section on interviewing for sample interviewing questions.)

3. Make an appointment with the person you want to interview as soon as you know your topic. It takes time to reach busy people, so be aware that you may not be able to schedule an appointment for several weeks from the time you call. Occasionally you will have to settle for a phone interview.

4. Explain the purpose of your interview to the people you want to get information from; always let people know that you would like to interview them for a class assignment. Most people are flattered if you tell them quite sincerely that they have some expertise that would be useful to you in writing your paper. Remember to respect people's privacy, however. If you are asked not to use the interviewee's name, discuss a particular topic, or reveal certain information, do exactly what you are requested to do.

5. Ask if you may use a tape recorder during the session. It is difficult to write down all the information you might need while conducting your interview, and you cannot depend on your memory to recall the details and sequence of events. If you use a tape recorder, write down key ideas during the most important part of the interview so you will be able to fast forward to those sections on the tape. That way you won't have to listen to hours of tape that may not contain information you can use in your paper.

6. Stick to the questions you prepared as much as possible to avoid recording long stories or lines of questioning that don't have much to do with your paper. On the other hand, be ready to let one question

lead to another if the interview seems to be going in an interesting direction that you hadn't anticipated.

7. Advise the person you are interviewing that you may need to call and verify information or ask follow-up questions. Occasionally you may want to schedule a second interview.

Preliminary writing is often one of the most difficult parts of the writing process, and that is certainly the case with projects that involve interviewing and other research. After conducting an interview, you are faced with piles of notes or several hours of tape recordings. How do you make sense of all this?

As soon as you can, organize the notes you took during the interview and transcribe parts of the tape that you might be able to use in your paper. Freewrite about your dominant impression of the interview. This impression may have to do with the person you interviewed or the events he or she related. Once you have that idea, write down what you remember about the interview that relates to that dominant impression. Refer to your notes once you have exhausted your memory and pick up any ideas that develop the dominant impression.

Use techniques for preliminary writing you have learned to expand your notes, and do an initial arrangement of material. Try cutting and pasting your notes and putting them in stacks according to topic and subtopic ideas. By this time you should have a list of ideas that you can arrange into an outline of the sequence of events you will discuss in the paper. Write a tentative thesis early in the process and select or reject material based on its relevance to that thesis. To check your progress, try answering these questions:

What's the main point or dominant impression?
What are my supporting points?
What point of view will I use?
Do I have enough information to develop my point?
Do I need further preliminary writing to gather additional details?

Additional Considerations for Organizing Ideas

Your job as interviewer and writer is to *make sense* of the details you have gathered. That means organizing details in a sequence that is easy to follow and explaining why things happened, what is important about them, and how they relate to the dominant impression or main point you plan to make. Like most narratives, oral histories usually follow the order of events as they happen in a person's life. Once in a while you may want to use a flashback to add interest or emphasis.

Additional Considerations for Writing a Fast Draft

When you are satisfied that you have an outline for your paper and enough evidence to develop ideas, write a draft. You may write the draft in one of two ways:

(1) write the essay quickly, knowing that you will revise later to add evidence you gathered in your interviews, or (2) write the draft slowly and carefully, gradually working in the information you gathered during the interviews.

Additional Considerations for Sharing Your Writing and for Making Final Revisions

When you revise your paper, be sure to identify the subject of your oral history. In the body of your essay, put quotation marks around words and phrases spoken by the person you interviewed. In addition to using direct quotes, you may **paraphrase,** or put your subject's ideas in your own words.

The notes below were taken by a student, Sam Masuno, during an interview with his mother. The first paragraph of his essay, "To Be Thankful," appears after the notes so that you can see how Sam incorporated into his paper the information he gathered during the interview.

INTERVIEWING NOTES
Born in Kure, Japan, during the war—February 22, 1943.
Kure made ships for Japan and was bombed constantly.
First memories are of the roar of planes, constantly flying. Heard them
    even as an infant lying in crib.
Was youngest in the family—had three older brothers and sisters. Had
    a nice home in Kure. Had to move when the bombings increased.
Mother bundled her up and strapped her to her back. Family literally
    ran from Kure, hoping the bombs would not hit them.
Father took wheelbarrow and filled it with prized possessions. He ran,
    guiding his family out of Kure. They ran to safety.

OPENING PARAGRAPH
    My mother, Naoko Uemitsu, was born in war-ravaged Japan on February 22, 1943. World War II roared in her ears as she lay in a crib in the ship-building city of Kure. Naoko lived in a nice Japanese home with her father, mother, two older brothers, and one older sister. Sadly, the bombs kept beating on the city of Kure, angrier day by day. The time arrived when it was too dangerous to stay, and the Uemitsu family moved. Naoko's mother ran with Naoko strapped on her back, bundled in lots of blankets. Naoko's father placed all the family's most prized possessions in a wheelbarrow, and led the family to safety.

Here is a checklist to use when revising your essay.

Checklist

❑ Does the essay have a main point or dominant impression? What is it? Have I adequately supported that point or impression?

❑ Is the point I am making in each paragraph expressed in a topic sentence or implied by the details and examples I have given?

❑ Would additional details, examples, quotes, or explanations make my point clearer?

❑ Do I include sufficient details and explanations to convey the importance of each particular person or event?

❑ In general, have I written a vivid account of a portion of this person's life?

❑ Do the paragraphs in my essay present a clear sequence of events, or do I need to change the order of a few paragraphs?

❑ Have I proofread my sentences carefully enough to catch words I omitted by mistake and any errors in punctuation, spelling, or sentence construction (such as fragments or run-on sentences)?

Once you have a revised draft of your paper, show it to the person you interviewed to make sure the facts, names, and occurrences are correct. People are usually pleased to see how interesting their lives seem when information about them is organized and edited by a careful writer.

Now read the complete essay that Sam Masuno wrote as a poignant tribute to his mother and grandmother.

To Be Thankful

My mother, Naoko Uemitsu, was born in war-ravaged Japan on February 22, 1943. World War II roared in her ears as she lay in a crib in the ship-building city of Kure. Naoko lived in a nice Japanese home with her father, mother, two older brothers, and one older sister. Sadly, the bombs kept beating on the city of Kure, angrier day by day. The time arrived when it was too dangerous to stay, and the Uemitsu family moved. Naoko's mother ran with Naoko strapped on her back, bundled in lots of blankets. Naoko's father placed all of the family's most prized possessions in a wheelbarrow and led the family to safety.

The Uemitsu family arrived in the peaceful countryside of Kurose many days later. They were tired, hungry, and scared but very happy to be alive. Naoko's father's parents lived on a farm in Kurose, and the family stayed there. This was a life Naoko had never experienced before—a lull in a raging storm. Her father (otōsan) began a job as a high-school principal, and Naoko's brothers and sister began to attend school once more. Naoko's mother (okāsan) was a faithful Japanese wife and mother and worked hard at raising the children. Life during wartime was very harsh even in Kurose. Distant bombings could be felt all day long. Food was very scarce and drinking water even scarcer, yet okāsan taught the Uemitsu children to be very humble and appreciate all of the little things in life. "Kansha, kansha," okāsan would say gently. "Be thankful, be thankful." Okāsan was very religious and repeatedly thanked God for blessing them with the incredible good fortune of living so well in the midst of a horrible war. "Our whole family is eating together," okāsan would say with tears in her eyes. "Kansha, kansha."

On August 6, 1945, the atomic bomb was dropped on the city of Hiroshima, fifty miles away from Kurose. Otōsan saw the nightmarish mushroom cloud that darkened the sky and was burdened with grief. That day was full of tears cried for friends and relatives who perished in Hiroshima. Naoko, who was only two years old, cried in her sleep.

After much confusion and devastation, the war finally ended and the Uemitsu family decided to move once more. Naoko was now six years old and she wanted to go to school. When the A-bomb was dropped, the city of Hiroshima was not destroyed entirely. In the middle of Hiroshima was Higeyama (little hill). To one side of the hill was utter destruction, but the other side, thanks to Higeyama, survived with only minor damage. The Uemitsu family moved in with an aunt who lived on the habitable side of Hiroshima. At such a young age, Naoko was shocked to see the hibakusha, the people who were deformed from the effects of the bomb. She was at first disgusted and frightened of their hideously melted faces and bodies. But okāsan taught her otherwise. "You appreciate people for how they look on the inside, not on the outside. These, too, are beautiful." Naoko took this to heart and overcame her fear of the hibakusha. In fact, Naoko began to help them in any way she could. She held their hands when they stumbled. She gave them water when they were thirsty. She would soothe them when they cried out in pain and loneliness. Naoko helped the hibakusha to momentarily forget the pain and smile. She was eager to let them know that people still listened and cared.

Naoko Uemitsu was born during World War II, an era of full of pain, confusion, and anger. But Naoko did not succumb to the bitterness of her surroundings. She learned to appreciate the little things in life—to always look at the brighter side. "Kansha, kansha," my mother says to this day. "Be thankful, be thankful."

—Sam Masuno

Questions for Discussion

1. What is the dominant impression in "To Be Thankful"? How does Masuno convey this impression?
2. What do you think his purpose was in writing this narrative? How well did he achieve it?
3. What do you remember reading about the United States attack on Hiroshima and Nagasaki, the bombings that ended World War II? What did Masumo's narrative add to your understanding of that event?
4. Describe the point of view Masumo uses in this narrative. How does he include Naoko's perspective?

TOPICS FOR WRITING

Topic 1.   Write an essay describing how your ancestors came to the United States. For information on your family's history, interview several family members. In your essay, identify your ancestors' country of origin, their reasons for coming to the United States, and what you know about their early adjustments.

Topic 2.   Go to the library at your school, the public library, or a local historical society and ask the librarian to help you locate the microfilm or microfiche for any newspaper printed on August 7, 1945. You might also look at articles printed one or two days later. Choose one article that covers the bombing of Hiroshima and write a paragraph or short paper in which you explain the main point the writer of the article makes about the bombing. Be sure to refer to the words and phrases that helped you find the writer's main point.

10

Self and Others

Probably it happened little by little, year by year, as we grew up and as we did all the things that adults do. And one day we woke up and realized that this wasn't the way we thought it would be. Our friends were gone. And we wondered what ever happened to those guys and girls, those friends who didn't stay friends forever.

—Art Jahnke

When someone "describes the world and you are not in it, there is a moment of psychic disequilibrium, as if you looked into a mirror and saw nothing."

—Adrienne Rich
(quoted in "Personal Politics: A Lesson in Straight Talk")

The readings in this chapter explore the individual's experience of self and others. Art Jahnke's "What Ever Happened to Friendship?" analyzes how once-precious friendships are lost. The authors of "Personal Politics: A Lesson in Straight Talk" and "Just Walk On By" write about their painful attempts to relate to others who view them as "different," even suspicious. This chapter also introduces techniques for classifying ideas in your writing. Selections from Art Jahnke's "What Ever Happened to Friendship?" illustrate some of the characteristics of essays that use classification as the dominant writing strategy.

CLASSIFYING

A common way of ordering experience is to classify similar experiences, ideas, and information in order to analyze the characteristics common to each category. In Art Jahnke's article, he analyzes the "ABCs of lost friendships" or the three ways we lose friends.

Characteristics of Classifying

Purpose, Audience, and Point of View

Like process analysis, classification essays need a purpose—a reason for grouping people, places, events, or objects into categories—and that purpose is usually stated in a thesis or implied in the body of the essay.

In the opening paragraphs of his essay, Art Jahnke establishes his point of view, audience, and purpose for writing "What Ever Happened to Friendship?"

> Once there were friends who were friends forever. Once there were lots of guys who were always there to shoot a few hoops, give us a lift downtown, or loan us a few bucks. And once there were lots of girls who would listen all night and never laugh, no matter how goofy or self-indulgent our complaints. We never worried about whether they would be there for us. What was there to worry about? There were lots of friends, and friends, true friends, were friends forever.
>
> But something happened. Maybe it happened when we went away to college. Maybe it happened when we got married. Or when we started working 40, 50, and 60 hours a week. Or had kids. Or got divorced, changed jobs, and moved to another town.
>
> Probably it happened little by little, year by year, as we grew up and as we did all the things that adults do. And one day we woke up and realized that this wasn't the way we thought it would be. Our friends were gone. And we wondered what ever happened to those guys and girls, those friends who didn't stay friends forever.
>
> This is a story about what went wrong while we were all so busy doing what was right: marrying and having families and

1

2

3

4

working the long days that would get us a home and get us ahead. . . . I'll try to tell you . . . what I know about the loss of friendship. . . . I'll put the different ways in which I have lost friends into three categories. The first, category A, of the ABCs of lost friends, is neglect. Here's how it works.

Jahnke writes in the first person about his experiences with losing friends. By using the pronoun "we," he makes a personal appeal to his readers and suggests that their experiences are probably similar to his own. Jahnke enhances this connection by explaining exactly what he intends to do: "I'll try to tell you . . . what I know about the loss of friendship." In addition, his examples identify the audience as anyone who has gone to college, married, divorced, had kids, worked long hours, moved, or changed jobs. In other words, he appeals to a broad reading population.

Art Jahnke's purpose is to explain what can go wrong with friendships. His thesis stated how he will discuss these losses: "I'll put the different ways in which I have lost friends into three categories." He mentions the first category— neglect—in the introduction. The other two categories, violation of personal rules and rejection of someone no longer liked, come up later in the essay.

Not all essays are as straightforward as Jahnke's, and in some essays, Jahnke's style of addressing the reader personally might not be appropriate. His style does, however, illustrate how audience, purpose, and point of view can work together in an essay.

Strong Support for Each Category

Experienced writers who discuss categories take care to provide adequate details, examples, definitions, and explanations for their categories. Not all categories will have equal importance in an essay, but each should have enough support to give readers a clear understanding of it.

Jahnke's discussion of his categories is lengthy and thorough. His explanations include personal experiences with the loss of friends and excerpts from interviews with experts and acquaintances. The following segment from his article illustrates the variety of sources he uses as evidence for the third category of lost friends. They include quotes from authorities on the subject of friendship, information gathered during interviews, the experience of a friend, his own experience, and an incident in the life of an acquaintance.

There is a third category, the C in the ABCs of lost friends. It's the fastest, dirtiest, and most painful way to go. Psychologist Paul Wright calls it "a negation or a denial of a friend's personalized interest." David D'Alessandro calls it betrayal, a violation of the rules. 41

"The rules of my friendships are very simple," said D'Alessandro. "They are based on Italian tradition. Unless I tell you otherwise, assume that anything I tell you is confidential. When I lived in New York, I had a very good friend, a roommate who broke a 42 confidence and told another friend something I did not want known. I moved out, and I haven't talked about it since."

It wasn't only macho Italian men who told me that they have no patience with friends who break the rules. A professional woman in her forties, call her woman A, told me this story. Her best friend, woman B, whom she had known for 10 years, betrayed confidences about woman A's future plans to a third person they both knew. When woman A found out, she didn't speak to woman B for five months, and then only after they had reaffirmed the rules of their relationship.   **43**

I heard stories about a different kind of betrayal: the betrayal that results from a failure to follow the rules of mutual aid. A friend told me that he had suffered months of shame because he wasn't there to help a friend weather an emotional breakdown. I know that scenario well. For years I watched from afar while a friend crept more deeply into drugs, from recreational use to finally being a junkie. I watched as his wife left him. I watched as he lost his job, and I watched as they took him away to prison for writing bad checks. Did my friend feel betrayed? He should have.   **44**

A businessman I know said he felt betrayed when a friend steadfastly refused to discuss his own divorce. "He walked out on his wife," the business man said. "Because of the close relationship I have had with him for 20 years, I tried repeatedly to reach out. There was no acknowledgment on his part of responsibility for his action or for the damage. I felt that he wasn't playing by the ground rules of the friendship. I had expectations that certain things would happen. It was his failure even to talk about it that bugged me, and now the relationship has been soured."   **45**

In his discussion of the second category of lost friendships—letting go of a friend—Jahnke *defines* friendship for the reader. Here again, he offers his definition as well as the definitions of experts who have written books on the subject of human relations. Jahnke defines friendship as "that voluntary, nonsensual love affair between two people." Robert Weiss, professor at the University of Massachusetts, offers this definition of a friend: "Essentially, it is someone we maintain a friendship with when there is no reason for doing so except for the relationship. There is no kinship obligation. It is not someone we work with, so there is no work obligation. It's not necessarily a neighbor, so there is no neighborhood obligation." In other words, the relationship is an end in itself. Jahnke uses these definitions in later discussions of what makes a good friendship and in interviews in which he asks people what they think friends do for each other.

Clear Organization

In most essays organized by categories of experience, writers save the most important point for the end of their paper. The logic behind this arrangement is that people are more likely to remember the last thing they read. The organization also adds drama to the paper because it builds to its strongest point.

Art Jahnke makes the order of his discussion clear in topic sentences. If you remember, he says, "The first, category A, of the ABCs of lost friends, is neglect." For the next thirteen paragraphs he explains how this particular abandonment occurs. He announces his second category with this topic sentence: "My second category in the ABCs of lost friends may be less lamentable than the first but no less saddening. It is letting go, cutting bait—deliberately blowing off a relationship." Twenty-two paragraphs later, and after much detailed support, he says, "There is a third category, the C in the ABCs of lost friends. It's the fastest, dirtiest, and most painful way to go. Psychologist Paul Wright calls it 'a negation or a denial of a friend's personalized interest.' David D'Alessandro calls it betrayal, a violation of the rules."

FOR PRACTICE

What transitional words and phrases link the three topic sentences discussed above? What pattern of organization do they suggest?

What Ever Happened to Friendship?
Art Jahnke

Art Jahnke is the Articles Editor at Boston *magazine and teaches journalism at Harvard University summer school. His work has appeared in many magazines and newspapers.*

Once there were friends who were friends forever. Once there were lots of guys who were always there to shoot a few hoops, give us a lift downtown, or loan us a few bucks. And once there were lots of girls who would listen all night and never laugh, no matter how goofy or self-indulgent our complaints. We never worried about whether they would be there for us. What was there to worry about? There were lots of friends, and friends, true friends, were friends forever. 1

But something happened. Maybe it happened when we went away to college. Maybe it happened when we got married. Or when we started working 40, 50, and 60 hours a week. Or had kids. Or got divorced, changed jobs, and moved to another town. 2

Probably it happened little by little, year by year, as we grew up and as we did all the things that adults do. And one day we woke up and realized that this wasn't the way we thought it would be. Our friends were gone. And we wondered what ever happened to those guys and girls, those friends who didn't stay friends forever. 3

This is a story about what went wrong while we were all so busy doing what was right: marrying and having families and working the long days that would get us a home and get us ahead. . . . I'll try to tell you . . . what I know 4 about the loss of friendship. . . . I'll put the different ways in which I have lost friends into three categories. The first, category A, of the ABCs of lost friends, is neglect. Here's how it works:

My oldest friend lives in eastern Connecticut, about an hour and 15 min-   5 utes from Boston. I've known this man since we were in the first grade, since we used to play with blocks together. In high school we caroused together: I remember my mother chastening him as he drove away from my house late one night, leaving me reeling in the driveway from too much beer.

After college we worked together as landscapers—sweating together, taking   6 down trees and putting up stone walls, pissing together, and talking about the weirdness of John Milton, whose works we had studied with the same professor. When I left that job and headed south, for Mexico, I quoted to him from a poem written by the Chinese poet Li Po to a friend about 1,200 years ago:

> And if you ask how I regret that parting:
> It is like flowers falling at Spring's end
> Confused, whirled in a tangle.
> What is the use of talking, and there is no end of
> talking,
> There is no end of things in the heart.

Is it true that there is no end of things in the heart? I don't know. But I   7 haven't seen my friend in five years. Because I moved? No. Because I got divorced? No. Because I remarried? No. It's because I haven't called him. Because I neglected to call.

Most of the people to whom I talked while researching this story were men   8 and women whom I had met in either social or professional settings and who had impressed me as thoughtful, articulate, and sane. One of the first was David D'Alessandro, 38, president of the corporate sector at John Hancock. D'Alessandro is an interesting guy. Around town, he has the reputation of being a tough wheeler-dealer who knows his mind and speaks it. Hancock hired him five years ago to move the company's image out of colonial times and into the modern age. He is credited with Hancock's decision to spend $10 million on the Boston Marathon and $7 million on TV spots during football bowl games. He took over Michael Dukakis's advertising campaign in the last months of the Duke's doomed quest. When I told him I wanted to talk about the importance of friends, he chuckled.

"It's funny you should ask about that," he said. "It's something that has   9 been on my mind a lot lately. Two years ago I realized that I had virtually no friends in Boston, yet male friendship is extremely important to me. I had just moved up here, and Boston is kind of a hard town to make friends in. I realized that the only people I really trusted were the people I grew up with in the old neighborhood."

When you're working 70 hours a week and have two young kids at home,   10 D'Allesandro said, it's hard to find the time it takes to nourish friendships. And it's easy to neglect old friends.

I talked to a lawyer in Cambridge, a friend of a friend, an introspective guy 11
with a preference for keeping his name out of print.

"I've got about three good friends," he told me. "Maybe a couple more. A 12
half dozen, and they are primarily from the old neighborhood."

His friends are, he said, the people he would turn to at the time of a per- 13
sonal calamity: when a marriage is in trouble or when a parent dies. The trouble with those relationships, he said, is that marriages don't go bad very often
and a parent dies only once. So there are many gaps between meaningful
exchanges with his friends. If he turned to friends only when he or they were
in need, how could he be sure that they would always be there?

"There is an understanding that they will be there," he told me, "and that 14
I will be there for them. I don't know how implicit it is, maybe it's an adolescent notion, but I think it's fairly clear.

"When I think about what I'm going to do this weekend, it usually involves 15
the kids," says this friend of a friend. "And if I'm not with the kids, then I want
to be with my wife. As is, we never have enough time together. I seldom see my
friends. I take my friends for granted, and when I think about that, I regret it."

Regret is a harsh word. It's a reminder of just how easily things go bad, of 16
how we miss what shouldn't be missed, how we fail to see the obvious. It is
also a subtle theme in a book I read: *Just Friends: The Role of Friendship in Our
Lives,* by Lillian B. Rubin. I tracked Rubin to Berkeley, where she is working
at the Institute for the Study of Social Change.

"One of the tragedies in our lives is that friendship is so undervalued as a 17
relationship of permanence," she told me. "Love relationships are so overvalued. Despite all of the evidence in our lives that it doesn't work, people are still
looking for that magical salvation from a love relationship, and they are ignoring the relationship that could offer them ongoing sustenance: friendship.
One of the sad things about friendship is that it often gets put on hold when
we get married or find a loved other.

"In childhood and in adolescence, friends are the people we turn to to help 18
us out of the family. That's what adolescent peer groups are about. They provide
a transition and give us the support that enables us to leave the family. It's ironic
that it is those very relationships that become the cause for our search for a new
family. When you start a family, you are supported by a sense that everybody is
doing it, and it is part of living—that it is disruptive not to do it. When the mating time comes, those close relationships tend to go by the boards."

My second category in the ABCs of lost friends may be less lamentable 19
than the first but no less saddening. It is letting go, cutting bait—deliberately
blowing off a relationship. Here's how it works:

I went back to my hometown a couple of years ago and looked up an old 20
friend, a neighborhood kid with whom I used to shoot baskets after school.
My idea was to relive old times. Maybe to revive the friendship.

We met at another friend's house, and he drove up in a car that was fast 21
and Italian and worth about 10 times what my car was worth. On his arm was
a woman who was approximately half his age. My old friend strolled in, sat
down, and set about laying down lines of cocaine. He talked for an hour or two

about how he had made his money, and when he was done I knew that I was not his friend anymore. I didn't want him for a friend.

Was I callous? Was I unduly judgmental? Was I being a prig? Should I   22
have made an allowance and exempted my old (former) friend from the value system to which I now subscribed? I think not.

I talked to David Ross, a kind of middle-ground friend, who is the director   23
of the Institute of Contemporary Art, and he told a similar story about an old friend of his who evolved into what Ross believes to be a less-than-respectable PR guy in New York. Ross no longer sees him, no longer wishes to.

Then a colleague at the office told me a story about an old friend of his   24
who, after divorcing his wife, turned into a first-class cad. Like me, and like Ross, my colleague blew off his old friend and believed he did the right thing. But it wasn't an easy decision. Friendship may not get the kind of fawning press that we heap on romantic love, but its virtues have been celebrated for thousands of years. A simple glance at the literature of Western civilization reveals centuries of reverence for friendship, from the Greek tale of Damon and Pythias to the biblical story of David and Jonathan to television's "Cagney and Lacey."

And still, despite its history, friendship—that voluntary, nonsexual love   25
affair between two people—perplexes social scientists no end. . . . Most of the social scientists I talked to couldn't even offer a definition of friendship.

I started with the psychology department at Harvard and was told that the   26
university has no professors whose expertise is friendship. I called Tufts, where the psychology department chairman, Walter Swap, told me that the best person in the Boston area to talk to about friendship was Zick Rubin, who, Swap said, was teaching at Brandeis. . . . But when I called Brandeis, I was told that Rubin had quit studying friendship to go to law school.

I tracked down Rubin's home number and called him anyway. He was   27
helpful and polite, but he didn't want to talk about friendship, he explained, because he had been away from his research for so long. Instead of giving me a definition of friendship, Rubin gave me a half dozen names and a few telephone numbers of academics who could help. The best, he said, may be Robert Weiss, a research professor at the University of Massachusetts and the author of *Loneliness: The Experience of Emotional and Social Isolation.* . . .

"It's very tough to say what a friend is," Weiss told me. "Essentially, it is   28
someone we maintain a relationship with when there is no reason for doing so except for the relationship. There is no kinship obligation. It is not someone we work with, so there is no work obligation. It is not necessarily a neighbor, so there is no neighborhood obligation. That is an enormous opportunity to define a relationship."

I asked Weiss if there were certain kinds of people who became friends   29
with each other. He said there were. "One recipe for friendship is the right mixture of commonality and difference," he said. "You've got to have enough in common so that you understand each other and enough difference so that there is something to exchange." . . .

When I asked several people what friends do for friends, they gave me one 30
of two answers: nothing or everything. What they meant is that friends lack
. . . specific responsibilities. They don't even have unspoken, understood roles,
as the members of most families do. In friendship, experts and most of the
people I spoke with insisted, there are no obligations. But there are expectations, enormous expectations—tougher, deeper, and longer lasting than in any
. . . relationships except perhaps those with family members. In fact, when
those relationships crack—when a parent dies or when a marriage falls
apart—a friend is expected to be there for emotional support.

"If I were seeking some feedback on a possible career change, or marital 31
issues, or worrying about a father's failing health, I would turn to a friend," a
40-year-old Cambridge businessman told me.

"I use friends to play back events in my life that I want to understand bet- 32
ter," Zella Luria, a psychologist at Tufts, told me. "Friendship is a way of comparing life's notes."

Luria said that she was not an expert on friendship but that she had read 33
a few books about it, and the thing that fascinated her was the alleged difference between friendships among men and friendships among women.

"I think men have been given a bum rap," Luria said. "But if what I read 34
about men's relationships is true, if there is really nothing more going on than
meets the eye, then it's very sad. Men are truly bereft."

I asked psychologist Lillian Rubin about that. 35

"Can you imagine a man telling a friend that his wife was leaving him 36
because she was dissatisfied with his sexual performance?" Rubin asked me.

"I doubt it," she said, answering her own question. "Not even in 37
Cambridge. But a woman would talk to a friend about that kind of thing. The
central difference between men friends and women friends is that men tend to
do things together, women tend just to *be* together. It isn't that they don't do
things, but in the process of just being together there is for women some kind
of intimate exchange. With men, relationships are based on a kind of nonver-
bal bonding, the bonding that goes on while shooting baskets or watching a
football game. One of those guys might have had some very bitter pill to swallow the day before—maybe with his wife or at work—but he is not likely to
mention it. Yet this is exactly what women will talk about.

"Women will turn to women for that kind of talk because it is something 38
that men do not do well," Rubin said. "Just look at the difference in the way
men and women use the telephone. If a man wants to make a tennis date, he'll
call up and say what time he wants to play and say, 'Meet you at the court.' If
a woman wants to do the same thing, she will call up and say, 'Hi, how are
you?' and talk for 20 minutes before making the date. Professional women will
go to great lengths to maintain friendships, even when it means calling somebody up at 11 o'clock, when both of them should be asleep.

"I'm living through a threat to my friendships right now," Rubin told me. 39
"I just got a job in New York, and it is playing havoc with my friends here, who
are feeling abandoned. I can hear their pain and their anger and their envy

because it's the idea that I'm leaving them for a new life. All that gets talked about.

"What is interesting about that is that for the woman, the one-on-one inti-   40
mate friendships become very important and they remain very important for the rest of their lives. But the men will remain dependent on the women in their lives for their emotional needs, so for the men friendships will never really regain that kind of ascendancy."

There is a third category, the C in the ABCs of lost friends. It's the fastest,   41
dirtiest, and most painful way to go. Psychologist Paul Wright calls it "a nega-tion or a denial of a friend's personalized interest." David D'Alessandro calls it betrayal, a violation of the rules.

"The rules of my friendships are very simple," said D'Alessandro. "They   42
are based on Italian tradition. Unless I tell you otherwise, assume that any-thing I tell you is confidential. When I lived in New York, I had a very good friend, a roommate who broke a confidence and told another friend some-thing I did not want known. I moved out, and I haven't talked about it since."

It wasn't only macho Italian men who told me that they have no patience   43
with friends who break the rules. A professional woman in her forties, call her woman A, told me this story. Her best friend, woman B, whom she had known for 10 years, betrayed confidences about woman A's future plans to a third person they both knew. When woman A found out, she didn't speak to woman B for five months, and then only after they had reaffirmed the rules of their relationship.

I heard stories about a different kind of betrayal: the betrayal that results   44
from a failure to follow the rules of mutual aid. A friend told me that he had suffered months of shame because he wasn't there to help a friend weather an emotional breakdown. I know that scenario well. For years I watched from afar while a friend crept more deeply into drugs, from recreational use to finally being a junkie. I watched as his wife left him. I watched as he lost his job, and I watched as they took him away to prison for writing bad checks. Did my friend feel betrayed? He should have.

A businessman I know said that he felt betrayed when a friend steadfastly   45
refused to discuss his own divorce. "He walked out on his wife," the business-man said. "Because of the close relationship I have had with him for 20 years, I tried repeatedly to reach out. There was no acknowledgment on his part of responsibility for his action or for the damage. I felt that he wasn't playing by the ground rules of the friendship. I had expectations that certain things would happen. It was his failure even to talk about it that bugged me, and now the relationship has been soured."

One thing that I heard over and over again from the men and women I   46
talked to was that it is easier to lose old friends than to make new ones—a sad formula for loneliness. . . .

The beginnings of my own friendships, I learned from psychologist Robert   47
Weiss, are dishearteningly typical. They start in the office or on one of the rac-quetball or squash courts at the YMCA.

"A man will have a tennis friend," Weiss said. "A friendship will start with   48
a small sense of reciprocity. There is almost always a sense of linkage that goes
with it. *You* bring the balls this time, and *I'll* bring them next time. Soon you
get a sense of the other person as a person, and you start to feel loyalties."

I know that. I see how a relationship grows. I learn that my partner is get-   49
ting divorced. He learns that I have been through a divorce. It's a sadness that
we share, our knowledge that love doesn't last forever. We both try to make it
easy on the kids, and sometimes we succeed. But are we friends yet, as in
"friends forever"? Maybe. I don't know. Both of us hardly have time to play
ball, let alone hang out and talk.

Is he someone I'll call late at night when something is troubling me?   50
Probably not. Probably, I'll do something else typical of men my age: I'll talk
to my wife. Will he call me? And if he does, will I listen? Do I really have the
time and energy to invest in a brand-new friendship? Does anyone?

After all, we're not kids anymore.   51

RESPONDING TO THE READING

Freewriting

Exercise 10a.   Freewrite about the passages you found most like your own
experiences of friendship. What about them seemed familiar?

Exercise 10b.   What does Jahnke assume will happen to most friendships?
Does your experience support or contradict his assumption?

Exercise 10c.   Are there additional categories you would like to add to
Jahnke's list of the ways in which we lose friendships?

Building Your Vocabulary

VOCABULARY LIST

Words to Look Up	My Definition	Dictionary Definition
self-indulgent (1)		
caroused (5)		
chastening (5)		
wheeler-dealer (8)		
colonial (8)		
introspective (11)		
calamity (13)		
implicit (14)		
permanence (17)		
sustenance (17)		

Words to Look Up	My Definition	Dictionary Definition
disruptive (18)		
by the boards (18)		
lamentable (19)		
callous (22)		
prig (22)		
cad (24)		
colleague (24)		
fawning (24)		
expertise (26)		
alleged (33)		
bereft (34)		
ascendancy (40)		
scenario (44)		
reciprocity (48)		

Questions for Discussion

1. Write a one-page summary of the main and supporting points in Art Jahnke's article. Which sections are most convincing? What writing strategies does he use most effectively?
2. What sources did Jahnke consult in his research for this article? Which of his sources gave you the most valuable information?
3. Notice that Jahnke does more than just list the categories of lost friendships. What subtopics does he explore for each? How do they add interest to his essay? How is each relevant to his overall discussion?
4. Which of the categories of lost friendships contains relationships that are most worth saving? Reread the examples in this section and suggest what might be done to save these friendships.

TOPICS FOR WRITING

Topic 1.   Think about Robert Weiss's definition of friendship as "someone we maintain a relationship with when there is no reason for doing so except for the relationship." Write a paper in which you classify the friendships you have had or have still. Freewrite to gather details about the characteristics of those friendships. Ask yourself these questions:

Why were you friends?
What did you see in each other? do together? talk about?
What qualities about the other person made you his or her friend?
In what interesting ways were you different?
What common ground did you share?
What did your friend add to your life, and you to his or hers, that made
   this friendship work?

Once you have lots of information, organize it by grouping similar elements among the friendships and developing a topic idea that characterizes each group—steadfast friends and friends who betrayed you are two examples. Focus on "nonsexual love affairs" you have had with friends.

Topic 2.   Jahnke quotes writer Lillian Rubin who argues that "friendship is so undervalued as a relationship of permanence," while "love relationships are so overvalued." Write a paper in which you offer evidence from your own experience that either supports or contradicts Rubin's evaluation of friendship and love relationships.

Topic 3.   Go over Deborah Tannen's findings (Chapter 11) about the way men communicate and their expectations about what will happen during a conversation (see pages 239–244). How is the information Jahnke quotes from Lillian Rubin on male friendships (paragraphs 38–40) similar to or different from Tannen's analysis?

Topic 4.   Write a paper in which you analyze how well Art Jahnke's depiction of the loss of friends parallels your own experience. Which instances correspond to your experience and observations? Which contradict them? Consider using a T-graph to help you generate and organize ideas. On the left side list incidents from Jahnke's article, and on the right list your own experiences, observations, and reactions.

Topic 5.   Certain friends are good for certain things. Examine your own life and the lives of people you know to write about the different needs we have for different kinds of friends. Give numerous examples of each to establish your categories clearly.

THE WRITING PROCESS: CLASSIFYING

The strategy of classifying ideas is somewhat familiar to you from your work with process analysis in Chapter 9. When describing the Lion Dance, Donald Inn grouped the players according to the action and function of each. Similarly, when you are classifying, you break a subject into categories of experience and analyze each in detail.

Additional Considerations for Developing a Topic

When you have a topic that asks you to classify experiences, people, or objects by category, think of specific details and events that you can group according to similar and contrasting qualities. Writing assignments in college sometimes ask you to analyze particular categories of experience. You might, for example, be asked to write a paper about different kinds of homeless people in the United States or effective strategies for solving math problems. If you must choose your own topic, the questions below and some of the topics that follow the readings in this chapter may help you find a good one.

> What subjects have you read about in magazines, newspapers, or books that interest you? Are there subject areas your instructors have covered that you would like to investigate?
>
> How can you break a subject into smaller categories?
>
> What kinds of teachers, students, partners, pets, doctors, or politicians are there?

Additional Considerations for Thinking about Your Audience

After developing a topic, ask yourself *What do I want to tell my readers about this topic?* You might want to inform your audience about your topic—the kinds of bosses you have had, for example—to warn them what to watch for (when looking for work in this instance), or how to handle certain people and situations. On the other hand, you might want to entertain your readers with humorous descriptions of the ridiculous people you have met at work or the boring jobs you have held in the last few years. Yet another purpose might be to evaluate your categories. You might, for example, categorize the types of colleges you are considering for transfer or those you investigated before making your present choice. In this case, your purpose might be to advise fellow students which colleges offer the greatest number of courses for a particular major or the most well-qualified faculty.

Regardless of your purpose, you must offer enough details to develop your categories and make them distinct from one another.

Additional Considerations for Preliminary Writing

Once you have given some thought to your audience and know your purpose for writing, break your topic into categories; use the techniques for preliminary writing—drawing an idea wheel, listing ideas, and asking questions—to help you gather information and evidence for discussing your categories. Don't overlook the possibility of interviewing experts or friends to gather additional material. The following questions may help you generate ideas:

> What are the characteristics of each category?
>
> What examples from your own experience or from interviews illustrate each?
>
> What details, features, actions, shapes, or experiences are unique to any particular category?
>
> What differences do you find among these categories that make them distinct?

When setting up categories and gathering details for discussion, consider drawing a graph to help you visualize your categories. Here is a three-column graph suggested by the three categories in Jahnke's essay:

Neglect	Letting Go	Betrayal

FOR PRACTICE

Use a separate sheet of paper to add the details Art Jahnke uses in his essay in the appropriate columns above.

Additional Considerations for Organizing Ideas

If you are comparing categories or evaluating which is the most advantageous, important, or interesting, organize your ideas by their importance, saving the category you want to emphasize until the end. Arranging categories from most to least familiar is another possible arrangement.

Some of the transitional words and phrases that should be useful for writing classification papers are listed below:

To order ideas in time or according to importance	after, before, briefly, by this time, currently or during, eventually, finally, first, now, later, meanwhile, next, presently, recently, second, so far, soon, then, third, when, while
To introduce examples	especially, for example, for instance, namely, for one thing, in particular
To show contrast	although, but, however, in contrast, more than, nevertheless, on the other hand, unlike, the most, one of the most, the best

Additional Considerations for Sharing Your Writing and Making Final Revisions

When revising your essay, you may wish to add the following questions to the checklist for revising found in Appendix C.

Checklist

- ❏ Does my thesis anticipate a classification essay?
- ❏ Is the reason for writing the essay clear?
- ❏ Are my categories distinct from one another?
- ❏ Are my categories developed adequately?
- ❏ Do I need more explanations to make one or more of the categories more convincing?

❏ How have I organized the categories?
❏ Have I used transitions and topic sentences between categories?
❏ Is the organization effective or should a category or two be rearranged?

FOR FURTHER READING

Personal Politics: A Lesson in Straight Talk
Lindsy Van Gelder

Lindsy Van Gelder, an editor and writer for **Ms.** *magazine, wrote this essay advising "straight" people how to feel more at ease when dealing with gay women. It appeared in the November 1987 issue of* **Ms.** *magazine.*

I'll begin at the beginning, when you and I first meet. Maybe we'll talk   1
about our work or the weather. But my antennae are out, and if it's a particularly delicate situation (someone I'm interviewing, say, or another parent at school), I may even have a knot in my stomach. I haven't had a casual conversation in nearly a decade, because I know what's coming: any minute now we'll hit the topic that to most Americans seems innocuous, friendly, getting-to-know-you. *The Family.*

Are you married? "Not legally," I may answer, "but I've been in a relation-   2
ship with Pamela since 1978." I've learned to say things like this in a perfectly natural tone of voice and to burble on a bit while you regain your composure. I've even started to refer to Pamela as my Life-Partner—even though I think it sounds like we run an insurance agency together—since I know that "lover," while an honorable term in the gay world, often falls upon straight ears as a synonym for someone I've had sex with a few times.

But unless you already have lesbian friends in your life (or you're gay   3
yourself), chances are that you're incredibly uncomfortable. At worst, you think I'm saying something hostile—or dirty. Sometimes you think I'm confiding a deep secret. If by some fluke it takes a few conversations before we get to this point, you might even feel vaguely betrayed, as if you'd been getting to know me under false pretenses (although this can still coexist with the thought that I should have kept my "private life" private). If you're a man, you might tell me that you're "disappointed" or that I don't "seem the type," and expect me to be flattered. If you're a woman, your first thought might be to wonder if I'm coming on to you (by mentioning my long-term committed relationship?). If you're basically a nice, liberal person—a potential friend—your impulse will be to want to do the right thing. But maybe you're not sure what that is—so you quickly change the subject.

My straight friend Jane says I'm usually silly to tell the truth, especially to 4
men. "He's really asking if you're available," she says. "So say yes, you're married." The problem with this, as Adrienne Rich has pointed out, is that
whether you're dark-skinned or disabled or a lesbian, when someone
"describes the world and you are not in it, there is a moment of psychic disequilibrium, as if you looked into a mirror and saw nothing." To collaborate
and agree that there's no one in the mirror—that we *do not exist,* are not real—
is what legions of closeted lesbians do, and it's a vicious cycle: how can a
group of phantoms ever hope to change anything?

Lesbians have a serious visibility problem, which is one of the reasons you 5
were surprised when you first met me. And it's not getting better, although
"gays" have surfaced all over the map lately because of AIDS awareness. My
own sense is that lesbians are even *less* visible than before—and if anything
we've been subsumed. (How many times have you read that "homosexuals"
are the major risk group?) Because of the times we live in, more of us also
seem to be hiding who we are. For all the most sexist reasons, this is distress-
ingly easy: a single man of a certain age might be presumed to be gay, especially if he has a roommate, but a woman is simply assumed to be saving her
(underpaid) pennies and waiting for Mr. Right.

So what I would hope you would do, first of all, is to remember that any 6
woman you meet might be a lesbian. By the same token, remember that any
lesbian you meet probably wants to be treated pretty much like any other
woman. When I mention Pamela, understand that she is as dear to me as any
boyfriend or husband, and if you would have asked me about *him,* don't
change the subject: ask about *her.*

But beyond that, I'm asking you not only for an awareness of the ways our 7
lives are alike, but the ways they're different. Please don't feel that you have to
pretend that my relationship is a clone of yours, exactly the same but with
Veronica instead of Archie. Lesbians *do* exist in a context of discrimination,
and like all minority groups, we have a culture of our own. Not only am I not
offended if you've thought or even just wondered about this; I'm relieved.

After all, if we're going to be friends, isn't it because we're interested in
each other's lives?

RESPONDING TO THE READING

Freewriting

Exercise 10d.   Describe your reaction to Lindsy Van Gelder's very personal
appeal.

Exercise 10e.   How effective is this article in gaining your understanding?

Building Your Vocabulary

VOCABULARY LIST

Words to Look Up	My Definition	Dictionary Definition
antennae (1)		
innocuous (1)		
composure (2)		
synonym (2)		
fluke (3)		
coexist (3)		
psychic (4)		
disequilibrium (4)		
collaborate (4)		
legions (4)		
subsumed (5)		
context (7)		
discrimination (7)		

Questions for Discussion

1. Who is Van Gelder writing for? Who is the "you" she addresses?
2. What is her purpose in writing this piece? How well does she accomplish this purpose?
3. How does she organize her article? Suggest an alternate arrangement. Which do you feel is most effective and why?
4. How does the title relate to the point of Van Gelder's essay? Explain the meaning of "Straight Talk."

TOPICS FOR WRITING

Topic 1.   Van Gelder quotes Adrienne Rich as saying that if someone "describes the world and you are not in it, there is a moment of psychic disequilibrium as if you looked into a mirror and saw nothing." Write a paper about a time when you felt left out in this profound way. When did this happen? How did it happen? How did you feel? Who or what made you feel this way? How did you handle the situation? How has your attitude toward the event changed?

Topic 2.   Think about a time you felt misunderstood. Write a letter to the person who misunderstood you, explaining the points of misunderstanding and your own position as clearly as you can. You may wish to freewrite first about what you remember. Then choose the crucial events that need

explaining and focus on them in your letter. Be sure to include a thesis that
carries the main idea you want to communicate.

Just Walk On By: A Black Man Ponders His Power to Alter Public Space
Brent Staples

*Brent Staples holds a Ph.D. in psychology from the University of Chicago and is
an editor for* The New York Times. *He wrote this article for* Ms. *magazine in
September, 1986.*

My first victim was a woman—white, well dressed, probably in her early 1
twenties. I came upon her late one evening on a deserted street in Hyde Park,
a relatively affluent neighborhood in an otherwise mean, impoverished section of Chicago. As I swung onto the avenue behind her, there seemed to be a
discreet, uninflammatory distance between us. Not so. She cast back a worried glance. To her, the youngish black man—a broad six feet two inches with
a beard and billowing hair, both hands shoved into the pockets of a bulky military jacket—seemed menacingly close. After a few more quick glimpses, she
picked up her pace and was soon running in earnest. Within seconds she disappeared into a cross street.

That was more than a decade ago. I was 22 years old; a graduate student 2
newly arrived at the University of Chicago. It was in the echo of that terrified
woman's footfalls that I first began to know the unwieldly inheritance I'd
come into—the ability to alter public space in ugly ways. It was clear that she
thought herself the quarry of a mugger, a rapist, or worse. Suffering a bout of
insomnia, however, I was stalking sleep, not defenseless wayfarers. As a softy
who is scarcely able to take a knife to a raw chicken—let alone hold it to a person's throat—I was surprised, embarrassed, and dismayed all at once. Her
flight made me feel like an accomplice in tyranny. It also made it clear that I
was indistinguishable from the muggers who occasionally seeped into the
area from the surrounding ghetto. That first encounter, and those that followed, signified that a vast, unnerving gulf lay between nighttime pedestrians—particularly women—and me. And I soon gathered that being perceived
as dangerous is a hazard in itself. I only needed to turn a corner into a dicey
situation, or crowd some frightened, armed person in a foyer somewhere, or
make an errant move after being pulled over by a policeman. Where fear and
weapons meet—and they often do in urban America—there is always the possibility of death.

In that first year, my first away from my hometown, I was to become thor- 3
oughly familiar with the language of fear. At dark, shadowy intersections in
Chicago, I could cross in front of a car stopped at a traffic light and elicit the
thunk, thunk, thunk, thunk of the driver—black, white, male, or female—

hammering down the door locks. On less traveled streets after dark, I grew accustomed to but never comfortable with people who crossed to the other side of the street rather than pass me. Then there were the standard unpleasantries with police, doormen, bouncers, cab drivers, and others whose business it is to screen out troublesome individuals *before* there is any nastiness.

I moved to New York nearly two years ago and I have remained an avid   4
night walker. In Central Manhattan, the near-constant crowd cover minimizes tense one-on-one street encounters. Elsewhere—visiting friends in SoHo, where sidewalks are narrow and tightly spaced buildings shut out the sky— things can get very taut indeed.

Black men have a firm place in New York mugging literature. Norman   5
Podhoretz in his famed (or infamous) 1963 essay, "My Negro Problem—And Ours," recalls growing up in terror of black males; they "were tougher than we were, more ruthless," he writes—and as an adult on the Upper West Side of Manhattan, he continues, he cannot constrain his nervousness when he meets black men on certain streets. Similarly, a decade later, the essayist and novelist Edward Hoagland extols a New York where once "Negro bitterness bore down mainly on other Negroes." Where some see mere panhandlers, Hoagland sees "a mugger who is clearly screwing up his nerve to do more than just *ask* for money." But Hoagland has "the New Yorker's quick-hunch posture for broken-field maneuvering," and the bad guy swerves away.

I often witness that "hunch posture," from women after dark on the war-   6
renlike streets of Brooklyn where I live. They seem to set their faces on neutral and, with their purse straps strung across their chests bandolier style, they forge ahead as though bracing themselves against being tackled. I understand, of course, that the danger they perceive is not a hallucination. Women are particularly vulnerable to street violence, and young black males are drastically overrepresented among the perpetrators of that violence. Yet these truths are no solace against the kind of alienation that comes of being ever the suspect, against being set apart, a fearsome entity with whom pedestrians avoid making eye contact.

It is not altogether clear to me how I reached the ripe old age of 22 with-   7
out being conscious of the lethality nighttime pedestrians attributed to me. Perhaps it was because in Chester, Pennsylvania, the small, angry industrial town where I came of age in the 1960s, I was scarcely noticeable against a backdrop of gang warfare, street knifings, and murders. I grew up one of the good boys, had perhaps a half-dozen fist fights. In retrospect, my shyness of combat has clear sources.

Many things go into the making of a young thug. One of those things is the   8
consummation of the male romance with the power to intimidate. An infant discovers that random flailings send the baby bottle flying out of the crib and crashing to the floor. Delighted, the joyful babe repeats those motions again and again, seeking to duplicate the feat. Just so, I recall the points at which some of my boyhood friends were finally seduced by the perception of themselves as tough guys. When a mark cowered and surrendered his money without resistance, myth and reality merged—and paid off. It is, after all, only

manly to embrace the power to frighten and intimidate. We, as men, are not supposed to give an inch of our lane on the highway; we are to seize the fighter's edge in work and in play and even in love; we are to be valiant in the face of hostile forces.

Unfortunately, poor and powerless young men seem to take all this non- 9 sense literally. As a boy, I saw countless tough guys locked away; I have since buried several, too. They were babies, really—a teenage cousin, a brother of 22, a childhood friend in his mid-twenties—all gone down in episodes of bravado played out in the streets. I came to doubt the virtues of intimidation early on. I chose, perhaps even unconsciously, to remain a shadow—timid, but a survivor.

The fearsomeness mistakenly attributed to me in public places often has a 10 perilous flavor. The most frightening of these confusions occurred in the late 1970s and early 1980s when I worked as a journalist in Chicago. One day, rushing into the office of a magazine I was writing for with a deadline story in hand, I was mistaken for a burglar. The office manager called security and, with an ad hoc posse, pursued me through the labyrinthine halls, nearly to my editor's door. I had no way of proving who I was. I could only move briskly toward the company of someone who knew me.

Another time I was on assignment for a local paper and killing time before 11 an interview. I entered a jewelry store on the city's affluent Near North Side. The proprietor excused herself and returned with an enormous red Doberman pinscher straining at the end of a leash. She stood, the dog extended toward me, silent to my questions, her eyes bulging nearly out of her head. I took a cursory look around, nodded, and bade her good night. Relatively speaking, however, I never fared as badly as another black male journalist. He went to nearby Waukegan, Illinois, a couple of summers ago to work on a story about a murderer who was born there. Mistaking the reporter for the killer, police hauled him from his car at gunpoint and but for his press credentials would probably have tried to book him. Such episodes are not uncommon. Black men trade tales like this all the time.

In "My Negro Problem—And Ours," Podhoretz writes that the hatred he 12 feels for blacks makes itself known to him through a variety of avenues—one being his discomfort with that "special brand of paranoid touchiness" to which he says blacks are prone. No doubt he is speaking here of black men. In time, I learned to smother the rage I felt at so often being taken for a criminal. Not to do so would surely have led to madness—via that special "paranoid touchiness" that so annoyed Podhoretz at the time he wrote the essay.

I began to take precautions to make myself less threatening. I move about 13 with care, particularly late in the evening. I give a wide berth to nervous people on subway platforms during the wee hours, particularly when I have exchanged business clothes for jeans. If I happen to be entering a building behind some people who appear skittish, I may walk by, letting them clear the lobby before I return, so as not to seem to be following them. I have been calm and extremely congenial on those rare occasions when I've been pulled over by the police.

And on late-evening constitutionals along streets less traveled by, I employ 14 what has proved to be an excellent tension-reducing measure: I whistle melodies from Beethoven and Vivaldi and the more popular classical composers. Even steely New Yorkers hunching toward nighttime destinations seem to relax, and occasionally they even join in the tune. Virtually everybody seems to sense that a mugger wouldn't be warbling bright, sunny selections from Vivaldi's *Four Seasons*. It is my equivalent of the cowbell that hikers wear when they know they are in bear country.

RESPONDING TO THE READING

Freewriting

Exercise 10f.   Do you sympathize with Brent Staples' dilemma? Why or why not?

Exercise 10g.   Have you had experiences similar to ones Staples describes in "Just Walk On By"? Were you the victim or the person someone else was trying to avoid?

Exercise 10h.   Freewrite about Staples' perspective as a "night walker." What point of view does he offer on the urban experience?

Building Your Vocabulary

VOCABULARY LIST

Words to Look Up	My Definition	Dictionary Definition
affluent (1)		
impoverished (1)		
discreet (1)		
uninflammatory (1)		
billowing (1)		
unwieldy (2)		
quarry (2)		
wayfarers (2)		
accomplice (2)		
indistinguishable (2)		
unnerving (2)		
dicey (2)		
errant (2)		
avid (4)		
taut (4)		
panhandlers (5)		
maneuvering (5)		
warrenlike (6)		
bandolier (6)		

lethality (7)
retrospect (7)
consummation (8)
intimidate (8)
flailings (8)
intimidation (9)
perilous (10)
ad hoc (10)
labyrinthine (10)
paranoid (12)
berth (13)
congenial (13)
constitutionals (14)

Questions for Discussion

1. What is Brent Staples' purpose in writing this article?
2. How do people misjudge him? How does his "unwieldy inheritance" affect their judgment?
3. Skim several issues of *Ms.* magazine from 1987 or 1988 to determine its principal audience. Examine the kinds of articles published and the kinds of advertisements the magazine carried. Then write a profile of the audience most likely to read *Ms.* Support your conclusion with evidence gathered from your research.
4. Why do you think the editors of *Ms.* think Staples' essay was appropriate for their magazine?
5. What does this article tell us about Staples himself in terms of his education, personality, and where he comes from? Why does he want the reader to know these things?
6. What, in Staples' estimation, causes young men to become "thugs"? Include an explanation of "the consummation of the male romance with the power to intimidate." What other reasons can you think of to explain violence against others?
7. What solutions does Staples propose for dealing with public stereotyping? Does he seem resigned to the way people stereotyped him? Explain your answer.

TOPICS FOR WRITING

Topic 1.   Brent Staples admits in his article that "the danger [women] perceive is not a hallucination." Write a paper advising women what precautions they should take to ensure their safety. Focus on two or three strategies that you consider most important and develop them in detail. You might consult your local police department for suggestions about what to do and how to judge the behavior of others. Check your suggestions to see that you have avoided stereotyping.

Topic 2.   Write an essay in which you analyze in detail one or two times in your life when you felt threatened or uncomfortable. Your essay should make some point about these experiences. To support that point, you will need to explain, as Brent Staples does, why these things happened, what you felt at the time, any long-term effects on your behavior, and the larger social situation that may have produced these experiences.

Student Writing

The Good Samaritans

A story about plundering marauders, a brutal beating, and uncaring bystanders usually doesn't convey a code of ethics, but in the parable of the Good Samaritan, these actions show how people are supposed to treat one another. In the parable, a Jewish merchant is robbed and left half dead by the road. First a priest and then a Levite (another religious man) walk to the other side of the road and ignore the injured man. Finally, a Samaritan, a known enemy of the Jews, aids the wounded man and nurses him back to health. At the end of this parable, as it is told in the New Testament, Christ asks, "Which of these three, in your opinion, was the neighbor of the robber's victim?" Of course his listeners answered, "The one who treated him with mercy." Then Christ gave the commandment, "Go and do likewise." Today, Christ's commandment often gets lost in a tangle of rules or stalled by the cumbersome hierarchy that modern Christian churches have erected. Consequently, instead of the churches living out their God's commandment, individuals are the ones who have been caring for the lowly with respect and dignity; individuals not institutions continue to make this world a better place.

In Calcutta, India, Mother Teresa spent her life healing the poor, the sick, and the abandoned. As a young woman teaching in Calcutta, she constantly came across people uncared for and dying in the street. In 1948 she began caring for the poor. Over the years her unrelenting work has brought worldwide attention not only to the plight of these homeless people, but also to the plight of the homeless around the world. She began a religious order, the Sisters of Charity, and built an international organization which now includes 335 orphanages, hospices, refugee centers, clinics, AIDS centers, and homes for the destitute in 66 countries on five continents.

Taking the lead in Poland, a shipyard worker, Lech Walesa, became a spokesman for his people. Poor working conditions became a vital concern to him when, in 1970, 22 workers were killed in an explosion. Walesa spoke out for justice in the workplace and soon had many supporters. The authorities ignored them until he and his followers called a general strike. The strike ended when the Polish army attacked the workers and left 45 dead in four cities. Walesa continued to lead the workers even though he lost his job and was jailed. On August 14, 1980, another strike was called and the nation united behind Walesa. The government gave in by the end of the month and signed an agreement that met the workers' demands. An election in Poland saw the Solidarity Party win a majority of the votes and take the leadership of its country.

During this time, Father Oscar Romero was leading his fight for the justice and dignity of the people of El Salvador. When Romero became Archbishop of the Catholic church, he was known as a mild and conservative priest. But when a fellow priest, Father Grande, along with two travelers, were ambushed and killed by government sympathizers, he knew he could no longer hide behind his office. He spoke out publicly for reform, went to prisons to protest the torturing of priests and common people, confronted the president-elect, and demanded reforms. He called the world's attention to the cold fact that 50,000 people have been murdered by government-sanctioned death squads in El Salvador over the past ten years. In 1980 Romero himself was murdered by an assassin.

All of these people in their own way have contributed to making the world a better place. They have done it with determination and boundless energy. The church hierarchy has come forward to help with funds now and then, but too often they advise caution or promise to "study" the issue. The leaders of the Christian community have got to stop walking by the victims of hunger and oppression. Until they do, the army of Samaritans will keep working, hoping for a brighter day, and treating all people with love, respect, and dignity.

—Stella Hallsted

Questions for Discussion

1. Who is the intended audience for "The Good Samaritans"?
2. What do you think was Stella Hallsted's purpose for writing this essay? How well does she achieve this purpose?
3. What does Hallsted suggest should be the role of religious institutions in helping poor and politically oppressed people in the world?
4. In your own opinion, what priorities should religious and/or governmental institutions set for helping people in need?
5. Discuss whether or not Hallsted's criticism applies to an organization, religious institution, or governmental agency with which you are familiar.

11

Men and Women

*Studying the way people talk convinced
me that male-female conversation is
cross-cultural communication.*

—*Deborah Tannen*

*Only men can initiate men, as only women
can initiate women. . . . Only men can change
the boy to a man. Initiators say that boys need
a second birth, this time a birth from men.*

—*Robert Bly*

The readings in this chapter examine relationships between the sexes and images of women. "Why Can't He Hear What I'm Saying?" by Deborah Tannen explains why misunderstandings may occur between men and women. In Gloria Naylor's "George and Ophelia," a dramatic account of a courtship, the writer explores some of the basic differences between men and women. The two remaining readings discuss cultural images of men and women. In "A Thinly Disguised Message," Deborah Marquardt examines the idealized view of women exploited by advertisements. In the last selection, "Iron John," Robert Bly uses a folk tale to propose a new, more self-assured identity for American men.

This chapter also introduces writing techniques for comparing and contrasting. Selections from Deborah Tannen's article, "Why Can't He Hear What I'm Saying?" are used to suggest techniques for writing about the differences between two subjects. The same techniques may be used to write about similarities between subjects.

COMPARING AND CONTRASTING

The author of *Gulliver's Travels*, Jonathan Swift, wrote: "Undoubtedly philosophers are in the right when they tell us that nothing is great or little otherwise than by comparison." Swift was saying that we can judge the true size of a thing only by comparing and contrasting it with other things. If, for example, we ask a six-foot man to stand beside a California redwood that measures ten feet in diameter and is three hundred feet tall, we get a much better idea of just how large the redwoods are. Similarly, to appreciate a certain condition, attitude, or event, we might compare it to something like or very unlike it.

Comparing and contrasting are familiar activities to anyone who has shopped for clothing, an automobile, or gifts for someone's birthday. More important decisions, such as what classes to take, which of two careers to pursue, or what school to attend also involve making comparisons; for decisions such as these, it is usually best to list what you know about your alternatives and then compare them to see which is the best choice.

If you have read Annie Dillard's "Self and World" and the discussion of analogy that follows it (Chapter 8), you have some idea of how comparisons work. You may recall that Dillard uses an analogy (shows how two things are alike or analogous) to compare the monster that enters her room at night to a segmented Chinese Dragon. She uses this more familiar creature to help describe the abstract shadow that streaks along the wall.

In extended comparisons, two subjects are discussed together in order to explore their similarities or differences. The following discussion uses Deborah Tannen's article, "Why Can't He Hear What I'm Saying?" to discuss techniques for comparing and contrasting.

Characteristics of Comparing and Contrasting

Point of View

Deborah Tannen writes about male and female ways of communicating from an objective point of view, although she does mention personal experiences when they clarify her ideas. She also addresses the audience directly because her purpose is to explain and explore. Here are the first three paragraphs of "Why Can't He Hear What I'm Saying?"

> You know the feeling: You meet someone for the first time, 1 and it's as if you've known each other all your lives. The conversation goes smoothly. You each know what the other means. You laugh at the same time. Your sentences are in perfect rhythm. You're doing everything right.
>
> But you also know the other feeling: You meet someone, you 2 try to be friendly, but everything goes wrong. There are uncomfortable silences. You fish for topics. You both start talking at the same time and then both stop. Whatever you do to make things better only makes them worse.
>
> Most talk falls somewhere between these two patterns. And, if 3 sometimes people say things that sound a little odd or if someone doesn't quite get our point, we let it go, the talk continues, and no one pays much attention. But, when the conversation is with the most important person in your life, the little hitches can become big ones, and you can end up in a dialogue of the second sort without knowing quite how you got there.

In the first two paragraphs, Tannen addresses the reader directly as "you" and describes two situations—one in which people are completely comfortable, the other in which absolutely everything goes wrong—likely to be familiar to her reader. In the third paragraph, she adopts the point of view of the examiner who will analyze situations where partners who care about each other show signs that they are not quite communicating.

A Purpose

It is extremely important that writers make clear, probably in an introductory paragraph, why they are making their comparison or contrast. They must communicate that purpose to the reader to prevent their essay from appearing random or their arguments from appearing without focus.

In nonfiction works, authors often explain their purpose for writing. Deborah Tannen, for example, explains that she became interested in the problems of how men and women communicate—or fail to communicate— because of a misunderstanding that arose between her and her ex-husband. Her purpose in writing "Why Can't He Hear What I'm Saying?" was to get couples to understand one another and be more tolerant of their differences. In her concluding paragraphs she makes that purpose clear:

> If you and your mate fight constantly about insignificant mat- 31
> ters, it's natural to assume something's wrong with him—or with
> you for having chosen him. But, when you begin to recognize the
> different ways men and women talk, you can begin to accept the
> differences between you in habits and assumptions about how to
> have a conversation, show interest, be considerate, and so on. And
> you can start to make the small, steady changes that will accommo-
> date two conflicting conversational styles.

In addition to a purpose, writers usually tell their readers not only what subjects they plan to compare or contrast but also the way they will draw those comparisons or contrasts. The plan or **thesis** that controls Tannen's essay is contained in paragraph 10.

> . . . Studying the way people talk convinced me that male-
> female conversation is cross-cultural communication. Culture,
> after all, is simply a network of habits and patterns based on past
> experience—and women and men have very different past experi-
> ences. Between the ages of five and fifteen, young girls and young
> boys are learning—mainly from their playmates—how to have con-
> versations, and during those years they play mostly with friends of
> their own sex. So it's not surprising that they learn different ways of
> having and using conversations.

Tannen explains that her essay will show that "male-female conversation" is based on very different assumptions about the way people communicate—assumptions that are so different that men and women might as well be from different cultures. Furthermore, she will show that these differences are caused by contrasting expectations that boys and girls develop in their gender-segregated play.

Supporting Details

Detailed writing is important for any writing strategy. One element that makes comparisons and contrasts different from other kinds of writing is that topics being compared or contrasted have matching subtopics, details, and examples that develop their similarities or differences. In objective writing—when the author's task is to explain similarities and differences—such matches are exact, and contrasts are stated clearly as we see in the following paragraphs from "Why Can't He Hear What I'm Saying?"

> Little girls tend to play in small groups or, even more com- 11
> mon, in pairs. Their social life usually centers around a best friend,

and friendships are made, maintained, and broken by talk, especially "secrets." The secrets themselves may or may not be important, but the fact of telling them is all-important. It's hard for newcomers to get into these tight groups, but anyone who is admitted is treated as an equal. Girls like to play cooperatively; if they can't cooperate, the group breaks up.

Little boys tend to play in larger groups, often outdoors, and   12
they spend more time doing than talking. It's easy for boys to get into a group, but once in they must jockey for status. One of the ways they do so is through talk—telling stories and jokes, arguing about who is best at what, challenging and sidetracking the talk of other boys and withstanding the others' challenges in order to maintain their own story and, consequently, their status.

The following T-graph (a graph shaped like a capital *T*) illustrates the contrasts Deborah Tannen makes between the play of little boys and little girls.

Little Girls	Little Boys
Play in small groups, have a "best friend"	Play in large groups
Use talk and secrets to keep friendships together	Spend more time doing than talking
Make it difficult to be admitted to the group	Make it easy to be admitted to the group
View those admitted as equal	Don't see members as equal
Play cooperatively	Compete with each other for status

Organization by Subject or Point-by-Point

Deborah Tannen's article illustrates the two main patterns writers use to organize comparisons: they may discuss one subject first, mentioning all its points and examples before going on to the second subject; or they may discuss one point about their first subject and then the same point about their second subject, and so forth. The preceding two paragraphs above about the differences between the play of little girls and little boys illustrate the first pattern; Tannen discusses all the points about girls' play first and then all the opposing points typical of little boys' play. The following paragraph, again from Tannen's article, illustrates the second organizational pattern:

When these boys and girls grow up into men and women, they   13
keep the divergent attitudes and habits they learned as children—which they don't recognize as such but simply take for granted as the way people talk. Women want their partners to be a new and improved version of a best friend. This gives them a soft spot for men who tell them secrets. As Jack Nicholson once advised a guy in a movie: "Tell her about your troubled childhood—that always gets 'em." Men, on the

other hand, expect to *do* things together and don't feel anything is missing if they don't have heart-to-heart talks all the time.

In this paragraph Tannen first discusses one point about women—how they
carry childhood expectations of their close friends into relationships with
men—and then applies the same point to men, explaining that in contrast to
women, they expect to "do" things and don't need intimate talk. This point-by-
point or alternating pattern is useful when writers have a lot of information to
convey because that way the reader doesn't have to remember the points the
writer made about the first topic before going on to the second.
    Regardless of the pattern of organization the writer chooses, the subtopics
mentioned for one topic must have a matching or contrasting point in the discussion of the second topic.

Using Transitions

Like causal analysis, comparisons can be quite complex, so it is essential that
writers be clear about when they are discussing one subject and when they
have moved to the other. In the paragraph in which Tannen discusses both
male and female expectations, she uses a transitional phrase to signal the
shift from women to men: "men, on the other hand, expect to *do* things
together. . . ." Here are a few additional transitional words and phrases that
you will find useful when discussing similarities or differences.

To Show Similarity	To Show Difference or Exception
similarly	in contrast
in the same way	on the other hand
at the same time	but
likewise	yet
too, also	however
equally	not as . . . as
furthermore	nevertheless
much in common	in spite of
much alike	although
	while

FOR PRACTICE

The full article by Deborah Tannen is reprinted on the following pages. After
reading it carefully, reread paragraphs 14 through 18 and underline transitional words that signal contrasts between what men and women expect of
each other.

Why Can't He Hear What I'm Saying?
Deborah Tannen

In the following excerpt from her book, That's Not What I Meant! How Conversational Style Makes or Breaks Your Relations with Others, *published in 1986, Deborah Tannen examines the reasons why men and women may have difficulty communicating.*

You know the feeling: You meet someone for the first time and it's as if 1 you've known each other all your lives. The conversation goes smoothly. You each know what the other means. You laugh at the same time. Your sentences are in perfect rhythm. You're doing everything right.

But you also know the other feeling: You meet someone, you try to be 2 friendly, but everything goes wrong. There are uncomfortable silences. You fish for topics. You both start talking at the same time and then both stop. Whatever you do to make things better only makes them worse.

Most talk falls somewhere between these two patterns. And, if sometimes 3 people say things that sound a little odd or if someone doesn't quite get our point, we let it go, the talk continues, and no one pays much attention. But, when the conversation is with the most important person in your life, the little hitches can become big ones, and you can end up in a dialogue of the second sort without knowing quite how you got there. Sometimes strains in a conversation reflect real differences between people—they are angry or at cross-purposes with each other. But at other times trouble develops when there really are no basic differences of opinion, when everyone is sincerely trying to get along. To say something and see it taken to mean something else; to try to be helpful and be thought pushy; to try to be considerate and be called cold—this is the type of miscommunication that drives people crazy. And it is usually caused by differences in conversational style.

I got hooked on linguistics, the study of language, the year my marriage 4 broke up. Seven years of living with the man I had just separated from had left me dizzy with questions about communication. What went wrong? Why did this wonderful, lovable man turn into a cruel lunatic when we tried to talk to each other? I remember one argument near the end of our marriage. It stuck in my mind because it was so painfully typical and because my frustration reached a new height. It was one of our frequent conversations about plans—in this case, about whether or not to accept an invitation to visit my sister.

Cozy in the setting of our home and willing to do whatever my husband 5 wished, I asked, "Do you want to go to my sister's?" He answered, "Okay." To me, "okay" didn't sound like a real answer; it seemed to indicate he was going along with something. So I said, "Do you really want to go?" He blew up. "You're driving me crazy! Why don't you make up your mind what you want?"

That explosion sent me into a tailspin. I was incredulous and outraged at 6 his seeming irrationality. "*My* mind? I haven't even said what I want. I'm willing to do whatever you want, and this is what I get?" I felt trapped in a theater of the absurd. I thought my husband was crazy and that I was crazy for having married him. He was always getting angry at me for saying things I'd never said or for not paying attention to things I was sure *he* had never said.

I had given up trying to solve these communication impasses but was still 7 trying to understand how they developed when I heard Professor Robin Lakoff lecture about indirectness at a linguistic institute at the University of Michigan. Lakoff explained that people prefer not to say exactly what they mean because they're concerned not only with the ideas they're expressing but also with the effect their words will have on those they're talking to. They want to maintain camaraderie, avoid imposing, and give (or at least appear to give) the other person some choice in the matter being discussed. And different people have different ways of achieving these potentially conflicting goals.

Suddenly I understood what had been going on in my marriage. I had 8 taken it for granted that I could say what I wanted and that I could ask my husband what he wanted and that he would tell me. When I asked if he wanted to visit my sister, I was seeking information about his preferences so I could accommodate them. *He* wanted to be accommodating, too, but he assumed that people don't just blurt out what they want. To him, that would be coercive because he found it hard to deny a direct request. So he assumed that talkers hint at what they want and listeners pick up on those hints.

A good way to hint is to ask question. When I asked my husband if he 9 wanted to go to my sister's, he assumed I was letting him know, indirectly, that *I* wanted to go. Since he agreed to give me what I wanted, I should have gracefully—and gratefully—accepted. When I then asked, "Are you sure you want to go?" he heard that I didn't really want to go and was asking him to let me off the hook. From my husband's point of view, I was being capricious while he was trying to be agreeable—exactly my impression, but with our roles reversed. The intensity of his explosion (and of my reaction) came from the cumulative effect of repeated frustrations like this.

Although these differences in attitudes toward questions and hints could 10 arise between any two people, perhaps it was not a coincidence that we were man and woman. Studying the way people talk convinced me that male-female conversation is cross-cultural communication. Culture, after all, is simply a network of habits and patterns based on past experience—and women and men have very different past experiences. Between the ages of five and fifteen, young girls and young boys are learning—mainly from their play-mates—how to have conversations, and during those years they play mostly with friends of their own sex. So it's not surprising that they learn different ways of having and using conversations.

Little girls tend to play in small groups or, even more common, in pairs. 11 Their social life usually centers around a best friend, and friendships are made, maintained, and broken by talk, especially "secrets." The secrets them-selves may or may not be important, but the fact of telling them is all-impor-tant. It's hard for newcomers to get into these tight groups, but anyone who is admitted is treated as an equal. Girls like to play cooperatively; if they can't cooperate, the group breaks up.

Little boys tend to play in larger groups, often outdoors, and they spend more time doing than talking. It's easy for boys to get into a group, but once in they must jockey for status. One of the ways they do so is through talk—telling stories and jokes, arguing about who is best at what, challenging and sidetracking the talk of other boys and withstanding the others' challenges in order to maintain their own story and, consequently, their status.

When these boys and girls grow up into men and women, they keep the divergent attitudes and habits they learned as children—which they don't recognize as such but simply take for granted as the way people talk. Women want their partners to be a new and improved version of a best friend. This gives them a soft spot for men who tell them secrets. As Jack Nicholson once advised a guy in a movie: "Tell her about your troubled childhood—that always gets 'em." Men, on the other hand, expect to *do* things together and don't feel anything is missing if they don't have heart-to-heart talks all the time.

If they do have heart-to-hearts, the meaning of those talks may be opposite for men and women. To many women, the relationship is working as long as they can talk things out. To many men, the relationship *isn't* working out if they have to keep talking it over. If she keeps trying to get things going to save the relationship and he keeps trying to avoid them because he sees them as weakening it, then each one's efforts to preserve the relationship appear to the other as reckless endangerment.

If talks (of any kind) do get going, men's and women's ideas about how to conduct them may be very different. For example, Dora is feeling comfortable and close to Tom. She settles into a chair after dinner and begins to tell him about a problem at work. She expects him to reassure her that he understands and that what she feels is normal and to return the intimacy by, perhaps, telling her a problem of his. Instead, Tom sidetracks her story, cracks jokes about it, questions her interpretation of the problem, and gives her advice about how to solve it and avoid such problems in the future.

All these responses, natural to men, are unexpected to women, who see them in terms of their own habits—negatively. When Tom comments on side issues or cracks jokes, Dora thinks he doesn't care about what she's saying and isn't really listening. If he challenges her interpretation of what went on, she feels he is criticizing her. If he tells her how to solve the problem, it makes her feel as if she's the patient to his doctor and that he's condescending. And, because he doesn't volunteer information about his problems, she feels he's implying he doesn't have any.

Her bid for intimacy ends up making her feel distant from him; she tries harder to regain intimacy the only way she knows how—by revealing more and more about herself; he tries harder by giving more insistent advice. The more problems she exposes, the more incompetent she feels, until they both see her as emotionally draining and problem-ridden. He wonders why she asks for his advice if she doesn't want to take it.

In a long-term relationship, a woman often feels, "After all this time, you 18
should know what I want without my telling you," whereas a man feels, "After
all this time, we should be able to tell each other what we want." These incongruent expectations pinpoint one of the key differences between men and
women. Communication is always a matter of balancing conflicting needs for
involvement and independence. Though everyone has both these needs,
women often have a relatively greater need for involvement and men a relatively greater need for independence. Being understood without saying what
you mean is the payoff of involvement; that's why women value it so highly.

Harriet complains to Morton, "Why don't you ask me how my day was?" 19
He replies, "If you have something to tell me, tell me. Why do you have to be
invited?" What he doesn't understand is that she wants an expression of interest, evidence that he cares how her day was, regardless of whether or not she
has something to tell.

A lot of trouble is caused between women and men by, of all things, pro- 20
nouns. Women often feel hurt when their partners use "I" or "me" in a situation in which they would use "we" or "us." When Morton announces, "I think
I'll go for a walk," Harriet feels specifically uninvited, though Morton later
claims she would have been welcome to join him. She feels locked out by his
use of "I" and his omission of an invitation: "Would you like to come?"

It's difficult to straighten out such misunderstandings because each per- 21
son feels convinced of the logic of his or her position and the illogic—or irre-
sponsibility—of the other's. Harriet knows that she always asks Morton how
his day was and that she'd never announce, "I'm going for a walk," without
inviting him to join her. If he talks differently to her, it must mean that he feels
differently. But Morton wouldn't feel unloved if Harriet didn't ask about his
day, and he would feel free to ask, "Can I come along?" if she announced she
was taking a walk. So he can't believe she is justified in having reactions he
knows he wouldn't have.

One of the commonest complaints wives have about their husbands is, 22
"He doesn't listen to me any more!" And a second is, "He doesn't talk to me any
more!" Since couples are parties to the same conversations, why are women
more dissatisfied with them than men?

The silent father was a presence common to the childhoods of many 23
women, and that image often becomes the model for the lover or husband.
But what attracts us can become flypaper to which we are unhappily stuck,
and many women who were lured to the strong, silent type as a lover find he's
turned into a lug as a husband. To a woman in a long-term relationship, male
silence may begin to feel like a brick wall against which she is banging her
head. These wives may be right in thinking that their husbands aren't listening
if the men don't value the telling of problems and secrets to establish rapport.
But some of the time men feel unjustly accused: "I *was* listening." And, some
of the time, they're right. They were.

Anthropologists Daniel Maltz and Ruth Borker report that women and 24
men have different ways of showing that they're listening. Women make—and
expect—more listening noises, such as "mhm" and "uh-huh." So, when a man

is listening to a woman telling him something, he's not likely to make enough such noises to convince her he's really hearing her. And, when a woman is listening to a man, making more "mhms" and "uh-huhs" than he expects or would use himself, he may get the impression she's impatient for him to finish or exaggerating her interest in what he's saying.

To complicate matters further, what women and men mean by such   25 noises may be different. Maltz and Borker contend that women tend to use these noises just to show they're listening and understanding, while men, in keeping with their different focus in communication, use them to show they agree. Women use the noises to indicate "I'm listening: go on," which serves the relationship level of talk; men use them to show what they think of what is being said, a response to the content of talk. So, when a man sits through his wife's talk, follows it, but doesn't agree with all she says, he's not going to shower her with "uh-huhs," and she's going to think he's not paying attention.

Sometimes, when men and women feel the other isn't paying attention,   26 they're right. And this may be because their assumptions about what's interesting are different. Muriel gets bored when Daniel goes on and on about the stock market. He gets bored when she goes on and on about the details of her day or the lives of people he doesn't even know.

It seems natural to women to tell and hear about what happened today, who   27 turned up at the bus stop, who called and what she said, not because these details are important in themselves but because the telling of them proves involvement—that you care about each other, that you have a best friend. Since men don't use talk for this purpose, they focus on the inherent insignificance of the details. What they find worth telling are facts about such topics as sports, politics, history, or how things work, and a woman listening to this kind of talk feels the man is lecturing her or being slightly condescending.

Women describing an experience often include reports of conversations.   28 Tone of voice, timing, intonation and wording are all re-created in the telling in order to explain—dramatize, really—the experience that is being reported. But most men aren't in the habit of reporting on conversations and are thus less likely to pay as much attention at the time they're going on. If men tell about an incident, they are more likely to give a brief summary instead of recreating what was said and how, and, if the woman asks, "What exactly did he say?" and "How did he say it?," the man probably can't remember.

These different habits have repercussions when a man and woman are   29 talking about their own relationship. She claims to recall exactly what he said, and she wants him to account for it. He can hardly do so because he has forgotten exactly what was said—if not the whole conversation. She secretly suspects he's only pretending not to remember; he secretly suspects that she's making up the details. So women's conversations with their women friends keep them in training for talking about their relationships with men, but many men come to such conversations with no training at all—and an uncomfortable sense that this really isn't their event.

Most of us expect our partners to be both lovers and best friends. Though   30 women and men may share fairly similar romantic expectations, they have very different ideas about how to be friends, and these are the differences that mount over time and can keep two people stewing in the juice of accumulated minor misunderstandings. Ironically, the big issues—values, interests, philosophies of life—can be talked about and agreed on. It is far harder to achieve harmony in the nuances of talk regarding simple day-to-day matters.

If you and your mate fight constantly about insignificant matters, it's nat- 31 ural to assume something's wrong with him—or with you for having chosen him. But, when you begin to recognize the different ways men and women talk, you can begin to accept the differences between you in habits and assumptions about how to have a conversation, show interest, be considerate, and so on. And you can start to make the small, steady changes that will accommodate two conflicting conversational styles.

Sometimes explaining assumptions can help. If a man starts to tell a 32 woman what to do to solve her problem, she may say, "Thanks for the advice, but I really don't want to be told what to do. I just want you to listen and say you understand." A man might want to explain, "If I challenge you, it's not to prove you wrong; it's just my way of paying attention to what you're telling me." Maybe you won't always correctly interpret your partner's intentions immediately, but you can remind yourself that, if you get a negative impression, it may not be what was intended.

Most of all, we have to give up our conviction that, as linguist Robin 33 Lakoff put it, "Love means never having to say 'What do you mean?'."

RESPONDING TO THE READING

Freewriting

Exercise 11a. Freewrite about experiences you have had that support or contradict ideas in Tannen's article.

Building Your Vocabulary

VOCABULARY LIST

Words to Look Up	My Definition	Dictionary Definition
hitches (3)		
cross-purposes (3)		
incredulous (6)		
camaraderie (7)		
preferences (8)		
accommodate (8)		
coercive (8)		
capricious (9)		
cross-cultural (10)		
divergent (13)		
endangerment (14)		

condescending (16)
incongruent (18)
rapport (23)
repercussions (29)
accumulated (30)
nuances (30)

Questions for Discussion

1. What is Deborah Tannen's purpose in writing this article?
2. Tannen uses the pronoun "you" in addressing the reader. Who is Tannen's intended audience?
3. Tannen argues that "differences in conversational style" between men and women cause miscommunication. What examples does she offer in support of this idea? Do you agree with her position?
4. Paraphrase Tannen's definition of culture in paragraph 10. Find another definition of culture in a dictionary or encyclopedia. How do they compare? How does Tannen's definition fit her purpose?
5. What connections does Tannen make between the "culture" learned as children and the adult behavior of men and women? What behavior does this early patterning cause?

TOPICS FOR WRITING

Topic 1.   Choose a spot for people-watching—an airport, a train station, a bus stop, a library, a shopping mall, a movie-theater lobby, a restaurant, a bar, or a coffee shop. Observe people carefully and record in your journal exactly what you see. Try to get more than just superficial descriptions. Look at the whole person and how he or she communicates. Examine such things as gestures, body movement, speech, and dress. Choose one or two of the people you observed. Then write an explanation of what they communicate to others and how they convey this message.

Topic 2.   Tannen's research shows that men and women (1) place different emphasis on involvement and independence, (2) learn different cultural patterns and habits as children, (3) have different ways to show they're listening, (4) make different assumptions about what is interesting, and (5) can learn to communicate.

Choose one of these ideas and write a paper about your own experience and observations on the subject.

Topic 3.   Interview half a dozen men and women, and ask them to discuss what they think are the four or five most common problems that occur when people try to communicate with their partner. Ask your interviewees for examples of the problems they mention and possible solutions. After gathering your information, write an essay in which you analyze the two or three problems that seemed most important to the people you interviewed. Include a description of each problem, a discussion of what causes the problem, and what might be done about it.

THE WRITING PROCESS: COMPARING AND CONTRASTING

In general, follow the steps in the writing process when making comparisons or contrasts. Writing techniques especially useful for comparing and contrasting are discussed below.

Additional Considerations for Developing a Topic

An important part of getting started on your comparison or contrast involves making sure that you can think of enough interesting points that the two people, events, situations, or objects you will analyze have in common. The best way to see if you can gather enough details about your two subjects is to do some preliminary writing before you decide on a topic.

Additional Considerations for Preliminary Writing

In order to determine whether you can generate the details you will need for your comparison or contrast, freewrite, draw an idea wheel, make a list, and ask yourself questions. Another useful tool for exploring similarities and differences is the T-graph, which allows you to visualize the similarities or differences between your subjects. One student who wanted to write about the contrast between her grandmother's shopping habits and her own drew the following T-graph:

Grandmother's Shopping Habits	**My Shopping Habits**
Arrives early to avoid crowds	Shop at noon because I like the crowds
Goes to lots of stores to look for sales and get the best bargains	Usually buy the first thing I see
Never buys more than one of anything	Own identical pairs of shoes in different colors

By drawing a T-graph like this one, you can quickly discover whether or not you have matching or contrasting points for your topics.

Additional Considerations for Thinking about Your Audience

You should ask yourself early in the writing process why you are writing your paper and what the point is that you want your comparison or contrast to make. You must communicate your purpose to your audience so they will know what they should be looking for in the comparison or contrast they are reading.

The student who wrote the preceding T-graph decided that her purpose was to describe how whimsical her shopping habits are when compared with those of her more conservative grandmother. Her next step was to turn that statement of purpose into a thesis: "My whimsical shopping habits are quite different from those of my conservative grandmother."

Additional Considerations for Organizing Ideas

The two organizational patterns you may choose for your comparison are (1) arrangement by subject or (2) point-by-point discussion. When details are arranged by subject, writers discuss all the points or ideas about one subject and then all the similar or contrasting points about the second subject. Writers who organize their papers using the point-by-point method make one point, comparing or contrasting both subjects together, and then a second and perhaps a third point about the two subjects. The following essays contrasting the student's shopping habits with her grandmother's illustrate these two arrangements.

1. ARRANGED BY SUBJECT

The gap between generations has no better example in my family than the one between my grandmother and me. In particular, my whimsical shopping habits are quite different from those of my conservative grandmother.

For one thing, Grandmother likes to shop early on weekdays to avoid the crowds. She is a frail woman who is deathly afraid of being knocked down by customers so intent on their shopping that they don't see her. By noon, Grandma has been to half a dozen stores, shopping for one particular article of clothing that she has seen on sale. As far as I know, she has never bought more than one of anything, regardless of the fact that it is on sale.

My shopping habits look thoughtless in comparison. I get up about 10:30 A.M. on weekends and arrive at my first store by noon. Unlike Grandmother, I shop during peak hours because I enjoy being in the middle of a crowd of eager shoppers; in their excitement I feel a kind of camaraderie. I let my enthusiasm carry me along and never bother planning what to buy. I usually pick up the first thing I see that appeals to me without giving much thought to whether I need it or not. Moreover, I usually have no idea what is on sale. If I happen to find a dress or pair of jeans I like that is marked down, I buy them instantly and consider myself lucky. In addition, I have none of Grandmother's reservations about buying several similar items. If I find something I really like, I will buy two or three if I can afford them. I have two pairs of the same style shoes, for example, because they fit me so well.

Family photographs show that my grandmother looked just like me when she was in her twenties. But if I were to judge by our shopping habits, I might question whether she and I are related at all.

FOR PRACTICE

Underline the points this student made in her essay about her grandmother's methods of shopping and then those about her own method of shopping. What do you notice about the sequence of ideas in the paragraphs on each subject?

2. DISCUSSED POINT-BY-POINT

The gap between generations has no better example in my family than the one between my grandmother and me. In particular, my whimsical shopping habits are quite different from those of my conservative grandmother.

For one thing, Grandmother likes to shop early on weekdays to avoid the crowds. She is a frail woman who is deathly afraid of being knocked down by customers so intent on their shopping that they don't see her. In contrast, I get up about 10:30 A.M. on weekends, the time I do most of my shopping, and arrive at my first store by noon, about the time my grandmother is ready to go home. Unlike Grandmother, I shop during peak hours because I enjoy being in the middle of a crowd of eager shoppers; in their excitement I feel a kind of camaraderie.

Grandmother is a very methodical shopper who knows exactly what she came to buy. By noon, Grandma has been to half a dozen stores, shopping for one particular article of clothing that she probably saw on sale. When I shop, I let my enthusiasm carry me along and never bother planning what to buy. As a result, I usually buy the first thing I see that appeals to me without giving much thought to whether I need it or not. Moreover, I usually have no idea what is on sale. If I happen to find a dress or pair of jeans I like that is marked down, I buy them instantly and consider myself lucky.

My grandmother and I differ in one other area as well. As far as I know, Grandmother has never bought more than one kind of anything, regardless of the fact that it is on sale. I am just the opposite. If I find something I really like, I will buy two or three if I can afford them. I have two pairs of the same style shoes, for example, because they fit so well.

Family photographs show that my grandmother looked just like me when she was in her twenties. But if I were to judge by our shopping habits, I might question whether she and I are related at all.

FOR PRACTICE

Underline the points in the second example that the student makes about her grandmother and herself; then compare this point-by-point discussion with the arrangement by subject that you read earlier. Which method of organization do you think is most effective and why?

Additional Considerations for Sharing Your Writing and Making Final Revisions

You may find the following checklist helpful when revising your essay. Put a check mark beside each question as you complete it.

Checklist

- ❑ Is the purpose for comparing or contrasting points about my subjects stated clearly in the introduction?
- ❑ What point of view have I adopted (first person or third person)?
- ❑ Have I maintained that perspective throughout the paper?
- ❑ Would additional details, examples, or explanations make any of the ideas I am comparing or contrasting more convincing?
- ❑ Is my paper's organizational pattern (arrangement of ideas by subject or point-by-point discussion) used consistently and clearly?
- ❑ Is each point I make about one subject matched by a corresponding point of comparison or contrast for my second subject?
- ❑ Do transitional words and phrases make it clear when I shift from one point of my comparison or contrast to another?
- ❑ Have I proofread carefully for sentence correctness, spelling, and punctuation?
- ❑ Overall, have I achieved my original purpose in comparing or contrasting my subjects?

FOR FURTHER READING

George and Ophelia
Gloria Naylor

Gloria Naylor has written several novels and short stories, including The Women of Brewster Place, *which was produced for television. The following excerpt from* Mama Day *traces the romance of George and Ophelia. Naylor writes this section as though*

George and Ophelia were writing letters to each other. Each shift in narration from George to Ophelia and back again is noted with an asterisk (*).

I woke up one morning, sometime in early November, and realized I   1
wanted to be with you for the rest of my life. Whether I could or not was
seriously open to question, but the desire was certainly there. From a child
I had to accept that some things you may want aren't meant for you—or
worse, not even good for you. I had wanted to know my parents, I had
wanted to be able to take part in sports. But none of that was to happen
because of reasons beyond my control, and being carefully trained not to let
that upset me, I made the best of it. The life I had, I had, and what I could
do, that was that. So the revelation about you that day wasn't earth shatter-
ing—and I had my usual shave and shower, fixed a bowl of oatmeal, and
went on to work—it was simply another item in a long list of things I had
wanted. But was it possible, could we live around each other? The rest of
your life seems like a long time when you're only thirty-one. We had to look
at each other and see if we could accept what was there—because that's
exactly what we were getting.

That was when I decided *not* to go out and buy the video cassette recorder.   2
I had been toying with the idea because the relationship was fairly new and
most women are so insecure in the beginning. They think it proves something
if they call on the spur of the moment—Could you come over?—and you do. It
only means that you came over, and if the weather's bad, you're wet. But I
enjoyed pampering them—a little time and silly little attentions, and they
would purr. Add some sort of personal gift to that now and then, and they'd
walk on water for you. They were happy, and I was happy because I couldn't
tolerate pouting. When a woman was screaming about the big things, I found
out she just wanted something small. That "you don't care" crap could be
nipped in the bud by randomly checking off days in your appointment calendar to have your secretary mail out a Hallmark card. That way you're "thinking" about her—whether you are or not.

Unfortunately, you and I were in the middle of the football season. A VCR   3
could have solved that. But if it was going to be possible to spend the rest of
my life with you, I might as well find out if you could accept me totally—and
that meant football. It wasn't a pastime, it was a passion. I didn't talk, I didn't
cuddle, I didn't want your hand on my crotch when the games were on—and
television was a poor second best to a live stadium. I was always fascinated
with the mechanics of the game, the mixture of science, raw strength, and a
touch of human unpredictability. It challenged me more than other sports,
with its infinite possibility of moves. Baseball and basketball were a linear display of skill and strength: if you thought fast and were strong and flexible, you
could endure. But football took that extra ounce from a man: when your physical frame is being beaten and slammed, you can simply become too tired to
think, to move. And sometimes your guts can even give out. So you keep going
because you keep going. It produces a high that's possible only when a man
has glimpsed the substance of immortality.

Since I couldn't be out on the fields in high school, I would help the coach   4
design plays, and he often listened to my suggestions because he said I had a
very rational mind. But there was nothing rational about what happened
when I became part of the crowd—and the bigger, the better. Unless you've
been there, you can't understand what it's like. Yet, even being there for someone like you wasn't enough—you'd only see twenty-two men on a field and sev-
enty-odd thousand screaming people. So why tell you what you couldn't
believe? The crowd became a single living organism—one pulse, one heartbeat, one throat. I've seen it bend down and breathe life into disheartened
players. I've seen it crush men with its hate. And I'm not talking in
metaphors—it could create miracles. It did at the Super Bowl in 1976. First
quarter and the Steelers were down seven-nothing to the Cowboys after only
five minutes of play. That can wreak havoc on a team's morale and throw a
whole game off. But my half of the crowd's body leaned forward as Terry
Bradshaw dropped back at the Cowboys' forty-eight and missiled the ball, too
high and heading out of bounds, on the right side. But there was the wide
receiver, Lynn Swann, his dark, lean body defying gravity as he leaped up—
caught it—and twisted midair to ram it down in bounds. A thirty-two-yard
gain. No, being there wasn't enough. You'd have to feel the force that sus-
pended almost two hundred pounds of flesh above the ground to believe that
we had willed him those wings.

I had gone to my first big game in 1968, the Jets against the Raiders in the   5
AFC championship, and I had been hooked on live games ever since. I had
made every AFC playoff and most of the NFCs even if they were on different
coasts. But if there was a conflict, or I couldn't get a flight to make both, the
AFC was my league, just like the Pats were my team—I guess I had a special
affinity for underdogs. I took a lot of kidding from Bruce about them. What do
you know about football? I'd say. I know a lot about losers, he'd answer, and
the New England Patriots are definitely that. But he shut up in '78 when they
took the Eastern division championship on a tie breaker over Miami. He had
no choice—I wouldn't let him get a word in edgewise for weeks. Of course,
they didn't make the final round of playoffs. But I still believed that I would
live to see them get to the Super Bowl. Maybe, as Bruce said, that was a bit too
much to ask. He and I had a good working relationship: we broke our butts
together and knew when it was time to go our separate ways—he in April for
the start of the trout season, and me in January for the end of the games.

That was the way it was, but more important, the way it was going to be.   6
And sure, I could give in to you that first year, get a VCR, and maybe only do
the Super Bowl on my vacation. But what about the next year and the next?
You were obsessed with the idea of my behavior spelling the ending of us, and
I was laying the groundwork for the beginning. So why didn't I just come right
out and tell you? Because I had my own insecurities as well. It was frightening, wanting you as much as I did. I couldn't imagine your being able to equal
that intensity, and I didn't even hope for that. Just some sign that I was beginning to matter, that I was special from the other men you'd known. And if
there were no signs of that, why give you carte blanche to hurt me—or worse,

despise me for my vulnerability? The more you were beginning to mean to me, the more close-mouthed I became, waiting. And waiting for what? Something more than temper tantrums about whether it was a Monday or Tuesday night I was free to see you—those weren't about me, they were about you. Even something more than the conditioned responses I knew I would receive by being thoughtful—that was about human nature. I guess I was waiting for some action—words would not suffice—that said, Yes, I'm doing this because he makes the difference.

*

You wouldn't talk to me. I don't mean when I was being irrational and 7
demanding—I deserved having the phone hung up on me then. But by the time the new year came, it was more than apparent that you were football. And I started trying to read the sports section although it confused the hell out of me. I even tried watching a game one night, but where's the fun in all of it when you can't see the ball? They line up, bend down, and all of a sudden they're in a pile, smelling each other's behinds. Okay, this was a part of your life I couldn't share and you seemed to prefer not talking about it. I could handle that, since I was bored by the whole subject anyway. But, George, there were too many other things we didn't talk about.

I had told you about where I grew up. I painted the picture of a small rural 8
community and my life with Grandma and Mama Day, so it seemed like any other small southern town and they two old ladies doting over the last grandchild. Of course, some things about Willow Springs you could never believe, but I showed you Candle Walk, we exchanged gifts that night instead of Christmas Eve. You thought it quaint and charming, and it was fun, undressing each other on the floor with all that soft light around us. But I did open up fully to share my feelings about my father running off and my mother dying so young. I talked to you about loneliness—all kinds. About my day-to-day frustrations with the job, the plans I had for my future—going back to college and getting a history degree. Not a marketable skill, but something I'd wanted to do. Coming from a place as rich in legend and history as the South, I'd always been intrigued by the subject. I talked and talked, but getting you to say anything about yourself was like pulling teeth. Oh, you'd hold a conversation—and you could make me laugh with the stories about some of your clients, about your partner's offbeat relatives, and the niece who put chewing gum in the filing cabinet.

And when I pressed you for *your* life, you'd say that you grew up in a boys' 9
shelter, that it was hard, working your way through Columbia and getting set up in your own business. You'd mention a woman named Mrs. Jackson sometimes. The world lost a lot when she died, you said. But you'd never talk about your *feelings* surrounding any of that. "Only the present has potential" is how you'd brush me off. Deal with the man in front of you. I was trying, George.

But what you didn't understand is that I thought you didn't trust me enough to share those feelings. A person is made up of much more than the "now." I had opened up to you about the frightened little girl inside of me because I'd finally come to believe that you would never hurt her. And the more I did that, the more you shut yourself off. I wasn't going to beg you to trust me. And since I refused to think of my life anymore without you in it, this was just the way it would have to be. But it was a bitter pill to swallow. I have to admit, sometimes it went down better than others. And the day I dropped by your office was not one of those better days.

It was so weird, walking back into that lobby, thinking about how it felt   10
the first time. It seemed as if I'd changed so much since then and it was only five months later. The next day you were going to Philadelphia for the playoffs and from there to San Diego, so you were working late to tie up loose ends. I was bringing you the T-shirt as a going-away present. I forgot who you said was playing who, or whose side you were on, so I just had printed up: HE'S MY FOOTBALL BABY. The broken elevator should have told me to turn around and go home. No need to meet you after work, you were coming over anyway. And your guilt about not spending a single day of your vacation with me would make you extremely nice. When I thought about how nice, I figured I'd meet you halfway and climb those steps.   11

I was out of breath by the fifth floor, and that's when I got my second warning: the exit door was locked, and I was trying to decide if it was worth it to go down one flight and try the other end of the building when a woman with curly red hair opened the door from the hall. Short and pretty. Blue-green eyes. And fine sprays of freckles over her nose and forehead. She said I was lucky she had worked overtime because the janitor always locked this stairwell door after a certain hour. I thanked her and stood there, looking at the stairway where she had disappeared, for a long, long time. When I finally made it into your office, the bag holding your T-shirt was small enough to fit between my fists.

"Why didn't you tell me Shawn worked in this building?"   12
"I didn't think it was relevant. How did you find out?"   13
"It's not *relevant*. But I'm sure that's the least of what you've been keeping   14
from me."
"I'm not going to start with you, Ophelia, okay? That part of my life is   15
over—she knows it, I know it, and you know it."
"I don't know anything, George. Not one goddammed thing. You see,   16
nothing about your life is relevant to me. I'm just someone you fuck when you have a mind to—I should start charging."
"You've got a dirty mouth, and I don't like that."   17
"I don't care what you like. Since when do you care about me—you sneak   18
around and hide things from me, you—"
"Ophelia, what difference did it make where she worked? If I still wanted   19
to see her, I could see her."
"I'm not talking about *her*."   20
"Then what are you talking about, or is this some new kind of tantrum to   21
take up my time because I'm going to the games?"

"Forget it, George. Just forget it. Here, I brought you—"   22

You ignored the bag on your desk. "No, I don't want to forget it. What do   23
I hide from you? You know as much about me as anyone."

"Then that's pathetic—because I don't know anything."   24

"This is getting us nowhere."   25

"That's where we've been for a while."   26

"Okay, Ophelia, what could you possibly need to know about me that I   27
haven't told you—my age, my background, you're standing in the place where
I work. The only thing left is my social security number and shoe size. So
come on—ask me a question. Any question. You've got my undivided attention. Ah, I see we have silence. That just shows you how ridiculous you can be
with absolutely no effort."

"And you can be one sarcastic son-of-a-bitch."   28

"You know I hate that word."   29

"Yeah, that I do know. And here's a question for you—why, George? Why   30
do you hate being called a son-of-a-bitch? A pompous, snide, uptight son-of-
a-bitch?"

Your face was unreadable as you put on your coat, picked up your brief-   31
case, and walked out. You had left my T-shirt on your desk. I walked out without it as well. You were nowhere in sight when I got to the outer hall. You
didn't call me that night, and you didn't answer your phone. I knew not to try
the next day; you were in Philadelphia. And from Philadelphia to San Diego.
Come hell or high water, you were going to the games. And when you got back
I would have to make the first call anyway. I suppose I owed you an apology,
but there was something that you owed me.

The third warning was my crushing disappointment when the phone rang   32
the next evening and it wasn't you. An old boyfriend. No, I wasn't doing a
thing. And sure, I'd like to have dinner. His place? Why not. Yes, I remembered where it was. Those seven blocks were long ones: four over to Riverside
Drive, and a left turn to go north. I pushed all of those warnings out of my
mind as I was passing Riverside Park. So when I reached his building, I didn't
hesitate before going in.

*

I came back from Philadelphia that night to answer your question. And   33
to ask you to marry me. Enough was enough. If we kept on like this, there
wasn't much hope for us. Somebody had to take the first chance. I had understood what you were saying in my office perfectly, but I didn't want to deal
with it. I wasn't going to let you manipulate me into opening up my guts
before I was ready. But the point was, when would I ever be ready? How frustrated would you have to get before I had this elusive guarantee from you that
I was seeking? It's funny, I was losing you because of my fear of losing you.
Star-crossed. Yeah, that's what we were. Always missing each other. That

weekend was a total bust. I didn't have the spirit to be racing to a plane out to California—it was hard enough concentrating on the game in front of me. It didn't matter that the Eagles had won. They were coming up against either Oakland or San Diego in the Super Bowl, and either of those teams could beat them with their hands behind their backs. Yeah, in two weeks it was going to be an AFC victory in New Orleans. I was charmed by that city, and maybe I could enjoy it again, once I got all of this straightened out with you.

New Orleans. Tampa. Miami. None of those cities seemed like the real 34 South. Nothing like the place you came from. I was always in awe of the stories you told so easily about Willow Springs. To be born in a grandmother's house, to be able to walk and see where a great-grandfather and even great-great-grandfather was born. You had more than a family, you had a history. And I didn't even have a real last name. I'm sure my father and mother lied to each other about even their first names. How would he know years later that I might especially wonder about his? When the arrangement is to drop twenty bucks on a dresser for a woman, you figure that's all you've left behind. I had no choice but to emphasize my nows, while in back of all that stubbornness was the fear that you might think less of me. But I was going to be a lot less without you in my life anyway. So here goes nothing, I thought, as I walked up Broadway toward your street.

I decided to phone from the corner first. I could have walked in with my 35 key, but I wanted to give you a chance to invite me up. At that moment, I needed all the encouragement I could get. No answer. I was about to redial when I spotted you across the avenue, heading west. I recognized the red cashmere coat I had given you for Christmas and that undeniably proud strut. Was she taking a walk? I thought. Going out to meet friends? By the time I'd made it across Broadway myself, you were turning the corner two blocks ahead onto Riverside Drive. Perhaps it was glimpsing the side of your face or a certain angle of your shoulders that gave me the feeling something wasn't right. I started to speed up. I turned the corner and was just about to call out when the door closed behind you in the lobby.

I waited all night. 36

*

It was a gray and cold morning when I came out of that building and saw 37 you standing there across the Drive, leaning against the promenade wall, your trench coat buttoned to the neck with the collar up. It didn't matter how you got there. All those months I had wondered, and this is how it ends. I was too drained to feel anything—shame, fear—when you finally walked over. Your face was still unreadable. And your voice was matter of fact when you took your hand out of your pocket and slapped the living daylights out of me.

"My mother was a whore. And that's why I don't like being called the son 38 of a bitch."

My eyes were still blurred. My bottom lip had been slammed against my 39
teeth and was starting to bleed. Your fingers were like a vise when they
gripped mine as you began dragging me up Riverside Drive to Harlem. We
reached the pier at 125th Street. Still crushing my hand, you pointed to a
brownstone across the way.

"I found out that's where I was born. She was fifteen years old. And she 40
worked out of that house. My father was one of her customers."

A deserted, crumbling restaurant stood near the pier. The side windows 41
had been broken, but across the front in peeling letters I could read, Bailey's
Cafe. And I could hear the cars moving above us on the overpass, the muddy
water hitting against the rocks, the sound of gulls.

"The man who owned this place found me one morning, lying on a stack 42
of newspapers. He called the shelter and they picked me up. I was three
months old."

We went past Bailey's Cafe to the edge of the pier. You finally let my hand 43
go, put yours back into your pocket, and stared into the water.

"Later, her body washed up down there. I don't have all the pieces. But 44
there are enough of them to lead me to believe that she was not a bitch."

You then looked me straight in the face.   45

"The last name I have was given to me at the shelter on Staten Island 46
where I lived until I was eighteen—Wallace P. Andrews. And how do I *feel*
about all this?"

You smiled. I guess I could call it a smile.   47

"I feel that men will often grow up thinking of women in the same way 48
they think of their mothers. You see, when I was growing up, there was no reason for me to neglect her on the days that would have been important: her
birthday, anniversary, or the second Sunday in May. I didn't forget to call now
and then to ask her how she was doing. I didn't find her demands annoying, or
her worries unnecessary. I was the kind of son who didn't refuse to share my
friends, my interests, or my hopes for the future with her. Yeah, that's pretty
close to the kind of son I was."

I don't know how long I closed my eyes, but when I opened them, I asked 49
you to marry me. Next week, you said, if I didn't mind spending my honeymoon in New Orleans.

RESPONDING TO THE READING

Freewriting

Exercise 11b.   Write steadily for fifteen minutes to record your initial reactions to "George and Ophelia." Which character do you find most sympathetic? How do you explain your reaction?

Exercise 11c.   What advice would you like to give either George or Ophelia?

Building Your Vocabulary

VOCABULARY LIST

Words to Look Up	My Definition	Dictionary Definition
unpredictability (3)		
infinite (3)		
linear (3)		
wreak havoc (4)		
carte blanche (6)		
vulnerability (6)		
suffice (6)		
doting (8)		
intrigued (8)		
snide (30)		
elusive (33)		
promenade (37)		

Questions for Discussion

1. Summarize the stages in the relationship between George and Ophelia.
2. In this story we learn that George, the first speaker, is not entirely sure about his relationship with Ophelia. Explain how he feels about her and what makes him unsure about their being together. Compare his situation to a similar experience of your own.
3. What uncertainties does Ophelia have about the relationship? Are her feelings justified?
4. What do you think of George's description of how he handles women (see paragraph 2)? What does he do with Ophelia that is different? How do you explain his change of tactics?
5. How does Ophelia's view of football differ from George's? Which comes closer to your view?

TOPICS FOR WRITING

Topic 1.   Write a paper that uses specific examples to define love. Try to develop *one* aspect of love in detail.

Topic 2.   On the first page of this selection from *Mama Day,* George explains how he treats women. Write a paper giving your own advice about how to get along with the opposite sex. Again, include real-life examples to convey your ideas.

Topic 3.   Early in the story George explains why he likes football. Pick a particular sport that you enjoy playing or watching and explain several reasons why you like it. Use details and explanations as George does to convince the reader that this sport is worth watching. If you dislike a sport, explain why you do; use examples to illustrate how your experience shaped your opinion.

Topic 4.   George describes how the crowd acts as a "single organism" during a football game. Write your own vivid description of the crowd at a concert, ball game, or other large gathering you have witnessed. Be sure to capture the mood(s) of the crowd. Note if that mood changed during the event. Tie your description to particular events as George does in paragraph 4.

Topic 5.   Write a comparison of two relationships you have had or observed. Describe in detail the similarities or differences between the relationships. Consider examining the way the relationships began, how they developed, the way the couples communicate, what they have in common, the partners' roles in the family, or their expectations and whether these are met. Your thesis should include the main point you want to make in this comparison. At the end of your discussion, come to some conclusion about the relative success of these relationships.

A Thinly Disguised Message
Deborah Marquardt

Deborah Marquardt is a freelance writer whose work has appeared in numerous publications, including The New York Times, McCall's, *and* Business Magazine. *In the following article, published in* Ms. *magazine, she describes the effects of advertising on women's image of themselves.*

The new svelte Betty Crocker looks as if she's never tasted an angel food   1
cake, much less a double fudge brownie, and the Campbell Kids have lost a lot of their baby-fat bounce. And when was the last time you saw a size 12 model smiling from the pages of a magazine?

If the media message is thin, thin, thin, and if the ordinary person is   2
exposed to 400 to 1,500 advertising messages per day, is it coincidence that medical specialists estimate—conservatively—that 12 percent of college-age females have serious eating disorders?

Two media researchers, armed with separate studies, think not. They   3
believe that many young women are literally dying to achieve the pervasive, incredibly thin image spawned by the advertising industry because women perceive these images as "standard" and "acceptable."

Linda Lazier-Smith, Ph.D., currently teaching advertising at the Ohio State   4
University in Columbus, and Alice Gagnard, Ph.D., at Southern Methodist University in Dallas, both became interested in the advertisements/anorexic

link through encounters with students. "I was teaching at Marquette University in Milwaukee when one of my students missed four weeks of school because she was hospitalized with anorexia," recalls Gagnard. "She described her reha- bilitation program in which she had to 'unlearn' how to look at the media."

Lazier-Smith had similar experiences at Indiana University in Bloom- 5 ington when she began lecturing students on media and societal expectations. Many young women in the room said, "I'm trying to be like those women."

Although the researchers approached their studies differently, the conclu- 6 sions were startlingly similar. Gagnard, in "From Feast to Famine: Depiction of Ideal Body Type in Magazine Advertising, 1950–1984," reviewed 961 half page or larger ads in *Ladies' Home Journal, Woman's Day,* and *McCall's* in the years 1950, 1960, 1970, and 1984. Her findings weren't surprising: most mod- els were young, white, and female. The use of thin models increased each decade since 1950, reaching 46 percent in the 1980s, while the use of over- weight and obese models decreased from 12 percent in 1950 to 3 percent in 1984. (Overweight male models were far more common in all decades.)

The models were also rated by trained researchers, and although the thin 7 models were judged to be more attractive and successful, the overweight and obese models were considered the happiest, revealing, Gagnard notes, the age-old "fat and jolly" stereotype. But she concludes that the advertising stud- ied shows "a reflection of our perpetuation of America's preoccupation with slimness."

Lazier-Smith asked three groups of young women to complete question- 8 naires to elicit attitudes on physical attractiveness, such as the existence of an "ideal body shape," and media influences in promoting it. Thirty high-school students, a group of college-age anorexics, and a group of Indiana University women students were asked to evaluate the successfulness and happiness of women models in print ads and to match models—who were extremely thin (anorexic shape), normal (size 12 to 14), or full-figured—with various occupa- tions and roles in commercials.

Most of the women surveyed agreed that there is an "ideal body shape in 9 American society to which women are expected to conform." Both the high schoolers (the high-risk age for anorexia) and anorexics selected body size and shape as the most important features in women, and the "ideal" woman for all three groups was a size seven and a half.

On the success scale, the thin models were overwhelmingly voted most 10 successful and the heavier models least. And when asked to match the models in the pictures with occupations or commercials, no one picked "average" size women. This startled Lazier-Smith above all. "Average is invisible. You have to be either extreme to be noticed."

In presentations to national professional organizations, both educators 11 have detected an interest in the findings, although they admit most people still aren't sensitive to eating disorders. "We would like to see more realism in ads," said Lazier-Smith. "That doesn't have to mean fat and ugly. We got away from asses and boobs and superwoman because women complained. We'd like an awareness in the ad community that the constant use of overthin models is totally unrealistic, that it's not necessary to sell products, and that it might be injuring young minds."

RESPONDING TO THE READING

Freewriting

Exercise 11d.   Freewrite about advertisements that have influenced you or someone you know.

Exercise 11e.   Freewrite about destructive or positive effects of advertising. Compare your ideas with those of your classmates.

Building Your Vocabulary

VOCABULARY LIST

Words to Look Up	My Definition	Dictionary Definition
pervasive (3)		
spawned by (3)		
anorexic (4)		

Questions for Discussion

1. What is the "thinly disguised" message conveyed by advertisements that use skinny models? Explain the possible meaning of the title.
2. Write a brief definition of anorexia. Who might be influenced by the advertisements that use "anorexic models" (sizes four through seven)? Have you known women or men who imitate models they see in advertisements?
3. Do you think advertising has the power to shape behavior as Marquardt's researchers suggest? Give your reasoning in either case.

TOPICS FOR WRITING

Several of the following topics ask you to analyze the images in advertisements, the audience they target, and their strategies for selling a particular product. Use the eight steps listed here as a guide for analyzing the messages in advertisements.

1. Study the advertisement(s) you have selected for several minutes.
2. Record your initial impressions of the action, wording, color, and design. Assess their impact on you.

3. Block off areas of the ad and describe what is in the background, the foreground, the area to the left, the area to the right, and the area in the center.
4. Write a brief description of what the people or objects in the ad look like and what they are doing.
5. Do you find anything appealing or offensive about the advertisement?
6. What do the words say? How are they making an appeal to a potential buyer?
7. What connections does the advertisement ask you to make between what is going on in the ad and the product being sold?
8. What audience is the advertisement targeting? How can you tell?

Topic 1. Select several ads that seem to reflect what Dr. Alice Gagnard calls "America's preoccupation with slimness." Study the ads for several minutes. Freewrite about your initial reactions to each advertisement's action, models, wording, color, and design. Block off sections of the ad, noting what is in the background, foreground, on the left or right, and in the center. Which of these areas catch your attention? Why? Note what the ads are selling, how models are posed, and what is said in the written portion of the ad. Select several advertisements and write a paper in which you explain the techniques the advertisers are using to sell their product.

Topic 2. Pick two advertisements and compare them on the basis of how they present the people in the ads. Do some freewriting about activities, positions, facial expressions, appearance of the models, language, and the overall arrangements of things. You might focus on ads that use particular groups of people like mothers, couples, rugged men, "liberated" women, cowboys, etc. In your paper, compare the ways these advertisements convey a dominant image of the people in them.

Topic 3. Compare two television or magazine advertisements—one that you find very pleasing, another that offends you in some way. Write a detailed explanation of what, exactly, causes you to respond as you do.

Topic 4. Examine magazine and television advertisements and reports on popular stars, and interview men and women you know to capture their idea of the ideal male. Once you have gathered your information, group the characteristics that appear most frequently, organize them according to their importance, and write a comparison between people's ideal and the "ideal male" portrayed by advertisers.

Topic 5. Use your own experience, observations, and reading to explore the idea that "there is an ideal body shape in American society to which women are expected to conform." What is the ideal image, and what do women do to achieve it? (Magazine, newspaper, and television advertisements are good sources for compiling this notion of an "ideal body.")

Topic 6.   Interview young men or women to find out whether they try to conform to an "image" projected in the media. Compare the extent to which these men and women are obsessed with such conformity. The following questions may help you gather information for your paper.

> What ideal(s) are they aiming for?
> What do they do to conform to that image or ideal?
> Do they make sacrifices to attain what they want? If so, what are they?
> How important is it to them to conform?
> Why is it important?

Iron John
Robert Bly

Until the publication of Iron John *in 1990, Robert Bly was best known for his poetry, for which he won a National Book Award in 1968, and his translations of Latin-American and other poems. In the following selection from the first chapter of* Iron John, *Bly explores the emotional and spiritual aspects of what it means to be a male in modern American culture. Bly contends that most American men have either developed an unnatural softness or have become savage and violent. He argues that men must set free their "Wild Man," his term for ancient male energy, if they want to become fully developed human beings.*

1   We talk a great deal about "the American man," as if there were some constant quality that remained stable over decades, or even within a single decade.

2   The men who live today have veered far away from the Saturnian, old-man-minded farmer, proud of his introversion, who arrived in New England in 1630, willing to sit through three services in an unheated church. In the South, an expansive, motherbound cavalier developed, and neither of these two "American men" resembled the greedy railroad entrepreneur that later developed in the Northeast, nor the reckless I-will-do-without culture settlers of the West.

3   Even in our own era the agreed-on model has changed dramatically. During the fifties, for example, an American character appeared with some consistency that became a model of manhood adopted by many men: the Fifties male.

4   He got to work early, labored responsibly, supported his wife and children, and admired discipline. Reagan is a sort of mummified version of this dogged type. This sort of man didn't see women's souls well, but he appreciated their bodies; and his view of culture and America's part in it was boyish and optimistic. Many of his qualities were strong and positive, but underneath

the charm and bluff there was, and there remains, much isolation, depriva-
tion, and passivity. Unless he has an enemy, he isn't sure that he is alive.

The Fifties man was supposed to like football, be aggressive, stick up for 5
the United States, never cry, and always provide. But receptive space or intimate space was missing in this image of a man. The personality lacked some
sense of flow. The psyche lacked compassion in a way that encouraged the
unbalanced pursuit of the Vietnam war, just as, later, the lack of what we
might call "garden" space inside Reagan's head led to his callousness and bru-
tality toward the powerless in El Salvador, toward old people here, the unem-
ployed, schoolchildren, and poor people in general.

The Fifties male had a clear vision of what a man was, and what male 6
responsibilities were, but the isolation and one-sidedness of his vision were
dangerous.

During the sixties, another sort of man appeared. The waste and violence 7
of the Vietnam war made men question whether they knew what an adult
male really was. If manhood meant Vietnam, did they want any part of it?
Meanwhile, the feminist movement encouraged men to actually look at
women, forcing them to become conscious of concerns and sufferings that the
Fifties male labored to avoid. As men began to examine women's history and
women's sensibility, some men began to notice what was called their *feminine*
side and pay attention to it. This process continues to this day, and I would say
that most contemporary men are involved in it in some way.

There's something wonderful about this development—I mean the prac- 8
tice of men welcoming their own "feminine" consciousness and nurturing it—
this is important—and yet I have the sense that there is something wrong. The
male in the past twenty years has become more thoughtful, more gentle. But
by this process he has not become more free. He's a nice boy who pleases not
only his mother but also the young woman he is living with.

In the seventies I began to see all over the country a phenomenon that we 9
might call the "soft male." Sometimes even today when I look out at an audience, perhaps half the young males are what I'd call soft. They're lovely, valuable people—I like them—they're not interested in harming the earth or starting wars. There's a gentle attitude toward life in their whole being and style
of living.

But many of these men are not happy. You quickly notice the lack of 10
energy in them. They are life-preserving but not exactly life-giving. Ironically,
you often see these men with strong women who positively radiate energy.
Here we have a finely tuned young man, ecologically superior to his father,
sympathetic to the whole harmony of the universe, yet he himself has little
vitality to offer. The strong or life-giving women who graduated from the sixties, so to speak, or who have inherited an older spirit, played an important
part in producing this life-preserving, but not life-giving, man.

I remember a bumper sticker during the sixties that read "WOMEN SAY 11
YES TO MEN WHO SAY NO." We recognize that it took a lot of courage to
resist the draft, go to jail, or move to Canada, just as it took courage to accept

the draft and go to Vietnam. But the women of twenty years ago were definitely saying that they preferred the softer receptive male.

So the development of men was affected a little in this preference. Non-   12
receptive maleness was equated with violence, and receptive maleness was
rewarded.

Some energetic women, at that time and now in the nineties, chose and   13
still choose soft men to be their lovers and, in a way, perhaps, to be their sons.
The new distribution of "yang"[1] energy among couples didn't happen by accident. Young men for various reasons wanted their harder women, and women
began to desire softer men. It seemed like a nice arrangement for a while, but
we've lived with it long enough now to see that it isn't working out.

I first learned about the anguish of "soft" men when they told their stories   14
in early men's gatherings. . . . When the younger men spoke it was not uncommon for them to be weeping within five minutes. The amount of grief and
anguish in these younger men was astounding to me.

Part of their grief rose out of remoteness from their fathers, which they   15
felt keenly, but partly, too, grief flowed from trouble in their marriages or relationships. They had learned to be receptive, but receptivity wasn't enough to
carry their marriages through troubled times. In every relationship something
fierce is needed once in a while: both the man and the woman need to have it.
But at the point when it was needed, often the young man came up short. He
was nurturing, but something else was required—for his relationship, and for
his life.

The "soft" male was able to say, "I can feel your pain, and I consider your   16
life as important as mine, and I will take care of you and comfort you." But he
could not say what he wanted, and stick by it. *Resolve* of that kind was a different matter. . . .

Finding Iron John

One of the fairy tales that speak of a third possibility for men, a third mode, is   17
a story called "Iron John" or "Iron Hans." Though it was first set down by the
Grimm brothers around 1820, this story could be ten or twenty thousand
years old.

As the story starts, we find out that something strange has been happen-   18
ing in a remote area of the forest near the king's castle. When hunters go into
this area, they disappear and never come back. Twenty others go after the
first group and do not come back. In time, people begin to get the feeling that
there's something weird in that part of the forest, and they "don't go there
anymore."

One day an unknown hunter shows up at the castle and says, "What can I   19
do? Anything dangerous to do around here?"

The King says: "Well, I could mention the forest, but there's a problem.   20
The people who go out there don't come back. The return rate is not good."

---

[1]The active, male principle in Chinese Taoist philosophy.

"That's just the sort of thing I like," the young man says. So he goes into   21
the forest and, interestingly, he goes there *alone*, taking only his dog. The
young man and his dog wander about in the forest and they go past a pond.
Suddenly a hand reaches up from the water, grabs the dog, and pulls it down.

The young man doesn't respond by becoming hysterical. He merely says,   22
"This must be the place."

Fond as he is of his dog and reluctant as he is to abandon him, the hunter   23
goes back to the castle, rounds up three more men with buckets, and then
comes back to the pond to bucket out the water. Anyone who's ever tried it will
quickly note that such bucketing is very slow work.

In time, what they find, lying on the bottom of the pond, is a large man   24
covered with hair from head to foot. The hair is reddish—it looks a little like
rusty iron. They take the man back to the castle, and imprison him. The King
puts him in an iron cage in the courtyard, calls him "Iron John," and gives the
key into the keeping of the Queen.

Let's stop the story here for a second.   25

When a contemporary man looks down into his psyche, he may, if condi-   26
tions are right, find under the water of his soul, lying in an area no one has visited for a long time, an ancient hairy man.

The mythological systems associate hair with the instinctive and the sex-   27
ual and the primitive. What I'm suggesting, then, is that every modern male
has, lying at the bottom of his psyche, a large, primitive being covered with
hair down to his feet. Making contact with this Wild Man[2] is the step the
Eighties male or the Nineties male has yet to take. That bucketing-out process
has yet to begin in our contemporary culture.

As the story suggests very delicately, there's more than a little fear around   28
this hairy man, as there is around all change. When a man begins to develop
the receptive side of himself and gets over his initial skittishness, he usually
finds the experience to be wonderful. He gets to write poetry and go out and
sit by the ocean, he doesn't have to be on top all the time in sex anymore, he
becomes empathetic—it's a new, humming, surprising world.

But going down through water to touch the Wild Man at the bottom of   29
the pond is quite a different matter. The being who stands up is frightening,
and seems even more so now, when the corporations do so much work to produce the sanitized, hairless, shallow man. When a man welcomes his respon-
siveness, or what we sometimes call his internal woman, he often feels
warmer, more companionable, more alive. But when he approaches what I'll
call the "deep male," he feels risk. Welcoming the Hairy Man *is* scary and
risky, and it requires a different sort of courage. Contact with Iron John

---

[2]In his introduction to *Iron John,* Robert Bly writes, "I speak of the Wild Man in this book, and
the distinction between the savage man and the Wild Man is crucial throughout. The savage
mode does great damage to soul, earth, and humankind; we can say that though the savage man
is wounded he prefers not to examine it. The Wild Man, who has examined his wound,
resembles a Zen priest, a shaman, or a woodsman more than a savage."

requires a willingness to descend into the male psyche and accept what's dark down there, including the *nourishing* dark. . . .

The Loss of the Golden Ball

Now back to the story.   30

One day the King's eight-year-old son is playing in the courtyard with the   31
golden ball he loves, and it rolls into the Wild Man's cage. If the young boy
wants the ball back, he's going to have to approach the Hairy Man and ask him
for it. But this is going to be a problem.

The golden ball reminds us of that unity of personality we had as chil-   32
dren—a kind of radiance, or wholeness, before we split into male and female,
rich and poor, bad and good. The ball is golden, as the sun is, and round. Like
the sun, it gives off a radiant energy from the inside.

We notice that the boy is eight. All of us, whether boys or girls, lose some-   33
thing around the age of eight. If we still have the golden ball in kindergarten, we
lose it in grade school. Whatever is still left we lose in high school. In "The Frog
Prince," the princess's ball fell into a well. Whether we are male or female, once
the golden ball is gone, we spend the rest of our lives trying to get it back.

The first stage in retrieving the ball, I think, is to accept—firmly, defi-   34
nitely—that the ball has been lost. Freud[3] said: "What a distressing contrast
there is between the radiant intelligence of the child and the feeble mentality
of the average adult."

So where is the golden ball? Speaking metaphorically, we could say that   35
the sixties culture told men they would find their golden ball in sensitivity,
receptivity, cooperation, and nonaggressiveness. But many men gave up all
aggressiveness and still did not find the golden ball.

The Iron John story says that a man can't expect to find the golden ball in   36
the feminine realm, because that's not where the ball is. A bridegroom secretly
asks his wife to give him back the golden ball. I think she'd give it to him if she
could, because most women in my experience do not try to block men's
growth. But she can't give it to him, because she doesn't have it. What's more,
she's lost her own golden ball and can't find that either.

Oversimplifying, we could say that the Fifties male always wants a woman   37
to return his golden ball. The Sixties and Seventies man, with equal lack of
success, asks his interior feminine to return it.

The Iron John story proposes that the golden ball lies within the magnetic   38
field of the Wild Man, which is a very hard concept for us to grasp. We have
to accept the possibility that the true radiant energy in the male does not hide
in, reside in, or wait for us in the feminine realm, nor in the macho/John
Wayne realm, but in the magnetic field of the deep masculine. It is protected
by the *instinctive* one who's underwater and who has been there we don't
know how long.

---

[3]Sigmund Freud (1856–1939), an Austrian physician, renowned for his theory of psychoanalysis.

In "The Frog Prince" it's the frog, the un-nice one, the one that everyone 39 says "Ick!" to, who brings the golden ball back. And in the Grimm brothers version the frog himself turns into the prince only when a hand throws him against the wall.

Most men want some nice person to bring the ball back, but the story 40 hints that we won't find the golden ball in the force field of an Asian guru or even the force field of gentle Jesus. Our story is not anti-Christian but pre-Christian by a thousand years or so, and its message is still true—getting the golden ball back is incompatible with certain kinds of conventional tameness and niceness.

The kind of wildness, or un-niceness, implied by the Wild Man image is 41 not the same as macho energy, which men already know enough about. Wild Man energy, by contrast, leads to forceful action undertaken, not with cruelty, but with resolve. . . .

The first step amounts to approaching the cage and asking for the golden 42 ball back. Some men are ready to take that step, while others haven't yet bucketed the water out of the pond—they haven't left the collective male identity and gone out into the unknown area alone, or gone with only their dog. . . .

Jung[4] remarked that all successful requests to the psyche involve deals. 43 The psyche likes to make deals. If part of you, for example, is immensely lazy and doesn't want to do any work, a flat-out New Year's resolution won't do any good. The whole thing will go better if you say to the lazy part: "You let me work for an hour, then I'll let you be a slob for an hour—deal?" So in "Iron John," a deal is made: the Wild Man agrees to give the golden ball back if the boy opens the cage.

The boy, apparently frightened, runs off. He doesn't even answer. Isn't 44 that what happens? We have been told so often by parents, ministers, grade-school teachers, and high-school principals that we should have nothing to do with the Wild Man that when he says "I'll return the ball if you let me out of the cage," we don't even reply.

Maybe ten years pass now. On "the second day" the man could be twenty- 45 five. He goes back to the Wild Man and says, "Could I have my ball back?" The Wild Man says, "Yes, if you let me out of the cage."

Actually, just returning to the Wild Man a second time is a marvelous 46 thing; some men never come back at all. The twenty-five-year-old man hears the sentence all right, but by now he has two Toyotas and a mortgage, maybe a wife and a child. How can he let the Wild Man out of the cage? A man usually walks away the second time also without saying a word.

Now ten more years pass. Let's say the man is now thirty-five . . . have you 47 ever seen the look of dismay on the face of a thirty-five-year-old man? Feeling overworked, alienated, empty, he asks the Wild Man with full heart this time: "Could I have my golden ball back?"

"Yes," the Wild Man says, "If you let me out of my cage." 48

[4]A Swiss psychiatrist (1875–1961) who explored the connections between the individual and universal experiences or "archetypes" common to many cultures and eras.

Now something marvelous happens in the story. The boy speaks to the   49
Wild Man, and continues the conversation. He says, "Even if I wanted to let
you out, I couldn't, because I don't know where the key is."

That's so good. By the time we are thirty-five we don't know where the key   50
is. It isn't exactly that we have forgotten—we never knew where it was in the
first place.

The story says that when the King locked up the Wild Man, "he gave the   51
key into the keeping of the Queen," but we were only about seven then, and in
any case our father never told us what he had done with it. So where is the
key? . . .

The Wild Man replies, "The key is under your mother's pillow."   52

The key is not inside the ball, nor in the golden chest, nor in the safe . . .   53
the key is under our mother's pillow—just where Freud said it would be.

Getting the key back from under the mother's pillow is a troublesome task.   54
Freud, taking advice from a Greek play,[5] says that a man should not skip over
the mutual attraction between himself and his mother if he wants a long life.
The mother's pillow, after all, lies in the bed near where she makes love to
your father. Moreover, there's another implication attached to the pillow.

Michael Meade, the myth teller, once remarked to me that the pillow is   55
also the place where the mother stores all her expectations for you. She
dreams: "My son the doctor." "My son the Jungian analyst." "My son the Wall
Street genius." But very few mothers dream: "My son the Wild Man."

On the son's side, he isn't sure he wants to take the key. Simply transfer-   56
ring the key from the mother's to a guru's pillow won't help. Forgetting that
the mother possesses it is a bad mistake. A mother's job is, after all, to civilize
the boy, and so it is natural for her to keep the key. All families behave alike:
on this planet, "The King gives the key into the keeping of the Queen." . . .

And the keys has to be *stolen*. . . . No mother worth her salt would give the   57
key anyway. If a son can't steal it, he doesn't deserve it.

"I want to let the Wild Man out!"   58

"Come over and give Mommy a kiss."   59

Mothers are intuitively aware of what would happen if he got the key: they   60
would lose their boys. The possessiveness that mothers typically exercise on
sons—not to mention the possessiveness that fathers typically exercise on
daughters—can never be underestimated.

The means of getting the key back varies with each man, but suffice it to   61
say that democratic or nonlinear approaches will not carry the day. One
rather stiff young man danced one night for about six hours, vigorously, and
in the morning remarked, "I got some of the key back last night." Another man
regained the key when he acted like a whole-hearted Trickster for the first
time in his life, remaining fully conscious of the tricksterism. Another man
stole the key when he confronted his family and refused to carry any longer
the shame for the whole family.

---

[5]Sophocles' *Oedipus Rex*.

We could spend days talking of how to steal the key in a practical way. The 62
story itself leaves everything open, and simply says, "One day he stole the key,
brought it to the Wild Man's cage, and opened the lock. As he did so, he
pinched one of his fingers.". . . The Wild Man is then free at last, and it's clear
that he will go back to his own forest, far from "the castle."

What Does the Boy Do?

At this point a number of things could happen. If the Wild Man returns to his 63
forest while the boy remains in the castle, the fundamental historical split in
the psyche between primitive man and the civilized man would reestablish
itself in the boy. The boy, on his side, could mourn the loss of the Wild Man
forever. Or he could replace the key under the pillow before his parents got
home, then say he knows nothing about the Wild Man's escape. After that sub-
terfuge, he could become a corporate executive, a fundamentalist minister, a
tenured professor, someone his parents could be proud of, who "has never
seen the Wild Man."

We've all replaced the key many times and lied about it. Then the solitary 64
hunter inside us has to enter into the woods once more with his body dog
accompanying him, and then the dog gets pulled down again. We lose a lot of
"dogs" that way.

We could also imagine a different scenario. The boy convinces, or imag- 65
ines he could convince, the Wild Man to stay in the courtyard. If that happened, he and the Wild Man could carry on civilized conversations with each
other in the tea garden, and this conversation would go on for years. But the
story suggests that Iron John and the boy cannot be united—that is, cannot
experience their initial union—in the castle courtyard. It's probably too close
to the mother's pillow and the father's book of rules.

We recall that the boy in our story, when he spoke to the Wild Man, told 66
him he didn't know where the key was. That's brave. Some men never address
a sentence to the Wild Man.

When the boy opened the cage, the Wild Man started back to his forest. 67
The boy in our story, or the thirty-five-year-old man in our mind—however
you want to look at it—now does something marvelous. He speaks to the Wild
Man once more and says, "Wait a minute! If my parents come home and find
you gone, they will beat me." That sentence makes the heart sink, particularly
if we know something about child-rearing practices that have prevailed for a
long time in northern Europe.

As Alice Miller reminds us in her book *For Your Own Good*, child psychol- 68
ogists in nineteenth-century Germany warned parents especially about *exuberance*. Exuberance in a child is bad, and at the first sign of it, parents should
be severe. Exuberance implies that the wild boy or girl is no longer locked up.
Puritan parents in New England often punished children severely if they acted
in a restless way during the long church services.

"If they come home and find you gone, they will beat me." 69

The Wild Man says, in effect, "That's good thinking. You'd better come   70
with me."

So the Wild Man lifts the boy up on his shoulders and together they go off   71
into the woods. That's decisive. We should all be so lucky.

As the boy leaves for the forest, he has to overcome, at least for the   72
moment, his fear of wildness, irrationality, hairiness, intuition, emotion, the
body, and nature. Iron John is not as primitive as the boy imagines, but the
boy—or the mind—doesn't know that yet.

Still, the clean break with the mother and father, which the old initiators   73
call for, now has taken place. Iron John says to the boy, "You'll never see your
mother and father again. But I have treasures, more than you'll ever need." So
that is that.

Going Off on the Wild Man's Shoulders

The moment the boy leaves with Iron John is the moment in ancient Greek life   74
when the priest of Dionysus[6] accepted a young man as a student, or the
moment in Eskimo life today when the shaman, sometimes entirely covered
with the fur of wild animals, and wearing wolverine claws and snake vertebrae
around his neck, and a bear-head cap, appears in the village and takes a boy
away for spirit instruction.

In our culture there is no such moment. The boys in our culture have a   75
continuing need for initiation into male spirit, but old men in general don't
offer it. The priest sometimes tries, but he is too much a part of the corporate
village these days.

Among the Hopis and other native Americans of the Southwest, the old   76
men take the boy away at the age of twelve and bring him *down* into the all-
male area of the kiva. He stays *down* there for six weeks, and does not see his
mother again for a year and a half.

The fault of the nuclear family today isn't so much that it's crazy and full   77
of double binds (that's true in communes and corporate offices too—in fact, in
any group). The fault is that the old men outside the nuclear family no longer
offer an effective way for the son to break his link with his parents without
doing harm to himself.

The ancient societies believed that a boy becomes a man only through rit-   78
ual and effort—only through the "active intervention of the older men."

It's becoming clear to us that manhood doesn't happen by itself; it doesn't   79
happen just because we eat Wheaties. The active intervention of the older men
means that older men welcome the younger man into the ancient, mytholo-
gized, instinctive male world.

One of the best stories I've heard about this kind of welcoming is one that   80
takes place each year among the Kikuyu in Africa. When a boy is old enough
for initiation, he is taken away from his mother and brought to a special place
the men have set up some distance from the village. He fasts for three days.

---

[6]The Greek god of wine associated with fertility, drunken revelry, and ritualistic dances.

The third night he finds himself sitting in a circle around the fire with the older men. He is hungry, thirsty, alert, and terrified. One of the older men takes up a knife, opens a vein in his own arm, and lets a little of his blood flow into a gourd or bowl. Each older man in the circle opens his arm with the same knife, as the bowl goes around, and lets some blood flow in. When the bowl arrives at the young man, he is invited to take nourishment from it.

In this ritual the boy learns a number of things. He learns that nourish- 81 ment does not come only from his mother, but also from men. And he learns that the knife can be used for many purposes besides wounding others. Can he have any doubt now that he is welcome among the other males?

Once that welcoming has been done, the older men teach him the myths, 82 stories, and songs that embody distinctively male values: I mean not competitive values only, but spiritual values. Once these "moistening" myths are learned, the myths themselves lead the young male far beyond his personal father and into the moistness of the swampy fathers who stretch back century after century.

In the absence of old men's labor consciously done, what happens? 83 Initiation of Western men has continued for some time in an altered form even after fanatics destroyed the Greek initiatory schools. During the nineteenth century, grandfathers and uncles lived in the house, and older men mingled a great deal. Through hunting parties, in work that men did together in farms and cottages, and through local sports, older men spent much time with younger men and brought knowledge of male spirit and soul to them.

Wordsworth,[7] in the beginning of "The Excursion," describes the old 84 man who sat day after day under a tree and befriended Wordsworth when he was a boy:

> He loved me; from a swarm of rosy boys
> Singled me out, as he in sport would say,
> For my grave looks, too thoughtful for my years.
> As I grew up, it was my best delight
> To be his chosen comrade. Many a time
> On holidays, we wandered through the woods . . .

Much of that chance or incidental mingling has ended. Men's clubs and 85 societies have steadily disappeared. Grandfathers live in Phoenix or the old people's home, and many boys experience only the companionship of other boys their age who, from the point of view of the old initiators, know nothing at all.

During the sixties, some young men drew strength from women who in turn 86 had received some of their strength from the women's movement. One could say that many young men in the sixties tried to accept initiation from women. But only men can initiate men, as only women can initiate women. Women can change the embryo to a boy, but only men can change the boy to a man. Initiators say that boys need a second birth, this time a birth from men. . . .

---

[7]William Wordsworth (1770–1850) was an English poet and leader of the Romantic movement in England.

RESPONDING TO THE READING

Freewriting

Exercise 11f.   Write about your observations of "soft" and aggressive males.

Exercise 11g.   Freewrite about portions of Bly's discussion that seemed to describe your own life or that were quite unlike your experience.

Building Your Vocabulary

VOCABULARY LIST

Words to Look Up	My Definition	Dictionary Definition
Saturnian (2)		
introversion (2)		
entrepreneur (2)		
mummified (4)		
dogged (4)		
receptive (5)		
psyche (5)		
callousness (5)		
hysterical (22)		
reluctant (23)		
mythological (27)		
skittishness (28)		
sanitized (29)		
magnetic field (38)		
alienated (47)		
guru (56)		
tenured (63)		
kiva (76)		
gourd (80)		
initiatory (83)		
incidental mingling (85)		

Questions for Discussion

1. What struck you about the style of writing or subject of Bly's work that is different from other kinds of reading you have done in this course?
2. The speech used by characters in Bly's story of the Wild Man is modern and matter-of-fact, unlike the more formal language typical of most fairy tales. Why do you think Bly updated the language? What effect does he achieve?

3. Comment on Bly's portrait of the nineties male in paragraph 10. What does "vitality" seem to mean here?
4. What is the significance of the golden ball in Bly's folk tale? In what sense are men and women still seeking it?
5. What does the boy's dog symbolize (paragraphs 21 and 64)? Why is it an important part of the boy's development that he lose his "dog"?
6. In the tale of Iron John, the boy's mother keeps the key to the Wild Man's cage under her pillow. What, according to Bly, is the psychological meaning of the key, and the fact that the boy's mother has it and keeps it under her pillow?
7. Reread passages where Bly applies this tale, which he says could be "ten or twenty thousand years old," to modern situations. Which of his explanations of the boy's journey did you find most or least appealing? Explain your reaction.

TOPICS FOR WRITING

Topic 1.   Pick one or two of the types of men Bly discusses and write an essay in which you briefly describe each type and explain which is the most accurate description of men based on your experience, observations, or interviews.

Topic 2.   Bly spends a lot of time discussing the mythological or archetypal life of men. Write an essay in which you describe the deep emotional or spiritual transformations you have witnessed in men or women.

Topic 3.   Write an essay in which you explore Bly's idea that "A mother's job is, after all, to civilize the boy." In what ways do mothers or other female figures "civilize" boys? Do fathers have a role to play in this civilizing process?

Topic 4.   What problems does Bly foresee for boys who grow up in all-female households? Write an essay in which you explain how your experiences, observations, or reading support or contradict Bly's insistence that boys need guidance from older males.

Topic 5.   Write an essay in which you examine the significance the story of Iron John might have for women. Be sure to explain what women can learn from the myth and give examples of behavior that the myth seems to recommend.

Student Writing

Relationships

In my life I have met many people, and out of these interactions I have found a few women that I wanted to get to know better. Although I don't do much conscious planning, I seem to go through certain stages in my progress from mild interest to love.

The first thing I do when entering a new relationship is to decide whether or not this woman makes me happy. Usually I make my decision very quickly without giving it much thought. One evening, for example, I may discover that my date is wearing a brightly colored dress that makes her look like Madonna or the gorgeous little sister of my last girlfriend. Suddenly I am convinced that this resemblance is the answer to my prayers. On one occasion in particular, I became deliriously happy because my date started staring at me for no reason, and when I turned to look back at her, she gave me a smile that could make roses bloom.

What follows this initial burst of happiness is a sickness that I call the "New Person Syndrome." This syndrome is a disease that undermines my objective mind and makes me act like a love-sick puppy. Basically this is the infatuation stage, and it is needed to keep me interested in my partner long enough to get through the other two characteristics of this phase—the insecurity and testiness.

Once the initial infatuation and uneasiness wear off, I volunteer to give up whatever freedom I have left because I am convinced that I'm in love. I rationalize giving up my independence by thinking romantic thoughts about me and my gal sitting on a hilltop, speaking in low voices, unable to take our eyes off each other. Since I am so in love, I give up time I would ordinarily spend with friends to become totally faithful to my girlfriend. Even though I may realize that I am in love with an ideal and not the person I am with, I still give up my independence in the name of love.

At this point in the relationship all the major sacrifices have been made and all that is left to deal with are a few difficulties like parental disapproval, quarrels over money, and disputes about seemingly insignificant things like who sleeps on which side of the bed. By parental disapproval, I am talking about trying to convince a pair of doting parents that I am a nice, responsible young man who is worthy of dating their daughter. On occasion I have worn my older brother's suit and tie, taken my girlfriend's whole family to dinner, or rented a limousine for the senior prom in order to impress her and her family. Money is always a problem, especially when I am trying to impress my girlfriend's parents. Finding someone who will loan me enough money to make a lasting impression on doubting parents requires a fair amount of conniving. The little things in a relationship are also important when you are adjusting to living with someone else. Figuring out which side of the bed belongs to whom sounds simple enough, but it's the kind of issue that reveals the first signs of conflict. How a couple works out the problem of perceived rights to an accustomed sleeping space will determine how other problems get solved later on. This phase of a relationship can be exciting as well as stressful. In my experience it is characterized by euphoria interspersed with headaches and sleepless nights.

Relationships that go beyond the "New Person Syndrome" usually go in one of several directions: toward indifference, mutual respect and friendship, or eventual commitment. I have avoided making too firm a commitment in any relationship because I have a lot of hard work ahead of me before I finish school. However, I have been lucky enough to develop one very strong friendship with a woman with whom I was once quite infatuated. Now we like to get together and talk about old times as well as more current issues in our lives. The remaining possibility—indifference—always takes me by surprise. I rarely see it coming, nor do I usually detect it in a partner. But if a relationship is headed for it, sooner or later deadly indifference will surface. When it does, I find it best not to question it but rather to pack my bags and leave my key at the door.

Any relationship is a lot of work because no two people are exactly alike. At times the whole business of relationships seems to be just one big hassle, but if you can weather these stormy seas, then you have a chance of developing a very close and caring relationship with someone who loves you.

—Dan Krum

Questions for Discussion

1. What do you think are strong points of Dan Krum's essay?
2. What suggestions do you have for revising it?
3. Write a letter advising Dan Krum what he might do differently at each of the stages of love he identifies. Be sure to explain why he should follow your advice.
4. Do you agree with Krum that relationships take a lot of hard work? Support your answer.

12

Immigrants

"Give me your tired, your poor,
Your huddled masses yearning to breathe free,
The wretched refuse of your teeming shore.
Send these, the homeless, tempest-tost to me.
I lift my lamp beside the golden door!"

—Emma Lazarus
(from the poem, "The New Colossus," engraved on the
pedestal below the Statue of Liberty)

These words carved into the base of the Statue of
Liberty speak to America's vision of itself. We
were, and still are, a nation of immigrants.

—Michael J. Mandel and Christopher Farrell

R eadings in this chapter present several views of the immigrant's experience. In the first selection, the authors of "The Immigrants: How They're Helping to Revitalize the U.S. Economy" analyze the effects that the recent wave of immigrants from Asia, Latin America, and Eastern Europe are having on the economy. Amy Tan gives a fictional account of adjustment to customs and ways of thinking in the United States. In "Walking in Lucky Shoes," Bette Bao Lord uses images of the shoes she and others like her have worn to discuss the difficulties and rewards that are part of the immigrant's experience.

"The Immigrants: How They're Helping to Revitalize the U.S. Economy" illustrates some of the characteristics of essays that use causal analysis as the dominant writing strategy.

EXPLAINING CAUSES AND EFFECTS

The work you have done in other chapters on process analysis, classifying, and comparing and contrasting will help you write about the causes of a certain event or the results of a particular action. At this point, drawing distinctions among these strategies might be helpful. Process analysis describes *how* things happen; causal analysis explains *why* they happen or what the *results* will be. Classifying involves grouping similar experiences, ideas, or behavior in order to discuss characteristics common to each category. Similarly, discussing causes or effects requires grouping events or behavior that *caused* something to happen, or that *resulted* from a particular action or circumstance. Comparing and contrasting involve discussing similarities and differences. Causal analysis employs these skills when *causes are weighed against effects* or important reasons and results are *compared* to those of lesser importance. As with other writing strategies, you should support your ideas with details and examples and present your ideas in a logical sequence.

Characteristics of Causal Analysis

Point of View

Writers who wish to analyze why a situation exists or examine its results may adopt a subjective (first person) or an objective (third person) point of view, depending on their topic. Lindo Sun, the character in "Memoirs of a Chinese Mother," the selection from Amy Tan's novel, *The Joy Luck Club*, narrates a first person account of the events that brought her to the United States and those that helped her assimilate or, as she puts it, lose her "Chinese face." The authors of "The Immigrants: How They're Helping to Revitalize the U.S. Economy," on the other hand, choose an objective point of view for discussing the reasons U.S. citizens may feel that it is not in the best interests of this country to accept more immigrants. More important, the writers of that article focus on the effects that the influx of immigrants is having on the American economy. What follows are the opening paragraphs of "The Immigrants."

Give me your tired, your poor,
Your huddled masses yearning to breathe free. . . .

> These words carved into the base of the Statue of Liberty speak to America's vision of itself. We were, and still are, a nation of immigrants. In the 1980s alone, a stunning 8.7 million people poured into the U.S., matching the great immigration decade of 1900–10. But with the country facing difficult economic and social problems, is it time to put aside our romantic past and kick away the immigrant welcome mat?
>
> A lot of Americans feel the answer is "yes." In a *Business Week*/Harris poll, 68% of respondents said today's immigration is bad for the country, even though most thought it was good in the past. President Bush has found it politically expedient to refuse refugees from Haiti. And in areas like recession-weary Southern California, immigrants are being blamed for everything from rising unemployment to a rocketing state budget deficit. "I understand, in the past, 'give me your tired, your poor.' Today, the U.S. has to look at our own huddled masses first," says former Colorado Governor Richard D. Lamm, who is running for the U.S. Senate.

In addition to establishing an objective point of view, these paragraphs clarify the kind of information the authors will use to support their discussion. In the opening paragraphs, they do not draw on their own experience to support their analysis. Instead, they rely on statistics, an example (former President Bush's refusal of asylum to Haitian refugees), and testimony—in this case the testimony of a former governor who represents one perspective on immigration. At other places in the article, the authors quote experts in a particular field.

A Main Point or Thesis

Authors of causal analysis need to identify clearly the causes or effects they will discuss. The first two paragraphs of "The Immigrants" introduce ideas that the writers address near the end of their article. The thesis or main point of the article appears at the beginning of paragraph 3: "But on balance, the economic benefits of being an open-door society far outweigh the costs. . ." This statement prepares the reader for an analysis of the positive effects that immigrants' entry into the United States have on the economy. We might also note that the authors use the thesis to answer the question raised at the end of the first paragraph: ". . . is it time to put aside our romantic past and kick away the immigrant welcome mat?" Their answer is "the economic benefits of being an open-door society far outweigh the costs."

Why do you think the authors of "The Immigrants" began their essay with a question? Why do you think they chose to answer that question in one of the early paragraphs of their article?

A Clear Sequence of Ideas

Clear organization is important in any paper, but it is imperative with writing strategies as complex as causal analysis. "The Immigrants" is a good example of how effective an analysis can be when the writers are able to make clear distinctions between effects and causes and address critics' concerns. Most of this article addresses the causes of current immigration patterns, skills levels of recent immigrants, and the effects their presence has on job competition and education. Transitional phrases signal movement from one topic to another. The following list shows the order in which the writers discuss their points.

> Refer to American tradition reflected in Emma Lazarus's famous poem (paragraph 1)
> Acknowledge opposition to immigration (paragraphs 2–3)
> Discuss **effects** of immigration in immigrants' contributions to high-tech industries and to the tax base (paragraphs 4–5)
> Discuss historical **causes** of recent immigration from Asia, Latin America, and Eastern Europe (paragraphs 6–9)
> Discuss varied skill levels of the new immigrants (paragraphs 10–12)
> Discuss **effects** of these workers' entry into the labor force (paragraphs 13–19)
> Discuss immigrants' positive **effects** on inner cities (paragraphs 21–22)
> Address the negative **effects** of immigrants who compete for low-skilled jobs (paragraphs 23–27)
> Discuss the **effects** immigrant children have on schools (paragraphs 28–29)
> Conclusion rephrases the thesis (paragraph 30)

Information Mapping

Another organizational technique deserves mention. Writers whose articles are several pages long often use a technique called information mapping, which involves the use of headings to guide the reader from one point to another. The authors of "The Immigrants" use six headings: "New Wave," "Talent Base," "Up the Ladder," "Urban Boosters," "Margin Dwellers," and "School Daze" to announce major topic breaks. Furthermore, these headings break up large blocks of writing and help the reader identify important points discussed in the article.

Clear Reasoning

Several techniques are involved when a writer presents a convincing, well-reasoned analysis of causes and effects. For one thing, ideas must have detailed support. As we saw in the opening paragraphs of "The Immigrants," evidence for causes and effects comes from statistics, examples, and testimony. In paragraph 5, statistics illustrate the amount of taxes collected from working immigrants; at the end of that paragraph, the authors quote sociologist John D. Kasarda to make their final point about the immigrants' contribution to the U.S. economy. The authors also rely on examples from the lives of immigrants, as in the discussion of the Indian entrepreneur in paragraph 12. Surveys conducted by *Business Week* (paragraph 2) and research done at universities (paragraphs 26 and 27) provide additional evidence.

Causal analysis examines more than one cause or effect. Few events in life have only one cause or produce a single effect. Writers of causal analysis recognize that they must discuss multiple causes and effects in order to do justice to the complexity of most topics. In "The Immigrants," for example, the writers examine several reasons why American citizens might feel threatened by these newcomers. Some are afraid that immigrants will compete for scarce jobs. Others fear they will place a tremendous burden on limited resources or exacerbate ethnic conflicts, especially in the inner cities. The authors also discuss causes of the current influx of Asian, Latin American, and Eastern European immigrants: the 1965 revision of the immigration laws and the passage of the Immigration Reform and Control Act, the end of the Vietnam War, the collapse of the Soviet Union, and economic problems in Latin America. The numerous effects of the government's accepting the numbers and kinds of immigrants it does is also examined in detail. These effects, both positive and negative, include the impact of immigrant workers on businesses, job competition, the tax base, the condition of inner cities, and the costs of social services like welfare and education.

For a causal analysis to be convincing, it must show the reader that the author has examined not only possible causes and effects but has also looked at the issue from several points of view. The authors of "The Immigrants" begin their article by acknowledging legitimate objections to the open-access attitude toward immigration that they feel is part of our heritage (paragraphs 1 through 3). They address these concerns in greater detail in paragraphs 23 through 29. At the end of the article they reach the conclusion that despite the costs of accommodating the new arrivals, "the positives far outweigh any short-term negatives."

The Immigrants: How They're Helping to Revitalize the U.S. Economy
Michael J. Mandel and Christopher Farrell

The authors of this article address the controversial question of whether the United States should reject its traditional role as a haven for immigrants. Their analysis of the positive effects new immigrant populations are having on the U.S. economy supports their position that America should preserve this vision of itself. This article first appeared in the July 13, 1992, issue of Business Week.

> *Give me your tired, your poor,*
> *Your huddled masses yearning to breathe free. . . .*

These words carved into the base of the Statue of Liberty speak to 1 America's vision of itself. We were, and still are, a nation of immigrants. In the 1980s alone, a stunning 8.7 million people poured into the U.S., matching the great immigration decade of 1900–10. But with the country facing difficult economic and social problems, is it time to put aside our romantic past and kick away the immigrant welcome mat?

A lot of Americans feel the answer is "yes." In a *Business Week*/Harris poll, 2 68% of respondents said today's immigration is bad for the country, even though most thought it was good in the past. President Bush has found it politically expedient to refuse refugees from Haiti.[1] And in areas like recession-weary Southern California, immigrants are being blamed for everything from rising unemployment to a rocketing state budget deficit. "I understand, in the past, 'give me your tired, your poor.' Today, the U.S. has to look at our own huddled masses first," says former Colorado Governor Richard D. Lamm, who is running for the U.S. Senate.

This rising resentment against immigrants is no surprise. The million or so 3 immigrants—including 200,000 illegals—that will arrive in the U.S. this year are coming at a time when unemployment is high and social services strained. Unlike past waves of immigration, the new immigrants are mainly from Asia and Latin America. And just like the American work force, these immigrants are split between the highly skilled and well-educated and those with minimal skills and little education. Hungry for work, the newcomers compete for jobs with Americans, particularly with the less skilled. The large number of untrained immigrants, especially those from Mexico, are finding it harder to move up the employment ladder than did past generations of newcomers. And in the cities, the new immigrants seem to inflame racial and ethnic conflicts.

But on balance, the economic benefits of being an open-door society far 4 outweigh the costs. For one thing, the U.S. is reaping a bonanza of highly educated foreigners. In the 1980s alone, an unprecedented 1.5 million college-educated immigrants joined the U.S. work force. More and more, America's

---

[1]President Clinton also denied Haitian refugees entry into the United States.

high-tech industries, from semiconductors to biotechnology, are depending on immigrant scientists, engineers, and entrepreneurs to remain competitive. And the immigrants' links to their old countries are boosting U.S. exports to such fast-growing regions as Asia and Latin America.

Even immigrants with less education are contributing to the economy as 5 workers, consumers, business owners, and taxpayers. Some 11 million immigrants are working, and they earn at least $240 billion a year, paying more than $90 billion in taxes. That's a lot more than the estimated $5 billion immigrants receive in welfare. Immigrant entrepreneurs, from the corner grocer to the local builder, are creating jobs—and not only for other immigrants. Vibrant immigrant communities are revitalizing cities and older suburbs that would otherwise be suffering from a shrinking tax base. Says John D. Kasarda, a sociologist at the University of North Carolina at Chapel Hill: "There is substantial evidence that immigrants are a powerful benefit to the economy, and very little evidence that they are negative."

In 1965, when Congress overhauled the immigration laws, nobody 6 expected this great tide of new immigrants. But that law made it easier to bring close relatives into the country and, influenced by the civil-rights movement, eliminated racially based barriers to immigration. Prior to that, it was difficult for anyone who was not European or Canadian to settle here. The result: a surge of immigrants from Asia and Latin America, especially from countries like South Korea and the Philippines that had close economic and military ties to the U.S. And once a group got a foothold in the U.S., it would continue to expand by bringing over more family members.

New Wave

The aftermath of the Vietnam War provided the second powerful source of 7 immigrants. Over the last 10 years, the U.S. granted permanent-resident status to about 1 million refugees, mostly from Vietnam, Cambodia, and Laos. And now the end of the cold war is tapping another immigrant stream: Over the last three years, the fastest growing group of new settlers has been refugees from Eastern Europe and the former Soviet Union.

Throughout the 1970s and 1980s, a total of some 5 million illegal immi- 8 grants from Mexico and other countries settled in the U.S., drawn by opportunity here and fleeing economic troubles at home. Many settled in Southern California and Texas. In 1986, Congress passed the Immigration Reform & Control Act (IRCA), which imposed penalties on employers who hired illegal immigrants but also gave amnesty to many illegal immigrants. About 2.5 million people have become permanent residents under the amnesty program. And the pending North American Free Trade Agreement, by strengthening economic ties between Mexico and the U.S., might very well increase illegal immigration in the short run rather than diminish it.

Opening the gates to Asians and Latin Americans dramatically altered the 9 face of immigration. In the 1950s, 68% of legal immigrants came from Europe or Canada. In the 1980s, that percentage fell to only 13%. Conversely, the proportion of legal immigrants coming from Latin America and Asia rose from 31% to 84%, including illegal aliens granted amnesty under the 1986 law.

As the ethnic mix of the new immigrants changed, so did their levels of skill.   10
At the low end, the plethora of low-wage service-sector jobs drew in a large number of unskilled, illiterate newcomers. About one-third of immigrant workers are high school dropouts, and one-third of those entered the U.S. illegally.

But the number of skilled immigrants has been increasing as well. "The   11
level of education of recent immigrants has definitely increased over the last 10 years," says Elaine Sorensen, an immigration expert at the Urban Institute. About one-quarter of immigrant workers are college graduates, slightly higher than for native-born Americans. Some groups, such as Indians, are on average much better educated than today's Americans. Observes Steven Newman, an executive at the New York Association for New Americans, which will resettle about 20,000 immigrants from the former Soviet Union this year, including many engineers, computer programmers, and other skilled workers: "The only thing they lack is English skills."

Talent Base

Even immigrants who were doing well in their home countries are being   12
drawn to the U.S. Take Subramonian Shankar, the 43-year-old president of American Megatrends Inc., a maker of personal-computer motherboards and software based in Norcross, Ga. He was director of personal-computer R&D[2] at one of India's largest conglomerates. Then in 1980, he came to the U.S. In 1985, he and a partner founded AMI, which last year had sales of $70 million and employed 130 workers, both immigrants and native-born Americans. "I couldn't have done this in India," says Shankar. "That's one good thing about America. If you're determined to succeed, there are ways to get it done."

And U.S. industry has been eager to take advantage of the influx. About   13
40% of the 200 researchers in the Communications Sciences Research wing at AT&T Bell Laboratories were born outside the U.S. In Silicon Valley, the jewel of America's high-tech centers, much of the technical work force is foreign-born. At Du Pont Merck Pharmaceutical Co., an $800 million-a-year joint venture based in Wilmington, Del., losartan, an antihypertensive drug now in clinical trials, was invented by a team that included two immigrants from Hong Kong and a scientist whose parents migrated from Lithuania. People from different backgrounds bring a richness of outlook, says Joseph A. Mollica, chief executive of Du Pont Merck, "which lets you look at both problems and opportunities from a slightly different point of view."

The next generation of scientists and engineers at U.S. high-tech compa-   14
nies will be dominated by immigrants. While about the same number of Americans are getting science PhDs, the number of foreign-born students receiving science doctorates more than doubled between 1981 and 1991, to 37% of the total. In biology, the hot field of the 1990s, the number of non-U.S.

---

[2]Research and development

citizens getting doctorates tripled over the last 10 years. And about 51% of computer-science doctorates in 1991 went to foreign-born students. "We are getting really good students—very, very smart people," says Victor L. Thacker, director of the office of international education at Carnegie Mellon University, which has doubled its foreign enrollment since 1985.

Up the Ladder

Attracted by the research opportunities and the chance to use what they know, about half of them stay in the U.S. after graduation, estimates Angel G. Jordan, a professor and former provost at Carnegie Mellon, who himself emigrated from Spain in 1956. And the 1990 changes to the immigration law, by increasing the number of visas for skilled immigrants, will increase the number of foreign graduates who remain in the U.S.   15

Besides boosting the nation's science and engineering know-how, the latest wave of immigrants is loaded with entrepreneurs. Korean greengrocers and other immigrant merchants are familiar sights in many cities, but the entrepreneurial spirit goes far beyond any one ethnic group or single line of business. Almost by definition, anyone who moves to a new country has a lot of initiative and desire to do well. Says Dan Danilov, an immigration lawyer based in Seattle: "They're willing to put in more hours and more hard work."   16

And do they work. Paul Yuan, for example, left Taiwan with his wife in 1975, seven days after their marriage, eventually settling in Seattle with several thousand dollars in life savings and no work visas. For two years Yuan, a college graduate, worked in Chinese restaurants. Then, in 1978, he became a legal resident and opened his own travel agency while working nights as a hotel dishwasher. Today, at age 43, Yuan owns a thriving Seattle travel business, and he and his family live in a $4 million house. In 1965, 21-year-old Humberto Galvez left Mexico City for Los Angeles. He started pumping gas and busing tables, working his way up the ladder, with a lot of bumps along the way. After starting, then selling, the chain of 19 "El Pollo Loco" charbroiled chicken restaurants in the Los Angeles area, he now owns six Pescado Mojado (wet fish) seafood diners, employing 100 workers.   17

Immigrant entrepreneurs have also made big contributions to the U.S. export boom. Businesses run by immigrants from Asia, for example, have ready-made connections overseas. Immigrants bring a global perspective and international contacts to insular American businesses. And it is not just Asians. From Poles to Mexicans, "the utility of the immigrant groups is that they bring their fearless spirit of competing globally," observes Michael Goldberg, dean of the University of British Columbia's business school.   18

That's certainly true for Benjamin and Victor Acevedo, two brothers whose family moved from Tijuana, Mexico, to California in 1960, when they were 3 and 8. In 1984, the Acevedos started up a wood-products company in the south San Diego community of San Ysidro, just across the U.S.-Mexico border. Cal-State Lumber Sales Inc. now commands 10% of the architectural molding market in the U.S. and had 110 employees and $147 million in sales   19 last year. And as long-term trade barriers with Mexico crumbled over the past few years, the Acevedos have been able to take advantage of their bicultural heritage. "My brother and I started shipping all over Mexico, and our export business boomed," says Ben Acevedo.

Urban Boosters

Perhaps the least-appreciated economic benefit from the new immigrants is   20
the contribution they are making to American cities. Immigrants have been drawn to the major metropolitan areas. They are invigorating the cities and older suburbs by setting up businesses, buying homes, paying taxes, and shopping at the corner grocery. In the past decade, population in the nation's 10 largest cities grew by 4.7%, but without new immigrants it would have shrunk by 6.8%, according to calculations done by *Business Week* based on the 1990 census. Almost a million immigrants came to New York City in the 1980s, more than offsetting the 750,000 decline in the rest of the city's population. Indeed, about a third of adults in New York, 44% of adults in Los Angeles, and 70% of adults in Miami are now foreign-born, according to the 1990 census.

Immigrants have turned around many a decaying neighborhood. Ten   21
years ago, Jefferson Boulevard in south Dallas was a dying inner-city business district filled with vacant storefronts. Today, there are almost 800 businesses there and on neighboring streets, and about three-quarters of them are owned by Hispanics, many of them first- and second-generation immigrants. "They were hungry enough to start their own businesses," says Leonel Ramos, president of the Jefferson Area Assn. And sociologist Kasarda adds: "There is a whole-multiplier effect throughout the community."

Moreover, immigrants provide a hardworking labor force to fill the low-   22
paid jobs that make a modern service economy run. In many cities, industries such as hotels, restaurants, and child care would be hard-pressed without immigrant labor. At the Seattle Sheraton, 28% of the hotel's staff of 650 is foreign-born, and most work in housekeeping, dish-washing, and other low-paying jobs. "We don't have American-born people apply for those positions," says Carla Murray, hotel manager for the Seattle Sheraton.

Margin Dwellers

But all the economic vitality immigrants add comes at a price. While econo-   23
mists and employers may celebrate industrious immigrants, many barely survive on the economy's margins. "They don't go to the doctor, don't buy insurance, don't buy glasses, don't buy anything you or I are used to," says Hannah Hsiao, head of the Employment Program at the Chinese Information & Service Center in Seattle. A firing, unpaid wages, a deportation, or some other calamity is always threatening. And racial discrimination makes their lot even harder, especially those who don't speak English. Some, like economist George J. Borjas of the University of California at San Diego, worry that these poor and unskilled immigrants are condemned to years of poverty.

In many cities, newcomers and long-time residents struggle over jobs and 24 access to scarce government resources. Immigrants are straining health and education services in some cities and suburbs. And many African-Americans believe the apparent success of immigrants is coming at their expense. In New York City, blacks picketed a number of Korean greengrocers. According to the *Business Week*/Harris poll, 73% of blacks said businesses would rather hire immigrants than black Americans.

The people hurt worst by immigrants are native-born high school 25 dropouts, who already face a tough time. They compete for jobs against a large number of unskilled immigrants, including illegals from Mexico and the Caribbean who are poorly educated, unable to start their own businesses, and willing to work harder for lower wages than most longtime residents.

For Americans who have at least a high school education, however, the 26 influx of immigrants hasn't had much negative impact. High school graduates, for example, saw their real wages decline by 10% in the 1980s. But almost all of that drop came from import competition and rising skill requirements of many jobs, and only a fraction from immigrant competition, according to a study by Borjas of UC, San Diego, and Richard Freeman and Lawrence Katz of Harvard University. "It is extremely convenient to point a finger at immigrants," says Muzaffar Chishti, director of the Immigration Project for the International Ladies' Garment Workers' Union in New York. "But the problems of black employment are outside the immigrant domain."

Moreover, for all their struggles, most immigrants are hardly wards of the 27 state. Illegals are not eligible for welfare, and even many legal immigrants shun it, fearing that it will make it harder to become a citizen in the future. A study by Borjas shows that in 1980—the latest national data available—only 8.8% of immigrant households received welfare, compared to 7.9% of all native-born Americans. And with the education and skill levels of immigrants rising in the 1980s, the expectations are that the spread between the two hasn't worsened and may have even narrowed. In Los Angeles County, for example, immigrants amount to 16% of the 722,000 people on Aid to Families with Dependent Children, the government's main welfare program. Yet immigrants are more than 30% of the county's population. "Immigrants benefit natives through the public coffers by using less than their share of services and paying more than their share of taxes," says Julian L. Simon, a University of Maryland economist.

School Daze

One real concern is whether urban school systems can handle the surge of 28 immigrant children. "The public school is the vehicle through which the child of immigrants becomes Americanized," says Jeffrey S. Passel, a demographer for the Washington-based Urban Institute. But in many cities, the task of educating immigrant students has become an enormous burden. In Los Angeles, 39% of the city's students don't speak English well, and in Seattle, 21% come from homes where English is not the family's first language. In the nation's capital, the school system is nearly overwhelmed by a huge number of Vietnamese, Haitians, and Salvadorean children. "If the school system is inadequate, then it's much more difficult to help immigrants move up the economic ladder," says Robert D. Hormats, vice-chairman of Goldman, Sachs International and head of the Trilateral Commission's working group on immigration.

City schools, despite the constraint of tight resources, are finding innova-   29
tive ways to reach immigrant children. In Seattle, about half the immigrant students speak such limited English that they qualify for a program where they are taught subjects in simplified English. The Los Angeles schools offer dual language classes in Spanish, Korean, Armenian, Cantonese, Filipino, Farsi, and Japanese. Other organizations, such as unions, are also teaching immigrants English. In New York, the Garment Workers Union, often called the immigrant union, offers English classes to its members and their families.

In the coming decade, it won't be easy to assimilate the new immigrants,   30
whether they come from Laos or Russia. But the positives far outweigh any short-term negatives. In today's white-hot international competition, the U.S. profits from the ideas and innovations of immigrants. And by any economic calculus, their hard work adds far more to the nation's wealth than the resources they drain. It is still those "huddled masses yearning to breathe free" who will keep the American dream burning bright for most of us.

RESPONDING TO THE READING

Freewriting

Exercise 12a.   Write your reaction to one or two of the ideas in "The Immigrants."

Exercise 12b.   Freewrite about immigrants you have known or have read about. Compare these examples to the profiles in "The Immigrants."

Building Your Vocabulary

VOCABULARY LIST

Words to Look Up	My Definition	Dictionary Definition
stunning (1)		
respondent (2)		
expedient (2)		
minimal (3)		
inflame (3)		
bonanza (4)		
unprecedented (4)		
semiconductors (4)		

biotechnology (4)
entrepreneurs (5)
vibrant (5)
sociologist (5)
substantial (5)
amnesty (8)
conversely (9)
plethora (10)
conglomerate (12)
influx (13)
doctorate (14)
initiative (16)
insular (18)
molding (19)
invigorate (20)
vitality (23)
deportation (23)
calamity (23)
wards (27)
coffers (27)
demographer (28)
assimilate (30)

Questions for Discussion

1. Describe the writing strategy that the authors of "The Immigrants" use in the first three paragraphs. Why do you think they waited until the fourth paragraph to state the thesis? Explain why you think this tactic is effective or ineffective.

2. Carefully reread the sequence of ideas from "The Immigrants" that are listed on page 280. Why do you think the writers chose this particular order? Rearrange sections of the article so paragraphs that discuss causes and effects appear in a different order. Is this new order more or less effective than the original arrangement of ideas? Explain your answer.

3. What reasons do the authors give in support of their position that immigrants have a positive effect on the American economy? Which reasons do you find most convincing and why? What examples of these or other effects have you seen?

4. What solutions to the negative effects of immigration do the writers discuss? How effective do you think they would be in answering critics' objections to immigration? Offer evidence in support of your answer.

5. Who might be the audience for the magazine *Business Week,* the periodical in which this article appeared? Refer to evidence from the article to help you describe these readers. How might the interests of this audience explain the writers' positive view of immigration?

TOPICS FOR WRITING

Topic 1.   Conduct your own survey of a dozen friends, relatives, or class-mates to examine their views of immigrants' effects on the economy. In the course of your interview, you might ask them (1) whether they think of immigrants as mostly skilled or unskilled, (2) whether immigrants contribute to or deplete the economy, and (3) whether the respondents or someone they know has had to compete with immigrants for jobs. Once you discover your inter-viewees' attitudes toward immigrants, ask them to explain what experiences or observations contributed to that attitude. Spend some time organizing the data you gathered and write an essay in which you categorize the attitudes you uncovered and explain two or three reasons why the respondents devel-oped these attitudes.

Topic 2.   Choose one or two of the effects discussed in "The Immigrants" that new arrivals have on the U.S. economy. Write an essay in which you examine the negative or positive side of those effects. Use your experiences, observations, readings, or interview notes to support your ideas.

Topic 3.   "The Immigrants" is written from the point of view of writers who are interested in ways to stimulate the American economy. Write an essay from a different perspective—perhaps that of unskilled American workers—and discuss several problems that immigrants might pose and what might be done to alleviate those problems.

THE WRITING PROCESS: CAUSAL ANALYSIS

Additional Considerations for Developing a Topic

The topics for writing in this chapter suggest several assignments for practicing causal analysis. To develop a topic of your own, you might examine journal entries that would lead to a discussion of causes or effects. Think of major events in your life or the lives of people you know. Pick one of these events and examine its causes or effects. Perhaps a local or national issue has piqued your curiosity recently. You might write about how it became an issue or what its effects have been. Another good tactic is to interview people you know about their relationships in order to discover what drew them to their current part-ners. When you have collected about half a dozen samples, write a paper exam-ining what caused the people you interviewed to choose certain mates. Group your information into two or three common reasons and write your analysis.

Additional Considerations for Thinking about Your Audience

It is helpful if you think about purpose, point of view, and thesis as you gather information and write your paper. Your purpose may change as you develop and organize your ideas; that's normal in writing. To keep your main point clear in your own mind, try answering the following questions before you begin writing, and revise them as your paper develops.

What causes or effects will I examine?
What is my purpose for writing about these causes or effects?
Who is my audience?
What point of view will I adopt?

Additional Considerations for Preliminary Writing

Use any of the preliminary writing techniques that work best for you. These additional questions may be useful:

What situation will you discuss?
What are some immediate causes or effects?
What do you think will be long-term or lasting causes or results?
Which cause is most important? Why?
How might physical conditions, events, behavior, attitudes, assumptions, laws, values, or regulations cause a situation to exist? How might one or more of these be the effects of a situation?
Are there other points of view you should consider when discussing causes or effects for this topic?
What additional causes or effects might these points of view suggest?
Do causes or effects follow one another in time, or, as in "The Immigrants," do some occur simultaneously?

Additional Considerations for Organizing Ideas

Several ways are available to organize a causal analysis. If the causes or results follow one another in time, you will probably want to use chronological order to arrange them. If, on the other hand, causes or effects occur simultaneously, as they do in "The Immigrants," then order of emphasis or importance works well. Here are a few possible patterns for cause-effect essays.

Pattern 1

1. Identify problem or event
   Thesis
2. Discuss causes of that problem or event
3. Conclusion

Pattern 2

1. Identify problem or event
   Thesis
2. Discuss effects of that problem or event
3. Conclusion

Pattern 3

1. Identify problem or event
   Thesis
2. Discuss effects of that problem or event
3. Discuss solutions
4. Conclusion

Pattern 4

1. Identify problem or event
   Thesis
2. Discuss effects of that problem or event
3. Discuss the causes of that problem or event
4. Discuss solutions
5. Conclusion

Additional Considerations for Writing a Fast Draft

As you write your essay, be careful not to settle for *one* cause or result. Only the simplest, and usually the least interesting, situation has merely one cause or effect. Even something that may seem straightforward may not really be so simple on closer examination.

Let's say, for example, that your cousin Max tripped on a skateboard left on a landing and fell down the stairs. What are the possible causes of his fall? The most immediate is the skateboard itself, but his own behavior might have contributed to the fall. Perhaps he was reading a book, thinking about something else, or simply not watching where he was going. He might, on the other hand, have been running to get somewhere and may not have seen the skateboard in time to avoid the accident. It's good practice when writing a causal analysis to consider as many possible causes or outcomes as you can. Once you have a list of these, choose the most important and most plausible for your essay.

Additional Considerations for Sharing Your Writing and Making Final Revisions

Use the checklist below when revising your paper.

Checklist

- ❏ Does the introduction present the essay's point of view and topic?
- ❏ Does my thesis state the causes or effects I will discuss?
- ❏ Is the point of view objective or subjective? Do I maintain this point of view throughout?
- ❏ Have I discussed a sufficient number of causes or effects, or are there others I should consider?

❏ Have I included enough support for the causes or effects I discuss?
❏ Is my paper organized clearly enough that the reader can follow my ideas?
❏ Do transitions make it clear when I shift from one cause or effect to another?
❏ Does my conclusion follow from the discussion of causes and effects?
❏ Have I proofread carefully for sentence correctness, spelling, and punctuation?

FOR FURTHER READING

Memoirs of a Chinese Mother
Amy Tan

The following narrative is taken from Amy Tan's novel, The Joy Luck Club. *Here, her character, Lindo Sun, describes her immigration from China to America. The person she addresses in this passage is Waverly Sun, her Chinese-American daughter, whose description of Chinatown appears in "Rules of the Game" in Chapter 8.*

It's hard to keep your Chinese face in America. At the beginning, before I 1 even arrived, I had to hide my true self. I paid an American-raised Chinese girl in Peking to show me how.

"In America," she said, "you cannot say you want to live there forever. If 2 you are Chinese, you must say you admire their schools, their ways of thinking. You must say you want to be a scholar and come back to teach Chinese people what you have learned."

"What should I say I want to learn?" I asked. "If they ask me questions, if 3 I cannot answer . . ."

"Religion, you must say you want to study religion," said this smart 4 girl. "Americans all have different ideas about religion, so there are no right and wrong answers. Say to them, I'm going for God's sake, and they will respect you."

For another sum of money, this girl gave me a form filled out with English 5 words. I had to copy these words over and over again as if they were English words formed from my own head. Next to the word NAME, I wrote *Lindo Sun.* Next to the word BIRTHDATE, I wrote *May 11, 1918,* which this girl insisted was the same as three months after the Chinese lunar new year. Next to the word BIRTHPLACE, I put down *Taiyuan, China.* And next to the word OCCUPATION, I wrote *student of theology.*

I gave the girl even more money for a list of addresses in San Francisco, 6 people with big connections. And finally, this girl gave me, free of charge, instructions for changing my circumstances. "First," she said, "you must find a husband. An American citizen is best."

She saw my surprise and quickly added, "Chinese! Of course, he must be 7 Chinese. 'Citizen' does not mean Caucasian. But if he is not a citizen, you should immediately do number two. See here, you should have a baby. Boy or girl, it doesn't matter in the United States. Neither will take care of you in your old age, isn't that true?" And we both laughed.

"Be careful, though," she said. "The authorities there will ask you if you   8
have children now or if you are thinking of having some. You must say no. You should look sincere and say you are not married, you are religious, you know it is wrong to have a baby."

I must have looked puzzled, because she explained further: "Look here   9
now, how can an unborn baby know what it is not supposed to do? And once it has arrived, it is an American citizen and can do anything it wants. It can ask its mother to stay. Isn't that true?"

But that is not the reason I was puzzled. I wondered why she said I should   10
look sincere. How could I look any other way when telling the truth?

See how truthful my face still looks. Why didn't I give this look to you?   11
Why do you always tell your friends that I arrived in the United States on a slow boat from China? This is not true. I was not that poor. I took a plane. I had saved the money my first husband's family gave me when they sent me away. And I had saved money from my twelve years' work as a telephone operator. But it is true I did not take the fastest plane. The plane took three weeks. It stopped everywhere: Hong Kong, Vietnam, the Philippines, Hawaii. So by the time I arrived, I did not look sincerely glad to be here.

Why do you always tell people that I met your father in the Cathay House,   12
that I broke open a fortune cookie and it said I would marry a dark, handsome stranger, and that when I looked up, there he was, the waiter, your father. Why do you make this joke? This is not sincere. This was not true! Your father was not a waiter, I never ate in that restaurant. The Cathay House had a sign that said "Chinese Food," so only Americans went there before it was torn down. Now it is a McDonald's restaurant with a big Chinese sign that says *mai dong lou*—"wheat," "east," "building." All nonsense. Why are you attracted only to Chinese nonsense? You must understand my real circumstances, how I arrived, how I married, how I lost my Chinese face, why you are the way you are.

When I arrived, nobody asked me questions. The authorities looked at my   13
papers and stamped me in. I decided to go first to a San Francisco address given to me by this girl in Peking. The bus put me down on a wide street with cable cars. This was California Street. I walked up this hill and then I saw a tall building. This was Old St. Mary's. Under the church sign, in handwritten Chinese characters, someone had added: "A Chinese Ceremony to Save Ghosts from Spiritual Unrest 7 A.M. and 8:30 A.M." I memorized this information in case the authorities asked me where I worshipped my religion. And then I saw another sign across the street. It was painted on the outside of a short building: "Save Today for Tomorrow, at Bank of America." And I thought to myself, This is where American people worship. See, even then I was not so dumb! Today that church is the same size, but where that short bank used to be, now there is a tall building, fifty stories high, where you and your husband-to-be work and look down on everybody.

My daughter laughed when I said this. Her mother can make a good joke. 14

So I kept walking up this hill. I saw two pagodas, one on each side of the 15
street, as though they were the entrance to a great Buddha temple. But when
I looked carefully, I saw the pagoda was really just a building topped with
stacks of tile roofs, no walls, nothing else under its head. I was surprised how
they tried to make everything look like an old imperial city or an emperor's
tomb. But if you looked on either side of these pretend-pagodas, you could see
the streets became narrow and crowded, dark, and dirty. I thought to myself,
Why did they choose only the worst Chinese parts for the inside? Why didn't
they build gardens and ponds instead? Oh, here and there was the look of a
famous ancient cave or a Chinese opera. But inside it was always the same
cheap stuff.

So by the time I found the address the girl in Peking gave me, I knew not 16
to expect too much. The address was a large green building, so noisy, children
running up and down the outside stairs and hallways. Inside number 402, I
found an old woman who told me right away she had wasted her time waiting
for me all week. She quickly wrote down some addresses and gave them to me,
keeping her hand out after I took the paper. So I gave her an American dollar
and she looked at it and said, "*Syaujye*"—Miss—"we are in America now. Even
a beggar can starve on this dollar." So I gave her another dollar and she said,
"Aii, you think it is so easy getting this information?" So I gave her another
and she closed her hand and her mouth.

With the addresses this old woman gave me, I found a cheap apartment on 17
Washington Street. It was like all the other places, sitting on top of a little
store. And through this three-dollar list, I found a terrible job paying me sev-
enty-five cents an hour. Oh, I tried to get a job as a salesgirl, but you had to
know English for that. I tried for another job as a Chinese hostess, but they
also wanted me to rub my hands up and down foreign men, and I knew right
away this was as bad as fourth-class prostitutes in China! So I rubbed that
address out with black ink. And some of the other jobs required you to have a
special relationship. They were jobs held by families from Canton and
Toishan and the Four Districts, southern people who had come many years
ago to make their fortune and were still holding onto them with the hands of
their great-grandchildren.

So my mother was right about my hardships. This job in the cookie factory 18
was one of the worst. Big black machines worked all day and night pouring little
pancakes onto moving round griddles. The other women and I sat on high stools,
and as the little pancakes went by, we had to grab them off the hot griddle just as
they turned golden. We would put a strip of paper in the center, then fold the
cookie in half and bend its arms back just as it turned hard. If you grabbed the
pancake too soon, you would burn your fingers on the hot, wet dough. But if you
grabbed too late, the cookie would harden before you could even complete the
first bend. And then you had to throw these mistakes in a barrel, which counted
against you because the owner could sell those only as scraps.

After the first day, I suffered ten red fingers. This was not a job for a stu- 19
pid person. You had to learn fast or your fingers would turn into fried

sausages. So the next day only my eyes burned, from never taking them off the pancakes. And the day after that, my arms ached from holding them out ready to catch the pancakes at just the right moment. But by the end of my first week, it became mindless work and I could relax enough to notice who else was working on each side of me. One was an older woman who never smiled and spoke to herself in Cantonese when she was angry. She talked like a crazy person. On my other side was a woman around my age. Her barrel contained very few mistakes. But I suspected she ate them. She was quite plump.

"Eh, *Syaujye,*" she called to me over the loud noise of the machines. I was   20 grateful to hear her voice, to discover we both spoke Mandarin, although her dialect was coarse-sounding. "Did you ever think you would be so powerful you could determine someone else's fortune?" she asked.

I didn't understand what she meant. So she picked up one of the strips of   21 paper and read it aloud, first in English: "Do not fight and air your dirty laundry in public. To the victor go the soils." Then she translated in Chinese: "You shouldn't fight and do your laundry at the same time. If you win, your clothes will get dirty."

I still did not know what she meant. So she picked up another one and   22 read in English: "Money is the root of all evil. Look around you and dig deep." And then in Chinese: "Money is a bad influence. You become restless and rob graves."

"What is this nonsense?" I asked her, putting the strips of paper in my   23 pocket, thinking I should study these classical American sayings.

"They are fortunes," she explained. "American people think Chinese peo-   24 ple write these sayings."

"But we never say such things!" I said. "These things don't make sense.   25 These are not fortunes, they are bad instructions."

"No, Miss," she said, laughing, "it is our bad fortune to be here making   26 these and somebody else's bad fortune to pay to get them."

So that is how I met An-mei Hsu. Yes, yes, Auntie An-mei, now so old-   27 fashioned. An-mei and I still laugh over those bad fortunes and how they later became quite useful in helping me catch a husband.

"Eh, Lindo," An-mei said to me one day at our workplace. "Come to my   28 church this Sunday. My husband has a friend who is looking for a good Chinese wife. He is not a citizen, but I'm sure he knows how to make one." So that is how I first heard about Tin Jong, your father. It was not like my first marriage, where everything was arranged. I had a choice. I could choose to marry your father, or I could choose not to marry him and go back to China.

I knew something was not right when I saw him: He was Cantonese! How   29 could An-mei think I could marry such a person? But she just said: "We are not in China anymore. You don't have to marry the village boy. Here every-body is now from the same village even if they come from different parts of China." See how changed Auntie An-mei is from those old days.

So we were shy at first, your father and I, neither of us able to speak to   30 each other in our Chinese dialects. We went to English class together, speak-ing to each other in those new words and sometimes taking out a piece of paper to write a Chinese character to show what we meant. At least we had that, a piece of paper to hold us together. But it's hard to tell someone's marriage intentions when you can't say things aloud. All those little signs—the teasing, the bossy, scolding words—that's how you know if it is serious. But we could talk only in the manner of our English teacher. I see cat. I see rat. I see hat.

But I saw soon enough how much your father liked me. He would pretend 31
he was in a Chinese play to show me what he meant. He ran back and forth, jumped up and down, pulling his fingers through his hair, so I knew— *mangjile!*—what a busy, exciting place this Pacific Telephone was, this place where he worked. You didn't know this about your father—that he could be such a good actor? You didn't know your father had so much hair?

Oh, I found out later his job was not the way he described it. It was not so 32
good. Even today, now that I can speak Cantonese to your father, I always ask him why he doesn't find a better situation. But he acts as if we were in those old days, when he couldn't understand anything I said.

Sometimes I wonder why I wanted to catch a marriage with your father. I 33
think An-mei put the thought in my mind. She said, "In the movies, boys and girls are always passing notes in class. That's how they fall into trouble. You need to start trouble to get this man to realize his intentions. Otherwise, you will be an old lady before it comes to his mind."

That evening An-mei and I went to work and searched through strips of 34
fortune cookie papers, trying to find the right instructions to give to your father. An-mei read them aloud, putting aside ones that might work: "Diamonds are a girl's best friend. Don't ever settle for a pal." "If such thoughts are in your head, it's time to be wed." "Confucius say a woman is worth a thousand words. Tell your wife she's used up her total."

We laughed over those. But I knew the right one when I read it. It said: "A 35
house is not a home when a spouse is not at home." I did not laugh. I wrapped up this saying in a pancake, bending the cookie with all my heart.

After school the next afternoon, I put my hand in my purse and then made 36
a look, as if a mouse had bitten my hand. "What's this?" I cried. Then I pulled out the cookie and handed it to your father. "Eh! So many cookies, just to see them makes me sick. You take this cookie."

I knew even then he had a nature that did not waste anything. He opened 37
the cookie and he crunched it in his mouth, and then read the piece of paper.

"What does it say?" I asked. I tried to act as if it did not matter. And when 38
he still did not speak, I said, "Translate, please."

We were walking in Portsmouth Square and already the fog had blown in 39
and I was very cold in my thin coat. So I hoped your father would hurry and ask me to marry him. But instead, he kept his serious look and said, "I don't know this word 'spouse.' Tonight I will look in my dictionary. Then I can tell you the meaning tomorrow."

The next day he asked me in English, "Lindo, can you spouse me?" And I 40
laughed at him and said he used that word incorrectly. So he came back and made a Confucius joke, that if the words were wrong, then his intentions must

also be wrong. We scolded and joked with each other all day long like this, and that is how we decided to get married.

One month later we had a ceremony in the First Chinese Baptist Church, 41 where we met. And nine months later your father and I had our proof of citizenship, a baby boy, your big brother Winston. I named him Winston because I liked the meaning of those two words "wins ton." I wanted to raise a son who would win many things, praise, money, a good life. Back then, I thought to myself, At last I have everything I wanted. I was so happy, I didn't see we were poor. I saw only what we had. How did I know Winston would die later in a car accident? So young! Only sixteen!

Two years after Winston was born, I had your other brother, Vincent. I 42 named him Vincent, which sounds like "win cent," the sound of making money, because I was beginning to think we did not have enough. And then I bumped my nose riding on the bus. Soon after that you were born.

I don't know what caused me to change. Maybe it was my crooked nose 43 that damaged my thinking. Maybe it was seeing you as a baby, how you looked so much like me, and this made me dissatisfied with my life. I wanted everything for you to be better. I wanted you to have the best circumstances, the best character. I didn't want you to regret anything. And that's why I named you Waverly. It was the name of the street we lived on. And I wanted you to think, This is where I belong. But I also knew if I named you after this street, soon you would grow up, leave this place, and take a piece of me with you.

RESPONDING TO THE READING

Freewriting

Exercise 12c.   Freewrite about Lindo Sun's experiences in America that you found most interesting or humorous.

Exercise 12d.   How are Lindo Sun's evaluations of American culture like or unlike your own?

Building Your Vocabulary

VOCABULARY LIST

Words to Look Up	My Definition	Dictionary Definition
pagoda (15)		
Mandarin (20)		
dialect (20)		

Questions for Discussion

1. What do you think Lindo Sun means when she says "It's hard to keep your Chinese face in America"? What does "face" seem to mean here?
2. Why is Lindo Sun telling this story of her immigration to the United States?
3. What can you tell about the relationship between Lindo Sun and the daughter for whom she writes this story?
4. What did you learn about Chinese thought and culture in this selection from Amy Tan's novel?
5. How do Lindo Sun's impressions of America compare to the perspective we get from Bette Bao Lord's "Walking in Lucky Shoes"?
6. This story is a companion for "Rules of the Game" in Chapter 8. What does this portrait of Lindo Sun add to the view of her we get through her daughter's eyes?

TOPICS FOR WRITING

Topic 1. Survey several people to see how they met their partners. Consider asking the following questions:

> Where did you meet?
> Was there something special about the place you met?
> Was the meeting arranged by either of you or did it happen by chance?
> What were your initial impressions of your partner?
> Did your perspective change after that first encounter?
> How did you eventually decide that the two of you should begin seeing each other?
> What is unusual or special about the way you relate to each other?

Choose the story that sounds the most interesting, arrange the details according to topic ideas, and write a narrative account of the meeting you chose. To avoid writing a dull account (this happened, then this happened, and so on), explore *why* things went as they did, what the individuals were thinking, how they responded to each other, and what they expected. Analogies, comparisons, and contrasts may add interest to your narrative.

Topic 2. Write an explanation of similarities and differences between the way Lindo Sun found a husband and some methods for finding a partner that are familiar to you.

Topic 3. Identify several instances when Lindo Sun criticizes what she sees in the United States. Then write a defense or criticism of her opinions. Use examples from your own observations to support your position.

Walking in Lucky Shoes
Bette Bao Lord

Bette Bao Lord is a novelist and essayist. Her most recent book is Legacies: A Chinese Mosaic. *In "Walking in Lucky Shoes," published in a 1992 issue of* Newsweek, Lord *uses images of shoes to characterize changes she and other immigrants have made as they adapted to life in the United States.*

I confess. Novelists have a fetish. We can't resist shoes. Indeed, we spend 1 our lives recalling the pairs we have shed and snatching others off unsuspecting souls. We're not proud. We're not particular. Whether it's Air Jordans or the clodhoppers of Frankenstein, Imelda's[1] gross collection or one glass slipper, we covet them all. There's no cure for this affliction. To create characters, we must traipse around and around in our heads sporting lost or stolen shoes.

At 8, I sailed for America from Shanghai without a passing acquaintance 2 of A, B or C, wearing scruffy brown oxfords. Little did I know then that they were as magical as those glittering red pumps that propelled Dorothy down the yellow brick road.

Only yesterday, it seems, resting my chin on the rails of the SS Marylinx, 3 I peered into the mist for *Mei Guo,* Beautiful Country. It refused to appear. Then, in a blink, there was the Golden Gate, more like the portals to Heaven than the arches of a man-made bridge.

Only yesterday, standing at PS 8 in Brooklyn, I was bewitched—others, 4 alas, were bothered and bewildered—when I proclaimed:

> I pledge a lesson to the frog of
>   the United States of America.
> And to the wee puppet for witch's hands.
>   One Asian, in the vestibule,
> with little tea and just rice for all.

Although I mangled the language, the message was not lost. Not on some- 5 one wearing immigrant shoes.

Only yesterday, rounding third base in galoshes, I swallowed a barrelful of 6 tears wondering what wrong I had committed to anger my teammates so. Why were they all madly screaming at me to go home, go home?

Only yesterday, listening in pink cotton mules to Red Barber broadcasting 7 from Ebbetts Field,[2] I vaulted over the Milky Way as my hero, Jackie Robinson,[3] stole home.

---

[1]As wife of former President Ferdinand Marcos of the Philippines, Imelda Marcos is reported to have owned thousands of pairs of shoes.

[2]Baseball stadium in Brooklyn, New York.

[3]The first African-American player in major league baseball.

Only yesterday, enduring the pinch of new Mary Janes at my grammar- 8
school graduation, I felt as tall as the Statue of Liberty, reciting Walt
Whitman:[4] "I hear America singing, the varied carols I hear . . . Each singing
what belongs to him or her and to none else. . . ."

Today I cherish every unstylish pair of shoes that took me up a road 9
cleared by the footfalls of millions of immigrants before me—to a room of my
own. For America has granted me many a dream, even one that I never dared
to dream—returning to the land of my birth in 1989 as the wife of the
American ambassador. Citizens of Beijing were astounded to see that I was
not a *yang guei ze*, foreign devil, with a tall nose and ghostly skin and bumpy
hair colored in outlandish hues, I looked Chinese, I spoke Chinese, and after
being in my company they accused me of being a fake, of being just another
member of the clan.

I do not believe that the loss of one's native culture is the price one must 10
pay for becoming an American. On the contrary, I feel doubly blessed. I can
choose from two rich cultures those parts that suit my mood or the occasion
best. And unbelievable as it may seem, shoes tinted red, white and blue go
dandy with them all.

Recently I spoke at my alma mater. There were many more Asian faces in 11
that one audience than there were enrolled at Tufts University when I
cavorted in white suede shoes to cheer the Jumbos to victory. One asked, "Will
you tell us about your encounters with racial prejudice?" I had no ready
answers. I thought hard. Sure, I had been roughed up at school. Sure, I had
failed at work. Sure, I had at times felt powerless. But had prejudice against
the shade of my skin and the shape of my eyes caused these woes? Unable to
show off the wounds I had endured at the hands of racists, I could only cite a
scene from my husband's 25th reunion at Yale eight years ago. Throughout
that weekend, I sensed I was being watched. But even after the tall, burly man
finally introduced himself, I did not recognize his face or name. He hemmed
and hawed, then announced that he had flown from Colorado to apologize to
me. I could not imagine why. Apparently at a party in the early '60s, he had
hectored me to cease dating his WASP classmate.

Someone else at Tufts asked, "How do you think of yourself? As a Chinese 12
or as an American?" Without thinking, I blurted out the truth: "Bette Bao
Lord." Did I imagine the collective sigh of relief that swept through the auditorium? I think not. Perhaps I am the exception that proves the rule. Perhaps
I am blind to insult and injury. Perhaps I am not alone. No doubt I have been
lucky. Others have not been as fortunate. They had little choice but to wear ill-
fitting shoes warped by prejudice, to start down a less traveled road strewn
with broken promises and littered with regrets, haunted by racism and awash
with tears. Where could that road possibly lead? Nowhere but to a nation,
divided, without liberty and no justice at all.

---

[4]Nineteenth-century American poet and author of *Leaves of Grass*, a seminal work in American
literature.

The Berlin wall is down, but between East Harlem and West Hempstead,[5] 13 between the huddled masses of yesterday and today, the walls go up and up. Has the cold war ended abroad only to usher in heated racial and tribal conflicts at home? No, I believe we shall overcome. But only when:

We engage our diversity to yield a nation greater than the sum of its parts. 14

We can be different as sisters and brothers are, and belong to the same 15 family.

We bless, not shame, America, our home. 16

A home, no doubt, where skeletons nest in closets and the roof leaks, 17 where foundations must be shored and rooms added. But a home where legacies conceived by the forefathers are tendered from generation to generation to have and to hold. Legacies not of gold but as intangible and inalienable and invaluable as laughter and hope.

We the people can do just that—if we clear the smoke of ethnic chauvin- 18 ism and fears by braving our journey to that "City Upon a Hill" in each other's shoes.

RESPONDING TO THE READING

Freewriting

Exercise 12e.   Freewrite about one or two of Bette Bao Lord's experiences that are like or distinctly unlike your own.

Exercise 12f.   Try to answer the question Lord was asked in paragraph 12: "How do you think of yourself?"

Building Your Vocabulary

VOCABULARY LIST

Words to Look Up	My Definition	Dictionary Definition
fetish (1)		
clodhoppers (1)		
traipse (1)		
portals (3)		
mangled (5)		
vaulted (7)		
alma mater (11)		
burly (11)		
hemmed and hawed (11)		
hectored (11)		

---

[5]Boundaries of African-American and Latino ghettos in upper Manhattan, New York City.

legacies (17)
tendered (17)
intangible (17)
inalienable (17)
chauvinism (18)

Question for Discussion

1. Reread Bette Bao Lord's version of the pledge of allegiance (paragraph 4). What might be "the message" to immigrants that she alludes to in paragraph 5?
2. Examine Lord's use of shoes to characterize experiences in America. How appropriate are these shoes for the occasions she mentions? How effective is this image in translating her experiences as an immigrant?
3. Toward the end of her essay, Lord uses several familiar phrases such as "the huddled masses," "without liberty and no justice at all," "to have and to hold." Why do you think she chose such phrases? How effective are they in communicating her ideas?
4. Why does Lord consider herself lucky? What does she say about those who have been less fortunate? Why do you think she mentions the unlucky ones?
5. Lord believes that immigrants can preserve their native culture and still become Americans. What evidence do you find that Lord has been able to retain her Chinese culture while embracing elements of American culture?
6. What advice does Lord offer in the last six paragraphs of her essay? What problems need to be solved if we are to take her advice?
7. What similarities or differences do you find between the writing and points of view in "Walking in Lucky Shoes" and Amy Tan's "Memoirs of a Chinese Mother"?

TOPICS FOR WRITING

Topic 1. Think about two or three important changes in your life. Choose one image (you might use clothing, the way you walk or talk, or hair style) that characterizes these changes. Write an essay in which you use this image to help explain the changes you made.

Topic 2. In paragraph 10 Bette Bao Lord says, "I do not believe that the loss of one's native culture is the price one must pay for becoming an American." Write an essay in which you discuss the problems that sometimes arise for Americans who embrace several cultures. You might read "Complexion" (Chapter 13), "The Shock of Alienation" (Chapter 14), "The

Struggle to Be an All-American Girl" (Chapter 16), or "The Arab's Image" (Chapter 17) to gather ideas for your discussion.

Topic 3.   Carefully examine the writing strategies Lord uses in "Walking in Lucky Shoes." Write an essay in which you compare these strategies to those Amy Tan uses to depict her character Lindo Sun in "Memoirs of a Chinese Mother."

Student Writing

Coming to America

When my parents came from Mexico to the United States, they had nothing to start with but determination. Both parents were determined that their children would have the opportunities they didn't have when they were growing up.

Not having much more than a third-grade education, my father started out working in the tomato fields in California. He would work fifteen hours a day, seven days a week while my mother stayed at home with seven children. Home at that time was a small two-room shack clustered with dozens of other two-room shacks where other farm workers' families lived. My father always saved one of his paychecks each month for investments, knowing that someday they would pay off. He cashed the other check for the things his family needed, like clothes for the children and food to feed us. Maybe once in a while we would get treated to ice cream at our local A & W.

My father managed to find a good career for himself working at a huge tomato plant in the town where we lived. He started at the bottom of the list of jobs the plant had available at that time. He took a slight pay decrease when he quit working in the tomato fields, but his new job had many benefits his family could use, like medical and dental plans. I was three when my father managed to save enough money to put down a deposit on a house. Having a foundation to build on, my parents quickly saved their money for future investments they planned to make.

Through several years of hard work, my father managed to go up the ladder of jobs the company offered. At first he was a member of the janitorial crew. Next he worked at cleaning the canning machines, making sure they were free of old pieces of tomato. While he had that job, he learned enough about state regulations and the way the assembly line was run that he was able to apply for and get a job as assistant foreman, the position he held when he retired. With each new job he got a little more money. He soon started investing in a college education for all his children. My father dreamed of giving his children a chance to go to college. It was soon to become a reality.

Now, 15 years later, my parents tell themselves how fortunate and happy they are to have four of their children holding college degrees from some of the finest universities in California and more to come. My parents often share tales with the family of how fortunate they feel for being where they are today and having built something from nothing because of their determination.

—Gabriel Ramirez

Questions for Discussion

1. What is the dominant impression Gabriel Ramirez creates with this portrait of his parents? What details help to create this impression?
2. Can you find a thesis statement that contains the main idea of the essay?
3. What suggestions for revision can you offer Gabriel Ramirez?
4. What do you know about your own parents' or guardians' early attempts to provide for their family's needs? How do their efforts compare with those of Ramirez's parents?
5. What comparisons can you make between the situations that Ramirez describes and a newspaper item, magazine article, novel, or short story you have read, or a television show or movie you have seen?

13

Between Two Cultures

*It is in these remote border
cities, far from national capitals,
that the United States and Mexico not
only meet but merge to form a new society.*

—*Marjorie Miller and Ricardo Chavira*

*What makes basketball the most intriguing of
sports is how . . . the punishing intensity of
"white" players and the dazzling moves of the
"blacks" can fit together, a fusion of cultures that
seems more and more difficult in the world
beyond the out-of-bounds line.*

—*Jeff Greenfield*

Ln a country with as much diversity among its people as this one, most of us have, at one time or another, been caught between the rhythms of a culture or value system that we have known since birth and those of another culture to which we may have to adapt. In this chapter you read about the cross-cultural experiences of Mexican Americans, European Americans, and African Americans. In "Border Culture," Marjorie Miller and Ricardo Chavira write about the mixed culture that thrives along the border shared by Mexico and the United States. In "Complexion," Richard Rodriguez fights the image of the Mexican laborer as he struggles to forge a new identity as a student and intellectual. Jeff Greenfield's "The Black and White Truth about Basketball" is about two distinct styles of the game, one "black," the other "white," whose players may come from either ethnic group.

The essays in this chapter employ several of the writing strategies introduced in earlier chapters, including narrating, describing, causal analysis, and comparing and contrasting. "Border Culture" presents an additional writing strategy—defining.

DEFINING

You have already seen defining used in earlier chapters to clarify terms. Art Jahnke, for example, in "What Ever Happened to Friendship?" offers several definitions of "friend." Most writers who use definition, whether as the principal writing strategy for their essay or for a small but important explanation of terms, answer this question: "What is _____?" (Fill in the blank.) In "Border Culture," for instance, the authors' definitions answer the question, "What is this border culture?"

Characteristics of Defining

A Purpose and Point of View

Usually the purpose of an essay that relies principally on defining is to explain what something means. Occasionally a definition may be used to argue a point, or it may be written to entertain, as is the case with David Owen's essay, "The Perfect Job" (Chapter 15). As with other writing strategies, authors choose either a first-person point of view or the more objective third-person perspective. In the sample essay, "Border Culture," Marjorie Miller and Ricardo Chavira write objectively in order to inform the reader about the uniqueness of the culture along the border between the United States and Mexico.

Use of Other Writing Strategies

In most cases, writers whose main purpose is to define a subject rely on other writing strategies to make that definition clear to the reader. Describing, giving examples, explaining, comparing and contrasting, or discussing causes and effects are common ways that writers use to define their subjects. Miller and Chavira's article, "Border Culture," illustrates each of these strategies.

USING DESCRIBING TO DEFINE.   Writers may choose to describe the characteristics of their topic; these descriptions may include qualities, behavior, size, or shape, depending on whether a commercial product, person, or object is being defined. In "Border Culture," because the authors are defining a place, they devote their opening paragraphs to a description of that place—the borderland between Mexico and the United States.

> Highway 80, a blacktop ribbon of road through scrub brush 1
> and hill after rugged hill, unfolds to the south toward Douglas. The
> windswept Arizona highway leads to the 1,900-mile border where
> Mexico and the United States stand face to face in a barren land.
> At the border, the highway joins a trio of narrow Mexican 2
> highways that also traverse the arid geography.
> But there are more than lonesome roads among the scrub 3
> brush. These Mexican and American highways form a network that
> connects far-apart towns and cities from San Diego to Brownsville,
> Texas; from Tijuana to Matamoros, Tamaulipas.

In these paragraphs the authors describe the physical characteristics of the borderlands; they are mostly barren and arid wastelands stretching between the towns and cities that comprise the border culture. As this description makes clear, the highways that form the boundaries of this area have all but invented the border culture in the sense that it could not exist without this vital network.

Once Miller and Chavira have described the landscape of the border for the reader, they write their thesis: "It is in these remote border cities, far from national capitals, that the United States and Mexico not only meet but merge to form a new society" (paragraph 4). Two paragraphs later the authors restate the thesis in more specific terms: "Here on the border a 200-year-old, upstart culture meets one with roots that predate Christ. Together they meld into a new, third culture of the borderlands that blurs the very border from which it was born" (paragraph 8).

USING EXAMPLES TO DEFINE.   Case studies and examples show the reader specific instances that clarify the meaning of a particular term or concept. In our sample article, Miller and Chavira define the border culture by offering cross-cultural examples of the people who live there.

> It [border culture] is a society of people like Elsa Vega and 5
> Celia Díaz, both of whom grew up south of the border, but now live
> north. It is people like Barney Thompson and William Arens, who
> married women from Tijuana but live in San Diego.

It is Robert Bracker, whose father built a store in Nogales, 6
Arizona, to serve Mexican customers, or Pablo Hourani, who lives
in Bonita and commutes south daily to run his family clothing business. Or Leobardo Estrada of Los Angeles, the grandson of Mexican
immigrants whose family still extends south to Tijuana.

USING EXPLAINING TO DEFINE.   Effective writing usually requires that
authors explain or interpret their examples for the reader. In paragraphs following their examples of the people who live along the border, Miller and
Chavira offer the following observations:

At the border, a wealthy technological superpower meets a 7
developing agricultural nation; a predominantly Anglo-Protestant
people encounters a society of *mestizos,* Indians, and Spanish
Catholics. . . .

The culture of the borderlands is a binational world where 12
Mexicans are becoming more Americanized and where Americans
are becoming more Mexicanized. It is an area, sometimes hundreds
of miles wide, where families, businesses, languages, and values
from the two countries often are entwined as tightly as the chain
link fence that attempts to separate them.

USING COMPARING AND CONTRASTING TO DEFINE.   Writers sometimes
explain how something is like or unlike the topic being defined. In "Border
Culture," for example, the authors use this strategy when contrasting the
diverse culture along the border with its opposite—a homogeneous culture.

Just as the border is not homogeneous, neither is it completely 39
unified.

Conflicts, clashes and contradictions have developed out of 40
the interaction between two such diverse peoples: Mexicans and
Americans.

On both sides of the border, there is the necessary mutual 41
dependence of neighbors. But respect and friendship often have
combined with resentment and racism to form a love-hate relationship.

There is suspicion and scorn on both sides.   42

Americans who value speed and efficiency often huff if 43
Mexican goods break down or service is slow; Mexicans, on the
other hand, sometimes turn up their noses at Americans whom they
feel are rushing through life too fast to appreciate living it.

Many Mexicans are envious of American wealth while, at the 44
same time, they are put off by the individualism, egotism, and selfishness that they believe goes with it. They are offended by
American haughtiness and bluntness.

A mythology has evolved on both sides that leads Americans to   45
believe all Mexican police will demand a bribe or throw them in jail,
and Mexicans to believe that U.S. businessmen always are honest
and that U.S. authorities always will deal with them fairly.

By using examples of people who are not part of the border culture, Miller
and Chavira suggest what the border culture *is* by showing the reader what
it is *not.* Furthermore, their illustrations of the antagonism between
Mexicans and citizens of the United States also show that the culture is not
harmonious.

USING CAUSAL ANALYSIS TO DEFINE.   Sometimes examining causes and
effects helps writers define their subject. Examining the history that produced
the border culture, for example, clarifies not only what it is, but why it exists
in its present form.

While some people who live in the border culture embrace it   33
as a positive and inevitable change, others are hostile toward it for
fear it will degrade their own culture.

The history of the border begins with such antagonism.   34

After a two-year war between Mexico and the United States,   35
the present-day border was drawn up, which cost Mexico nearly
half its territory. Mutual hate and distrust poisoned relations, and
for years after the conquest Americans and Mexicans launched
cross-border raids against each other.

Mexico later decided to put up the only barrier it had—peo-   36
ple—to prevent Americans from capturing more land by simply
moving onto it. The government in the 1930s made it a national policy to entice Mexicans to move north—ironically, by offering them
access to cheap American goods.

More recently, Mexicans in the interior have chastised those   37
northern Mexicans for becoming too Americanized and too dependent on American goods.

Today, many Mexicans see the cultural encroachment of   38
the United States in Mexico as a further "occupation" of their
country. Many Americans, on the other hand, fear that Mexicans
are slowly reconquering the Southwest with *their* cultural encroachment.

Notice that this look at history employs narration to tell what happened along
the border in years past. Transitions in each topic sentence ("after a two-year
war," "Mexico later decided," "more recently," and "today") link events in this
chronological arrangement smoothly.

Border Culture
Marjorie Miller and Ricardo Chavira

Marjorie Miller and Ricardo Chavira, staff writers for the San Diego Union, *wrote this article about the mixing of Mexican and U.S. cultures along their common border. Their article appeared in the* San Diego Union *December 26, 1983, under the title "A Unique Culture Grows in the Desert."*

Highway 80, a blacktop ribbon of road through scrub brush and hill after 1 rugged hill, unfolds to the south toward Douglas. The windswept Arizona highway leads to the 1,900-mile border where Mexico and the United States stand face to face in a barren land.

At the border, the highway joins a trio of narrow Mexican highways that 2 also traverse the arid geography.

But there are more than lonesome roads among the scrub brush. These 3 Mexican and American highways form a network that connects far-apart towns and cities from San Diego to Brownsville, Texas; from Tijuana to Matamoros, Tamaulipas.

It is in these remote border cities, far from national capitals, that the 4 United States and Mexico not only meet but merge to form a new society.

It is a society of people like Elsa Vega and Celia Díaz, both of whom grew 5 up south of the border, but now live north. It is people like Barney Thompson and William Arens, who married women from Tijuana but live in San Diego.

It is Robert Bracker, whose father built a store in Nogales, Arizona to 6 serve Mexican customers, or Pablo Hourani, who lives in Bonita and commutes south daily to run his family clothing business. Or Leobardo Estrada of Los Angeles, the grandson of Mexican immigrants whose family still extends south to Tijuana.

At the border, a wealthy technological superpower meets a developing 7 agricultural nation; a predominantly Anglo-Protestant people encounters a society of *mestizos*, Indians, and Spanish Catholics.

Here on the border a 200-year-old, upstart culture meets one with roots 8 that predate Christ. Together they meld into a new, third culture of the borderlands that blurs the very border from which it was born.

This barren land has been fertile ground after all, fertile for a culture that 9 has flourished in part because of its isolation. The border culture has had room to grow in the desert.

It has grown in Mexican cities like Mexicali, where the land once belonged 10 to American developers, and in Tijuana, which was so isolated that until the 1940s Tijuanans had to pass through the United States to visit their mainland.

It has grown in American cities like Laredo and Calexico, where the main- 11 stream is a Hispanic majority.

The culture of the borderlands is a binational world where Mexicans are 12 becoming more Americanized and where Americans are becoming more Mexicanized. It is an area, sometimes hundreds of miles wide, where families, businesses, languages, and values from the two countries often are entwined as tightly as the chain link fence that attempts to separate them.

While not all of the cities and the 7 million people who live along the 13 U.S.–Mexico boundary belong to the binational culture, there is a border society that is distinct from Mexico and the United States.

In parts, the border culture reaches as far north as Santa Barbara and San 14 Antonio, Texas, as far south as La Paz in Baja California Sur, and Chihuahua City, Chihuahua.

In a few instances, the borderlands culture crops up like an island far from 15 the international boundary, such as in Chicago—where Mexican immigrants have converted old neighborhoods into replicas of border communities.

By and large, the culture clings to the area along the U.S.–Mexico border, 16 where people might live in one country and work or go to school in another.

It is where Americans and Mexicans intermarry and have children who 17 are dual citizens for the first 18 years of their lives, until they must choose one country or the other.

It is a region where the people speak English and Spanish and often a 18 third language, Spanglish, that is a hybrid of the two.

And it is a society where certain businesses exist simply because the bor- 19 der exists—businesses like currency exchange houses, import-export broker-age firms, and drive-through Mexican car insurance agencies—and where businessmen must learn to operate in two cultures so that after years of doing so they become bicultural.

The border society is made up of towns and cities that experience interna- 20 tional issues, like illegal immigration, as local problems. Pollution, sewage, and natural disasters affect Mexican and American border cities equally, because such problems do not respect an international boundary.

Society on the border is united by footbridge, ferry and bus; by bilingual 21 radio and television; by millions of people who legally cross the border hun-dreds of times each year, and by countless others who cross illegally.

It is a society in which the local economies on each side of the border 22 often are more attached to one another than to the mother country's.

It is a society that is slightly scorned by both Mexico and the United States 23 for its unconventional behavior.

Even some of the cities have blended. Take Calexico and Mexicali—on 24 opposite sides of the border, but both named by the Colorado Land River Co. from the words California and Mexico. And cities such as Columbus, New Mexico, and its neighbor Palomas, Chihuahua, that have merged in other ways, helping to sustain each other.

Many Columbus residents have family in Palomas, while nearly half of 25 Columbus' schoolchildren are from the border's other side. Columbus pro-vides the Mexican town with ambulance and fire services. Mexicans com-monly use the hospital on the U.S. side, the only one in the area.

On the other hand, Palomas is still the place where Columbus residents go 26 to eat bargain-priced steak dinners and drink hearty Mexican beer. And despite Mexico's ailing economy, Columbus still relies on Mexican shoppers to spend money in the U.S. town.

But this binational blend is not spread evenly along the boundary. The border society is not homogeneous.   27

The border region is the wealthiest in Mexico, but one of the poorest regions of the United States.   28

Its people are a mix of pioneers who have called the frontier home for generations, and a generation of new settlers who arrived yesterday from Ohio or Oaxaca, from Michigan or Michoacan.   29

There are people living along the boundary line who are so oblivious to the new, third culture that they might be nearer the Canadian border. There are fourth, fifth, sixth cultures, such as that of the Kickapoo Indians in Texas, the Chinese of Mexicali, the Filipinos of San Ysidro, that exist under the umbrella of the border society. And there are differences between urban and rural people, the rich and poor, Texans and Californians.   30

In fact, those who are totally immersed in the border culture are a minority. Far greater are the numbers who dip in and out, whose cross-border experience might be limited to occasional shopping or dining in the other country, whose cross-cultural experience might be limited to Mexicans seeing an American movie or to San Diegans living next door to a family whose mother tongue is Spanish.   31

Some might be touched by the border only because they work with Americans or employ a Mexican. But inevitably, bits and pieces of the culture rub off—exposure to another language or lifestyle, a conversion from dollars to pesos or kilometers to miles, a sketchy knowledge of the history of another country, a familiarity with its holidays and traditions.   32

While some people who live in the border culture embrace it as a positive and inevitable change, others are hostile toward it for fear it will degrade their own culture.   33

The history of the border begins with such antagonism.   34

After a two-year war between Mexico and the United States, the present-day border was drawn up, which cost Mexico nearly half its territory. Mutual hate and distrust poisoned relations, and for years after the conquest Americans and Mexicans launched cross-border raids against each other.   35

Mexico later decided to put up the only barrier it had—people—to prevent Americans from capturing more land by simply moving onto it. The government in the 1930s made it a national policy to entice Mexicans to move north—ironically, by offering them access to cheap American goods.   36

More recently, Mexicans in the interior have chastised those northern Mexicans for becoming too Americanized and too dependent on American goods.   37

Today, many Mexicans see the cultural encroachment of the United States in Mexico as a further "occupation" of their country. Many Americans, on the other hand, fear that Mexicans are slowly reconquering the Southwest with *their* cultural encroachment.   38

Just as the border is not homogeneous, neither is it completely unified.   39

Conflicts, clashes and contradictions have developed out of the interaction 40
between two such diverse peoples: Mexicans and Americans.

On both sides of the border, there is the necessary mutual dependence of 41
neighbors. But respect and friendship often have combined with resentment
and racism to form a love-hate relationship.

There is suspicion and scorn on both sides. 42

Americans who value speed and efficiency often huff if Mexican goods 43
break down or service is slow; Mexicans, on the other hand, sometimes turn
up their noses at Americans whom they feel are rushing through life too fast
to appreciate living it.

Many Mexicans are envious of American wealth while, at the same time, 44
they are put off by the individualism, egotism, and selfishness that they believe
goes with it. They are offended by American haughtiness and bluntness.

A mythology has evolved on both sides that leads Americans to believe all 45
Mexican police will demand a bribe or throw them in jail, and Mexicans to
believe that U.S. businessmen always are honest and that U.S. authorities
always will deal with them fairly.

U.S. police along the border patrol America's underbelly. It is 1,900 miles 46
of largely unprotected boundary that is vulnerable to anyone determined
enough to enter or to bring something into the country.

Even in an era of sophisticated electronic surveillance, millions of people 47
and billions of dollars of narcotics find their way north, while stolen cars,
high-tech equipment, and top-secret defense documents flow south. It is that
permeability that scares Americans.

Mexicans, meanwhile, have heard horror stories about discrimination in 48
the United States and for that reason some are wary of going north.

Americans continue to picture the Mexican border as replete with good- 49
time towns of sleazy, honky-tonk bars where anything is for sale for the right
price. Some of that does exist, yet Americans played a large role in the creation of that Mexico in the '20s and '30s during Prohibition.

While spending their dollars for fun, Americans developed a double stan- 50
dard, frowning on Mexico for being "that kind of place."

Mexicans invoked their own double standard, profiting from the indulgence 51
while disapproving of Americans for acting as they would not act at home.

Misconceptions and misunderstandings about border life still exist, but 52
they are not unique to the border. They exist away from the border—in
Mexico City and Washington, D.C., among other places.

For all that border residents criticize each other, however, they are 53
becoming more tolerant of each other and more alike.

U.S. border residents who do business in Mexico learn to temper some of 54
their American straightforwardness with a little Mexican graciousness.
Mexican businessmen learn to speed up their timetables to meet Americans'
habits, so that a 2 P.M. lunch in Tijuana becomes a noon lunch in San Diego.

American hostesses who invite guests from south of the border learn to 55
time their evenings accordingly, because one never knows how long it will
take to cross the border.

Many border Mexicans want their children schooled in the United States 56
to learn English, but send them to Catholic schools to make sure they preserve
traditional values of family, religion, and respect.

A few Americans send their children south to learn proper Spanish.   57

Tastes have changed along the U.S. border.   58

From California to Texas, tacos and burritos have become as American as 59
apple pie—so American, in fact, that the way they are prepared is foreign to
many Mexicans from the interior.

While Mexican restaurants are just now becoming an expensive fad in 60
New York, rare is the shopping mall or hotel center along the border without
at least one Mexican restaurant—fast-food or fancy.

And products from both countries intermingle easily on supermarket 61
shelves for people whose tastes include chilies and Idaho potatoes, tortillas
and grits.

Some holidays are heartily celebrated on both sides of the border. In the 62
United States, Cinco de Mayo has become the St. Patrick's Day of the
Southwest. Border Mexicans have become attuned to American holidays such
as July Fourth, Labor Day, and Memorial Day, if only because they mean
added business over long weekends.

U.S. sports teams in the borderlands are vigorously supported by thou- 63
sands of Mexican fans. While Mexicans head north to see football and baseball, Americans head south for bullfights, cockfights, and jai alai.

For residents of the binational society, the border is united by cooperation 64
among peoples through charity and neighborliness, among businesses
through joint ventures, and governments through joint projects.

Despite the rugged terrain of scrub brush and fear, the border is not a bar- 65
rier but a network of relationships and opportunities: The people who strad-
dle the boundary guarantee that the border society will continue to grow in
the desert.

RESPONDING TO THE READING

Freewriting

Exercise 13a.   Freewrite about a mixing of cultures you have observed.
How did it affect the people involved?

Exercise 13b.   Freewrite about differences between the culture of the
United States that Miller and Chavira describe and another culture with
which you are familiar.

Building Your Vocabulary

VOCABULARY LIST

Words to Look Up	My Definition	Dictionary Definition
traverse (2)		
arid (2)		

Questions for Discussion

1. Why do you think the authors wrote this article? What "tone" or "attitude" do they adopt toward their topic? Cite evidence of this tone in their article.
2. "Border Culture" was originally published in a newspaper. To make the article easy to read, the editors made paragraph breaks every few sentences. Find topic sentences in the article and indicate in the margins of your textbook where paragraph breaks might be if Miller and Chavira had used the standard paragraph format introduced in Chapter 3.
3. What is unique about the region Miller and Chavira describe?
4. What do you see as positive or negative about mixing cultures?
5. What examples are most effective in depicting the blending of cultures and communities along the border? What makes them effective?
6. Are there hostile reactions to this blending of cultures? How do the authors explain this resistance?
7. Describe a peaceful or antagonistic meeting of two cultures that you have observed.

TOPICS FOR WRITING

Topic 1. Pick two or three other articles from a chapter in Part Two that illustrate a blending of cultures. You might, for example, choose "Complexion," which appears later in this chapter, "The Immigrants" from Chapter 12, or readings in Chapter 16—"The Struggle to Be an All-American Girl," "It's Not Just Anglo-Saxon," or "Western Values Are Central." First identify the cultures involved; then examine how each article depicts either a peaceful blending or an antagonistic meeting of two cultures.

Topic 2. Freewrite about the neighborhood where you live or one you know well. Where do your neighbors come from? What culture do they seem to belong to? How do they get along with one another? When you have gathered lots of information, examples, incidents, and descriptions concerning the people in your neighborhood, write a paper explaining how different people with different styles, values, and perhaps different cultures live together there.

THE WRITING PROCESS: DEFINING

The steps in the writing process will prove useful if defining is the dominant writing strategy for a paper you wish to write. The following considerations will help you apply the writing process to the task of defining a subject.

Additional Considerations for Developing a Topic

If you write an essay that relies principally on defining to develop ideas, it is best to choose a topic for which you can find specific examples to illustrate your points. The topic you choose should hold some interest for you so that it will keep your attention; this way you will be less likely to put off writing your paper.

Additional Considerations for Preliminary Writing

To generate ideas for your definition, you might ask yourself the following questions. They will help you explore other possible writing strategies for writing your definition.

> What parts, sections, or categories will you describe?
> What examples illustrate your subject?
> How might discussing causes or effects help you define your subject?
> Does your subject serve a purpose or have a particular function that
> might help you define it?
> What else does it resemble?
> What is its opposite?

As you generate ideas and information for your essay, keep in mind that you should use dictionary definitions sparingly and only if you refer to them directly in your paper. Edit these definitions carefully to avoid introducing unnecessary ideas or ideas that are too abstract to illustrate easily.

Additional Considerations for Organizing Ideas

Order of importance and chronological arrangement are common ways to organize ideas in an essay whose purpose is to define.

Additional Considerations for Sharing Your Writing and Making Final Revisions

These following checklist will help you revise your essay for effective focus, organization, and development. Put a check mark beside each question as you revise.

Checklist

- ❏ Do I have a thesis that announces my topic and purpose for writing?
- ❏ Is my point of view subjective (first person) or objective (third person)?
- ❏ Have I provided enough background information for the reader?
- ❏ Is the point I am making in each paragraph expressed in a topic sentence or implied by the details and examples I have given?
- ❏ What other writing strategies do I use (examples, explanation, comparison, contrast, cause, effect)? Do these strategies help me clarify my subject?
- ❏ Do any paragraphs need additional examples or explanations?
- ❏ How have I organized the essay? Do some ideas or paragraphs seem out of order and need rearranging?
- ❏ Have I proofread my sentences carefully enough to catch spelling and punctuation errors and words I may have omitted by mistake, and to find sentence errors I sometimes make (such as fragments or run-on sentences)?

FOR FURTHER READING

Complexion
Richard Rodriguez

Richard Rodriguez, whose parents emigrated from Mexico, distinguished himself as a student of English literature. He attended Stanford and Columbia universities, earned a doctorate from the University of California at Berkeley, and received a fellowship to attend the Warburg Institute in London. In this selection from Hunger of Memory, *Rodriguez writes about his and his family's assimilation into Anglo-American culture.*

Visiting the East Coast or the gray capitals of Europe during the long 1 months of winter, I often meet people at deluxe hotels who comment on my complexion. (In such hotels it appears nowadays a mark of leisure and wealth to have a complexion like mine.) Have I been skiing? In the Swiss Alps? Have I just returned from a Caribbean vacation? No. I say no softly but in a firm voice that intends to explain: My complexion is dark. (My skin is brown. More exactly, terra-cotta in sunlight, tawny in shade. I do not redden in sunlight. Instead, my skin becomes progressively dark; the sun singes the flesh.)

When I was a boy the white summer sun of Sacramento would darken me   2
so, my T-shirt would seem bleached against my slender dark arms. My mother
would see me come up the front steps. She'd wait for the screen door to slam
at my back. "You look like a *negrito*," she'd say, angry, sorry to be angry, frustrated almost to laughing, scorn. "You know how important looks are in this
country. With *los gringos* looks are all that they judge on. But you! Look at
you! You're so careless!" Then she'd start in all over again. "You won't be satisfied till you end up looking like *los pobres* who work in the fields, *los
braceros*."

(*Los braceros:* Those men who work with their *brazos*, their arms; Mexican   3
nationals who were licensed to work for American farmers in the 1950s. They
worked very hard for very little money, my father would tell me. And what
money they earned they sent back to Mexico to support their families, my
mother would add. *Los pobres*—the poor, the pitiful, the powerless ones. But
paradoxically also powerful men. They were the men with brown-muscled
arms I stared at in awe on Saturday mornings when they showed up downtown like gypsies to shop at Woolworth's or Penney's. On Monday nights they
would gather hours early on the steps of the Memorial Auditorium for the
wrestling matches. Passing by on my bicycle in summer, I would spy them
there, clustered in small groups, talking—frightening and fascinating men—
some wearing Texas *sombreros* and T-shirts which shone fluorescent in the
twilight. I would sit forward in the back seat of our family's '48 Chevy to see
them, working alongside Valley highways: dark men on an even horizon, loading a truck amid rows of straight green. Powerful, powerless men. Their fascinating darkness—like mine—to be feared.)

"You'll end up looking just like them." . . .   4

Dark skin was for my mother the most important symbol of a life of   5
oppressive labor and poverty. But both my parents recognized other symbols
as well.

My father noticed the feel of every hand he shook. (He'd smile some-   6
times—marvel more than scorn—remembering a man he'd met who had soft,
uncalloused hands.)

My mother would grab a towel in the kitchen and rub my oily face sore   7
when I came in from playing outside. "Clean the *graza* off of your face!"
(*Greaser!*)

Symbols: When my older sister, then in high school, asked my mother if   8
she could do light housework in the afternoons for a rich lady we knew, my
mother was frightened by the idea. For several weeks she troubled over it
before granting conditional permission: "Just remember, you're not a maid. I
don't want you wearing a uniform." My father echoed the same warning.
Walking with him past a hotel, I watched as he stared at a doorman dressed
like a Beefeater. "How can anyone let himself be dressed up like that? Like a
clown. Don't you ever get a job where you have to put on a uniform." In sum-
mertime neighbors would ask me if I wanted to earn extra money by mowing
their lawns. Again and again my mother worried: "Why did they ask *you?*

Can't you find anything better?" Inevitably, she'd relent. She knew I needed the money. But I was instructed to work after dinner. ("When the sun's not so hot.") Even then, I'd have to wear a hat. *Un sombrero de* baseball.

(*Sombrero.* Watching gray cowboy movies, I'd brood over the meaning of the broad-rimmed hat—that troubling symbol—which comically distinguished a Mexican cowboy from real cowboys.) 9

From my father came no warnings concerning the sun. His fear was of dark factory jobs. He remembered too well his first jobs when he came to this country, not intending to stay, just to earn money enough to sail on to Australia. (In Mexico he had heard too many stories of discrimination in *los Estados Unidos.* So it was Australia, that distant island-continent, that loomed in his imagination as his "America.") The work my father found in San Francisco was work for the unskilled. A factory job. Then a cannery job. (He'd remember the noise and the heat.) Then a job at a warehouse. (He'd remember the dark stench of old urine.) At one place there were fistfights; at another a supervisor who hated Chinese and Mexicans. Nowhere a union. 10

His memory of himself in those years is held by those jobs. Never making money enough for passage to Australia; slowly giving up the plan of returning to school to resume his third-grade education—to become an engineer. My memory of him in those years, however, is lifted from photographs in the family album which show him on his honeymoon with my mother—the woman who had convinced him to stay in America. I have studied their photographs often, seeking to find in those figures some clear resemblance to the man and the woman I've known as my parents. But the youthful faces in the photos remain, behind dark glasses, shadowy figures anticipating my mother and father. 11

They are pictured on the grounds of the Coronado Hotel near San Diego, standing in the pale light of a winter afternoon. She is wearing slacks. Her hair falls seductively over one side of her face. He appears wearing a double-breasted suit, an unneeded raincoat draped over his arm. Another shows them standing together, solemnly staring ahead. Their shoulders barely are touching. There is to their pose an aristocratic formality, an elegant Latin hauteur. 12

The man in those pictures is the same man who was fascinated by Italian grand opera. I have never known just what my father saw in the spectacle, but he has told me that he would take my mother to the Opera House every Friday night—if he had money enough for orchestra seats. ("Why go to sit in the balcony?") On Sundays he'd don Italian silk scarves and a camel's hair coat to take his new wife to the polo matches in Golden Gate Park. But one weekend my father stopped going to the opera and polo matches. He would blame the change in his life on one job—a warehouse job, working for a large corporation which today advertises its products with the smiling faces of children. "They made me an old man before my time," he'd say to me many years later. Afterward, jobs got easier and cleaner. Eventually, in middle age, he got a job making false teeth. But his youth was spent at the warehouse. "Everything changed," his wife remembers. The dapper young man 13 in the old photographs yielded to the man I saw after dinner: haggard, asleep on the sofa. During "The Ed Sullivan Show" on Sunday nights, when Roberta Peters or Licia Albanese would appear on the tiny blue screen, his head would jerk up alert. He'd sit forward while the notes of Puccini sounded before him ("Un bel dí.")

By the time they had a family, my parents no longer dressed in very fine 14 clothes. Those symbols of great wealth and the reality of their lives too noisily clashed. No longer did they try to fit themselves, like paper-doll figures, behind trappings so foreign to their actual lives. My father no longer wore silk scarves or expensive wool suits. He sold his tuxedo to a secondhand store for five dollars. My mother sold her rabbit fur coat to the wife of a Spanish radio station disc jockey. ("It looks better on you than it does on me," she kept telling the lady until the sale was completed.) I was six years old at the time, but I recall watching the transaction with complete understanding. The woman I knew as my mother was already physically unlike the woman in her honeymoon photos. My mother's hair was short. Her shoulders were thick from carrying children. Her fingers were swollen red, toughened by house-cleaning. Already my mother would admit to foreseeing herself in her own mother, a woman grown old, bald and bowlegged, after a hard lifetime of working.

In their manner, both my parents continued to respect the symbols of 15 what they considered to be upper-class life. Very early, they taught me the *pro-pria* way of eating *como los ricos*. And I was carefully taught elaborate formu-las of polite greeting and parting. The dark little boy would be invited by class-mates to the rich houses on Forty-fourth and Forty-fifth streets. "How do you do?" or "I am very pleased to meet you," I would say, bowing slightly to the amused mothers of classmates. "Thank you very much for the dinner; it was very delicious."

I made an impression. I intended to make an impression, to be invited 16 back. (I soon realized that the trick was to get the mother or father to notice me.) From those early days began my association with rich people, my fasci-nation with their secret. My mother worried. She warned me not to come home expecting to have the things my friends possessed. But she needn't have said anything. When I went to the big houses, I remembered that I was, at best, a visitor to the world I saw there. For that reason, I was an especially watchful guest. I was my parents' child. Things most middle-class children wouldn't trouble to notice, I studied. Remembered to see: the starched black and white uniform worn by the maid who opened the door; the Mexican gar-deners—their complexions as dark as my own. (One gardener's face, glassed by sweat, looked up to see me going inside.)

"Take Richard upstairs and show him your electric train," the mother 17 said. But it was really the vast polished dining room table I'd come to appraise. Those nights when I was invited to stay for dinner, I'd notice that my friend's mother rang a small silver bell to tell the black woman when to bring in the food. The father, at his end of the table, ate while wearing his tie. When I was not required to speak, I'd skate the icy cut of crystal with my eye; my gaze would follow the golden threads etched onto the rim of china. With my mother's eyes I'd see my hostess's manicured nails and judge them to be marks of her leisure. Later, when my schoolmate's father would bid me goodnight, I would feel his soft fingers and palm when we shook hands. And turning to leave, I'd see my dark self, lit by chandelier light, in a tall hallway mirror. . . .

Throughout adolescence, I felt myself mysteriously marked. Nothing else 18 about my appearance would concern me so much as the fact that my complexion was dark. My mother would say how sorry she was that there was not money enough to get braces to straighten my teeth. But I never bothered about my teeth. In three-way mirrors at department stores, I'd see my profile dramatically defined by a long nose, but it was really only the color of my skin that caught my attention.

I wasn't afraid that I would become a menial laborer because of my skin. 19 Nor did my complexion make me feel especially vulnerable to racial abuse. (I didn't really consider my dark skin to be a racial characteristic. I would have been only too happy to look as Mexican as my light-skinned older brother.) Simply, I judged myself ugly. And, since the women in my family had been the ones who discussed it in such worried tones, I felt my dark skin made me unattractive to women.

Thirteen years old. Fourteen. In a grammar school art class, when the 20 assignment was to draw a self-portrait, I tried and I tried but could not bring myself to shade in the face on the paper to anything like my actual tone. With disgust then I would come face to face with myself in mirrors. With disappointment I located myself in class photographs—my dark face undefined by the camera which had clearly described the white faces of classmates. Or I'd see my dark wrist against my long-sleeved white shirt.

I grew divorced from my body. Insecure, overweight, listless. On hot sum- 21 mer days when my rubber-soled shoes soaked up the heat from the sidewalk, I kept my head down. Or walked in the shade. My mother didn't need anymore to tell me to watch out for the sun. I denied myself a sensational life. The normal, extraordinary, animal excitement of feeling my body alive—riding shirtless on a bicycle in the warm wind created by furious self-propelled motion—the sensations that first had excited in me a sense of my maleness, I denied. I was too ashamed of my body. I wanted to forget that I had a body because I had a brown body. I was grateful that none of my classmates ever mentioned the fact.

I continued to see the *braceros,* those men I resembled in one way and, in 22 another way, didn't resemble at all. On the watery horizon of a Valley afternoon, I'd see them. And though I feared looking like them, it was with silent envy that I regarded them still. I envied them their physical lives, their freedom to violate the taboo of the sun. Closer to home I would notice the shirtless construction workers, the roofers, the sweating men tarring the street in front of the house. And I'd see the Mexican gardeners. I was unwilling to admit the attraction of their lives. I tried to deny it by looking away. But what was denied became strongly desired.

In high school physical education classes, I withdrew, in the regular com-   23
pany of five or six classmates, to a distant corner of a football field where we
smoked and talked. Our company was composed of bodies too short or too
tall, all graceless and all—except mine—pale. Our conversation was usually
witty. (In fact we were intelligent.) If we referred to the athletic contests
around us, it was with sarcasm. With savage scorn I'd refer to the "animals"
playing football or baseball. It would have been important for me to have
joined them. Or for me to have taken off my shirt, to have let the sun burn dark
on my skin, and to have run barefoot on the warm wet grass. It would have
been very important. Too important. It would have been too telling a gesture—to admit the desire for sensation, the body, my body.

Fifteen, sixteen. I was a teenager shy in the presence of girls. Never dated.   24
Barely could talk to a girl without stammering. In high school I went to several
dances, but I never managed to ask a girl to dance. So I stopped going. I cannot
remember high school years now with the parade of typical images: bright
drive-ins or gliding blue shadows of a Junior Prom. At home most weekend
nights, I would pass evenings reading. Like those hidden, precocious adoles-
cents who have no real-life sexual experiences, I read a great deal of romantic
fiction. "You won't find it in your books," my brother would playfully taunt me
as he prepared to go to a party by freezing the crest of the wave in his hair with
sticky pomade. Through my reading, however, I developed a fabulous and
sophisticated sexual imagination. At seventeen, I may not have known how to
engage a girl in small talk, but I had read *Lady Chatterley's Lover.*

It annoyed me to hear my father's teasing: that I would never know what   25
"real work" is; that my hands were so soft. I think I knew it was his way of
admitting pleasure and pride in my academic success. But I didn't smile. My
mother said she was glad her children were getting their educations and
would not be pushed around like *los pobres.* I heard the remark ironically as a
reminder of my separation from *los braceros.* At such times I suspected that
education was making me effeminate. The odd thing, however, was that I did
not judge my classmates so harshly. Nor did I consider my male teachers in
high school effeminate. It was only myself I judged against some shadowy,
mythical Mexican laborer—dark like me, yet very different.

Language was crucial. I knew that I had violated the ideal of the *macho* by   26
becoming such a dedicated student of language and literature. *Machismo* was
a word never exactly defined by the persons who used it. (It was best described
in the "proper" behavior of men.) Women at home, nevertheless, would repeat
the old Mexican dictum that a man should be *feo, fuerte, y formal.* "The three
F's," my mother called them, smiling slyly. *Feo* I took to mean not literally ugly
so much as ruggedly handsome. (When my mother and her sisters spent a
loud, laughing afternoon determining ideal male good looks, they finally settled on the actor Gilbert Roland, who was neither too pretty nor ugly but had
looks "like a man.") *Fuerte,* "strong," seemed to mean not physical strength as

much as inner strength, character. A dependable man is *fuerte*. *Fuerte* for that reason was a characteristic subsumed by the last of the three qualities, and the one I most often considered—*formal*. To be *formal* is to be steady. A man of responsibility, a good provider. Someone *formal* is also constant. A person to be relied upon in adversity. A sober man, a man of high seriousness.

I learned a great deal about being *formal* just by listening to the way my 27 father and other male relatives of his generation spoke. A man was not silent necessarily. Nor was he limited in the tones he could sound. For example, he could tell a long, involved, humorous story and laugh at his own humor with high-pitched giggling. But a man was not talkative the way a woman could be. It was permitted a woman to be gossipy and chatty. (When one heard many voices in a room, it was usually women who were talking.) Men spoke much less rapidly. And often men spoke in monologues. (When one voice sounded in a crowded room, it was most often a man's voice one heard.) More important than any of this was the fact that a man never verbally revealed his emotions. Men did not speak about their unease in moments of crisis or danger. It was the woman who worried aloud when her husband got laid off from work. At times of illness or death in the family, a man was usually quiet, even silent. Women spoke up to voice prayers. In distress, women always sounded quick ejaculations to God or the Virgin; women prayed in clearly audible voices at a wake held in a funeral parlor. And on the subject of love, a woman was verbally expansive. She spoke of her yearning and delight. A married man, if he spoke publicly about love, usually did so with playful, mischievous irony. Younger, unmarried men more often were quiet. (The *macho* is a silent suitor. *Formal*.)

At home I was quiet, so perhaps I seemed *formal* to my relations and other 28 Spanish-speaking visitors to the house. But outside the house—my God!—I talked. Particularly in class or alone with my teachers, I chattered. (Talking seemed to make teachers think I was bright.) I often was proud of my way with words. Though, on other occasions, for example, when I would hear my mother busily speaking to women, it would occur to me that my attachment to words made me like her. Her son. Not *formal* like my father. At such times I even suspected that my nostalgia for sounds—the noisy, intimate Spanish sounds of my past—was nothing more than effeminate yearning.

High school English teachers encouraged me to describe very personal 29 feelings in words. Poems and short stories I wrote, expressing sorrow and loneliness, were awarded high grades. In my bedroom were books by poets and novelists—books that I loved—in which male writers published feelings the men in my family never revealed or acknowledged in words. And it seemed to me that there was something unmanly about my attachment to literature. Even today, when so much about the myth of the *macho* no longer concerns me, I cannot altogether evade such notions. Writing these pages, admitting my embarrassment or my guilt, admitting my sexual anxieties and my physical insecurity, I have not been able to forget that I am not being *formal*.

So be it. 30

RESPONDING TO THE READING

Freewriting

Exercise 13c.   Freewrite about a few passages from "Complexion" that fascinated or disturbed you in some way. Explain your choices.

Exercise 13d.   Write about the sources of alienation in your life.

Exercise 13e.   Freewrite for several pages about the ways in which Rodriguez's relationship to each of his parents was similar to or different from your relationship to your parents.

Exercise 13f.   How did Rodriguez's teachers encourage him? What kind of encouragement or discouragement have you received from teachers in your high-school or college classes?

Building Your Vocabulary

VOCABULARY LIST

Words to Look Up	My Definition	Dictionary Definition
terra-cotta (1)		
tawny (1)		
uncalloused (6)		
stench (10)		
hauteur (12)		
appraise (17)		
precocious (24)		
audible (27)		
mischievous (27)		
irony (27)		

Questions for Discussion

1. Write an outline of the scenes Rodriguez describes in "Complexion." Occasionally he leaves extra space between paragraphs to indicate breaks between sections in his essay. What is the effect of using these gaps in place of transitional phrases?
2. Which cultures clash in "Complexion"? How is Richard Rodriguez both connected to and alienated from each?
3. How does Rodriguez's thinking reflect the values and concerns of his parents? How does he use them to measure himself?

4. What is Rodriguez's purpose for writing his observations? Is his attitude toward his experiences and observations humorous, critical, angry, informative, curious, bitter, or does some other emotion come to mind?
5. What writing strategy does Rodriguez use to convey his parents' disappointments in life? How effective is it?
6. What is your general impression of Richard Rodriguez? Which passages contributed to this impression?
7. Ask someone in your class who has a Catholic background to explain the term *confession*. In what way might "Complexion" be read as a "confession"?

TOPICS FOR WRITING

Topic 1.   Rodriguez explains some of the uncertainties he has about himself and other people, particularly the *braceros*. Write a paper in which you illustrate one or two of the conflicts or contradictions in your own life. These may involve uneasy feelings about other people or doubts about yourself.

Topic 2.   Rodriguez writes about his "association with rich people" and his fascination with their "secret." Examine several television shows and magazine advertisements to find characterizations or images of the rich. Write a paper in which you illustrate a few of the more frequent images of the rich that you find.

Topic 3.   Rodriguez mentions characteristics of Latin *machismo* (*feo, fuerte,* and *formal*) as appealing to Hispanic women like his mother. Write a paper explaining some of the characteristics that you find most appealing in a partner. In writing your paper, be sure to give actual examples and explain *why* you find a particular behavior, attitude, or personality type appealing.

Topic 4.   Conduct four or five interviews to discover how the people you select have been affected, either negatively or positively, by their parents. Find out how their parents affected their self-esteem, views of others, or attitudes toward work and school. Write an essay examining two or three important ways these people have been influenced by their parents.

Topic 5.   Find two photographs of one or both of your parents or two photographs of your guardian taken several years apart. Analyze the differences you see. Discuss not only age differences but also changes in attitude, lifestyle, or values suggested by the photographs.

Topic 6.   Rodriguez tells us that he says very little when he is at home, but is extremely talkative at school. Like Rodriguez, most of us have different personalities for different occasions. You might, for example, behave one way at home and act quite differently at work and school. Write an essay in which you describe two different "faces" or "selves" you present to the world.

The Black and White Truth about Basketball
Jeff Greenfield

Jeff Greenfield is a columnist, a sportswriter, and an analyst for ABC News. He has written several books on sports, the media, and politics. When "The Black and White Truth about Basketball" was first published in Esquire *in 1975, Greenfield was both praised and criticized for his views. He was asked to write an updated version in 1989.*

The dominance of black athletes over professional basketball is beyond 1 dispute. Two-thirds of the players are black, and the number would be greater were it not for the continuing practice of picking white bench warmers for the sake of balance. Over the last two decades, no more than three white players have been among the ten starting players on the National Basketball Association's All-Star team, and in the last quarter century, only two white players—Dave Cowens and Larry Bird of the Boston Celtics—have ever been chosen as the NBA's Most Valuable Player.

And at a time when a baseball executive can lose his job for asserting that 2 blacks lack "the necessities" to become pro sports executives and when the National Football League only in 1989 had its first black head coach, the NBA stands as a pro sports league that hired its first black head coach in 1968 (Bill Russell) and its first black general manager in the early 1970s (Wayne Embry of the Milwaukee Bucks). What discrimination remains—lack of equal opportunity for speaking engagements and product endorsements—has more to do with society than with basketball.

This dominance reflects a natural inheritance: Basketball is a pastime of 3 the urban poor. The current generation of black athletes are heirs to a tradition more than half a century old. In a neighborhood without the money for bats, gloves, hockey sticks and ice skates, or shoulder pads, basketball is an eminently accessible sport. "Once it was the game of the Irish and Italian Catholics in Rockaway and the Jews on Fordham Road in the Bronx," writes David Wolf in his brilliant book, *Foul!* "It was recreation, status, and a way out." But now the ethnic names have been changed: Instead of the Red Holzmans, Red Auerbachs, and the McGuire brothers, there are Julius Ervings and Michael Jordans, Ralph Sampsons and Kareem Abdul-Jabbars. And professional basketball is a sport with national television exposure and million-dollar salaries.

But the mark on basketball of today's players can be measured by more 4 than money or visibility. It is a question of style. For there is a clear difference between "black" and "white" styles of play that is as clear as the difference between 155th Street at Eighth Avenue and Crystal City, Missouri. Most simply (remembering we are talking about culture, not chromosomes), "black" basketball is the use of superb athletic skill to adapt to the limits of space imposed by the game. "White" ball is the pulverization of that space by sheer intensity.[1]

It takes a conscious effort to realize how constricted the space is on a basketball court. Place a regulation court—ninety-four by fifty feet—on a football field, and it will reach from the back of the end zone to the twenty-one-yard line; its width will cover less than a third of the field. On a baseball diamond, a basketball court will reach from home plate to first base. Compared to its principal indoor rival, ice hockey, basketball covers about one-fourth the playing area. Moreover, during the normal flow of the game, most of the action takes place on the third of the court nearest the basket. It is in this dollhouse space that ten men, each of them half a foot taller than the average man, come together to battle each other.

There is, thus, no room; basketball is a struggle for the edge: the half step with which to cut around the defender for a lay-up, the half second of freedom with which to release a jump shot, the instant a head turns allowing a pass to a teammate breaking for the basket. It is an arena for the subtlest of skills: the head fake, the shoulder fake, the shift of body weight to the right and the sudden cut to the left. Deception is crucial to success; and to young men who have learned early and painfully that life is a battle for survival, basketball is one of the few pursuits in which the weapon of deception is a legitimate tactic rather than the source of trouble.

If there is, then, the need to compete in a crowd, to battle for the edge, then the surest strategy is to develop the *unexpected:* to develop a shot that is simply and fundamentally different from the usual methods of putting the ball in the basket. Drive to the hoop, but go under it and come up the other side; hold the ball at waist level and shoot from there instead of bringing the ball up to eye level; leap into the air, but fall away from the basket instead of toward it. All these tactics, which a fan can see embodied in the astonishing play of the Chicago Bulls' Michael Jordan, take maximum advantage of the crowding on the court. They also stamp uniqueness on young men who may feel it nowhere else.

"For many young men in the slums," David Wolf writes, "the school yard is the only place they can feel true pride in what they do, where they can move free of inhibitions and where they can, by being spectacular, rise for the moment against the drabness and anonymity of their lives. Thus, when a player develops extraordinary 'school yard' moves and shots . . . [they] become his measure as a man."

---

[1]This distinction has nothing to do with the question of whether whites can play as "well" as blacks. In 1987, the Detroit Pistons' Isiah Thomas quipped that the Celtics' Larry Bird was "a pretty good player," but would be much less celebrated and wealthy if he were black. As Thomas later said, Bird is one of the greatest pro players in history. Nor is this distinction about "smart," although the Los Angeles Lakers' Magic Johnson is right in saying that too many journalists ascribe brilliant strategy by black players to be solely due to "innate" ability. (Author's note.)

So the moves that begin as tactics for scoring soon become calling cards.   9
You don't just lay the ball in for an uncontested basket; you take the ball in
both hands, leap as high as you can, and slam the ball through the hoop. When
you jump in the air, fake a shot, bring the ball back to your body, and throw
up a shot, all without coming back down, you have proven your worth in
uncontestable fashion.

This liquid grace is an integral part of "black" ball, almost exclusively the   10
province of the playground player. Some white stars like Bob Cousy, Billy
Cunningham, and Doug Collins had it, and the Celtics' Kevin McHale has it
now: the body control, the moves to the basket, the free-ranging mobility.
Most of them also possessed the surface ease that is integral to the "black"
style; an incorporation of the ethic of mean streets—to "make it" is not just to
have wealth but to have it without strain. Whatever the muscles and organs
are doing, the face of the "black" star almost never shows it. Magic Johnson of
the Lakers can bring the ball downcourt with two men on him, whip a pass
through an invisible opening, cut to the basket, take a return pass, and hit the
shot all with no more emotion than a quick smile. So stoic was San Antonio
Spurs' great George Gervin that he earned the nickname "Ice Man."
(Interestingly, a black coach like former Celtics' coach K. C. Jones exhibited
far less emotion on the bench than a white counterpart like Dick Motta or Jack
Ramsey.)

If there is a single trait that characterizes "black" ball it is leaping abil-   11
ity. Bob Cousy, ex-Celtic great and former pro coach, says that "when
coaches get together, one is sure to say, 'I've got the one black kid in the
country who can't jump.' When coaches see a white boy who can jump or
who moves with extraordinary quickness, they say, 'He should have been
born black, he's that good.'"

Don Nelson, now a top executive with the Golden State Warriors, recalls   12
that back in 1970, Dave Cowens, then a relatively unknown graduate of
Florida State, prepared for his rookie pro season by playing in the Rucker
League, an outdoor competition in Harlem playgrounds that pits pros against
college kids and playground stars. So ferocious was Cowens's leaping ability,
Nelson says, that "when the summer was over, everyone wanted to know who
the white son of a bitch was who could jump so high." That's another way to
overcome a crowd around the basket—just go over it.

Speed, mobility, quickness, acceleration, "the moves"—all of these are   13
catch-phrases that surround the "black" playground athlete, the style of play.
So does the most racially tinged of attributes, "rhythm." Yet rhythm is what
the black stars themselves talk about: feeling the flow of the game, finding the
tempo of the dribble, the step, the shot. It is an instinctive quality (although it
stems from hundreds of hours of practice), and it is one that has led to difficulty between system-oriented coaches and free-form players. "Cats from the
street have their own rhythm when they play," said college dropout Bill
Spivey, onetime New York high school star. "It's not a matter of somebody setting you up and you shooting. You *feel* the shot. When a coach holds you back,
you lose the feel and it isn't fun anymore."

When legendary Brooklyn playground star Connie Hawkins was winding   14
up his NBA career under Laker coach Bill Sharman, he chafed under the
methodical style of play. "He's systematic to the point where it begins to be a
little too much. It's such an action-reaction type of game that when you have
to do everything the same way, I think you lose something."

There is another kind of basketball that has grown up in America. It is not   15
played on asphalt playgrounds with a crowd of kids competing for the court;
it is played on macadam driveways by one boy with a ball and a backboard
nailed over the garage; it is played in gyms in the frigid winter of the rural
Midwest and on Southern dirt courts. It is a mechanical, precise development
of skills (when Don Nelson was an Iowa farm boy, his incentive to make his
shots was that an errant rebound would land in the middle of chicken drop-
pings). It is a game without frills, without flow, but with effectiveness. It is
"white" basketball: jagged, sweaty, stumbling, intense. Where a "black" player
overcomes an obstacle with finesse and body control, a "white" player reacts
by outrunning or overpowering the obstacle.

By this definition, the Boston Celtics are a classically "white" team. They   16
rarely suit up a player with dazzling moves; indeed such a player would probably make Red Auerbach swallow his cigar. Instead, the Celtics wear you
down with execution, with constant running, with the same play run again
and again and again. The rebound by Robert Parrish triggers the fast break, as
everyone races downcourt; the ball goes to Larry Bird, who pulls up and takes
the shot or who drives and then finds Reggie Lewis or Kevin McHale free for
an easy basket.

Perhaps the most definitively "white" position is that of the quick for-   17
ward, one without great moves to the basket, without highly developed shots,
without the height and mobility for rebounding effectiveness. So what does
he do?

He runs. He runs from the opening jump to the final buzzer. He runs up   18
and down the court, from base line to base line, back and forth under the basket, looking for the opening, the pass, the chance to take a quick step, the high-
percentage shot. To watch San Antonio's Mark Olberding or Detroit's Bill
Lambeer, players without speed or obvious moves, is to wonder what they are
doing in the NBA—until you see them swing free and throw up a shot that,
without demanding any apparent skill, somehow goes in the basket more frequently than the shots of many of their more skilled teammates. And to have
watched the New York Knicks' (now U.S. Senator) Bill Bradley, or the Celtics'
John Havlicek, is to have watched "white" ball at its best.

Havlicek or Lambeer, or the Phoenix Suns' Kurt Rambis, stands in dra-   19
matic contrast to Michael Jordan or to the Philadelphia 76ers' legend, Julius
Erving. Erving had the capacity to make legends come true, leaping from the
foul line and slam-dunking the ball on his way down; going up for a lay-up,
pulling the ball to his body, and driving under and up the other side of the rim,
defying gravity and probability with impossible moves and jumps. Michael
Jordan of the Chicago Bulls has been seen by thousands spinning a full 360
degrees in midair before slamming the ball through the hoop.

When John Havlicek played, by contrast, he was the living embodiment of   20
his small-town Ohio background. He would bring the ball downcourt, weaving left, then right, looking for a path. He would swing the ball to a teammate,
cut behind the pick, take the pass, and release the shot in a flicker of time. It
looked plain, unvarnished. But it was a blend of skills that not more than half
a dozen other players in the league possessed.

To former pro Jim McMillian, a black who played quick forward with   21
"white" attributes, "it's a matter of environment. Julius Erving grew up in a
different environment from Havlicek. John came from a very small town in
Ohio. There everything was done the easy way, the shortest distance between
two points. It's nothing fancy; very few times will he go one-on-one. He hits
the lay-up, hits the jump shot, makes the free throw, and after the game you
look up and say, 'How did he hurt us that much?'"

"White" ball, then, is the basketball of patience, method, and sometimes   22
brute strength. "Black" ball is the basketball of electric self-expression. One
player has all the time in the world to perfect his skills, the other a need to
prove himself. These are slippery categories, because a poor boy who is black
can play "white" and a white boy of middle-class parents can play "black." Bill
Cartwright of the Chicago Bulls and Steve Alford of the Golden State Warriors
are athletes who seem to defy these categories.

And what makes basketball the most intriguing of sports is how these   23
styles do not necessarily clash; how the punishing intensity of "white" players and the dazzling moves of the "blacks" can fit together, a fusion of cultures that seems more and more difficult in the world beyond the out-of-
bounds line.

RESPONDING TO THE READING

Freewriting

Exercise 13g.   Freewrite about basketball games you have seen that either
confirm or contradict Jeff Greenfield's theory that there are two styles of play
in basketball.

Exercise 13h.   What do you think readers find controversial about
Greenfield's discussion of "black" and "white" basketball?

Building Your Vocabulary

VOCABULARY LIST

Words to Look Up	My Definition	Dictionary Definition
dispute (1)		
endorsements (2)		

eminently (3)
chromosomes(4)
pulverization (4)
constricted (5)
inhibitions (8)
drabness (8)
anonymity (8)
uncontestable (9)
integral (10)
exclusively (10)
ferocious (12)
macadam (15)
incentive (15)
errant (15)
finesse (15)
execution (16)
embodiment (20)

Questions for Discussion

1. Who is Greenfield's audience? What appeal might his essay have for readers who do not know much about basketball?
2. How does Greenfield define "black" and "white" basketball? If you know something about basketball, discuss whether his definitions are accurate based on your knowledge of the game.
3. What evidence does Greenfield offer in support of his claim that basketball "is a pastime of the urban poor" (paragraph 3)? Do you find his explanations convincing?
4. Why does Greenfield describe the size of a basketball court in such detail? How does this description serve his thesis?
5. What is the origin of the two styles of basketball? How do these origins help explain the characteristics of each?
6. What strategies does Greenfield use to avoid making racial generalizations? How successful is he in avoiding such stereotypes?
7. If you have seen the movie *White Men Can't Jump*, discuss ways that it supports or contradicts Greenfield's theory of "black" and "white" basketball.

TOPICS FOR WRITING

Topic 1.   Study the behavior or "style" of two athletes, sports announcers, musicians, or television personalities. Write an essay in which you compare or contrast their styles. Be sure to discuss how their styles affect their work.

Topic 2.   Observe the teaching styles of two of your instructors or freewrite about the styles of two supervisors you have worked for. Write a comparison of these two styles; in your conclusion mention which of the two you think is most effective and include a brief explanation of your choice.

Topic 3.   Write an essay in which you compare Greenfield's discussion of "black" and "white" basketball to the way basketball is played in the movie *White Men Can't Jump.*

Student Writing

Can You Really Go Back Home?

I was born in Georgia and raised in South Carolina. On the farm I learned to grow vegetables, milk cows, and gather eggs. These were all the basic skills for survival. We had outdoor toilets and wood-burning cook stoves to cook on.

At the age of eleven, I moved to the city. I saw my first escalator and first indoor toilet. The biggest department store I had ever seen in my life was Woolworth's five-and-dime. Talk about home sweet home—you could just turn me loose in that place.

When I started to school in the city, I had one problem: no one could understand anything I said. My speech sounded like something out of Huckleberry Finn—taters, maters, that-there, shornuff, and pert near. I remember someone asking me what time it was, and I said, "It's pert near four o'clock." I took speech classes and just about drove my teacher mad. It took about three years for me to get proper English down. I still slip up now and then.

I was grown and married when I went back home. It was such a shock. The house seemed smaller. The old dirt road we used to pedal the vegetable cart down was paved. Even my grandparents seemed shorter. The old water well out back was covered and water was now being piped into the house. Grandpa said, "Girl, what happen to ya! Ya sound like a damn Yankee!" I just started laughing and said, "No, Grandpa, it's called schooling. I went to school and learned the proper way to speak English." He just looked at me with those eyes. "Twerent nothing wrong with the way ya spoke before, girl. Just sound high fluten now is all."

As I looked around, I could see the slow pace of life. Such an easy going, laid back kind of feeling. There sat Grandpa under the shade of a tree, leaning back in his chair, with his shoes off. The crops were in; the sun was going down. It was time to rest before starting the new day.

As I looked around, I thought about my life. How different things were in town. Everyone there was in such a hurry. Here, there was all the time in the world. In town, everyone was chasing the dollar. Here, people were just scratching a living out of the ground.

I took a good look at my grandfather. He couldn't read; he could barely sign his name. I thought how blessed I am to be able to read. As I sat down beside my grandfather and read him some poems, he looked at me and smiled. "You can give the city your head, girl, but don't let it take your heart." I didn't know what he meant then, but I think I do now.

—Norma Davis

Questions for Discussion

1. What is Norma Davis's main point in this essay?
2. What is the most effective section of her narrative for you? Explain your reasons for selecting this passage. Can you think of ways that Davis might strengthen her essay?
3. Explain the effect of using her family's speech in her narrative. Do you think this technique enhances or detracts from the essay? Why, in either case?

14

Evaluating Experience

Experience everywhere taught the foreign-born that they were expected to do what they could not do—to live like others.

—Oscar Handlin

I think the real trouble between the races in America is that the races are not just races but competing power groups.

—Shelby Steele

Thistitle chapter presents a variety of essays, articles, and narratives derived from people's religious and cultural experiences. These readings invite evaluation in several ways. Black Elk's "The First Cure" introduces the religious values of the Oglala Sioux. "The Shock of Alienation," from Oscar Handlin's book *The Uprooted*, evaluates Anglo-American attempts to define the term *American.* Handlin explains what such definitions meant to people who, by their culture or their appearance, did not fit these definitions. Finally, Shelby Steele examines individuals' preconceptions about race and the way those preconceptions can trap both whites and blacks in a struggle for power. He argues that people's stereotypical versions of each other prevent them from judging others by the content of their character, as Martin Luther King, Jr. proposed, not the color of their skin.

Passages from a student essay, "Hypocrisy," are used to illustrate the characteristics of evaluating, the writing strategy introduced in this chapter. An example of a film critique appears at the end of the chapter under "Student Writing."

EVALUATING

Evaluate literally means to judge the value or worth of something. People use evaluation techniques every day. In order to make decisions about whether to take a particular class, buy one car instead of another, or recycle newspapers, people must evaluate their choices. When writers evaluate an experience they usually discuss either the value that experience had for them or ways that it proved harmful. To evaluate a subject (such as a painting, a movie, a restaurant, or a car), it is important to identify strengths or weaknesses of that subject based on standards that help the writer judge the subject's effectiveness, quality, or value. In the following paragraphs, passages from "Hypocrisy," an essay by a student writer, illustrate some of the writing techniques common to evaluations.

Characteristics of Evaluating

A Distinct Point of View and Purpose

In "Hypocrisy," Jamie Myers adopts a first person point of view in order to evaluate the extent to which her mother is actually "religious." That point of view and purpose are clear in the opening sentences of Myers' essay:

> My mother feels that she is securely in God's hands. She goes   1
> to church three times a week and gives ten percent of her income to
> church work. In her mind, this is what a good Christian does.
> However, I see major differences between what my mother does
> and what Christian values teach.

As she tells us, Myers plans to show the discrepancy between Christian values familiar to her and her mother's actions.

Clear Criteria or Standards

Identifying distinct, believable criteria for evaluating a subject is the key to writing effective evaluations. Jamie Myers evaluates her mother's behavior on the basis of Christian principles of fair-mindedness, appreciation of other people, and love of one's family. The following chart clarifies the relationships among judgment, criteria, and supporting evidence in Myers' essay.

EVALUATION

Evaluative Judgment	Criteria for Judgment	Supporting Evidence
My mother says she is a Christian, but she doesn't behave like one.	Her definition of a Christian is too narrow.	Church attendance is her main measure of a Christian.
	She shows prejudice.	Prejudiced against son-in-law—a Mexican—and her grandson's friends—one of mixed race, the other a Chinese American.
	She has a poor attitude toward her family.	Finds it difficult to show her children respect and love—must take drugs to stand being around them.

Detailed Support for Criteria

Depending on their topic, writers may rely on the detailed information typical of describing, narrating, comparing, process or causal analysis, explaining, or classifying as long as such information contributes to the evaluation they are making. Jamie Myers, for example, describes specific events to illustrate her claim that her mother behaves hypocritically. She also explains how her mother's behavior differs from the values her religion teaches. Myers' discussion of her mother's prejudiced attitudes toward other people illustrates Myers' use of describing, explaining, and contrasting.

> Along with my mother's dogmatic insistence on church atten- 3
> dance, I cannot accept her prejudice against people from non-
> European cultures who don't share her beliefs or whose skin color
> is darker than hers. I find her attitude toward some of her own
> family members particularly disgusting. One of my stepsisters is

married to a Mexican. My mother and her husband are always making racist jokes about "stupid Mexicans," in spite of the fact that they have grandchildren whose heritage is part Mexican. One of my other sisters' sons lives with my mother, and he complains that she does not like his friends because one is Chinese American and the other is racially mixed. She keeps telling him to "pick better friends." I would think that Christians aren't supposed to judge their friends or neighbors, especially for such superficial reasons, if they truly follow the teaching "Judge not lest ye be judged."

Clear Connections between Criteria and Evidence

Unless the primary writing strategy is narrating, writers need to explain the connection between their criteria and the examples that illustrate them. Jamie Myers makes such connections quite clear. In these sample paragraphs notice how Myers links her judgment of her mother's behavior to her own understanding of Christian values.

> . . . I would think that Christians aren't supposed to judge their 3 friends or neighbors, especially for such superficial reasons, if they truly follow the teaching "Judge not lest ye be judged."
> . . . It seems to me that loving one's children should be just as 4 Christian a value as honoring one's father and mother. But where my mother is concerned, she dreads rather than loves being with us. . . .
> I always thought of God as love and light, but when people tell 5 me they are in God's hands, or they are walking in God's light, I expect to see God in their interactions with other people. There is a feeling—call it peace or concern for others—that I feel when God is present in a person, and if this feeling is not present, spirituality isn't there either. It has been a long time since I have gotten that feeling from my mother. She says she has God in her heart, but I don't see Him in her actions. . . .

Organizing Ideas by Order of Importance

When evaluating a subject, writers frequently rely on chronological order or they arrange criteria by their order of importance. You can see this second pattern in the opening paragraph and topic sentences of Jamie Myers' essay.

> My mother feels that she is securely in God's hands. She 1 goes to church three times a week and gives ten percent of her income to church work. In her mind, this is what a good Christian does. However, I see major differences between what my mother does and what Christian values teach. For one thing, she

narrow-mindedly thinks that whether or not a person goes to church on Sunday is the most important measure of a true Christian. Nor does it seem to me at all Christian that my mother is prejudiced against people who happen to belong to ethnic groups different from her own. Finally, if she is such a good Christian, why is it so hard for her to show respect and love to her own children? To me, a good Christian thinks and behaves a little differently.

   I object to my mother's insistence that people can't be truly religious unless they attend church every Sunday. (topic sentence for paragraph 2)

   Along with my mother's dogmatic insistence on church attendance, I cannot accept her prejudice against people from non-European cultures who don't share her beliefs or whose skin color is darker than hers. (topic sentence for paragraph 3)

   My mother's dogmatism and prejudice are very hard for me to take, but worst of all is her inability to show respect and love to her own children. (topic sentence for paragraph 4)

At the beginning of each paragraph, Myers makes clear to her readers the criteria she is using to evaluate her mother's behavior. To prepare the reader for her discussion, she mentions each criterion in her introduction.

FOR PRACTICE

Identify transitions in the topic sentences above that signal Jamie Myers' shift from one topic to the next.

Hypocrisy
Jamie Myers

   My mother feels that she is securely in God's hands. She goes to church 1
three times a week and gives ten percent of her income to church work. In her mind, that is what a good Christian does. However, I see major differences between what my mother does and what Christian values teach. For one thing, she narrow-mindedly thinks that whether or not a person goes to church on Sunday is the most important measure of a true Christian. Nor does it seem to me at all Christian that my mother is prejudiced against people who happen to belong to ethnic groups different from her own. Finally, if she is such a good Christian, why is it so hard for her to show respect and love to her own children? To me, a good Christian thinks and behaves a little differently.

   I object to my mother's insistence that people can't be truly religious 2
unless they attend church every Sunday. I once pointed out that it takes more than church attendance to make a good Christian. I told my mother about one

of my classmates at school who spends two days a month working as a volunteer in a local soup kitchen that, on an average, feeds 400 homeless people each day. I also mentioned a friend of mine who volunteers for the county's literacy program. My friend has worked with six people in the last two years and has enabled them to read for the first time in their lives. Although my mother admitted that these two people were doing good work, she refused to accept the idea that they could be fully authentic Christians because they don't go to church. I have been around some of the people who are in their pews every Sunday morning. Several of them spend their time talking about how much other people need to reform. One woman in particular who is my mother's good friend gossips continually about what other members of the church are or are not doing. It saddens me to think that my mother has been so influenced by these hypocrites that she cannot recognize true Christian charity.

Along with my mother's dogmatic insistence on church attendance, I cannot accept her prejudice against people from non-European cultures who don't share her beliefs or whose skin color is darker than hers. I find her attitude toward some of her own family members particularly disgusting. One of my stepsisters is married to a Mexican. My mother and her husband are always making racist jokes about "stupid Mexicans," in spite of the fact that they have grandchildren whose heritage is part Mexican. One of my other sister's sons lives with my mother, and he complains that she does not like his friends because one is Chinese American and the other racially mixed. She keeps telling him to "pick better friends." I would think that Christians aren't supposed to judge their friends or neighbors, especially for such superficial reasons, if they truly follow the teaching "Judge not lest ye be judged."   3

My mother's dogmatism and prejudice are very hard for me to take, but worst of all is her inability to show respect and love to her own children. It seems to me that loving one's children should be just as Christian a value as honoring one's father and mother. But where my mother is concerned, she dreads rather than loves being with us. In order for her to maintain her composure when her children are present, she takes tranquilizers. Without drugs she becomes hysterical. Even cooking dinner with her daughters is a major ordeal for her. Last Christmas my sister Jeannie and I were helping her prepare dinner. My mother was going to cook some hard-boiled eggs. Jeannie made several suggestions that she felt would help make the eggs come out perfect, but my mother became insulted and stormed off to the bathroom to cry. This year she said very little to any of us because she was too high on tranquilizers to carry on a conversation.   4

I always thought of God as love and light, but when people tell me they are in God's hands, or they are walking in God's light, I expect to see God in their interactions with other people. There is a feeling—call it peace or concern for others—that I feel when God is present in a person, and if this feeling is not present, spirituality isn't there either. It has been a long time since I have gotten that feeling from my mother. She says she has God in her heart, but I don't see Him in her actions. She would have to do a lot of changing before I could believe in her brand of Christianity.   5

Questions for Discussion

1. How does Jamie Myers defend her position that her mother's actions are hypocritical? Which of her arguments is most or least convincing? Explain your response.
2. Can you offer wholehearted support for Myers' critique of her mother's behavior, or are there points with which you disagree? Explain the basis for your disagreement.

THE WRITING PROCESS: EVALUATING

The steps in the writing process are useful for completing any writing assignment, including one that requires you to evaluate a subject. The discussion below presents particular considerations for adapting the writing process to the task of evaluating.

Additional Considerations for Developing a Topic

If you have difficulty finding a subject to evaluate, the following suggestions may prove helpful.

> Think of policies, procedures, or attitudes at work or school that you think need changing.
> Ask yourself what hobbies, goals, or jobs you have judged harshly or favorably.
> Consider writing about a law passed by Congress or your state legislature that you have criticized or applauded.
> Try to recall a performance, movie, or piece of music that affected you either positively or negatively.
> Study the strengths and weaknesses of several colleges you have considered attending.

Additional Considerations for Preliminary Writing

Once you have picked a topic, use the steps in the writing process to gather information, organize your ideas, and revise your paper. The preliminary writing questions below should prove helpful as you evaluate your topic.

> Who or what is your topic? What background will the reader need to have in order to understand this topic?
> What are the characteristics—both positive and negative—of your topic?
> Is there anything you might compare it to that would help you show the positive or negative side of your topic?
> What is your main criticism or praise of this topic?

If witnesses or experts can provide information on your topic, contact such people for an interview. If, for example, you are evaluating programs at a particular college, you might interview counselors at your school or call a professor in a department or program in which you are interested. If you use ideas or information from people you interview, be sure to acknowledge them with lead-ins like "According to Stephanie Brophie, advisor at the University of Colorado ..." or "Jacqueline McKnight, a nurse-practitioner at the University Medical Center, says . . ."

Additional Considerations for Organizing Ideas

Organizing ideas by importance or by putting them in chronological order are common ways to arrange details when you are evaluating. But before you choose your organizational pattern, you must have a clear idea of the criteria you will use to evaluate your topic. Following are criteria commonly used to evaluate places, events, movies and other forms of entertainment, and people's behavior.

Criteria for Evaluating Places

> Quality of the location
> Who is there and what they are doing
> What goes on in that place
> What is positive or negative about being there
> How it is better or worse than other places

Criteria for Evaluating Events

> Details about what happened
> The people involved and their motives
> The circumstances surrounding the event
> How this event compares with other events
> The positive or negative outcome of the event
> The effects of this event on other events or on the people involved

Criteria for Evaluating Movies or Television Shows

> The nature of the subject and theme
> Who the characters are
> What they are like
> The dialogue they use
> Whether they are realistic, appealing, and convincing
> How setting or special effects are used

Criteria for Evaluating Music or Live Performances

> The audience for the music
> The appropriateness of the music for that audience

The effectiveness of words and instrumentation
How this music or performance is like or unlike others you have seen
Whether or not the performance is what you expected
Positive or negative effects of the music or the performance

Criteria for Evaluating People's Behavior

Performance
Actions
Attitude toward certain events or other people
Taste or preferences
Similarities or differences when compared to other people

If you decide to evaluate people, avoid taking a point of view that is too personal, that sounds petty, or that offers a stereotypical or narrow view of your subject. Instead, evaluate your subject's performance, attitude, or other behavior using appropriate examples as evidence of what this person does. For an example of an essay that evaluates a person's behavior, look again at Jamie Myers' essay, "Hypocrisy," at the beginning of this chapter. An additional sample evaluating a movie appears at the end of this chapter under "Student Writing."

Additional Considerations for Sharing Your Writing and Making Final Revisions

When revising essays, the questions for sharing essays in Appendix C are always helpful. The checklist below gives you additional ideas for revising.

Checklist

- ❑ Is my point of view clearly expressed?
- ❑ Does my thesis predict the criteria I actually use?
- ❑ Are my criteria and supporting ideas developed adequately?
- ❑ Have I made it clear to the reader where one criteria ends and another begins?
- ❑ Do I need to add transitional words or phrases to clarify the essay's organization?

FOR FURTHER READING

The First Cure
Black Elk

Black Elk was an Oglala chief and medicine man who watched the destruction of his people at the hands of the invading whites or "Wasichu." When he was an old man,

Black Elk met John G. Neihardt, who wrote down the chief's words in a book entitled
Black Elk Speaks: Being the Life Story of a Holy Man of the Oglala Sioux, *published*
in 1932. In the chapter preceding "The First Cure," Black Elk described how his visions
told him he would be a great healer of his nation. In the excerpt that follows, he talks
about his beliefs and describes the first time he used his powers.

After the heyoka ceremony, I came to live here where I am now between   1
Wounded Knee Creek and Grass Creek. Others came too, and we made these
little gray houses of logs that you see, and they are square. It is a bad way to
live, for there can be no power in a square.

You have noticed that everything an Indian does is in a circle, and that is   2
because the Power of the World always works in circles, and everything tries
to be round. In the old days when we were a strong and happy people, all our
power came to us from the sacred hoop of the nation, and so long as the hoop
was unbroken, the people flourished. The flowering tree was the living center
of the hoop, and the circle of the four quarters nourished it. The east gave
peace and light, the south gave warmth, and west gave rain, and the north
with its cold and mighty wind gave strength and endurance. This knowledge
came to us from the outer world with our religion. Everything the Power of
the World does is done in a circle. The sky is round, and I have heard that the
earth is round like a ball, and so are all the stars. The wind, in its greatest
power, whirls. Birds make their nests in circles, for theirs is the same religion

AN INDIAN WAY OF
WRITING A NAME. IT
INDICATES BLACK ELK.

as ours. The sun comes forth and goes down again in a circle. The moon does the same, and both are round. Even the seasons form a great circle in their changing, and always come back again to where they were. The life of a man is a circle from childhood to childhood, and so it is in everything where power moves. Our tepees were round like the nests of birds, and these were always set in a circle, the nation's hoop, a nest of many nests, where the Great Spirit meant for us to hatch our children.

But the Wasichus have put us in these square boxes. Our power is gone   3 and we are dying, for the power is not in us any more. You can look at our boys and see how it is with us. When we were living by the power of the circle in the way we should, boys were men at twelve or thirteen years of age. But now it takes them very much longer to mature.

Well, it is as it is. We are prisoners of war while we are waiting here. But   4 there is another world.

It was in the Moon of Shedding Ponies (May) when we had the heyoka cer-   5 emony. One day in the Moon of Fatness (June), when everything was bloom- ing, I invited One Side to come over and eat with me. I had been thinking about the four-rayed herb that I had now seen twice—the first time in the great vision when I was nine years old, and the second time when I was lamenting on the hill. I knew that I must have this herb for curing, and I thought I could recognize the place where I had seen it growing that night when I lamented.

After One Side and I had eaten, I told him there was an herb I must find,   6 and I wanted him to help me hunt for it. Of course I did not tell him I had seen it in a vision. He was willing to help, so we got on our horses and rode over to Grass Creek. Nobody was living over there. We came to the top of a high hill above the creek, and there we got off our horses and sat down, for I felt that we were close to where I saw the herb growing in my vision of the dog.

We sat there awhile singing together some heyoka songs. Then I began to   7 sing alone a song I had heard in my first great vision:

"In a sacred manner they are sending voices."

After I had sung this song, I looked down towards the west, and yonder at   8 a certain spot beside the creek were crows and magpies, chicken hawks and spotted eagles circling around and around.

Then I knew, and I said to One Side: "Friend, right there is where the herb   9 is growing." He said: "We will go forth and see." So we got on our horses and rode down Grass Creek until we came to a dry gulch, and this we followed up. As we neared the spots the birds all flew away, and it was a place where four or five dry gulches came together. There right on the side of the bank the herb was growing, and I knew it, although I had never seen one like it before, except in my vision.

It had a root about as long as to my elbow, and this was a little thicker 10 than my thumb. It was flowering in four colors, blue, white, red, and yellow.

We got off our horses, and after I had offered red willow bark to the Six   11
Powers, I made a prayer to the herb, and said to it: "Now we shall go forth to
the two-leggeds, but only to the weakest ones, and there shall be happy days
among the weak."

It was easy to dig the herb, because it was growing in the edge of the clay   12
gulch. Then we started back with it. When we came to Grass Creek again, we
wrapped it in some good sage that was growing there.

Something must have told me to find the herb just then, for the next   13
evening I needed it and could have done nothing without it.

I was eating supper when a man by the name of Cuts-to-Pieces came in,   14
and he was saying: "Hey, hey, hey!" for he was in trouble. I asked him what
was the matter, and he said: "I have a boy of mine, and he is very sick and I am
afraid he will die soon. He has been sick a long time. They say you have great
power from the horse dance and the heyoka ceremony, so maybe you can save
him for me. I think so much of him."

I told Cuts-to-Pieces that if he really wanted help, he should go home   15
and bring me back a pipe with an eagle feather on it. While he was gone, I
thought about what I had to do; and I was afraid, because I had never cured
anybody yet with my power, and I was very sorry for Cuts-to-Pieces. I
prayed hard for help. When Cuts-to-Pieces came back with the pipe, I told
him to take it around to the left of me, leave it there, and pass out again to
the right of me. When he had done this, I sent for One Side to come and
help me. Then I took the pipe and went to where the sick little boy was. My
father and my mother went with us, and my friend, Standing Bear, was
already there.

I first offered the pipe to the Six Powers, then I passed it, and we all   16
smoked. After that I began making a rumbling thunder sound on the drum.
You know, when the power of the west comes to the two-leggeds, it comes
with rumbling, and when it has passed, everything lifts up its head and is glad
and there is greenness. So I made this rumbling sound. Also, the voice of the
drum is an offering to the Spirit of the World. Its sound arouses the mind and
makes men feel the mystery and power of things.

The sick little boy was on the northeast side of the tepee, and when we   17
entered at the south, we went around from left to right, stopping on the west
side when we had made the circle.

You want to know why we always go from left to right like that. I can tell   18
you something of the reason, but not all. Think of this: Is not the south the
source of life, and does not the flowering stick truly come from there? And
does not man advance from there toward the setting sun of his life? Then
does he not approach the colder north where the white hairs are? And does
he not then arrive, if he lives, at the source of light and understanding,
which is the east? Then does he not return to where he began, to his second
childhood, there to give back his life to all life, and his flesh to the earth
whence it came? The more you think about this, the more meaning you will
see in it.

As I said, we went into the tepee from left to right, and sat ourselves down 19
on the west side. The sick little boy was on the northeast side, and he looked
as though he were only skin and bones. I had the pipe, the drum, and the four-
rayed herb already, so I asked for a wooden cup, full of water, and an eagle
bone whistle, which was for the spotted eagle of my great vision. They placed
the cup of water in front of me; and then I had to think awhile, because I had
never done this before and I was in doubt.

I understood a little more now, so I gave the eagle bone whistle to One 20
Side and told him how to use it in helping me. Then I filled the pipe with red
willow bark, and gave it to the pretty young daughter of Cuts-to-Pieces, telling
her to hold it, just as I had seen the virgin of the east holding it in my great
vision.

Everything was ready now, so I made low thunder on the drum, keeping 21
time as I sent forth a voice. Four times I cried "Hey-a-a-hey," drumming as I
cried to the Spirit of the World, and while I was doing this I could feel the
power coming through me from my feet up, and I knew that I could help the
sick little boy.

I kept on sending a voice, while I made low thunder on the drum, saying: 22
"My Grandfather, Great Spirit, you are the only one and to no other can any
one send voices. You have made everything, they say, and you have made it
good and beautiful. The four quarters and the two roads crossing each other,
you have made. Also you have set a power where the sun goes down. The two-
leggeds on earth are in despair. For them, my Grandfather, I send a voice to
you. You have said this to me: The weak shall walk. In vision you have taken
me to the center of the world and there you have shown me the power to make
over. The water in the cup that you have given me, by its power shall the dying
live. The herb that you have shown me, through its power shall the feeble walk
upright. From where we are always facing (the south), behold, a virgin shall
appear, walking the good red road, offering the pipe as she walks, and hers
also is the power of the flowering tree. From where the Giant lives (the north),
you have given me a sacred, cleansing wind, and where this wind passes the
weak shall have strength. You have said this to me. To you and to all your
powers and to Mother Earth I send a voice for help."

You see, I had never done this before, and I know now that only one power 23
would have been enough. But I was so eager to help the sick little boy that I
called on every power there is.

I had been facing the west, of course, while sending a voice. Now I 24
walked to the north and to the east and to the south, stopping there where
the source of all life is and where the good red road begins. Standing there,
I sang thus:

> "In a sacred manner I have made them walk.
> A sacred nation lies low.
> In a sacred manner I have made them walk.

> A sacred two-legged, he lies low.
> In a sacred manner, he shall walk."

While I was singing this I could feel something queer all through my body,   25
something that made me want to cry for all unhappy things, and there were
tears on my face.

Now I walked to the quarter of the west, where I lit the pipe, offered it to   26
the powers, and, after I had taken a whiff of smoke, I passed it around.

When I looked at the sick little boy again, he smiled at me, and I could feel   27
that the power was getting stronger.

I next took the cup of water, drank a little of it, and went around to where   28
the sick little boy was. Standing before him, I stamped the earth four times.
Then, putting my mouth to the pit of his stomach, I drew through him the
cleansing wind of the north. I next chewed some of the herb and put it in the
water, afterward blowing some of it on the boy and to the four quarters. The
cup with the rest of the water I gave to the virgin, who gave it to the sick little
boy to drink. Then I told the virgin to help the boy stand up and to walk
around the circle with him, beginning at the south, the source of life. He was
very poor and weak, but with the virgin's help he did this.

Then I went away.   29

Next day Cuts-to-Pieces came and told me that his little boy was feeling   30
better and was sitting up and could eat something again. In four days he could
walk around. He got well and lived to be thirty years old.

Cuts-to-Pieces gave me a good horse for doing this; but of course I would   31
have done it for nothing.

When the people heard about how the little boy was cured, many came to   32
me for help, and I was busy most of the time.

This was in the summer of my nineteenth year (1882), in the Moon of   33
Making Fat.

RESPONDING TO THE READING

Freewriting

Exercise 14a.   Freewrite about what you learned by reading "The First
Cure."

Exercise 14b.   Which passages did you find most powerful? Why?

Exercise 14c.   What sort of person was Black Elk? What were his beliefs?
What did he value most?

Building Your Vocabulary

VOCABULARY LIST

Words to Look Up	My Definition	Dictionary Definition
lamenting (5) magpies (8) sage (12)		

Questions for Discussion

1. Black Elk "spoke" his words to John Neihardt, and through a translator, Neihardt wrote his story. Who did Black Elk consider his audience?
2. Why do you think Black Elk told the events in "The First Cure" to Neihardt? What did he hope to show?
3. Black Elk's narrative uses a flashback to convey the healing of the young boy. How do this flashback and the information that precedes it shape our understanding of Black Elk's message?
4. How does Black Elk's healing power rely on his knowledge of man's connection to nature?
5. What other elements of the Native American faith are mentioned in Black Elk's tale? How are they like or unlike the religion most familiar to you?

TOPICS FOR WRITING

Topic 1.   Write a paper explaining your religious beliefs to someone whose beliefs are different from your own. You may want to interview a spokesperson of your religion—a priest, rabbi, or minister—or a person who has studied this religion carefully to get a better understanding of particular rituals, practices, beliefs, or symbols.

Topic 2.   Write an explanation of how Black Elk's beliefs compare to your own. Use a T-graph to help you discover points of similarity and difference.

Topic 3.   Pick a religion you know little about, preferably one that has followers in your community. Interview a few people from that faith, including a religious spokesperson, if possible (see the techniques for interviewing discussed in Chapter 9). To supplement this information, look up articles on the computerized data system or *Readers' Guide to Periodical Literature* in your school or local library. Take the information you gather, organize ideas, and draft an information paper about your topic.

The Shock of Alienation
Oscar Handlin

This selection is from The Uprooted, *a study of the immigrant experience during the late 1800s. Oscar Handlin offers the historian's perspective on the hostility that met immigrants and other peoples considered "foreign" or different by Anglo-Americans. His study, which won the Pulitzer Prize in 1952, is valuable for its perspective on the origins of ethnic conflict in the United States.*

As the nineteenth century moved into its last quarter, a note of petulance 1
crept into the comments of some Americans. . . . It was a long time now that the melting pot had been simmering, but the end product seemed no closer than before. The experience of life in the United States had not broken down the separateness of the elements mixed into it; each seemed to retain its own identity. Almost a half-century after the great immigration of Irish and Germans, these people had not become indistinguishable from other Americans; they were still recognizably Irish and German. Yet even then, newer waves of newcomers were beating against the Atlantic shore. Was there any prospect that all these multitudes would ever be assimilated, would ever be Americanized?

A generation earlier such questions would not have been asked. 2
Americans of the first half of the century had assumed that any man who subjected himself to the American environment was being Americanized. Since the New World was ultimately to be occupied by a New Man, no mere derivative of any extant stock, but different from and superior to all, there had been no fixed standards of national character against which to measure the behavior of newcomers. The nationality of the new Republic had been supposed fluid, only just evolving; there had been room for infinite variation because diversity rather than uniformity had been normal.

The expression of doubts that some parts of the population might not 3
become fully American implied the existence of a settled criterion of what was American. There had been a time when the society had recognized no distinction among citizens but that between the native and the foreign-born, and that distinction had carried no imputation of superiority or inferiority. Now there were attempts to distinguish among the natives between those who really belonged and those who did not, to separate out those who were born in the United States but whose immigrant parentage cut them off from the truly indigenous folk.

It was difficult to draw the line, however. The census differentiated after 4
1880 between natives and native-born of foreign parents. But that was an inadequate line of division; it provided no means of social recognition and offered no basis on which the *true Americans* could draw together, identify themselves as such.

Through these years there was a half-conscious quest among some 5
Americans for a term that would describe those whose ancestors were in the

United States before the great migrations. Where the New Englanders were, they called themselves Yankees, a word that often came to mean non-Irish or non-Canadian. But Yankee was simply a local designation and did not take in the whole of the old stock. In any case, there was no satisfaction to such a title. Its holders were one group among many, without any distinctive claim to Americanism, cut off from other desirable peoples prominent in the country's past. Only the discovery of common antecedents could eliminate the separations among the really American.

But to find a common denominator, it was necessary to go back a long 6 way. Actually no single discovery was completely satisfactory. Some writers, in time, referred to the civilization of the United States as Anglo-Saxon. By projecting its origins back to early Britain, they implied that their own culture was always English in derivation, and made foreigners of the descendants of Irishmen and Germans, to say nothing of the later arrivals. Other men preferred a variant and achieved the same exclusion by referring to themselves as "the English-speaking people," a title which assumed there was a unity and uniqueness to the clan which settled the home island, the Dominions, and the United States. Still others relied upon a somewhat broader appellation. They talked of themselves as Teutonic and argued that what was distinctively American originated in the forests of Germany; in this view, only the folk whose ancestors had experienced the freedom of tribal self-government and the liberation of the Protestant Reformation were fully American.

These terms had absolutely no historical justification. They nevertheless 7 achieved a wide currency in the thinking of the last decades of the nineteenth century. Whatever particular phrase might serve the purpose of a particular author or speaker, all expressed the conviction that some hereditary element had given form to American culture. The conclusion was inescapable: to be Americanized, the immigrants must conform to the American way of life completely defined in advance of their landing.

There were two counts to the indictment that the immigrants were not so 8 conforming. They were, first, accused of their poverty. Many benevolent citizens, distressed by the miserable conditions in the districts inhabited by the laboring people, were reluctant to believe that such social flaws were indigenous to the New World. It was tempting, rather, to ascribe them to the defects of the newcomers, to improvidence, slovenliness, and ignorance rather than to inability to earn a living wage.

Indeed to those whose homes were uptown the ghettos were altogether 9 alien territory associated with filth and vice and crime. It did not seen possible that men could lead a decent existence in such quarters. The good vicar on a philanthropic tour was shocked by the moral dangers of the dark unlighted hallway. His mind rushed to the defense of the respectable young girl: *Whatever her wishes may be, she can do nothing—shame prevents her from crying out.* The intention of the reformer was to improve housing, but the summation nevertheless was, *You cannot make an American citizen out of a slum.*

The newcomers were also accused of congregating together in their own   10
groups and of an unwillingness to mix with outsiders. The foreign-born flocked to the great cities and stubbornly refused to spread out as farmers over the countryside; that alone was offensive to a society which still retained an ideal of rusticity. But even the Germans in Wisconsin and the Scandinavians in Minnesota held aloofly to themselves. Everywhere, the strangers persisted in their strangeness and willfully stood apart from American life. A prominent educator sounded the warning: *Our task is to break up their settlements, to assimilate and amalgamate these people, and to implant in them the Anglo-Saxon conception of righteousness, law, and order.*

It was no simple matter to meet this challenge. The older residents were   11
quick to criticize the separateness of the immigrant but hesitant when he made a move to narrow the distance. The householders of Fifth Avenue or Beacon Street or Nob Hill could readily perceive the evils of the slums but they were not inclined to welcome as a neighbor the former denizen of the East Side or the North End or the Latin Quarter who had acquired the means to get away. Among Protestants there was much concern over the growth of Catholic, Jewish, and Orthodox religious organizations, but there was no eagerness at all to provoke a mass conversion that might crowd the earlier churches with a host of poor foreigners. When the population of its neighborhood changed, the parish was less likely to try to attract the newcomers than to close or sell its buildings and move to some other section.

Indeed there was a fundamental ambiguity to the thinking of those who   12
talked about "assimilation" in these years. They had arrived at their own view that American culture was fixed, formed from its origins, by shutting out the great mass of immigrants who were not English or at least not Teutonic. Now it was expected that those excluded people would alter themselves to earn their portion in Americanism. That process could only come about by increasing the contacts between the older and the newer inhabitants, by sharing jobs, churches, residences. Yet in practice, the man who thought himself an Anglo-Saxon found proximity to the other folk just come to the United States uncomfortable and distasteful and, in his own life, sought to increase rather than to lessen the gap between his position and theirs.

There was an escape from the horns of this unpleasant dilemma. It was   13
tempting to resolve the difficulty by arguing that the differences between Americans on the one hand and Italians or Jews or Poles on the other were so deep as to admit of no conciliation. If these other stocks were cut off by their own innate nature, by the qualities of their heredity, then the original breed was justified both in asserting the fixity of its own character and in holding off from contact with the aliens.

Those who wished to support that position drew upon a sizable fund of   14
racialist [racist] ideas that seeped deep into the thinking of many Americans toward the end of the nineteenth century. From a variety of sources there had

been accumulated a body of doctrine that proclaimed the division of humanity into distinct, biologically separate races.

In the bitter years of controversy that were the prelude to the Civil War, 15 there were Southerners who had felt the urgency of a similar justification. The abolitionists had raised the issue of the moral rightness of slavery, had pronounced it sinful to hold a fellow man in bondage. Sensitive to the criticism but bound in practice to his property, the plantation owner was attracted by the notion that the blacks were not his fellow men. Perhaps, as George Fitzhugh told him, the Negroes were not really human at all, but another order of beings, condemned by their natures to a servile status.

During the tragic reconstruction that followed the peace the argument 16 acquired additional gravity. The formal, legal marks of subordination were gone; it was [all] the more important to hold the colored people in submission by other means. Furthermore the section was now under the control of a national authority, dominated by Northern men; the vanquished faced the task of convincing the victors of the essential propriety of the losing cause.

For years after the end of the war, Southerners directed a stream of dis- 17 cussion across the Mason-Dixon line. Through their writing and talking ran an unvarying theme—the Negro was inherently inferior, did not need or deserve, could not use or be trusted with, the rights of humans. It did not matter how many auditors or readers were persuaded, the very agitation of the question familiarized Americans with the conception of race.

Eastward from the Pacific Coast came a similar gospel, also the product of 18 local exigencies. Out of the dislocating effects of depression in 1873 and of the petering-out of the mining economy, there had developed in California a violent anti-Chinese movement. Those who regarded the Oriental as the source of all the state's difficulties were not content with what discriminatory measures the legislature could enact. They wished no less than the total exclusion of the Chinese.

Satisfaction of that demand could come only from the Federal Congress; 19 and to get Congress to act, it was necessary to persuade representatives from every section of the reality of the menace. The attack upon the little brown rice-eaters, congenitally filthy and immoral, had the same consequences as the Southern charges against the Negro; it made current the notion of ineradicable race differences.

A third problem brought the prestige of many influential names to the 20 support of the idea. The War with Spain had given the United States substantial new overseas possessions, government of which posed troublesome problems. In the traditional pattern of American expansion, additional lands were treated as territories, held in a transitional stage until the time when they would become states. But their residents were citizens, endowed with all the rights of residents of the older part of the Union.

Substantial bodies of opinion opposed the extension of such treat- 21 ment to the newly acquired islands. The proponents of navalism and of an aggressive imperialism, businessmen interested in the possibilities of profitable investments, and Protestant clergymen attracted by the possibility of converting large numbers of Catholics and heathen preferred to have the conquered areas colonies rather than territories, preferred to have the inhabitants subjects rather than citizens protected by the Constitution. To persuade the nation that such a departure from past policy was appropriate, the imperialists argued that the conquered peoples were incapable of self-government; their own racial inferiority justified a position of permanent subordination.

By 1900, the debates over the Negro, the Chinese, and the Filipino had   22
familiarized Americans with the conception of permanent biological differences among humans. References to the "realities of race" by then had taken on a commonplace, almost casual quality. Early that year, for instance, a distinguished senator, well known for his progressive temperament and scholarly attainments, spoke exultantly of the opportunities in the Philippines and in China's limitless markets. *We will not renounce our part in the mission of our race, trustee of the civilization of the world. God has not been preparing the English-Speaking and Teutonic People for one thousand years for nothing. He has made us the master organizers to establish system where chaos reigns. He has marked the American People as the chosen nation to finally lead in the regeneration of the world.*

These ideas were unsystematic; as yet they were only the unconnected   23
defenses of specific positions. But there were not lacking men to give these rude conceptions a formal structure, to work them up into a scientific creed.

Sociology toward the end of the century, in the United States, was only   24
just emerging as a discipline of independent stature. The certitude with which its practitioners delivered their generalizations covered its fundamental immaturity of outlook. The American social scientists approached their subject through the analysis of specific disorders: criminality, intemperance, poverty, and disease. Everywhere they looked they found immigrants somehow involved in these problems. In explaining such faults in the social order, the scholar had a choice of alternatives: these were the pathological manifestations of some blemish, either in the nature of the newcomers or in the nature of the whole society. It was tempting to accept the explanation that put the blame on the outsiders.

From the writings of the Europeans Gobineau, Drumont, and   25
Chamberlain, the sociologists had accepted the dictum that social characteristics depended upon racial differences. A succession of books now demonstrated that flaws in the biological constitution of various groups of immigrants were responsible for every evil that beset the country—for pauperism, for the low birth rate of natives, for economic depressions, for class divisions, for prostitution and homosexuality, and for the appearance of city slums.

Furthermore, the social scientists of this period were not content with aca-   26
demic analysis. They were convinced their conclusions must be capable of practical application and often became involved in the reform movements

which, by planning, hoped to set right the evils of the times. The sociologist eager to ameliorate the lot of his fellow men by altering the conditions of their lives found the newcomers intractable, slow to change, obstacles in the road to progress. Since few among these thinkers were disposed to accept the possibility they might themselves be in error, they could only conclude the foreigners were incapable of improvement. From opposite ends of the country, two college presidents united in the judgment that the immigrants were *beaten men from beaten races, biologically incapable of rising, either now or through their descendants, above the mentality of a twelve-year-old child.*

The only apparent solution was in eugenics, the control of the composition of the population through selection of proper stocks based on proper heredity. A famous social scientist expressed it as his considered opinion that *race differences are established in the very blood. Races may change their religions, their form of government, and their languages, but underneath they may continue the PHYSICAL, MENTAL, and MORAL CAPACITIES and INCAPACITIES which determine the REAL CHARACTER of their RELIGION, GOVERNMENT, and LITERATURE.* Surface conformity would only conceal the insidious subtle characteristics that divided the native from the foreign-born. **27**

The fear of everything alien instilled by the First World War brought to fullest flower the seeds of racist thinking. Three enormously popular books by an anthropologist, a eugenist, and a historian revealed to hundreds of thousands of horrified Nordics how their great race had been contaminated by contact with lesser breeds, dwarfed in stature, twisted in mentality, and ruthless in the pursuit of their own self-interest. **28**

These ideas passed commonly in the language of the time. No doubt many Americans who spoke in the bitter terms of race used the words in a figurative sense or in some other way qualified their acceptance of the harsh doctrine. After all, they still recognized the validity of the American tradition of equal and open opportunities, of the Christian tradition of the brotherhood of man. Yet, if they were sometimes troubled by the contradiction, nevertheless enough of them believed fully the racist conceptions so that five million could become members of the Ku Klux Klan in the early 1920's. **29**

Well, a man who was sixty then had seen much that was new in his lifetime; and though he had not moved from the town of his birth, still his whole world had wandered away and left him, in a sense, a stranger in his native place. He too knew the pain of unfamiliarity, the moments of contrast between what was and what had been. Often he turned the corner of some critical event and confronted the effects of an industrial economy, of an urban society, of unsettled institutions, and of disorderly personal relationships. And, as he fought the fear of the unknown future, he too yearned for the security of belonging, for the assurance that change had not singled out him alone but had come to the whole community as a meaningful progression out of the past. **30**

It was fretfully hard, through the instability of things, to recognize the signs of kinship. In anxious dread of isolation the people scanned each other **31** in the vain quest for some portentous mark that would tell them who belonged together. Frustrated, some created a sense of community, drew an inner group around themselves by setting the others aside as outsiders. The excluded became the evidence of the insiders' belonging. It was not only, or not so much, because they hated the Catholic or Jew that the silent men marched in hoods, but because by distinguishing themselves from the foreigner they could at last discover their common identity, feel themselves part of a meaningful body.

The activities of the Klan were an immediate threat to the immigrants and   32
were resisted as such. But there was also a wider import to the movement. This was evidence, at last become visible, that the newcomers were among the excluded. The judgment at which the proponents of assimilation had only hinted, about which the racist thinkers had written obliquely, the Klan brought to the open. The hurt came from the fact that the mouthings of the Kleagle[1] were not eccentricities, but only extreme statements of beliefs long on the margin of acceptance by many Americans. To the foreign-born this was demonstration of what they already suspected, that they would remain as alienated from the New World as they had become from the Old.

Much earlier the pressure of their separateness had begun to disturb the   33
immigrants. As soon as the conception of Americanization had acquired the connotation of conformity with existing patterns, the whole way of group life of the newcomers was questioned. Their adjustment had depended upon their ability as individuals in a free society to adapt themselves to their environment through what forms they chose. The demand by their critics that the adjustment take a predetermined course seemed to question their right, as they were, to a place in American society.

Not that these people concerned themselves with theories of nationalism,   34
but in practice the hostility of the "natives" provoked unsettling doubts about the propriety of the most innocent actions. The peasant who had become a Polish Falcon or a Son of Italy, in his own view, was acting as an American; this was not a step he could have taken at home. To subscribe to a newspaper was the act of a citizen of the New World, not of the Old, even if the journal was one of the thousand published by 1920 in languages other than English. When the immigrants heard their societies and their press described as un-American they could only conclude that they had somehow become involved in an existence that belonged neither in the old land nor in the new.

Yet the road of conformity was also barred to them. There were matters in   35
which they wished to be like others, undistinguished from anyone else, but they never hit upon the means of becoming so. There was no pride in the surname, which in Europe had been little used, and many a new arrival was willing enough to make a change, suitable to the new country. But August

---

[1]A Kleagle is an official of the Klan; the word is formed by combining *Klan* and *eagle*.

Björkegren was not much better off when he called himself Burke, nor the Blumberg who became Kelly. The Lithuanians and Slovenes who moved into the Pennsylvania mining fields often endowed themselves with nomenclature of the older settlers, of the Irish and Italians there before them. In truth, these people found it difficult to know what were the "American" forms they were expected to take on.

What they did know was that they had not succeeded, that they had not   36
established themselves to the extent that they could expect to be treated as if they belonged where they were.

If he was an alien, and poor, and in many ways helpless, still he was   37
human, and it rankled when his dignity as a person was disregarded. He felt an undertone of acrimony in every contact with an official. Men in uniform always found him unworthy of respect; the bullying police made capital of his fear of the law; the postmen made sport of the foreign writing on his letters; the streetcar conductors laughed at his groping requests for directions. Always he was patronized as an object of charity, or almost so.

His particular enemies were the officials charged with his special over-   38
sight. When misfortune drove him to seek assistance or when government regulations brought them to inspect his home, he encountered the social workers, made ruthless in the disregard of his sentiments by the certainty of their own benevolent intentions. Confident of their personal and social superiority and armed with the ideology of the sociologist who had trained them, the emissaries of the public and private agencies were bent on improving the immigrant to a point at which he would no longer recognize himself.

The man who had dealings with the social workers was often sullen and   39
uncooperative; he disliked the necessity of becoming a case, of revealing his dependence to strangers. He was also suspicious, feared there would be no understanding of his own way of life or of his problems; and he was resentful, because the powerful outsiders were judging him by superficial standards of their own. The starched young gentleman from the settlement house took stock from the middle of the kitchen. Were there framed pictures on the walls? Was there a piano, books? He made a note for the report: *This family is not yet Americanized; they are still eating Italian food.*

The services are valuable, but taking them is degrading. It is a fine thing to   40
learn the language of the country; but one must be treated as a child to do so. *We keep saying all the time, This is a desk, this is a door. I know it is a desk and a door. What for keep saying it all the time? My teacher is a very nice young lady, very young. She does not understand what I want to talk about or know about.*

The most anguished conflicts come from the refusal of the immigrants to   41
see the logic of their poverty. In the office it seems reasonable enough: people incapable of supporting themselves would be better off with someone to take care of them. It is more efficient to institutionalize the destitute than to allow them, with the aid of charity, to mismanage their homes. But the ignorant poor insist on clinging to their families, threaten suicide at the mention of the Society's refuge, or even of the hospital. What help the woman gets, she is still

not satisfied. Back comes the ungrateful letter. *I don't ask you to put me in a poorhouse where I have to cry for my children. I don't ask you to put them in a home and eat somebody else's bread. I can't live here without them. I am so sick for them. I could live at home and spare good eats for them. What good did you give me to send me to the poorhouse? You only want people to live like you but I will not listen to you no more.*

A few dedicated social workers, mostly women, learned to understand the   42
values in the immigrants' own lives. In some states, as the second generation became prominent in politics, government agencies came to co-operate with and protect the newcomers. But these were rare exceptions. They scarcely softened the rule experience everywhere taught the foreign-born, that they were expected to do what they could not do—to live like others.

For the children it was not so difficult. They at least were natives and could   43
learn how to conform; to them the settlement house was not always a threat, but sometimes an opportunity. Indeed they could adopt entire the assumption that national character was long since fixed, only seek for their own group a special place within it. Some justified their Americanism by discovery of a colonial past; within the educated second generation there began a tortuous quest for eighteenth-century antecedents that might give them a portion in American civilization in its narrower connotation. Others sought to gain a sense of participation by separating themselves from later or lower elements in the population; they became involved in agitation against the Orientals, the Negroes, and the newest immigrants, as if thus to draw closer to the truly native. Either course implied a rejection of their parents who had themselves once been green off the boat and could boast of no New World antecedents.

The old folk knew then they would not come to belong, not through their   44
own experience nor through their offspring. The only adjustment they had been able to make to life in the United States had been one that involved the separateness of their group, one that increased their awareness of the differences between themselves and the rest of the society. In that adjustment they had always suffered from the consciousness they were strangers. The demand that they assimilate, that they surrender their separateness, condemned them always to be outsiders. In practice, the free structure of American life permitted them with few restraints to go their own way, but under the shadow of a consciousness that they would never belong. They had thus completed their alienation from the culture to which they had come, as from that which they had left.

RESPONDING TO THE READING

Freewriting

Exercise 14d.   Freewrite about the sections of Handlin's descriptions in "The Shock of Alienation" that struck you as most relevant to attitudes you see today.

Building Your Vocabulary

VOCABULARY LIST

Words to Look Up	My Definition	Dictionary Definition
petulance (1)		
derivative (2)		
extant (2)		
imputation (3)		
parentage (3)		
indigenous (3)		
differentiated (4)		
designation (5)		
variant (6)		
exclusion (6)		
appellation (6)		
Teutonic (6)		
indictment (8)		
improvidence (8)		
slovenliness (8)		
vicar (9)		
philanthropic (9)		
aloofly (10)		
assimilate (10)		
amalgamate (10)		
proximity (12)		
conciliation (13)		
propriety (16)		
exigencies (18)		
ineradicable (19)		
proponents (21)		
imperialism (21)		
exultantly (22)		
certitude (23)		
dictum (25)		
ameliorate (26)		
intractable (26)		
eugenics (27)		
insidious (27)		
portentous (31)		
eccentricities (32)		
surname (35)		
rankled (37)		
acrimony (37)		
emissaries (38)		
destitute (41)		
tortuous (43)		
antecedents (43)		
connotation (43)		

Questions for Discussion

1. Write a one-page summary of the thesis and main points in Oscar Handlin's essay. What problems confronted those defining themselves as "fully" or "truly American"?
2. What definitions were used to identify the true "American"? What is Handlin's opinion of such definitions? Locate passages that convey his opinion.
3. What misunderstandings occurred between immigrants and Anglo-Americans? How might they have been avoided?
4. Paraphrase the "fundamental ambiguity" that Handlin describes in attitudes toward immigrants (paragraph 12).
5. What "evidence" did Anglo Americans use to justify their attitudes toward African Americans and immigrants? What does Handlin think of these arguments?

TOPICS FOR WRITING

Topic 1.   Handlin uncovers various sources of racism and ethnic prejudice in the United States. Pick one of these prejudices, and use it to interpret current attitudes toward immigrants or ethnic populations. What parallels exist to this turn-of-the-century attitude? What, if anything, has changed? When you write your paper, use specific examples with well-thought-out explanations to support your ideas. Consider interviewing people to gather information.

Topic 2.   Identify the criteria used by some Americans to judge whether or not an immigrant had been "Americanized." Use these criteria and add others of your own to evaluate current judgments about what constitutes "American" culture, thinking, or behavior, and what does not.

I'm Black, You're White, Who's Innocent?
Race and Power in an Era of Blame
Shelby Steele

Shelby Steele is a professor of English at San Jose State University in California. His essays have appeared in several national magazines, and he has received awards for his writing, including a National Book Critics Circle Award for The Content of Our

Character: A New Vision of Race in America, *published in 1990. This widely read book has many supporters and numerous detractors. Some of Steele's critics believe he has betrayed the African-American community because of his stand against affirmative action. Others accuse him of underestimating the barriers that racism and economic hardships present for many African Americans. In the following excerpt from the first essay in this popular and controversial book, Steele examines race relations as a power struggle to determine which of the two racial groups—black or white—is innocent and, therefore, morally superior to the other.*

It is a warm, windless California evening, and the dying light that covers the redbrick patio is tinted pale orange by the day's smog. Eight of us, not close friends, sit in lawn chairs sipping chardonnay. A black engineer and I (we had never met before) integrate the group. A psychologist is also among us, and her presence encourages a surprising openness. But not until well after the lovely twilight dinner has been served, when the sky has turned to deep black and the drinks have long since changed to scotch, does the subject of race spring awkwardly upon us. Out of nowhere the engineer announces, with a coloring of accusation in his voice, that it bothers him to send his daughter to a school where she is one of only three black children. "I didn't realize my ambition to get ahead would pull me into a world where my daughter would lose touch with her blackness," he says. 1

Over the course of the evening we have talked about money, past and present addictions, child abuse, even politics. Intimacies have been revealed, fears named. But this subject, race, sinks us into one of those shaming silences where eye contact terrorizes. Our host looks for something in the bottom of his glass. Two women stare into the black sky as if to locate the Big Dipper and point it out to us. Finally, the psychologist seems to gather herself for a challenge, but it is too late. "Oh, I'm sure she'll be just fine," says our hostess, rising from her chair. When she excuses herself to get the coffee, the psychologist and two sky gazers offer to help. 2

With four of us now gone, I am surprised to see the engineer still silently holding his ground. There is a willfulness in his eyes, an inner pride. He knows he has said something awkward, but he is determined not to give a damn. His unwavering eyes intimidate even me. At last the host's head snaps erect. He has an idea. "The hell with coffee," he says. "How about some of the smoothest brandy you've ever tasted?" An idea made exciting by the escape it offers. Gratefully, we follow him back into the house, quickly drink his brandy, and say our good-byes. 3

An autopsy of this party might read: death induced by an abrupt and lethal injection of the American race issue. An accurate if superficial assessment. Since it has been my fate to live a rather integrated life, I have often witnessed sudden deaths like this. The threat of them, if not the reality, is a part of the texture of integration. In the late 1960s, when I was just out of college, I took a delinquent's delight in playing the engineer's role, and actually developed a small reputation for playing it well. Those were the days of flagellatory white guilt; it was such great fun to pinion some professor or housewife or, best of 4 all, a large group of remorseful whites, with the knowledge of both their racism and their denial of it. The adolescent impulse to sneer at convention, to startle the middle-aged with doubt, could be indulged under the guise of racial indignation. And how could I lose? My victims—earnest liberals for the most part—could no more crawl out from under my accusations than Joseph K. in Kafka's *Trial*[1] could escape the amorphous charges brought against him. At this odd moment in history the world was aligned to facilitate my immaturity.

About a year of this was enough: the guilt that follows most cheap thrills   5 caught up to me, and I put myself in check. But the impulse to do it faded more slowly. It was one of those petty talents that is tied to vanity, and when there were ebbs in my self-esteem the impulse to use it would come alive again. In integrated situations I can still feel the faint itch. But then there are many youthful impulses that still itch, and now, just inside the door of midlife, this one is least precious to me. . . .

I think those who provoke this sort of awkwardness are operating out of a   6 black identity that obliges them to badger white people about race almost on principle. Content hardly matters. (For example, it made little sense for the engineer to expect white people to anguish terribly much over his decision to send his daughter to school with *white* children.) Race indeed remains a source of white shame; the goal of these provocations is to put whites, no matter how indirectly, in touch with this collective guilt. In other words, these provocations I speak of are *power* moves, little shows of power that try to freeze the "enemy" in self-consciousness. They gratify and inflate the provocateur. They are the underdog's bite. And whites, far more secure in their power, respond with a self-contained and tolerant silence that is itself a show of power. What greater power than that of nonresponse, the power to let a small enemy sizzle in his own juices, to even feel a little sad at his frustration just as one is also complimented by it. Black anger always, in a way, flatters white power. In America, to know that one is not black is to feel an extra grace, a little boost of impunity.

I think the real trouble between the races in America is that the races are   7 not just races but competing power groups—a fact that is easily minimized, perhaps because it is so obvious. What is not so obvious is that this is true quite apart from the issue of class. Even the well-situated middle-class (or wealthy) black is never completely immune to that peculiar contest of power that his skin color subjects him to. Race is a separate reality in American society, an entity that carries its own potential for power, a mark of fate that class can soften considerably but not eradicate.

The distinction of race has always been used in American life to sanction   8 each race's pursuit of power in relation to the other. The allure of race as a human delineation is the very shallowness of the delineation it makes. Onto

---

[1]Franz Kafka (1883–1924), an Austrian-Czech writer known for his unsettling tales of guilt and alienation. In *The Trial* Joseph K. is an accused man who battles an indifferent bureaucracy that never reveals the crime he is supposed to have committed.

this shallowness—mere skin and hair—men can project a false depth, a system of dismal attributions, a series of malevolent or ignoble stereotypes that skin and hair lack the substance to contradict. These dark projections then rationalize the pursuit of power. Your difference from me makes you bad, and your badness justifies, even demands, my pursuit of power over you—the oldest formula for aggression known to man. Whenever much importance is given to race, power is the primary motive.

But the human animal almost never pursues power without first convincing himself that he is *entitled* to it. And this feeling of entitlement has its own precondition: to be entitled one must first believe in one's innocence, at least in the area where one wishes to be entitled. By innocence I mean a feeling of essential goodness in relation to others and, therefore, superiority to others. Our innocence always inflates us and deflates those we seek power over. Once inflated we are entitled; we are in fact licensed to go after the power our innocence tells us we deserve. In this sense, *innocence is power*. Of course, innocence need not be genuine or real in any objective sense, as the Nazis demonstrated not long ago. Its only test is whether or not we can convince ourselves of it. 9

I think the racial struggle in America has always been primarily a struggle for innocence. White racism from the beginning has been a claim of white innocence and therefore of white entitlement to subjugate blacks. And in the sixties, as went innocence so went power. Blacks used the innocence that grew out of their long subjugation to seize more power, while whites lost some of their innocence and so lost a degree of power over blacks. Both races instinctively understand that to lose innocence is to lose power (in relation to each other). To be innocent someone else must be guilty, a natural law that leads the races to forge their innocence on each other's backs. The inferiority of the black always makes the white man superior; the evil might of whites makes blacks good. This pattern means that both races have a hidden investment in racism and racial disharmony despite their good intentions to the contrary. Power defines their relations, and power requires innocence, which, in turn, requires racism and racial division. 10

I believe it was his hidden investment that the engineer was protecting when he made his remark—the white "evil" he saw in a white school "depriving" his daughter of her black heritage confirmed his innocence. Only the logic of power explained his emphasis—he bent reality to show that he was once again a victim of the white world and, as a victim, innocent. His determined eyes insisted on this. And the whites, in their silence, no doubt protected their innocence by seeing him as an ungracious troublemaker, his bad behavior underscoring their goodness. What none of us saw was the underlying game of power and innocence we were trapped in, or how much we needed a racial impasse to play that game. 11

When I was a boy of about twelve, a white friend of mine told me one day that his uncle, who would be arriving the next day for a visit, was a racist. 12

Excited by the prospect of seeing such a man, I spent the following afternoon hanging around the alley behind my friend's house, watching from a distance as this uncle worked on the engine of his Buick. Yes, here was evil and I was compelled to look upon it. And I saw evil in the sharp angle of his elbow as he pumped his wrench to tighten nuts. I saw it in the blade-sharp crease of his chinos, in the pack of Lucky Strikes that threatened to slip from his shirt pocket as he bent, and in the way his concentration seemed to shut out the human world. He worked neatly and efficiently, wiping his hands constantly, and I decided that evil worked like this.

I felt a compulsion to have this man look upon me so that I could see evil— 13 so that I could see the face of it. But when he noticed me standing beside his toolbox, he said only, "If you're looking for Bobby, I think he went up to the school to play baseball." He smiled nicely and went back to work. I was stunned for a moment, but then I realized that evil could be sly as well, could smile when it wanted to trick you.

Need, especially hidden need, puts a strong pressure on perception, and 14 my need to have this man embody white evil was stronger than any contravening evidence. As a black person you always hear about racists but rarely meet any who will let you know them as such. And I needed to incarnate this odious category of humanity, those people who hated Martin Luther King, Jr., and thought blacks should "go slow" or not at all. So, in my mental dictionary, behind the term "white racist," I inserted this man's likeness. I would think of him and say to myself, "There is no reason for him to hate black people. Only evil explains unmotivated hatred." And this thought soothed me; I felt innocent. If I hated white people, which I did not, at least I had a reason. His evil commanded me to assert in the world the goodness he made me confident of in myself.

In looking at this man I was *seeing for innocence*—a form of seeing that 15 has more to do with one's hidden need for innocence (and power) than with the person or group one is looking at. It is quite possible, for example, that the man I saw that day was not a racist. He did absolutely nothing in my presence to indicate that he was. I invested an entire afternoon in seeing not the man but in seeing my innocence through the man. *Seeing for innocence* is, in this way, the essence of racism—the use of others as a means to our own goodness and superiority.

The loss of innocence has always to do with guilt, Kierkegaard[2] tells us, 16 and it has never been easy for whites to avoid guilt where blacks are concerned. For whites, *seeing for innocence* means seeing themselves and blacks in ways that minimize white guilt. Often this amounts to a kind of white revisionism, as when President Reagan declared himself "color-blind" in matters of race. The President, like many of us, may have aspired to racial

---

[2]Søren Kierkegarrd (1813–1855), Danish philosopher.

color blindness, but few would grant that he ever reached this sublimely guilt-less state. His statement clearly revised reality, moved it forward into some heretofore unknown America where all racial determinism would have vanished. I do not think that Ronald Reagan was a racist, as that term is commonly used, but neither do I think that he was capable of seeing color without making attributions, some of which may have been negative—nor am I, or anyone else I've ever met.

So why make such a statement? I think Reagan's claim of color blindness 17 with regard to race was really a claim of racial innocence and guiltlessness—the preconditions for entitlement and power. This was the claim that grounded Reagan's campaign against special entitlement programs—affirmative action, racial quotas, and so on—that black power had won in the sixties. Color blindness was a strategic assumption of innocence that licensed Reagan's use of government power against black power.

I do not object to Reagan's goals in this so much as the presumption of 18 innocence by which he rationalized them. I, too, am strained to defend racial quotas and any affirmative action that supersedes merit. And I believe there was much that Reagan had to offer blacks. His emphasis on traditional American values—individual initiative, self-sufficiency, strong families—offered what I think is the most enduring solution to the demoralization and poverty that continue to widen the gap between blacks and whites in America. Even his de-emphasis of race was reasonable in a society where race only divides. But Reagan's posture of innocence undermined any beneficial inter-action he might have had with blacks. For blacks instinctively sense that a claim of racial innocence always precedes a power move against them. Reagan's pretense of innocence made him an adversary and made his quite reasonable message seem vindictive. You cannot be innocent of a man's prob-lem and expect him to listen.

I'm convinced that the secret of Reagan's "Teflon" coating, his personal 19 popularity apart from his policies and actions, was his ability to offer main-stream America a vision of itself as innocent and entitled (unlike Jimmy Carter, who seemed to offer only guilt and obligation). Probably his most far-reaching accomplishment was to reverse somewhat the pattern by which innocence came to be distributed in the sixties, when outsiders were innocent and insiders were guilty. Corporations, the middle class, entrepreneurs, the military—all villains in the sixties—either took on a new innocence in Reagan's vision or were designated as protectors of innocence. But again, for one man to be innocent, another man must be bad or guilty. Innocence imposes—*demands*—division and conflict, a right/wrong view of the world. And this, I feel, led to the underside of Reagan's achievement. His posture of innocence drew him into a partisanship that undermined the universality of his values. He couldn't sell these values to blacks because he made blacks into the bad guys and outsiders who justified his power. It was humiliating for a black person to like Reagan because Reagan's power was so clearly derived from a distribution of innocence that left blacks with less of it and the white man with more.

Black Americans have had to find a way to handle white society's pre- 20 sumption of racial innocence whenever they have sought to enter the American mainstream. Louis Armstrong's[3] exaggerated smile honored the presumed innocence of white society—*I will not bring you your racial guilt if you will let me play my music.* Ralph Ellison[4] calls this "masking"; I call it bargaining. But whatever it's called, it points to the power of white society to enforce its innocence. I believe this power is greatly diminished today. Society has reformed and transformed—Miles Davis[5] never smiles. Nevertheless, this power has not faded altogether and blacks must still contend with it.

Historically, blacks have handled white society's presumption of inno- 21 cence in two ways: they have bargained with it, granting white society its innocence in exchange for entry into the mainstream, or they have challenged it, holding that innocence hostage until their demand for entry (or other concessions) was met. A bargainer says, *I already believe you are innocent (good, fairminded) and have faith that you will prove it.* A challenger says, *If you are innocent, then prove it.* Bargainers *give* in hope of receiving; challengers *withhold* until they receive. Of course, there is risk in both approaches, but in each case the black is negotiating his own self-interest against the presumed racial innocence of the larger society.

Clearly, the most visible black bargainer on the American scene today is 22 Bill Cosby. His television show has been a perfect formula for black bargaining in the eighties. The remarkable Huxtable family—with its doctor/lawyer parent combination, its drug-free, college-bound children, and its wise yet youthful grandparents—is a blackface version of the American dream. Cosby is a subscriber to the American identity, and his subscription confirms his belief in its fair-mindedness. His vast audience knows this, knows that Cosby will never assault their innocence with racial guilt. Racial controversy is all but banished from the show. The Huxtable family never discusses affirmative action.

The bargain Cosby offers his white viewers—*I will confirm your racial* 23 *innocence if you accept me*—is a good deal for all concerned. Not only does it allow whites to enjoy Cosby's humor with no loss of innocence, but it actually enhances their innocence by implying that race is not the serious problem for blacks that it once was. If anything, the success of this handsome, affluent

---

[3]One of the better-known American jazz musicians, Louis "Satchmo" Armstrong (1900–1971), a brilliant cornet and trumpet player.

[4]American novelist and essayist, Ralph Ellison (1914–1994) wrote *The Invisible Man*, which won the National Book Award in 1953.

[5]Miles Davis (1926–1991), a trumpet player and composer whose innovations influenced many musicians in the 1960s and '70s.

black family points to the fair-mindedness of whites who, out of their essential goodness, changed society so that black families like the Huxtables could succeed. Whites can watch "The Cosby Show" and feel complimented on a job well done.

The power that black bargainers wield is the power of absolution. On 24 Thursday nights, Cosby, like a priest, absolves his white viewers, forgives and forgets the sins of the past. And for this he is rewarded with an almost sacrosanct status. Cosby benefits from what might be called the gratitude factor. His continued number-one rating may have something to do with the (white) public's gratitude at being offered a commodity so rare in our time; he tells his white viewers each week that they are okay, and that this black man is not going to challenge them.

When a black bargains, he may invoke the gratitude factor and find himself 25 cherished beyond the measure of his achievement; when he challenges, he may draw the dark projections of whites and become a source of irritation to them. If he moves back and forth between these two options, as I think many blacks do today, he will likely baffle whites. It is difficult for whites either to accept or reject such blacks. It seems to me that Jesse Jackson is such a figure—many whites see Jackson as a challenger by instinct and a bargainer by political ambition. They are uneasy with him, more than a little suspicious. His powerful speech at the 1984 Democratic Convention was a masterpiece of bargaining. In it he offered a King-like vision of what America could be, a vision that presupposed Americans had the fair-mindedness to achieve full equality—an offer in hope of a return. A few days after this speech, looking for rest and privacy at a lodge in Big Sur, he and his wife were greeted with standing ovations three times a day when they entered the dining room for meals. So much about Jackson is deeply American—his underdog striving, his irrepressible faith in himself, the daring of his ambition, and even his stubbornness. These qualities point to his underlying faith that Americans can respond to him despite race, and this faith is a compliment to Americans, an offer of innocence.

But Jackson does not always stick to the terms of his bargain as Cosby 26 does on TV. When he hugs Arafat,[6] smokes cigars with Castro, refuses to repudiate Farrakhan,[7] threatens a boycott of major league baseball or, more recently, talks of "corporate barracudas," "pension-fund socialism," and "economic violence," he looks like a challenger in bargainer's clothing, and his positions on the issues look like familiar protests dressed in white-paper

---

[6]Yasir Arafat (1929–), leader of the Palestinian Liberation Organization (PLO) since 1969. As chairman of the PLO, Arafat fought to replace the state of Israel with a Palestinian state. In 1987 he softened his position and supported the establishment of a Palestinian state independent of Israel. Arafat's support for Saddam Hussein during the Persian Gulf War cost him a great deal in American sympathy for the Palestinian cause. Since Shelby Steele published *The Content of Our Character,* Yasir Arafat and Israeli Prime Minister Yitzhak Shamir signed their historic peace agreement on September 13, 1993.

[7]Louis Farrakhan (1933–), leader of the Nation of Islam. Critics often accuse Farrakhan and his aides of making anti-Semitic remarks.

formality. At these times he appears to be revoking the innocence so much else about him seems to offer. The old activist seems to come out of hiding once again to take white innocence hostage until whites prove they deserve to have it. In his candidacy there is a suggestion of protest, a fierce insistence on his *right* to run, that sends whites a message that he may secretly see them as a good bit less than innocent. His dilemma is to appear the bargainer while his campaign itself seems to be a challenge.

There are, of course, other problems that hamper Jackson's bid for the   27 Democratic presidential nomination. He has held no elective office, he is thought too flamboyant and opportunistic by many, there are rather loud whispers of "character" problems. As an individual, he may not be the best test of a black man's chances for winning so high an office. Still, I believe it is the aura of challenge surrounding him that hurts him most. Whether it is right or wrong, fair or unfair, I think no black candidate will have a serious chance at his party's nomination, much less the presidency, until he can convince white Americans that he can be trusted to preserve their sense of racial innocence. Such a candidate will have to use his power of absolution; he will have to flatly forgive and forget. He will have to bargain with white innocence out of genuine belief that it really exists. There can be no faking it. He will have to offer a vision that is passionately raceless, a vision that strongly condemns any form of racial politics. This will require the most courageous kind of leadership, leadership that asks all the people to meet a new standard.

Now the other side of America's racial impasse: How do blacks lay claim   28 to their racial innocence?

The most obvious and unarguable source of black innocence is the vic-   29 timization that blacks endured for centuries at the hands of a race that insisted on black inferiority as a means to its own innocence and power. Like all victims, what blacks lost in power they gained in innocence—innocence that, in turn, entitled them to pursue power. This was the innocence that fueled the civil rights movement of the sixties and that gave blacks their first real power in American life—victimization metamorphosed into power via innocence. But this formula carries a drawback that I believe is virtually as devastating to blacks today as victimization once was. It is a formula that binds the victim to his victimization by linking his power to his status as a victim. And this, I'm convinced, is the tragedy of black power in America today. It is primarily a victim's power, grounded too deeply in the entitlement derived from past injustice and in the innocence that Western/Christian tradition has always associated with poverty.

Whatever gains this power brings in the short run through political action,   30 it undermines in the long run. Social victims may be collectively entitled, but they are all too often individually demoralized. Since the social victim has been oppressed by society, he comes to feel that his individual life will be improved more by changes in society than by his own initiative. Without realizing it, he makes society rather than himself the agent of change. The power he finds in his victimization may lead him to collective action against society, but it also encourages passivity within the sphere of his personal life.

Not long ago, I saw a television documentary that examined life in 31
Detroit's inner city on the twentieth anniversary of the riots there in which
forty-three people were killed. A comparison of the inner city then and now
showed a decline in the quality of life. Residents feel less safe, drug trafficking
is far worse, crimes by blacks against blacks are more frequent, housing
remains substandard, and the teenage pregnancy rate has skyrocketed.
Twenty years of decline and demoralization, even as opportunities for blacks
to better themselves have increased. This paradox is not peculiar to Detroit.
By many measures, the majority of blacks—those not yet in the middle class—
are further behind whites today than before the victories of the civil rights
movement. But there is a reluctance among blacks to examine this paradox, I
think, because it suggests that racial victimization is not our real problem. If
conditions have worsened for most of us as racism had receded, then much of
the problem must be of our own making. To admit this fully would cause us to
lose the innocence we derive from our victimization. And we would jeopardize
the entitlement we've always had to challenge society. We are in the odd and
self-defeating position in which taking responsibility for bettering ourselves
feels like a surrender to white power.

So we have a hidden investment in victimization and poverty. These dis- 32
tressing conditions have been the source of our only real power, and there is
an unconscious sort of gravitation toward them, a complaining celebration of
them. One sees evidence of this in the near happiness with which certain black
leaders recount the horror of Howard Beach, Bensonhurst,[8] and other recent
instances of racial tension. As one is saddened by these tragic events, one is
also repelled at the way some black leaders—agitated to near hysteria by the
scent of victim power inherent in them—leap forward to exploit them as evidence of black innocence and white guilt. It is as though they sense the decline
of black victimization as a loss of standing and dive into the middle of these
incidents as if they were reservoirs of pure black innocence swollen with
potential power.

Seeing for innocence pressures blacks to focus on racism and to neglect the 33
individual initiative that would deliver them from poverty—the only thing that
finally delivers *anyone* from poverty. With our eyes on innocence we see
racism everywhere and miss opportunity even as we stumble over it. About 70
percent of black students at my university drop out before graduation—a
flight from opportunity that racism cannot explain. It is an injustice that
whites can see for innocence with more impunity than blacks can. The price
whites pay is a certain blindness to themselves. Moreover, for whites seeing
for innocence continues to engender the bad faith of a long-disgruntled
minority. But the price blacks pay is an ever-escalating poverty that threatens
to make the worst off a permanent underclass. Not fair, but real.

---

[8]Racially motivated attacks on African Americans occurred in these areas of New York in 1986
(Howard Beach) and 1989 (Bensonhurst).

Challenging works best for the collective, while bargaining is more the   34
individual's suit. From this point on, the race's advancement will come from
the efforts of its individuals. True, some challenging will be necessary for a
long time to come. But bargaining is now—today—a way for the black individual to *join* the larger society, to make a place for himself or herself.

"Innocence is ignorance," Kierkegaard says, and if this is so, the claim of   35
innocence amounts to an insistence on ignorance, a refusal to know. In their
assertions of innocence both races carve out very functional areas of ignorance for themselves—territories of blindness that license a misguided pursuit
of power. Whites gain superiority by not knowing blacks; blacks gain entitlement by not seeing their own responsibility for bettering themselves. The
power each race seeks in relation to the other is grounded in a double-edged
ignorance of the self as well as of the other.

The original sin that brought us to an impasse at the dinner party I men-   36
tioned occurred centuries ago, when it was first decided to exploit racial difference as a means to power. It was a determinism that flowed karmically
from this sin that dropped over us like a net that night. What bothered me
most was our helplessness. Even the engineer did not know how to go forward. His challenge hadn't worked, and he'd lost the option to bargain. The
marriage of race and power depersonalized us, changed us from eight people
to six whites and two blacks. The easiest thing was to let silence blanket our
situation, our impasse.

I think the civil rights movement in its early and middle years offered the   37
best way out of America's racial impasse: in this society, race must not be a
source of advantage or disadvantage for anyone. This is fundamentally a
moral position, one that seeks to breach the corrupt union of race and power
with principles of fairness and human equality: if all men are created equal,
then racial difference cannot sanction power. The civil rights movement was
conceived for no other reason than to redress that corrupt union, and its guid-
ing insight was that only a moral power based on enduring principles of justice, equality, and freedom could offset the lower impulse in man to exploit
race as a means to power. Three hundred years of suffering had driven the
point home, and in Montgomery, Little Rock, and Selma, racial power was the
enemy and moral power the weapon.

An important difference between genuine and presumed innocence, I   38
believe, is that the former must be earned through sacrifice while the latter is
unearned and only veils the quest for privilege. And there was much sacrifice
in the early civil rights movement. The Gandhian principle of nonviolent resistance that gave the movement a spiritual center as well as a method of protest
demanded sacrifice, a passive offering of the self in the name of justice. A
price was paid in terror and lost life, and from this sacrifice came a hard-
earned innocence and a credible moral power.

Nonviolent passive resistance is a bargainer's strategy. It assumes the   39
power that is the object of the protest has the genuine innocence to respond
morally, and puts the protesters at the mercy of that innocence. I think this
movement won so many concessions precisely because of its belief in the

capacity of whites to be moral. It did not so much demand that whites change as offer them relentlessly the opportunity to live by their own morality—to attain a true innocence based on the sacrifice of their racial privilege, rather than a false innocence based on presumed racial superiority. Blacks always bargain with or challenge the larger society; but I believe that in the early civil rights years, these forms of negotiation achieved a degree of integrity and genuineness never seen before or since.

In the mid-sixties all this changed. Suddenly a sharp *racial* consciousness **40** emerged to compete with the moral consciousness that had defined the movement up to that point. Whites were no longer welcome in the movement, and a vocal "black power" minority gained dramatic visibility. Increasingly, the movement began to seek racial as well as moral power, and thus it fell into the fundamental contradiction that plagues it to this day. Moral power precludes racial power by denouncing race as a means to power. Now suddenly the movement itself was using race as a means to power and thereby affirming the very union of race and power it was born to redress. In the end, black power can claim no higher moral standing than white power.

It makes no sense to say this shouldn't have happened. The sacrifices that **41** moral power demands are difficult to sustain, and it was inevitable that blacks would tire of these sacrifices and seek a more earthly power. Nevertheless, a loss of genuine innocence and moral power followed. The movement, splintered by a burst of racial militancy in the late sixties, lost its hold on the American conscience and descended more and more to the level of secular interest-group politics. Bargaining and challenging once again became racial rather than moral negotiations.

You hear it asked, why are there no Martin Luther Kings around today? I **42** think one reason is that there are no black leaders willing to resist the seductions of racial power, or to make the sacrifices moral power requires. King understood that racial power subverts moral power, and he pushed the principles of fairness and equality rather than black power because he believed those principles would bring blacks their most complete liberation. He sacrificed race for morality, and his innocence was made genuine by that sacrifice. What made King the most powerful and extraordinary black leader of this century was not his race but his morality.

Black power is a challenge. It grants whites no innocence; it denies their **43** moral capacity and then demands that they be moral. No power can long insist on itself without evoking an opposing power. Doesn't an insistence on black power call up white power? (And could this have something to do with what many are now calling a resurgence of white racism?) I believe that what divided the races at the dinner party I attended, and what divides them in the nation, can only be bridged by an adherence to those moral principles that disallow race as a source of power, privilege, status, or entitlement of any kind. In our age, principles like fairness and equality are ill-defined and all but drowned in relativity. But this is the fault of people, not principles. We keep them muddied because they are the greatest threat to our presumed innocence and our selective ignorance. Moral principles, even when somewhat ambiguous,

have the power to assign responsibility and therefore to provide us with knowledge. At the dinner party we were afraid of so severe an accountability.

What both black and white Americans fear are the sacrifices and risks that   44
true racial harmony demands. This fear is the measure of our racial chasm.
And though fear always seeks a thousand justifications, none is ever good
enough, and the problems we run from only remain to haunt us. It would be
right to suggest courage as an antidote to fear, but the glory of the word might
only intimidate us into more fear. I prefer the word effort—relentless effort,
moral effort. What I like most about this word are its connotations of every-
dayness, earnestness, and practical sacrifice. No matter how badly it might
have gone for us that warm summer night, we should have talked. We should
have made the effort.

RESPONDING TO THE READING

Freewriting

Exercise 14e.   Freewrite about ideas in Shelby Steele's article that you find
most appealing or ones that made you angry. What experiences have you had
that contributed to your response?

Exercise 14f.   Freewrite about possible conversations the dinner guests in
Steele's story might have had in response to the engineer's comment about his
daughter losing her Black heritage by attending a predominantly white school.

Building Your Vocabulary

VOCABULARY LIST

Words to Look Up	My Definition	Dictionary Definition
chardonnay (1)		
autopsy (4)		
flagellatory (4)		
remorseful (4)		
guise (4)		
amorphous (4)		
facilitate (4)		
badger (6)		
provocation (6)		
provocateur (6)		
impunity (6)		
eradicate (7)		
sanction (8)		
allure (8)		
delineation (8)		
dismal (8)		

attribution (8)
malevolent (8)
ignoble (8)
precondition (9)
entitlement (9)
subjugate (10)
impasse (11)
compulsion (13)
contravening (14)
incarnate (14)
odious (14)
revisionism (16)
racial determinism (16)
attributions (16)
presumption (18)
supersedes (18)
adversary (18)
vindictive (18)
sacrosanct (24)
irrepressible (25)
flamboyant (27)
opportunistic (27)
absolution (27)
collectively entitled (30)
initiative (30)
individually demoralized (30)
jeopardize (31)
repelled (32)
hysteria (32)
long-disgruntled (33)
ever-escalating (33)
breach (37)
sanction (37)
redress (37)
integrity (39)
subverts (42)
chasm (44)
antidote (44)
intimidate (44)
relentless (44)
connotations (44)

Questions for Discussion

1. Who is the primary audience for this reading selection? What passages suggest this readership? What other readers might Shelby Steele have had in mind?

2. Why does Steele begin his analysis of race relations with the anecdote of the dinner party? How effective is this opening and other narrative examples he includes in his chapter?

3. Role-play a few of the dialogues that you and your classmates wrote in response to Exercise 14f.

4. Why do you think Shelby Steele refers to his role as racial monitor in the late 1960s (paragraphs 4 and 5)? How does this discussion add to our understanding of Steele and his purpose in writing?

5. What does Steele mean when he says that "Black anger always, in a way, flatters white power" (paragraph 6)? Do you agree with this position?

6. What is Steele's purpose in writing "I'm Black, You're White, Who's Innocent?" What alternative does he propose for replacing the current struggle for power?

7. Use your own words to explain what Steele means when he says, "I think the racial struggle in America has always been primarily a struggle for innocence." How are power and innocence connected? What evidence does Steele offer to support his claim? Do you find it convincing?

8. How does "seeing for innocence" work for whites? for blacks?

9. What criteria does Steele use to evaluate Reagan's claim that he is "'color blind' in matters of race"? How does Steele connect this claim to the fact that Reagan was popular with so many Americans?

10. What are the good points that Steele discusses about Reagan's goals with regard to African Americans? What criticisms does he offer of Reagan's attitude toward African Americans?

11. What are "bargainers" and "challengers" in Steele's view? Examine key words in the examples he gives of Bill Cosby and Jesse Jackson to determine how this writer feels about the role of bargainer. In what way does Steele think Martin Luther King, Jr. was a bargainer (paragraphs 37 through 39)? Do you foresee problems for African Americans who play this role? Offer a few examples of people you know or have read about who are either bargainers or challengers and explain how you feel about these figures.

12. What does Steele mean by "victimization" (paragraphs 31 through 34)? What problems does he see for African Americans because of their history as social victims? What quality does he think should replace the victims' stance that he feels African Americans have unwittingly assumed? Do you think, as several of Steele's critics do, that he is blaming the victims for a predicament caused by whites?

13. What value does Steele find in the civil rights movement? What has happened to that movement in his view? How do you feel about his position?

14. When reevaluating the scene with which he opens his chapter, Steele says, "No matter how badly it might have gone for us that warm summer night, we should have talked. We should have made the effort" (paragraph 44). What is Steele's motive in recommending this course of action? What effect might more talk and more effort have produced?

TOPICS FOR WRITING

Topic 1. Read Dr. King's "Letter from the Birmingham Jail" in Chapter 18 and write an essay in which you evaluate King's letter as a statement of "genuine innocence" rather than "racial privilege."

Topic 2. Several African-American writers, including Julian Bond, a civil rights activist and former state Senator in Georgia, have argued that affirmative action programs allow blacks to receive equal consideration as job applicants. Find three or four articles that present differing positions on affirmative action. Write an essay in which you evaluate the arguments in at least one of these articles. Try to use criteria suggested by the other articles you have read to write your evaluation.

Topic 3. Choose one or two individuals in the media or whom you know personally and write an essay in which you discuss characteristics that make these individuals either "bargainers" or "challengers." Be sure to identify the characteristics you will discuss and include supporting examples and analysis.

Topic 4. If you have read about or witnessed ethnic conflicts in your school, neighborhood, or city, interview as many of the people involved in those conflicts as you can, and consult local newspapers for additional information. Then write an essay in which you explain the situation, analyze the sources of the conflict, and propose solutions.

Student Writing: Evaluating a Movie

Love and War: An Evaluation of <u>Dr. Zhivago</u>

   <u>Dr. Zhivago,</u> the movie based on a novel by Boris Pasternak, is a well-made movie. It is artistically filmed and makes good use of shots of the Russian countryside during different seasons. The handling of the movie's complex plot, however, stands out as its greatest achievement. The director, David Lean, uses his main characters, Dr. Zhivago, played by Omar Sharif, and Lara, played by Julie Christie, to effectively tell two stories. The first is a rich-boy, poor-girl love story. The second follows the Bolshevik Revolution. Lean sometimes gets too heavy-handed, and he occasionally overstates his point, but as a whole, <u>Dr. Zhivago</u> is an entertaining movie that tells both of its stories well.

The audience follows the movie's double plot mainly through the eyes of the main character—Dr. Zhivago himself. We see the love between Lara and Zhivago develop at the same time as the revolution is brewing. The relationship and the revolution seem to be born together and develop together; Zhivago's first indication that an insurrection might be possible and his first view of Lara happen almost simultaneously. On the same evening he discovers this beautiful woman who will haunt his dreams, he walks into the street and is nearly trampled by horses ridden by the Czar's troops who are chasing a band of rebels. The stories are constantly intertwined in this fashion. Later, one of Lara's shy, seemingly inconsequential suitors becomes a general in the Bolshevik Army and is instrumental in persecuting the lovers. Then, too, as the rebels struggle for control of the countryside and the revolution slowly gains momentum, Zhivago and Lara struggle and grow in their love. Certainly the revolution shapes the lives of these two lovers who are eventually swept up in the general chaos. They are torn apart, then brought back together several times by the jealous general and other forces of the revolution.

The director also brings the two plots together when he uses the characters to show the feelings of the common people during the revolution. Like most Russians under the cruel Czar Nicholas II, Zhivago starts out believing that a change might be good for his country, and for this reason, he is not initially opposed to the revolt. But through his eyes we see the ugliness that develops. The Bolsheviks first take over Zhivago's house, then steal his possessions. Through his eyes we see the fear and despair of people swept up in something they don't understand and cannot control. As Zhivago loses control over his life, the entire Russian population experiences homelessness, exile, and starvation to one degree or another.

Another tactic successfully used by the director is the filming of beautiful scenes with Zhivago and Lara in the Russian countryside as a commentary on the contrasting ugliness of the war. At one point in the movie, Zhivago and Lara retreat to a house in the Caucasus Mountains. It is snowing as Zhivago arrives for the rendezvous with his lover; they enjoy each other for several days in that glorious world full of glittering snow and bright sunshine until the war tears them apart once more. In another, even more pointed scene, the Czarist troops battle with the Bolsheviks in a field of golden wheat. As the wheat blows gently and peacefully in the wind, the grisly battle claims hundreds of lives. At one point a group of young boys are mistaken for soldiers and massacred by the Red Army. As they lie bleeding in the field, the camera shows acres and acres of beautiful, moving wheat, a sad commentary on their tragedy.

The negative points of the movie are few, but they do detract from its overall effectiveness. The first is the overuse of the theme music, "Lara's Song." It is a lovely, haunting tune, but it is just used too often. Whenever Zhivago sees Lara or even thinks of her, we hear this music. After a while, it becomes intrusive. A little more restraint would have made it a little easier to listen to. Second, the director sometimes feels compelled to hit the audience over the head with his point about the evils of the Russian Revolution. For one thing, he portrays Lara's ex-lover as one of the coldest, most evil men I have seen in movies. One scene in particular typifies him; he is standing in the locomotive of a fast-moving train (symbolic of the revolution itself?) staring straight ahead, jaw set, arms at his sides, as though he had turned into a robot. In another scene, a group of soldiers in the Red Army attack a group of peasants who are marching to protest the lack of food in their village. The Bolshevik soldiers run them down in the street, killing unarmed women and children. We see their deaths through Zhivago's eyes, which register the disgust and horror of the doctor—a man whose duty is to save lives. True, the director wants to make his point that the people have become the innocent victims in this brutal, wrong-headed revolution. However, most people and situations are not all evil or all good, and a little subtlety would still have made the point, and perhaps been more true to life.

Putting these few flaws aside, this movie is very enjoyable. The love story is moving, and the characters are generally believable. You really care what happens to them because they are warm, troubled, and suffering people. Who can watch the end where Zhivago dies before reaching Lara after so many years of separation without crying? If a love story can make you cry like that, it must be a success.

—Sheryl Little

Questions for Discussion

1. What criteria does Sheryl Little use to evaluate *Dr. Zhivago?* How does she organize her discussion?
2. Which of her arguments do you find most convincing? Explain your choice.

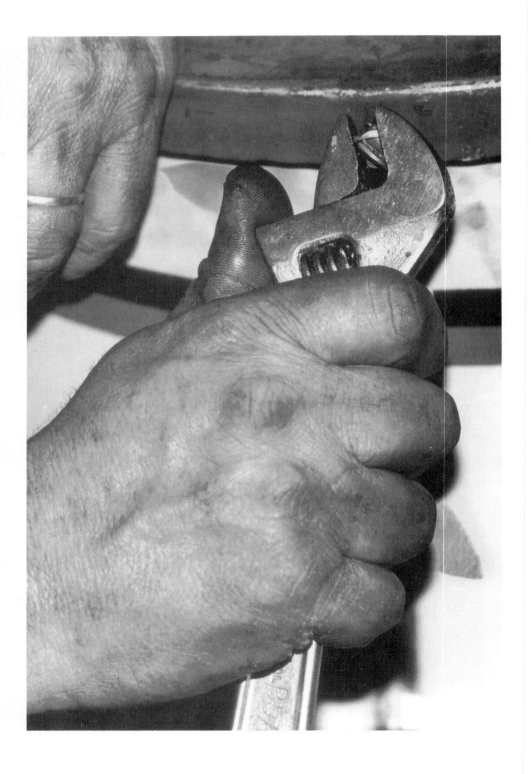

15

The Work Place

*To get the workforce we need,
we're going to have to create the environment
that develops the potential in people.*

—Evon Emerson

*The problem with history is that it's written
by college professors about great men.
That's not what history is.
History's a hell of a lot of little people
getting together and deciding they want
a better life for themselves and their kids.*

—Bill Talcott (quoted in "The Organizer")

Lhe readings in this chapter provide a variety of perspectives on some of the problems associated with working as well as solutions for dealing with those problems. In the first selection, "The Workforce and the Future of Business," Evon Emerson focuses on ways to address problems that businesses will face given that the current working population is aging, and that more women with families, unskilled and untrained workers, and a growing number of immigrants are entering the workforce. In an interview conducted by Studs Terkel, Bill Talcott discusses his life-long effort to organize workers to fight for better wages, benefits, and working conditions. Thi Nga Tran's poem, "Jobs," shows how difficult it can be for immigrants to find work in the United States. The last essay, "The Perfect Job" by David Owen, presents a humorous look at jobs the author would like to have.

This chapter also introduces techniques for writing essays that identify a problem and suggest solutions. Passages from Evon Emerson's "The Workforce and the Future of Business" employ several of the techniques that are common to problem-and-solution papers.

PROBLEM SOLVING

We often call on skills we have been developing since childhood to identify problems in our lives and to consider them closely enough to propose solutions that will solve those problems. The child who is not doing well in school, the indifferent teacher, crime in our neighborhood, and water shortages caused by a drought are samples of problems we may face at some time in our lives. We can solve some of these problems ourselves. A child may need more help with his homework. Talking with the teacher during an office hour may help a student understand or even change an instructor's attitude. Other problems—such as crime and water shortages—must be solved collectively.

When writers decide which problems to explore, they must keep in mind that not every problem has a solution. In the example of the drought, the problem might be that rainfall in southeastern Iowa is 16 inches below normal. That is one problem human beings cannot solve directly because it involves forces that are beyond our control. We might, however, restate the problem as a shortage of water for irrigation and domestic use. In this case, we are much more likely to have a problem we can solve. One solution to this problem, for example, might be to locate a water source and negotiate a contract for purchasing water. We might also try rationing the amount of water allocated to each resident and farmer in the affected area. As this example shows, writers should reject problems that seem unsolveable in favor of those with feasible solutions.

Good problem-solving papers depend on the effective use of several writing strategies. **Describing** the problem in detail helps demonstrate its seriousness. Identifying problems that have realistic solutions depends on the writer's ability to **evaluate** a situation and **propose solutions.** The writer must also judge the relative merits of those solutions based on short- and long-term **effects** he or she can foresee and propose solutions that are most likely to solve those problems. The solutions a writer proposes will be most convincing if they are supported by clear **explanations** and **examples** that show how the solutions will be put into effect and what results the reader can reasonably expect.

Characteristics of Problem Solving

A Clear Purpose and Point of View

Usually the purpose of an essay that uses problem solving as a major writing strategy is to identify problems to be solved and to offer solutions that readers are likely to accept. An additional purpose might be to inspire readers to take a particular action or work toward solving the problem.

In "The Workforce and the Future of Business," Evon Emerson responds to what she considers short-sighted advice about how to improve the American economy. She takes issue with the "wise owls" who tell us that the survival of American businesses depends on increasing the number of goods we produce and improving the quality of services we offer. Emerson argues that we won't improve the quality of goods and services until we find solutions for three problems with the American workforce that she believes must be solved if the economy is to enjoy long-term health.

Emerson uses the first person point of view ("The reason I like this story . . ."; "I suggest . . ."; and "I believe . . .") to personalize the essay and to clarify that the ideas she presents are her own. As president of the National Association of Bank Women, Emerson writes as an expert in managing and financing businesses and corporations. Her position shows that she has received recognition as a leader and spokesperson for a national organization of bankers, and further clarifies her point of view.

A Sense of Audience

To persuade an audience to accept a solution as valid or to take action, the writer must address the audience directly, in terms that are likely to convince. In Evon Emerson's article, she makes a point of addressing both managers and employees about how to prepare for increasing competition. In paragraph 2, for example, she makes suggestions to "business executives" and "business professionals." She also discusses the workers' roles in preparing for economic changes. In paragraph 27, she points out that "Developing the workforce is not just the boss' responsibility. It's up to all of us." Her question, "What can each of us do?" is followed by a list of four changes workers must make if the partnership between managers and employees is to work well for everyone. Her solutions are likely to appeal to management and workers because she asks both sides to make difficult changes.

In appealing to a broad audience Emerson begins her essay with a story.

> Once upon a time, there was a young frog who became wor- 1
> ried about the number of his fellow frogs being eaten by snakes. So
> he went to the wise old owl and asked, "Owl, what can I do to avoid
> being eaten by a snake?" The owl thought for a moment, then
> advised, "Fly away." The little frog was thrilled; he now had the
> solution to the problem facing all the frogs. Then, one day, he got
> caught by a snake. He tried to fly away, but couldn't. As the snake
> was getting ready to swallow him, the frog called out to the owl for
> help. The owl just shrugged and said, "Sorry. I only deal with con-
> cepts, not reality."

Her opening makes the reader think about supposedly wise business advice and the danger of following it blindly, especially if the advice has not been tested for feasibility. The story also helps Emerson establish a no-non-sense, practical tone. To maintain that tone, Emerson avoids sounding angry or unreasonable about the problems she discusses. Instead, she maintains a common-sense approach and promises realistic solutions.

Emerson also shows that she is willing to accommodate her audience to make sure they understand connections she wants them to see. In paragraph 2, for example, she clarifies the connection between the story and her purpose for writing when she explains:

> The reason I like this story is that we each can read whatever 2
> message we want in it, because, especially these days, we all feel like
> threatened frogs sometimes. Yet, as much as we may sympathize
> with him, that little frog was a co-conspirator in his own demise—
> he was guilty of some fatally short-term thinking.

Emerson assures the reader that the insecurity of the work place makes us "all feel like threatened frogs sometimes." Later in the article she points out that, like the frog, we bear some responsibility for what happens to us.

In paragraph 3 Emerson connects the story to her subject more explicitly.

> Everyone in business today is hearing the advice of a lot of 3
> owls on what we should do to solve our economic problems. In
> considering these recommendations, we should avoid shortsighted
> strategic plans which fail to recognize that the workforce is the key
> to corporate success or failure. I suggest that business executives
> can add to their corporate planning in order to maximize the
> potential of their workforce and minimize exposure to long-term

disaster. To get the workforce we need, we're going to have to create the environment that develops the potential in people. In addition, business professionals actively must become involved in shaping social policy.

In moving the reader from the entertaining but pointed story of the frog and the owl, Emerson makes this smooth transition to her thesis: "To get the workforce we need, we're going to have to create the environment that develops the potential in people. In addition, business professionals actively must become involved in shaping social policy."

Clear Statement of the Problem

For proposals to be taken seriously, writers must identify problems clearly and convey the importance of those problems to their readers. To isolate the problem with which she is most concerned, Emerson asks the question "Where will we get the workforce we need to compete and succeed in the 1990's?" (paragraph 14). Her discussion of two trends in the working population—"the workforce is aging" and "the pool of young people is shrinking"—help convince the reader that we are facing a serious problem. To further clarify the problem, Emerson points out that "75% of the people who will be employed in the year 2000 are working today" (paragraph 16). In other words, only 25% of the workers employed at the turn of the century will be young people entering the workforce for the first time. Armed with this information, Emerson concludes: "We won't be able to find the number of eager entry-level young people our businesses have depended on in the past because they're not there."

Reference to Authorities

By referring to an authority who has studied the problem writers want to discuss, they add credibility to their position. Emerson's analysis of the problems businesses must face is based on a study of the workforce completed by "the prestigious Hudson Institute"[1] for the U.S. Department of Labor. This study identified several trends in the workforce, two of which Emerson uses in her analysis of problems employers will face in the year 2000—"the workforce is aging," and "the pool of young people is shrinking."

Reliance on Examples

Examples that illustrate problems and solutions are essential if readers are to understand the severity of a problem or appreciate the merit of a particular solution. In Emerson's article, for instance, to support her idea that businesses

---

[1]A research group specializing in reports for U.S. governmental agencies.

are not addressing the problem of a declining workforce adequately she gives three examples of "de-motivators" that hamper a manager's ability to make more products and give better service: "stress from constantly changing demands and jobs; lack of recognition for the people who are doing twice as much work with half the staff; and fear of the unknown when companies restructure without telling their managers what the new corporate goals are" (paragraph 6). When she discusses how difficult it has become to find teenagers to take entry-level jobs, Emerson cites the example of McDonald's recruitment of seniors in their fast-food restaurants (paragraph 12). Such examples help the reader appreciate the employment problem Emerson sees.

Reliance on Statistics

Once Emerson establishes that the number of available workers is shrinking and that solutions tried have so far been shortsighted, she is ready to discuss ways to bring the new populations—women, the disadvantaged, and immigrants—into the workforce and to keep them employed. Statistics help Emerson establish the importance of these populations and the problems they pose for employers. For example, she reports that "70 percent of the workforce and more than 40 percent of management in financial institutions is women," then concludes that "a new employee or manager is likely to be a woman." Having established the importance of women in the work place, Emerson stresses the importance of helping women solve problems of child care and equal pay—issues that must be addressed if women are to stay on the job.

Presenting Feasible Solutions

EVALUATING LESS FEASIBLE SOLUTIONS.   To convince an audience that their solutions are the most plausible, writers often discuss other less feasible solutions by way of comparison. For example, when Emerson examines short-term solutions to the problem that "the pool of young people is shrinking," she mentions the practice of some businesses who are "eliminating middle management" in an effort to "streamline operations" and "to get rid of older, more 'difficult' employees." Although this solution has the immediate effect of saving money and aggravation, it assumes that younger people being hired will eventually fill those middle-management positions. Emerson shows the impracticality of this assumption by noting that the younger people these strategists expect are simply "not there" (paragraph 12).

To illustrate the difficulty of finding these expected qualified workers, Emerson cites the McDonald's recruitment of seniors and mentions banks like those in the New England states that have been forced to raise the salaries for tellers because of the lack of applicants. In a later paragraph Emerson points out that her proposals for educating the disadvantaged tap "an increasingly important segment of our emerging workforce," one that is ignored by the short-term solutions of hiring seniors and raising salaries to entice the few skilled workers (paragraph 24). In addition, such a solution will help make

American companies competitive in both the domestic and international marketplace (paragraph 25).

In the last three paragraphs of her article Emerson mentions the problem of getting consensus or agreement on the employment issues she discusses. How might this mention of consensus contribute to the feasibility or reasonableness of her position?

CONVINCING EVIDENCE.   To help her establish the practicality of her own solutions, which involve recruiting from three different populations—women, the disadvantaged, and immigrants—and paying attention to these workers' needs, Emerson establishes logical connections between the success of American companies and the success and well-being of individual workers. When she discusses the disadvantaged, for example, Emerson relies on statistics to establish that this is a large, untapped source for workers—1 million of the new workers needed by American businesses "can't read, write, or count" (paragraph 24). Her solution to this problem is "to raise the level of literacy."

To show that her solution is feasible, Emerson proposes what she feels are realistic goals for businesses: "We must be prepared to train entry-level people to the skill level we need on the job and recognize that remedial-level training may be necessary before developing the higher-level skills needed in high-technology areas." She continues with the statement that business leaders must participate more in the community, encourage people to develop their skills, and insist on better schools and better education that will give workers the communications and math skills they need.

A Clear Sequence of Ideas

As with papers explaining causes and effects, as well as essays that rely on comparing and contrasting, problem-solving essays ask that the reader follow some fairly complex reasoning. For example, readers must be able to see connections between problems and solutions, sort out supporting evidence, separate competing solutions, and agree with the writer's proposal. As a result, problem-solving essays must have a clear organizational pattern if the writer expects his or her readers to follow such a complex sequence of ideas.

The organizational pattern in Emerson's essay is one of several patterns writers use to organize an analysis of problems and solutions. The sequence of ideas in her essay "The Workforce and the Future of Business" appears in the following list:

Presents the problem of "wise owls" who propose impractical solutions (paragraphs 1 through 6)

Identifies the problem of getting an adequate workforce (paragraphs
    3 and 7)
Discusses trends in the workforce (paragraphs 8 through 13)
Proposes solutions for businesses to implement (paragraphs 14
    through 26)
Discusses what workers can do to solve the problem (paragraphs
    27 through 31)
Concluding statements (paragraphs 32 through 34)

FOR PRACTICE

How does Emerson's discussion of trends in the workforce prepare the reader
for her discussion of how to solve problems workers might bring to the job?

The Workforce and the Future of Business
Evon Emerson

*Ms. Emerson is president of a consulting firm that designs marketing strategies for
banking and other companies that provide financial services. She is also president of the
National Association of Bank Women. In this article, which appeared in* USA Today *in
November 1988, Emerson insists that businesses must invest in the training and
education of their workers and that workers must lower their expectations if America is
to compete in the international marketplace.*

Once upon a time, there was a young frog who became worried about the   1
number of his fellow frogs being eaten by snakes. So he went to the wise old
owl and asked, "Owl, what can I do to avoid being eaten by a snake?" The owl
thought for a moment, then advised, "Fly away." The little frog was thrilled; he
now had the solution to the problem facing all the frogs. Then, one day, he got
caught by a snake. He tried to fly away, but couldn't. As the snake was getting
ready to swallow him, the frog called out to the owl for help. The owl just
shrugged and said, "Sorry. I only deal with concepts, not reality."

The reason I like this story is that we each can read whatever message we   2
want in it, because, especially these days, we all feel like threatened frogs
sometimes. Yet, as much as we may sympathize with him, that little frog was
a co-conspirator in his own demise—he was guilty of some fatally short-term
thinking.

Everyone in business today is hearing the advice of a lot of owls on what   3
we should do to solve our economic problems. In considering these recommendations, we should avoid shortsighted strategic plans which fail to recognize that the workforce is the key to corporate success or failure. I suggest that
business executives can add to their corporate planning in order to maximize
the potential of their workforce and minimize exposure to long-term disaster.

To get the workforce we need, we're going to have to create the environment that develops the potential in people. In addition, business professionals actively must become involved in shaping social policy.

Two of the most popular buzz words in the financial services industry 4 today are productivity and quality service. They're used a lot in other businesses, too. The wise old owl tells us that these are two concepts we need to make into reality in order to compete and survive. I believe there is much truth in that advice, but we must look for the truth beyond the buzz words.

Productivity and quality service only will be achieved by and through each 5 employee. If they don't fly, neither will the company. However, many companies are having difficulty getting their middle management to accept and carry out their strategic plans. Because of the tremendous amount of restructuring, mergers, and consolidation in financial services and other industries, confusion, frustration, and stress are common at all levels, especially among management.

Consider some important de-motivators to managers' productivity and 6 service: stress from constantly changing demands and jobs; lack of recognition for the people who are doing twice as much work with half the staff; and fear of the unknown when companies restructure without telling their managers what the new corporate goals are.

In order to accomplish corporate strategic goals, companies must take a 7 hard look at who will achieve them. They also should act now to make sure they have the workforce they need to survive and prosper in the future.

The prestigious Hudson Institute did a study in 1987 for the U.S. 8 Department of Labor. *Workforce 2000* identified some important trends. Many people already are aware of them, but may not have thought of their implications yet.

Trends and Implications

Trend number 1: the workforce is aging. What does that portend for a compa- 9 ny's planning? It means that management in financial services and other businesses is facing a dilemma. The workforce now in place has been responsible for most success to date. They're the ones with the Puritan work ethic. They're at all levels of the company, but particularly at the upper levels of middle management.

Today, many business needs are changing and the workforce must adjust 10 and learn and use new skills. Yet, as employees age, they can become less adaptable and less willing to relocate or retrain.

What's the short-term solution many institutions are using? They're elimi- 11 nating middle management—not only to streamline operations, but also to get rid of older, more "difficult" employees. This saves money and aggravation, and opens up opportunities for younger people just coming into the company.

Which leads me to trend number 2: the pool of young people is shrinking. 12 The last of the baby boom is already in the workplace and the baby bust is coming of age. We won't be able to find the numbers of eager entry-level young people our businesses have depended on in the past because they're not there. Meanwhile, many of those who *are* there don't have the fundamental communications and math skills they need to do the jobs available. Service businesses like financial services are the most affected by this baby bust and the failure of our educational system. Look at the way McDonald's is recruiting senior citizens to sell hamburgers; they can't get teenagers. In some areas of the country, like New England, banks are paying top dollar for tellers and can't fill positions because the workforce pool for that level of job barely exists.

Short-term solutions that financial organizations are applying to this   13
problem include raising salaries to attract the small number of eligible employees, or investing heavily in technology to reduce their dependence on people.

The central problem businesses are facing and will continue to confront is   14
this: Where will we get the workforce we need to compete and succeed in the 1990's? Unlike the old owl in the story, I deal in reality as well as concepts. The solutions I have to offer to the workforce shortage problem will enable a company to succeed, but they are varied, aren't simple, and aren't easy. They are meant for both the short and long haul, and require courage and commitment from individuals and corporations.

The workforce for the successful company for the 1990's and beyond will   15
come from the current workforce, women, the disadvantaged, and immigrants. To make that workforce—and therefore the company—successful, we will have to motivate, retrain, and re-educate the current workforce; face up to a number of social and economic issues affecting current and potential workforces; and recognize that the company actively must become involved in shaping public policy.

Look at the current workforce and consider that 75% of the people who   16
will be employed in the year 2000 are working today. This means that the productivity of the current labor force, not the emerging one, will determine a company's competitiveness.

Even if the managers in a company are willing to change to meet the com-   17
pany's needs, that step often is difficult. If, at the same time, they see a cap on salaries and upward advancement, lateral or downward mobility, and increased workloads and responsibilities, they can lose their motivation. They even can lose their loyalty to the company, especially if they can't or don't see its long-term viability. They are operating on career expectations of the 1960's and 1970's.

It is essential for everyone in business to find ways to re-educate our cur-   18
rent workforce to the new economic and career realities. People must learn to expect to change jobs, companies, and even careers more than once in their working lives. Therefore, management must help them understand that they constantly must reinvest in themselves by learning new skills. It also must help them by providing access to skills training.

The challenge to managers is to create among the current workforce a new   19
understanding of career potential; help people through feelings of fear, anger, and disappointment; and, above all, recognize and devote resources to dealing

with the human element of change. The success of our companies is at stake in how well the current workforce does.

Already, 70% of the workforce and more than 40% of management in financial institutions is women. In the 1990's, as many as two-thirds of the new entrants in the workforce will be women. By the year 2000, most of the women of working age will be employed.   20

What this means is that a new employee or manager is likely to be a woman. In a tight employment environment, we will have to compete to recruit and retain women, who will be the largest segment of the emerging workforce. To compete successfully, we are going to have to come to grips with economic issues which currently limit women's ability to work to their full potential. That means we no longer can avoid dealing with pressing social issues like pay equity, child care, dependent care, or parental leave. Neither can we look the other way as women walk away from corporate executive positions because they are not treated fairly or can't see a challenging future in their companies.   21

Imagine that you have a son and a daughter in high school today. By the year 2000, both of them will be working because they have to. Assuming both have the same education and credentials, your daughter will be earning 74 cents to every dollar your son earns. She probably will have at least one child and, because she is underpaid for the work she does, won't be able to afford decent child care. If this occurs, what's going to happen to your grandchild? Now multiply your imaginary daughter by 49,000,000 working women. What is being done to meet their economic needs and their growing demand for justice?   22

I am not advocating any particular solution to these issues, although the National Association of Bank Women is beginning to examine some of those that appear to be the most promising. I am saying that the day of reckoning is here; management has to address these issues actively as an economic imperative.   23

I mentioned the disadvantaged. They are an increasingly important segment of our emerging workforce and one which we can not afford to ignore, but let's not whitewash the truth. Many Americans are illiterate and incapable of doing simple computations. Today, the shocking truth is that American businesses will have to hire 1,000,000 new workers who can't read, write, or count.   24

The disadvantaged constitute an enormous, unused pool of available entry-level workers. If our companies are to survive through the competitive abilities of our workforce, not only in this country, but in the international marketplace, we must raise the level of literacy. We must be prepared to train entry-level people to the skill level we need on the job, and recognize that remedial-level training may be necessary before developing the higher-level skills needed in high-technology areas. Business executives historically have been community leaders. It is in our self-interest to demand that schools educate our children and to make ourselves available to our communities to help develop a total environment for encouraging human potential.   25

Finally, we should not overlook the latent ability of immigrants as valued   26
members of our workforce. In the last 20 years, more and more young people
in developing nations have attended college. Our international economy, with
its increased trade and travel, has lowered our borders. Immigration means
more and better-educated workers now can compete for jobs in this country.
It is in our interests to make sure that immigration policies help us in our
search for qualified employees and that our internal management policies
accommodate different cultures and styles.

Expectations and Solutions

Developing the workforce is not just the boss' responsibility. It's up to all of us.   27
What can each of us do?

First, be open to change, and recognize new demands and realities. Learn   28
the new skills you need to know, and use them. Be versatile and flexible.

Second, change career expectations. Many companies don't have tradi-   29
tional hierarchies or corporate ladders straight to the top anymore. Lateral
moves within a company and moves into important new areas of business are
increasingly important strategies. If you find that your company, for whatever
reason, isn't able to give you the position you want, the right move is not to sit
around and feel sorry for yourself. Instead, it's smart to look around for what
you want elsewhere, then make it happen.

Third, child care, dependent care, and the other important issues of today   30
are not going to solve themselves. Moreover, they're not the sole responsibility
of management. If employers aren't doing anything about them, maybe it's
because employees never said they wanted something done, or maybe those in
charge aren't being told by their employees what would be most helpful.
Speaking up and making your needs known is the first step toward improving
a situation. It also helps to make yourself available to work together with your
company, and your community, to find solutions that will work for everyone.

Finally, be open to and supportive of others. The workforce is going to be   31
different from what we've known. We won't be able to find lots of people who
are exactly like us. I think that's just fine. We should all be open to new faces,
experiences, and ideas. That cooperation and initiative will help make our
businesses and our society better places to be.

I said my solutions wouldn't be easy. I don't have all the answers. There is   32
no consensus on these issues. Until we have one, we will have to grope our
own ways to individual solutions. However, time is not on our side. Good people are leaving business, are frustrated, or can't get in.

Richard Fitzwater of the U.S. Comptroller's Office uses a remarkable anal-   33
ogy when he talks about the difficulties of reaching consensus on an issue. He
poses this question: What piece of legislation passed through Congress in the
shortest amount of time? It wasn't the declaration of war against Japan after
Pearl Harbor or the Bank Holiday Act of 1933. It was the bill that made black-
outs of televised football games illegal when those games are sold out.
Fitzwater points out that the reason this piece of legislation moved so fast

through Congress was that there was nearly unanimous consensus on it. Lack of consensus, he says, can mean failure to take action. Yet, we can't afford to wait for consensus because we can't afford not to act immediately.

Today, it takes real courage to pick up the ball in the face of great odds and to be willing to run with it, especially when you don't know if you've got a team behind you. There is no consensus today on what business's most pressing needs and problems are. The workforce issues and needs I've identified are not high on most wise owls' agendas, though I hope to see them emerge soon. If they don't, we all will have to face them in a few years, at the disadvantage of time gone by, and perhaps in competition with countries and businesses that were not shortsighted and who saw the need and addressed the issues sooner.

RESPONDING TO THE READING

Freewriting

Exercise 15a.   Freewrite about problems with workers or managers that you have observed. Were those problems addressed? If so, how?

Exercise 15b.   How well have managers accommodated the needs of workers in places you have worked? What might have been done differently?

Building Your Vocabulary

VOCABULARY LIST

Words to Look Up	My Definition	Dictionary Definition
co-conspirator (2)		
demise (2)		
shortsighted (3)		
productivity (4)		
buzz words (4)		
mergers (5)		
consolidation (5)		
restructure (6)		
prestigious (8)		
adaptable (10)		
relocate (10)		
executive positions (21)		
credentials (22)		
reckoning (23)		
imperative (23)		
hierarchies (29)		
consensus (32)		

Questions for Discussion

1. What did you find appealing about the story of the frog and the wise owl? What do you think its effect might be on each of Emerson's readers— business executives, managers, and employees?
2. What social policies does Emerson want business professionals to support? What other groups might support or oppose these policies? What reasons might these opposing groups have for voicing opposition?
3. Identify the problems with the workforce that Emerson thinks American businesses and corporations will face in the future. Which of these problems have you observed? Which do you think is the most serious? Why?
4. How effectively does Emerson demonstrate problems in the American workforce, problems that are likely to increase in the next century? Can you think of anything else she might have said to help convince her audience that these problems are serious and must be addressed immediately?
5. Emerson identifies several short-term solutions to problems she discusses in paragraphs 9 through 13. What possible flaws or merits do you see in her strategies?
6. What does Emerson mean by "the human element of change" (paragraph 19)? What do you think employers should do to help workers face this "element of change" in their lives?
7. Why do you think Emerson addresses the reader directly in paragraph 22? How effectively does the story she tells demonstrate her point?
8. What long-term solutions to the problems of the workforce does Emerson propose? What are the advantages or disadvantages of implementing these solutions in places you have worked or in employment situations with which you are familiar?
9. Which of the long-term solutions that Emerson discusses do you think is the most feasible? Explain your choice.

TOPICS FOR WRITING

Topic 1.   Think of a supervisor whose management style you disliked. Write a paper explaining what you would do differently if you were in charge. In your paper you will want to clarify the problems with your supervisor's management style and explain the changes you would make and why you would make them.

Topic 2.   Identify a serious problem that exists where you work now or have worked in the past. Explain the causes of that problem and propose solutions. Choose the solution that you think would work best and explain why you think it would address the problem.

Topic 3. Write an analysis of several management styles you have observed. You might wish to write a detailed explanation of two or three styles, or an information paper describing several management styles. In either case, focus on what makes each style effective or ineffective. Come to some conclusion about which of the styles is most effective and why.

Topic 4. Do some research to discover a problem faced by employers or workers. You might consider discussing protective tariffs, uncooperative employees, or high wages as business concerns, or lack of advancement or health benefits as problems employees often face.

THE WRITING PROCESS: PROBLEM SOLVING

For essays that identify problems and propose solutions, writers must define problems clearly, evaluate those problems well, judge possible outcomes of solutions, and explain why certain solutions are more realistic than others. The success of papers that call for such in-depth analysis depends on how well writers select a problem, gather information, find and evaluate possible solutions, and provide enough support to convince readers that the solutions presented are feasible.

Additional Considerations for Developing a Topic

Your instructor may assign one of the topics in this chapter that asks you to write about a problem for which you have solutions. Freewriting you do for readings in this chapter or for the chapter on evaluation might generate ideas for problems you wish to discuss and proposals you would like to make. If you have difficulty finding a problem you feel comfortable discussing or one you genuinely care about, ask yourself the following questions:

> What are a few of the problems you are aware of in your neighborhood? What can you and your neighbors do to solve them?
> In reading the local newspaper lately, have you been able to identify problems in your community that interest you or involve you personally?
> What can students, teachers, administrators, or other professionals do to solve a campus issue that you feel is not being properly addressed?
> Imagine that you have been promoted to an important management position where you work. What would you change, how would you make your changes, and what would be the result(s)?
> What problems seem to recur in your own life? What solutions might you use to solve them once and for all, or at least alleviate them?

Additional Considerations for Thinking about Your Audience

Because your audience must agree that the problem you identify is real and your solutions are viable, you need to make the problem as understandable as you can, given the knowledge and interest of the readers you are targeting. A good idea is to do what you can to appeal to the reader's self-interest, or interest in the community or the environment.

When considering the tone or attitude you will adopt in your paper, a common-sense, practical voice is usually the most convincing. That often means choosing a problem that allows you to remain as objective and neutral about your topic as you can.

Additional Considerations for Preliminary Writing

Identifying the Problem

To help you identify the problem clearly, you might ask yourself the following questions:

> What is the problem I have identified?
> Who or what is involved in this problem?
> What evidence do I have to support the idea that a problem exists?
> Who can I interview with first-hand knowledge of this problem or who might have an interesting perspective on it? If so, who are they, and how can I find them?

Discovering Solutions

Use freewriting techniques to list all the solutions to the problem that you can think of or that others have suggested to you. The questions below might help you find solutions you have not considered.

> What seems to have caused this problem? How might these causes be eliminated or at least reduced?
> What are characteristics of this problem? Does it have an economic, emotional, or ethical aspect? Is there anything about the problem that doesn't make sense?
> What makes this a problem?
> What solutions seem to address costs associated with this problem?
> How might the emotional, ethical, or irrational aspect of the problem be solved?
> Could the problem be addressed by any of the following:
> - Education or training
> - Information to make people better informed
> - Higher fees or a tax increase
> - Lower fees or a tax decrease

- Greater incentives to change attitudes or behavior
- Fundraising
- Community involvement
- Eliminating unnecessary steps
- Acknowledging that some elements of the problem will not change

Imagine what the situation might be like in ten years if nothing is done about the problem. What courses of action might ensure that the situation will either improve or at least not get worse?

Evaluating Solutions

Once you have a list of possible solutions, you are in a position to weigh the advantages and disadvantages of each. The following questions offer specific criteria for judging the merits of each solution; they also can help you determine how relevant a solution is to the problem, how practical a solution is, and the benefits or the harm that will likely result from it.

What benefits might result from eliminating one of the causes of this problem?

What additional problems might this solution create? How easy would they be to solve?

Are there elements of the problem that this solution does not address? What might be done about them?

What costs might be associated with this problem?

Who would be responsible for carrying out this plan? Is it reasonable to expect it will be done?

Has this solution worked in other situations? Is it reasonable to expect that something similar might happen here?

What action might the readers take to help solve this problem?

Additional Considerations for Organizing Ideas

Put simply, papers relying principally on problem solving include an identification of a problem, evidence that this problem exists, a proposal to solve the problem, and evidence that this proposal will work. In addition to these elements, writers may present competing solutions and evaluate their effectiveness. They might also advise their readers about what they can do to help solve the problem. For a reader to follow such a complex analysis, ideas must follow a clear organizational pattern. Several possible patterns for problem solving essays are listed below. The second pattern is similar to the one Evon Emerson uses in her article.

Pattern 1

1. Identify the problem
2. Discuss causes of the problem

3. Discuss ways to address those causes
4. Conclusion

Pattern 2

1. Identify the problem
2. Discuss weakest solutions
3. Discuss causes of the problem
4. Propose solution(s) or actions to be taken
5. Conclusion

Pattern 3

1. Identify the problem
2. Discuss weakest solutions
3. Defend most feasible solution
4. Discuss how the solution can be put into effect
5. Discuss outcome of the solution

When organizing your essay, you can also select elements in two or three of these patterns to form your own outline.

Additional Considerations for Sharing Your Writing and Making Final Revisions

Use the checklist below when revising your paper.

Checklist

- ❑ Does the opening paragraph(s) present the essay's purpose and point of view?
- ❑ Are the problems I discuss identified clearly?
- ❑ Will these problems seem real enough to my audience?
- ❑ Does my thesis anticipate solutions to the problems I discuss?
- ❑ Are the solutions I propose clearly linked to the problems I identify?
- ❑ Are these solutions convincing and presented with a reasonable tone?
- ❑ Is my paper organized clearly enough that the reader can follow my ideas?
- ❑ Do transitions make it clear when I shift from one problem or solution to another?
- ❑ Does my conclusion follow from the discussion of problems and solutions?
- ❑ Have I proofread carefully for sentence correctness, spelling, and punctuation?

FOR FURTHER READING

The Organizer
Studs Terkel

In the following interview, Bill Talcott describes his experiences as a labor organizer. This interview appears in Studs Terkel's book, Working: People Talk about What They Do All Day and How They Feel about What They Do, *published in 1972.*

My work is trying to change this country. This is the job I've chosen. When 1 people ask me, "Why are you doing this?" it's like asking what kind of sickness you got. I don't feel sick. I think this country is sick. The daily injustices just gnaw on me a little harder than they do on other people.

I try to bring people together who are being put down by the system, left 2 out. You try to build an organization that will give them power to make the changes. Everybody's at the bottom of the barrel at this point. Ten years ago one could say the poor people suffered and the middle class got by. That's not true any more.

My father was a truck driver with a sixth-grade education. My uncle was 3 an Annapolis graduate. My father was inarticulate and worked all his life with his hands. My uncle worked all his life with his mouth and used his hands only to cut coupons. My father's problem was that he was powerless. My uncle's problem was that he was powerless, although he thought he was strong. Clipping coupons, he was always on the fringe of power, but never really had it. If he tried to take part in the management of the companies whose coupons he was clipping, he got clipped. Both these guys died very unhappy, dissatisfied with their lives.

Power has been captured by a few people. A very small top and a very big 4 bottom. You don't see much in-between. Who do people on the bottom think are the powerful people? College professors and management types, the local managers of big corporations like General Motors. What kind of power do these guys really have? They have the kind of power Eichmann[1] claimed for himself. They have the power to do bad and not question what they're told to do.

I am more bothered by the ghetto child who is bitten by rats than I am by 5 a middle-class kid who can't find anything to do but put down women and take dope and play his life away. But each one is wasted.

I came into consciousness during the fifties, when Joe McCarthy[2] was 6 running around. Like many people my age—I'm now thirty-seven—I was

---

[1]Adolf Eichmann, an official in Nazi Germany responsible for the extermination of millions of European Jews.

[2]A United States Senator who, in the early 1950s, led a campaign against government officials he claimed were Communist subversives. Never able to prove his allegations, he was censured for his conduct in 1954.

aware something was terribly wrong. I floundered around for two years in college, was disappointed, and enlisted in the army. I was NCO[3] for my company. During a discussion, I said if I was a black guy, I would refuse to serve. I ended up being sent to division headquarters and locked up in a room for two years, so I wouldn't be able to talk to anybody.

At San Francisco State, I got involved with the farm workers movement. I would give speeches on a box in front of the Commons. Then I'd go out and fight jocks behind the gym for an hour and a half. (Laughs.) In '64, I resigned as student body president and went to Mississippi to work for SNCC.[4] I spent three years working in the black community in San Francisco.   7

At that point, I figured it was time for me to work with whites. My father was from South Carolina. We had a terrible time when I visited—violent arguments. But I was family. I learned from that experience you had to build a base with white people on the fringe of the South. Hopefully you'd build an alliance between blacks and whites. . . .   8

I came to East Kentucky with OEO.[5] I got canned in a year. Their idea was the same as Daley's.[6] You use the OEO to build an organization to support the right candidates. I didn't see that as my work. My job was to build an organization of put-down people, who can *control* the candidates once they're elected.   9

I put together a fairly solid organization of Appalachian people in Pike County. It's a single industry area, coal. You either work for the coal company or you don't work. Sixty percent of its people live on incomes lower than the government's guidelines for rural areas.   10

I was brought in to teach other organizers how to do it. I decided these middle-class kids from Harvard and Columbia were too busy telling everybody else what they should be doing. The only thing to do was to organize the local people.   11

When I got fired, there were enough people to support me on one hundred dollars a month and room and board. They dug down in their pockets and they'd bring food and they'd take care of me like I was a cousin. They felt responsible for me, but they didn't see me as one of them. I'm not an Appalachian, I'm a San Franciscan. I'm not a coal miner, I'm an organizer. If they're gonna save themselves, they're gonna have to do it themselves. I have some skills that can help them. I did this work for three years.   12

The word organizer has been romanticized. You get the vision of a mystical being doing magical things. An organizer is a guy who brings in new members. I don't feel I've had a good day unless I've talked with at least one new person. We have a meeting, make space for new people to come in. The   13

---

[3]Non-Commissioned Officer.

[4]Student Nonviolent Coordinating Committee.

[5]Office of Economic Opportunity.

[6]Richard Daley, Mayor of Chicago from 1955 to 1975.

organizer sits next to the new guy, so everybody has to take the new guy as an equal. You do that a couple of times and the guy's got strength enough to become part of one group.

You must listen to them and tell them again and again they are important, 14 that they have the stuff to do the job. They don't have to shuck themselves about not being good enough, not worthy. Most people were raised to think they are not worthy. School is a process of taking beautiful kids who are filled with life and beating them into happy slavery. That's as true of a twenty-five-thousand-dollar-a-year executive as it is for the poorest.

You don't find allies on the basis of the brotherhood of man. People are 15 tied into their immediate problems. They have a difficult time worrying about other people's. Our society is so structured that everybody is supposed to be selfish as hell and screw the other guy. Christian brotherhood is enlightened self-interest. Most sins committed on poor people are by people who've come to help them.

I came as a stranger but I came with credentials. There are people who 16 know and trust me, who say so to the others. So what I'm saying is verifiable. It's possible to win, to take an outfit like Bethlehem Steel and lick 'em. Most people in their guts don't really believe it. Gee, it's great when all of a sudden they realize it's possible. They become alive.

Nobody believed PCCA[7] could stop Bethlehem from strip mining. Ten 17 miles away was a hillside being stripped. Ten miles away is like ten million light years away. What they wanted was a park, a place for their kids. Bethlehem said, "Go to hell. You're just a bunch of crummy Appalachians. We're not gonna give you a damn thing." If I could get that park for them, they would believe it's possible to do other things.

They really needed a victory. They had lost over and over again, day after 18 day. So I got together twenty, thirty people I saw as leaders. I said, "Let's get that park." They said, "We can't." I said, "We can. If we let all the big wheels around the country know—the National Council of Churches and everybody start calling up, writing, and hounding Bethlehem, they'll have to give us the park." That's exactly what happened. Bethlehem thought: This is getting to be a pain in the ass. We'll give them the park and they'll shut up about strip mining. We haven't shut up on strip mining, but we got the park. Four thousand people for Pike County drove up and watched those bulldozers grading down that park. It was an incredible victory.

Twenty or thirty people realized we could win. Four thousand people 19 understood there was a victory. They didn't know how it happened, but a few of 'em got curious. The twenty or thirty are now in their own communities trying to turn people on.

We're trying to link up people in other parts of the state—Lexington, 20 Louisville, Covington, Bowling Green—and their local issues and, hopefully, bind them together in some kind of larger thing.

---

[7]Pike County Citizens' Association.

When you start talking to middle-class people in Lexington, the words are 21
different, but it's the same script. It's like taking a poor person in Pike County
or Mississippi. The schools are bad. Okay, they're bad for different reasons—
but the schools are bad.

The middle class is fighting powerlessness too. Middle-class women, who 22
are in the Lexington fight, are more alienated than lower-class women. The
poor woman knows she's essential for the family. The middle-class woman
thinks, If I die tomorrow, the old man can hire himself a maid to do everything
I do. The white-collar guy is scared he may be replaced by the computer. The
schoolteacher is asked not to teach but to baby-sit. God help you if you teach.
The minister is trapped by the congregation that's out of touch with him. He
spends his life violating the credo that led him into the ministry. The policeman has no relationship to the people he's supposed to protect. So he
oppresses. The fireman who wants to fight fires ends up fighting a war.

People become afraid of each other. They're convinced there's not a damn 23
thing they can do. I think we have it inside us to change things. We need the
courage. It's a scary thing. Because we've been told from the time we were
born that what we have inside us is bad and useless. What's true is what we
have inside us is good and useful.

In Mississippi, our group got the first black guy elected in a hundred 24
years. In San Francisco, our organization licked the development agency
there. We tied up two hundred million dollars of its money for two years, until
the bastards finally came to an agreement with the community people. The
guy I started with was an alcoholic pimp in the black ghetto. He is now a
Presbyterian minister and very highly respected.

I work all the way from two in the morning until two the next morning 25
seven days a week. (Laughs.) I'm not a martyr. I'm one of the few people I
know who was lucky in life to find out what he really wanted to do. I'm just
havin' a ball, the time of my life. I feel sorry for all these people I run across all
the time who aren't doing what they want to do. Their lives are hell. I think
everybody ought to quit their job and do what they want to do. You've got one
life. You've got, say, sixty-five years. How on earth can you blow forty-five
years of that doing something you hate?

I have a wife and three children. I've managed to support them for six 26
years doing this kind of work. We don't live fat. I have enough money to buy
books and records. The kids have as good an education as anybody in this
country. Their range of friends runs from millionaires in San Francisco to
black prostitutes in Lexington. They're comfortable with all these people. My
kids know the name of the game: living your life up to the end.

All human recorded history is about five thousand years old. How many 27
people in all that time have made an overwhelming difference? Twenty?
Thirty? Most of us spend our lives trying to achieve some things. But we're not
going to make an overwhelming difference. We do the best we can. That's
enough.

The problem with history is that it's written by college professors about 28
great men. That's not what history is. History's a hell of a lot of little people

getting together and deciding they want a better life for themselves and their kids.

I have a goal. I want to end my life in a home for the aged that's run by the state—organizing people to fight 'em because they're not running it right. (Laughs.)   29

RESPONDING TO THE READING

Freewriting

Exercise 15c.   Freewrite about the passages in this interview that interested, moved, or angered you in some way.

Building Your Vocabulary

VOCABULARY LIST

Words to Look Up	My Definition	Dictionary Definition
inarticulate (3)		
verifiable (16)		

Thinking about Words

Talcott says that his uncle "clipped coupons," but "if he tried to take part in the management of the companies whose coupons he was clipping, he got clipped." How is Talcott using the word *clipped* here?

Questions for Discussion

1. Terkel's interview with the organizer opens with a startling statement: "My work is to change this country." What does Talcott want to change? Briefly state what seems to have motivated Talcott to do this kind of work.
2. After reading Talcott's article, use your own words to write a definition of what an organizer does.
3. What has Talcott done to change things? What is your opinion of the changes he has made? What experiences have you had that helped to shape your opinion?
4. What difference does Talcott see between himself and other people and organizations that claim to help the poor? How do you explain his effectiveness?

5. Why do you think Talcott said, "If I were a black guy, I'd refuse to serve" [in the Army]?
6. What does Talcott mean when he says that "Christian brotherhood" in the U.S. means little more than "enlightened self-interest"? Do you agree with his criticism? Explain why you agree or disagree.

TOPICS FOR WRITING

Topic 1.   In paragraphs 11 through 21 Talcott explains what he did to organize the coal miners in Pike County, Kentucky. Write a summary of the stages he went through in this process. In your summary focus on what he does to bring people together and how he gains their confidence.

Topic 2.   Freewrite for several sessions about experiences in your life that either support or contradict Talcott's statements that "Most people were raised to think they are not worthy" and "School is a process of taking beautiful kids who are filled with life and beating them into happy slavery" (paragraph 14). Pick out the instances that you think will be the most promising for developing into a paper that either illustrates or contrasts with Talcott's ideas about the way children are raised.

Topic 3.   Talcott says "I'm one of the few people I know who was lucky in life to find out what he really wanted to do." He goes on to say, "I think everybody ought to quit their job and do what they want to do. You've got one life. You've got, say, sixty-five years. How on earth can you blow forty-five years of that doing something you hate?" Freewrite about these ideas. Do they make sense to you or not? Why in either case? What problems do you see in following Talcott's advice? How might these problems be overcome?

Topic 4.   Interview someone who has or used to have an interesting job. Develop a list of questions that will help you get information for your paper about this person's experience.

Jobs
Tran Thi Nga

The following poem appears in the collection of writings titled Shallow Graves: Two Women and Vietnam, *written in collaboration with Wendy Wilder Larson.*

> We took the jobs available.   *1*
> My son-in-law, who had a law degree,
> sold the Electrolux vacuum cleaner
> demonstrated door to door.

American people are afraid of Asians.   5
They would not let him in.

My sons worked as mechanics,
sold gasoline at night for extra money
until they were robbed.
My daughter worked in a training program   10
for a cosmetics company.
Bao and my sister started a small grocery store
near the university, selling notebooks, cigarettes,
cookies, ice cream, newspapers for the students.

My brother is an electrician.   15
My daughter-in-law stayed home
to cook and watch the babies.
We all studied English at night.
One of our friends in Saigon
was Chief Justice of the Supreme Court.   20
He was trained in France
spoke four languages.

He wrote me:
"I am a watchman in Houston.
When they hired me,   25
they felt uneasy with my title,
called me a telephone operator.
When anyone knocks on the door
of the company, I open it.
They call me a telephone operator,   30

but to tell you the truth,
I am a watchman."

From what I have seen in the States,
education means less than in my country.
There, if you are well educated,   35
you are sure of a high position and respect.
We say with the Chinese,
*"Learn to handle a writing brush
and you will not handle a begging bowl."*
Here a skilled worker makes a lot of money.   40
America is an industrial society.

RESPONDING TO THE READING

Freewriting

Exercise 15d.   Write about your initial reactions to several passages in this poem.

Exercise 15e.   Write a note to Tran Thi Nga explaining why her family has had difficulty finding jobs they were trained for in their country, and what you think they should do.

Questions for Discussion

1. Use your own words to restate this Chinese saying: "Learn to handle a writing brush / and you will not handle a begging bowl." How well does this idea fit the experience of Tran Thi Nga and her family?
2. Why did Tran's family have such a difficult time getting jobs that they were trained for—indeed, getting any jobs at all?
3. Tran says, "From what I have seen in the States / education means less than in my country." What is her evidence for making this statement? Do you agree with her conclusion? Why or why not?

TOPIC FOR WRITING

Topic 1.   Write a paper explaining whether or not Americans seem to value education. For evidence, draw on your own experience and interview family members, friends, teachers, or fellow students. Be sure to include examples of how education is or is not valued.

The Perfect Job
David Owen

David Owen wrote this humorous look at jobs for the Atlantic Monthly, *March 1990. He writes regularly for* The New Yorker *and is also the author of* The Walls Around Us *and* The Man Who Invented Saturday Morning.

The perfect job—the one you would have if you could have any job in the world—what would it be?   1

The most nearly perfect part of any less-than-perfect job is usually the   2 occasional hour in which you are able to pretend that you are doing the job when in fact you are reading a magazine and eating candy. The rest of the office is throbbing frantically, but you are sitting quietly at your desk and learning interesting facts about Fergie and that guy who put his wife in the wood chipper. The perfect job would feel like that, but all the time.

The trouble with less-than-perfect jobs is that they usually don't swoop 3 you up and fling you through your day. That is, you don't very often look up at the clock to find out how many minutes past eleven it is and discover that it's five and time to go home. That's what the perfect job would be like. The time would zoom by, the way it does when you are going through some old boxes and suddenly discover that they are filled with artifacts from the Pilgrim days.

Well, I've thought about this a lot (while I was supposed to be doing 4 something else), and I've narrowed down my choice of the perfect job to five possibilities:

- Doing an unbelievably great cleanup of my basement, and organizing 5 my workshop so that I know exactly where everything is, and drawing up a lot of plans to show how I might expand my workshop so that it would fill the entire basement instead of only the third that it fills now, and buying every conceivable kind of woodworking tool and finding exactly the perfect place to keep each one, but never actually getting around to doing any woodworking projects.
- Doing the *Times* crossword puzzle and watching MTV while listening to 6 people I knew in college discuss their marital problems on the other side of a one-way mirror.
- Sorting my children's vast Lego collection—by type, size, and color— 7 into muffin tins and other containers while my children nearby happily build small vehicles and structures without hitting each other or asking me for something to eat.
- Setting the prison sentences of criminals convicted in highly publicized 8 court cases; making all parole decisions for these people; receiving daily updates on how they spend their time in jail.
- Touring the houses of strangers and looking through their stuff while 9 they're not there. If I were driving along and happened to see a house that looked interesting, I could pull over and let myself in with a set of master keys. If the people happened to be there, I could spray them with a harmless paralyzing gas that would prevent them from remembering that I had read their diaries and checked to see whether they were making efficient use of their limited amount of storage space, which they probably wouldn't have been.

All these jobs, as I see them, would require a full complement of office 10 supplies: every conceivable kind of clip and clasp, name-brand ball-point pens, ungunked-up bottles of correction fluid, ammo-like refills for various desktop mechanisms, and cool, smooth, hard pads of narrow-lined paper. I guess I would also need a fax machine and a staff of cheerful recent college graduates eager to do my bidding. Plus a really great benefits program that would pay not only for doctors and prescription drugs but also for things like deodorant.

Recently I've begun to think that my *real* perfect job would probably con- 11
sist of all five of my *possible* perfect jobs, one for each weekday. That way I
would never have to lie awake at night wondering whether sorting my children's Legos would have made me happier than snooping through people's tax
returns. Then, on weekends, I could hang around my house, drinking beer and
watching golf tournaments on TV. I would seem to be having a really great
time, but in reality I would be counting the hours until Monday and just itch-
ing to get back to work.

RESPONDING TO THE READING

Freewriting

Exercise 15f.   Freewrite about an unforgettable job you've had; it may be
unforgettable because it was funny, boring, or horrible. Record what was
memorable about it.

Exercise 15g.   What is your idea of "the perfect job"? How does it compare
to David Owen's list of jobs he would like to have?

Building Your Vocabulary

VOCABULARY LIST

Words to Look Up	My Definition	Dictionary Definition
artifacts (3)		
complement (10)		

Questions for Discussion

1. Owen speculates that for most of his readers "the perfect part of any less-
   than-perfect job is usually the occasional hour in which [they] are able to
   pretend that [they] are doing the job when in fact [they] are reading a
   magazine and eating candy." Is there a grain of truth in what Owen says,
   or is this *nothing* like your idea of a perfect moment on the job?
2. Based on the information he gives and the attitude he projects, what can
   you conclude about the personality that David Owen assumes in writing
   this article? What do you think was his purpose in writing "The Perfect
   Job"?
3. Which of Owen's "jobs" seems most appealing? Least appealing? Explain
   your response.

TOPICS FOR WRITING

Topic 1. David Owen gives us a very different view of work than we are used to getting. After rereading his examples of "perfect jobs," determine the ways in which his "perfect jobs" are different from most jobs. Use specific examples of jobs you have had or know about to illustrate these differences.

Topic 2. Write a detailed account of a job that either "swoop[ed] you up and [flung] you through your day" so you hardly noticed that time had passed, or, on the other hand, dragged by so slowly that time seemed to stand still. Explain in detail why the job had the effect it had.

Topic 3. Write a paper in which you answer David Owen's question: "The perfect job . . . what would it be?" Consider Owen's idea that the perfect job would make time pass so quickly that you'd think it was just past eleven when you "discover that it's five and time to go home" (paragraph 3). You might reread the article to see what ideas it gives you and then ask yourself the following questions:

> How would I like to spend my day? What, exactly, would I be doing?
> What am I curious about? What do I hope to learn?
> Where would I work? What would the surroundings be like?
> Would I have any coworkers? What would they be like?

Consider making a visit to the career center on campus to survey job possibilities. When you get ready to write your paper, choose a "voice"—a tone you want to establish (serious, comic, or absurd). Maintain that tone throughout your paper as you illustrate your idea of "the perfect job."

Student Writing

Emergency Room

I work at Mercy General Hospital. I am an emergency room technician. My duties consist of assessing the patient's life history and chief complaint of illness; documenting blood pressure, temperature, and pulse rate; and assisting the doctors and nurses with resuscitating patients who have suffered cardiac arrest—a heart attack in layman's terms.

The emergency room is an in- and out-patient clinic for those people who feel they cannot wait for an appointment with their regular doctor and for trauma patients brought by ambulance to the emergency room. In the emergency room, I have been exposed to many situations that challenged my

knowledge of the human body and tested my patience and my desire to care
for sick people. At other times my experiences have overwhelmed my soul
with feelings of gratitude for being in such an occupation.

During emergency situations, I have assisted with procedures that have
given me a good understanding of the structure of the human body. For
instance, if a patient cannot be stabilized on our level of emergency care, we
cannot transport him to surgery. At this point, the attending cardiac surgeon
prepares for open heart surgery in the emergency room. He starts by cutting
the epidermis, or outer layer of skin, with a scalpel, and then while I suction
away blood and bits of loose skin with a long, plastic tube, he cuts the
exposed subdermal part of the skin. He then carves the fat away while cutting his way into the sternum and rib cage with a long-nosed tool that resembles a pair of bolt cutters. Shaping and twisting his way through the exposed
sternum, the surgeon reveals the thin lining of the pleural sac which covers
the heart and lungs. After cutting the thin sack, he grasps the unoxygenated,
bluish gray heart and starts to massage the flaccid organ while searching for
the right location to insert a pacemaker. Wiring and twisting in the pacemaker, the surgeon carefully sutures in the pacer like a mechanic tightening
a spark plug into a motor. After setting a rhythm for the pacer, he sutures
in long hooked tubings and attaches the patient to a life-support machine
until further surgery can be done. Although the physician is getting the glory
for his work, it is worthwhile just being there observing and learning.

When I work with patients in the emergency room who are conscious, I
have to be compassionate toward each one. However, I find it very difficult
to maintain my professionalism with especially difficult patients. For example, I once had to deal with a patient who was brought in for care because he
had fallen on broken glass while being arrested for public drunkenness. It
must have been 3:30 in the morning—my time for feeling grouchy—when the
nurse asked me to help her draw blood for an alcohol-level exam. The
patient—an irritable alcoholic—was being very uncooperative, and while he
resisted, he called me every filthy racial name he could think of. I patiently
explained that if he didn't cooperate, we would have no choice but to restrain
him with force. He then proceeded to spit on me, so I forced him onto a gur-
ney and stuffed a towel in his mouth while the nurses tied his hands to the
rail. I was later angry at myself, but I had no other alternative because we
had no time to waste. Those sorts of incidents make me want to get out of
this work altogether.

Fortunately, the rewarding experiences outweigh the unpleasant times.
Special holidays really touch me when I see patients having to be

hospitalized; I think of who might be in the waiting room anticipating good or bad news when they should be at home celebrating and rejoicing. For instance, a patient had stopped breathing at 11:30 P.M. one Christmas Eve. As I ran past the waiting room toward the patient, who had gone into cardiac arrest, I saw the family members pounding on the closed door, demanding to know what was wrong. One of the sobbing members of the family grabbed me, but I shrugged away and entered the room, committed to saving the woman's life. While assisting with artificial resuscitation, I looked down and noticed that this comatose woman was as old as my own grandmother. I felt a sense of sadness come over me as I repeated over and over in my head, "You have to make it! You have to make it!" I felt so helpless, knowing that this was all we could do for her and that at this point her survival would be determined by fate alone. By 11:59 we had no rhythm and at 12:00 A.M. the physician called off the artificial support and drugs that were being pumped into her heart. Several seconds later, she miraculously produced a rhythm on her own and at that moment the puzzled doctor ordered the drugs and life support to be continued and asked the surgery room to prepare for an emergency bypass. While washing up, I wondered if I had just witnessed an act of God; after all, it was Christmas morning. Why couldn't it have been?

Throughout the emotional stress and thankless moments of working in a hospital, the true meaning of gratitude comes at the end of a shift when I go home with more knowledge and understanding of the human body, or when the alcoholic nods a thank you on his way out the door, or when I see the smiles and dried tears of the family that was able to enjoy life with their grandmother through one more Christmas.

—Ernesto Morales

Questions for Discussion

1. What experiences of working in a hospital does Morales emphasize? How do they compare to your own ideas about hospitals?
2. How would you react if you were placed in each of the situations that Morales describes?

More Student Writing

Gloria Moulder wrote the following essay after gathering information about the experiences of female police officers from books, magazines, journals, and personal interviews. The sources she refers to in her essay are listed under "Works Cited" at the end of her paper. After each piece of information she uses, Moulder encloses in parentheses the name of the author of the article or

book and the page number where she found the information. She omits page
references if her information came from an interview. When she mentions the
author elsewhere in her paragraph, she puts only the page number of the reference in parentheses.

Women in Law Enforcement

For many years women have been working in police departments as secretaries and dispatchers. With the advent of Affirmative Action and the hope
of equal opportunity for women in the workforce, some women who are
already employees of police departments, as well as applicants from outside
departments, want to become police officers. But women who choose this profession face strong opposition from various sources. Administrators, for
example, are apt to encourage women to stay in their traditional roles. Male
officers often believe that women are incapable of performing the duties of a
police officer. But the most strident protests may come from family members
who find it difficult to accept a female family member as a police officer.

Women began looking for careers as police officers in the early part of
this century. In a study conducted for the California Command College,
Robert G. Norman reports:

> Historically, police departments began hiring women officers for
> specialized duties early in this century—the most memorable being
> Mrs. Alice Stebbins Wells with the Los Angeles Police Department in
> 1910—yet full integration into the service did not occur until the
> 1970s (62).

Although police departments sometimes allowed an exceptional woman to join
the force, few women actually became officers until departments were legally
required to provide them equal access to jobs. The 1972 Equal Employment
Opportunity Act and the Crime Control Act of 1973 meant that women could
no longer be denied jobs as police officers on the basis of their gender
(Norman 62).

Passing laws to ensure equal hiring does not necessarily mean that police
departments can suddenly achieve gender equity and employ an equal number of women as men. As late as 1987, fifteen years after the Civil Rights
Act became law, Robert Norman reported that in California, a progressive
state in these matters, only 10% of the police officers were women. Women
compose about 51% of the state's population. The discouraging news for
women is that only 64, or 1.6%, held any of the 4,000 managerial positions

(63). The situation for women in the Denver police force looks even worse. In June 1987, 8% of that city's police officers were women, and only one of the 160 detectives was a woman (Blair 56). The research team of Rebecca Warner and Brent Steel predict that nationwide, the most women can hope for is that by the turn of the century they will hold 10 to 15% of the jobs as police officers and only 5% of the administrative positions (300).

Why does the situation look so grim for women who choose careers in law enforcement? Probably the most obvious obstacle is the attitude of their male counterparts. Women who apply for jobs as police officers face the stereotypical view that women are too fragile and helpless to make good police officers. This view has been perpetuated by managers and police officers alike. Studies conducted in the late 1950s and early '80s show little change in attitudes toward women held by male officers and administrators. Women who tried to advance from secretary or dispatcher were accused of being "unwomanly," physically weak, or "emotionally unstable." Their most strident critics declared that women are "'dangerous to the lives of police officers and the public at large'" (Warner 296). One female officer who found fellow officers hostile, reported that men made it clear to her that a man should have been hired in her place. They let her know their feelings by calling her "Trixie," a pet name usually reserved for prostitutes. "Every time I came into a room where more than one male officer was gathered, they started telling dirty jokes or talking about how stupid women are" (Presler). Scenes like these are repeated all over the country. One male administrator admitted that "'If a woman officer went out tomorrow and saved six male officers' lives, the men would call her a superwoman, but it wouldn't change many attitudes'" ("Women Cops" 58).

In some cases, reluctance to give women the training that male officers receive has the effect of reinforcing the stereotypes about women as weaklings and ineffectual members of the force. Sociologist Patricia Weiser Remmington reports that the female officers she studied in 1980 "were not trained in the martial arts or encouraged to handle tough assignments" ("Women Cops" 58). This lack of training and encouragement left them feeling unprepared for potentially violent situations. As a result, they went out of their way to avoid confrontation and "sometimes deliberately drove slowly to a potentially violent call" (58). Even tougher women, like Barbara Schein, who entered the New Jersey City Police Department after twenty years of trying, can experience terrible isolation. The only female in her class at the police academy, Schein found herself alone much of the time: "I had to change in the women's bathroom, while everyone else just changed right there in the gym. . . . I ran alone and ate lunch by myself" (Abrahams 140).

In such a male-dominated, sometimes hostile, field, family support is crucial for the women who choose a career in law enforcement. All too often, however, women meet opposition rather than enthusiasm when they announce their choice of careers. Frank Harris, for example, admitted that while he could support the idea of women becoming police officers, he could not accept his little sister's decision to become one. In an effort to talk Karen Harris out of her decision, Frank tried to frighten her by asking, "How many men would want to say they were dating a cop?" (7). While it is understandable that family members wouldn't want their loved ones choosing such a dangerous career, they are more likely to think a son but not a daughter is capable of managing confrontations. Wendy Ridley, for example, has a brother who became a detective with a local police force with only minor protests from his father. When Wendy announced that she had been accepted into an junior training program with the same department, her father flatly refused to let her participate. He felt that his son could take care of himself, but his daughter would always need to be protected (Ridley).

The irony is that women are perfectly capable of completing the difficult training required by police academies. Moreover, they have skills that are proving valuable in police work. Barbara Schein, for example, completed an obstacle course with a few cracked ribs but said nothing because "'If they saw you in pain,' she figured, 'you'd be out.'" (Abrahams 140). Several studies have shown that women perform their duties as police officers as competently as do their fellow male officers[1] (Norman 65). Women are also generally skillful negotiators. A Time magazine article entitled "Women Cops on the Beat" points out that "they are better than men in talking people out of violence." In a rather backhanded comment, Police Sergeant Earl Sargent quips, "'Just as you don't have to teach a man how to fight . . . you don't have to teach a woman how to talk'" (58).

Unjust though it may be, it is likely that women in law enforcement will continue to face opposition from members of the institution they serve and from family members, especially fathers and brothers. As in any male-dominated profession that pays well and carries prestige, women will have to endure at least some harassment if they want to break into the profession. With time, sensitive media reporting, and the appearance of positive images of female officers like those on the old Hill Street Blues series, women and men will one day work together as equals.

—Gloria Moulder

---

[1] Norman cites studies by Block and Anderson, 1974; Sherman, 1975; California Highway Patrol, 1975; Bartlett and Rosenblum, 1977; and Sichel, 1978.

Works Cited

Abrahams, Andrew. "Barbara Schein Finally Gets a Shot at Walking the Beat." People 4 May 1987: 139–40.

Blair, Gwenda. "The Case of the Ski-Mask Rapist." Woman's Day. 1 June 1987: 56–61.

Harris, Frank. "My Sister, the Cop" Essence July 1989: 6–7.

Norman, Robert H. "Women Peace Officers: Law Enforcement's Resource of the Future". Journal of California Law Enforcement 23 (1989): 62–66.

Presler, Viola. Telephone interview. 1 December 1990.

Ridley, Wendy. Personal interview. 28 November 1990.

Warner, Rebecca L., and Brent S. Steel. "Affirmative Action in Times of Fiscal Stress and Changing Value Priorities: The Case of Women in Policing." Public Personnel Management 18 (1989): 192–307.

"Women Cops on the Beat." Time 10 March 1989: 58.

Questions for Discussion

1. Identify elements of causal analysis and problem solving in Gloria Moulder's essay.
2. Does Moulder make points that are well-supported? What ideas might be strengthened?
3. Are the arguments in "Women in Law Enforcement" organized well or might paragraphs be arranged more effectively?
4. Has gender equity been a problem at places where you have worked?

Getting an Education

The challenge facing America will be the shaping of a truly common public culture, one responsive to the long-silenced cultures of color.

—Henry Louis Gates, Jr.

It is necessary to place Western civilization and the culture to which it has given rise at the center of our studies, and we fail to do so at the peril of our students, country, and the hopes for a democratic, liberal society.

—Donald Kagan

Lhe readings in this chapter explore a variety of points of view on getting an education. In "The Struggle to Be an All-American Girl," Elizabeth Wong describes how she felt about her life as a student in a Chinese school in Chinatown and in an American public school. David Pierpont Gardner discusses what schools have done, are doing, and should do to educate our children. Langston Hughes finds common experiences and economic differences between he and his white teacher and classmates in "Theme for English B." In "Whose Culture Is It, Anyway?" Henry Louis Gates, Jr. and Donald Kagan offer their ideas about what should be taught in our schools.

This chapter also discusses techniques for drawing inferences based on careful observation of details and illustrates how writers use inductive and deductive reasoning to structure their arguments. "The Struggle to Be an All-American Girl" provides the model for drawing inferences from what you read. David Gardner's article, "If We Stand, They Will Deliver," offers examples of inductive reasoning, or basing conclusions on information and observations, and deductive reasoning, drawing conclusions based on a premise or assumption.

DRAWING INFERENCES

The practice you receive in this chapter in drawing inferences should help you with the complex inferential reasoning required for such writing strategies as causal analysis (Chapter 12), evaluating (Chapter 14), and problem solving (Chapter 15). The first step is to clarify what we mean by observations and inferences. Additional discussion shows you how to make careful observations about what you see and what you read in order to draw sound conclusions from factual evidence.

Observations that you might use in your writing are always based on details and factual information about which there can be little debate. If, for example, you are walking down the street at 9 A.M. on a weekday, and you decide to record your observations of a woman who is walking toward you, you might list the following details:

1. A woman is walking toward me.
2. She glances at buildings and other people as she walks.
3. She is wearing shorts and a T-shirt.
4. She smiles at me as she passes by.

Any two people could make and record these observations, and agree on their validity.

Inferences, by contrast, are conclusions that you draw based on the factual information you have at hand. In the example of the woman walking down the street, you might conclude from fact 3 that she is dressed too casually to be on her way to work. You might also conclude that because she takes the time to look at the buildings and people around her, she may be from out of town, and is, perhaps, a tourist on vacation. Because she smiles at you as she passes, you may infer that she is an open and friendly person. Your inference that she is friendly is reinforced by the idea that she is on vacation and is having a good time. These are plausible conclusions based on your observations about the woman. To ensure that your reasoning is as sound as it can be, your inferences should be directly connected to the details and facts you observe.

Making observations about photographs is an especially useful way of practicing inferential thinking because, unlike the details in written language, the details in photographs are visual and, therefore, easier to discover. When making observations about a photograph, you will want to study the photo for a few minutes; observe it systematically, scanning from left to right, top to bottom, or edge to center; and notice any people, animals, or objects you see. Ask yourself questions about what you are seeing: what kind of clothing are the people wearing? what are they doing? what are their facial expressions? how are they interacting? To practice thinking inferentially, use a T-graph and record details you observe about a photo in the left-hand column, leaving the column on the right for inferences. If you are working with a partner or doing an exercise like this in class, compare your list of observations with those of your classmates to be sure you have recorded all the important details. Once you have a complete list of details, fill in the right side of the T-graph by asking yourself what inferences you can draw that match the details you have listed in the left-hand column.

Sample T-Graph

Look carefully at the photograph of a man and a young boy on bicycles that appears on page 420. Details and inferences that we might draw from the photograph are listed in the following T-graph. Next, practice drawing inferences in Exercises 16a and 16b.

Details	Inferences
A little boy and a man are riding their bicycles.	
The little boy is following closely behind the man.	The man is probably the little boy's father or guardian.
Both are wearing helmets.	
Both are wearing long-sleeved shirts.	
The man is looking at the road ahead.	
His face is relaxed; he has a half-smile on his face.	The man is pleased with his son's progress.
The little boy is also looking ahead; his lips are pressed firmly together.	The little boy is working hard to keep up with his father.

FOR PRACTICE

Exercise 16a.   Take at least five minutes to study one of the photographs that appears at the beginning of each chapter in Part Two. Then, in your note-book or journal, make an initial list of all the details you find. Once you complete your list, draw a T-graph and include the most important details in the left-hand column. To the right, list inferences or conclusions you reached based on these details. After completing your lists, write a paragraph in which you describe this photograph for someone who has not seen it.

Exercise 16b.   Choose two additional photographs from among those that appear at the beginning of the chapters in Part Two and apply the steps for drawing inferences discussed above. Don't forget to study each photograph, list details, and connect inferences to details. Write a journal entry in which you discuss which of these photographs is the most thought-provoking. Explain your choice.

Drawing Inferences from Details in Your Reading

Many of the critical thinking tasks you face in college will require you to pick out details, draw conclusions or inferences, and respond to them in some way.

Your technique for gathering information from written material is much the same as the technique you use when observing details in photographs—your inferences are based on the factual information you have read. Here again, your conclusions will be plausible if they are directly connected to the details and facts you can point to in the text.

We can put these ideas into practice by looking at passages from Elizabeth Wong's essay, "The Struggle to Be an All-American Girl." A careful reading of the sights and smells that Wong associates with the Chinese school she attended helps us infer her attitude toward that school. Her description of the walk to school and her impressions of the principal and the auditorium where she had her Chinese classes appear early in her essay:

> Forcibly, she [her mother] walked us the seven long, hilly 3
> blocks from our home to school, depositing our defiant, tearful
> faces before the stern principal. My only memory of him is that he
> swayed on his heels like a palm tree, and he always clasped his
> impatient, twitching hands behind his back. I recognized him as a
> repressed maniacal child killer, and knew that if we ever saw his
> hands, we'd be in big trouble.
>
> We all sat in little chairs in an empty auditorium. The room 4
> smelled like Chinese medicine, an imported, faraway mustiness.
> Like ancient mothballs or dusty closets. I hated that smell. . . .
> There was a stage far to the right, flanked by an American flag and
> the flag of the National Republic of China, which was also red,
> white, and blue, but not as pretty.

The details Wong includes in her descriptions allow us to draw a number of inferences. The children's tears and defiance when their mother forces them to walk the "seven long, hilly blocks" to school show how much they hate attending Chinese school. Going to the school is a punishment for them, and the "stern principal" who meets them is like an extension of their mother's harshness. Wong remembers the principal's "impatient, twitching hands [clasped] behind his back" and how she thought of him as "a repressed maniacal child killer." As a child, she concluded that "if we ever saw his hands, we'd be in big trouble." From these details and the judgment Wong made of the principal we can infer that she was terrified of him. Her description of his hands conveys her irrational fear that he is a crazed killer of children. We can conclude that for Wong, having to go to Chinese school was like being threatened with murder.

Wong also remembers that in their makeshift school the students "sat in little chairs in an empty auditorium." The contrast between the size of the chairs and the unfilled auditorium suggests how small and alone Wong felt. The building did not seem child-sized at all to her and, like the principal, it was intimidating.

The sense of smell dominates the rest of Wong's descriptions of the Chinese school and the American public school she attended as well. She tells us that at the Chinese school "the [auditorium] smelled like Chinese medicine, an imported faraway mustiness." Wong associates the Chinese school with the smell of medicine, which no child likes to take. She suggests that the school itself is like some awful medicine that is being forced upon her and the other children. The room's "faraway" smell equates it with the distant culture of China and also suggests that the children's Chinese heritage is far away in the sense that they do not see it as relevant to their lives in the United States. The comparison Wong makes between the smell of the room and "ancient moth-balls" is also appropriate because it makes a connection between ancient Chinese tradition and the smell of mothballs, as though that tradition were safe from moths or anything else that might devour it; at the same time Wong associates it with the unpleasant smell of old clothes kept in mothballs. With a second comparison to "dusty closets," a smell she hates, Wong again suggests that like the closet, the tradition is dusty and old. We might also remember that Wong was just a child when she attended this school and as a child, she was new to the world as well as being in a country that was new to her and her family. The old ways were bound to feel alien to someone ready to experience "crisp, new scents." The exotic "soft French perfume" of her public school teacher captures her romantic attitude toward the Anglo-European tradition she wants to adopt.

Exercise 16c.   Read one of the essays in this chapter or in Chapter 9. Select a passage that you think would be a good one to use for practice at drawing inferences, and using the discussion of Elizabeth Wong's essay in the preceding section as an example, explain what the details suggest in the passage you selected.

Now, as you read the entire text of Elizabeth Wong's essay, "The Struggle to Be an All-American Girl," look for more details that reinforce the inferences we have already made about her experiences as a child living in Chinatown.

The Struggle to Be an All-American Girl
Elizabeth Wong

Elizabeth Wong is a playwright currently living and working in New York. She wrote these memories of her childhood for the Los Angeles Times.

It's still there; the Chinese school on Yale Street where my brother and I   1
used to go. Despite the new coat of paint and the high wire fence, the school I knew ten years ago remains remarkably, stoically the same.

Every day at 5 P.M., instead of playing with our fourth- and fifth-grade   2
friends or sneaking out to the empty lot to hunt ghosts and animal bones, my brother and I had to go to Chinese school. No amount of kicking, screaming, or pleading could dissuade my mother, who was solidly determined to have us learn the language of our heritage.

Forcibly, she walked us the seven long, hilly blocks from our home to   3
school, depositing our defiant, tearful faces before the stern principal. My only
memory of him is that he swayed on his heels like a palm tree, and he always
clasped his impatient, twitching hands behind his back. I recognized him as a
repressed maniacal child killer, and knew that if we every saw his hands, we'd
be in big trouble.

We all sat in little chairs in an empty auditorium. The room smelled like   4
Chinese medicine, an imported faraway mustiness. Like ancient mothballs or
dusty closets. I hated that smell. I favored crisp new scents. Like the soft
French perfume that my American teacher wore in public school.

There was a stage far to the right, flanked by an American flag and the flag   5
of the Nationalist Republic of China, which was also red, white, and blue, but
not as pretty.

Although the emphasis at the school was mainly language—speaking,   6
reading, writing—the lessons always began with an exercise in politeness.
With the entrance of the teacher, the best student would tap a bell and everyone would get up, kowtow, and chant, "*Sing sun ho,*" the phonetic for "How
are you, teacher?"

Being ten years old, I had better things to learn than ideographs copied   7
painstakingly in lines that ran right to left from the tip of a *moc but,* a real ink
pen that had to be held in an awkward way if blotches were to be avoided.
After all, I could do the multiplication tables, name the satellites of Mars, and
write reports on *Little Women* and *Black Beauty.* Nancy Drew, my favorite
book heroine, never spoke Chinese.

The language was a source of embarrassment. More times than not, I had   8
tried to dissociate myself from the nagging, loud voice that followed me wherever I wandered in the nearby American supermarket outside Chinatown. The
voice belonged to my grandmother, a fragile woman in her seventies, who
could outshout the best of the street vendors. Her humor was raunchy, her
Chinese rhythmless, patternless. It was quick, it was loud, it was unbeautiful.
It was not like the quiet, lilting romance of French or the gentle refinement of
the American. South Chinese sounded pedestrian. Public.

In Chinatown, the comings and goings of hundreds of Chinese on their   9
daily tasks sounded chaotic and frenzied. I did not want to be thought of as
mad, as talking gibberish. When I spoke English, people nodded at me, smiled
sweetly, said encouraging words. Even the people in my culture would cluck
and say that I'd do well in life. "My, doesn't she move her lips fast," they'd say,
meaning that I'd be able to keep up with the world outside Chinatown.

My brother was even more fanatical than I about speaking English. He   10
was especially hard on my mother, criticizing her, often cruelly, for her pidgin
speech—smatterings of Chinese scattered like chop suey in her conversation.
"It's not 'What it is,' Mom," he'd say in exasperation. "It's 'What *is,* what *is,*
what *is!*'" Sometimes, Mom might leave out an occasional "the" or "a," or perhaps a verb of being. He would stop her in mid-sentence: "Say it again, Mom.
Say it right." When he tripped over his own tongue, he'd blame it on her: "See,
Mom, it's all your fault. You set a bad example."

What infuriated my mother most was when my brother cornered her on 11
her consonants, especially *r*. My father had played a cruel joke on Mom by
assigning her an American name that her tongue wouldn't allow her to say. No
matter how hard she tried, "Ruth" always ended up "Luth" or "Roof."

After two years of writing with a *moc but* and reciting words with multi- 12
ples of meanings, I finally was granted a cultural divorce. I was permitted to
stop Chinese school.

I thought of myself as multicultural. I preferred tacos to egg rolls; I 13
enjoyed Cinco de Mayo more than Chinese New Year.

At last, I was one of you; I wasn't one of them. 14

Sadly, I still am. 15

RESPONDING TO THE READING

Freewriting

Exercise 16d.   Freewrite about a "cultural divorce" or rejection of values
or cultural practices that you have experienced.

Exercise 16e.   Freewrite about teachers you have had who are similar to
either the "child-killer" principal or the perfumed American teacher in Wong's
essay.

Building Your Vocabulary

VOCABULARY LIST

Words to Look Up	My Definition	Dictionary Definition
stoically (1)		
dissuade (2)		
forcibly (3)		
flanked (5)		
kowtow (6)		
dissociate (8)		
raunchy (8)		
lilting (8)		
pidgin (10)		
exasperation (10)		
infuriated (11)		

Questions for Discussion

1. What is gained and what is lost in the process of Americanization that
    Elizabeth Wong describes?

2. What does Wong mean when she says she was granted a "cultural divorce" (paragraph 12)? Do you think this was a positive separation? Why or why not?
3. What does Wong consider her identity now, if not strictly Chinese? How is it like or unlike your own?
4. How do you explain the sadness she expresses in the last line of her article? What is the effect of adding this line to the narrative?

TOPICS FOR WRITING

Topic 1.   Write a paper in which you explain under what circumstances, if any, children should be forced to do things they don't want to do, as Wong was forced to go to Chinese school in the hopes of preserving the family's Chinese heritage in America. Some of the topics you might consider include taking music lessons, playing in organized sports like little league, and attending religious or language schools. To gather information for this paper, consider interviewing members of your family, friends, or students in other classes whose opinions you value.

Topic 2.   We all enjoy feeling that we "belong" to certain groups as well as to the larger culture around us. But as Wong points out, assimilation may bring unforeseen costs. What, in your experience, are the costs of "belonging"? The advantages? Do some freewriting about your own experience and observations to gather information. You might also interview people to draw on their experiences.

Topic 3.   Write an essay explaining the similarities and differences between Elizabeth Wong's early schooling and your own. Compare or contrast your teachers, your after-school activities, your parents' attitudes, or the atmosphere of the schools you attended with Wong's experiences.

INDUCTIVE REASONING

If you have worked through the discussion on drawing inferences at the beginning of this chapter, you are ready to examine **inductive reasoning** in writers' works. When writers reveal to their readers how facts, examples, case studies, personal experience, observations, statistics, data from surveys, or expert testimony led them to reach a particular conclusion, they are writing inductively.

In his article, "If We Stand, They Will Deliver," David Pierpont Gardner examines evidence that led he and the co-authors of "A Nation At Risk," a report issued by the U.S. Department of Education, to conclude that if schools are not improved the middle class may demand that public funds be used to finance private as well as public schools. He relies on statistics, a case study, and facts to support the idea that students are not receiving an adequate education. In the third paragraph of his article, Gardner says that scores on Scholastic Aptitude tests taken from 1963 to 1980 fell steadily:

> Average verbal scores fell over 50 points and mathematics scores dropped nearly 40 points. Nearly 40 percent [of the 17-year-olds who took the test] could not draw inferences from written material, only one-fifth could write a persuasive essay and only one-third could solve a math problem requiring several steps.

The increasingly poor performance during this 17-year period forms the basis of Gardner's inference that the students who took these tests in 1980 "did not possess the higher intellectual skills they needed."

Gardner and other members of the commission responsible for the report "A Nation At Risk" studied the courses of study at several high schools in New England and concluded from these **case studies** that "the curriculum had been diluted over time." He then explains how the commission's analysis led to this conclusion. For one thing, by examining students' transcripts, the commission found that the courses students took did not appear to be guided by a clear goal: "Schools made little distinction between the significance of a course in bachelor living compared with one in English composition." The kinds of classes students took also revealed that "the proportion of graduating students who had taken a general course of study—neither college preparatory nor vocational—had increased from 12 percent in 1964 to 42 percent in 1979." This **statistic** supports Gardner's claim that the college curriculum was watered down between 1963 and 1980. Finally, Gardner paraphrases Tom Wicker, an editor for *The New York Times*, to add the opinion of an **expert:** "We had been expecting less of our students and they had been giving it to us." In addition, Gardner opens his essay with the **testimony** of former Secretary of Education Terrell Bell to emphasize the risk that public schools will face if we do not work to improve them. As former President of the University of California and chair of the National Commission on Excellence in Education, Gardner is himself an expert on the subject of education and what needs to be done to better prepare students for higher education or for vocational careers.

Gardner refers to a **fact** in paragraph 5 to underscore another problem that may have contributed to the poor achievement of our high school students in recent years. Students in the United States, he informs us, spend an average of 180 days in school each year as compared to other industrial counties where students are required to be in school 200 to 220 days. This disadvantage is compounded by the fact that school days are shorter in this country than they are in other industrialized countries.

FOR PRACTICE

Why do you think Gardner chose not to include data to support his claim that American students spend fewer hours a day in school than do students in industrialized countries? Would his point have been more convincing if he had?

Chapter 16 • *Getting an Education*   **427**

DEDUCTIVE REASONING

Unlike inductive reasoning, characterized by presenting evidence for the conclusions drawn, **deductive reasoning** follows a series of conclusions based on a general statement or assumption. Usually the general statements that provide the foundation for the writer's conclusions have come from an inductive process that the writer may not state. For example, David Gardner argues deductively in paragraph 9:

> Clearly, if the influence of the home is either hostile or contrary to what the school is attempting to accomplish, the home influence will, over time, tend to overpower the school, not the other way around—notable exceptions notwithstanding.

Gardner's chain of reasoning can be rewritten in the three-part pattern characteristic of deductive logic:

1. Because the influence of the home is stronger than that of the school;
2. When the influence of the home is hostile or contrary to what the school is attempting to accomplish;
3. The home influence will, over time, overpower the school's influence.

The conclusion in the third statement is based on the assumption that what happens to a child at home is more important than what happens to the student at school. Even though Gardner does not state that assumption, the idea is implied in his argument. If the reader does not accept Gardner's premise that what happens to children at home has a stronger influence on them than what happens at school, the reader will not find the argument convincing.

Unlike the inductive technique Gardner uses elsewhere in his article, this deductive reasoning does not mention the evidence he uses to arrive at the conclusion in statement 3. Instead, he relies on the reader's acceptance of the first statement, called the "major premise" in formal logic; the other two statements, the "minor premise" and "conclusion," follow logically from the first statement.

FOR PRACTICE

What is the assumption or major premise behind Gardner's statement "If we expect much of them [students] they will give us much in return"?

Some deductive arguments appear in one or more series of ideas connected logically. We find two such logical chains in Gardner's argument:

> If at home or in the community the work of the school is regarded with indifference, then whatever the level of dedication, commitment and ability possessed by the teachers, the salvage rate will be low. In contrast, if students come principally from homes where

there are books, a respect for education and learning, and reason-able expectations about how students spend their time, the salvage rate will be much higher.

Both conclusions—the salvage rate will be low or high depending on parental or community interest in learning—are based on Gardner's earlier premise that the influence of the home determines how well a child does in school. Once again, this argument can be written in a deductive format, this time with the same premise used above followed by two other conditions and a conclusion:

1. Because the influence of the home is stronger than that of the school;
2. When the work of the school is regarded with indifference at home or in the community;
3. It doesn't matter whether the teachers are dedicated, committed, and effective (because)
4. The salvage rate will be low anyway.

Gardner adds a second chain of reasoning in contrast to the reasoning above.

1. Because the influence of the home is stronger than that of the school;
2. When students come principally from homes where there are books, a respect for education and learning, and reasonable expectations about how students spend their time;
3. The salvage rate will be much higher.

Whether the reader accepts the premise of an argument has to do with the reader's own experience, observations, reading, and outside information. For this reason, writers who use deductive logic run the risk that their premise, and hence the argument as a whole, will not be accepted as true.

FOR PRACTICE

For a deductive argument to be convincing, the reader must accept the writer's initial assumption. Examine Gardner's premise that the parents and community's attitude toward school affects whether a student will do well in the classroom. Use your own experience and observations to decide whether this statement is true or false. Be sure you have enough appropriate examples to make your own position convincing.

If We Stand, They Will Deliver
David Pierpont Gardner

In the following article published in 1990, David Gardner comments on the state of education in 1983, the year he helped write "A Nation At Risk." He also outlines improvements that have been made in the seven years since the report was published

and identifies issues that have not been addressed. Gardner is past President of the
University of California. He chaired the U.S. Department of Education's Commission on
Excellence, which published "A Nation At Risk."

When then-Secretary of Education Terrell Bell asked me to chair the National 1
Commission on Excellence in Education, his plea was, in effect, that "We have one
last chance to set things right. If we fail to engage the active support and involvement of middle-class America in improving our schools, they will withdraw their
support from the public schools." The consequence, he believed, was that there
would be a demand for changes in the tax laws facilitating a major shift in students from public to private education, leaving only the poor and a dispropor-
tionate share of minorities in poorly-supported public schools. This would stratify
our society, he was convinced, in ways hurtful to the nation's well-being and the
future economic, social, and political strength of our country.

In response to this concern, we issued a call for reform entitled, "A Nation 2
At Risk." Although the response to the Commission's report has been more
encouraging than discouraging, the risk still remains today. As a matter of fact,
in absolute terms of comparative performance scores with other advanced
industrial nations, we are worse off today than we were in 1980.

The Way We Were

The indicators of risk we found in 1980 were truly alarming. The College 3
Board's Scholastic Aptitude Test (SAT) scores showed a virtually unbroken
decline since 1963. Average verbal scores had fallen over 50 points and math-
ematics scores dropped nearly 40 points. Many 17-year-olds did not possess
the higher intellectual skills they needed. Nearly 40 percent could not draw
inferences from written material, only one-fifth could write a persuasive essay
and only one-third could solve a math problem requiring several steps.

In preparing "A Nation At Risk," we studied transcripts of students from 4
the New England states who completed high school between 1964 and 1981.
What we found was that the curriculum had been diluted over time; the core
had been weakened and the peripheral had ascended; and academic and intellectual expectations had deteriorated. It was not obvious which courses in the
high-school curriculum were intended to be appetizers and desserts and
which were intended to be the main course: Schools made little distinction
between the significance of a course in bachelor living compared with one in
English composition. The proportion of graduating students who had taken a
general course of study—neither college preparatory nor vocational—had
increased from 12 percent in 1964 to 42 percent in 1979. Moreover, during
this same period of time, grade point averages increased while performance
declined. As Tom Wicker put it in *The New York Times*, we had been expecting
less of our students and they had been giving it to us.

Further, we had, and still have, fewer school days in the year than any 5
other advanced industrial country in the world—180 on average, whereas the
average for the advanced industrial countries ranges between 200 and 220.

Moreover, the average school day had shortened relative to other advanced industrial countries. In brief, we were spending less time in school and what time we were spending was focused on a diluted curriculum further weakened by diminished academic and intellectual expectations.

The Way We Are

In many respects, the general response to the call of "A Nation At Risk" has 6 been encouraging. Since the report was issued in 1983, there has been a sig- nificant increase in the number of college students who have chosen teaching as their profession, and they are, on average, better prepared and drawn from a more promising portion of the undergraduate student body than has been true for many years. In real terms, teacher compensation has risen nearly 20 percent since 1981 and is as high now as it has been, on average, in the U.S. for 30 years. A number of able and committed governors, including Bill Kean in New Jersey, Bill Clinton in Arkansas, and Lamar Alexander in Tennessee took the lead in school reform in their states. And the business community has finally interested itself in educational reform, though it is not altogether cer- tain about how best to respond.

Since the Commission's report was issued, it has also been encouraging to 7 note a significant increase in the percentage of students taking more demand- ing courses as suggested in "A Nation at Risk"—what we called the "New Basics." More than 40 states increased the requirements for high-school grad- uation. A significantly smaller proportion of students today are in a "general track" program, and a much larger proportion are in college preparatory or vocational programs. SAT and ACT scores rose from the early to mid-1980s, though they have since plateaued. And there have been even more substantive improvements in the test scores of minority students, especially blacks. But we still have a very long way to go.

The Way We Should Be

At the end of "A Nation At Risk," there is a small section entitled "A Word to 8 Parents." While parents have a right to demand for their children the best our schools and colleges can provide, we also said that this right carries a double responsibility: "You must be a living example of what you expect your chil- dren to honor and to emulate [and] you bear a responsibility to participate actively in your child's education."

If I were issuing "A Nation At Risk" today, I would write a much more 9 extended letter to parents and move it more to the front of the report. Clearly, if the influence of the home is either hostile or contrary to what the school is attempting to accomplish, the home influence will, over time, tend to overpower the school, not the other way around—notable exceptions notwithstanding.

Indeed, as it now stands, our classrooms tend to reflect conditions prevailing 10 in the larger society, e.g., the disintegration of the nuclear family, the high degree of mobility—and sometimes rootlessness—that characterizes our society, and the erosion of community life. It is not easy for teachers to motivate students to learn if learning is not respected in the home. If at home or in the community the work of the school is regarded with indifference, then whatever the level of dedication, commitment and ability possessed by the teachers, the salvage rate will be low.

In contrast, if students come principally from homes where there are **11** books, a respect for education and learning, and reasonable expectations about how students spend their time, the salvage rate will be much higher. Although students from these different home environments may have equal opportunity on paper, or under the law, there is no equality in reality. Schools cannot solve these problems alone, nor should they be expected to. The failures and shortcomings of our society cannot be placed at the doorstep of the nation's schools. They have a role to play, but they cannot play it on a field where only the schools have fielded a team.

In Japan, the average class size is 37 while ours is 24. One reason the **12** Japanese can teach 37 students and attain a higher level of performance than here is because there is more respect for the school and the teacher in Japan than is true in this country. There is both societal and parental support for schooling in Japan, and neither the home nor the school would be willing to tolerate or accommodate the disruptions and disciplinary problems that disproportionately occupy the time and attention of our teachers and hinder the average student's opportunity to learn.

The expectations we have of our students is also a crucial factor. What **13** message have we been giving our students over the years as their grades have risen and their performance has fallen? The question is rhetorical. As with our children, we do our students no favor by expecting less of them than they are able to give. If we expect much of them, they will give us much in return. If we stand, they will deliver. If we expect little of them, they will have contempt both for what we are asking them to do and, in the end, for us.

RESPONDING TO THE READING

Freewriting

Exercise 16f. Freewrite about the course of study at your high school. Were you and other students following a plan or academic schedule when you selected classes each semester?

Exercise 16g. What is the most important problem with the classes you have taken in elementary school, high school, or college? What makes this problem so important? What are possible solutions?

Exercise 16h. To what extent were you and other members of your family encouraged to attend school? Who or what did you find most encouraging?

Building Your Vocabulary

VOCABULARY LIST

Words to Look Up	My Definition	Dictionary Definition
facilitate (1)		
disproportionate (1)		
stratify (1)		
absolute (2)		
indicators (3)		
virtually (3)		
curriculum (4)		
diluted (4)		
peripheral (4)		
ascended (4)		
vocational (4)		
significant (6)		
compensation (6)		
"general track" (7)		
substantive (7)		
extended (9)		
notable (9)		
notwithstanding (9)		
disintegration (10)		
erosion (10)		
salvage rate (10)		
societal (12)		
accommodate (12)		
disproportionately (12)		
crucial (13)		
rhetorical (13)		
contempt (13)		

Thinking about Words

As you saw in Annie Dillard's "Self and World" in Chapter 8, writers sometimes use comparisons or **analogies** to make their points. In David Gardner's "If We Stand, They Will Deliver," the author draws the analogy between classes in a high-school curriculum and courses on a dinner menu: "It was not obvious which courses in the high-school curriculum were intended to be appetizers and desserts and which were intended to be the main course." This analogy helps the reader understand the next statement Gardner makes: "Schools made little distinction between the significance of a course in bachelor living compared with one in English composition."

FOR PRACTICE

Which of these two courses is the "appetizer" and which is the "main course"—bachelor living or English composition?

Questions for Discussion

1. Terrell Bell seems to refer to the school voucher system in the quote that David Gardner includes in paragraph 1 of "If We Stand, They Will Deliver." Identify the assumption that lies behind the chain of reasoning in this paragraph. Might one make an alternate assumption?
2. Express the following description of the courses offered at high schools in New England in your own words: "The core had been weakened and the peripheral had ascended." You might first try to determine what Gardner means by "core" ("core" what?) and "peripheral" ("peripheral" what?).Why might this distinction between bachelor living and English composition be an important one to make?
3. Compare your answers to Exercise 16f with other students in the class. Work with classmates to write an inductive argument that reaches a conclusion about how conscientious the high schools they attended were about offering an academic or vocational plan as opposed to a general, less focused course of study.
4. Discuss advantages and disadvantages in the courses of study that Gardner mentions—academic, vocational, and general.
5. In paragraphs 6 and 7 Gardner discusses the progress that has been made since the report "A Nation at Risk" appeared in 1983. Based on the accomplishments he mentions, what were some of the recommendations in that report?
6. Why do you think Gardner wants to write a longer letter to parents and insert it at the beginning of "A Nation at Risk"? How important have parents been in supporting education in your community or school? How strong is parental influence when compared to the influence of friends, teachers, and the child's neighborhood or community?
7. What is Gardner's purpose in comparing classrooms in the United States to those in Japan? How does this comparison relate to his point about parents' influence on a child's attitude toward school?
8. Why do some educators think it is important to compare students' performance on tests taken in the United States to the performance of students on exams in other industrialized nations? What might be the value or drawback to making such comparisons?

TOPICS FOR WRITING

Topic 1.   If you completed discussion question 3, write an essay in which you use the information you have gathered to evaluate how well courses of study in local high schools prepare students for a vocation or for entry into college. Use examples from your classmates' experiences to support your evaluation.

Topic 2.   Interview several parents, teachers, and fellow college students to determine what they think the parents' role should be in educating their children. Write an essay in which you classify these roles in order of importance and explain in detail what activities and commitments each required.

Topic 3.   Do some freewriting on what you have heard about the voucher system, one possible change in school funding that would allow some parents to make a direct payment of public funds to the public or private school they want their children to attend. Consult the *Readers Guide to Periodical Literature* or a computerized index of newspaper and magazine articles to locate information on the voucher system. Then write a summary of supporting and opposing arguments.

Theme for English B
Langston Hughes

Langston Hughes was an important writer during the Harlem Renaissance—a period in the 1920s when African-American art, music, and literature flourished. He wrote these memories of his days as a student at Columbia University in New York. The word colored *is considerably dated and no longer an acceptable term.*

The instructor said,

> *Go home and write*
> *a page tonight.*
> *And let that page come out of you—*
> *Then, it will be true.*   5

I wonder if it's that simple?
I am twenty-two, colored, born in Winston-Salem.
I went to school there, then Durham, then here
to this college on the hill above Harlem.
I am the only colored student in my class.   10
The steps from the hill lead down into Harlem,
through a park, then I cross St. Nicholas,
Eighth Avenue, Seventh, and I come to the Y,
the Harlem Branch Y, where I take the elevator
up to my room, sit down, and write this page: 15

It's not easy to know what is true for you or me

at twenty-two, my age. But I guess I'm what
I feel and see and hear, Harlem, I hear you:
hear you, hear me—we two—you, me, talk on this page.
(I hear New York, too.) Me—who?   *20*

Well, I like to eat, sleep, drink, and be in love.
I like to work, read, learn, and understand life.
I like a pipe for a Christmas present,
or records—Bessie,[1] bop, or Bach.
I guess being colored doesn't make me *not* like   *25*
the same things other folks like who are other races.
So will my page be colored that I write?

Being me, it will not be white.
But it will be
a part of you, instructor.   *30*
You are white—
yet a part of me, as I am a part of you.
That's American.
Sometimes perhaps you don't want to be a part of me.
Nor do I often want to be a part of you.   *35*

But we are, that's true!
As I learn from you,
I guess you learn from me—
although you're older—and white—
and somewhat more free.   *40*

This is my page for English B.

RESPONDING TO THE READING

Freewriting

Exercise 16i.   What perspective does Hughes offer on his relationship to his teacher? Freewrite about your relationships to teachers or classmates. Do they contain elements of discomfort?

Exercise 16j.   Write a response of your own to the assignment Hughes and his classmates were given:

---

[1]Bessie Smith (1898?–1937), influential blues singer of the Harlem Renaissance.

> *Go home and write*
> *a page tonight.*
> *And let that page come out of you—*
> *Then, it will be true.*

Share your responses with classmates.

Questions for Discussion

1. Describe the situation in Langston Hughes' poem. Who is speaking? What do we know about him?
2. Why does Hughes ask "Is it that simple?" to complete the teacher's assignment? What makes the task complex?
3. Who is Hughes' audience? Is there more than one?
4. Summarize the walk Hughes takes from school to his home in Harlem. Why do you think he includes this walk in the poem?
5. What is the main point Hughes conveys in this "Theme for English B"?
6. How well does his poem satisfy the teacher's assignment? Was that his main intent, or did he have an additional purpose?

TOPICS FOR WRITING

Topic 1.   Write a paper describing your own relationship to school (either high school or college). You may wish to discuss how comfortable or uncomfortable you feel in particular classes with particular teachers or students. You could also focus on your relationship to students and teachers in sports, drama, or other school activities.

Topic 2.   Write a paragraph or short essay giving reasons why you are going to college. Consider what experiences and people influenced your decision. Use details, examples, and explanations to explain your choice.

Topic 3.   Reread your freewriting notes for Exercise 16f. Then use the writing process to develop a more formal response to the teacher's assignment. If you are so moved, you might attach a poem that expresses the truth that "comes out of you."

Whose Culture Is It, Anyway?

The following pieces appeared as companion articles in The New York Times *in May 1991. They represent two views of what should be taught in college courses.*

It's Not Just Anglo-Saxon
Henry Louis Gates, Jr.

*Professor Gates is a W.E.B. Du Bois professor of humanities at Harvard. He writes in
defense of a multicultural approach to college studies.*

DURHAM, N.C.

I recently asked the dean of a prestigious liberal arts college if his school 1
would ever have, as Berkeley has, a 70 percent nonwhite enrollment. "Never," he
replied. "That would completely alter our identity as a center of the liberal arts."

The assumption that there is a deep connection between the shape of a 2
college's curriculum and the ethnic composition of its students reflects a dis-
quieting trend in education. Political representation has been confused with
the "representation" of various ethnic identities in the curriculum.

The cultural right wing, threatened by demographic changes and the 3
ensuing demands for curricular change, has retreated to intellectual protec-
tionism, arguing for a great and inviolable "Western tradition," which contains the seeds, fruit and flowers of the very best thought [written] or uttered
in history. (Typically, Mortimer Adler has ventured that blacks "wrote no good
books.") Meanwhile, the cultural left demands changes to accord with population shifts in gender and ethnicity. Both are wrongheaded.

I am just as concerned that so many of my colleagues feel that the ratio- 4
nale for a diverse curriculum depends on the latest Census Bureau report as I
am that those opposed see pluralism as forestalling the possibility of a com-
munal "American" identity. To them, the study of our diverse cultures must
lead to "tribalism" and "fragmentation."

The cultural diversity movement arose partly because of the fragmenta- 5
tion of society by ethnicity, class and gender. To make it the culprit for this
fragmentation is to mistake effect for cause. A curriculum that reflects the
achievement of the world's great cultures, not merely the West's, is not "politicized"; rather it situates the West as one of a community of civilizations. After
all, culture is always a conversation among different voices.

To insist that we "master our own culture" before learning others—as 6
Arthur Schlesinger, Jr. has proposed—only defers the vexed question: What
gets to count as "our" culture? What has passed as "common culture" has been
an Anglo-American regional culture, masking itself as universal. Significantly
different cultures sought refuge underground.

Writing in 1903, W.E.B. Du Bois expressed his dream of a high culture 7
that would transcend the color line: "I sit with Shakespeare and he winces
not." But the dream was not open to all. "Is this the life you grudge us," he concluded, "O knightly America?" For him, the humanities were a conduit into a
republic of letters enabling escape from racism and ethnic chauvinism. Yet no
one played a more crucial role than he in excavating the long buried heritage
of Africans and African-Americans.

The fact of one's ethnicity, for any American of color, is never neutral: One's 8
public treatment, and public behavior, are shaped in large part by one's

perceived ethnic identity, just as by one's gender. To demand that Americans shuck their cultural heritages and homogenize themselves into a "universal," WASP culture is to dream of an America in cultural white face, and that just won't do.

So it's only when we're free to explore the complexities of our hyphenated   9
culture that we can discover what a genuinely common American culture might actually look like.

Is multiculturalism un-American? Herman Melville didn't think so. As he   10
wrote: "We are not a narrow tribe, no. . . . We are not a nation, so much as a world." We're all ethnics; the challenge of transcending ethnic chauvinism is one we all face.

We've entrusted our schools with the fashioning and refashioning of a   11
democratic polity. That's why schooling has always been a matter of political judgment. But in a nation that has theorized itself as plural from its inception, schools have a very special task.

Our society won't survive without the values of tolerance, and cultural tol-   12
erance comes to nothing without cultural understanding. The challenge facing America will be the shaping of a truly common public culture, one responsive to the long-silenced cultures of color. If we relinquish the ideal of America as a plural nation, we've abandoned the very experiment America represents. And that is too great a price to pay.

RESPONDING TO THE READING

Freewriting

Exercise 16k.   Freewrite about what Henry Gates might mean by "our hyphenated culture." How well does this term describe your own experience?

Exercise 16l.   What courses have you had that offered a non-European approach to the subject matter? Would you recommend that other students take these courses? Explain your recommendation.

Building Your Vocabulary

VOCABULARY LIST

Words to Look Up	My Definition	Dictionary Definition
prestigious (1)		
liberal arts (1)		
disquieting (2)		
demographic (3)		
ensuing (3)		
inviolable (3)		
pluralism (4)		
culprit (5)		

politicized (5)
conduit (7)
chauvinism (7)
excavating (7)
theorized (11)
inception (11)
relinquish (12)

Questions for Discussion

1. Why does Gates disagree with the assumption that a college's curriculum has a "deep connection to the ethnic composition of its students"? What alternative does he propose?
2. What did Arthur Schlesinger, Jr. mean when he said we should "master our own culture" before learning others (paragraph 6)? Identify another possible meaning for the phrase "our own culture."
3. Gates says, "We're all ethnics: the challenge of transcending ethnic chauvinism is one we all face." How does his claim that everyone is "ethnic" serve Gates's argument? Why is it important to him that we learn to transcend "ethnic chauvinism"? Can you think of specific ways for people to make this transformation?
4. Identify several key assumptions that Gates makes in his article. What examples can you offer that either support or contradict these assumptions?
5. Discuss possible ways to promote cultural understanding.

TOPICS FOR WRITING

Topic 1. Write an essay in which you examine the "multicultural" content of a few of the liberal arts courses at your college. As you prepare to write your paper, evaluate the courses you have taken in terms of the variety of cultural perspectives they offer. Interview students and instructors to determine their experience.

Topic 2. Choose a culture that is not familiar to you that you would like to explore. The traditions discussed in Chapter 9 might give you ideas about possible topics. Find information in the library or by interviewing people who have studied the culture or who have this cultural identification. Write a paper in which you explain one or two areas of the culture in some depth.

Western Values Are Central
Donald Kagan

Donald Kagan is dean of Yale College. The following article appeared in The New York Times *as a companion to Henry Gates's article, "It's Not Just Anglo-Saxon." Kagan's piece is an excerpt from a speech delivered to Yale's freshman class.*

NEW HAVEN

Americans do not share a common ancestry and a common blood. What 1
they have in common is a system of laws and beliefs that shaped the establishment of the country, a system developed within the context of Western civilization.

It should be obvious, then, that all Americans need to learn about that civ- 2
ilization to understand our country's origins and share in its heritage, purposes and character.

At present, however, the study of Western civilization is under attack. We 3
are told we should not give a privileged place in the curriculum to the great
works of its history and literature. At the extremes of this onslaught, the civilization, and its study, is attacked because of its history of slavery, imperialism, racial prejudice, addiction to war, its exclusion of women and people not
of the white race from its rights and privileges.

Some criticize its study as narrow, limiting, arrogant and discriminatory, 4
asserting that it has little or no value for those of different cultural origins.
Others concede the value of the Western heritage but regard it as only one
among many, all of which have equal claim to our attention.

These attacks are unsound. It is necessary to place Western civilization 5
and the culture to which it has given rise at the center of our studies, and we
fail to do so at the peril of our students, country and the hopes for a democratic, liberal society.

The assault on Western civilization badly distorts history. Its flaws are real 6
enough, but they are common to almost all the civilizations on any continent
at any time in history.

What is remarkable about the Western heritage is the important ways in 7
which it has departed from the common experience. More than any other, it
has asserted the claims of the individual against those of the state, limiting its
power and creating a realm of privacy into which it cannot penetrate.

By means of the philosophical, scientific, agricultural and industrial revo- 8
lutions in the West, human beings have been able to produce and multiply the
things needed for life so as to make survival and prosperity possible for ever-
increasing numbers, without rapacious wars and at a level that permits dignity and independence. It is the champion of representative democracy as the
normal way for human beings to govern themselves. It has produced the theory and practice of the separation of church from state, protecting each from
the other and creating a free and safe place for the individual conscience.

At its core is a tolerance and respect for diversity unknown in most cul- 9
tures. One of its most telling characteristics is its encouragement of criticism
of itself and its ways. The university itself, a specially sheltered place for such
self-examination, is a Western phenomenon only partially assimilated in other
cultures.

Western culture and institutions are the most powerful paradigm in the 10
world. As they increasingly become the objects of emulation by peoples everywhere, their study becomes essential for those of all nations who wish to
understand their nature and origins.

Happily, student bodies have grown vastly more diverse. Less happily, stu- 11
dents see themselves increasingly as parts of groups, distinct from other
groups. They often feel pressure to communicate mainly with others like
themselves in the group and to pursue intellectual interests that are of particular importance to it. But a liberal education needs to bring about a challenge
to the ideas, habits and attitudes students bring with them.

Take pride in your family and in the culture they and your forebears have 12
brought to our shores. Learn as much as you can about that culture. Learn as
much as you can of what the particular cultures of others have to offer. But do not
fail to learn the great traditions that are the special gifts of Western civilization.

RESPONDING TO THE READING

Freewriting

Exercise 16m.   Freewrite about courses you have taken whose material is
primarily "Western" in Kagan's sense of the word. Did you find the courses
rewarding, or was the subject matter limiting in some way?

Exercise 16n.   What courses have you taken in high school or college that
caused you to change your thinking or attitude about a subject?

Building Your Vocabulary

VOCABULARY LIST

Words to Look Up	My Definition	Dictionary Definition
onslaught (3)		
imperialism (3)		
concede (4)		
unsound (5)		
peril (5)		
liberal (5)		
rapacious (8)		
conscience (8)		
assimilated (9)		
paradigm (10)		
emulation (10)		

Questions for Discussion

1. What reasons does Kagan give for seeing "Western civilization and the
    culture to which it has given rise" as the centerpiece of college studies? Do

you find his arguments convincing? Explain your answer. How would Henry Gates respond to Kagan's reasoning?

2.   What are some of the "great traditions of Western civilization" that you have studied? Discuss traditions of non-Western cultures that might also be considered "great."

3.   Kagan says that "a liberal education needs to bring about a challenge to the ideas, habits, and attitudes students bring with them." What courses have challenged you in one or more of these ways?

4.   On what points does Donald Kagan seem to disagree with Henry Gates? What assumptions does each make in presenting his argument? Do they seem to agree on any points?

TOPICS FOR WRITING

Topic 1.   Write an essay in which you discuss contributions a non-European people has made to American culture. You might interview an American history teacher or an instructor in art, music, or humanities to discover a topic that interests you.

Topic 2.   Use a computerized magazine index to find other articles that argue for either culturally diverse studies or a primarily Western curriculum on college campuses. Write an essay in which you present one or two of the major arguments and supporting discussion on both sides. In your conclusion state what you think is the best alternative for college studies.

Student Writing

The Truth about High School

The drill team places third in a statewide competition. A math teacher retires after thirty years of service. The homecoming queen blows kisses to the crowd after the last important game of the season. The principal congratulates the debate team for defeating the school's cross-town rival. Three hundred smiling faces crowd the stage as the new high school graduates wait for their diplomas. A local track star gets a full-tuition scholarship to the University of Southern California. These are the memories that many older Americans have of high school days—the wholesome images reported in the local newspapers. But what really goes on in the halls and cafeterias of today's high schools? The sad truth is that gang fights and drug deals are commonplace, and school authorities have little or no control over the situation.

My high school was dominated by the Bloods, a notorious California gang. Everybody who belonged to the gang wore red. If the Bloods suspected a student of belonging to the Crips, a rival gang, they would do everything they could to make him get out of their territory. Once my cousin was wearing blue jeans and a blue shirt, the Crips' color. The Bloods attacked him on the way home, and he spent the next two weeks in the hospital. Such incidents were so common that black and brown practically became the school colors.

While these random fights were hard to take, there was an even worse problem—drugs being sold and used openly. It was a common sight in my school to see one student buying drugs from another. I sometimes smelled marijuana in the halls or the boys' bathroom. Once while I was looking for a book, I saw three students—one male and two females—snorting cocaine in the library.

The strangest thing is that nobody wants to talk about these problems, let alone do anything about them. The teachers are often too afraid of their students to say much. Even if they saw gang members selling drugs, they would just look the other way because they don't want to get these violent characters mad at them. The principal will call the police if a major fight breaks out or a student gets crazy from the drugs he or she has taken. But most of the time the drug deals and casual use don't get much attention.

If other schools have the problems mine did, there isn't much hope for getting a high-school education. Few students can concentrate well enough to learn anything because they are either loaded or terrified. In fact, most of the students are intent on surviving the experience so they can find a job or get some real education at a college or trade school.

—Thomas Carbone

QUESTIONS FOR DISCUSSION

1. Identify the thesis of Carbone's essay. How well does it express the ideas that follow?
2. Examine the evidence Carbone uses to support his points. Does he offer enough examples to make his evaluation of his high school convincing? Where might the essay benefit from more detailed discussion?
3. Could Carbone have suggested solutions to the problems or specific actions to be taken to give his essay a more hopeful ending?
4. What sources might Carbone have consulted to give his essay a more objective point of view?

17

Examining Stereotypes

*A social norm that is prejudiced against women
instills in them a fear of not being accepted by
family and peers if they break that norm.*

—*Bruce Ogilvie*

*If the U.S. believes in the cause of truth
and in the importance of peace
and brotherhood among peoples,
it must attempt to change its image of Arabs.*

—*Mustafa Nabil*

The authors whose work appears in this chapter take a stand against stereotypical notions of particular groups of people. In "Speaking of Stereotypes," for example, Bruce Ogilvie would like to correct what he considers a stereotypical view of female athletes. Maya Angelou writes her "Song for the Old Ones" as a tribute to older blacks who suffered a great deal because of prejudices against which they had no defense. Mustafa Nabil uses his article "The Arabs' Image" to describe the image that many people in the United States have of Arab Americans and Islamic peoples. In "C'mon, They Don't All Drive Fast Cars!" Roy Blount, Jr., writes a humorous account of the unflattering image of Southerners presented in several television programs.

This chapter also introduces techniques for taking a stand on an issue. Selections from Bruce Ogilvie's "Speaking of Stereotypes" illustrate techniques for writing effective essays that take a clear position on a subject.

TAKING A STAND

Readings in this chapter introduce some of the essential components of persuasive writing—they identify an unfair situation and make a rational, at times personal, appeal to the reader. In "Speaking of Stereotypes," the sample article for this chapter, Bruce Ogilvie expresses the unfairness of judging female athletes as "unfeminine."

Characteristics of Essays That Take a Stand

A Reasonable Point of View

Even though writers have strong feelings about their topics, they must avoid lecturing their readers or relying on unsupported assumptions to make their case. If you consider your own experience, the reasons for taking such precautions become clear. In all probability, you are not convinced by parents', bosses', teachers', or other authority figures' arguments unless they offer evidence to support their claims. Similarly, a writer who appears demanding (you better listen to me) or pompous (you're foolish not to believe me) rarely makes the reader receptive to his or her position. A much more effective approach involves explaining the experience or knowledge that motivated a writer to take a particular stand. Bruce Ogilvie adopts this reasonable approach in his essay, "Speaking of Stereotypes." In his opening paragraph he explains how his observations prompted him to write about the unfounded prejudices against women athletes:

> As a guest on nearly 30 radio and television talk shows 1
> throughout the country over the past five weeks, I gained insight
> into the prejudice and ignorance that still surrounds women

athletes. It has become clear to me that although there is some data on physiological differences between the sexes that affect athletic capabilities, there is a serious lack of data on social differences that affect women's participation in sports.

The phrases "I gained insight into . . . ," "It has become clear to me . . . ," and "There is a serious lack of data . . . " establish Ogilvie as a reasonable person who has come to a rational conclusion based on careful observation. This tone works well when writers wish to take a stand on an issue. Ogilvie also makes his point of view clear; he speaks from personal experience, but he is not writing about himself as a victim of this stereotype. Instead, he writes as a professional and a lecturer who is knowledgeable about sports. In fact, he is a professor emeritus in psychology at San Jose State University and has served as a consultant to professional and nonprofessional teams, including several United States Olympic teams.

A Problem or Source of Unfairness

A writer who takes a strong stand on an issue must explain the problem or source of unfairness clearly, in case the reader is not aware of it. In his article, Bruce Ogilvie identifies stereotyping of female athletes as an unfair situation: "I gained insight into the prejudice and ignorance that still surrounds women athletes." His position on this problem is that while "some data" show that body type and biological differences between men and women may affect their performance, there is no scientific evidence to suggest that women should not become athletes. Rather, purely "social differences"—that is, the way men and women are supposed to act in this culture—often prevent women from competing. The unfounded prejudice against women who become athletes is the target of Ogilvie's criticism.

Ogilvie's lecture tour provided him with further evidence that the problem exists: he observed it in the attitude of the audience who attended his lectures:

> The best example of the prevailing ignorance and sex-role 4 stereotyping that I heard during my talks was the frequent question, "Doesn't participation in highly competitive athletics make a woman less feminine?" Any deviation from culturally defined "women's" qualities of passivity, dependence, and inclination for emotionality rather than rationality was abhorrent to my audiences. Women bodybuilders and field-event participants were the most common targets.

Ogilvie quotes the most common question asked by his audience and explains the prejudice it reveals. The implied judgment of women, as he says earlier, has nothing to do with "data" and everything to do with what this culture defines as acceptable behavior for women—"passivity, dependency, and . . .

emotionality rather than rationality." That attitude, in Ogilvie's view, goes to the heart of the problem.

Convincing Evidence

Essays that take a stand must offer convincing examples, case studies, or explanations to illustrate that the problem they identify is a serious one and that the solutions offered are valid. In Ogilvie's essay, he argues that the assumptions people make about women's anatomical inferiority are wrong. In fact, when physical differences do exist between males and females, they can just as easily be in the woman's favor.

> . . . A recent article in *The Physician and Sports Medicine* sum- 2
> marized the effect of distance running on male and female physiol-
> ogy and concluded that differences in oxygen utilization, heat reten-
> tion, and heat convection do exist. It was suggested that the female
> may even have a slight advantage over the male in her capacity to
> dissipate heat. This is the kind of data that encouraged authorities to
> finally accept the women's marathon as an Olympic event.

After introducing the idea that no biological proof shows that participating in sports might be harmful for women (and to the contrary, that they might have physiological advantages over their male counterparts), Ogilvie examines the real motivations for discouraging women from participating in sports.

> For years women were warned of the dangers vigorous activ- 3
> ity would present to their reproductive organs. There was no physi-
> ological data to support that contention; it was merely an excuse to
> maintain a social norm that did not allow women the kind of
> aggression and physical activity that sports call for. This kind of
> social bias ultimately has psychological effects: a social norm that
> is prejudiced against women instills in them a fear of not being
> accepted by family and peers if they break that norm. It has taken
> years to refute such beliefs and we have made some progress, but
> we still have a lot of ground to cover on the road to understanding.

Reference to Causes or Effects

When exposing what they consider an unfounded assumption, prejudice, or behavior, writers often show the underlying causes of such a stance or discuss its harmful effects. Ogilvie uses both strategies in his article. First, as we have seen, he identifies cultural stereotyping as the cause of prejudice against female athletes. He proposes that this social bias is strong enough to prevent women from becoming athletes because they fear "not being accepted by family and peers."

Solutions

Writers often stress an alternative point of view on an issue to help the reader imagine how to exchange stereotypical views for a more reasonable perspective. This strategy often means appealing to common sense and the reader's concept of fairness. In "Speaking of Stereotypes," Bruce Ogilvie uses these tactics when mentioning the way he thinks young women deserve to be treated in this culture—equally and without gender-bias.

> Ideally women should enjoy a fairly androgynous upbringing, 5 with primary role models who do not see human experience in terms of gender-appropriate behavior. Childhood should be like a smorgasbord from which one is relatively free to make selections according to her inclinations or talents. Perhaps many elite women athletes had this kind of healthy home environment since, as adults, they tend to be very self-directed.

Ogilvie proposes other ways to counteract traditional stereotypical views of women: providing young women with role models who are successful athletes and educating people about the value of sports in building self-esteem:

> As in many aspects of our society, there is a great need for— 6 and unfortunate dearth of—athletic pioneers who can serve as models for female children. The 1983 Miller Lite Report on American Attitudes Toward Sports produced proof of just this lack. When children were asked to name their primary athletic role model, 98 percent of the males readily named a successful male athlete; less than 8 percent of the females had formed such an identification.
>
> We need to strive to educate those who don't understand that 7 there are positive psychological changes that accompany physical fitness and competitive sports. Although we cannot expect prejudice to disappear immediately, our influence could cause a moment's reflection, even the beginning of awareness.

Ogilvie hopes that his essay is instrumental in at least making the reader aware that prejudices against female athletes exist and that they are unfair and erroneous.

Speaking of Stereotypes
Bruce Ogilvie

Bruce Ogilvie is professor emeritus at San Jose State University, in San Jose, California. He also has been an adviser to several U.S. Olympic teams as well as a consultant for teams involved in professional sports. In this article written for Women's Sports, *Ogilvie examines the image of the female athlete.*

As a guest on nearly 30 radio and television talk shows throughout the 1
country over the past five weeks, I gained insight into the prejudice and ignorance that still surrounds women athletes. It has become clear to me that
although there is some data on physiological differences between the sexes
that affect athletic capabilities, there is a serious lack of data on social differences that affect women's participation in sports.

For example, a recent article in *The Physician and Sports Medicine* sum- 2
marized the effects of distance running on male and female physiology and
concluded that differences in oxygen utilization, heat retention, and heat con-
vection do exist. It was suggested that the female may even have a slight
advantage over the male in her capacity to dissipate heat. This is the kind of
data that encouraged authorities to finally accept the women's marathon as an
Olympic event.

For years women were warned of the dangers vigorous activity would pre- 3
sent to their reproductive organs. There was no physiological data to support
that contention; it was merely an excuse to maintain a social norm that did
not allow women the kind of aggression and physical activity that sports call
for. This kind of social bias ultimately has psychological effects: a social norm
that is prejudiced against women instills in them a fear of not being accepted
by family and peers if they break that norm. It has taken years to refute such
beliefs and we have made some progress, but we still have a lot of ground to
cover on the road to understanding.

The best example of the prevailing ignorance and sex-role stereotyping that 4
I heard during my talks was the frequent question, "Doesn't participation in
highly competitive athletics make a woman less feminine?" Any deviation from
culturally defined "women's" qualities of passivity, dependency, and inclination
for emotionality rather than rationality was abhorrent to my audiences. Women
bodybuilders and field-event participants were the most common targets.

Ideally women should enjoy a fairly androgynous upbringing, with pri- 5
mary role models who do not see human experience in terms of gender-appro-
priate behavior. Childhood should be like a smorgasbord from which one is
relatively free to make selections according to her inclinations or talents.
Perhaps many elite women athletes had this kind of healthy home environment since, as adults, they tend to be very self-directed.

As in many aspects of our society, there is a great need for—and unfor- 6
tunate dearth of—athletic pioneers who can serve as models for female children. The 1983 Miller Lite Report on American Attitudes Toward Sports
produced proof of just this lack. When children were asked to name their
primary athletic role model, 98 percent of the males readily named a successful male athlete; less than 8 percent of the females had formed such an
identification.

We need to strive to educate those who don't understand that there are 7
positive psychological changes that accompany physical fitness and competitive sports. Although we cannot expect prejudice to disappear immediately, our influence could cause a moment's reflection, even the beginning of
awareness.

RESPONDING TO THE READING

Freewriting

Exercise 17a.   Freewrite about portions of Bruce Ogilvie's essay that you found most or least convincing. Explain your response.

Exercise 17b.   Do male athletes suffer from stereotyping? What is characteristic of such attitudes? What are possible negative effects?

Building Your Vocabulary

VOCABULARY LIST

Words to Look Up	My Definition	Dictionary Definition
physiological (1)		
retention (2)		
convection (2)		
dissipate (2)		
vigorous (3)		
instills (3)		
refute (3)		
abhorrent (4)		
androgynous (5)		
gender-appropriate (5)		
smorgasbord (5)		
dearth (6)		

Questions for Discussion

1. What distinction does Ogilvie make between "physiological" and "social" differences between the sexes? Why is this distinction important to his discussion?
2. What social demands keep women from participating in sports? What is Ogilvie's opinion of these demands? Do you agree with his position?
3. What solutions does Ogilvie propose to the problem of stereotyping female athletes? Which solution seems most reasonable to you and why?
4. Why does Ogilvie mention the statistics on male and female role models among sports figures (paragraph 6)? How does this information support his position?
5. Ogilvie contends that people must understand that there are "positive psychological changes that accompany physical fitness" and participation in "competitive sports." Specifically, what are these benefits?

TOPICS FOR WRITING

Topic 1.   Write an explanation of the problems faced by women athletes you know. If you are an athlete yourself, draw on your own experience as well. Interview female coaches, strong runners, or swimmers you knew in high school or have met in college. What barriers have they overcome? What attitudes did other men and women have toward them?

Topic 2.   Write a paper in which you make a case for the positive and/or negative effects of doing physical exercise or participating in competitive sports. You might interview athletes in your classes, relatives, or friends who participate in sports.

Topic 3.   Write a paper exposing the stereotypes of male athletes, either professional or amateur. What evidence do you have that such stereotypes exist? Why are they harmful? What can people do to counter them?

THE WRITING PROCESS: TAKING A STAND

Essays that ask a reader to listen to the writer's side of an issue also require that the writer clearly express his or her conviction about the subject. Because commitment to a topic and a clearly stated position are essential for the success of essays that take a stand, the following discussion emphasizes the beginning stages of the writing process and pays attention to possible ways of organizing ideas.

Additional Considerations for Developing a Topic

To achieve the high degree of commitment to your position necessary for writers of essays that take a stand on an issue, it is imperative that you choose a topic that evokes strong feelings for you. If you have difficulty finding a topic you genuinely care about, ask yourself the following questions:

> What are a few of the problems you are aware of in your neigh-
> borhood? What can you and your neighbors do to solve them?
> In reading the local newspaper lately, have you been able to identify
> issues in your community that interest or involve you personally?

What can students, teachers, administrators, or other professionals do
to solve a campus issue that you feel is not being properly addressed?
Imagine that you have been promoted to an important management
position where you work. What would you change, how would you
make your changes, and what would be the result?

Once you have chosen a topic, use the following questions to help clarify
your position:

What is my topic? Why have I chosen it? What convictions about it do
I hold?
Does my approach to this topic come from personal experience, or am
I writing about a situation I feel strongly about but which does not
affect me personally?
What is my purpose for writing this paper?

Additional Considerations for Thinking about Your Audience

For essays that take a firm stand against prejudice, stereotyping, or other misconceptions about people, it is important to maintain a reasonable stance
even though you feel strongly about your position. Assume that your audience
is sensitive, intelligent, and reasonable, and just needs to be informed about
the situation that you judge to be unfair.

Additional Considerations for Preliminary Writing

As you begin gathering information for your essay, consider interviewing people who have some experience or expertise related to your topic. They can provide insights, details, examples, and solutions that might offer valuable support for your position. As always, you need to introduce comments and ideas
from your sources with phrases like "According to Iva Kicksman. . . ."
The following questions will help you fill out lists of ideas, draw an idea
wheel, and conduct an interview:

Why do you feel strongly about this situation?
Who does this prejudice or problem affect? How are they affected?
What examples illustrate serious consequences of this problem?
What are possible causes? Are some more important than others? Why
do you think so?
How can the difficult or harmful situation you are writing about be
changed? Who can effect these changes?

Additional Considerations for Organizing Ideas

The following outline offers one possible way of organizing a paper that takes a stand. Corresponding ideas in Ogilvie's article are noted in parentheses.

I. Introduction
   A. Present your own point of view.
   B. Identify the situation you support or reject. (Ogilvie objects to prejudice against female athletes.)
II. Explain why the attitude or situation you are writing about creates a problem.
   A. Show causes and effects. (The cause of the problem Ogilvie is addressing is the social stereotyping of women; the effect of this attitude is that qualified women may choose not to participate in sports.)
III. Suggest ways to counter prejudices. (Ogilvie suggests that young girls should have equal access to sports and that people should be taught the benefits of participating in sports.)
IV. Conclusion

Additional Considerations for Sharing Your Writing and Making Final Revisions

Use the checklist below to find areas in your paper that need revising.

Checklist

- ❑ Have I defined the problem or situation clearly for the reader?
- ❑ Have I maintained a calm, reasonable tone throughout the essay?
- ❑ Have I presented sufficient examples and explanations to make my case?
- ❑ If I discuss causes, are they clearly related to the situation? Are some more important than others? Have I given these proper emphasis?
- ❑ If I have discussed effects, have I explained how they contribute to the seriousness of the situation?
- ❑ Have I offered solutions or alternative ways of thinking about the problem I identify? Have I shown that they are practical, reasonable solutions?
- ❑ Have I organized the paper so the reader can distinguish problems from solutions?
- ❑ Have I proofread carefully for sentence errors I commonly make, and for mistakes in spelling and punctuation?

FOR FURTHER READING

Song for the Old Ones
Maya Angelou

Maya Angelou is a distinguished lecturer, poet, essayist, and playwright. She has written a five-volume autobiography that begins with the volume titled I Know Why the Caged Bird Sings. *For President Clinton's inauguration on January 20, 1993, Angelou recited "On the Pulse of Morning," a poem she composed for the occasion. In the following poem from* I Pray My Wings Are Gonna Fit Me Well, *Angelou honors the "old ones" who have suffered for the sake of generations to come.*

My Fathers sit on benches
    their flesh count every plank
    the slats leave dents of darkness
deep in their withered flanks.

They nod like broken candles   *5*
    all waxed and burnt profound,
    they say "It's understanding
that makes the world go round."

There in those pleated faces
    I see the auction block   *10*
    the chains and slavery's coffles
the whip and lash and stock.

My Fathers speak in voices
    that shred my fact and sound
    they say "It's our submission   *15*
that makes the world go round."

They used the finest cunning
    their naked wits and wiles
    the lowly Uncle Tomming
and Aunt Jemimas' smiles.   *20*

They've laughed to shield their crying
    then shuffled through their dreams
    and stepped 'n fetched a country
to write the blues with screams.

> I understand their meaning   *25*
>   it could and did derive
>   from living on the edge of death
> They kept my race alive.

RESPONDING TO THE READING

Freewriting

Exercise 17c.   Angelou's poem is a powerful expression of human survival. How do you account for its power?

Exercise 17d.   Freewrite about possible meanings of the two quotes Angelou attributes to "the old ones" (lines 7 through 8, and 15 and 16).

Building Your Vocabulary

VOCABULARY LIST

Words to Look Up	My Definition	Dictionary Definition
flanks (4)		
coffles (11)		
submission (15)		

Questions for Discussion

1. What impression of the "old ones" do we get in the first two stanzas (lines 1 through 8)? How does our picture of them change in the course of the poem? What is Angelou's final evaluation?
2. What emotions does Angelou feel for these "old ones"? How does she convey those emotions?
3. In lectures she has given, Angelou has told her audience that we have all been paid for by ancestors who endured humiliation, changes of fortune, displacement, hardships, and prejudice. How have her ancestors "paid for" her? What debts do you owe your own people?
4. Uncle Tom and Aunt Jemima are stereotypes of African Americans. What characteristics of blacks do these stereotypes assume? How have "the old ones" used these misconceptions as masks to help them survive? What is the truth behind the masks that the "old ones" present to the world?

TOPICS FOR WRITING

Topic 1.   Write a paper explaining the debt you owe the "old ones" in your family. Interview family members whose memories will help you gather details. What pressures or indignities did they bear? What ideals or motivations drove them?

Topic 2.   Think of circumstances when you acted in a particular way in order to please the people you were with or those observing you. Write an essay in which you either defend or criticize your actions.

Topic 3.   Based on your own experience, feelings, and observations, write about the psychological, economic, or personal value of belonging to a certain ethnic or cultural group.

The Arabs' Image
Mustafa Nabil

In this article, Mustafa Nabil describes the superficial image most Americans have of Arab Americans and Islamic peoples in general. Nabil's article first appeared in Al Mussawar, *a weekly publication in Cairo. The following excerpt from his article was printed in* World Press Review *in June, 1986.*

Arab Americans are mounting a campaign against the anti-Arab bias of the American media and of American society at large. Leading the protest are the Society of Arab Americans, founded in 1972, and the American-Arab Anti-Discrimination Committee, formed in 1980. The Arab-Israeli conflict and the oil crisis of the 1970s have exacerbated an atmosphere of hostility toward Arabs who have chosen to make their home in the U.S. 1

There are more than one million Arab Americans, 90 percent of them 2 Christian and 10 percent Moslem. Arab immigration to the U.S., which has increased over the past century, first occurred from Lebanon during the era of Ottoman rule.[1] Most early immigrants were merchants and traders with little education.

More recently, many Arab students who were sent to the U.S. to study 3 chose to stay after completing their education. The Arab "brain drain" reached its peak in 1968–71, when Egypt alone lost some 7,000 professionals, many of them doctors, to the United States.

All that the average American ever hears about Arab countries concerns 4 their polygamy, the status of their women, and the Islamic movements behind

[1]The Ottomans were Turks who ruled an empire (1300–1918) that included areas of modern Europe, Asia, and North Africa.

the Iranian revolution. Americans see Arabs as desert bedouins in flowing robes. Such stereotypes do not make distinctions between rich and poor Arab countries, or between Arabs who have lived since the dawn of history on the banks of rivers where they planted crops, and those who are desert nomads. American portrayals of Arabs take no account of the universities and research centers all over the Arab World, or of the programs of economic growth and social development there.

The American media choose to ignore all of this, preferring the racist car-   5
icatures that spring from Western chauvinism that holds the civilizations of the East in contempt. In television, probably the medium that most strongly influences U.S. public opinion, hardly a week goes by without its portraying the Arabs in a negative and bigoted fashion on series like *Vegas* or *Hawaii Five-O.*

On such programs—and on commercials—Arabs appear as blood-thirsty   6
terrorists and dissolute tribal sheiks who squander their vast wealth among the women of their harems. The scriptwriters apparently get their informa-tion, more imaginary than real, straight from the *Arabian Nights*[2] and the tales of Ali Baba.[3]

In a major American newspaper a political cartoon depicts a huddle of   7
obese emirs, surrounded by belly dancers, as they munch huge mutton chops and toss a single dry bone to a starving boy—who symbolizes the plight of Africa. The message: Arabs plunder the world and care for nothing but danc-ing girls.

The U.S. film industry also has played on the negative stereotypes of   8
Arabs. In American movies the Sahara is a mysterious and dangerous setting where Americans fall into the clutches of evil bedouin sheiks.

U.S. research centers now are offering programs to spread knowledge of other   9
cultures and countries to the American public. These centers have translated and published foreign works of literature. The Department of Middle Eastern Studies at the University of Washington in Seattle conducts seminars for teachers in the hope that public-school systems will expand their study of for-eign cultures and rectify anti-Arab stereotypes.

Los Angeles, where more than 250,000 Arabs live, has an Arab-American   10
television station. It is run by Wahib Baqtar, a young Egyptian trained as an architectural engineer. Baqtar reports that the station avoids discussions of political matters and Arab disputes. Its schedule does include programs on places of historical and cultural significance to Arabs.

If the U.S. believes in the cause of truth and in the importance of peace   11
and brotherhood among peoples, it must attempt to change its image of

---

[2]A collection of tales chiefly from Arabia, India, and Persia.

[3]One of the better-known characters from the *Arabian Nights;* Ali Baba gains entry to a cave filled with treasure by saying the magic words "Open Sesame."

Arabs. That imagery takes root in U.S. classrooms, where the minds of a new generation are shaped, and flourishes in its media.

RESPONDING TO THE READING

Freewriting

Exercise 17e.   Freewrite about the associations you have with the words *Arab, Iraqi,* or *Moslem.* What are the sources of your images of Arabic peoples?

Exercise 17f.   Freewrite about the information Mustafa Nabil offers in his attempt to broaden his readers' views of Arabs.

Building Your Vocabulary

VOCABULARY LIST

Words to Look Up	My Definition	Dictionary Definition
exacerbated (1)		
polygamy (4)		
bedouins (4)		
caricatures (5)		
chauvinism (5)		
obese (7)		
emirs (7)		

Questions for Discussion

1. Give several of Mustafa Nabil's examples of how the media perpetuate stereotypes of Arabs. What additional illustrations can you offer?
2. According to Nabil, what is being done to broaden Americans' view of Arabs? Do you see any evidence that these efforts are succeeding?
3. Who are the characters in the advertisement for nuclear power on page 460? Describe their positions and expressions. How do these images and the words in the ad play on Americans' fears? Based on your reading of Nabil's article, what do you think would be the Arab response to this advertisement?

IMPORTED OIL STRENGTHENS OUR TIES TO THE MIDDLE EAST.

Last year, almost 40 percent of all the oil we used came from foreign countries. Much of that from the unstable Middle East. And this dependence on foreign oil is growing.

The more we use nuclear energy, instead of imported oil, to generate electricity, the less we have to depend on foreign nations.

The 110 nuclear electric plants in the U.S. have cut our foreign oil dependence by over three billion barrels since the first Arab oil embargo. And they have cut foreign oil payments by over 100 billion dollars.

But 110 nuclear plants will not be enough to meet our growing electricity demand. More plants are needed.

If we are going to keep our energy future in our own hands, we need to rely more on energy sources we can count on, like nuclear energy.

For a free booklet on nuclear energy, write to the U.S. Council for Energy Awareness, P.O. Box 66103, Dept. AY01, Washington, D.C. 20035.

U.S. COUNCIL FOR ENERGY AWARENESS

Nuclear energy means more energy independence.

As seen in February 1989 issues of TIME, Sports Illustrated, Newsweek, U.S. News & World Report, The Wall Street Journal, The New York Times, The Washington Post, Forbes, The Economist, State Legislatures, and National Journal, March 1989 issues of Reader's Digest, National Geographic, Smithsonian, Business Week, The Leadership Network, and Governing, and the April 1989 issue of Good Housekeeping.

TOPICS FOR WRITING

Topic 1.   Using evidence from Mustafa Nabil's article and your own observations, write a paper in which you evaluate the media's portrayal of Arabs. You may use examples from television programs, commercials, news stories, political cartoons, comic strips, or movies to make your case.

Topic 2.   Write a paper in which you analyze the tactics used by the U.S. Council for Energy Awareness (a group representing the nuclear power industry) to promote nuclear power. (See the advertisement on page 460.)

Topic 3.   Identify another target of stereotypical attitudes. Explain what the stereotype is, how and where it is perpetuated, and why it is unreasonable to hold such a stereotype.

C'mon, They Don't All Drive Fast Cars!
Roy Blount, Jr.

Roy Blount, Jr. is a humorist and satirist. He wrote the following article on the stereotypes of Southerners common to television programs. The article appeared in a 1980 issue of TV Guide.

In the movie "Smokey and the Bandit," which has spawned so many situation comedies about good ol' boys in good ol' car wrecks, Burt Reynolds, playing a Southerner, and Sally Field, playing a Northerner, compare their cultures. Reynolds admits his ignorance of Elton John and she hers of Waylon Jennings. Since they are walking together near a Southern crick, the Field character is the more embarrassed. Reynolds observes, "When you say something, it depends on what part of the country you're standing in as to whether you're dumb or not." 1

In the country of television, things that Southerners say tend to be fairly dumb. In *The Dukes of Hazzard* and *The Misadventures of Sheriff Lobo* you can calibrate how much of a bungler a character is by the strength of his Southern accent. The dashing Bo and Luke Duke might as well be from La Jolla; but Boss Hogg sounds like he studied elocution under Jeeter Lester. No wonder the Carter Administration has had such a hard time getting respect. 2

I am from the South myself. I have heard a lot of Southerners say dumb things, and I have said some. But I wouldn't be entirely surprised to see data indicating that as many lame remarks per capita occur in California and New York as in, say, the Ozarks. Yet no ethnic group associated with California, New York, or any other part of the world has ever been so ill-served by a situation comedy as Ozark mountain whites in *The Beverly Hillbillies*, which is still to be seen in reruns even though it is just as stereotypical and much less funny 3 than *The Amos and Andy Show,* or *The Goldbergs,* or *Life with Luigi,* none of which are likely to be revived. (Ray Charles, incidentally, says that *Amos and Andy* was his favorite radio show.)

Neither *Petticoat Junction, Carter Country, Green Acres,* nor *The Kallikaks* 4 was exactly a tribute to my region, but the very title *Beverly Hillbillies* is an ethnic slur. Would you call a series about a black family moving to a posh suburb of Detroit *Negrosse Pointe?* This is from a recent TV GUIDE listing for *The Misadventures of Sheriff Lobo:* "A dimwitted hillbilly inadvertently gets involved in an armored-car robbery." Is there any other ethnic term that would be preceded by "dimwitted" in a national magazine today? "There are no indications of a glimmer of intelligence in the lead characters of *The Dukes of Hazzard,*" said producer Paul Picard, after he got the first five shows in the can. "Eventually there will be some."

But I am not out to purge the videoways of anti-redneck (there's another 5 term that people toss around loosely) bias. I guess us Crackers are just too lazy to take on a job like that. And I didn't like it when I read the other day that the Machinists Union is training monitors all over the country to document complaints that TV news shows contribute to the low image of unions and workers in the public mind. I don't doubt that the machinists can make a good case, but when it comes to the media, "monitor" is a bad word to me like "scab" or "hillbilly."

If I were a monitor I would have to admit that not every Southerner on TV 6 is supposed to be a fool. No doubt it is a feather in my ethnic cap for a Southerner to have achieved such a prominent position in the New York Police Department as Joe Don Baker did in the recently canceled *Eischied.* I liked the fact that even though Eischied was Southern, he wasn't called Elroy or Dwayne (or Joe Don).

I also have to admit that *The Waltons* doesn't debase the Southern image. 7 Of course now that the grandparents have passed on none of the Waltons *sounds* Southern, but they are supposed to be living in the hills of Virginia. And the Waltons are nice high-type folks.

So nice and so high type, in fact, that I would like to sic the Ewings of 8 *Dallas* on them. Sometimes I entertain the idea that the young Waltons grew up, moved to Texas, struck oil, got mean, and became the Ewings. At any rate it would be interesting to sit both families down at the same dinner table and see whether good or evil would prevail.

My bet is on J.R. I could never be a good media policeman because J.R., a 9 Southwesterner and as nasty a person as ever came into my living room, is my favorite TV character. I am proud that a part of the old Confederacy can produce such a snake. My least favorite TV character of recent years is not Sheriff Lobo's buffoonish Deputy Perkins but John-Boy Walton. I don't care what part of the country John-Boy is allegedly from, I want to see J.R. set him up in business and ruin him.

You might say that J.R. and the other residents of *Dallas*—even *Miss Ellie* 10 is sometimes mean—draw upon stereotypical notions of the city, but at least J.R. isn't dumb or sweet. And at least he isn't forever totaling his automobile.

During the *credits* of *Lobo,* eight or 10 cars are smashed. The last time I   11
watched that program, an armored car rammed a truck full of chickens.
Perkins drove his cruiser through a billboard and the bad guys' green sedan
rammed a split-rail fence—and then a tank crumbled the jailhouse wall and
squashed a police car and demolished a privy. At the conclusion a watertower
was shot down with a cannon and a still full of money was blown to
smithereens.

I have two reservations about such humor. One: I hate to see perfectly   12
good privies, watertowers, stills and trucks full of chickens destroyed. My
other reservation is that I think vehicles in motion stopped being funny when
they started attaining speeds of over 15 miles an hour.

The South after all does have forms of entertainment other than reckless   13
driving. For one thing, there's talking. Whatever else so-called Southern TV
shows ought to be they shouldn't be weak in the area of storytelling. *The Dukes
of Hazzard* has no verbal richness at all, and for every two head-on collisions
in *Lobo,* there is maybe one good flavorful remark, like "Them boys is dumber
than a two-dollar dog," or "It was so cold where he growed up they used to
have to use a car battery to jump-start the hunting dogs."

Deputy Perkins does sometimes have a way with words. Once when he   14
thought he was going to have to leave law enforcement, he lamented, "I'll have
to go back to my old job at the Dairy Queen, wearing one of them silly paper
hats." Much as I regret that the essential media image of the Southerner is a
dumb and/or mean deputy sheriff, I can't entirely dislike Perkins.

But what good talk there is in *Lobo* is overwhelmed by the silly plots, thin   15
characters and grinding of sheet metal. Remember *The Andy Griffith Show?*
There were Andy and Barney Fife and Opie and Gomer and Aunt Bee and all
sorts of interesting out-of-towners coming in on the bus to be brought gently
down to earth. Andy wouldn't have let anybody drive like a maniac in
Mayberry.

The only thing wrong with *The Andy Griffith Show* was that it was too   16
sane. If you want to confirm your feeling that the South is a crazy place, I recommend an occasional dose of *Hee Haw,* the white-face minstrel show that is
too ethnic for the networks, but thrives in syndication.

Hee Haw is truly awful—awful enough sometimes to be Southern folk   17
humor at its best. Junior Samples, who is often seen lying in the yard in a pile
of pigs and relatives, comes running inside crying, "Daddy, there's an animal
out there that's over 60 feet high, he's all blue, with fire all up and down him.
What is it?"

"I don't rightly know, Junior," comes the answer from Daddy, who hasn't   18
been roused to open his eyes, "but you sure don't see many of 'em around
here."

In New York, an animal like that would drive everybody crazy. They'd all   19
be out trying to interview it, or consulting their psychiatrists about it, or blaming it on the Mafia or the police or the air or various ethnic groups or the
mayor. But down where Junior and his Daddy live, there is a willingness to
accept strangeness, enjoy it and not mess with it too much.

"You know these girlie shows they got in town?" Junior said once. "Daddy   20
told me I ought never to go to 'em. I might see something Daddy didn't want
me to see. So I decided to go to one. Sure enough, I saw something Daddy
didn't want me to see. I saw Daddy, right there in the front row."

There you go: there's the generation gap bridged, and also the pornogra-   21
phy question taken care of. You don't find that kind of perspective, that kind
of continuity, in big Northern cities. Once on *Hee Haw*, somebody held up a
fairly new-looking ax and said, "This belonged to George Washington."

"That was George Washington's ax?" somebody obligingly inquired.   22

"Yep. Course it's had three new heads and four new handles since he   23
had it."

Another time, somebody playing the *Hee Haw* equivalent of Walter   24
Cronkite confined his entire newscast to this announcement: "The news was
pretty much the same today, only it happened to different people."

Also on *Hee Haw*, somebody once said: "She's a real lady. I haven't ever   25
seen her when she wasn't breathing through her nose."

How are you going to monitor something like that? I don't want televi-   26
sion's portrayal of the South to be cleaned up: I'd just like to see it slowed
down, brought in off the highway for longer stretches and given some breathing room. And I'd like to see a special in which Eischied and Sheriff Andy
return, enlist Junior Samples as a consultant, and try to deal with J.R. They
wouldn't be able to *reform* him, of course.

RESPONDING TO THE READING

Freewriting

Exercise 17g.   What television series do you recall that has Southern characters? What are they like? What do they typically do or say on the series?

Building Your Vocabulary

VOCABULARY LIST

Words to Look Up	My Definition	Dictionary Definition
calibrate (2)		
elocution (2)		
posh (4)		
inadvertently (4)		
monitors (5)		
buffoonish (9)		
allegedly (9)		
smithereens (11)		

minstrel (16)
syndication (16)

Questions for Discussion

1. According to Roy Blount, Jr. how is the Southerner usually portrayed on television? Compare or contrast his analysis with your own image of Southerners. What are the sources of your image?
2. What reasons does Blount give for criticizing or praising particular portraits of Southerners?
3. Which of the following best describes Blount's attitude toward television's depiction of Southerners: angry, humorous, sarcastic, serious, bitter, nostalgic? Which phrases or passages are representative of this tone?

TOPICS FOR WRITING

Topic 1.   Watch a few prime-time television shows with an eye toward examining the way they portray women, fathers, the elderly, or members of a particular ethnic group. Arrange your evidence in order of emphasis, decide the point you want to make, and draft your paper. (Note: You may wish to explore the *positive* image promoted by a few programs.)

Topic 2.   Write a paper evaluating the use of stereotypical images of Native Americans in sports or advertising. You might reread "The Tonto Syndrome" in Chapter 2 or use other magazine articles for ideas.

Topic 3.   Think of television programs or movies you have seen, articles you have read, or conversations you have heard that expressed very narrow views of a certain group of people. (The elderly, homeless people, or members of a particular ethnic population are a few of the possible groups you might choose.) Write a paper in which you take a strong stand against such stereotypes. To support your position, draw on your own experience and knowledge of people who belong to the group you are writing about but do not fit the stereotype.

Student Writing

And "How!"

I am a Menominee Indian. When informed of this fact, most non-native people give a predictable response: "My great-great grandfather on my mother's side knew a woman whose aunt taught music to the second cousin of one of the tribal chief's daughters who was married to a man who actually fought at the Battle of the Big Horn." Or perhaps they have just read an article in Smithsonian Magazine about a tribe who lived before dirt was invented and proceed to ask me obscure questions regarding the mating customs and net weaving techniques of the indigenous coastal tribes. "Yes, they mated while they were weaving." How should I know? Ask me about Menominees. Would they ask an African American about Kunta Kinte or an Irish American if they eat "Lucky Charms" in Ireland? Where do these ridiculous presumptions come from?

As a young "squaw," my mother took me to the Indian Museum in Sacramento near Sutter's Fort. This was to be an enlightening experience for both of us for we were not prepared to see the remains of an ancient tribesman encased in an undignified display as a museum curio.

"Why don't they bury this person, Mother? Why is this jewelry pinned to the wall? Why do they have baskets and beads under these glass cases, Mother?" What's the big deal anyway, I thought to myself. We have this stuff all over the place at home.

As we walked outside to the park and sat down under a tree, my mother explained. "Someday we will go downtown to the old cemetery, dig up some white people, and put them in a glass case. We will go to Sears, purchase Teflon cookware and Tupperware and arrange them around a place setting of Corning dishes. We'll build a house in the suburbs, put a car in the driveway and sprinklers on the lawn, and we'll call it the 'Sacramento Caucasian Museum of History.' Maybe, then, they will realize the injustice of this."

Thirty years later, I was to take my own daughter to the same Indian Museum. "Mom, there's a porcupine quill necklace over here that looks just like the one grandma gave you. Hey, we've got stuff like this at home. What's the big deal, anyway? Grandma's got this stuff all over the place. Why didn't they bury this guy? Oh, yea, my teacher wants to know if you'll come to class and talk about Columbus and the Indians."

"Tell her I'll stop by on my way back from Sears."

"What?"

"Someday we'll go downtown to the old cemetery. . . ."

—Rebecca Valencia

Questions for Discussion

1. Characterize the author's attitude in this essay. What words or phrases convey this attitude?

2. What does Rebecca Valencia feel is unjust about the displays in the Indian Museum? Describe your own reactions to a similar display.

Gary Gilbert wrote the following essay after gathering information about the experiences of interracial couples from magazine articles and personal interviews. The articles and interview notes he refers to in his essay are listed under "Works Cited" at the end of his paper. After each piece of information he used, Gilbert enclosed in parentheses the name of the author of the article and the page number where he found the information. He omitted page numbers if his information came from an interview. When he mentioned the author elsewhere in his paragraph, he put only the page number in parentheses.

Love in Black and White

Blacks and whites who marry face many problems during their lives together. Historically, interracial marriages were prohibited by law during the eighteenth and early nineteenth centuries. The popular theory of the time was that interracial marriages would spell the destruction of the white race. Although the United States' Census reveals that interracial marriages are increasing slightly nationwide, these couples continue to experience discrimination, public and private ridicule, and sometimes even violence.

One problem interracial couples have is finding a place to live. Many realtors and landlords refuse to rent to them. To counteract this form of racism, the white partner must secure the home before introducing the landlord or realtor to his or her spouse. Betty Jones and her black husband, Don, needed a larger home for themselves and their four children. Betty ventured out alone looking for adequate housing, making no mention that her husband was black, and relying on her intuition to detect whether a landlord or realtor might be prejudiced against an interracial couple. After finding the perfect home in South Natomas, she returned to fill out the necessary papers. Everything looked promising—until her husband showed up for the final signing of the contract. At that point, they were informed that South Natomas, built with a good deal of private money, had restrictive covenants and was to be a segregated community (Jones). Although completely illegal, such practices prevent interracial couples, as well as all blacks, from living where they choose.

Racial insults are the most common form of racism for bi-racial couples. For instance, it is not uncommon for the white wife of a black man to be called "white tramp," "jungle bunny," or numerous other racist names. Gillian Goldson reported her surprise when she and her husband were dining in Forest Park, Georgia, and a total stranger came up to whisper "nigger lover" in her ear (Turner 41). In spite of the fact that most of these comments come from whites, including friends and family members of the white partner, whites are not the only ethnic group that disapproves of interracial marriage.

Women of color are now beginning to openly express their disgust with black men who marry white women. Typically these women ask insulting questions like "Why are you wasting your life on that white tramp when you could be enjoying your life with a woman who won't be giving birth to little zebras?" Their comments are generally made out of frustration because black women outnumber eligible black males by a ratio of six to one. In light of these circumstances, women of color are turning to relationships with white males themselves in order to find love, comfort, and companionship (Randolph 162).

For most interracial couples, it is really not the insults from strangers that hurt most. Rather, it is the disfavor of family members that is so piercing. Black parents' disapproval of interracial marriage stems from the fact that they fear for their child's opportunity for success since white America discriminates against bi-racial couples so intensely. Apparently, most whites still believe that people should marry within their own race. When comparing the white and black communities on the issue, however, the researcher finds the black community far more receptive and accepting of whites becoming members of the family. The reaction of John Cox's father to John's black fiancée is a case in point. "It was not a good scene," is all John will say (Gardner 270). Chuck Bronz's mother sat down with her future black daughter-in-law and asked, "Why don't you marry your own kind?" (Kantrowitz 40). The period of adjustment for black parents of interracial couples is usually shorter and less turbulent. In contrast, white parents are more likely to abandon or disown their children for marrying blacks. Consider the plight of the Garretts. May Garrett and her black husband, Frank, met and married in March, 1983, despite their parents' disapproval. Because of her marriage to Frank, May's parents have refused to talk to her. As a final gesture of their disgust over May's marriage, they had her removed from their will (Garrett).

This strong reaction to interracial marriages may come from an attitude similar to the one mentioned by Augustina Barbera, Director of Psychology at Ohio State University. She has found some agreement among people she interviewed who think that black men are marrying white women to "get back" at white men (285). While it is a fact that black men are marrying white women over blacks in increasing numbers, those "numbers" are still quite small—half of one percent, according to the 1986 Census (Kantrowitz 40). Moreover, this reasoning is based on the uncomfortable assumption that such marriages must be made out of something other than love. The most obvious reason why people marry is the one most often overlooked in discussing interracial marriages: Black men are not marrying white women as a way of getting back at whites but because they sincerely love them. Perhaps Deborah Mathis, a black woman whose husband is white, says it best: "I didn't do this in rejection of anybody or to prove a point. It boils down to two people who got married for the same reasons that people have been doing it for forever—because we love each other" (Turner 44).

Racial violence, the most serious threat to interracial couples, is generally on the rise in America. This type of violence is society's way of releasing its hatred and racist attitudes against individuals who have defied racial injustice by marrying across racial lines. As the Gregorys discovered, these beliefs can assume a very threatening form. This couple made the mistake of stopping for ice cream in rural Mississippi. Before they got to the door, Josephine, a black American, and her white husband, Patrick, were met by "A white man wielding a four-by-four" (Turner 44). Luckily, they were able to get away in their car unharmed. In spite of the fact that many interracial couples like the Gregorys consider their love bigger than life, the fact remains that America is not yet ready to accept the idea that a black man should be free to marry a white woman (Levin 94).

Acts of racial violence against interracial marriages are becoming more common in cities where the overall ethnic breakdown is 75% white and the thought of blacks and whites marrying is considered racially unacceptable. According to Klanwatch, racial hate groups such as the Ku Klux Klan and WAR (White Aryan Resistance), have increased their acts of harassment against bi-racial couples nationwide (Turner 48). The following example tells the story of what one family had to endure because of their black-white marriage.

Elmo Seay and his white wife, Susan, had just recently moved to a community two miles outside of Atlanta, Georgia. They soon became victims of white supremacist groups when their home was first vandalized, then fire-bombed (Turner 42). Another couple, who wish to remain anonymous, had a similar experience when they moved into a predominantly white community. Their new neighborhood seemed the perfect place to live and raise their four children, until the night of August 4, 1989. As the entire family lay asleep on a warm summer night, they were suddenly awakened at one A.M. to find their living room a blazing inferno. As they gathered the children and ran out of the house, they were instantly met by a group of angry whites yelling, "Get out of our neighborhood you nigger-lover, and take that black bitch and those half-breed kids with you." Within twenty-four hours of this incident they were gone.

Although the White Aryan Resistance and other hate-groups continue to attempt to destroy bi-racial marriages by the use of force, their efforts are failing since many of these couples are receiving assistance from other interracial couples and support groups like the Atlanta-based Interracial Families Alliance. Public officials and religious leaders have also been helpful in condemning racist assaults.

Racism is one of the most dreaded terms in today's society; its effects on interracial marriages can be devastating. But there are things that can be done to halt the public's disapproval of interracial marriage and the racial violence that is being perpetrated against mixed-race couples. First, blacks and whites must begin to educate their children to respect the cultural differences of others and to appreciate individuals instead of hating a certain race. Next, we must welcome partners of family members who have decided to marry across racial lines. When difficulties arise, and they certainly will, we should encourage these couples to seek counseling from professionals who are trained in dealing with the problems of bi-racial couples. Because they will need ongoing support, these couples should join groups such as the Atlanta-based Interracial Families Alliance or, like the Bronz family of Westchester, New York, they should relocate to an interracial neighborhood and make friends with other bi-racial couples (Kantrowitz 40). Last of all, instead of harassing and complicating their marriages with our own racist insecurities, we should be assisting these couples to maintain their beautiful and unusual marriages.

—Gary Gilbert

Works Cited

Barbera, Augustina. "America's Viewpoint of Interracial Marriage: Can They Survive?" Women's World Magazine, December 1979: 282–87.

Gardner, Ralph. "Cosmo's Update on Interracial Marriage." Cosmopolitan Magazine, November 1989: 268–72.

Garrett, May and Frank. Personal interview. 5 December 1990.

Jones, Betty. Personal interview. 12 December 1990.

Kantrowitz, Barbera. "Colorblind Love: One Group of Friends Still Lives the Dream." Newsweek Magazine, March 1988: 40–42.

Levin, Norma. "Love in Black and White: Bi-racial Marriages in the Twin Cities Metropolitan Area." St. Paul Magazine, August 1987: 72–79.

Randolph, Laura. "Black Women—White Men: What's Going On?" Ebony Magazine, March 1989: 42–44.

Tucker, Dorothy. "Guess Who's Coming to Dinner Now." Essence Magazine, April 1987: 45–49.

Turner, Renee D. "Interracial Couples in the South: Attitudes Are Changing on Once Illegal Marriages of Blacks to Whites." Ebony Magazine, June 1990: 41–46.

Questions for Discussion

1. What is Gary Gilbert's purpose for writing his essay?
2. Evaluate several of Gilbert's arguments. Which do you find most effective? Explain your choice.

18

Against Injustice

*Injustice anywhere is a threat
to justice everywhere.*

—*Martin Luther King, Jr.*

*Perhaps the question of eliminating
homelessness in America ultimately comes
down to fulfilling our part of a bargain.*

—*Charles E. King*

T he previous chapter features articles by writers taking a stand against various forms of stereotyping. The writers in this chapter present their cases against other forms of social injustice. Martin Luther King, Jr. explores a nonviolent solution to racial injustice. Charles E. King, the author of "Homelessness in America," argues that we have a responsibility to provide shelter for the homeless. And finally, Cesar Chavez criticizes farmers whose use of pesticides endangers the health of their workers.

This chapter introduces techniques used in writing persuasive essays. Passages from Martin Luther King's "Letter from the Birmingham Jail" illustrate some of the techniques that writers use to write persuasively.

PERSUADING

The writing techniques discussed in Chapter 17 for developing a topic and generating ideas for papers that take a stand will be useful as you write more formal persuasive essays. Additional considerations for presenting rational, emotional, and moral appeals include a clear purpose and audience, a debatable thesis, a reasonable approach to the topic, an appeal to emotions, an appeal to moral values, and, as always, a clear organization.

Characteristics of Persuading

A Clear Purpose and Audience

The purpose of persuasive essays is often to convince the reader to take a particular stand on an issue or to take action to remedy a situation. In his "Letter from the Birmingham Jail," Martin Luther King, Jr.'s immediate purpose is to defend himself against the accusations that the sit-ins and marches he organized in an effort to integrate public facilities in Birmingham, Alabama, were "unwise and untimely." King addresses his letter to the four bishops, three ministers, and one rabbi who made the statement, but his answers have had a much wider audience. The letter was published in 1963 in a collection of King's essays entitled *Why We Can't Wait*. In the intervening thirty years, "The Letter from the Birmingham Jail" has become standard reading in many high-school and college classes.

A Debatable Thesis

For a topic to be suitable for a persuasive paper, it must be "debatable"; this means it must be possible for someone to take an opposing position on the issue. For example, an essay arguing that funding for programs that target disabled children and adults should be increased might have this thesis: the amount this state budgets for services to the disabled should be increased. This thesis is debatable because a writer who opposes this solution could take this position: the amount this state budgets for services to the disabled should *not* be increased. Taxpayers or groups that compete for funds might take this second position.

The following examples will help you distinguish between the thesis for a persuasive essay and thesis statements used for other writing strategies. Debatable thesis statements have a check (✓) beside them.

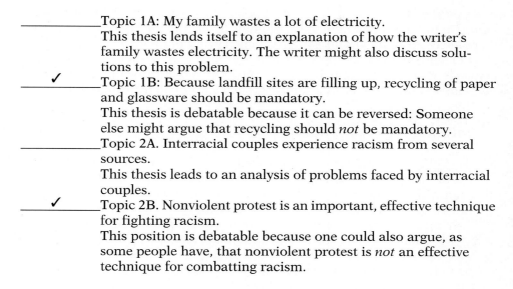

_____Topic 1A: My family wastes a lot of electricity.
This thesis lends itself to an explanation of how the writer's family wastes electricity. The writer might also discuss solutions to this problem.

✓_____Topic 1B: Because landfill sites are filling up, recycling of paper and glassware should be mandatory.
This thesis is debatable because it can be reversed: Someone else might argue that recycling should *not* be mandatory.

_____Topic 2A. Interracial couples experience racism from several sources.
This thesis leads to an analysis of problems faced by interracial couples.

✓_____Topic 2B. Nonviolent protest is an important, effective technique for fighting racism.
This position is debatable because one could also argue, as some people have, that nonviolent protest is *not* an effective technique for combatting racism.

FOR PRACTICE

Identify the thesis statements below that are debatable, and, consequently, suitable for a persuasive paper. For statements that are *not* debatable, note the writing strategy you would use to develop them. The first one is done for you.

_____1. Some businesses work to defeat gun control for several reasons. *I would* explain *why certain businesses support the quick sale of handguns.*

_____2. Laws should provide much stricter regulations for the use of firearms.

_____3. The United States has accumulated the most advanced weapons system the world has ever seen.

_____4. Teen suicide can be prevented if we learn to read the signs.

_____5. AIDS, often called the modern plague, has an obscure beginning and a tragic history.

_____6. Several important reasons justify why school lunch programs should not be cut from the Federal budget.

A Reasonable Approach to the Topic

In order to be persuasive, writers make rational, moral, and emotional appeals to their readers. Writers have several ways of demonstrating that their position is reasonable.

A REASONABLE TONE.   To write persuasively, an author, although convinced of his or her position, must maintain an overall tone of reasonableness. As pointed out in the discussion on taking a stand in Chapter 17, a self-righteous or narrow-minded approach may intimidate an audience, but it won't convince them. In the opening of the letter he wrote from the Birmingham jail, Martin Luther King, Jr. establishes such a rational, measured tone.

> My Dear Fellow Clergymen:
>
> While confined here in the Birmingham city jail, I came across   1
> your recent statement calling my present activities "unwise and
> untimely." Seldom do I pause to answer criticism of my work and
> ideas. If I sought to answer all the criticisms that cross my desk, my
> secretaries would have little time for anything other than such cor-
> respondence in the course of the day, and I would have no time for
> constructive work. But since I feel that you are men of genuine
> good will and that your criticisms are sincerely set forth, I want to
> try to answer your statement in what I hope will be patient and rea-
> sonable terms.

King acknowledges that his critics are "men of genuine good will" whose "criticisms are sincerely set forth," and he promises to be "patient and reasonable" in his response. He thereby establishes himself as someone who respectfully disagrees with his opponents and will remain reasonable in his rebuttal of their arguments.

A CLEAR POSITION.   Readers need to know exactly what position the writer will defend and how that position will be supported. King makes it clear that his letter is an answer to a "recent statement" signed by several clergymen who assert that his nonviolent protests are "unwise and untimely." His letter answers each of their objections in turn, and in the process, presents his own positions on the issues they raise.

OPPOSING POINTS OF VIEW.   Writers of persuasion often introduce opposing arguments and offer their own objections or counterarguments. In so doing, they anticipate objections that their readers may share. The tactic also shows that the writer examined the issue from several perspectives before reaching a reasonable conclusion. In his letter from jail, King presents and then refutes each of his opponents' arguments against nonviolent protest. A few of his rebuttals are illustrated in the following discussion of evidence.

SEVERAL KINDS OF EVIDENCE.   Support for ideas is always an important element in an essay, but because persuasive essays try to convince the reader to change a position or to take action on a particular issue, solid evidence is literally the heart of persuasive writing. Facts, case studies, personal experience, and the opinions of witnesses or authorities provide convincing support. King uses each of these sources of evidence. He counters with facts his opponents' accusation that he is an "outsider" who has come to Birmingham to make trouble:

> I think I should indicate why I am here in Birmingham, since 2 you have been influenced by the view which argues against "outsiders coming in." I have the honor of serving as president of the Southern Christian Leadership Conference, an organization operating in every southern state, with headquarters in Atlanta, Georgia. We have some eighty-five affiliated organizations across the South, and one of them is the Alabama Christian Movement for Human Rights. Frequently we share staff, educational, and financial resources with our affiliates. Several months ago the affiliate here in Birmingham asked us to be on call to engage in a nonviolent direct-action program if such were deemed necessary. We readily consented, and when the hour came we lived up to our promise. So I, along with several members of my staff, am here because I was invited here. I am here because I have organizational ties here.

Next, King explains the biblical authority for his actions in Birmingham, and cites biblical precedent. Because his audience consists of four bishops, three ministers, and a rabbi, the Bible is completely appropriate as an "authority" for his actions, one that his clerical readers respect.

> But more basically, I am in Birmingham because injustice is 3 here. Just as the prophets of the eighth century B.C. left their villages and carried their "thus saith the Lord" far beyond the boundaries of their home towns, and just as the Apostle Paul left his village of Tarsus and carried the gospel of Jesus Christ to the far corners of the Greco-Roman world, so am I compelled to carry the gospel of freedom beyond my own home town. Like Paul, I must constantly respond to the Macedonian call for aid.

Appeal to Emotions

Although it should be used sparingly, an appeal to readers' emotions can sometimes be quite effective. In some of the most persuasive writing in the English language, King makes an emotional appeal to his readers when he gives examples of the injustices suffered by black Americans and mentions the feeling of "nobodiness" that results from such treatment.

> We have waited for more than 340 years for our constitutional   10
> and God-given rights. The nations of Asia and Africa are moving
> with jetlike speed toward gaining political independence, but we
> still creep at horse-and-buggy pace toward gaining a cup of coffee
> at a lunch counter. Perhaps it is easy for those who have never felt
> the stinging darts of segregation to say, "Wait." But when you have
> seen vicious mobs lynch your mothers and fathers at will and
> drown your sisters and brothers at whim; when you have seen hate-
> filled policemen curse, kick, and even kill your black brothers and
> sisters; when you see the vast majority of your twenty million Negro
> brothers smothering in an airtight cage of poverty in the midst of an
> affluent society; when you suddenly find your tongue twisted and
> your speech stammering as you seek to explain to your six-year-old
> daughter why she can't go to the public amusement park that has
> just been advertised on television, and see tears welling up in her
> eyes when she is told that Funtown is closed to colored children,
> and see ominous clouds of inferiority beginning to form in her little
> mental sky, and see her beginning to distort her personality by
> developing an unconscious bitterness toward white people; when
> you have to concoct an answer for a five-year-old son who is asking:
> "Daddy, why do white people treat colored people so mean?"; when
> you take a cross-country drive and find it necessary to sleep night
> after night in the uncomfortable corners of your automobile
> because no motel will accept you; when you are humiliated day in
> and day out by nagging signs reading "white" and "colored"; when
> your first name becomes "nigger," your middle name becomes
> "boy" (however old you are), and your last name becomes "John,"
> and your wife and mother are never given the respected title "Mrs.";
> when you are harried by day and haunted by night by the fact that
> you are a Negro, living constantly at tiptoe stance, never quite
> knowing what to expect next, and are plagued with inner fears and
> outer resentments; when you are forever fighting a degenerating
> sense of "nobodiness"—then you will understand why we find it dif-
> ficult to wait. There comes a time when the cup of endurance runs
> over, and men are no longer willing to be plunged into the abyss of
> despair. I hope, sirs, you can understand our legitimate and
> unavoidable impatience.

Appeal to Moral Values

In "Letter from the Birmingham Jail," King uses the clergymen's own moral principles and the religious foundations on which their churches are based to criticize their position.

> I have heard numerous southern religious leaders admonish 25
> their worshipers to comply with a desegregation decision because it
> is the law, but I have longed to hear white ministers declare: "Follow
> this decree because integration is morally right and because the
> Negro is your brother." In the midst of blatant injustices inflicted
> upon the Negro, I have watched white churchmen stand on the side-
> line and mouth pious irrelevancies and sanctimonious trivialities. In
> the midst of a mighty struggle to rid our nation of racial and eco-
> nomic injustice, I have heard many ministers say: "Those are social
> issues, with which the gospel has no real concern." And I have
> watched many churches commit themselves to a completely other-
> worldly religion which makes a strange, un-biblical distinction
> between body and soul, between the sacred and secular.
> I have traveled the length and breadth of Alabama, Missi- 26
> ssippi, and all the other southern states. On sweltering summer
> days and crisp autumn mornings I have looked at the South's beau-
> tiful churches with their lofty spires pointing heavenward. I have
> beheld the impressive outlines of her massive religious-education
> buildings. Over and over I have found myself asking: "What kind of
> people worship here? Who is their God?" . . .
> . . . So often the contemporary church is a weak, ineffectual 29
> voice with an uncertain sound. So often it is an archdefender of
> the status quo. Far from being disturbed by the presence of the
> *church*, the power structure of the average community is consoled
> by the church's silent—and often even vocal—sanction of things
> as they are.
> But the judgment of God is upon the church as never before. If 30
> today's church does not recapture the sacrificial spirit of the early
> church, it will lose its authenticity, forfeit the loyalty of millions,
> and be dismissed as an irrelevant social club with no meaning for
> the twentieth century.

As far as King is concerned, the white churches have betrayed their moral trust by their passive acceptance of overtly racist practices.

A Clear Organization

Persuasive essays have several possible patterns for organization, some of which are illustrated in the discussion of the writing process that appears later in this chapter. Generally, writers who use persuasive techniques acknowledge and rebut at least a few opposing arguments. Martin Luther King wrote "Letter from the Birmingham Jail" as a rebuttal to criticisms of his decision to organize nonviolent demonstrations. In his letter, he responds carefully to each of his critics' objections.

> You may well ask: "Why direct action? Why sit-ins, marches, 6 and so forth? Isn't negotiation a better path?" You are quite right in calling for negotiation. Indeed, this is the very purpose of direct action. Nonviolent direct action seeks to create such a crisis and foster such a tension that a community which has constantly refused to negotiate is forced to confront the issue. It seeks so to dramatize the issue that it can no longer be ignored. My citing the creation of tension as part of the work of the nonviolent-resister may sound rather shocking. But I must confess that I am not afraid of the word "tension." I have earnestly opposed violent tension, but there is a type of constructive, nonviolent tension which is necessary for growth. Just as Socrates felt that it was necessary to create a tension in the mind so that individuals could rise from the bondage of myths and half-truths to the unfettered realm of creative analysis and objective appraisal, so must we see the need for nonviolent gadflies to create the kind of tension in society that will help men rise from the dark depths of prejudice and racism to the majestic heights of understanding and brotherhood.

In this excerpt, King answers his opponents' questions, explains his own position, notes a historical parallel to Socrates, and reaffirms his own moral goal.

Letter from the Birmingham Jail
Martin Luther King, Jr.

As founding president of the Southern Christian Leadership Conference, Dr. Martin Luther King, Jr. (1928-1968) led the nonviolent movement to desegregate the South. The efforts of King and his followers culminated in the Civil Rights Act of 1964 and the 1965 Voting Rights Act. After the passage of the Civil Rights Act, King received the Nobel Peace Prize, and more recently, his birthday has been declared a national holiday. He wrote the "Letter from the Birmingham Jail" to eight clergymen—four bishops, three ministers, and a rabbi—who had criticized him for resorting to civil disobedience in his fight against segregationist policies in the South. Dr. King worked for civil rights causes until his death at the hands of an assassin on April 4, 1968.

April 16, 1963

My Dear Fellow Clergymen:

While confined here in the Birmingham city jail, I came across your recent 1 statement calling my present activities "unwise and untimely." Seldom do I pause to answer criticism of my work and ideas. If I sought to answer all the criticisms that cross my desk, my secretaries would have little time for anything other than such correspondence in the course of the day, and I would have no time for constructive work. But since I feel that you are men of genuine good will and that your criticisms are sincerely set forth, I want to try to answer your statement in what I hope will be patient and reasonable terms.

I think I should indicate why I am here in Birmingham, since you have 2 been influenced by the view which argues against "outsiders coming in." I have the honor of serving as president of the Southern Christian Leadership Conference, an organization operating in every southern state, with headquarters in Atlanta, Georgia. We have some eighty-five affiliated organizations across the South, and one of them is the Alabama Christian Movement for Human Rights. Frequently we share staff, educational, and financial resources with our affiliates. Several months ago the affiliate here in Birmingham asked us to be on call to engage in a nonviolent direct-action program if such were deemed necessary. We readily consented, and when the hour came we lived up to our promise. So I, along with several members of my staff, am here because I was invited here. I am here because I have organizational ties here.

But more basically, I am in Birmingham because injustice is here. Just as 3 the prophets of the eighth century B.C. left their villages and carried their "thus saith the Lord" far beyond the boundaries of their home towns, and just as the Apostle Paul left his village of Tarsus and carried the gospel of Jesus Christ to the far corners of the Greco-Roman world, so am I compelled to carry the gospel of freedom beyond my own home town. Like Paul, I must constantly respond to the Macedonian call for aid.

Moreover, I am cognizant of the interrelatedness of all communities and 4 states. I cannot sit idly by in Atlanta and not be concerned about what happens in Birmingham. Injustice anywhere is a threat to justice everywhere. We are caught in an inescapable network of mutuality, tied in a single garment of destiny. Whatever affects one directly, affects all indirectly. Never again can we afford to live with the narrow, provincial "outside agitator" idea. Anyone who lives inside the United States can never be considered an outsider anywhere within its bounds.

You deplore the demonstrations taking place in Birmingham. But your 5 statement, I am sorry to say, fails to express a similar concern for the conditions that brought about the demonstrations. I am sure that none of you would want to rest content with the superficial kind of social analysis that deals merely with effects and does not grapple with underlying causes. It is unfortunate that demonstrations are taking place in Birmingham, but it is even more unfortunate that the city's white power structure left the Negro community with no alternative. . . .

You may well ask: "Why direct action? Why sit-ins, marches, and so forth? 6 Isn't negotiation a better path?" You are quite right in calling for negotiation. Indeed, this is the very purpose of direct action. Nonviolent direct action seeks to create such a crisis and foster such a tension that a community which has constantly refused to negotiate is forced to confront the issue. It seeks so to dramatize the issue that it can no longer be ignored. My citing the creation of tension as part of the work of the nonviolent-resister may sound rather shocking. But I must confess that I am not afraid of the word "tension." I have earnestly opposed violent tension, but there is a type of constructive, nonviolent tension which is necessary for growth. Just as Socrates[1] felt that it was necessary to create a tension in the mind so that individuals could rise from the bondage of myths and half-truths to the unfettered realm of creative analysis and objective appraisal, so must we see the need for nonviolent gadflies to create the kind of tension in society that will help men rise from the dark depths of prejudice and racism to the majestic heights of understanding and brotherhood.

The purpose of our direct-action program is to create a situation so crisis-   7
packed that it will inevitably open the door to negotiation. I therefore concur with you in your call for negotiation. Too long has our beloved Southland been bogged down in a tragic effort to live in monologue rather than dialogue.

One of the basic points in your statement is that the action that I and my   8
associates have taken in Birmingham is untimely. Some have asked: "Why didn't you give the new city administration time to act?" The only answer that I can give to this query is that the new Birmingham administration must be prodded about as much as the outgoing one, before it will act. . . . My friends, I must say to you that we have not made a single gain in civil rights without determined legal and nonviolent pressure. Lamentably, it is an historical fact that privileged groups seldom give up their privileges voluntarily. Individuals may see the moral light and voluntarily give up their unjust posture; but, as Reinhold Niebuhr[2] has reminded us, groups tend to be more immoral than individuals.

We know through painful experience that freedom is never voluntarily   9
given by the oppressor; it must be demanded by the oppressed. Frankly, I have yet to engage in a direct-action campaign that was "well timed" in the view of those who have not suffered unduly from the disease of segregation. For years now I have heard the word "Wait!" It rings in the ear of every Negro with piercing familiarity. This "Wait" has almost always meant "Never." We must come to see, with one of our distinguished jurists, that "justice too long delayed is justice denied."

We have waited for more than 340 years for our constitutional and God-   10
given rights. The nations of Asia and Africa are moving with jetlike speed toward gaining political independence, but we still creep at horse-and-buggy pace toward gaining a cup of coffee at a lunch counter. Perhaps it is easy for those who have never felt the stinging darts of segregation to say, "Wait." But

---

[1]Greek philosopher (470?–399 B.C.) whose outspoken criticism of the government in Athens led to his imprisonment and eventual death.

[2]American theologian, 1892–1971.

when you have seen vicious mobs lynch your mothers and fathers at will and drown your sisters and brothers at whim; when you have seen hate-filled policemen curse, kick, and even kill your black brothers and sisters; when you see the vast majority of your twenty million Negro brothers smothering in an airtight cage of poverty in the midst of an affluent society; when you suddenly find your tongue twisted and your speech stammering as you seek to explain to your six-year-old daughter why she can't go to the public amusement park that has just been advertised on television, and see tears welling up in her eyes when she is told that Funtown is closed to colored children, and see ominous clouds of inferiority beginning to form in her little mental sky, and see her beginning to distort her personality by developing an unconscious bitterness toward white people; when you have to concoct an answer for a five-year-old son who is asking: "Daddy, why do white people treat colored people so mean?"; when you take a cross-country drive and find it necessary to sleep night after night in the uncomfortable corners of your automobile because no motel will accept you; when you are humiliated day in and day out by nagging signs reading "white" and "colored"; when your first name becomes "nigger," your middle name becomes "boy" (however old you are), and your last name becomes "John," and your wife and mother are never given the respected title "Mrs."; when you are harried by day and haunted by night by the fact that you are a Negro, living constantly at tiptoe stance, never quite knowing what to expect next, and are plagued with inner fears and outer resentments; when you are forever fighting a degenerating sense of "nobodiness"—then you will understand why we find it difficult to wait. There comes a time when the cup of endurance runs over, and men are no longer willing to be plunged into the abyss of despair. I hope, sirs, you can understand our legitimate and unavoidable impatience.

You express a great deal of anxiety over our willingness to break laws. This 11
is certainly a legitimate concern. Since we so diligently urge people to obey the Supreme Court's decision of 1954 outlawing segregation in the public schools, at first glance it may seem rather paradoxical for us consciously to break laws. One may well ask: "How can you advocate breaking some laws and obeying others?" The answer lies in the fact that there are two types of laws: just and unjust. I would be the first to advocate obeying just laws. One has not only a legal but a moral responsibility to obey just laws. Conversely, one has a moral responsibility to disobey unjust laws. I would agree with St. Augustine that "an unjust law is no law at all."

Now, what is the difference between the two? How does one determine 12
whether a law is just or unjust? A just law is a man-made code that squares with the moral law or the law of God. An unjust law is a code that is out of harmony with the moral law. To put it in the terms of St. Thomas Aquinas: An unjust law is a human law that is not rooted in eternal law and natural law. Any law that uplifts human personality is just. Any law that degrades human personality is unjust. All segregation statutes are unjust because segregation distorts the soul and damages the personality. It gives the segregator a false sense of superiority and the segregated a false sense of inferiority.

Segregation, to use the terminology of the Jewish philosopher Martin Buber,[3] substitutes an "I-it" relationship for an "I-thou" relationship and ends up relegating persons to the status of things. Hence segregation is not only politically, economically, and sociologically unsound, it is morally wrong and sinful. Paul Tillich has said that sin is separation. Is not segregation an existential expression of man's tragic separation, his awful estrangement, his terrible sinfulness? Thus it is that I can urge men to obey the 1954 decision of the Supreme Court, for it is morally right; and I can urge them to disobey segregation ordinances, for they are morally wrong.

Let us consider a more concrete example of just and unjust laws. An 13 unjust law is a code that a numerical or power majority group compels a minority group to obey but does not make binding on itself. This is *difference* made legal. By the same token, a just law is a code that a majority compels a minority to follow and that it is willing to follow itself. This is *sameness* made legal.

Let me give another explanation. A law is unjust if it is inflicted on a minor- 14 ity that, as a result of being denied the right to vote, had no part in enacting or devising the law. Who can say that the legislature of Alabama which set up that state's segregation laws was democratically elected? Throughout Alabama all sorts of devious methods are used to prevent Negroes from becoming registered voters, and there are some counties in which, even though Negroes constitute a majority of the population, not a single Negro is registered. Can any law enacted under such circumstances be considered democratically structured? . . .

I hope you are able to see the distinction I am trying to point out. In no 15 sense do I advocate evading or defying the law, as would the rabid segregationist. That would lead to anarchy. One who breaks an unjust law must do so openly, lovingly, and with a willingness to accept the penalty. I submit that an individual who breaks a law that conscience tells him is unjust, and who willingly accepts the penalty of imprisonment in order to arouse the conscience of the community over its injustice, is in reality expressing the highest respect for law.

Of course, there is nothing new about this kind of civil disobedience. It 16 was evidenced sublimely in the refusal of Shadrach, Meshach, and Abednego[4] to obey the laws of Nebuchadnezzar, on the ground that a higher moral law was at stake. It was practiced superbly by the early Christians, who were willing to face hungry lions and the excruciating pain of chopping blocks rather than submit to certain unjust laws of the Roman Empire. To a degree, academic freedom is a reality today because Socrates practiced civil disobedience. In our own nation, the Boston Tea Party represented a massive act of civil disobedience.

---

[3]Israeli philosopher and theologian (1878–1965) associated with religious Existentialism.

[4]The three Hebrew prophets in *The Book of Daniel* who emerged from the "fiery furnace" unharmed.

We should never forget that everything Adolf Hitler did in Germany was 17 "legal" and everything the Hungarian freedom fighters did in Hungary was "illegal." It was "illegal" to aid and comfort a Jew in Hitler's Germany. Even so, I am sure that, had I lived in Germany at the time, I would have aided and comforted my Jewish brothers. If today I lived in a Communist country where certain principles dear to the Christian faith are suppressed, I would openly advocate disobeying that country's antireligious laws.

I must make two honest confessions to you, my Christian and Jewish 18 brothers. First, I must confess that over the past few years I have been gravely disappointed with the white moderate. I have almost reached the regrettable conclusion that the Negro's great stumbling block in his stride toward freedom is not the White Citizen's Counciler or the Ku Klux Klanner, but the white moderate, who is more devoted to "order" than to justice; who prefers a negative peace which is the absence of tension to a positive peace which is the presence of justice; who constantly says: "I agree with you in the goal you seek, but I cannot agree with your methods of direct action"; who paternalistically believes he can set the timetable for another man's freedom; who lives by a mythical concept of time and who constantly advises the Negro to wait for a "more convenient season." Shallow understanding from people of good will is more frustrating than absolute misunderstanding from people of ill will. Lukewarm acceptance is much more bewildering than outright rejection. . . .

You speak of our activity in Birmingham as extreme. At first I was rather 19 disappointed that fellow clergymen would see my nonviolent efforts as those of an extremist. I began thinking about the fact that I stand in the middle of two opposing forces in the Negro community. One is a force of complacency, made up in part of Negroes who, as a result of long years of oppression, are so drained of self-respect and a sense of "somebodiness" that they have adjusted to segregation; and in part of a few middle-class Negroes who, because of a degree of academic and economic security and because in some ways they profit by segregation, have become insensitive to the problems of the masses. The other force is one of bitterness and hatred, and it comes perilously close to advocating violence. It is expressed in the various black nationalist groups that are springing up across the nation, the largest and best-known being Elijah Muhammad's Muslim movement. Nourished by the Negro's frustration over the continued existence of racial discrimination, this movement is made up of people who have lost faith in America, who have absolutely repudiated Christianity, and who have concluded that the white man is an incorrigible "devil."[5]

I have tried to stand between these two forces, saying that we need emu- 20 late neither the "do-nothingism" of the complacent nor the hatred and despair

---

[5]King refers to the Black Muslim movement which flourished in the 1960s. Malcolm X, an eloquent spokesman for that movement, originally accepted Elijah Muhammad's teaching that the white man was the devil.

of the black nationalist. For there is the more excellent way of love and nonviolent protest. I am grateful to God that, through the influence of the Negro church, the way of nonviolence became an integral part of our struggle.

If this philosophy had not emerged, by now many streets of the South 21 would, I am convinced, be flowing with blood. And I am further convinced that if our white brothers dismiss as "rabble-rousers" and "outside agitators" those of us who employ nonviolent direct action, and if they refuse to support our nonviolent efforts, millions of Negroes will, out of frustration and despair, seek solace and security in black nationalist ideologies—a development that would inevitably lead to a frightening racial nightmare.

Oppressed people cannot remain oppressed forever. The yearning for free- 22 dom eventually manifests itself, and that is what has happened to the American Negro. Something within has reminded him of his birthright of freedom, and something without has reminded him that it can be gained. Consciously or unconsciously, he has been caught up by the *Zeitgeist,*[6] and with his black brothers of Africa and his brown and yellow brothers of Asia, South America, and the Caribbean, the United States Negro is moving with a sense of great urgency toward the promised land of racial justice. If one recognizes this vital urge that has engulfed the Negro community, one should readily understand why public demonstrations are taking place. The Negro has many pent-up resentments and latent frustrations, and he must release them. So let him march; let him make prayer pilgrimages to the city hall; let him go on freedom rides—and try to understand why he must do so. If his repressed emotions are not released in nonviolent ways, they will seek expression through violence; this is not a threat but a fact of history. So I have not said to my people: "Get rid of your discontent." Rather, I have tried to say that this normal and healthy discontent can be channeled into the creative outlet of nonviolent direct action. And now this approach is being termed extremist.

But though I was initially disappointed at being categorized as an extrem- 23 ist, as I continued to think about the matter I gradually gained a measure of satisfaction from the label. Was not Jesus an extremist for love: "Love your enemies, bless them that curse you, do good to them that hate you, and pray for them which despitefully use you, and persecute you." Was not Amos an extremist for justice: "Let justice roll down like waters and righteousness like an ever-flowing stream." Was not Paul an extremist for the Christian gospel: "I bear in my body the marks of the Lord Jesus." Was not Martin Luther[7] an extremist: "Here I stand; I cannot do otherwise, so help me God." And John Bunyan: "I will stay in jail to the end of my days before I make a butchery of my conscience." And Abraham Lincoln: "This nation cannot survive half slave and half free." And Thomas Jefferson: "We hold these truths to be self-evident,

---

[6]German for the "spirit of the age"; the way of thinking that is characteristic of a particular era.

[7]Martin Luther's protests against the Catholic church started the Protestant movement in Europe.

that all men are created equal . . ." So the question is not whether we will be extremists, but what kind of extremists we will be. Will we be extremists for hate or for love? Will we be extremists for the preservation of injustice or for the extension of justice? In that dramatic scene on Calvary's hill three men were crucified. We must never forget that all three were crucified for the same crime—the crime of extremism. Two were extremists for immorality, and thus fell below their environment. The other, Jesus Christ, was an extremist for love, truth and goodness, and thereby rose above his environment. Perhaps the South, the nation and the world are in dire need of creative extremists. . . .

I came to Birmingham with the hope that the white religious leadership of 24
this community would see the justice of our cause and, with deep moral con- cern, would serve as the channel through which our just grievances could reach the power structure. I had hoped that each of you would understand. But again I have been disappointed.

I have heard numerous southern religious leaders admonish their wor- 25
shipers to comply with a desegregation decision because it is the law, but I have longed to hear white ministers declare: "Follow this decree because inte- gration is morally right and because the Negro is your brother." In the midst of blatant injustices inflicted upon the Negro, I have watched white church- men stand on the sideline and mouth pious irrelevancies and sanctimonious trivialities. In the midst of a mighty struggle to rid our nation of racial and economic injustice, I have heard many ministers say: "Those are social issues, with which the gospel has no real concern." And I have watched many churches commit themselves to a completely other-worldly religion which makes a strange, unbiblical distinction between body and soul, between the sacred and the secular.

I have traveled the length and breadth of Alabama, Mississippi and all the 26
other southern states. On sweltering summer days and crisp autumn morn- ings I have looked at the South's beautiful churches with their lofty spires pointing heavenward. I have beheld the impressive outlines of her massive religious-education buildings. Over and over I have found myself asking: "What kind of people worship here? Who is their God? Where were their voices when the lips of Governor Barnett dripped with words of interposition and nullification? Where were they when Governor Wallace gave a clarion call for defiance and hatred? Where were their voices of support when bruised and weary Negro men and women decided to rise from the dark dungeons of com- placency to the bright hills of creative protest?"

Yes, these questions are still in my mind. In deep disappointment I have 27
wept over the laxity of the church. But be assured that my tears have been tears of love. There can be no deep disappointment where there is not deep love. Yes, I love the church. How could I do otherwise? I am in the rather unique position of being the son, the grandson, and the great-grandson of preachers. Yes, I see the church as the body of Christ. But, oh! How we have blemished and scarred that body through social neglect and through fear of being nonconformists.

There was a time when the church was very powerful—in the time when   28
the early Christians rejoiced at being deemed worthy to suffer for what they
believed. In those days the church was not merely a thermometer that
recorded the ideas and principles of popular opinion; it was a thermostat that
transformed the mores of society. Whenever the early Christians entered a
town, the people in power became disturbed and immediately sought to con-
vict the Christians for being "disturbers of the peace" and "outside agitators."
But the Christians pressed on, in the conviction that they were "a colony of
heaven," called to obey God rather than man. Small in number, they were big
in commitment. They were too God-intoxicated to be "astronomically intimidated." By their effort and example they brought an end to such ancient evils
as infanticide and gladiatorial contests.

Things are different now. So often the contemporary church is a weak,   29
ineffectual voice with an uncertain sound. So often it is an archdefender of the
status quo. Far from being disturbed by the presence of the church, the power
structure of the average community is consoled by the church's silent—and
often even vocal—sanction of things as they are.

But the judgment of God is upon the church as never before. If today's   30
church does not recapture the sacrificial spirit of the early church, it will lose
its authenticity, forfeit the loyalty of millions, and be dismissed as an irrelevant social club with no meaning for the twentieth century. Every day I meet
young people whose disappointment with the church has turned into outright
disgust. . . .

I hope the church as a whole will meet the challenge of this decisive hour.   31
But even if the church does not come to the aid of justice, I have no despair
about the future. I have no fear about the outcome of our struggle in
Birmingham, even if our motives are at present misunderstood. We will reach
the goal of freedom in Birmingham and all over the nation, because the goal
of America is freedom. Abused and scorned though we may be, our destiny is
tied up with America's destiny. Before the pilgrims landed at Plymouth, we
were here. Before the pen of Jefferson etched the majestic words of the
Declaration of Independence across the pages of history, we were here. For
more than two centuries our forebears labored in this country without wages;
they made cotton king; they built the homes of their masters while suffering
gross injustice and shameful humiliation—and yet out of a bottomless vitality
they continued to thrive and develop. If the inexpressible cruelties of slavery
could not stop us, the opposition we now face will surely fail. We will win our
freedom because the sacred heritage of our nation and the eternal will of God
are embodied in our echoing demands.

Before closing I feel impelled to mention one other point in your state-   32
ment that has troubled me profoundly. You warmly commended the
Birmingham police force for keeping "order" and "preventing violence." I
doubt that you would have so warmly commended the police force if you had
seen its dogs sinking their teeth into unarmed, nonviolent Negroes. I doubt
that you would so quickly commend the policemen if you were to observe
their ugly and inhumane treatment of Negroes here in the city jail; if you were

to watch them push and curse old Negro women and young Negro girls; if you were to see them slap and kick old Negro men and young boys; if you were to observe them, as they did on two occasions, refuse to give us food because we wanted to sing our grace together. I cannot join you in your praise of the Birmingham police department. . . .

I wish you had commended the Negro sit-inners and demonstrators of 33 Birmingham for their sublime courage, their willingness to suffer and their amazing discipline in the midst of great provocation. One day the South will recognize its real heroes. They will be the James Merediths, with the noble sense of purpose that enables them to face jeering and hostile mobs, and with the agonizing loneliness that characterizes the life of the pioneer. They will be old, oppressed, battered Negro women, symbolized in a seventy-two-year-old woman in Montgomery, Alabama, who rose up with a sense of dignity and with her people decided not to ride segregated buses, and who responded with ungrammatical profundity to one who inquired about her weariness: "My feets is tired, but my soul is at rest." They will be the young high-school and college students, the young ministers of the gospel and a host of their elders, courageously and nonviolently sitting in at lunch counters and willingly going to jail for conscience' sake. One day the South will know that when these disinherited children of God sat down at lunch counters, they were in reality standing up for what is best in the American dream and for the most sacred values in our Judaeo-Christian heritage, thereby bringing our nation back to those great wells of democracy which were dug deep by the founding fathers in their formulation of the Constitution and the Declaration of Independence.

Never before have I written so long a letter. I'm afraid it is much too long 34 to take your precious time. I can assure you that it would have been much shorter if I had been writing from a comfortable desk, but what else can one do when he is alone in a narrow jail cell, other than write long letters, think long thoughts, and pray long prayers?

If I have said anything in this letter that overstates the truth and indicates 35 an unreasonable impatience, I beg you to forgive me. If I have said anything that understates the truth and indicates my having a patience that allows me to settle for anything less than brotherhood, I beg God to forgive me.

I hope this letter finds you strong in the faith. I also hope that circum- 36 stances will soon make it possible for me to meet each of you, not as an integrationist or a civil-rights leader but as a fellow clergyman and a Christian brother. Let us all hope that the dark clouds of racial prejudice will soon pass away and the deep fog of misunderstanding will be lifted from our fear-drenched communities, and in some not too distant tomorrow the radiant stars of love and brotherhood will shine over our great nation with all their scintillating beauty.

Yours for the cause of Peace and Brotherhood,
MARTIN LUTHER KING, JR.

RESPONDING TO THE READING

Freewriting

Exercise 18a.   Based on what you have just read about segregation in the South, describe the situation blacks faced when Dr. King wrote his "Letter from the Birmingham Jail."

Building Your Vocabulary

VOCABULARY LIST

Words to Look Up	My Definition	Dictionary Definition
affiliated (2)		
deemed (2)		
cognizant (4)		
interrelatedness (4)		
mutuality (4)		
agitator (4)		
grapple (5)		
appraisal (6)		
gadflies (6)		
query (8)		
prodded (8)		
lamentably (8)		
ominous (10)		
concoct (10)		
harried (10)		
terminology (12)		
relegating (12)		
existential (12)		
estrangement (12)		
rabid (15)		
anarchy (15)		
paternalistically (18)		
repudiated (19)		
emulate (20)		
blatant (25)		
pious (25)		
irrelevancies (25)		
sanctimonious (25)		
interposition (26)		
nullification (26)		
clarion (26)		
laxity (27)		
nonconformists (27)		
mores (28)		

intimidated (28)
infanticide (28)
gladiatorial (28)
archdefender (29)
forfeit (30)
provocation (33)
scintillating (36)

Questions for Discussion

1. Who was Dr. King's audience? Which of his arguments do you think were the most convincing for them?
2. Which of the issues Dr. King raises might apply to the country as a whole as well as to the community of Birmingham, Alabama?
3. Dr. King argues that the black community has been as patient as it can be in the struggle for equality. What evidence does he offer in support of his position? Do you find it convincing?
4. How does Dr. King distinguish between just and unjust laws (paragraphs 12 through 15)? Do you agree with his distinction? Why or why not?
5. State in your own words the purpose of nonviolent direct action (paragraphs 6 through 7). Might other situations be appropriate for this method of protest? Explain your response.
6. Why does Dr. King consider the white moderate a greater "stumbling block" to freedom than more open racists like the members of the White Citizens Council or the Ku Klux Klan (see paragraph 18)?
7. What does Dr. King mean when he accuses the church of being an "archdefender of the status quo" (see paragraph 29)? Is his statement accurate today? Are you aware of churches that work actively for social change?

TOPICS FOR WRITING

Topic 1. Write a paper arguing whether certain circumstances justify breaking a law. Consider, as does Dr. King, which laws, if any, one might break and why you think such an act would be justified.

Topic 2. Write a paper in which you identify a situation that you consider unjust and explain why it is unjust. Then propose solutions for changing this situation. As you discuss solutions, explain how they will make a difference.

Topic 3. If you belong to a church or temple, write a letter to its religious leader evaluating what the church is doing for the community's homeless, disadvantaged, working poor, or other people in need. You may rely on your own knowledge, but also interview ministers, priests, rabbis, or members of the congregation to find out what they do and how effective their work has been.

THE WRITING PROCESS: PERSUADING

The guidelines for using the writing process to take a stand (Chapter 17) also work well for essays that attempt to persuade the reader that the writer's argument is a valid one, one worth adopting. Organizing and revising persuasive essays, however, are two areas that deserve additional comment.

Additional Considerations for Organizing Ideas

Two organizational patterns presented in earlier chapters—chronological, order of emphasis and importance—also inform essays based on argument. In addition, most arguments devote some time to the presentation and refutation of opposing views. The number of opposing arguments you present determines which of the following organizational patterns is most appropriate for your paper.

1. Presenting opposing arguments first

   I. Introduction
       A. Clarify the situation or problem
          1. Thesis states the position you will defend
  II. Body Paragraphs
       A. Opposing argument
          1. Rebuttal and support
       B. Opposing argument
          1. Rebuttal and support
       C. Your argument
          1. Support
       D. Your argument
          1. Support
 III. Conclusion

2. Presenting your arguments first

   I. Introduction
       A. Clarify the situation or problem
          1. Thesis states the position you will defend
  II. Body Paragraphs
       A. Your argument
          1. Support
       B. Your argument
          1. Support
       C. Your argument
          1. Support
       D. Opposing argument

1. Rebuttal and support
III. Conclusion

3. Presenting opposing arguments throughout

I. Introduction
   A. Clarify the situation or problem
      1. Thesis states the position you will defend
II. Body Paragraphs
   A. Opposing argument
      1. Rebuttal and support
   B. Opposing argument
      1. Rebuttal and support
   C. Opposing argument
      1. Rebuttal and support
   D. Opposing argument
      1. Rebuttal and support
III. Conclusion

Additional Considerations for Sharing Your Writing and Making Final Revisions

Checklist

❑ Is my thesis debatable?
❑ Have I stated my position clearly in the introduction?
❑ Is my position consistent throughout the paper?
❑ Have I considered opposing points?
❑ Are rebuttals reasonable and well-supported?
❑ Are any discussions unduly brief or unsupported? What additional support can I add to these paragraphs?
❑ Have I checked the paper for spelling and any sentence errors that give me trouble?

FOR FURTHER READING

Homelessness in America
Charles E. King

Charles King holds an undergraduate degree in history at the University of Arkansas. This article on homelessness won first place in the North American Essay Contest sponsored by The Humanist Magazine.

In recent years, greater media attention to the problem of homelessness in   1
America has helped to bring to the attention of the public the magnitude of the

homelessness problem and to break some of the traditional stereotypes of homeless persons. Articles in *Time, Newsweek, The New Yorker,* and other popular periodicals, extensive coverage of the Yonkers housing discrimination suit, and special reports on local and national news programs have helped, at least, to raise public consciousness.

Such media attention is certainly not unwarranted. The Department of 2 Housing and Urban Development's 1984 report on homelessness, perhaps the most statistically reliable source to date, included five hundred telephone interviews and visits to 184 randomly selected shelters in sixty metropolitan areas. The report concluded that, in the United States, there are 200,000 to 600,000 homeless persons, with the most accurate range being 250,000 to 350,000. Other sources—such as Mitch Snyder of the Community for Creative Nonviolence, one of the nation's leading homeless advocacy groups—give figures as high as three million persons.

Even more startling than the sheer magnitude of the homeless problem 3 itself are the demographics of the homeless population. With the move toward de-institutionalization in the past three decades, the percentage of the homeless mentally ill has risen sharply. In 1955, the population of public psychiatric hospitals was 559,000, but by 1981 that figure had dropped to around 122,000, accounting for the American Psychiatric Association's estimate that 20 to 50 percent of homeless persons are seriously mentally ill.

Children, too, account for a growing percentage of the homeless. If one may 4 extrapolate from figures in a Pennsylvania study by Temple University, as much as 15 percent of the homeless population may be children under five years of age. And in a recent Harvard University study of 151 children living with their families in shelters, nearly half of them of preschool age showed at least one developmental lag on the Denver Developmental Screening Test, and one-third had two or more lags. According to Ellen Bassuk, a homelessness researcher, "Many were depressed and anxious and had severe learning difficulties; 43 percent had repeated a grade, and about one-fourth were in special classes."

Perhaps surprisingly, a Baltimore study conducted by the National 5 Institute of Mental Health showed that one-half to two-thirds of the homeless persons surveyed had completed high school, and 25 to 30 percent had completed college. Similarly, 22 percent of the homeless persons polled in a recent U.S. Conference of Mayors survey had full- or part-time jobs. Although studies disagree on exact figures, it is clear that the stereotype of the "bum," the uneducated free-loader who chooses to be homeless—if it ever were an accurate portrayal—certainly no longer fits.

In a political system in which policy decisions are made according to 6 strictly utilitarian criteria, questions of the magnitude of the homeless problem and the profile of the shelter population are important. Even though the efforts of the media must be lauded for helping to make homelessness a political issue, concentrating on numbers and percentages in recent reportage has necessarily obscured what may well be some of the central questions of the homeless problem: What, in more human terms, does it mean to be homeless, and why ought we help the homeless in the first place?

It is of more than semantic significance, I think, that we call these people 7
"homeless" instead of "houseless" or "shelterless." In our culture, the idea of a
home connotes more than just a physical shelter. A *home* offers a sense of
security, of permanence, of one's own *space*. In fact, where we live, where we
are *from*, is often the quintessential source of our self-identity. Perhaps the
defining characteristic of homelessness, which often seems to be ignored, is
the homeless person's total lack of support—physical, financial, emotional,
spiritual. As writer David Whitman has said, the homeless are decidedly different from other poor persons in at least one significant respect: "They are
profoundly alone."

That at least *something* should be done to aid the homeless no longer seems 8
to be a serious point for debate. Liberals and conservatives alike advocate, in
greater or lesser degrees, job training programs, housing projects, and other
forms of aid, and only the most uninformed persons still speak of the entire
homeless population as "bums." But even to persons actively involved in seeking solutions to the homeless problem, nagging questions often arise: Why
ought we help the homeless in the first place, and how can we convince others
that *they* ought to be concerned? Responses to these questions vary. Churches
seem to donate to shelter programs perhaps in part as an exercise in Christian
charity, and attempt—as Jesus did—to see God in the hungry, the thirsty, and
the naked. Secular groups, though, often rely upon appeals to basic human
compassion or, in some cases, to enlightened self-interest—approaches that
have little moral impact on the compassionless or the unenlightened.

But these approaches aside, perhaps the question of eliminating home- 9
lessness in America ultimately comes down to fulfilling our part of a bargain—to undertaking a kind of social contract. Inasmuch as we benefit from
our choice to live in a society that encourages economic competition and
rewards personal initiative, it is incumbent on us to help those who have
somehow been left behind in the race for economic success. And considering
the alienation of the poor from the sources of political and economic power—
their inability to represent themselves in the political forums that we have created—a fundamental maxim becomes clear: If we accept the benefits of the
system, we must necessarily accept the responsibilities.

Still, by many accounts the prospects for eliminating homelessness are 10
rather bleak. One recent study shows that the United States will need 7.5 million new low-income housing units by the year 2000, and a report from the
General Accounting Office estimates that 240,000 to 890,000 low-income
units could be lost by 1995 to landlords' renting them at prevailing market
rates. An additional 800,000 could disappear by 2005. Yet, in the face of
decreased funding and housing availability, there has been an average
increase of 31 percent in the number of families requesting shelter space during 1986 and 1987. The 1983 American Housing Survey (the latest data available) reported that almost seven million renter households spend more than
one-half their income on housing. One more rent increase and these people,
too, will join the ranks of the homeless.

Since homelessness is not a monolithic problem, any comprehensive solu-   11
tion must address substance abuse, mental illness, disease, and the plethora of
other social ills that have become results—if not causes—of homelessness. But
it is clear that the solution must begin with our going beyond the numbers and
percentages, understanding what being homeless means in human terms, and
agreeing that "securing the blessings of liberty" is as much the job of individuals as it is the task of the federal government. We must affirm, with Peter
Marin of *Harper's,* that responding to the problem of homelessness in America
does not translate into the language of "conservatives" or "liberals."
Homelessness, in its most fundamental terms, is "the *sum total* of our dreams,
policies, intentions, errors, omissions, cruelties, kindnesses, all of it recorded
in flesh, in the life of the street."

RESPONDING TO THE READING

Freewriting

Exercise 18b.   What are your impressions of homeless people? Who are
they? What are they like? What sort of background are they likely to have?

Exercise 18c.   Freewrite about facts or ideas that you found disturbing in
Charles King's article on homelessness.

Building Your Vocabulary

VOCABULARY LIST

Words to Look Up	My Definition	Dictionary Definition
unwarranted (2)		
demographics (3)		
de-institutionalization (3)		
psychiatric (3)		
extrapolate (4)		
utilitarian (6)		
magnitude (6)		
lauded (6)		
reportage (6)		
semantic (7)		
quintessential (7)		
incumbent (9)		
maxim (9)		

Questions for Discussion

1. According to the statistical reports that Charles King cites, who are the homeless people in this country? How do the facts compare to your original impressions of the homeless (see Exercise 18b)?
2. Which of the groups listed were you surprised to learn were homeless? What do you think might have put them in that situation?
3. Paraphrase King's definition of homelessness. Why did he include this definition in his argument?
4. What does King mean when he says, "If we accept the benefits of a system, we must necessarily accept the responsibilities" (paragraph 9)? What are the "benefits" we enjoy by living in the economic and political system of the United States? Can you think of other benefits that he did not mention? What does King see as our responsibilities? Do you agree with his position?

TOPICS FOR WRITING

Topic 1. Do some research on the idea of the social contract originated by John Locke. Write a paper explaining how Charles King used Locke's theory to argue that we are socially responsible for the homeless.

Topic 2. Conduct interviews to find out what local organizations and governmental agencies are doing about the problem of homelessness in your area or in an urban area close to you. Who is active (church groups, volunteers, schools, social service agencies, businesses, etc.)? What do they provide for the homeless? How effective are they? Are problems involved with helping the homeless? If so, do plans exist to overcome them? After you have collected your information, write a paper in which you evaluate which of these strategies seems to be most effective.

My Anger and Sadness over Pesticides
Cesar Chavez

Cesar Chavez was founder and president of the United Farm Workers of America. Chavez's death in April 1993 was hastened by his practice of fasting in protest against agricultural policies he felt ignored the welfare of farm workers. This article is adapted from a speech he delivered in 1989 at Pacific Lutheran University in Tacoma, Washington. It was one of his first public appearances after ending his thirty-six day fast in protest of pesticide use in California.

What is the worth of a man or a woman? What is the worth of a farm worker? How do you measure the value of a life? 1

Ask the parents of Johnnie Rodriguez. Johnnie Rodriguez was not even a   2
man; Johnnie was a 5-year-old boy when he died after a painful two-year battle against cancer. Like all farm workers, his parents, Juan and Elia, are
exposed to pesticides and other agricultural chemicals. Elia worked in the
table grapes around Delano in the Valley until she was eight months pregnant
with Johnnie.

Juan and Elia cannot say for certain if pesticides caused their son's can-   3
cer. But neuroblastoma is one of the cancers found in McFarland, a small
farm town only a few miles from Delano, where the Rodriguezes live.
"Pesticides are always in the fields and around the towns," Johnnie's father
told us. "The children get them when they play outside, drink the water, or hug
you after you come home from working in fields that are sprayed.

"Once your son has cancer, you hope it's a mistake, you pray," Juan says.   4
"He was a real nice boy. He took it strong and lived as long as he could."

I keep a picture of Johnnie Rodriguez. He is sitting on his bed, hugging his   5
Teddy bears. His sad eyes and cherubic face stare out at you. The photo was
taken four days before he died.

Johnnie Rodriguez was one of 13 McFarland children diagnosed with can-   6
cer in recent years; and one of six who have died from the disease. With only
6,000 residents, the rate of cancer in McFarland is 400 percent above normal.

The chief source of carcinogens in this and other farming communities   7
are pesticides from the vineyards and fields that encircle them. Health experts
think the high rate of cancer in McFarland is from pesticides and nitrate-con-
taining fertilizers leaching into the water system from surrounding fields.

Last year California's Republican governor, George Deukmejian, killed a   8
modest study to find out why so many children are dying of cancer in
McFarland. "Fiscal integrity" was the reason he gave for his veto of the $125,000
program, which could have helped 84 other rural communities with drinking
water problems.

Last year, as support for our cause grew, Gov. Deukmejian used a   9
statewide radio broadcast to attack the grape boycott. There is no evidence to
prove that pesticides on grapes and other produce endanger farm workers or
consumers, Deukmejian claimed.

Ask the family of Felipe Franco.   10

Felipe is a bright 7-year-old. Like other children, he will some day need to   11
be independent. But Felipe is not like other children: He was born without
arms and legs.

Felipe's mother, Ramona, worked in the grapes near Delano until she was   12
in her eighth month of pregnancy. She was exposed to Captan, known to
cause birth defects and one of the pesticides our grape boycott seeks to ban.
"Every morning when I began working I could smell and see pesticides on the
grape leaves," Ramona said.

Like many farm workers, she was assured by growers and foremen how   13
the pesticides that surrounded her were safe, that they were harmless "medicine" for the plants. Only after Ramona took her son to specialists in Los
Angeles was she told that the pesticides she was exposed to in the vineyards

caused Felipe's deformity. The deep sadness she feels has subsided, but not the anger.

Felipe feels neither anger nor sadness. He dreams of what only a child can hope for: Felipe wants to grow arms and legs. "He believes he will have his limbs *someday*," his mother says. "His great dream is to be able to move around, to walk, to take care of himself." 14

Our critics sometimes ask: Why should the United Farm Workers worry about pesticides when farm workers have so many other more obvious problems? 15

But what good does it do to achieve the blessings of collective bargaining and make economic progress for people when their health is destroyed in the process? If we ignored pesticide poisoning, then all the other injustices our people face would be compounded by an even more deadly tyranny. The farm workers' collective bargaining agenda also includes protecting consumers from dangerous pesticides. 16

"Don't worry," the growers say. "The UFW misleads the public about the dangers of pesticides," the Table Grape Commission says. "Gov. Deukmejian's pesticide safety system protects workers," the Farm Bureau proclaims. 17

Ask the family of Juan Chabolla. 18

Juan Chabolla collapsed after working in a field sprayed only an hour before with Monitor, a deadly pesticide. But instead of rushing Juan to a nearby hospital, the grower drove him 45 miles across the U.S.-Mexico border and left him in a Tijuana clinic. He was dead on arrival. 19

Just after Juan died, Deukmejian vetoed a modest bill, strongly opposed by agribusiness, that would have required growers to post warning signs in fields where dangerous pesticides are applied. 20

Two hundred and fifty million pounds of pesticides are applied each year to crops in California; in 1986, 10 million pounds went on grapes, the state's largest fruit crop. It receives more restricted-use pesticides than any other fresh food crop. 21

About one-third of grape pesticides are known carcinogens—like the chemicals that may have afflicted Johnnie Rodriguez. Others are teratogens—birth defect-producing pesticides—that doctors think deformed Felipe Franco. 22

Pesticides cause acute poisoning—of the kind that killed Juan Chabolla— and chronic, long-term effects such as we're seeing in communities like McFarland. In 1987 and 1988, entire crews of grape workers—hundreds of people—were poisoned after entering vineyards containing toxic residues. In all those episodes, the grapes had been sprayed weeks before. All the *legal* requirements were followed. 23

Illegal use of pesticides is also commonplace. Grape growers have been illegally using Fixx, a growth enhancer, for 20 years. Another illegal pesticide, Acephate, which causes tumors, has also been used on grapes. Over 2,000 consumers were poisoned in 1984 after eating watermelons illegally sprayed with Aldicarb. And these are only cases where growers were *caught* applying illegal chemicals. 24

Use of pesticides are governed by strict laws, agribusiness says. Growers   25
argue reported poisonings involved only 1 percent of California farm workers
in 1986.

But experts estimate that only 1 percent of California pesticide illness or   26
injury is reported. The underreporting of pesticide poisoning is flagrant, and
it is epidemic. A World Resources Institute study concludes that 300,000 farm
workers are poisoned each year by pesticides in the United States. Even the
state Department of Food and Agriculture reported that total pesticide poisoning of farm workers rose by 41 percent in 1987.

Yet the United Farm Workers aren't sincere when we raise the pesticide   27
issue, grape growers complain. They won't admit that the first ban on DDT,
Aldrin, and Dieldrin in the United States was not by the Environmental
Protection Agency in 1972, but in a United Farm Workers contract with a
grape grower in 1967.

Who will protect farm workers from poisoning if it isn't the farm workers'   28
union? The Environmental Protection Agency is in bed with the same agricultural and chemical interests they are supposed to regulate.

Agribusiness lobbied mightily to exclude farm workers from federal job   29
safety and health laws. And they won.

The agrichemical industry is out to maximize profits. Using smaller   30
amounts of safer chemicals more wisely is not in the interest of chemical companies. There is nothing wrong with pesticides, they claim; the blame rests
with abuse and misuse of pesticides. It's like the National Rifle Association
saying, "Guns don't kill people, people kill people."

Most physicians farm workers see won't even admit their patients' problems   31
are caused by pesticides. They don't know much about pesticides; the signs and
symptoms of acute pesticide poisoning are similar to other illnesses. Doctors
who work for growers—and most rural physicians—won't take a stand.

Workers endure skin irritations and rashes that none of us would tolerate.   32
They continue to work because they desperately need the money. They don't
complain out of fear of losing their jobs.

Farm workers aren't told when pesticides are used. They rarely have   33
health insurance. They are cheated out of worker compensation benefits by
disappearing labor contractors or foremen who intimidate people into not filing claims.

In the old days, miners would carry birds with them to warn against poi-   34
son gas. They hoped the birds would die before the miners.

Farm workers are society's canaries. Farm workers—and their children—   35
demonstrate the effects of pesticide poisoning before anyone else. But the
unrestrained use of agricultural chemicals is like playing Russian Roulette
with the health of both farm workers *and* consumers. So much of so many
pesticides are used and so little is known about them. Hundreds of farm pesticides leave residues on food; most can't be detected by commonly used tests.
Many can't be detected by any test at all. And 44 percent of the pesticides
applied on grapes—pesticides that can't be detected by tests used to check for
toxic residues—pose potential health hazards for humans.

The truth is *we do not know* if pesticide residues on the food you buy in 36
supermarkets cause cancer, birth defects, and other tragedies. And EPA has
made no effort to encourage the use of safer alternatives to toxic pesticides.

The chemical companies have convinced the growers—and they want us 37
to believe—that if it wasn't for them, the whole world would succumb to
malaria and starvation. But pesticides haven't worked. Crop loss to pests is as
great or greater than it was 40 years ago. Pesticides haven't changed anything
because Darwinian evolution has favored pests of all kinds with this enormous ability to resist and survive.

There are mosquitoes that can survive any combination of pesticides 38
delivered in any dose. There is a startling resurgence of malaria around the
world. And it's much worse now because 40 years ago we relied entirely on a
chemical solution. We ignored alternatives: draining ponds, dredging ditches,
observing sound crop practices, encouraging use of natural predators. And in
the long run, more lives will be lost, because for 30 years we also stopped
developing malaria vaccines.

People thought pesticides were the cure-all—the key to an abundance of 39
food. They thought pesticides were the solution, but they were the problem.

The problems are the huge farms, this mammoth agribusiness system, the 40
pressure on the land from developers not allowing the land to lay fallow and
rest, the abandonment of cultural practices that have stood the test of centuries: crop rotation, diversification of crops.

The problem is monoculture—growing acres and acres of the same crop; 41
disrupting the natural order of things; letting insects feast on acres and acres of
a harem of delight—and using pesticides that kill *off* their natural predators.

The chemical companies believe in the Domino Theory: All chemicals are 42
threatened if any chemical is questioned. No matter how dangerous it may be.

But at what cost? The lives of farm workers and their children who are 43
suffering? The lives of consumers who could reap the harvest of pesticides 10,
20 years from now? The contamination of our ground water? The loss of our
reverence for the soil? The raping of the land? People forget that the soil is our
sustenance. It is a sacred trust. It is what has worked for us for centuries. It is
what we pass on to future generations. If we continue in this thoughtless submission to pesticides—if we ruin the top soil—then there will not be an abundance of food to bequeath our children.

Farm workers and consumers cannot get pesticide regulation because 44
those who make the rules are captives of the bankrupt 40- and 50-year policies
that have been shown not to work.

So they don't ban the worst of these poisons because some farm workers 45
might give birth to a deformed child. So they don't imperil millions of dollars
in profits today because, some day, some consumers might get cancer.

The growers, the chemical companies, and the bureaucrats say these are 46
acceptable levels of exposure.

Acceptable to whom? . . . 47

The misery that pesticides bring farm workers—and the dangers they 48
pose to all consumers—will not be ended with more hearings or studies. The

solution is not to be had from those in power because it is they who have
allowed this deadly crisis to grow. The answer lies with you and me. It is with all
men and women who share the suffering and yearn with us for a better world.

Our cause goes on in hundreds of distant places. It multiplies among thou-   49
sands and then millions of caring people who heed through a multitude of
simple deeds the commandment set out in the book of the Prophet Micah, in
the Old Testament: "What does the Lord require of you, but to do justice, to
love kindness, and to walk humbly with your God."

RESPONDING TO THE READING

Freewriting

Exercise 18d.   Summarize what you learned about labor conditions in the
farming communities of California's Central Valley. Describe your reaction to
Chavez's position.

Building Your Vocabulary

VOCABULARY LIST

Words to Look Up	My Definition	Dictionary Definition
cherubic (5)		
carcinogens (7)		
diversification (40)		

Questions for Discussion

1. What is Chavez's purpose for writing this article? Which argument best supports this purpose?
2. How does the fact that he is head of the United Farm Workers affect his argument?
3. Who is the audience for this article? What clues in the article point to this audience?
4. Which techniques for writing argument does Chavez use most effectively? Explain what makes particular passages convincing.
5. Identify opposing arguments. How does Chavez counter those arguments? Is his method effective? Why or why not?
6. At what point does Chavez show that pesticide use might affect a broader population, not just farm workers? Why do you think he added this group to his discussion?
7. What solutions does Chavez propose for the problems associated with pesticide use?

8. After reading this article, what is your feeling about the use of certain pesticides? Has Chavez convinced you to take action? Why or why not?

TOPICS FOR WRITING

Topic 1.   Do some research on pesticide use in a particular agricultural area, not necessarily California. Be sure to include articles and interviews, if possible, that justify the use of pesticides as well as those that warn against their use. After gathering information, write a paper in which you argue against the use of particular pesticides or defend the farmer's use of them.

Topic 2.   If you believe strongly in a social cause, do some investigation and write an argument in which you (1) define the issue clearly, (2) offer rebuttals to opposing arguments, and (3) propose solutions to solve the injustice you have identified.

Student Writing

Linda Lozano wrote the following essay after gathering information from books and magazine articles about how difficult it is for a single parent—usually a mother—to collect child support payments from a former spouse. She listed the books and articles that provided details or commentary for her paper in the "Works Cited" section at the end. In the body of her essay, Lozano enclosed in parentheses the name of the author of the book or article she used and the page number where she found the information. When she mentioned the author's name elsewhere in her paragraph, she put only the page number in parentheses.

Fathers Should Pay

    The child support system in the United States is a disgrace. Fathers make their payments about half the time (Simpson 65). But even if the money comes, it is often less than the required amount or comes too infrequently to keep the family living above the poverty level. It's not that the fathers can't pay; in fact the incomes of separated families are often so unequal that "the wife and children have to live at 48 percent of their previous income level while the husband has two hundred percent of his former financial capacity" (Lieberman 24). It is not surprising that female-headed households are three times more likely to live at the poverty level or below than male-headed households (Lieberman 21). There is a definite problem here. What can be done about it? Automatic wage and benefit deductions, and, if necessary, imprisonment, will greatly increase the collection of child support payments. Basing support payments on the actual cost of raising a child (instead of just the father's income) and automatically adjusting awards every year for cost of living increases would allow children of single mothers to live above the poverty level. Federal legislation must be passed to enforce these improvements.

Once a woman gets a judgment requiring her husband to pay child support, the amount allotted to the family should be deducted each month from his paycheck. Of course, many men think that automatic deductions from wages and benefits is much too drastic a measure and argue to keep the voluntary system that operates in most states. One father in New York, for example, challenged automatic deductions from his paychecks as violating his due process rights. The court did not agree. It ruled that his making child support payments served a greater public good and, hence, precluded his right to a hearing (Lieberman 84). There are other good reasons for instituting wage deductions. For one thing, it would free the over-burdened court system to handle other issues because suits over delinquent payments would be fewer (Simpson 65). It would also establish a precedent. As Merrily Burch, a Wisconsin prosecutor put it, "For the father who's mistakenly giving priority to his car payments, withholding has made a tremendous difference. He can't spend what he doesn't see" (Whitman 22).

The most drastic solution of all is to arrest fathers who do not obey the court order to support their families. The biggest argument against imprisoning these fathers is that they can't pay while in jail. But in all but a few cases this tactic has proven effective in collecting back payments. For example, Arlin Cole stated that he couldn't afford $100 a week to help provide for his three children. His ex-wife took him to court many times and finally, in April 1986, he was sentenced to five months in jail. He was released only ten days later when he was suddenly able to pay the $2,800 he owed. As David Whitman points out, "Men are more likely to be arrested for failing to pay a parking ticket than for not sending money to their families" (22). In his studies, Connecticut Attorney General Joseph Lieberman found that the fear of being incarcerated convinced many fathers to make payments. There are few fathers who have gotten a judgment against them who are genuinely unable to pay or who are so poor that the threat of imprisonment doesn't substantially increase the frequency and amount of their payments (Lieberman 97).

Although automatic wage deductions and threat of imprisonment will greatly increase collection of child support payments, more must be done.

Child support payments must be based upon what it actually costs to raise a child instead of the amount the father is paid. If the father lived at home, he would be providing a home, food, and clothing for his child, no matter what his income, but "child support awards are generally not consistent with the real cost of raising children . . . [Judges] are more concerned with the father's ability to continue living adequately than with what it actually costs to raise children. They consider income more than costs" (Lieberman 19, 20). Divorced women struggle every day with problems of survival and worry each month whether they'll have enough money to pay the bills. They rarely receive even half of what it costs to raise a child. Right now, the average payment for one child is sixteen dollars a week (Whitman 25). Many states have guidelines for setting fees, but no minimum. Besides, it is always the judge's choice to follow the guidelines or not. When they are enacted, they don't affect old cases. A mother must return to court to try to receive amounts within the new guidelines and then it is still up to the judge whether she gets the increase or not. If a minimum payment were set that would cover at least half the cost of raising a child, the courts could guarantee that fewer children would be raised in poverty.

One more improvement that needs to be made in the child support system is that there needs to be automatic yearly cost of living increases. Besides the fact that the necessities of life cost more each year, the cost of raising a child increases with age. Teenagers eat more, wear more expensive clothes, and have more recreational expenses than younger children. One college instructor jokingly advises parents to begin a savings account when a child is born and to use the money to feed and clothe him or her when the child becomes a teenager (Waite). Although humorous, this is no exaggeration. The State of Indiana has shown other states the way in this procedure. A father appealed an order that modified payments each year by the percentage change in the Consumer Price Index. He argued that the automatic changes infringed on his right to be heard by a judge. This was the court's answer:

> We approve the court's order prescribing an adjustment in the amount of child support . . . because the provision (1) gives due regard to the actual needs of the child, (2) uses readily available objective information, (3) requires only a simple calculation, (4) results in judicial economy, (5) reduces expenses for attorney fees, (6) in no way infringes upon the right of the custodial parent or the noncustodial parent to petition the court . . . (Lieberman 45).

Other states would do well to follow Indiana's example. Families headed by single mothers desperately need these steps to correct abuses in the child support system. The time and money needed to implement these measures will be well spent. If we make sure that mothers and their children have enough money to live above the poverty level, Aid to Families with Dependent Children (welfare) payments will decrease (Simpson 65). Statistics show that "for every dollar spent by the Office of Child Support Enforcement, about three dollars in child support has been collected" (Takas 58). Very few governmental agencies can report such efficiency. The American public will save money, but more importantly, our children will be saved.

—Linda Lozano

Works Cited

Lieberman, Joseph I. Child Support in America. New Haven: Yale University Press, 1986.

Simpson, Peggy. "Making Sure Dad Pays Up." Ms. Magazine, May 1988:65.

Takas, Marianne. "Collecting Child Support—Why Uncle Sam Won't Help." Vogue, November 1987: 58.

Waite, Ava Craig. "Family and Consumer Science 34." Sacramento City College, Spring 1988.

Whitman, Davis. "The Children Who Get Cut Out." U.S. News and World Report, 12 October, 1987: 24–25.

_____. "The Word to Deadbeat Dads: Pay Up." U.S. News and World Report, 1 December, 1986: 22.

Questions for Discussion

1. Identify the techniques for writing persuasion that Linda Lozano uses in her essay.
2. Which of Lozano's arguments do you find most convincing? least convincing? Why in either case?
3. What issues might be raised by the writer of an essay entitled "In Defense of Fathers"?

PART THREE

Revising Sentences: A Writing Skills Workbook

19

Recognizing Verbs

A s you have seen, proofreading is an important step in the writing process. Part Three of this book gives you a review of basic sentence patterns and grammar that will help you understand how to construct sentences correctly. Exercises in Chapters 19–26 give you practice in identifying the building blocks of the sentence (the subject, verb, and modifying phrases), and in clarifying connections between the elements of sentences and paragraphs. Additional exercises introduce sentence combining techniques that will help you add variety to the way you construct sentences as well as give you practice constructing correct sentences. Chapter 27 provides a summary of rules for spelling, punctuation, and capitalization. As you complete chapters in Part Three, you should gain greater confidence in your ability to write correct, even powerful, sentences.

THE PRESENT TENSE

A **subject** and **verb** are part of every sentence you will ever write. The subject tells who or what you are writing about. The verb is the heartbeat of the sentence—it provides action or says something about the subject. It may describe what the subject is doing, what it is like, or what is said about it. Verbs you will work with in this chapter are written in the past, present, or future tenses.

Study the following sentences about waking up in the morning. The verbs are underlined twice:

1. At 7 A.M. my nagging alarm clock buzzes me awake.
2. I poke my nose out of the covers into the freezing air.
3. I shake like a house in an earthquake.

4. I <u>pour</u> myself out of my nice, warm waterbed.
5. My teeth <u>chatter</u> like castanets.

In the sentences you just read, the words identified as verbs are alike in that they are in the **present tense,** they provide the action in the sentence, and they tell us what the subject is doing.

Checking for Verbs

The **verb** helps anchor a sentence in time. When we refer to the tense of a written verb, we literally mean the "time" in which it is written—past, present, or future. If you aren't sure whether or not a word is the verb in the sentence, use the following test to see if it can be written in the past, present, and future tenses.

The Verb Test

To find the verb in the sentence, *Sometimes, dirty water floods my grandmother's bathroom floor,* try changing the tense of any words that you think might be the verb. If, for example, you think that the action in the sentence is the flooding, then try putting the word *floods* in the past, present, and future tenses:

> Today dirty water *floods* her bathroom floor.
> Yesterday dirty water *flooded* her bathroom floor.
> Tomorrow dirty water *will flood* her bathroom floor.

Because you can write flood in these three tenses and have the sentences make sense, *flood* is indeed the verb you were seeking.

If you have trouble finding the verb in the sentence, *Luckily, I know something about plumbing,* use this test on words you think might be verbs. Let's say that you think the word *luckily* sounds like a verb, and you write something like this:

> Today I *luckily* I know something about plumbing.
> Yesterday I *luckilied* I know something about plumbing.
> Tomorrow I *will luckily* I know something about plumbing.

The fact that these sentences don't make sense tells you that the word *luckily* is *not* a verb because it cannot change tense, so you must keep looking. (*Luckily* is actually an adverb used as an introductory word to modify the sentence.)

Perhaps the next word you check in this sentence about plumbing is *know.* This time the test looks like this:

Today I *know* something about plumbing.
Yesterday I *knew* something about plumbing.
Tomorrow I *will know* something about plumbing.

The test shows that *know* is a word that can change tense; therefore, it is a verb.
    Try this test whenever you are not sure whether a particular word in a sentence is a verb. It may not work for you 100 percent of the time, but it is generally a good guide. Use this test to help you find verbs in some of the following exercises.

Exercise 19a.   Read the following sentences carefully. Then underline the verbs twice. The first sentence is done for you.

Immigrants

1. Immigrants come to the United States for many reasons.
2. Sometimes people suffer economic hardships in their home country.
3. Low salaries in their homeland make it difficult to feed a family.
4. Perhaps the immigrants' families lack clothing or shelter.
5. Political oppression contributes to people's problems in some countries.
6. Individuals from the wrong tribe or political party experience persecution, detention, or even torture.
7. These immigrants seek political protection in the United States.
8. Limited educational opportunities provide another reason for immigrating to this country.
9. Some schools in foreign countries stress rote memorization, an unimaginative and boring method of instruction.
10. People from other countries often associate improved economic and educational opportunities with immigration to the United States.

Verb Forms in the Present Tense

The following table illustrates the possible forms of three regular verbs—*grow, run,* and *wait*—written in the present tense. The *s* on the end of the third-person singular form is underlined for you.

	Present Tense Singular			Present Tense Plural	
		grow			
Subject	*Verb*		*Subject*	*Verb*	
I	grow		we	grow	
you	grow		you	grow	
he/she/it	grows		they	grow	
		run			
Subject	*Verb*		*Subject*	*Verb*	
I	run		we	run	
you	run		you	run	
he/she/it	runs		they	run	
		wait			
Subject	*Verb*		*Subject*	*Verb*	
I	wait		we	wait	
you	wait		you	wait	
he/she/it	waits		they	wait	

The third-person singular form—he, she, it—in the present tense often gives students trouble because it ends in *s,* even though it is singular.

> **Rule to Remember: Verbs written in the third person, present tense (the *he/she/it* form) always end in *s*.**

The verb *be* is irregular in the present tense. That means that the base or core of the word changes forms. The verb *be* is conjugated below with the irregular forms underlined for you.

	Present Tense Singular			Present Tense Plural	
		be			
Subject	*Verb*		*Subject*	*Verb*	
I	am		we	are	
you	are		you	are	
he/she/it	is		they	are	

Notice that the third-person singular form still ends in *s.*

THE PAST TENSE

The underlined verbs in the following sentences are written in the **past tense.**

1. At seven years of age, I took horseback riding lessons.
2. My instructor started me on "Coco," a little Shetland pony.
3. At first I had trouble with her.
4. She challenged me.
5. But after about two months, I wanted a bigger horse, a "real" horse.

Verb Forms in the Past Tense

Verbs in the past tense are regular or irregular. For regular verbs written in the past tense, add an *-ed* ending. Irregular verbs change form in the past tense and must be memorized. The following chart lists the infinitive and past tense forms of common irregular verbs. The past participles are used with helping verbs.

Infinitive	Past Tense	Past Participle
to become	became	become
to begin	began	begun
to bite	bit	bitten, bit
to blow	blew	blown
to break	broke	broken
to bring	brought	brought
to buy	bought	bought
to catch	caught	caught
to choose	chose	chosen
to come	came	come
to do	did	done
to draw	drew	drawn
to drink	drank	drunk
to drive	drove	driven
to eat	ate	eaten
to fall	fell	fallen
to find	found	found
to fly	flew	flown
to forget	forgot	forgotten
to freeze	froze	frozen
to get	got	got, gotten
to give	gave	given
to go	went	gone
to grow	grew	grown
to hear	heard	heard
to hide	hid	hidden
to hold	held	held

Infinitive	Past Tense	Past Participle
to keep	kept	kept
to know	knew	known
to lay	laid	laid
to lead	led	led
to leave	left	left
to lie	lay	lain
to lose	lost	lost
to pay	paid	paid
to prove	proved	proved, proven
to ride	rode	ridden
to ring	rang	rung
to rise	rose	risen
to run	ran	run
to say	said	said
to see	saw	seen
to shake	shook	shaken
to sing	sang, sung	sung
to sink	sank, sunk	sunk
to sit	sat	sat
to speak	spoke	spoken
to stand	stood	stood
to steal	stole	stolen
to swim	swam	swum
to take	took	taken
to tear	tore	torn
to throw	threw	thrown
to wear	wore	worn
to write	wrote	written

Exercise 19b.   In the sentences below, change any present tense verbs you find to the past tense. The verb in the first sentence is changed for you.

The Wedding Picture

showed

1. One precious photograph in my mother's photo album ~~shows~~ my father as a young, all-American boy on his wedding day.
2. He has a weekend pass from the Army for this special occasion.
3. He wears light-colored plaid pants with a navy sports jacket.
4. A bright red carnation adorns one of his lapels.
5. My mother stands right next to him.
6. In contrast with my dad, her skin has the dark tones of her native Hawaii.
8. She holds a bouquet of orchids.

WORE
9. She wears a white minidress and heels with bows.
10. They both have bright, eager eyes.
HAD

Exercise 19c. Now comes the creative part. Read the following sentences to get a sense of what they mean. Then fill in the blanks with verbs in the past tense. Possible answers for the first sentence are provided for you.

Old Stories

1. When I was a child, my father _____ to talk about the old days.

   Possible Anwers:
   When I was a child, my father <u>loved</u> to talk about the old days.
   or
   When I was a child, my father <u>used</u> to talk about the old days.
   or
   When I was a child, my father <u>wanted</u> to talk about the old days.

2. He _____ my sister and me crazy with talk about walking to school in 30-degree weather during a snowstorm.

3. He was always telling us that *his* father never ___WALKED___ *him* to school.

4. Actually, I ___WAS___ listening to stories about the good old days.

5. But sometimes I ___TALKED___ about my father's stories.

6. After all, he ___WAS___ on the plains of North Dakota.

7. On a "good" day in winter, the temperature _____ to 5 degrees below zero.

8. I _____ that my father probably _____ about walking to school in a blizzard.

9. But I don't care. I just ___KEPT___ remembering those stories he ___TOLD___ me when I was a child.

Exercise 19d. Now add past tense verbs to the following paragraph. Try to make your verbs as lively as you can.

The Nightmare

Early this morning the alarm _____ , and I _____ with a start, _____ with sweat. I _____ a bad dream with horror. Homeless and jobless, I _____ the streets during the day. I

_____ the shopping malls and movie theaters, a ghostly figure in tattered jeans and a sweat-soaked shirt. Without a job, I _____ on benevolent strangers to give me food or coins. If they _____ , I _____ for the nearest soup kitchen and _____ a meal donated by one of the charity organizations in town. At night I _____ under bridges or by the river. With only a thin blanket to cover me, I _____ and _____ all night. The hard ground _____ me from getting a full night's sleep. Happily, the dream _____ , and I _____ my alarm clock telling me it was time to get ready for school.

THE FUTURE TENSE

The verbs that are underlined below are written in the **future tense.** These verbs describe what the subject will be doing or will be like in the future.

   1. I can tell this <u>will be</u> another bad day for Raphael.
   2. He <u>will</u> not <u>get</u> to work on time.
   3. He <u>will reach</u> the highway during rush hour.
   4. He <u>will</u> probably <u>be</u> at least an hour late for work.

Notice that words like *not* and *probably* may come between the helping verb *will* and the verb. (See pages 525–526 for more work with helping verbs.)

Verb Forms in the Future Tense

The future tense uses the helping verb *will* and the base form of a verb (the infinitive without the word *to*). When the verb is negative, *will* may be written as *won't*.

Exercise 19e.   Read the following sentences carefully; then change the underlined verbs in the present tense to the future tense. The first sentence is done for you.

Routine

will do   will be   will do

1. The activities I ~~do~~ today ~~are~~ much like the things I ~~do~~ every day.
2. The sound of my blaring alarm <u>awakens</u> me at 5 A.M.   *will wake*
3. I *will sit* <u>sit</u> on the edge of my bed for five minutes or so, trying to remember what day it is.

will claw

4. One of my three cats claws his way up my leg.
5. I *will stumble* stumble down to the kitchen to give the cats their food.
6. I am still half-asleep as I take my morning shower.
7. But soon after my shower I am able to think clearly again.

will be

will be

WRITING EXERCISE

Exercise 19f.   Write at least ten sentences describing one of the following:

> a friend opening an unusual gift (use the past, present, or future)
> an event that happened on the first day of school (use the past tense)
> a memorable moment or a first date (use the past, present, or future)

When you have finished writing, underline the verbs in the sentences twice.

20

Working with Verbs and Subjects

This chapter gives you practice identifying verbs and subjects in several sentence patterns. In some exercises, you will work with sentences that have multiple verbs and subjects. Other exercises ask you to use linking verbs and auxiliary verbs to form sentences. You also will learn to identify subjects and verbs in commands, in questions, and in sentences with introductory phrases.

IDENTIFYING VERBS AND SUBJECTS

Read these two sentences carefully. The verbs are underlined twice.

1. In my younger years I <u><u>did</u></u> a lot of irresponsible things.
2. My older brothers <u><u>got</u></u> me into a lot of trouble.

Let's go over these two sentences to explore the relationship between the subject and the verb.

1. In my younger years, I <u><u>did</u></u> a lot of irresponsible things.
   Who or what *did a lot of irresponsible things?* __YOUNGER YEARS__
2. My older brothers <u><u>got</u></u> me into a lot of trouble.
   Who or what *got me into trouble?* __BROTHERS__

Rule to Remember: The "who" or "what" doing the action, being described, or being talked about in a sentence is the subject.

Questions to Help You Find Verb and Subject

Use the following questions to help you locate the verb and the subject in a sentence:

1. Which word can change tense in the sentence?
2. Who or what does the verb part of the sentence describe or refer to?

Exercise 20a. Use the questions you just read to locate the verb and the subject in the following sentences. Underline subjects once and verbs twice. The first sentence is done for you.

Coaching Tactics

1. The football <u>coaches</u> in high school and college <u>emphasize</u> very different things.

2. In high school, the coaches concentrate mostly on the emotional well-being of the players.

   Which word can change tense in this sentence? _____ *COACHES*
   Who or what did the "concentrating"? _____ *PLAYERS*

3. They pay less attention to a player's mastery of skills.

   Which word can change tense in this sentence? _____ *PAU*
   Who or what did the "paying"? _____ *PLAYERS*

4. College coaches, however, stress the accuracy of the plays.

   Which word can change tense in this sentence? _____ *STRESS*
   Who or what did the "stressing"? _____ *COACHES*

Exercise 20b. Underline the subjects once and the verbs twice in the following sentences. The first one is done for you.

Wearing a Tie

1. Yesterday afternoon <u>I</u> <u>turned</u> the corner near my house.
2. <u>I</u> <u>saw</u> a tall man struggling with his necktie.
3. First the <u>man</u> <u>tugged</u> at it.

4. Then he fussed with it.
5. Finally, the man tore at the knot.
6. He yanked the tie off his neck.
7. Then he stuffed it into his shirt pocket.

Multiple Subjects

When two nouns are used as the subject of a sentence, they form a **compound subject.** The compound subjects in the sentences below are underlined once; the verbs are underlined twice.

1. At fourteen or fifteen years of age, the teenage boy or girl grows extremely restless.
2. Parents and teachers are no longer respected authorities.
3. Family and friends often look at these teenagers suspiciously.

Exercise 20c.   Underline the subjects in the following sentences once and the verbs twice. Watch for multiple subjects. The first sentence is done for you. Notice that the word *high* in the first sentence is an adjective modifying the noun *school.* It tells you what kind of school the writer is discussing.

College: The Big Change

1. High school and college have very little in common.
2. Teachers and counselors treat students more like extended family in high school.
3. Time constraints and class size prevent most college teachers from giving a lot of personal attention to their students.
4. Campus activities and weekend dates get the most attention in high school.
5. In contrast, college freshmen and sophomores spend most of their time studying and attending classes.

Forming Sentences with Multiple Subjects

You may find in your own writing that you can combine several short, choppy sentences by creating one longer sentence with a multiple subject. This pattern is illustrated in the following examples. The subjects are underlined for you.

Janet performs well on the trapeze. Algernon does too.

It is easy to combine these two short sentences to make one smooth sentence by combining the subjects.

Janet and Algernon perform well on the trapeze.

Notice that the third-person singular verb *performs* becomes the plural *perform* in the rewritten sentence, the word *and* joins the subjects of the new sentence, and there is no comma in front of *and*. Let's add a third sentence and combine it with the first two.

> Janet and Algernon perform well on the trapeze. Charla performs with them.

Here are the three sentences combined:

> Janet, Algernon, and Charla perform well on the trapeze.

Notice that we've added commas to separate the subjects because commas are used to separate *three* items in a series. The comma preceding the third item is optional, but once you begin using it, use it throughout your paper.

Exercise 20d.   Combine the groups of sentences below to make a single, fluid sentence. Underline all the subjects once in both the sentences you are given and in the sentence you create. Remember that if you have three subjects, you need to add commas. The first sentence is done for you.

Some Vacation

1. Michael Lee goes camping in winter. His wife Sara goes with him.

Combined: Michael Lee and his wife Sara go camping in winter.

2. Jennifer the cat stays home when the Lees go camping. Their lizard, Frederick, stays home, too. _____

_____

3. However, Wendell the turtle goes with them. The golden retriever they have also goes with them. Even Frisky Boy the parrot goes with them. _____

_____

4. They pack plenty of food for this menagerie. They take uncontaminated water for drinking. _____

_____

5. Since the campground has electricity, the Lees bring along their television. They also bring along a huge portable radio. They bring along the cassette tape deck, too.

Multiple Verbs

When two verbs in a sentence have the same subject, they form a **compound verb.** The compound verb in the sentence below is underlined twice, the subject once.

> The businessman yanked the tie off his neck and stuffed it into his shirt pocket.

The student who wrote this sentence wanted to describe *two* actions that the man (the subject) performed: first he "yanked the tie off his neck"; then he "stuffed it into his shirt pocket."

Exercise 20e.   Read the following sentences carefully and identify the verbs in each. Test any words you aren't sure about by trying to put them in the past, present, and future tenses. Underline each verb twice. Be sure to read the *whole* sentence to catch all the verbs. The first sentence is done for you.

I Prefer Contacts

1. Contact lenses make me look attractive and give me a good image of myself.
2. Regular glasses, on the other hand, clutter up my face and make me look too serious.
3. Besides, glasses get dirty easily and fog up in cold weather.
4. But my tears wash the contact lenses naturally and keep them dust-free.

Forming Sentences with Multiple Verbs

Carefully read the following sentences. The verbs are underlined twice for you.

> I run to my bicycle. I jump over the handlebars.

We can combine these short sentences to make one longer sentence in the following way:

> I run to my bicycle and jump over the handlebars.

Notice that the second *I* is omitted in the rewritten sentence, the word *and* joins the two parts of the new sentence, and there is no comma in front of *and.* Let's add a third sentence and combine it with the first two.

> I run to my bicycle and jump over the handlebars. I hit the seat hard.

Here are the three sentences combined:

> I run to my bicycle, jump over the handlebars, and hit the seat hard.

Notice that the *I* in the third sentence has been omitted in the new sentence and that commas separate the verb phrases because there are *three* items in a series.

Exercise 20f.   Combine the verbs in these short sentences to make a single, fluid sentence. Be sure to drop the second subject, add *and*, and place commas if you have three items in a series. Underline all the verbs twice in both the sentences you are given and in the sentences you create. The first one has been done for you.

The Wild Ride

1. I tear out of the driveway. I race up the street.

    Combined: I tear out of the driveway and race up the street.

2. A giant bulldog crouches on the sidewalk. He looks ready to attack me.

    _____

3. He growls at me. He snarls at me.

    _____

4. He jumps at me. He rips off half of my left pants leg.

    _____

5. I huff as fast as I can. I puff as fast as I can. I pedal as fast as I can.

    _____

6. I hit a truck. I fly over the hood!

    _____

7. I get right up. I scream like a banshee all the way.

    _____

Linking Verbs

So far you have been working with verbs that show movement or action in the sentence. The underlined verbs in the sentences below are different from verbs like *crouches, growls, jumps,* or *rips* because they show a state or condition rather than an action.

1. My father is very old fashioned.
2. My mother and brother are ill.
3. My aunt is angry.

The verb *be*, and other verbs like *become, feel, turn, look, seem, smell, appear, taste,* and *sound* are **linking verbs.** That means they link or join the subject of a sentence to a word or group of words that describe it.

The linking verbs in the following sentences are underlined twice and subjects are underlined once. The word or words that describe the subject are placed in brackets. You will see that the descriptive words, usually called **subject complements,** always answer a question about the subject. These descriptive words are called "complements" because they complete the meaning of the subject.

     complement   *complement*
1. It is [the Fourth of July, 1989,] and I look [beautiful.]
   What day is it? *the Fourth of July*
   What do I look like? *beautiful*

      complement
2. Today is [my wedding day.]
   What day is it? *my wedding day*

     complement   *complement*
3. My dress is [a peach color] and looks [like an April garden.]
   What color is my dress? *peach color*
   What does it look like? *like an April garden*

Exercise 20g.   Read the following sentences and underline the linking verbs twice and the subjects once. Place the subject complements in brackets. The first sentence has been marked as an example.

An Admirable Athlete

1. My friend Michelle is [short] and appears [fragile.]
2. But Michelle is a star softball player.
3. First of all, she is an excellent hitter.
4. She is also extremely supportive of the other team members.
5. If another player looks angry or depressed, Michelle is always sympathetic.
6. Her secret is her appreciation of other people's feelings.

Auxiliary or Helping Verbs

Compare the verbs in the following pairs of sentences. In the second sentence in each pair helping verbs have been added and the main verb has been changed to its *-ing* form. This -ing form is called the **present participle.**

  A giant bulldog crouches on the sidewalk.
  A giant bulldog is crouching on the sidewalk.
  I wear regular glasses.

I am wearing regular glasses.

Marlease watches the man at the bus stop.

Holden is watching the man at the bus stop.

The word *is,* a form of the verb *be,* serves as a "helping" verb in the sense that it "helps" to complete the verb.

Exercise 20h. Read the following sentences. Then underline the complete verb (helping verb plus present participle) twice. The first sentence is done for you.

The Class Clown

1. The picture of my best friend, Lon, is facing me as I glance through the pages of my high-school yearbook.
2. In one of the first pictures, he is clowning with me and other members of the yearbook staff.
3. In this picture, two straws are sticking out of each of his nostrils.
4. His eyes are hiding behind two cups from an egg carton.
5. He is looking at me from the two bulging eyeballs drawn on each cup.

The following list shows the two parts of each of the verbs in these five sentences:

Helping Verb	**The -ing Verb Form (present participle)**
is	facing
is	clowning
are	sticking
are	hiding
is	looking

You will frequently see some form of the verb *be* in combination with a participle. The same verbs may be written in the past tense or in the future tense as you see in the following tables.

PAST TENSE

Helping Verb	**The -ing Verb Form (present participle)**
was	facing
was	clowning
were	sticking
were	hiding
was	looking

FUTURE TENSE

Helping Verb	The -ing Verb Form (present participle)
will be	facing
will be	clowning
will be	sticking
will be	hiding
will be	looking

Other common helping verbs in English are forms of *have* and *do*. The following list illustrates how these verbs might combine with the verb *see: have seen, had seen, will have seen; have been seen, had been seen, will have been seen;* and *do see, does see, did see*. Other auxiliary verbs like *will* and *been; could, can,* and *may; would* and *should;* and *may, might,* and *must* are also used frequently. These verbs do not change form as do the verbs *have, be,* and *do*.

Exercise 20i.   Underline the verbs in the following sentences twice. Check carefully to make sure you underline the complete verb. The first sentence is done for you.

The Class Clown

1. In a second photograph of Lon, he is mimicking Mr. Ames, our math teacher.
2. He is standing with his feet shoulder-width apart.
3. He has rounded his shoulders to make himself look hunchbacked.
4. He is bending his knees.
5. No one could guess his real age.
6. He could easily be mistaken for an old man with chronic arthritis.

Exercise 20j.   Examine the following sentences carefully. Underline the verbs twice, watching for helping verbs. The first sentence is done for you.

Mother Is an Actress

1. My mother is studying to be an actress.
2. She will sometimes act like a madwoman by running wildly through the house.
3. She doesn't seem to pay attention to anyone but herself.
4. I should never have told anyone about her new career in acting.
5. My friends have been coming to the house daily to watch her perform.

Exercise 20k.   Read the paragraphs below carefully. Then underline all the subjects once and the verbs twice. If you have trouble finding the verbs, test particular words to see if they change tense. Also check for multiple subjects and verbs.

Fans

The fans at a baseball game are sometimes obnoxious. I remember one terrible game last fall. The unruly crowd intimidated the losing team by booing and yelling obscenities at them.

Grandfather

The most important person in my family was my grandfather. He taught me many things. As a young man he lived in Mexico. He built the town cathedral and many of the streets and houses in his town. He was certainly a genius. He was a plumber, an electrician, a carpenter, and a contractor. He even practiced medicine. Sometimes he let poorer relatives stay with him and then helped them find a place of their own. He helped my grandmother with the household chores. His family always had plenty to eat. I have immense respect for my grandfather, Salcedo Gutierrez.

Remembering Home

I remember Winchester Street, Chicago. That was the street I lived on. We called it the "block at the end of the world." Both early and late in the day, we could look down that street and see nothing but darkness. It was a perfect place for our wild adventures. Every afternoon after school we walked up that block. Dogs and cats darted in and out of traffic. Trash lay everywhere.

A big empty house stood right in the middle of the block with no other houses around it. That was the "witch house." No one had bothered to paint or fix it up in twenty years. We had to be careful, though. The boards on the porch were dry and old. Sometimes they crumbled beneath our feet. We threw parties in that house and played lots of loud music with no fussy neighbors to disturb us. I have lots of wonderful memories of that remote little block.

Verbs and Subjects in Commands

Examine the following sentences carefully. They are written in the imperative or command form. The verbs in these sentences are underlined twice.

1. Don't give up.
2. Never take your freedom lightly.
3. Go to the window and look at the sunshine.

The subject in an imperative sentence is "you"—the person spoken to. If we wanted to indicate the subject for these sentences, we could write it after the sentence as in the following examples:

1. Don't give up. (You)

2. Never <u>take</u> your freedom lightly. (You)
3. <u>Go</u> to the window and <u>look</u> at the sunshine. (You)

It probably seems impolite to your ears, as it does to most English-speakers, to say "You come to the window." That's why sentences like these give the listener a command without including the subject. The subject, then, is implied but not stated.

Exercise 20l.   Underline the verbs in the following commands, and, in parentheses, write the implied subject at the end of the sentence. The first one is done for you. Notice that like other sentences, commands may have more than one verb.

Girl

1. <u>Wash</u> the white clothes on Monday and <u>put</u> them on the stone heap. (You)
2. Don't walk bareheaded in the hot sun.
3. Cook pumpkin fritters in very hot sweet oil.
4. Soak salt fish overnight before you cook it.
5. Don't eat fruits on the street—flies will follow you.

Verbs and Subjects in Questions

Compare these pairs of sentences. Subjects and verbs are underlined for you.

<u>I</u> <u>became</u> an actor.
Why <u>did</u> <u>I</u> <u>become</u> an actor?

<u>I</u> <u>was</u> afraid of the elephant's feet.
<u>Was</u> <u>I</u> afraid of the elephant's feet?

<u>I</u> <u>will do</u> something after graduation.
What <u>will</u> <u>I</u> <u>do</u> after graduation?

Notice that the subject and verb change positions when the sentences are rewritten as questions. In the case of the examples with *did I become and will I do,* the subject comes between the two parts of the verb.

Exercise 20m.   Rewrite the following sentences as questions. The first one is changed for you.

The Coach

1. Mr. Corona is my son's soccer coach.

   <u>Who is Mr. Corona?</u>

2. He is a tall, heavy Caucasian man.

_____

3. He weighs about a hundred and seventy pounds.

_____

4. He is forty-two years old.

_____

5. He is giving out trophies to the best soccer teams.

_____

Differentiating Verbs and Subjects from Introductory Words and Phrases

Many sentences in English begin with introductory phrases. Usually these phrases simply add information. When the adverb *here* or *there* begins a sentence or a clause within a sentence, it is important not to mistake these adverbs for the subject of the sentence. Study the following sentences; some begin with introductory phrases, others illustrate the placement of verbs and subjects in clauses that begin with *here* or *there*. The verbs and subjects in these sentences are underlined for you.

1. Here we are on San Fernando Road, not too far from Los Angeles.
2. In the mid-1920s, my great-grandfather brought his family to this place.
3. There were very few cars on the streets then.
4. In fact, there were no streets to speak of.
5. For many years, streets were made of dirt or gravel, rather than asphalt.

Exercise 20n.   Underline the subject once and the verb twice in the rest of these sentences about Los Angeles.

1. In 1925, Los Angeles was nothing like the huge megalopolis it is today with 8 million people and nearly as many cars.
2. There were certainly no freeways then.
3. Instead of sitting in traffic jams, Los Angelinos rode the "Red Cars," which were part of a system of streetcars that ran from the San Fernando Valley to San Diego.
4. In the late 1940s, there was a rush in Southern California to buy automobiles.
5. By the mid-1950s, most families owned at least one car.

6. Slowly but surely, cities began pulling up the old streetcar tracks or paving over them.

7. With the rail system out, the people of Los Angeles lost one of the best transportation systems in the country.

> **Rule to Remember: The adverbs *here* and *there* can never be the subject of a sentence.**

WRITING EXERCISES

Exercise 20o.   Imagine that you are telling a young child how to make breakfast. Decide what food you want the child to prepare, and write directions for him or her using commands to give your instructions.

Exercise 20p.   Write a one- or two-page journal entry about something that is important in your life right now. You might write about a situation at work, problems that a friend or relative is having, a current relationship, an activity at school, or a class you like or dislike. Use the present tense as you describe this situation.

Exercise 20q.   Rewrite the journal entry you wrote for Exercise 20p above as though this event happened last year. Be sure to change all present tense verbs to the past tense as you rewrite.

21

Revising for Verb-Subject and Noun-Pronoun Agreement

Whenever you write, connections between subjects and verbs, and those between nouns and the pronouns that refer to them, must be clear to your reader. To give them that clarity, subjects and verbs, and nouns and pronouns must agree in number. In other words, if a subject is singular, the verb must also be singular; if a noun is plural, any pronouns that refer to it must be plural as well. In this chapter you will practice making these elements in your sentences uniformly plural or singular.

MAKING VERBS AND SUBJECTS AGREE

To make clear connections between the subjects and verbs in your sentences, both words must agree in number. That means they must both be *either* plural *or* singular. If one is plural and the other singular, the result is an **agreement** error.

Using Third-Person Singular Verbs

Writers can avoid making many errors in verb-subject agreement by reviewing the verb forms in the present tense.

Present Tense Singular		Present Tense Plural	
Subject	*Verb*	*Subject*	*Verb*
I	live	we	live
you	live	you	live
he/she/it	lives	they	live

> **A Reminder: Verbs in the third-person present tense always end in *s*.**

Exercise 21a.   Put a check (✓) next to the sentences in the following pairs that express the correct relationship between the subject and verb. The first pair is marked for you.

Planting

_____Freida plant her garden every spring.
_____✓_____Freida plants her garden every spring.

_____William sometimes mixes up the seeds.
_____✓_____William sometimes mix up the seeds.

_____When spring come, the flowers blooms in the wrong places.
_____✓_____When spring comes, the flowers bloom in the wrong places.

Exercise 21b.   In this exercise, change the verbs in parentheses to their present tense, singular forms to make the sentences complete. The first one is written for you.

1. The architecture of a culture _____ its soul. *(to reflect)* The architecture of a culture <u>reflects</u> its soul.

2. Tracy __works__ well with the models she photographs. *(to work)*

3. The photograph of her mother <u>showed</u> much compassion. *(to show)*

4. When a student __gets__ confused about an assignment, it is best to ask the instructor for help. *(to get)*

5. Sometimes the homework for a class __seems__ too difficult, and a student __needs__ a little extra help. *(to seem, to need)*

6. In this case, a campus tutoring center or the help of another student often __makes__ the difference between passing or failing a course. *(to make)*

Exercise 21c.   In the following sentences, change the underlined subjects and verbs from singular to plural. The first one is done for you.

Pick Your Video Store

1. When a <u>customer</u> <u>enters</u> a video store, the first thing <u>he</u> or she <u>notices</u> is how it is organized.

   Changed: <u>When customers enter a video store, the first thing they notice is how it is organized.</u>

2. It is important to note whether the <u>video</u> <u>is</u> <u>shelved</u> according to topic.

   there are important notes, whether Videos are shelve according to topics.

3. The <u>manager</u> at my video store <u>sorts</u> the titles alphabetically as well.

   managers   sorts

4. The <u>procedure</u> for reshelving used videos <u>is</u> also important.

   PROCEDURES   are

5. If a <u>clerk</u> <u>does</u> not <u>rewind</u> the video when it comes back to the store, the next customer has the frustration of having to rewind it at home.

   CLERKS   REMINDS

6. If a <u>movie</u> <u>has</u> <u>been</u> <u>used</u> too much, the tracking will be off a little or a strip of distortion may appear at the top.

   movies   HAD BEEN USE

7. The rental <u>fee</u> <u>is</u> another consideration when choosing a video store.

   fees ARE

8. If the <u>price</u> <u>is</u> too high, the <u>customer</u> <u>is</u> not likely to rent movies more than once a week.

   PRICES are   customers ARE

Exercise 21d.   Locate the verbs and subjects in the following sentences and change them from plural to singular. The first sentence is done for you.

Fur the Sake of Argument

1. The fur industries have developed elaborate traps for catching animals.

   Changed: The fur industry has developed elaborate traps for catching animals.

2. The leg-holding traps with pads are supposedly "kinder" to animals than most.

   legholdings trap

3. According to trappers, animals feel a numbness in the leg but no pain.

   to a trapper animal numbness

4. But the paddings do not prevent animals from suffering broken bones, severed tendons, and the like.

   But the padding do not prevent, an animal from suffering broken bone, severed tendon, and the like.

5. Steel traps, banned in many countries, are still used frequently in the United States.

   Steel trap, banned in country, is still used frequently in U.S.

6. When trapped, water animals often drown or die a slow death from exposure.

   When trapped, a water animals often drown or die a slow death from exposure

7. Animals have been known to chew off a leg or paw to get free of the trap.

   An animal has been known to chew off a leg or paw to get free of the traps

8. Advocates of these and other traps are probably more interested in business than in the animals' suffering.

   The advocate of this and other trap is probably more interested in business than in animal suffering

Exercise 21e.   To practice making verbs and subjects agree, change the underlined verbs in the following paragraph from the past to the present tense. Check all the verbs in each sentence to make sure they are written in the present tense and in the correct form (plural or singular) to agree with their subjects. The first sentence is rewritten for you. Use your own paper for this exercise.

Just Say No and Mean It

Women played a secondary role in a male-dominated world and were taught subservience to men. [Women play a secondary role in a male-dominated world and are taught subservience to men.] Rape represented [REPRESENT] the ultimate surrender of any remaining power, autonomy, and control. The surrender was [WERE] not by choice, but was [WERE] usually made to ensure survival. By destroying a woman's feelings of personal power and self-worth, the rapist hoped [HOPES] to gain [DOES] a sense of his own power and worth, and to take from the woman what he did not already feel [FELT] in himself. Rape occurred [OCCURRS] any time a person was forced [WERE FORCE] or coerced, physically or verbally, into sexual contact with another person. That assailant was [WERE] often a friend, an acquaintance, an employer or fellow employee, or a husband. The fact of acquaintance rape was ignored [WERE IGNORE] or denied [DENY] by most people. Even the women themselves did not identify their experiences as rape. [DOES   IDENTIFIES]

Exercise 21f.   Rewrite the verbs in the essay below in the present tense. This time they are not underlined, so you need to check the sentences carefully to find all the verbs and to make them agree in number with their subjects. The first sentence is rewritten for you. Use your own paper for this exercise.

Groupies

There were many different groups on high-school campuses. [There are many different groups on high-school campuses.] You could find them standing together in closed circles all over campus. The two groups most students wanted to join were the "cool" ones—the fashion group and the jock group. Everyone avoided the "nerd" group, the group that went to college and made something of themselves.

The fashion group thought they had it all. They dressed in name-brand clothes that their parents bought for them. These teens hung out together and talked about how everyone else dressed. Many people wanted to join this crowd. But it really wasn't worth it. Most of them were just snobs.

The most talked-about group were the jocks. They were completely unlike the fashion-conscious kids on campus. They wore sweats to school and didn't really care what they looked like. They knew it didn't matter how they looked; it was how they played the game that mattered.

The nerd group was not very popular. But they were the smartest people. They did not wear the cool clothes or play sports. Instead, they paid little attention to their clothes and studied all the time. Unlike the other two groups, they were not worried about trying to impress people. They were too busy thinking about the future.

Prepositional Phrases

One kind of agreement error occurs when students confuse the noun in a prepositional phrase with the subject of the sentence. To understand this problem better, we will identify the prepositional phrases in the following sentences and examine their structure.

In the sentences below, the subjects are underlined once, the verbs twice. The troublesome prepositional phrases come between the subjects and verbs.

1. The fans at most games are really rowdy.
2. Some of the more boisterous people throw food.
3. Others in the crowd yell at the top of their lungs.
4. Silence during plays is not necessarily a good sign.
5. The emotions among enthusiastic fans are always lying just below the surface.

The first prepositional phrase in each of these sentences describes the noun that precedes it. In sentence 1, for example, *at most games* describes which *fans. Of the more boisterous people* in sentence 2 describes *some.* In sentence 3, *in the crowd* refers to *others.* Notice, too, that the prepositional phrases also contain nouns—*games, people,* and *crowd.* These nouns are not, however, the subject of the sentence in which they appear because the noun in a prepositional phrase can *never* be the subject of a sentence.

Let's look at some of the prepositional phrases in the sentences above a little more closely. They are listed below.

> at most games
> of the more boisterous people
> in the crowd
> during plays
> among enthusiastic fans

Each of these phrases follows a basic pattern:

Preposition	Adjective(s)	Noun
at	most	games
of	the more boisterous	people
in	the	crowd
during		plays
among	enthusiastic	fans

You can see from this list that a preposition and a noun appear in every prepositional phrase. Some prepositional phrases also contain adjectives— words that clarify or modify the noun in that phrase. In the prepositional phrase *at most games,* for example, the word *most* is an adjective because it tells us which *games.* In the same way, *the more boisterous* describes *people, the* refers to *crowd,* and *enthusiastic* modifies *fans.* Notice, however, that the prepositional phrase *during plays* contains no adjective: not all prepositional phrases contain adjectives.

The following is a list of commonly used prepositions:

about	beside	next
above	between	of
across	beyond	off
after	by	on
against	down	out
along	during	outside
among	for	over
around	from	through
as	in	to
at	inside	toward
before	into	under
behind	like	up
below	near	with
beneath		

Rather than try to memorize these prepositions, learn to recognize them as the short words that appear in the pattern typical of prepositional phrases. It is also helpful to know that prepositional phrases often indicate direction (like *around, to, toward,* and *through*), or location in time or space (like *under, behind, inside,* and *outside*).

> **Rule to Remember: The noun in a prepositional phrase is *never* the subject of the sentence.**

Agreement errors are often created because the noun in a prepositional phrase is mistaken for the subject of the sentence. Correct any agreement errors you find in the following exercise. If you have difficulty finding the subject of a sentence, try crossing out prepositional phrases.

Exercise 21g.   Read the following sentences carefully. Cross out any prepositional phrases you find. Then underline the subject in each sentence once and the verb twice. The first sentence is done for you.

1. The man ~~of my dreams~~ likes to cook.
2. ~~Several~~ of the jugglers own parrots.
3. ~~That clever~~ Queen of Hearts tricked Alice.

4. Films by Spike Lee have become popular.
5. In front of the building down the block a gigantic pencil is sticking out of the grass.
6. The hours before dawn make me most uneasy.

Exercise 21h.   In the following sentences about sports fans, the subjects and verbs do not agree in number. Correct the sentences to make their subjects and verbs either plural or singular. If you are having trouble finding the subjects, try crossing out the prepositional phrases and underlining the subjects and verbs. The first sentence is done for you.

In the Crowd

1. The time between plays bore even the most loyal fan.

    Corrected: The time between plays bores even the most loyal fan.

2. The benches beside the field is sometimes very uncomfortable.

    THE BENCH IS SOMETIMES VERY UNCOMFORTABLE.

3. A sign of dissatisfaction are the "thumbs down" gesture.

    _____

4. The person next to you decide to yell every few minutes.

    THE PERSON YELLS EVERY FEW MINUTES

5. At times, boxes of popcorn comes flying through the air.

    THE BOXY OF POPCORN CAME FLYING THROUGH THE AIR.

6. The moments after a bad play is the hardest to take.

    _____

7. Sometimes the coach of a team get pretty angry about a bad play.

    _____

Exercise 21i.   Create your own sentences using prepositional phrases. To make this task easier, you might focus on a single subject. Wherever possible, make your prepositional phrases modify the subjects of your sentences. Refer to the preceding list of prepositions as you write.

1. _____

    _____.

2. _____

    _____.

3. _____

    _____.

4. _____

_____ .

5. _____

_____ .

Indefinite Pronouns

Indefinite pronouns used as subjects of sentences may cause errors in agreement. These pronouns are always singular and take singular verbs. In the following sentences the subjects are underlined once and the verbs twice. Notice that the verbs in these sentences are singular.

> Someone is listening at the door.
> Everybody at this meeting has something to say.
> Each of Paula's answers makes sense to the other students.
> Neither of Rodney's classes requires much homework.

> **Rule to Remember: When the following indefinite pronouns are used as subjects, they are *always* singular and take singular verbs.**

anybody	everything
anyone	neither
anything	nobody
each	nothing
either	somebody
every	someone
everybody	something
everyone	

These words express singular ideas in English. Think of *anyone,* for example, as referring to *any one person,* and *each* as referring to *each and every answer.*

Exercise 21j.   Write the proper present tense verb form in the following sentences. Verbs at the end are listed in the order you will use them. Keep in mind that an *s* on the end of a verb in the third-person present tense makes the verb singular. You may need to refer to the preceding list of indefinite pronouns for help in choosing the proper verb form. The first sentence in this exercise is written as a sample.

Anthropology Class

1. Everyone in Mr. Herzog's anthropology class _____ the subject.

   (to love)

   Everyone in Mr. Herzog's anthropology class loves the subject.

2. Each of the students __HAD__ seen an ancient skull of Cro-Magnon man. *(to have)*

3. The instructor, Mr. Herzog, makes the lectures so vivid that nobody __GETS__ bored. *(to get)*

4. The anthropology class is also interesting because someone always __ASKED__ an interesting question that __LEADS__ to a good discussion. *(to ask, to lead)*

5. Mr. Herzog makes the whole class feel so comfortable that nobody __BEEN__ afraid to ask questions. *(to be)*

6. In addition, each of the two books for the course __INCLUDES__ several fascinating articles about major debates between anthropologists. *(to include)*

7. Either of the two books __HAVE__ enough information to keep me reading for several years. *(to have)*

8. Neither textbook __CONTAINS__ information that __BEEN__ commonly known. *(to contain, to be)*

9. Each of the chapters __INCLUDES__ detailed examples of the subjects it __COVERS__. *(to include, to cover)*

10. Anybody who __PLANS__ to take anthropology __NEEDS__ to enroll in Mr. Herzog's class. *(to plan, to need)*

Study the following pairs of sentences. Whether the verbs are plural or singular depends on the noun in the prepositional phrase that follows the subject. Verbs in these sentences are underlined twice and the subjects once.

Some of the dollars never get to the bank.
Some of the money never gets to the bank.

In the first sentence, *some* refers to a number of dollars; in this case, *some* could also be expressed as a specific number (three dollars, six dollars, fifty dollars, and so forth) and is, therefore, a plural or count noun. In the second sentence, *some* refers to an amount of money, something you cannot count. In this case, *some* is a singular noun.

> **Rule to Remember: When *all, any, most, none,* or *some* refer to how many (the number of X), use a plural verb. When these words refer to the amount of something, they take a singular verb.**

Exercise 21k. Study the next two sentences and answer the questions that follow.

1. None of the candidates want to debate the parking problem downtown.

    Is the verb in this sentence singular or plural? _____PLURAL_____

    What makes it singular or plural?_____PROBLEM_____

2. None of the homework makes sense to Fred.

    Is the verb in this sentence singular or plural? _____SINGULAR_____

    What makes it singular or plural? _____MAKES_____

Exercise 21l. Write the correct form of the verb in parentheses. Reread the explanations on the preceding page if you have difficulty writing the verb. Use the present tense throughout.

1. Most of the students here _____BEEN_____ serious about their studies. *(to be)*

2. Any of the vitamins you want _____ available without a prescription. *(to be)*

3. Any of the medication for heart disease _____NEEDS_____ to be prescribed by a doctor. *(to need)*

4. Some of the houses in rural areas _____COSTED_____ from $20,000 to $50,000. *(to cost)*

5. Most of the property in the city _____SELLS_____ for $75,000 to $100,000. *(to sell)*

6. None of the land _____ for sale at the moment. *(to be)*

7. Realtors are angry because all the building permits _____HAS_____ been issued for the year, and none _____ presently available for new construction. *(to have, to be)*

8. All members of the City Council _____VOTES_____ against proposals to increase the number of building permits. *(to vote)*

9. Any attempt to change their minds _____ENDS_____ in defeat. *(to end)*

10. Some contractors _____ACCEPTS_____ defeat and _____LOOKS_____ forward to next year's building season. *(to accept, to look)*

Subjects Joined by *or* or *nor*

Chapter 20 explains that sentences may contain compound subjects joined by the conjunction *and*. Compare the sentences below to see the way in which the conjunctions *and* or *or* are used to join parts of a compound subject.

1. Either "Rapunzel" or "The Fairy Prince" is required reading for my folklore class.
2. Neither an evil stepmother nor wicked sisters have much chance of being liked.
3. Neither wicked sisters nor an evil stepmother has much chance of being liked.

> **Rule to Remember: When *or* or *nor* joins parts of a compound subject, the verb agrees with the subject closer to the verb.**

Exercise 21m.   Write the correct form of the verb in parentheses in the space provided. Be sure the verb you write is plural or singular to match the subject.

Fairy Tales

1. Most fairy tales _____ about princes, kings, queens, and princesses. *(to be)*

2. Either the prince or king in the tale _____ the beautiful female. *(to marry)*

3. Sometimes characters metamorphose in fairy tales, and either the princess or the prince _____ into a bird or frog. *(to turn)*

4. Leprechauns and elves also _____ the woods in fairy tales. *(to inhabit)*

5. But neither the wise old leprechaun nor the bands of elves _____ much more than a supporting role in most stories. *(to have)*

6. They exist mainly to assist the real hero or heroine of the story because neither the princess nor her admirers ever _____ from their adventures without help. *(to return)*

MAKING NOUNS AND PRONOUNS AGREE

Like subjects and verbs, pronouns and the nouns they refer to (called **antecedents**) must agree in number. If the noun is plural, the pronoun must also be plural; if the noun is singular, any pronoun that refers to it must be singular as well.

In the sentences that follow, arrows connect pronouns to their antecedents.

1. In many older films, male characters have a cigarette in their hands in most of the scenes.
   Are the noun and pronoun singular or plural? _____

2. In many older films, the male lead has a cigarette in his hand in most of the scenes.
   Are the noun and pronoun singular or plural? _____

> **Rule to Remember: A pronoun must agree with its antecedent.**

Exercise 21n.   Write the correct pronoun in the blanks below. Your choices are listed in parentheses at the end of the sentence.

The Changing Image of Smokers

1. Whereas cigarettes once gave a movie-character sex appeal, _____ are now smoked mostly by villains. *(it/they)*

2. In most of the spy thrillers, the agents from Russia or China smoke _____ cigarettes in full view of rival American agents. *(his or her/their)*

3. No self-respecting U.S. agent would dare smoke in front of _____ enemy. *(his or her/their)*

4. Even the antihero in most mass-market movies refuses to take a cigarette if is _____ offered one. *(he or she/they)*

5. In some films, a character who has obvious mental problems smokes _____ favorite cigarettes during tense moments. *(his or her/their)*

6. This pressure to change the image of the movie hero comes from the movement in our culture to eliminate smoking and to see _____ as characteristic of only the most despicable characters. *(it/them)*

7. Although it is true that smoking does pose health hazards, nobody should lose completely _____ right to smoke. *(his or her/their)*

Exercise 21o.   In the following sentences about working, nouns and pronouns do not always agree in number. Locate any agreement errors in these sentences and make both the nouns and the pronouns that refer to them uniformly singular or plural. Two possible corrections are given for the first sentence.

Working

1. If <u>someone</u> really <u>wants</u> to do something well, <u>they</u> <u>must</u> <u>work</u> hard.
   Corrected: <u>If someone really wants to do something well, he or she must work hard.</u>
   Corrected: <u>If individuals really want to do something well, they must work hard.</u>

2. A person can gain self-respect, regardless of what their job is, by working hard. _____

   _____

3. When a new employee is hired, it is important that they be shown around and helped with the tasks they don't understand. _____

   _____

4. Even the most seasoned worker needs help from their fellow workers once in a while. _____

   _____

5. Anyone who has been asked to work with a self-absorbed co-worker knows how unpleasant they can be. _____

   _____

6. If someone decides to quit their job, they must take full responsibility for that decision._____

7. A car salesperson has to keep their quota of sales. If they don't, they will not get much of a commission at the end of the month. _____

   _____

8. Realtors, who work under similar pressure, push themselves to sell as many houses as they can. _____

   _____

9. Salespeople sometimes quit because he or she finds the competition too stressful. He or she may discover that the money doesn't compensate for the amount of pressure they face. _____

   _____

10. When an advertiser puts an ad on television, they always make working in fast-food restaurants seem better than it really is. _____

   _____

WRITING EXERCISE

Exercise 21p.   Write two paragraphs about a major change that has taken place in your life in the past year or two. In paragraph one, describe what your life was like before the change; in the second paragraph, discuss what is happening now as a result of the change.

22

Coordinating Conjunctions and Other Connecting Words

Part of effective proofreading means making sure that ideas in your sentences are connected correctly. To help you make those connections, this chapter introduces you to clauses—the basic units of thought in any sentence. Exercises in this chapter ask you to use coordinating conjunctions and transitional words called conjunctive adverbs to link clauses logically in sentences.

CONNECTING INDEPENDENT CLAUSES

Like a sentence, a clause has a subject and a verb. Only two types of clauses occur in English—independent clauses and dependent clauses.

The first clause we will discuss is the **independent** clause, also called a **main clause.** We call this clause independent because it could be written by itself as a sentence.

Coordinating Conjunctions

Coordinating conjunctions are commonly used to join ideas in independent clauses. The example below shows how two sentences can be rewritten as independent clauses joined by a comma and the coordinating conjunction *but*. To emphasize this pattern, the independent clauses in the sample sentence are enclosed in brackets and the coordinating conjunction is circled.

I waved to Melissa. She didn't see me.

independent clause   *coordinating conjunction*   *independent clause*

[I waved to Melissa,]   [she didn't see me.]

The next section contains a list of coordinating conjunctions, their function, and samples of how they may be used. The explanations in brackets clarify the meaning of each coordinating conjunction. Use this list to make logical connections between short, choppy sentences in your own writing.

Coordinating Conjunctions

for—shows a reason or cause
>I am going back to school part-time, for [because, for this reason] I expect to get a better job with a college education.

and—adds the ideas together
>My starting salary is $4.50 an hour, and [plus, in addition] I will get a raise every three months.

nor—the least common coordinating conjunction; keeps the second independent clause negative
>I was not content to work for $4.25 an hour, nor [he or she wasn't either] was my boss willing to raise my salary.

but—shows a contrast or makes an exception
>I actually liked the work at the gas station, but [even so] I think my time is worth more than minimum wage.

or—gives a choice or alternative
>Last month I told my boss at Rick's Chevron to give me a raise, or [as an alternative] I would look for another job.

yet—like "but," draws a strong contrast
>My current job as a dishwasher and cook at a Chinese restaurant keeps me in the kitchen most of the time, yet [in spite of this] I get to talk to customers occasionally.

so—shows a consequence or result
>My old boss would not give in, so [as a result] I looked for and got a new job.

One good way to remember these seven coordinating conjunctions is by memorizing the word formed by the first letter in each:

For And Nor But Or Yet So = FANBOYS

Exercise 22a.   Complete this exercise by underlining verbs twice and subjects once, and by *circling* the words that join the two independent clauses. The first sentence is done for you.

Knowing When to Quit

1. I actually liked the work at the gas station, (but) my time is worth more than minimum wage.
2. I was not content to work for $4.25 an hour, nor was my boss willing to raise my salary.
3. He would not give in, so I looked for and got a new job.
4. My current job as dishwasher and cook at a Chinese restaurant keeps me in the kitchen most of the time, yet I get to talk to customers occasionally.
5. My starting salary is $4.50 an hour, and I will get a raise every three months.
6. I am going back to school part-time, for I expect to get better and better jobs with a college education.

Exercise 22b.   Add commas and coordinating conjunctions to the following sentences. Be sure that the conjunction you choose links the ideas in the two clauses logically; refer to the list of coordinating conjunctions if necessary. In some sentences, several conjunctions may work logically. The first sentence has been completed for you.

On the Spot

1. It was a muggy Monday morning,____and____I was in no mood to work.

2. My math teacher was busily going over the homework assignment _____so_____ I just sat in my seat thinking about how good it would feel to be in bed.

3. Suddenly she called on me to answer _____ I could feel my heart pounding.

4. My hand began to shake from nervousness _____ I was really scared.

5. At the time a few things were going through my mind: I could tell her that I had done the work _____ I didn't understand it _____ I could just refuse to do the work.

6. The work was absolutely no problem _____ I had done my home-work in thirty minutes.

7. At this point I was going through real emotional turmoil. I knew what was right _____ I didn't know exactly how to act on it.

8. This was the first time in my life that I had felt so unsure about anything _____ it frightened me.

9. I had to do something _____ I quickly considered how disap-pointed my teacher would be if I refused to do the problems.

10. Then it occurred to me that it would not hurt me to share my knowledge with the class _____ I took a deep breath and began to answer the question correctly.

11. In spite of my anxiety, this experience was good _____ I was able to return to my desk with the feeling that I had contributed some-thing valuable to the class _____ I hadn't betrayed my own intel-ligence.

Exercise 22c. Add your own independent clauses to complete the follow-ing sentences. The first one is done as a sample. Notice that commas precede the coordinating conjunctions.

Worried

1. I used to dread the first day in a new school, for <u>I was worried that I would</u> <u>not be able to find my classes or find any of my old friends.</u>

2. I tried and tried to get to bed early the night before my first day at school, but _____

    _____

3. I would lie awake wondering what would happen if I could not find my classes, and _____

    _____

4. By the time morning finally came, I was always a wreck, yet _____

    _____

5. Once I got to school, I usually felt better, for _____

_____

6. Then, too, as soon as I got my schedule, I bought my new books, and

_____

7. Now that I am in college, I have a little more confidence about that open-

ing day of school, so _____

_____

Exercise 22d.   Write five sentences in which you connect two independent clauses with a comma and coordinating conjunction. Use your own paper for this exercise.

Transitional Words (Conjunctive Adverbs)

In Chapter 4 you saw how transitional words and phrases add coherence to paragraphs by showing logical connections between ideas. Some of these transitions (also called **conjunctive adverbs**) are used in combination with a semicolon to join two independent clauses. The following sentence illustrates this pattern. The clauses are enclosed in brackets and the transitional word is circled for you.

[For years, women have been working in police departments as secretaries and dispatchers]; however, [they are no longer satisfied with these roles.]

Common transitions and the logical connection they express are listed below.

To add ideas:	use *also, besides, furthermore, moreover*
To order ideas in time:	use *finally, hence*
To emphasize:	use *certainly, actually*
To show contrast:	use *however, nevertheless*
To show similarity:	use *similarly*
To draw conclusions or show results:	use *consequently, therefore, thus, then, of course, as a result, unfortunately*

Exercise 22e.   Complete the following sentences by adding a transitional word to connect the two independent clauses. Notice that a semicolon precedes the transition and a comma follows the transition. The first sentence is completed for you.

Campus Events

1. Sometimes events on campus really interest Juan;   actually,   he finds the

celebration of Hispanic culture quite exciting.

2. Juan's chemistry teacher encourages the class to attend cultural events; _____ , she occasionally lets him leave class to participate in such activities.

3. She definitely appreciates his interest in such events; _____ , Juan must agree to make up any classwork he might miss.

4. Juan always waits by the fountain in the quad; _____ , he can catch his girl friend Judy as she comes from class.

5. Ti Lee, a friend of Juan's, likes to attend these events with his friend; _____ , he sometimes has to leave campus before a performance begins.

6. Poetry readings and loud music bore Judy; _____ , she sometimes leaves these events early.

Exercise 22f.   Complete the following sentences by adding a clause that works logically with the rest of the sentence. The first one has been completed for you.

Television

1. Some writers have called excessive television-viewing "addictive" behavior; furthermore, they argue that watching television impairs our ability to think and reason.

2. It is true that as a nation, we watch many hours of television a week; consequently, _____

3. It is not clear that watching five hours of television a day is as harmful as taking drugs; certainly, _____

4. I have never known anyone who stayed home from work to watch television; however, _____
_____

5. _____ ;
consequently, television can draw the whole family together.

6. Some elderly or severely disabled people cannot go to a movie or nice restaurant for entertainment; therefore, _____
_____

Exercise 22g.   Use a transition to connect the following pairs of sentences. The first two are joined for you.

Women in Law Enforcement

1. Female friends usually support women who want to become police officers. Family members may find it more difficult to accept an aunt, sister, or daughter as a police officer.
   Combined: <u>Female friends usually support women who want to become police officers; however, family members may find it more difficult to accept an aunt, sister, or daughter as a police officer.</u>

2. Executives view women as fragile and helpless. They are unwilling to employ women as police officers.

   _____

   _____

3. Women who are hired are not always given the same treatment as male officers. These women are expected to perform at least as well as the men who shun them.

   _____

   _____

4. Some officers refuse to be paired with a female. Male officers may stop eating at coffee shops or restaurants where female officers congregate.

   _____

   _____

5. The Equal Employment Opportunity Act of 1972 forced police departments to hire women as officers. Women continue to be underrepresented.

   _____

   _____

6. Training programs for female police officers sometimes ignore the martial arts. Women officers are forced to avoid potentially dangerous situations.

   _____

   _____

7. Parents are likely to discourage women from entering such a dangerous profession. They think that their sons are capable of handling conflicts, even violence.

   _____

   _____

8. Studies have shown that women officers are just as effective as men. There is no logical reason not to hire them.

   _____

   _____

9. In some cases, female officers have been able to break up fights or avoid violence in situations where a male officer could expect a confrontation. Such situations suggest that women can contribute a great deal to a police department.

   _____

   _____

10. Women officers are particularly effective in cases of domestic violence. When the department receives calls about suspected child abuse, the chief is likely to send women to investigate.

    _____

    _____

WRITING EXERCISE

Exercise 22h.   Use the sentence patterns you practiced in this chapter to write a paragraph on one of the following topics. Use coordinating conjunctions and transitional phrases (conjunctive adverbs) in at least five sentences. When you have finished, circle the punctuation and coordinating conjunctions that join each independent clause.
   1. Describe one or two unusual or frustrating experiences that happened to you during the first few weeks of this term.
   2. Write about a time when you were under tremendous pressure. Be sure to write in enough detail to recreate the experience for your reader.
   3. Discuss an event in your life that you found particularly rewarding.

23

Subordinating Conjunctions and Relative Pronouns

In this chapter you will work with the second kind of clause found in English sentences—the dependent or subordinate clause. Any clause that begins with a subordinating conjunction is a **subordinate** or **dependent clause** because it cannot stand by itself as a sentence. Instead, it is attached to an independent clause. The exercises in this chapter give you practice in using subordinating conjunctions and relative pronouns to make logical connections between the clauses in sentences.

CONNECTING DEPENDENT AND INDEPENDENT CLAUSES

Read the following sentence carefully. Can you find the coordinating conjunction?

> A big city can seem like an impersonal place, for it takes a long time to meet new friends.

Now read this second sentence. Notice that like the preceding sentence, it has two clauses.

> A big city can seem like an impersonal place because it takes a long time to meet new friends.

What word joins the two clauses in the second sentence? _____ In the second sentence, the word *because* is a **subordinating conjunction.** It makes the clause *it takes a long time to meet new friends* state the reason why *a big city can seem like an impersonal place.*

The list below contains subordinating conjunctions and gives ways that they might be used to link clauses.

Subordinating Conjunctions

> **as, because**—shows a reason or cause
> **although, even though**—denotes a contrast or exception
> **in order that, so that**—indicates a consequence or result
> **as if, if, provided that, unless**—states a condition
> **where, wherever**—shows location
> **after, before, since, until, when, while**—denotes a sequence in time

Although this list does not include all of the words that function as subordinating conjunctions, it does give you the most common ones.

Patterns of Subordination

The two patterns for combining dependent and independent clauses are explained below. The order of the elements in the first pattern is independent clause, conjunction, dependent clause. The order in the second pattern is conjunction, dependent clause, independent clause. Both patterns are correct, but notice that the idea in the second clause receives the most emphasis because it is the last thing the reader sees. Keep this notion of emphasis in mind when you choose one pattern over the other.

The two sentences below illustrate the first pattern for combining dependent and independent clauses—independent clause + subordinating conjunction + dependent clause. Clauses are enclosed in brackets and the subordinating conjunctions are circled for you.

independent clause *subordinating conjunction* *dependent clause*

[Not everyone is friendly]   [(when) you first move to a big city.]

independent clause *subordinating conjunction* *dependent clause*

[A big city can be an impersonal place]   [(because) it takes a long time to meet new friends.]

The conjunctions in these two sentences provide the logical connection between the clauses. In the first sentence, *when* tells us that moving to a big city is the time that *not everyone is friendly.* In the second sentence, *because* gives the reason why *a big city can be an impersonal place.*

Notice that when a dependent clause follows a main clause, as in the sentences on the preceding page, it is usually *not* preceded by a comma. This pattern differs from the punctuation with *for, and, nor, but, or, yet,* and *so* where commas precede these coordinating conjunctions. (Consult Chapter 22 for a discussion of how to punctuate clauses linked by coordinating conjunctions.)

Exercise 23a.   Put brackets around the clauses in the sentences below and circle the subordinating conjunctions. The first sentence is done for you.

Mr. Fish

1. [I went to a fish market with my mom every Sunday morning] (when) I was a little girl in Hong Kong.]
2. We never bought fish anywhere else once my mother found this market.
3. I called the owner of the market Mr. Fish although that was not his real name.
4. I gave him that name myself because I thought he was the president of fish.
5. One Sunday morning my mom and I went to the market to buy food while my grandmother watched my little brother.
6. On our way home, we had gotten about fifty feet from the shop when we heard a loud crash.
7. We would have probably been injured badly if we had stayed in the shop a minute longer.

The two sentences below illustrate the other pattern for combining a dependent and an independent clause—subordinating conjunction + dependent clause + independent clause. In this pattern, the dependent clause *precedes* rather than follows the independent clause, as the following samples show. The clauses in these sentences are enclosed in brackets, and the subordinating conjunctions are circled for you.

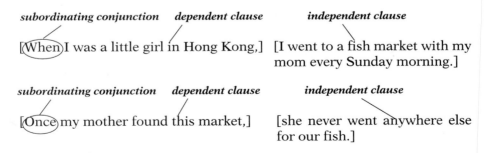

subordinating conjunction   dependent clause   *independent clause*

[(When) I was a little girl in Hong Kong,] [I went to a fish market with my mom every Sunday morning.]

subordinating conjunction   dependent clause   *independent clause*

[(Once) my mother found this market,]   [she never went anywhere else for our fish.]

Both of the subordinating conjunctions here, *when* and *once,* are words that connect the dependent and independent clauses by showing how the two relate to each other in time. In the first sentence, *when* connects a time in the writer's life (her childhood in Hong Kong) to a specific activity (the Sunday morning trip to the fish market with her mother). In the second sentence, *once* shows how one event follows another in time: first mother found the fish market; after that she never went anywhere else to shop for fish.

Notice, too, that the dependent clauses, *when I was a little girl in Hong Kong* and *once my mother found this market,* precede their independent clauses. In this sentence pattern, a comma follows the dependent clause.

> **Rule to Remember: When a subordinate clause comes *before* an independent clause in a sentence, it is *followed* by a comma. When it follows an independent clause, a comma is not usually needed.**

Exercise 23b. Put brackets around the clauses in the sentences below and circle the subordinating conjunctions. Add punctuation if the dependent clause comes first in the sentence. The first one is done for you.

The Test

1. [(When) I was about ten years old,] [my friends dared me to steal some candy.]
2. Because I wanted to fit in with the crowd I went along with what they told me to do.
3. Even though I was afraid of getting caught I was even more frightened of these big sixth graders.
4. Everybody looked up to these guys because they were the best in sports.
5. If they liked you they would let you play with their brand new toys.
6. Of course when I tried to steal the candy I was caught by the store owner.
7. After committing that little crime I changed my life for the better.
8. I realized that these guys weren't really the "in-crowd" if they had to steal to prove themselves.

Exercise 23c. Fill in an appropriate subordinating conjunction to link the clauses in the sentences below. Make sure that the word you choose makes sense in the sentence as a whole. You may wish to consult the preceding list of subordinating conjunctions. Be sure to add commas where you need them. The first sentence is completed for you.

One Teacher's Story

1. In the early 1970s, teaching positions were cut in the school district where I worked <u>because</u> enrollment had dropped.

2. _____ several hundred teachers, young and old, had assembled in the gym each of us picked a number to determine which classes we could have and how often we could teach.

3. That year we got our classes by lottery _____ I suspected that the real reason they used a lottery in assigning classes was to encourage some of us to retire.

4. _____ I managed to stay in the district three more tough, miserable years I sometimes wonder how I did it.

5. The first year I worked as a relief teacher _____ teachers who didn't like their assignments could be excused from a class.

6. _____ the sun came up in the morning, I was getting ready for my early morning physical education class.

7. Most children were cooperative and behaved nicely _____ one horrible morning.

8. _____ the class left for their second period, I noticed a child hanging around the entrance to the classroom.

9. I had the feeling she was watching for somebody _____ she kept peering around the corner into the class.

10. I learned the reason for my caution _____ later that day she punched a little boy in the stomach.

Exercise 23d.   To practice connecting clauses logically, combine the following sentences. To do this, make one of the sentences a dependent clause and join it to the remaining independent clause. As you write your sentences, think about which idea you want to subordinate and which is most appropriate for the main clause. Add commas as you need them. The first pair is combined for you.

Playing Santa

1. I had the opportunity to play Santa Claus.

   I worked for the Department of Parks and Recreation.

   Combined: When I worked for the Department of Parks and Recreation, I had the opportunity to play Santa Claus.

2. I made my first visit.

   I felt very nervous.

   _____

   _____

3. I saw the first child.

   I realized how much fun being Santa Claus was going to be.

   _____

   _____

4. The children see Santa.

   They can't believe he is there talking to them and passing out gifts.

   _____

   _____

5. I invited the children to sit on Santa's lap.

   They could tell Santa what they wanted for Christmas.

   _____

   _____

6. The children always told me they had been good.

   They acted like animals.

   _____

   _____

7. The entertaining part began.

   I listened to their requests.

   _____

   _____

8. I had studied Sears' catalogs.

   I knew about all the latest toys.

   _____

   _____

9. I never promised to bring anything.

   It would have been impossible, for example, to provide them with a little brother, a pony, or a car—things some of them wanted.

_____

_____

10. I was finished.

   Then old Santa got a hug and an "I love you, Santa."

_____

_____

Exercise 23e.   In the following sentences, the dependent clauses are sup-
plied for you. Add your own ideas in a main clause that completes the sentence. The first sentence is completed for you.

1. When I enrolled at City College, <u>my goal was to graduate and become an</u>

   <u>accountant.</u>

2. Once I took a computer class, _____

   _____.

3. Although I was bored with math in high school, _____.

4. _____because I want to make my

   parents proud of me.

5. Since I live with my parents, _____

   _____.

6. When I got my first job, _____

   _____.

7. _____although

   I am worth more than minimum wage.

8. If I continue going to school, _____

   _____.

Exercise 23f.   Use your own paper for this exercise. Write a paragraph on
one of the topics listed below. Use at least five sentences that combine dependent and independent clauses. Try to use both of the two possible patterns discussed in this chapter. Be sure to punctuate your sentences correctly. When
you have finished writing, go back over your paragraph and put brackets
around independent and dependent clauses. Then circle the subordinating
conjunctions.

   1. a difficult parting
   2. shopping for a special occasion

3. an offensive advertisement
4. a favorite television program
5. your least favorite member of the family

Relative Pronouns

When writers need to clarify an idea or identify a person more precisely, they use a **relative clause.** The relative clause in the following sentence is placed in brackets.

> My uncle, [who raises hogs for a living,] taught me the care and feeding of these misunderstood animals.

Notice that the relative clause *who raises hogs for a living* interrupts the independent clause *my uncle taught me the care and feeding of these misunderstood animals.* The relative pronoun, *who,* refers to *uncle;* the clause *who raises hogs for a living* says something about what this *uncle* does. In addition, because *who* refers to *uncle,* it is singular; that means the verb *raises* must be singular as well to agree with *uncle,* the singular subject of the sentence.

> **Rule to Remember: Relative clauses modify nouns. The verbs in these clauses agree with the noun that the clause modifies.**

The three common relative pronouns are *who, that,* and *which.* In this special kind of dependent clause, *who, that,* and *which* are the subjects of the clauses in which they appear. Here again, the verbs in these clauses agree in number with the noun the clause modifies. The arrows in the following sentences illustrate how *that* and *which* are connected to the nouns they modify.

> My uncle has almost two hundred hogs and pigs [that are waiting to be sold or roasted.]

> He has to mend the fences, [which the hogs love to charge,] at least once a month.

Exercise 23g.   Complete the relative clauses in the following sentences. The first one is completed for you.

Raising Hogs

1. The hogs that <u>my uncle raises</u> are some of the most interesting animals I have ever seen.

2. My hog-raising uncle, who _____
   _____, showed me what hogs do to keep warm.

3. When it gets cold, which _____
   _____, hogs lie on top of one another to keep warm.

4. Most human beings, who _____
   _____, could never be so close together for that long.

5. If the temperature dips below freezing, which _____
   _____, we light a fire to keep them warm.

Definition and Non-Definition Clauses

The following sentences and explanations illustrate the use of relative pronouns in definition and non-definition clauses. The relative clauses are
enclosed in brackets.

> People [who marry in their teens] often divorce in their twenties.

In this sentence, the relative clause *who marry in their teens* defines which people often divorce in their twenties. Notice that no commas are used to separate
this definition clause from the rest of the sentence. Here is the same sentence
without the relative clause.

> People often divorce in their twenties.

This second sentence has a completely different meaning from the first. It says
that people in general get divorced in their twenties, but the author really
wanted to refer only to a certain group of people—those *who marry in their
teens*. Therefore, the relative clause defines or restricts the meaning of *people*.
Without it, the original point of the sentence is lost.

> **Rule to Remember: A relative clause that *defines* the meaning of
> the noun it modifies is *not* set off by commas.**

In the next sample sentence, the relative clause (in brackets) does not
define the meaning of the noun it modifies.

> My sons, [who are three and four years of age,] are having a terrible time
> getting along with one another.

The relative clause *who are three and four years of age* refers to *my sons* but does not define or restrict that term. For that reason, commas are used to separate it from the rest of the sentence.

Here is the same sentence written without the relative clause.

My sons are having a terrible time getting along with one another.

In this sentence and in the sample above that included a relative clause, the writer makes the point that the sons are having trouble getting along. The author used the relative clause *who are three and four years of age* to make an additional comment, but *my sons* is a term that is specific enough to convey the meaning of the sentence without further elaboration.

Rule to Remember: A relative clause that *does not* define or limit the noun it modifies *is* set off by commas.

To become more familiar with clauses that define and those that do not, study the sentences below and the explanations that follow them. Relative clauses are enclosed in brackets.

My uncle John, [who is wearing a clown costume,] is visiting from France.

When a noun-subject is already defined by modifying words, as in *my uncle John,* the relative clause that follows it is *not* essential to its meaning and is, therefore, set off by commas.

In the next sentence, the relative clause *is* essential to the meaning of the noun it modifies.

The man *who is wearing the clown costume* is my uncle John.

Because the reader does not know which man the writer means, the relative clause is essential for defining *man.* Consequently, *no* commas are used.

Occasionally relative clauses may be definition or non-definition clauses, depending on the writer's meaning. The sentences below illustrate this possibility. Again, relative clauses are placed in brackets.

Older students, [who have a reason for being in school,] tend to work very hard.

In the preceding sentence, the writer includes commas; consequently, the relative clause does not define only those older students *who have a reason for being in school.* Instead, the writer implies that *all* older students *have a reason for being in school.* Compare this sentence about older students with the one below:

> Older students who have a reason for being in school tend to work very hard.

This writer does not assume that all older students *have a reason for being in school.* Instead, the focus is on a particular group of older students—those *who have a reason for being in school.*

Exercise 23h.   In the following sentences, enclose the relative clauses in brackets and add commas when the clauses do not define the noun to which they refer.

War

1. The combat soldier who knows what war is like has a much better idea of how frightening, chaotic, and horrifying it is.
2. Men and women who are soldiers cannot really be trained for actual combat.
3. In any ground war, invading soldiers who are keyed up from battle can mistake ordinary citizens for the enemy.
4. Bombings of civilian targets which have military significance are inevitable in war.
5. One thing is certain; men and women who live in a village or city inside a war zone must leave that place or die.

Exercise 23i.   Combine the following sentences. Use definition and non-definition clauses as appropriate, adding punctuation as needed. The first group is combined for you, and the relative clause is enclosed in brackets.

A Former President

1. Jimmy Carter is a former President.

   Most people living in the United States know that.

   Combined: <u>Most people [who live in the United States] know that Jimmy Carter is a former President.</u>

2. As Governor of Georgia, Carter reduced the number of the state agencies.

   He was determined to cut costs.

   _____

   _____

3. As President, Carter had a few setbacks.

    He had difficulty communicating with leaders in Congress.

    _____

    _____

4. His plans were never quite acceptable at the Capitol.

    His plans were designed for state agencies.

    _____

    _____

    _____

5. The economy was weakened during his administration.

    It suffered from both stagnation and inflation.

    _____

    _____

    _____

6. Carter's aides did not understand congressional traditions.

    They lost substantial support for his programs.

    _____

    _____

    _____

7. His foreign policy advisers did a much better job.

    They engineered the treaty that resulted from the Camp David accords
    between Israel and Egypt.

    _____

    _____

    _____

Exercise 23j.   Write a paragraph describing an activity with which you are
familiar. Use definition and non-definition clauses in at least five of your
sentences.

The following chart is a reminder of the connections you can make using
the conjunctions and relative pronouns you have studied thus far. Use them to
complete the next exercise.

WORDS THAT SHOW CONNECTION

Relationship	Coordinating Conjunctions	Subordinating Conjunctions	Relative Pronouns	Conjunctive Adverbs
To modify persons			who	
To modify things			that, which	
To add ideas	and			moreover
To compare		as		
To contrast	but, yet nor	although even though		nevertheless
To show cause or result	so for	because in order that so that		consequently therefore
To show choice	or			
To show condition		as if, if provided that unless		
To show location		where wherever		
To show sequence in time		after, before since, until when, while		

[handwritten annotations: "DEPENDENT CLAUSES", "COMPLEX SENT", "COMPOUND SENT, LINK→(;)", "COMPOUND SENTENCES", "COMPLEX SENTENCES", "INTRO :", "auxiliary verbs"]

Exercise 23k.   Use coordinating or subordinating conjunctions, or relative pronouns to combine the following sentences. Add commas where needed. The first two are done for you with the connecting words circled and the clauses in brackets.

Childhood in Germany

1. Wanda Schmit was a child living in Germany.

   World War II broke out in 1939.

   Combined: Wanda Schmit was a child living in Germany [(when) World War II broke out in 1939.]

2. Her father held an important post in Hamburg.

   He was sent to the front immediately.

   He was a mechanical engineer.

   Combined: Her father, [(who) held an important post in Hamburg,] was sent to the front immediately [(because) he was a mechanical engineer.]

3. Wanda was only eight years old.

She was caught in the major seaboard city of Hamburg.
The city had strategic importance.

_____

_____

_____

4. Most of the men in the city were sent into battle.
   The women, including mothers, were assigned to factories and offices.

_____

_____

5. Schools and churches were not really prepared for their task.
   They assumed the task of caring for the thousands of children left alone eight to ten hours a day.

_____

_____

6. Hamburg was a major port.
   It became a target for allied bombs.
   Germany began its fourth year of war.

_____

_____

7. Food quickly became scarce.
   The bombings and transference of supplies to the soldiers left severe shortages.

_____

_____

8. The city's occupants were mostly women and children.
   They often found themselves running to protective shelters and cellars for cover.

_____

_____

9. The bombing attacks were aimed at the German industries in Hamburg.
   They increased in the last years of the war.
   The children had to be moved to the farmlands of Southern Germany.

_____

_____

_____

WRITING EXERCISE

Exercise 23l.   Write a paragraph on one of the topics listed below. The paragraph should contain a variety of conjunctions and relative pronouns that link ideas in your sentences. When you are finished, check to make sure you have punctuated correctly; then circle the conjunctions and relative pronouns you used to join the clauses in your sentences.

1. how you were affected by the war in the Persian Gulf
2. soap operas
3. winning a lottery
4. something unique about you
5. a song that stays with you

24

Correcting Fragments and Run-on Sentences

I n this chapter you will identify and correct three kinds of fragments: those that lack a subject or verb, those that lack a complete verb (infinitive and -ing fragments), and those that result from writing dependent clauses as though they were sentences (subordination fragments). You will also practice recognizing and correcting another common error—run-on sentences.

CORRECTING FRAGMENTS WITH WORDS OMITTED

A **fragment** is a group of words that is written as though it were a complete sentence, but it is *not* a sentence because it lacks a subject or complete verb, or is a dependent clause. One common kind of fragment is a group of words masquerading as a sentence but missing a subject or verb. Read the following fragments carefully to see that words have been omitted. Notice, too, how confusing this sentence error can be for a reader.

> Poppies that in the summer are rare. (fragment)
> Unfortunately, never nest in my trees. (fragment)

In the first fragment, the writer meant to add the verb *grow* to produce the sentence *Poppies that grow in the summer are rare*. We must add the subject *robins* to the second fragment to create the sentence, *Unfortunately, robins never nest in my trees*.

Exercise 24a.   Some of the items below are fragments because a verb has been omitted. Add appropriate verbs to change fragments into complete sentences. Mark double underlines under any verbs you add. The first sentence is done for you.

Companion

1. Animals very important to us. Animals <u><u>are</u></u> very important to us.
2. Sometimes they lifelong, loyal companions.

   _____

3. Dogs in particular loyal to their masters.

   _____

4. My dog Sheila seems to sympathize with my pain.

   _____

5. She her sorrowful head in my lap when I am sick or upset.

   _____

Exercise 24b.   Some of the items below are fragments because a subject has been omitted. Add appropriate subjects to make complete sentences. Underline added subjects once. The first sentence is done for you.

My Parents' Divorce

1. Stood in the kitchen in shock. <u>I</u> stood in the kitchen in shock.
2. My father had just told me a story.

   _____

3. Told me an incredible story.

   _____

4. Were getting a divorce.

   _____

5. Many things went through my mind.

   _____

6. Was time for them to make a change in their lives.

   _____

Exercise 24c.   Correct the following fragments by supplying missing subjects or verbs. In the first five sentences the blanks tell you where to add a subject or verb. In the last three sentences you will need to locate the missing word yourself. The first sentence is completed for you.

Who's Getting Married?

1. Today, men and women in the United States _____ at an older age than they did twenty years ago.

   Today, men and women in the United States <u>marry</u> at an older age than they did twenty years ago.

2. Job situations _____ a lot to do with men's decisions.

3. _____ is not as easy to find employment as it was in the eighties.

4. _____ may not want the responsibility of having a family until they are financially ready.

5. Some men and women in their twenties and thirties _____ that getting married means losing their freedom.

6. Seems too restrictive and demanding for many couples.

7. Many couples, therefore, together before marriage.

8. Occasionally, have children, raise those children, and never get married.

> **Rule to Remember: A group of words that is missing a subject or verb is a fragment. To correct these fragments, add the missing subject or verb.**

CORRECTING INFINITIVE AND -ING FRAGMENTS

Fragments are also created when the writer uses an infinitive, a verb form like *to be, to seek,* or *to stammer,* in place of a complete verb. (These verbs are occasionally used incorrectly without the *to.*) Another kind of fragment occurs when writers use an -ing verb form without a helping verb. Samples of each kind of fragment are shown below.

Infinitive Fragments

> Daniel *be* the foremost sky diver in northern Utah.
> Felicia, a hot dog vendor, *to run* after a non-paying customer.

Two alternatives for correcting these kinds of fragments are listed below.

1. Change the infinitive to a past, present, or future tense verb.

    Daniel is the foremost sky diver in northern Utah.
    Felicia, a hot dog vendor, ran after a non-paying customer.

2. Add a conjugated verb to the sentence before the infinitive.

    Daniel wants to be the foremost sky diver in northern Utah.
    Felicia, a hot dog vendor, had to run after a non-paying customer.

-ing Fragments

Reggie *singing* in the living room.

The robins that lived in the tree next door *leaving* their nest early in the morning.

To correct these fragments you can do one of the following:

1. Replace the -ing form by putting the verb in the past, present, or future tense.

            sings
    Reggie sang in the living room.
            will sing

    The robins that lived in the tree next door left their nest early in the morning.

2. Add a helping verb.

    Reggie is singing in the living room.
           was singing

    The robins that lived in the tree next door were leaving their nest early in the morning.

Exercise 24d.   Some of the items below are fragments because they contain either infinitives or -ing forms instead of complete verbs. Add appropriate verbs to make complete sentences; mark any verbs you add with double underlines. The first sentence is done for you.

The World of Reading

1. The world be literally an open book to a reader. The world <u>is</u> literally an open book to a reader.

2. A reader wishing to go to the lush rain forests of Brazil, the savannas of Central Africa, or the Himalayas._____

   _____

3. Tales from the Maori of New Zealand or the nomads of North Africa to await the reader interested in human culture. _____

   _____

4. The story of Lucy, the oldest human-like creature in the world, to lure the reader into the study of anthropology. _____

   _____

5. Of course other worlds besides travel and anthropology may stir the human imagination. _____

   _____

6. Novels, for example, introducing the reader to the suffering, joys, humiliation, and triumph of the human experience._____

   _____

7. Tolstoy's *The Death of Ivan Ilyich* immortalizing the tale of a man who undergoes a spiritual awakening just before his death. _____

   _____

8. Chinua Achebe tells the story of native Nigerians' struggle against English colonialism._____

   _____

Rule to Remember: To correct infinitive fragments, (1) rewrite the infinitive in the past, present, or future tense, or (2) add a conjugated verb to the sentence. To correct -ing fragments, (1) change the -ing form to the past, present, or future tense, or (2) keep the -ing verb and add a helping verb to make it complete.

CORRECTING SUBORDINATION FRAGMENTS

A **subordination fragment** results from writing a dependent or relative clause as though it were a separate sentence. Such fragments may occur when writers experiment with a variety of ways of connecting ideas. Practice correcting fragments in the following exercises; and, more importantly, look for them in your own writing.

The following examples illustrate how fragments are created when a relative clause or a dependent clause is written as though it could stand as a complete sentence. The fragments are underlined for you.

> Last night I saw Sara. <u>Who hasn't spoken to me in ten years.</u>
> <u>After Barley went home.</u> Wanda started having a great time.

In order to express the connection between these fragments and the independent clauses written next to them, the two elements need to be joined as in the following corrected sentences.

> Last night I saw Sara, who hasn't spoken to me in ten years.
> After Barley went home. Wanda started having a great time.

Two additional ways of correcting fragments involve creating an independent clause or adding words to complete an independent clause. To correct the fragment *Small mammals that are usually the owl's prey,* you could omit the relative pronoun *that.*

> Small mammals are usually the owl's prey.

A second way of fixing the same fragment about the owl completes the fragment by adding a new idea.

> The owl hunts for small mammals that are usually its prey.

Rule to Remember: Correct a subordination fragment by (1) joining it to an independent clause; (2) omitting the relative pronoun (or subordinating conjunction) to create an independent clause; or (3) adding words that complete the clause.

Exercise 24e.   Use any of the three methods listed above to rewrite fragments you find in the following sentences. A few sentences are correct. Use your own paper for this exercise.

America the Beautiful

1. The United States has some of the most spectacular scenery in the world. Partly because so much land has been preserved in state and national parks.
2. Yosemite National Park, for example, has magnificent vistas with El Capitan and Yosemite Falls in the background.
3. Before the tragic fire that burned thousands of acres of forest. Yellowstone was the most popular of the national parks.
4. Old Faithful still gushes. Despite the tragic change in the landscape for much of the park.
5. The peace and quiet in any of these parks is indeed a national treasure. That even the most high-strung visitor can't help but appreciate.
6. And don't forget about the wildlife.
7. If you are camping and especially lucky. You may see an eagle or hear a coyote.

Exercise 24f. Rewrite the following paragraphs, correcting any fragments you find.

A Place I Call Home

As I was turning on to Sunset Drive, I felt as if I was turning back the hands of time. A time when I was safe, free of worry, so carefree and so innocent. At that moment I had forgotten. That I was twenty years old, engaged, struggling to pay the rent, worrying about my GPA, and most of all worrying about all those bills. I just to sit back and take a ride down memory lane. Suddenly I had this incredible feeling, Feeling the street knew me, And was wrapping itself around me and giving me a welcome-home hug. I had not realized just how homesick I really was.

Problems with Mass Transit

Currently, the mass-transit system in this city leaves much to be desired. For one thing, when I called the bus company for information on my bus route. I had to stay on the line for seven minutes before I got the schedule I needed. In another instance, requesting a schedule by mail. I called and left my name and address. Which the recorded message instructed me to do. Several weeks to pass without my receiving any information. As if my message had been ignored. After a second request, I received a map. But still no schedule. I finally to pretend I had a rotary phone in order to speak with an operator.

Because of the frustrations I suffered with the automated information system, I thought the bus drivers might be better sources of information. To my disappointment. This is not what I found. Instead, the drivers to be insensitive and their information misleading. For instance, one day when I was getting off the train to take bus #94. To my surprise I saw the #94 at the stop earlier than the scheduled time. The driver informed me that the bus was, indeed, #94, but failed to tell me its direction. As a result, ended up on the other side of town. The worst of it was that I had to pay for another ticket to go in the opposite direction. Because the driver refused to give me a transfer for the ride back.

CORRECTING RUN-ON SENTENCES

Run-ons are incorrectly written sentences in which independent clauses are put together with a comma or no punctuation at all. **Run-on sentences** are also called **fused sentences** or **comma splices.** As you practice using sentence patterns that might be new to you, you may find yourself writing quite a few run-on sentences. Don't be discouraged; the fact that you are writing run-ons is a positive sign that you are willing to take risks as you attempt to connect ideas in new ways.

Study the following reasons why you might be mistaking run-ons for correct sentences; then try correcting your own run-ons in some of the ways suggested.

If you are using a lot of run-on constructions, you may be misusing transitional words and expressions like *however, besides, therefore,* and *then.*

> Jason usually gets to class early **as a result** he gets involved in some stimulating conversations. (run-on)

Like the othe r transitional phrases listed in the discussion in Chapter 22, *as a result,* when used within a sentence, is preceded by a semicolon. It may also begin a new sentence, in which case it is followed by a comma.

> Jason usually gets to class early; **as a result,** he gets involved in some stimulating conversations.

> Jason usually gets to class early. **As a result,** he gets involved in some stimulating conversations.

Some run-on constructions may result from the fact that you are trying to suggest connections between closely related ideas.

> Rhonda enjoys her history class, the teacher encourages class discussion. (run-on)

Two independent clauses may be joined by a semicolon to suggest a logical or sequential connection:

> Rhonda enjoys her history class; the teacher encourages class discussion.

In this case, the semicolon indicates that the second clause explains why Rhonda enjoys her history class. The following corrected sentences express that causal relationship more explicitly by using conjunctions to join the clauses.

> Rhonda enjoys her history class, **for** the teacher encourages class discussion.

> Rhonda enjoys her history class **because** the teacher encourages class discussion.

Finally, run-ons may be appearing in your writing because you are trying to show a contrast or opposition between ideas.

> Lucilla broke her leg last week, she continues to attend class. (run-on)

A conjunction or transition can express this opposition.

> Lucilla broke her leg last week, **yet** she continues to attend class.

> Lucilla broke her leg last week; **however,** she continues to attend class.

> **Although** Lucilla broke her leg last week, she continues to attend class.

Rule to Remember: A run-on sentence can be corrected by using one of the following patterns:

1. **independent clause + comma + coordinating conjunction + independent clause**
2. **dependent clause + comma + independent clause**
3. **independent clause + dependent clause (no comma)**
4. **independent clause + semicolon + independent clause**
5. **sentence + period + sentence**

Complete the exercises below to practice spotting run-on sentences when you revise your own writing.

Exercise 24g.   Correct any run-on sentences you find in this exercise. Pay attention to the logical connections you make as you revise. The first sentence is corrected for you.

Cartoon Violence

1. Each morning, children have a little violence with their breakfast _∧^{as} the robotic heroes of "Robotech," "Voltron," and "Thunder Cats" demonstrate how to blow up bad robots and erring planets.

2. Other programs, such as "He-Man" and "She-Ra, Princess of Power," offer shallow versions of men and women, these cartoon characters are little more than sex symbols.

3. To be heroic, men must be muscular, women must be big-breasted and skinny.

4. Cartoons are teaching little boys to be warriors while little girls are learning to be sexy.

5. Most cartoon characters fight continually they rarely exchange words with their enemies.

6. In these cartoons, children learn that situations can be solved with violence, no one is required to negotiate or compromise with anyone believed to be evil.

Exercise 24h.   Make logical connections between ideas in any run-on sentences you find in this exercise. Use any of the sentence patterns you have studied to make your revisions. Some sentences are correct.

Toys and Children's Play

1. Toys do not challenge children's imaginations they are merely an imitation of what the kids have seen in cartoons.

2. Children learn to imitate what they see on television, they simply recreate what they see on "Teenage Mutant Ninja Turtles" or "Voltron."

3. Fewer and fewer children play with building blocks or Legos® to create a house or small town they rarely think of building a space ship or igloo out of cardboard boxes.

4. In the old days, parents helped their children build forts and houses out of wood or paper mâché today, dolls and robots come with their own town houses and space stations.

5. Teachers are complaining about their pupils' behavior, they contend that children are imitating the violence they see in cartoons.

6. The Teenage Mutant Ninja Turtles, for example, solve problems by hitting and kicking, the child reasons that problems are best solved by force.

7. Little boys are now fighting over little girls, this degree of sexual rivalry is new in elementary classrooms.

8. Cartoon mania is affecting performance in other ways as well. In today's crowded classrooms, teachers spend much of their time just getting the children to calm down.

9. Not much learning can take place in a classroom full of ninjas and robotic warriors, teachers are convinced that parents must help.

10. There are many things parents can do to get more involved in their child's behavior, they can regulate hours for watching television, for one thing.

11. In addition, parents can spend more time with their children so that they can help with school projects.

12. Parents can ask to see their child's homework assignments, that way they can be sure he or she is doing schoolwork.

WRITING EXERCISE

Exercise 24i.   Write one or two paragraphs on the following topics. As you revise, make sure you have used a variety of sentence patterns and that clauses are combined correctly.

1. Describe the sort of imaginative play you did as a child.
2. Write your observations about how television influences children or adults you know.
3. Describe one or two unusual or frustrating experiences that happened to you during the first few weeks on a new job.
4. Summarize the plot of a novel you have read or a movie you have seen.

25

Making Logical Connections

Learning to incorporate a variety of sentence patterns into your writing will increase your ability to express your thoughts in complex ways. It will also make your writing more interesting to read. With that in mind, exercises in this chapter give you practice in combining ideas in ways that present additional possibilities for choosing sentence patterns. You will also learn techniques for checking your sentences to ensure that they are correctly written.

PHRASES IN A SERIES

Unlike a clause, a **phrase** lacks a complete verb, a subject, or both. In Chapter 21 you studied one kind of phrase—the prepositional phrase. These, and other phrases, may be connected in a series as long as all items in the series have the same structure (that is, they are all prepositional phrases, -ing phrases or other verb phrases, and so on). In the explanation and exercises that follow, you will practice combining such phrases correctly.

Prepositional Phrases

The prepositional phrases in the following sentences describe the objects on Tina's hat:

> Tina decorated her hat with a peacock feather.
> She decorated her hat with a small pearl pin.
> She decorated her hat with a tiny Chinese dragon.

We can combine these sentences and write a more interesting, less monotonous sentence by joining the prepositional phrases.

> Tina decorated her hat with a peacock feather, a small pearl pin, and a tiny Chinese dragon.

Similarly, subjects, other nouns in a sentence, and verb phrases may be combined to form a single sentence.

Exercise 25a. Combine each of the following groups of sentences into a single sentence. The first is done as a sample.

1. Sal sent a letter of complaint to his congressman.

   He sent a copy to his senator.

   He sent a copy to the president.

   Combined: <u>Sal sent letters of complaint to his congressman, his senator, and the president.</u>

2. Beverly wanted enough money to live on.

   Beverly wanted a house to live in.

   Beverly wanted a modest car to drive.

   _____

   _____

3. The raging gorilla made the zoo a noisy place.

   The squawking macaws made the zoo a noisy place.

   The roaring lions made the zoo a noisy place.

   _____

   _____

4. My elderly aunt loves to eat peaches in summer.

   She loves to eat boysenberries in fall.

   She loves to eat red apples in winter.

   _____

   _____

5. Heavy rain made the trip to Kansas a nightmare for Dorothy.

   Violent tornadoes also made the trip a nightmare.

A high wind made the trip a nightmare.

_____

_____

Verb Phrases

Writers often use a series of verb phrases to describe more than one activity. In the following example, several sentences are combined to make a single description.

> My friend Switzer insists on jogging in the morning before work.
> He insists on working out at noon.
> He insists on playing racquetball or tennis at night.

Combined: My friend Switzer insists on jogging in the morning before work, working out at the gym at noon, and playing racquetball or tennis at night.

Exercise 25b.   Form a single sentence by joining the verb phrases in the following groups of sentences. Use the sample above as a model.

The Poor in Honduras

1. In Honduras, diseases are rampant.

   They are difficult to treat.

   They are often deadly.

   _____

   _____

2. People in the Agwan Valley are living in cardboard houses.

   They eat whatever they can scratch out of the soil.

   _____

   _____

3. Devoted Hondurans minister to their families' needs.

   They treat illnesses with home remedies.

   They share the little food they have.

   _____

   _____

4. In the last decade, the poverty in Honduras has increased among farmers.

   The poverty has spread to some members of the middle class.

   The poverty has even affected some professionals.

   _____

   _____

   _____

CORRECTING ILLOGICALLY JOINED SENTENCES

When you combine phrases, you achieve greater sentence variety and usually make your writing more interesting to read. It is important, however, to check the phrases being combined to ensure that they all have the same form. Such correctly combined phrases are considered to be **parallel.** Study this example:

> I caught Greg in a moment of weakness as he was watching television, munching corn nuts, and ignored his homework.

Underline any phrases that don't seem to fit in the sentence. The following breakdown of the phrases in this sentence will clarify its structure:

> I caught Greg in a moment of weakness as he was
>
> > watching television
> > munching corn nuts
> > and
> > ignored his homework

Notice that the last three ideas in the sentence are written in a series; all three must work logically with the helping verb *was* for the phrases to be parallel. *Was watching television* and *was munching corn nuts* make sense, but *was ignored his homework* does not. That is because it does not fit the pattern of the -ing ending established by the other two verb phrases. Phrases written in a series like this express a close connection between like ideas. If one of the forms is incorrect, that connection is lost or confused.

   To clarify the relationship between the ideas in this sentence, we can rewrite it in one of several ways. Here are two possible corrections.

> I caught Greg in a moment of weakness as he was watching television, munching on corn nuts, and *ignoring* his homework.

> I caught Greg in a moment of weakness as he was watching television and munching on corn nuts; *he had ignored his homework.*

In the first sentence, the verb *ignored* is changed to match the pattern in the other two verb phrases. The second sentence links *watching* and *munching,* and puts *ignored* in a clause by itself.

Rule to Remember: All phrases connected in a series must be written in the same form.

Exercise 25c.   Identify any forms in the following sentences that are not parallel. Rewrite them to fit logically with the rest of the sentence. You can add, delete, or change words as necessary. Put a C beside any sentences that are correctly written. In the first sentence, the correction is highlighted for you.

Hiding Well

1. My friend George is a master at deceiving people about his reading difficulties, at pretending he understands what he reads, and convince his teachers he knows more than he does.
   Corrected: <u>My friend George is a master at deceiving people about his reading difficulties, at pretending he understands what he reads, and **at convincing** his teachers he knows more than he does.</u>

2. To cover up, he coaxes his friends and classmates to do his homework, type his papers, but not learning anything himself.
   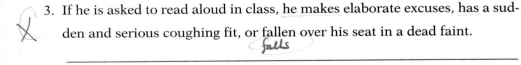
   To cover up, he coaxes his friends and classmates to do his homework, type his papers, but doesn't learn anything himself.

3. If he is asked to read aloud in class, he makes elaborate excuses, has a sudden and serious coughing fit, or ~~fallen~~ falls over his seat in a dead faint.

   _____

   _____

4. His teachers have gotten the message and no longer call on him to read.

   _____

   _____

5. If he goes to a party or dines out, George has to cover up his ignorance of many vocabulary words.

   _____

   _____

6. Sometimes he simply acts as though he is not interested in the conversation or having too much fun to be bothered.

_____

_____

7. Occasionally he slips and misinterprets what someone has asked and responding to a completely different question.

_____

_____

8. I have seen the time when such exchanges have become quite heated, feathers have gotten ruffled, and George to leave early.

_____

_____

9. There's a great deal about George that I appreciate—his love of sports and his devotion to friends are just two of them.

_____

_____

10. But for his own sake, George should think about getting into a reading program, start off slowly at first, and improving his reading skills gradually.

George should think about getting into a reading
program, start off slowly at first, and improving
his reading skills gradually for his own sake.

Connecting Other Verb Phrases Correctly

Writers use other phrases created from verb forms to add meaning to or modify the subjects in a sentence. Consider the examples below.

> Denise took a chemistry test at eight o'clock this morning.

To clarify the condition Denise was in when she took the test, the author of the sentence might add a verb phrase.

> Exhausted from studying, Denise took a chemistry test at eight o'clock this morning.

> Denise, exhausted from studying, took a chemistry test at eight o'clock this morning.

The -ing verb form (the present participle) is also used in verb phrases that modify nouns.

> While studying for an algebra test, Jackson gained a new understanding of the word *stressed*.

The infinitive form of a verb is the final kind of verb phrase that can be used to modify a noun.

> To get a good grade on his psychology test, Kenji reviewed his notes.

Exercise 25d.   Use any of the three kinds of phrases illustrated above and combine the following groups of sentences. First write the second sentence as a verb phrase (use an infinitive, an -ing form or an -ed form); then combine it with the first sentence. Two sample groups are combined for you.

> Jason tried to start his car but discovered it had a dead battery.
> Jason was running late this morning.
>
> Combined: Running late this morning, Jason tried to start his car but discovered it had a dead battery.

Notice that the subject and helping verb must be dropped to connect these ideas in one sentence.

> Jason took a taxicab to his mechanic's shop.
> He intended to get his money back for the battery.
>
> Combined: Intending to get his money back for the battery, Jason took a taxicab to his mechanic's shop.

In this example, *intended* changes to *intending* to create a logical combination with *Jason took a taxicab to his mechanic's shop*.

My Dad

1. My dad was a very jolly man in his later years.

   He resembled Santa Claus.

   My Dad was a very Jolly Man in his later years, ResembliNg Santa Claus.

   _____

2. My dad was a sawyer.

   He worked in saw mills most of his life.

My dad was a sawyer, working in saw mills most of his life.

3. He would fly the airplane he bought with a few of his buddies.

   He went between mill towns.

   He would fly the airplane he bought with a few of his buddies, going between mill towns.

4. My family used his plane to go shopping sometimes.

   We were living miles from any large towns.

   We lived miles from any large town, My family used his plane to go shopping sometimes.

5. My dad would pile us into his plane and take off for Montana or the Southwest.

   He wanted to go on vacation.

   Wanting to go on vacation, my Dad would pile us into his plane and take off for Montana or the Southwest.

6. He also flew us to the Oregon coast in the summer.

   He wanted to enjoy a different kind of scenery.

   Wanting to enjoy a different kind of scenery, he also flew us to the Oregon coast in the summer.

7. I now realize that his memory lives on in my heart.

   I was saddened by his death three years ago.

   Saddened by his death three years ago, I now realize that his memory lives on in my heart.

Connecting Dangling Modifiers

A verb phrase that is illogically connected to the main clause creates a **dangling modifier.** In the following example, the first sentence makes a logical connection between the ideas in its verb phrase and those in the main or independent clause. The second sentence does not. Arrows indicate connections between the subjects and the introductory verb phrases.

To become more muscular, John started lifting weights every morning.

> To become more muscular, weights were lifted every morning.

Both sentences begin with the phrase *To become more muscular.* In the first sentence, this phrase modifies *John,* thereby clarifying the fact that he started lifting weights to become more muscular. In the second sentence, however, the phrase modifies the noun *weights.* Because it does not make sense to say that weights want to become more muscular, the second sentence is an example of an illogical or "dangling" modifier.

Dangling or illogical phrases may appear at the end of a sentence as well as at the beginning:

> Devita's parents were careful not to wake her while sleeping so soundly.

In this case, the subject of the sentence, *parents,* is the subject of both *were careful not to wake her* and *while sleeping so soundly.* This dangling modifier creates the illogical situation of having Davita's parents be asleep at the same time they are trying not to waken their daughter. Here is a corrected version of this dangling modifier:

> Devita's parents were careful not to wake her while she was sleeping so soundly.

> **Rule to Remember: Verb phrases placed at the beginning or end of a sentence must have a logical connection to the subject in the independent clause.**

When you find dangling modifiers in your writing, use one of the two easy ways to fix them.

To use the first method, create a dependent clause. This solution gives the phrase a subject and complete verb, and clarifies its connection to the independent clause. Consider the following example:

> After dropping his backpack, **Lamar's books** went tumbling down the stairs. (dangling modifier)

To correct this error, give the phrase a subject to make it a dependent clause and to keep the emphasis in the main clause on the falling books.

> After **Lamar** dropped his backpack, his books went tumbling down the stairs.

To use the second method, create a new subject and verb for the main clause.

After dropping his backpack, **Lamar watched** his books go tumbling down the stairs.

This time the subject *Lamar's books* has been changed to *Lamar* and the verb *watched* has been added. With these changes the subject now works logically with both the phrase at the beginning of the sentence and the independent clause.

Notice that these methods of correcting illogical modifiers change the meaning and emphasis in the sentence. Be aware of these subtle changes in meaning as you revise your own writing.

Exercise 25e.   In the following sentences, modifying phrases may be written illogically. Rewrite sentences that contain errors. More than one answer may be correct. The first one is rewritten for you.

The Will of a Champion

1. Earning millions of dollars in prize money, boxing was good to Sugar Ray Leonard. (dangling modifier)

   Corrected: <u>While he was earning millions of dollars in prize money, boxing was good to Sugar Ray Leonard.</u>

2. At first Leonard's opponents were defeated, unbeaten fight after fight.

   _____

   _____

3. To earn an Olympic gold medal in Montreal in 1976, his skills were the best *he had his best skills ever.* they had ever been.

   _____

   _____

4. Unable to imagine a life without boxing, Sugar Ray avoided the idea of retiring season after season.

   _____

   _____

5. The ring called him back again and again, refusing to retire for good.

   _____

   _____

6. Determined to overcome the odds against him, defeat was not on his mind when he fought twenty-three-year-old Mike Norris.

   _____

   _____

7. When beaten every round of his last fight, even his most ardent fans had to admit that Leonard's once-great boxing career was over.

   _____

   _____

WRITING EXERCISE

Exercise 25f.   Describe an activity that happens repeatedly in your life or a dream that keeps recurring. Use the techniques for connecting ideas you have learned in this and previous chapters to vary the patterns of the sentences you write.

26

Consistency of Person and Tense

The chapters in Part Three illustrate how important it is to maintain clear connections between words and ideas in your sentences. Consistency in your use of pronouns and tense is also important for establishing a clear focus in any paper you write. Losing this consistency results in confusing shifts in point of view (from *I* to *he,* for example) and tense (from past to present). This chapter gives you practice recognizing this kind of consistency and making corrections whenever such consistency is lost.

CONSISTENCY OF PERSON

The review of pronoun forms in this section will help you identify the point of view in any piece of writing and recognize when a writer has shifted from that point of view.

PRONOUNS

Pronoun Form	Singular	Plural
first person	I	we
second person	you	you
third person	he/she/it	they

When drafting a paper, writers sometimes use the pronouns, *I, we, you,* and *they* at random. Such random use of pronouns is referred to as a **pronoun shift.** These shifts are confusing because they make it difficult for readers to tell what point of view the writer is trying to establish. An author must decide whether to adopt a personal point of view (using the first person, *I*), to write objectively (using *he/she/they/it*), or to address the reader directly (using *you*). These distinctions are not inflexible, however. The writer may, for example, use his or her own experience to illustrate a point in an otherwise objective paper.

The following sentences illustrate the confusion that occurs when the point of view or "voice" is not used consistently in a paragraph.

> Despite the efforts of the American Cancer Society and the American Lung Association, we Americans continue to smoke. I am more likely to be a smoker if I am a teenager, but you should not forget that the middle-aged and elderly also keep lighting cigarettes.

The writer of this paragraph will communicate ideas more clearly if she chooses a single point of view. The following is one possible revision:

> Despite the efforts of the American Cancer Society and the American Lung Association, many Americans continue to smoke. Americans are more likely to smoke if they are teenagers, but it should not be forgotten that the middle-aged and elderly also keep lighting cigarettes.

In this revision, the point of view is objective because it uses the third person *(he, she, it, they)* throughout. Here is a second revision:

> Despite the efforts of the American Cancer Society and the American Lung Association, we Americans continue to smoke. We are more likely to be smokers if we are teenagers, but we should not forget that as middle-aged and elderly adults, we also keep lighting cigarettes.

This second revision uses the first-person plural pronoun, *we,* to make a more personal appeal to the reader.

No single point of view will be appropriate all the time. Sometimes it is best to write about something using your own voice (*I*). On other occasions, you will want to be more objective about what you write. The important thing is to avoid confusing shifts among points of view. The best way to avoid that problem is to decide what point of view you will use before you begin writing.

Exercise 26a.   The following sentences form a single paragraph. They have been separated for ease in correcting. Read all of them before deciding which point of view to use. Change any pronouns that are not consistent with your choice.

Memories of Uncle Hugh and Aunt Florence

1. Years ago, before they sold their land to a developer whose company leveled their farm house, you could visit my great aunt and uncle.

2. To us, their house was like a grand palace, and my uncle was a nobleman who could have been driven about in a limousine.

3. Actually, Uncle Hugh was a humble man, a man who would take me into the fields to pick strawberries, who would help you fill your bucket to the brim.

4. Then, too, my great-aunt Florence was as fine a woman as I have ever known.

5. I remember her playful sense of humor most of all, and one could not imagine a more patient teacher.

6. When I was four and one's fingers barely reached the keys, Aunt Florence gave me my first lesson on her grand piano that sat in her living room.

7. The cold, ivory key keys came alive when she played them, and people could hear the sounds of a musical waterfall throughout the house.

Exercise 26b. Decide whether the following paragraphs should be written from a personal point of view *(I)*, an objective point of view *(he, she, it)*, or as a direct address to the reader *(you)*. Change pronouns that are not consistent with the point of view you have chosen. More than one choice is possible; what matters is that you use the pronouns consistently.

Autocross Racing

You can learn to autocross at the autocross school in town. Taught by experts, the courses teach a driver that autocross racing is fun, but challenging. After a single lesson, you can tell that autocross involves much more than showing off hot cars. Much skill is required to drive the course safely and effectively.

Autocross itself is a miniature race course marked by little orange cones. A large parking lot usually provides a good site for the course. You are put into two groups for "run" purposes. Engine size, type of tires, and the make and year of your car determine drivers' class designations. One by one, the drivers in each group take three laps: one is for practice and two are timed. Our ultimate goal is to turn in the fastest time in your class.

The differences between an autocross race and normal, everyday driving make them like night and day. When driving normally, for example, one turns a corner by letting up on the gas, stepping on your brakes, turning the wheel, and accelerating out of the turn. In autocross, on the other hand, the driver must approach the corner with one foot on the gas, then take the foot off the gas while braking hard and fast. Instead of waiting to come out of the turn, you punch the gas pedal and accelerate around the corner. In short, the driver attacks the course and controls it with his car.

CONSISTENCY OF TENSE

Like consistency of person, consistency of tense is important for the coherence and readability of your papers. The examples below illustrate this point. Study the underlined verbs in the following sentences:

> The student who studies is like the squirrel who prepares for winter. When the cold weather hit, or the teacher gave a test, both the squirrel and the student are ready.

The writer of these sentences shifts from the present tense (*studies, is, prepares*) to the past tense (*hit, gave*) and back to the present tense (*are*). The reader is bound to be confused because what begins as a lesson about the importance of keeping up with one's studies becomes a description of a past event. In this revised version, notice how much easier it is to understand the comparison.

> The student who studies is like the squirrel who prepares for winter. When the cold weather hits, or the teacher gives a test, both the squirrel and the student are ready.

Like consistency of person, consistency of tense is important to ensure that the time frame or sequence of events is clear to the reader. For ensuring such consistency, the writer must decide which tense—past, present, or future—controls each paragraph. An author recounting the events that led to the decision to become a machinist will write in the past tense. A writer wishing to describe the most impressive displays at the Smithsonian Institute in

Washington, D.C., may choose the present tense in order to recreate the experience for the audience. The writer may refer to something that happened before or after the basic tense of the paragraph but will return to that basic tense immediately after the reference.

Use the following exercises to practice proofreading for consistency of tense.

Exercise 26c. Study the paragraphs below. Look for clues that will help you decide whether to use the past, present, or future as the basic tense for the second paragraph. Change verbs as needed to make them consistent with the basic tense. The first paragraph uses the past tense.

Brother's Power

My older brother used to bully me unmercifully when we were children. He knew that as his younger sister, I worship him, and he can get me to do whatever he wants. I did exactly what he told me to do until the day he made me beat up a kid he doesn't like. At first I refused to do what he asks, but eventually, in a fit of rage at my brother, I run over and punch my brother's rival in the nose. That day I swore I will never do my brother's bidding again.

Now, choose a basic tense for the following paragraph and make all the verbs consistent with that tense.

Raising Money

Several ways are available for volunteer or nonprofit organizations to raise money. Auctions and bake sales were important sources of income for church organizations and groups like the Girl Scouts. Telephone and mail solicitation work best for large, national organizations, although these activities return cash only a small percentage of the time. It was expensive to use the mails, too, even though community organizations can mail letters and announcements for free. Of course, the costs of printing letters and fliers must be budgeted. Someone had to volunteer to stuff envelopes, as well.

Exercise 26d. Decide the most appropriate tense for the following paragraphs. Then change any verbs you find that shift from that tense.

Roommate

I had a close friend who tried and succeeded in ruining our friendship. When we met in January, I enjoy Ruth's company every time we are together. We hang out at coffee shops, go clothes shopping, and rode our bikes in the park. After a few months of this acquaintance, we move in together, thinking we will get along just fine. We have so many goals in common. We are both in school, we were practical, and we both agree about most political issues.

Living together is fine at first, until Ruth began hiding important things by lying. I told her there were certain things I will not tolerate as her roommate, but she ignores me. She tells me that she has plenty of money in the bank, and she didn't. She also tells me what a good line of credit she had, and that wasn't true. The first time she lied, I overlooked it, but when she continued, I become frustrated. Then our friendship became worse because I felt I can no longer trust her. We talked about what had happened and where things went wrong and agree that the best thing to do was move away from each other.

WRITING EXERCISE

Exercise 26e.   Write a paragraph or short essay on one of the topics below. When you edit your paper, check for consistency of person and tense.

1. Write a short essay describing the driving styles of several people you know.
2. Think of a time when you were little and you stood up for yourself. Compare that event to a more recent example of standing up for yourself or something you believe in. Explain similarities or differences between the two events.
3. Write a short paper in which you compare your initial impression of someone to a later opinion of that person.

27

Mechanics: A Few
Basic Rules for Writers

This chapter summarizes some of the basic rules covering the mechanics of the sentence. These include rules for using commas, semicolons, colons, and apostrophes, and for correcting spelling and capitalization. Refer to these rules when you proofread your papers.

PUNCTUATION

Commas

This section summarizes seven of the basic rules for using commas. Several examples follow each rule. Most of these rules will be familiar to you if you have worked through the chapters in Part Three.

Rule 1. Commas are used to separate three items in a series.

Tina decorated her hat with a peacock feather, a small pearl pin, and a tiny Chinese dragon.

Janet, Algernon, and Charla perform well on the trapeze.

I caught Greg in a moment of weakness as he was watching television, munching corn nuts, and ignoring his homework.

Rule 2. Commas are used after introductory words and phrases.

In the mid-1920s, my great-grandfather brought his family to Los Angeles.

Slowly but surely, cities began pulling up the old streetcar tracks.

Exhausted from her studying, Denise took a chemistry test at 8 A.M.

Rule 3. A comma precedes a coordinating conjunction.

I waved to Melissa, but she didn't see me.

I am going back to school part-time, for I expect to get a better job with a college education.

It was a muggy Monday morning, and I was in no mood to work.

Rule 4. A comma follows an introductory dependent clause.

When I worked for the Department of Parks and Recreation, I had the opportunity to play Santa Claus.

Although the children always told me they had been good, they acted like animals.

Because I had studied Sears' catalogs, I knew about all the latest toys.

Rule 5. Commas separate non-definition relative clauses—clauses that do not define the noun they modify.

My Uncle John, who is wearing a clown costume, is visiting from France.

The combat soldier, who knows what war is like, has a good idea of how frightening, chaotic, and horrifying it is.

The economy, which suffered from stagnation and inflation, was weakened during Carter's administration.